Hungarian Goulash

Hungarian Goulash

A HISTORICAL MEMOIR

Robert Hajdu

ISBN: 098644670X
ISBN 13: 9780986446702

Moreover, I had constantly been preoccupied by that accumulation of knowledge which I had pursued for decades, and which served as a substitute or compensatory memory.

W.G. Sebald, *Austerlitz*

Table of Contents

Maps and Illustrations

Part I

CHAPTER 1

Handing Off

I CAME TO AMERICA WITH my family at age fourteen in 1956. It was the time of the Hungarian Revolution, an event not much remembered today, although then a headline-grabber around the world for a little more than two weeks. But we did not emigrate on account of the revolution, as did so many others anxious to cheat the repression that was sure to follow or escape the retribution that was being visited upon the participants already. For we had not been participants. We had been revolutionaries only in our sentiments, fellow travelers on the return trip at the most.

The revolution made it possible for us to leave, but nothing more. So in terms of the logic of events, it was just a necessary precondition, and in terms of experience, just the opportunity. And, obviously, emigration and immigration are a more complicated business than that. You don't just pick up and go because you can. You don't just throw together the few belongings you can carry and set out one morning to transplant yourself and your so-called loved ones to a distant part of the world, playing cat-and-mouse to the death with the border patrol along the way – not just because you have the opportunity. In order to do that, you need also, first, a propulsive force like the Tatar at your back, to use a common Hungarian expression that harkens back to the smart pace at which the Magyars of the 13th-century fled the slash-and-burn invasion of the country by Ogedei, son of Genghis Khan, and second, the dogged determination that will keep you moving right up to the doorstep of what you yourself finally accept as a new permanent home. Only if you have these things too is an opportunity to go of any value at all.

The first shots of the revolution were fired on October 23, 1956. That was less than a month before my 14th birthday and less than a year after I had started wearing long pants and, in a related development, as they say, discovered girls. Early that September I had entered secondary school, in Hungary known as *gymnasium*. I was an excellent student, smart and bookish and popular among the goody two-shoes, but otherwise a disgrace of a boy. I was unathletic and weak and a physical coward, and the butt of many that's-not-funny jokes among the guys on the street. I had always been a bit chubby, although by this time I was already on the way to being tall like my father, and despite myself even somewhat strapping. My teens were good in this respect. They were one of a handful of leaner periods that punctuated a life of soft and fat, which ended only some years ago when finally I became devoted to daily sweat-sessions at a gym of a very different kind.

Even at fourteen I was already very independent-minded. Rose, my mother, often told the story of how one day, still back in the old country, when she said to me, "Well, that's the way you were raised," I respectfully demurred, "You mean that's the way I raised myself." For even before the transplantation, before she and Leslie, my father, officially became aliens, I had never had the desire to be or become like them, like either one of them. All in all, I knew very little about their lives and understood even less. I did live in fear of him and in obedience to her, and was thoroughly enmeshed in the family dynamics, but my ideas, and already then I lived mostly in my head – my ideas I picked up in school and learned mostly from books. The best I can remember, I never ever discussed these ideas at home or anywhere else either with anyone. It's not that I was reclusive or weird, not at all. I was no absent-minded professor in short pants. But I had no one to confide in, and maybe no desire either to confide. What were my ideas like? All I can say is that when I was about twelve, I read a lengthy fictionalized biography of the great Flemish painter Rubens, which deeply impressed me. The name of the book was *It's Good to Be*

Alive. During the next couple of years, without ever mentioning it to anyone, I thought often and at length about how I too could live my life so that being alive would feel good.

Rose, 49 in 1956, was five feet seven or maybe five eight, but she struck you as even taller on account of the conscious dignity and the pride even that she carried herself with. She had an indomitable will and she always got her way. Later on Marika sometimes even referred to her as Iron Rose. She just knew what she wanted and she simply did not budge. And if you challenged her, her anger could bring down a crushing silence on the whole house. She wore her hair in a fashionable permanent wave, the same brown as her eyes. She was still beautiful, although increasingly by then there was a heaviness and fatigue about her features that was not the work of time alone. Indeed, her life was hard and had always been. But she was strong and very womanly. If I make myself think about it, and it ain't easy, I have to conclude that she would have been a nice solid armful if ever she let herself be embraced. But it was rare that she did. Certainly my own arms, which seem to go prosthetically insensate when I step into this particular imaginary situation – they have no memory of her whatsoever. To put it as I first did only when she was already on her deathbed, Rose actually did not like physical contact. That should help explain, I think, how I also became not much of a hugger. We called her *Anyu*, the Hungarian word for mom.

Rose was born in a tiny village in eastern Hungary soon after the turn of the 20th century. Her first loss came early. Her mother died in childbirth when Rose was three. Then when she was eleven, her favorite stepbrother perished in the influenza epidemic of 1918, and her father followed to the grave when she herself was in her late twenties and had just recently gone up to work in Budapest. She was the chief of household staff for a well-to-do widowed lady, a Mrs. Frankel, who did not call her Rose, as you would a servant, but Miss rather, as you would an English governess. And there was a baronet in the wings, you almost expected her to say when telling this story, waiting to ask for her hand. Despite Rose's having just started on the job, Mrs. Frankel gave her leave to rush to

Debrecen to see her gravely ill father. But, alas, train service between the capital and the country's second city was so hit-or-miss those days that he had already departed when the freshly-orphaned feet touched down on the platform. Rose related these events many times, although just about never anything else from those years, and I always got the impression that her father's death hit her like an avalanche. As if it dammed up and buried whatever may still have been soft and vulnerable in her. Then – and I know I'm making the march of death relentless – then during the war she lost her other brothers, and soon after that the great trauma of her early years was reprised when she lost a sister to childbirth, so that by 1948 of the original nine Ferencz siblings there remained just four girls. Two in the Bronx, and Rose and Erzsi in Budapest. And, I almost forgot, there was also my grandmother, also in New York after 1953, the stepmother Rose still had as a parent, whom I rarely saw and more rarely yet made contact with. Ever strangers to each other we remained, she and I.

Leslie and Rose were a much more troubled couple in 1956 than they would be later in their so-called golden years, the times most vivid in my memory. But I can't possibly forget that the first two decades of their relationship were ghastly. They had by the time of the revolution survived the serial murder-attempts of the Nazi persecutions, and then endured a savage mauling at the hands of the Communists. And, worse than that I dare say, their marriage was a reciprocal torture-chamber, if you can picture something like that, a state of being in which simultaneously the two of them were torturing each other. During my childhood, the only things I ever saw or heard pass between them were glances that seared like hot irons and words the struck like rubber truncheons. They lived a stormy, emotionally devastating stalemate. For many years I held Leslie responsible for all this. After all, he was the tireless philanderer, the conjugal criminal repeatedly charged and convicted of unspecified crimes in open family court, where the children had to hear Rose's indignant allusions to her injuries. For she always made sure we were on her side. Well, she didn't have anything to worry about. She had treated me from the first I would think as completely her own, and would have even if

Leslie had not been away someplace like Siberia first as a forced-labor conscript and then as a prisoner of war. And so she treated Marika too I suppose, and in addition she was also even-tempered even if imperious and cold, whereas he was loving but also gruff and frightening like an untamed force. I was easily taken in, not only because I was a child, but also because in her life *I* was the most important person, and vice versa of course, me and all my smarty-pants ways.

But, really, Leslie also gave me no choice. The man – only 43 in 1956—had an uncontrollable temper. True, a wife like Rose had to contribute plenty to the unrelenting build-up of steam inside him, but that I didn't realize until much later. In any case, he exploded regularly, flying into fits of screaming and storming about, huge and menacing, a wounded grizzly, a looming figure of violence and terror. But for one very brief spanking of Marika, no more than three slaps, not once did he actually lay a hand on us, not even a little finger, but he had been a semi-professional boxer in his prime, a heavyweight, and as a volatile man with powerful fists he himself worried about the damage he could inflict. At best only a B-movie character, but just the thing to terrify children. Somehow even the tufts of curly ginger hair below his knuckles seemed to proclaim that he was something of a wild beast. His raised voice plunged the boy I was into a choking panic and sent me in frantic search of the maternal shelter. He scared me. I feared him. And then I hated him. We called him *Apu*.

As was the fashion back then, Leslie wore a brown fedora, a hat of soft felt with a low crown that you crease down the middle with the edge of your palm and dimple at its prow with thumb and forefinger, and with also an ample but not floppy brim that you turn down a bit over your brow and up a bit in the back. You've seen Humphrey Bogart do it, and I can still see Leslie too in my mind's eye going through that little drill before geometrically positioning the thing on his head. I don't recall anymore what coat-closet arrangements we had, but apparently the fedora did not have its own assigned place, or maybe not one immediately convenient, and so it happened a few times when I was even ten that, unwatchful and bouncing with childish energy, I threw myself onto a chair and right onto the paternal headgear already occupying it. Splat! Each time I would realize my mistake immediately of course, but it was already too late, for by then Leslie would be unleashed. Then my face would turn ashen, my stomach would clench and I would jump as if I had absent-mindedly leaned back against a hot radiator. He would snatch the pathetic felt pancake from under me, hold it up in a gesture of display, like Rigoletto holds up Gilda's just-lifeless body, and let out a bellow of pain, loss and rage. At once I would be reduced to a cringing, quivering lump of fear. Helplessly, my upraised hands would try to shield me and wordlessly plead my case, but in a series of violent gusts, he called down the gods' fury on my stupidity, my carelessness, my distractedness, my failure to pay attention, my refusal to behave like a normal person, my running about like a chicken without a head, and then he would stalk off in defeat, a man betrayed by life, all the time trying to resuscitate the limp wreck in his hand.

There was finally my sister, Marika, ten-and-a-half in late 1956 and very cute. It is only when I try to bring her into focus now that I realize the vagueness of my memories of her back then as a distinct personality. But of course she was still only a child and, admittedly, from my own perspective the least significant figure on the family stage. What I do remember are many, many details, snippets of quite ordinary scenes, and I know that we were usually allies, and always Rose's loyal troops, that Marika received her own dose of insufficiently benign parenting, and that we played together a lot. But we also bickered and pushed and shoved plenty, and I also did find her a pest. Pretty routine stuff I would think between siblings. Although I also recall Rose's frequent lament: "if only I had children who love each other."

So that was the family, a household of secular but not entirely faithless Jews, survivors and to all appearances not very badly damaged victims of the Holocaust, and their children. A family in which each relationship was either a cauldron or an ice-pit, a smothering or a being kept at bay by the business-end of that old lance-like infantryman's weapon called the pike. I myself was then already not inclined to be miserable, but in general there was unhappiness aplenty to go around. We labored under what, by today's standards at least, would be a complete lack of self-awareness. Like most everyone else, we also suffered from fear and want and the reliably punishing totalitarian circumstances, and hoped for something better but were unable to imagine what, when suddenly the world about us went up in flames. We had not anticipated the revolution. We had not been able to read its premonitory signs, or if we had been able then we had *dared* not. But if it succeeded, the uprising, as unbelievable as that was, who knew how things could change even for us? Out with those damn Communists, Leslie must have been cursing his persecutors. I want my factory back! And Rose had to suspect that with a little more money there'd be still more philandering, but it would be good anyway, she had to admit, for the children especially. Although thinking that far ahead was simply pointless, all you could do was hope, and at least it was a relief that for once the uproar was not an expression of the locally popular enthusiasm to annihilate us and our kind. But could this really be happening, armed resistance, a demand for change, an appeal for decency? It makes your head spin, as they say. It really does.

Many of those who participated in the revolution later assisted in boosting it, like saints in a Renaissance ascension, into the historical firmament. They were certain that there it would glitter and blaze forever. For them, those thirteen days had been a time of unmatched glory and national self-affirmation, and a time of unparalleled heartbreak too of course. But I myself was not among those people. On the contrary you can even say, as long as you're careful not to suggest that I had been *against* the revolution. For I hadn't at all. It was just that I had not been a freedom fighter. I had been too much under Rose's thumb to have been one even if I had been otherwise inclined. So, as I've said, at the time I had been no more than an enthusiastic well-wisher, and even afterwards I was never an *ex post facto* champion of the cause. Indeed, when the thing actually happened I had kept very much to myself, then from its aftermath I had escaped, and then from its memory I had finally *estranged* myself. Always I distanced myself from the event. Somehow, I felt *compelled* to distance myself from it.

My professional life – graduate school at Princeton, Ph.D. in medieval history, the years of teaching at City College in New York, then unemployment, Columbia Law School and about three decades of practicing real estate law – through all the years of such a professional life, times and places other than postwar Hungary occupied me always. As a historian I have tried in my mind to resurrect various bygone worlds, but never that one. Foolishly, I now admit, I considered the revolution in particular too paltry a subject for my endeavors, too ephemeral and insignificant an event, something that could not even qualify as the kind of uprising you remember at least for its exotic name, like the Boxer Rebellion, for example, or the Sepoy Mutiny or the Sicilian Vespers. Of course, even if that had been true, I could still have chosen the revolution as my field of specialization, or some other aspect of the Hungarian past, but I wanted none of that. And never mind that I knew the language, which is an advantage no one should fail to exploit. To my mind that would have just cheapened the whole enterprise, and even marked me as to-my-taste too Hungarian. So it was out of the question for me to become a historian either of Hungary or of Eastern Europe. I'm ashamed to say it now, but I even looked down on the acquaintances I briefly had who did specialize in Hungarian history. To me it had no appeal, and I myself cultivated a general *ignorance* of the subject beyond what I remembered from elementary school. How should *I* know this or that?

But as it usually happens in such cases I think, I did not *completely* repress the past. For some reason – not to foreclose the possibility of a later reclaiming maybe, or not to seem overly anxious to forget, or something else maybe, I don't know – I always commemorated the revolution. Every year on October 23rd, *sotto voce* I remarked on the anniversary. That was my regular celebration, my whisper of a celebration. But that was all, because after the earliest days, after I learned English and was then pretty much done talking about the deathless historical events that had, as everybody in a shorthand sort of way spoke and thought, landed me on these shores – after that the select few whom I would impress into sharing the commemoration already knew better than to pick up the cue. Only my two sons, Ari and Pete, my stepsons actually, ever did. They were eleven and twelve or so when it happened, we were sitting around the dinner table talking four ways, Ari on my right, Pete on my left, Barbara, their mother and my dear wife, across from me. Some of the best times of *my* life those dinners were. Then still the boys thought parents pretty cool and gladly took that whisper for what appeared to be conversational bait. A couple of times at least they actually asked what the Hungarian revolution had been, but each time I fielded the question with my usual three-sentence synopsis and tagged them out at first. Soon even they understood how things stood.

So I distanced myself from the revolution, and I distanced myself from the rest of Hungarian history too. And the estrangement, indeed the self-estrangement, extended its negative embrace to much else too, to all of my childhood, to the first half of my parents' lives, to all that could be known about my aunts and uncles and cousins, to all of my ancestors, and to just about everything I had had a personal connection with back then. I felt no *attachment* to any of those people or things and no curiosity about them either. Grandparents I won't even mention, for I hardly ever knew anyone who belonged to what for me was, until now that I myself have reached the age for it, not much more than an abstract relationship. I did not keep my origins secret of course, like characters have occasion to sometimes in Victorian novels, never indeed have I been ashamed of being an immigrant or reluctant to talk about being one either. I just hardly ever thought about the actors and events of those years, and certainly never tried to piece them together, to stitch them together into a story of some sort, to connect them to, or identify how they were discontinuous from, what came after. America and adulthood – did they really follow on the heels of Hungary and childhood? Am I really the descendant of my forebears, I who would not devote so much as a passing thought to who or what they may have

been? I obviously have an avid interest in the past and the often prank-
ishly transformative action of time, and I've long been a devoted reader
of Proust, but my own early years and those who came before me I had
always kept out of my mind's reach and grasp.

But all of this changed after Leslie died in 2001. In the midst of the
grief and the dislocation of routine, for each his or her own, I was overcome by unfamiliar feelings. One day, with no apparent cause, I suddenly
realized how thoroughly *rootless* I was. All at once, my deracinated life was
revealed to me, and I felt like some kind of *Luftmensch*, a levitated, rari-
fied, living-suspended-in-the-air being. And suddenly I also felt a pang:
the ache that rightly should accompany such a revelation for anyone still
addicted to oxygen. The emigration of course, I thought ruefully, that's
the price it has exacted. But then immediately I came clean. By itself, I
acknowledged, emigration can't account for such a brutal disconnection.
For emigrants need not be rootless. Indeed, how many refuse ever to
feel themselves at all removed from the native soil, and how many others
reterritorialize the new land and replant themselves in it? And how many
are there also who manage somehow to be attached to both this and that?
So something else had to explain my only-one-day-a-year-off forsaking
and discarding. Was it masochism then or was it self-defense, and how
did my early years contribute to it, I kept wondering. And what role did
the history of my family play, and what the history of my countrymen, and
what the history of my race?

It was the wish to answer these questions and, more than that, the
wish to deny their premise, to somehow graft life onto the severed roots
after all, and it was other things too. I'll never unravel exactly how it
happened. I can only say that soon after that bitter reckoning I found
myself, fairy-tale-like, as if awakened from a long trance. I saw that the
background scenery on the stage of my life had shifted, and with it came
all the corrections in perspective you would expect. What had been, as it
were, deepest in all that I had lived had just been absorbed, like a scrim at
the opera, into something still deeper and wider and, yes, truer. I found
myself gaining a new dimension, as it were, and with it a new attitude.

Now I was in the grip of a very different compulsion, one of action rather than resistance, of wanting rather than the decades of rejecting and refusing, a compulsion just the opposite of the one that had consigned me to the deep-freeze of self-alienation for so long. Now I just wanted to connect, and so desperately that time and again the thought of connecting, the anticipation of connecting, the imaginary rehearsals of connecting brought tears to my eyes. I guess Leslie had handed off the baton, and it was my family now and my history.

And just as I had thrown the past away with both hands, so now I wanted to snatch it back. Urgently and undeniably, with one hand I now wanted to reconnect with my *personal* past: revive old memories, awaken old tastes and smells and fears and loves, find traces of what had been my childhood or like my childhood, embrace relatives – the meager family I had here and there, especially Rózsi, my aunt in Budapest – be with them again and get from them whatever help I could in filling in the rapidly metastasizing blank spaces in the collective memory. My childhood, as you know already, had been no paradise, but now I wanted desperately to regain it as if it had. And with the other hand, with that I wanted to reconnect with my *historical* past: learn about the times that I and my family had lived through, acquaint myself with Hungarian history beyond the Austro-Hungarian-Empire and Eastern-European-satellite labels, and grasp the shifting meanings of being Hungarian through the ages. Desirous of the previously dreaded consequences, for I must indeed have dreaded them, now I wanted to ride through my own past on the so-called juggernaut of time.

And given my avocation of writing essays, stories, fictions and articles – the tasty side dish I always consumed with my lawyerly meat and potatoes – you won't be surprised to hear that very quickly then my urges consolidated into a scheme to write a book about all that would come out of my researches and rediscoveries. All at once, my mind, off to the races, was hot on the track of a single long story that reveals all that can still be known about what I was back then, what blessings and burdens I received by way of an inheritance, as well as the historical phenomena that shaped me and my family going back as far and spread as broadly as memory it-self, with maybe an assist even from my groping imagination. So what I'm offering you here is not at all the usual childhood memoir, but a hybrid rather of personal experiences and what is commonly known as history. This approach, as you will see, is absolutely necessary for the 1940s and 50s, because then historical events routinely manhandled my life. But my historical accounts will stray well beyond the necessary. And the reason for *that* is to be found not in my subject but in my ambitions. You see, I am firmly convinced that by themselves my personal recollections are not rich enough for my purposes here. So in order for my story to have the proper scope and heft, to realize its most pleasing contours and most ap-pealing contents, to challenge and reward from beginning to end – in a word, for my story to succeed, into the soup of those recollections I will throw some dumplings of history. As if I were making goulash.

This is how I suddenly became involved in a new project. This is why, for the time being at least, I stacked up, labeled and boxed my notes and sketched-out chapters on Chartres cathedral, the project I was work-ing on at that moment, slipped the boxes in the file-drawer next to my other unpublished and even unfinished manuscripts, and as if with the turn of a dial, refocused my enthusiasm and my energies. Then with hands and feet on controls and eyes on gauges, as if about to launch an expedition to a distant galaxy, I started the engines. I reorganized my bookshelves to create a section for Hungary and communism and the Holocaust, from the Internet and the 42nd Street library's catalogues I distilled a custom-made bibliography, I bought a couple of dozen books, some of them online from a bookseller in Budapest, and from Rose I started collecting information about the old days. She was still much haunted by Leslie's presence then – for life had indeed handed her a comeuppance, and the stronghold in which she had walled up her af-fections had finally succumbed to his half-century's siege – and she was tearfully happy to recall their long intertwined lives. Well, some parts of their lives anyway. She cherished the hours we reminisced together, and I did too. I still do.

And then very quickly, and as the most natural and obvious thing in the world, I decided to take a trip to Hungary. At the time I had not been back to the old country for almost thirty years. Three decades that for me were the broad midsection of life, I hope, and for the country the decline and disintegration of one social system and the breaking out of its egg of another. But in 2002, in July, after visiting in France, I left Barbara in Paris and flew to Budapest. I was going there, *expressly*, to recapture the past, as much of it and as well as possible. But how, I had asked myself right after booking the flight on MALÉV, the Hungarian airline. How will I entice antiquated memories, deaf-eared like cats sleeping in dusty nooks, to heed my call? How will I roll away the boulders that seal the cave of repressed traces of the past? Proustian expeditions can be tricky, especially if Proust's sources and resources are not at your disposal. And then what about things… well, I can't just say forgotten, so I'll say things never noted or acknowledged? But of course I had no answers to these questions. I knew only one thing, that while there I would have to be constantly striving to reclaim a long-fallowed identity. That in everything I saw and did in Budapest, I would have to try to be sprung-from-the-local-soil Hungarian. And so, other than my credit cards and everyday necessities, I took nothing of my American life with me. Not even Barbara, as I just said. I would have left even my English thoughts in *la belle France*, were they not the only thoughts I have.

Stepping into the plane, I grabbed one of the free Hungarian newspapers piled high on a rack to the right. I sat down and, with a little more difficulty than I had expected, started in my mind to sound out the syllables of the headlines and to listen to whatever I could catch of the ambient Hungarian conversations. I stole a glance at this or that speaker, considered whether he or she looked Hungarian, and wasn't at all sorry that *I* didn't. I was going to speak Hungarian to the stewardesses and wondered if they would think I was a native or not. Will I be exposed? Of having done what? As people were settling down, I calmed and coached myself – push the paper down into the pouch in front of you, just say what you have to, don't stare at the woman slamming down the overhead compartment doors – and where I had an opportunity for a casual word I chose to speak it even when a simple nod of the head would have done. That was good! You're just like the blond girl across the aisle and the guy in the jeans, just another fellow Hungarian, even if you do also have your little secret identity. Great! Everything was going well! But then along came the cart with the drinks, the usual selection, mostly French products flying out of Paris, and I almost choked on the *jus de pomme*. For apple juice was unknown in my childhood. As was fruit juice in general. I looked up into the expectant face bending toward me, exhaled some Hungarian hot air, stammered like a minor ordering a martini, swallowed twice, and then as the good humor on the stewardess's face began to turn to alarm, I made my request in French.

In my backpack, I had a copy of *Toldi*, the Hungarian national epic. Its author, János Arany, was a prominent Hungarian poet of the 19th century, but the narrative itself is about Miklós Toldi, a historical figure of the 14th century. I had first read the poem, about 200 eight-line stanzas with rhymes that lock like a mortise and tenon, in the 5th or 6th grade. The story is told as if at a campfire of shepherds on the Great Hungarian Plain, and concerns the younger brother of a noble family, a country-bumpkin warrior of prodigious strength, and how he manages, despite his firstborn brother's calumniations, to become King Louis the Great's champion in the chivalric clashes that back then were the tie-breakers in European warfare and dynastic rivalries. In the climactic scene, a great tournament in Buda, Miklós manfully defeats the foreign knight who had already dispatched all his home-grown challengers and so could hurl his insults at the Hungarian nation with impunity. In my boyhood Toldi had thrilled me with his unaffected directness and his exploits, and apparently I also liked the idea of a national epic, for while still in high school in the Bronx and wanting to read my new homeland's equivalent of *Toldi*, I persisted my way through *The Song of Hiawatha*. Although that of course is hardly the same thing. In any case, in anticipation of the trip, I revived my moribund memory of *Toldi*, someplace in New York found an inexpensive paperback edition of it, and finally on the plane cracked the binding.

By the time we started our descent, I had tears in the corners of my eyes and was already reading quite fluently. I was also confident that some things within me were still genuinely Hungarian.

But then soon I realized that as much as I had changed, I had changed hardly more than Budapest itself. You see, my plans on arrival were to pick up where I had left off not thirty but almost fifty years earlier, to fit together the present and the stump of a rudely amputated past like the two halves of a medieval chirograph – as if that required nothing more than just my wanting it so. Well, at every turn I was frustrated. For one thing, there had been my fervently visualized anticipation of simply stepping back into the physical world of the 1950s. In 1974 during my prior visit, when I didn't care much about that step, I still could have taken it, or sort of, but not in 2002 anymore. No way! I should have but hadn't foreseen the effects of the transformational fury of the intervening three decades. For during that generation's-worth of time even what had not been obliterated had by and large been remade into something else. Buildings had acquired new skin, the streets new guts. Remnants and remainders still did delight me with gratifying frequency, but mostly they just affirmed that that world had passed. For another thing, I could not find any former friends quadrupled in age, or any teachers or neighbors or anyone. Nobody! That too I should have expected, for I know only too well that the modern world changes so rapidly in part at least because people pursue their own modern lives, changing their circumstances if allowed like they change their shirts, leaving behind no trail to follow for the casual inquirer who himself had slipped off to another continent half a century earlier. You can call it the devastation of time or the irrepressible workings of the human life force – in either case the outcome is the overwhelming transience that confronted me. In the company of the few relatives who remained, I soon realized that even the few popular songs of the early 1950s that I still remember had faded long ago for the culture's actual carriers, so that each time after just a few bars of name-that-tune I let my lone voice trail off in embarrassment.

But notwithstanding my sobering failures nor the feeling that I was a space traveler returning to Earth from the time-warp of Einsteinian velocities, it was a giddy two weeks. Actually, it was exhilaration without end. I loved being in Budapest. I also loved speaking Hungarian from the first minute to the last. And I loved being whatever I was there, obviously not Hungarian but half transplant rather and half fruit of the fatherland, one part make-believe, the other true-to-the-bone, and impossible to say which part was which. If not exactly roots, I at least found a few abandoned wormholes that I could then imagine myself slinking through, down to or toward the evermore impenetrable core of the past. The personal and the historical past. In 2003 I returned and completed my retrospective fact-finding and feelings-retrieval. Since then, I've been going back pretty much annually in the most agreeable company of my American wife.

In any case, by the time the plane was landing I had already put the apple-juice fiasco behind me, and I was all atwitch with anticipation. But if I had had to say which siren song of my imagination was the sweetest, what I was looking forward to the most, I certainly would *not* have named Rózsi. Even though my then 88-year-old aunt did keep barging into my thoughts. She was the oldest of Leslie's three sisters and the only one of the four siblings still alive. But she and I had never had any kind of a connection, no meta-biological bond between us whatsoever. After the emigration, I had seen her only on the two visits she made to New York during the 60s and on my own two visits to Hungary, pretty much on the heels of hers. Of course, she had news of me over the years from Leslie's letters to her, and I of her from her letters to him, but theirs was the sporadic correspondence of two people who find both the written word and the international postal system much too impersonal. I also spoke to her after Leslie died. I had volunteered to bear the grim tidings, but we had only a short, almost perfunctory call. And that was it: the sum total of our planetary crossings for more than 45 years. Barely more than greetings. Of the conversation of life, little more than the punctuation.

I had never liked Rózsi very much, not when I was a boy and not during the trans-Atlantic drop-ins. I had always found her bossy and manipulative and given to talking down to you – she spoke even to her peers as if they were *children* – and she had also had a relationship with Leslie reminiscent of those California brushfires you hear about on the news, raging flames always in at least one new spot before all the old ones had been put out. So when I made my plans, I didn't even call her. I saw no need to. I didn't require her help with arrangements and wanted to avoid her interfering in my plans. This was *my* project, and I was going to go about it *my* way! I was also still keeping my distance I guess, as I had for 45 years, or indeed 60, never mind all my *urges* of the moment to the contrary. But I intended to get in touch with her immediately of course, as soon as I had put my bags down in my short-rent apartment, that is, and I knew that I could always find her at home.

You see, Rózsi was blind. She had been for a good 25 years by then and progressively losing her sight for the 25 or 30 before that. I had always thought that she had been injured during the war, a fragment of something to the head or a blow of some sort in a blasted bomb shelter. And that's what Rose had believed too to the end of her own life. But the actual story, as I soon found out from Cousin Gyuri, another nephew of hers, was much less romantic. It was just macular degeneration, first striking about mid-life, when she was 34 or 35, during the late 40s. So what then accounts for the muddle, I asked myself right away and was amused when quickly I came to the following conclusions: Quite plausibly, Rózsi had at first just gussied up the truth in order to aggrandize herself, but once the light of the world started slipping away from her in earnest, she realized that the facts sufficed just as they were, without embellishment. But just as plausibly, Rose and Leslie had considered it inappropriate to talk to the children about such a terrible disease, had satisfied our curiosity with the theoretically less scary cover story of the war, and then after a while had themselves forgotten what they had once known. Now, what is intriguing here is that the actuality of these two deceptions is about equally likely, for each would in fact have been in character for its perpetrator, as verified in each case by a salient family trait. The urge to self-aggrandize ruled all the Hónig children all their lives long. (Leslie was born Hónig László.) As for the Ferencz children, or those of them whom I've known at all, they habitually strove to control reality by whitewashing it, by painting it anodyne and neutral, by neutering it even I would have to say if I were to take prudish Rose as representative of her cohort. So the question must go on unanswered forever.

Rózsi lived alone. She had been briefly married but had lost her husband during the war, and she never married again on account of being fiercely independent and knowing that dependence, a ready trap for any blind person, would in marriage be impossible to resist. But through the years she always had a man waiting on her and catering to her needs. So it was when I was a boy, and so it remained, I've been told, right through the decades, right until a few years before my first visit in 2002 when the last of her steady Galahads became too infirm to discharge his duties. When the shadow of death at least did them part. The actual nature of these liaisons I was never able to grasp, and even now that I know the so-called facts of life, I still can't. All I know is that the gentlemen were accomplished, elegant and even dashing figures, and that they had other women in their lives too. But clearly she wasn't just a mistress. Were these perhaps financial arrangements then? A combination of the financial and the sexual? What else could it have been? Well, some kind of love of course. It sounds strange I know, but I can easily imagine these men getting no other recompense for their liege services than her words of gratitude and the privilege, of each during his own tenure, of being *uniquely* devoted to her. Somehow, I think, Rózsi managed to make her life, which already was so many other things, into a chivalric romance too.

On account of her handicap, the Communists had grudgingly granted Rózsi a dispensation from the rule against private ownership of enterprises. As far back as the 50s, she had been among the very few citizens of the capital who ran their own businesses. For half a century she had a little shop, very much like a French *tabac*, where she had leave to sell cigarettes and cigars, postage stamps and lottery tickets, and where, in defiance of what even at best was an unpleasant police state, she also sold many things not within the purview of her license. She stocked bobby-pins and lipstick and ball-point pens and hair nets and items of baby clothing and whatever other things considered luxury goods in that drab world she could connive to have friends and acquaintances bring or send to her from America. And she connived tirelessly, for after the mid-60s there never seemed to be any shortage of ex-Hungarians willing to take the risk of and pocket the gains from providing the merchandise required for a sizable operation. She did very well. She was an excellent businesswoman. She had brains and she had nerve. If I may indulge in one of those counterfactual moments historians find so tempting these days: what kind of life would she have had had she not been fated to a creeping blindness? Well, totalitarianism was clearly contrary to her instincts, but still I think she would have made one hell of a high-muck-a-muck Communist.

Once at least, as I understand, she was charged with black-marketeering and arrested. But even then she did not stumble. She sized up the corrupt legal system and the perversion of justice it added up to, and in a fit of self-righteousness, and with more than a modicum of shrewdness, concluded that no one could be more effective as her advocate than she herself. So the blind middle-aged Jewish widow disdained the idea of hiring a lawyer and defended herself in court. I imagine her wearing dark glasses that flash under the merciless courtroom lights, as, Bette-Davis-style you might say with Dylan, and aptly so, for this indeed was taking place on Desolation Row – as she rises and with exaggeratedly faltering steps approaches the bench, faces a little too high up and a little too far to the left, and pretty much dares the court to punish her. As her defense she recites her *curriculum vitae*, appropriately edited for the occasion of course. Behold, the ravages of life, individual and collective! In the end, she shamed them into letting her walk.

Hungary is a small country in Eastern Europe, just to the east of the continent's German-speaking center and at the western edge of the vast territories occupied by the Slavic peoples. The Danube River, one of the mighty waterways of the world, flows east out of Germany, through Austria and then for about a hundred miles along Hungary's northern border, then it makes a sharp right turn, flows directly south right through the whole country, right into Serbia and then again east out to the Black Sea. Just south of that sharp right turn, Budapest straddles the river. Buda is on the western bank, hilly and green, Pest on the eastern, flat and clad mostly in concrete. The two halves of the city are quite distinct, like Manhattan and Brooklyn you're likely to think, and indeed so if you don't get too carried away. Buda is quite elegantly urban near the river, more suburbanish as you go further west, and beyond that a still wooded, hill-and-dale area, with village-like clumps of houses, a few shops here and there along the main roads, and packs of modest vacation homes like clusters of leaves around the tips of a tree's smallest branches. Seen from a low-flying plane, the verdant hills parallel the riverbank, running in four or five lines of two or three little elongated protuberances each, gentle bumps rising to a pretty much regulation height of 1,200 feet. They seem like old-lady aunts watching from their easy-chairs as their vigorous nephew prances by, flashing in the noonday sun like the Knight of the Mirrors whom Don Quixote so quickly unhorses.

Rózsi lived in Pest, had lived there most of her life, in a congested, heart-of-the-city neighborhood, in a building blackened by soot, as is so much in that country because of the still common use of coal for heating. But she also had a cottage in the outer reaches of the Buda hills, to which she was transported usually in early June to spend the summer reclining in a recliner on the tiny but completely private terrace of a tiny one-room house with a tiny kitchen and bathroom on one side. Although she saw, as it were, only with flat taps of her extended hands, she commanded all in her realm there, she could get around by herself, go to the bathroom and go to bed and get up and get dressed, and almost every day she also had at least one visitor, the very part-time housekeeper if no one else. The visitors brought requested provisions, the occasional tasty surprise, and other things Rózsi required, books on tape, for example, and in general kept the household going. During that first Hungarian trip, I made almost daily visits to the cottage and quickly accepted my place within the ranks of the provisioners. You approach the house by walking down from the top of a hill and along a narrow footpath to the gate, and then up a steep flight of stairs to the terrace, which is thus perched above what is below it and below what is above, as if floating in mid-air, far removed you might think from the world of alienation, emigration and exile I was avidly seeking, but actually better situated for dealing with such things up there in the clear air and away from the violent historical currents gusting all about the city.

It was on our second afternoon together that Rózsi began seducing me. Suddenly, in the middle of a bit of boastful family history, I understood her to be offering me her friendship and affection. Instinctively, doors slammed inside me, lights went out, gates crashed down. I had not expected anything like this, and had certainly never wanted it. So I just squirmed and hesitated, absurdly hoping that she'd pick up my signals, but after two heartbeats she just went on as if silence were all she had been looking for. Only later in the day did I manage to give my instincts enough time off to consider the merits of her proposal and my own purposes as well. And then I promptly admitted to myself that she was indeed an intelligent, well-spoken, well-informed old woman, who by dint of the blindness itself saw life, or some aspects of it anyway, more clearly than others. True, the will to control still governed her sentiments, and what she proffered as wisdom was often no more than an experience meaningful only to her. But still, I now liked her. And the following afternoon I found myself better disposed to her suit. I enjoyed her Middle-European cynicism and humor, and even accepted at face value her sometimes self-deprecating manner. And so I liked her even more.

But it was only the day after that, as I reflected on our multiplying conversations, that suddenly I understood the extraordinary role she was playing in my life and would also play in my project. Rózsi, I reminded myself, had had a significant part in my boyhood and no part at all in what followed. While everyone else had been busy with the usual sublunary hustling, *vis-à-vis* me at least she had remained stuck in the 1950s.

And so, with her I could step back into the past. For me she was a living connection to the past of a kind you hardly ever encounter. Like nothing else, her voice, her vibes, her views raised from apparently inaccessible depths the sunken reality for which I, flea-bitten-like, was scratching the surface. So how could I resist her? That day, as twilight, unseen by her I realized, descended on us, she made a little speech about one person being important to another and then said: "For example, *we* matter to *each other*, don't you agree?" I did. Readily.

Until the day before she died in 2008, Rózsi continued to live alone. She had not been up to the demands of the summer relocation for the three previous years already, especially not after her beloved cat had, in an exquisite display of ante-mortem animal tact, disappeared into the hills. But the routine in the city was maintained. If somebody dropped out of the helpmeet line-up, as could happen for various reasons such as illness, some other kind of hardship or, most often, a falling out – for until the end Rózsi remained an uncompromising mistress – she put the world on emergency alert and always managed somehow to recruit a replacement. If necessary she even cut him or her a slice of the black-market pie, which would be served of course only after her demise. That's why I worked so hard all my life, she would say each time she indentured another volunteer, so that I would have what I need in my old age. I last saw her a few months before the end. She was stretched out on her recliner as always, her eyes closed as was usual, her hair still a steel-gray thicket of spikes, but now for the first time she did show a little willingness to adulterate logic, intellect and calculation with a few pinches of sentiment. It was eerie, the way the exposed bone-structure of her face conjured up Leslie. When I said goodbye and reminded her that on the morrow I would be flying to New York, she gave my hand a squeeze and said "I hope we don't see each other again."

During that first trip already I realized that Rózsi connected me to my personal past as Rose and Leslie themselves never had. For many reasons – some that I have already suggested and others that I hope to reveal hereafter, some that afflicted only individuals and others that plagued the whole family – through the decades always the four Hajdus stuck together very closely, at times too closely even, I regret to say. We were a unit sufficient onto ourselves, a family that would not let in anyone else and shut out, to various, barely tolerable degrees, all aunts and uncles and cousins. So outside that four-sided circle Rózsi was actually the first blood-relation towards whom I ever developed a family feeling. And, as a consequence of that, she was also the one who finally made it possible for me to have and love other blood-relations too, which now I do and love to do, the one who in this way succeeded in actually undoing Leslie and Rose's insistent mal-teachings and counter-examples. Which is just as you would expect, given how unlike them she was. For she was not secretive or up-tight or unable to either muster the empathy or wield the social skills you need for an intimate bond with another, as they were. And she was also not insular or isolated, but blessed with many friends and open to the new. So whereas Rose and Leslie made me feel that family attachments are shackles, Rózsi – just like Barbara and the boys, although not *nearly* as dramatically as they – she made me experience them as silken filaments linking arms and hearts through space and time. And for me she also demonstrated the proposition that even by itself heredity *is* a link to the past.

And that's not even all. For Rózsi connected me not only to the personal but also to the historical past. Born in 1914, she lived through most of Europe's bestial 20th century, herself becoming something like a figure of history, by which I don't mean a historical figure. When she recounted some of the memorable events of her life, over and over I just could not resist thinking that they had also been the memorable events of millions of other lives. Then her inexhaustible resourcefulness and feline instinct for survival seemed to become inconsequential, and I saw her as actually typical and representative, a creature swept along rather than deliberately striding down her own path. Then I understood that indeed she was speaking in the voice of her generation of Hungarians and Jews, of a certain kind among Hungarians and Jews of her generation, that is, and she was speaking of events and experiences that still serve as historical

emblems of their times. Then she was a reminder to me of just how cruelly and relentlessly history had pounded that generation, the generation
that produced me, into its forms and its deformities.

The pleasures of my daily visits to the cottage actually began with the
journey there. I hadn't rented a car for my two weeks because I was staying downtown, and with Budapest's great public transportation system I
never even considered taking a cab. So each day I boarded the tram in
Pest and rode it to its last stop in Buda, then a bus up into the hills, and
then another bus that plies a winding road along some crests to about
half a mile from my destination, with just a level hike ahead of me then.
I loved sitting by the window of tram or bus, watching Hungarian life
humming and gritting its teeth about me. Open-eyed I absorbed the
outside scenery, and from behind hooded lids my fellow passengers. I
may have appeared just another local straphanger, but, like on the flight
from Paris, I was an ogler and an eavesdropper, an intercontinental interloper even. I snap-shot the myriad passing frames of cityscape, and in my
head I replayed phrases I just heard uttered, trying to match the present
to some past or giving up in frustration. Abiding fascination it was, that
daily journey. On the tenth roundtrip still, new marvels of construction,
architectural and linguistic, were beguiling me.

One afternoon, I climbed onto the second bus right behind a dozen
or so college-age kids, boys and girls, dressed for summer fun, garish
bags hanging off their shoulders, pool and sports equipment bulging
from the bags. One of the girls was beautiful, with short dark hair, dark
eyes, soft curves of tanned flesh bursting from a white tank-top, and not
even a hint of self-consciousness. I couldn't stop staring at her. They
were, all of them, those with stubbly chins and those with shaved under-
arms, laughing and chatting, flirting, showboating and outdoing each
other, buzzing with excitement. They were casually physical, mostly in
an athletic rather than a sexual way, everything I had never been and
had thought I'd never be. They were older than I had been back then,
but from the heights of my accumulated years the lowlands of youth then
appeared conveniently uniform. I saw them as the rejuvenated objects of

my passionate adolescent envy, as the more adventurous and less inhibited teenagers of street and schoolyard, and once again I felt my long-ago shortcomings paralyzing me. I tasted, like I used to, the stale breath of timidity.

They streamed out of the bus at the first stop, at the entrance to a camp originally built for the Pioneers, the Communist youth organization. Immediately, two of the guys began to dribble a soccer ball from foot to foot even as they continued to make their way toward the gate, never letting the ball drop, doing turns and spins here and there and lunges too, but always keeping the ball in the air and talking all the time to the young beauty, who in turn walked and stopped and walked alongside them in her own playful way, skipping and leaping as if the zest for life had all by itself made her lighter than air and, as you may have imagined for yourselves already, her breasts with her.

The bus moved off. I kept reshuffling the just-departed images of youth, rerunning the whole scene again and again, as if that would keep my impressions from melting like Hungarian *gelato* under the July sun. I signaled for the next stop and stepped down to the exit door. Just ahead, where the cog railway the Pioneers had built to take them to the Pioneer camp crosses the road, some minor construction had closed down one lane. Once-white sawhorses marked off the site, their legs leaning at drunken angles, their crossbars festooned with flashing red lights. The bus stopped to make way for oncoming traffic.

I found myself looking at a ditch dug alongside the railway and at a bedraggled, heat-prostrated man standing a little more than knee deep in it at its near end. With a mud-encrusted shovel, the man was scraping some clumps of dirt from the bottom of the crude furrow, chipping others off the sides, and piling all the debris into a small wheelbarrow standing just a step or two away from him. An *entr'acte* of performance art it was in the midst of this most recent episode of my Budapest Yesterday and Today show. I watched. The man now laid the shovel aside, lifted the level-full barrow by its green-painted handles and slowly pushed off with the load of dirt. But here an unexpected complication revealed itself: the ditch turned out to vary in depth along its length. So the laborer, as he proceeded, first sank into the earth up to mid-thigh, then he rose a little, and then sank down again, this time almost up to his waist, sinking always faster of course than rising. Then, having reached the other end of the ditch, with sudden vigor he snatched the handles upright and spilled the dirt right in front of his own feet. Slowly then he wiped his brow, stuffed the bandana back into his pocket, rotated the belly-up barrow *en pointe*, as it were, sidled by it, lowered it with a crash, and promptly set out on the return trip. He carried on with the weary struggle as if already a denizen of Dante's inferno, again rising and sinking, and again gaining altitude always more slowly than losing it.

It was a bizarre scene. Baffling. What is that man doing, I wondered as the bus finally lurched forward. Why shift dirt around a ditch? What sense does that make? And why is the ditch so up-and-down crazy any-way? That's not how you dig! But then I forgot all these questions and puzzles as in a flash the metaphorical potential of the situation dazzled me. Can't you see, even at a glance, how the scene comes at life from so many compelling, thought-provoking, discomfiting directions? What re-ally good material it is? Well, that vignette was speaking to *me*, calling out to me, showering its meanings all over me. In the ditch life was nothing but preparation for the grave; in the ditch all your efforts were revealed to be absurd; in the ditch everything always was just repetition and tread-ing water; and that didn't even exhaust the subject.

For the scene owed its impact on *me* to something else yet. I saw it as *still another* profound verdict on life. Keep in mind that during that first visit my project was still in its first bloom, and I was like a man who had just discovered a great treasure or solved one of the great mysteries of life. My excitement at being in Hungary was *more* than redoubled by the thrill of my undertaking. I couldn't wait to get up in the morning. At dawn, and in July in Budapest that is an hour more remarkable to be rising than to be retiring at, I was already sitting with my cup of tea by the open window, fleshing out the prior day's skeletal notes. From day to day my involvement with gathering and processing all the data about the city and the family and the language, and with intimations of the past in general, kept intensifying, and everything I encountered turned out to have a direct bearing on my efforts. And so, for me, the man in the ditch and his absurdist exertions epitomized above all my own project and immediately became something like an infrastructure for my rapidly rising mental reconstructions. For me that scene demonstrated nothing so much as the role of the historical in life, how we sink into it sometimes more, sometimes less deeply – during much of my childhood, for example, it was up to my little ears – all the meanwhile struggling to hold on to the sometimes seemingly ample, sometimes more crimped freedom to live our lives as a *personal, private* endeavor.

Of course, I've always known that to one degree or another every human life is a product of its times. How then could mine not have been so too? And even if that fact of life were not self-evident, haven't my circumstances always rubbed my nose in it? As a historian, early on I came upon Theodor Adorno's somewhat clunky observation that "the illusory importance and autonomy of private life conceals the fact that [actually] private life drags on only as an appendage of the social process," and then I proceeded to develop the tools of trade I needed to make my work reflect that. And so, habitually I've thought about historical deeds and doers in a deep temporal perspective, as parts of processes, as defined by the web of societal causes and effects in which they were enmeshed. And before that, even before college I was already an emigrant, and very much a refugee from Communism, and thus a member of a *historically* defined group. And before that even, always, I was a child of Rose and Leslie, and they could not, even with all their secretiveness, prevent the unavoidable historical corollaries of that fact of life from coming to my attention. And more cogently still, and seemingly inescapably, I was born a Jewish boy in Hungary in 1942! Born to be *prey*! Shoved into world-historical brutality and genocidal persecution while still slick with blood and slime!

And yet, and yet, in the face of all this evidence to the contrary, or maybe in panicky denial of it actually, I had never accepted the inseparableness of the personal and the historical as being applicable to *myself,* as I've known it to be applicable to everyone else. Always, I was unable or unwilling to see my own life as part of this inextricability, this ever-changing, often malignant, periodically annihilating interplay. My rootlessness did not allow me to do otherwise. I could not become attached to or feel embedded in anything, not even a historical context. There had to have been complex reasons for this, which I would like to illuminate if I can a little at least by and by. But for now I will plead only the obvious: utterly rootless is what I have always been and needed to be, attached to nothing more personal or specific than Western civilization. That, evidently, is how I always felt the most comfortable in the world. So I always just routinely disowned everything and gloried in my real or imagined freedom and was rootless. Myself alone, I believed implicitly, the times did not make. Only now, at the last minute as it were, am I, a historian, trying to lay claim to what actually was mine all along, am I finally extending my historical awareness to my own existence, and in the process submitting to the truth of social life, which is pretty much the only life there is.

I first felt the ditch-digger's verdict applying to my own life, or had a premonition of it, that is, in 1999 or 2000, a year or two even before Leslie died, when I first started reading W.G. Sebald. He is a supreme master of this theme, although that is only one of the many reasons he occupies such an exalted place in my literary pantheon. But it was not until I met Rózsi again on the magic mountain that I actually encountered someone who both lived life on the terms of that verdict and allowed that manner of living to be an acknowledged reality. And then in short order came my experience with the man in the ditch, and that completed my education. My sentimental education concluded with that very scene from my sentimental journey to Hungary. I was ready to go home to America and do whatever I could to assure that Rose, during however much time she still had left, shared with me all the still-remembered details of how history had had its way with her and with Leslie. And I knew that I myself would never climb out of the ditch now.

Imagine what a *bouleversement*, as Barbara, who lived in France for many years, would say, what an upheaval of habits and tendencies this project represents for me. What distances within me had to collapse, what obstacles had to come tumbling down! But here I am, and a better man for it I'm convinced. I have reclaimed the past, to the extent that was still possible, or possible for me at least. I have, as it were, reconceived both those fourteen years and what preceded them, and in many respects I have conceived them for the first time. Indeed, I have heeded the ancient but ever unexpressed injunction: historian, heal thyself! For it *has* been a healing for me, as a historian and as a human being, even if right until it started I had hardly even been aware of the wounds festering my life long.

My work has progressed well, although it has been and is a tremendous undertaking. But I love it. As you will see, I have been as assiduous in learning as I had been through decades in remaining ignorant. I have read books and old newspapers, visited museums, questioned Rose and her sister Anci, the only one of *her* siblings still alive, and Rózsi and cousins Gyuri and Pista in Budapest. I have made myself into a bit of an expert in the historical episode of the revolution, and in much else too about the country and its people and the history of its Jews. I have also considered how best to present all of this. How to make the most of my many-colored material and weave my memories and the circumstances whose impact I blithely disregarded for most of my life into one continuous whole. And so, here it is, and it begins at a beginning.

CHAPTER 2

Growing Up Alien

MY EARLIEST MEMORY OF THE world beyond the family is of a spring Sunday in 1948, a sunny morning very soon after we moved into the cooperative apartment that Rose and Leslie had just bought and that would be our home until we left Budapest for good in 1956 in the aftermath of the revolution. The apartment was in Pest in the XIIIth district. Across the street from it sprawled a large urban lot, almost square in shape. Only two small six-story apartment buildings, very much like our own, with only three nice but not lavish apartments per floor, occupied non-adjacent sections of it. The rest of it was vacant land.

In the winter of '45, during the siege of Budapest, the Red Army repeatedly bombed the city and reduced much of it to wreckage, to pyramids alternating with craters, as if in some primitive mining operation. Our future neighborhood suffered too, although what later was to be our own building, put up in 1942, happened to escape the destruction. But even three years later all around devastation was evident. I am out on our fifth-floor balcony on that Sunday morning, observing a world that gleams as when clouds part after a shower, with light and darkness butting up against each other across a trespass-defying line. I am watching our new neighbors milling about like ants, clearing out the deeply-pocked mounds of rubble that make up most of the square block in front of me. Men stamp and tamp vigorously, securing footholds on the slopes, then raise their pickaxes overhead until they almost topple backwards, then bring them down to dislodge chunks of concrete, bricks iced like cakes with mortar, beams and planks I now imagine to have been bristling with twisted nails. Then they move on, yielding their places to other men and women, who quickly sort and carry away the pieces of debris, separating the bricks into the whole and the damaged, and stacking or throwing them into wagons that cart them off. The good ones for reuse; the bad ones to be abandoned to whatever fate a compulsively unwasteful world might have deemed appropriate for shards of brick. It is a group performance choreographed, as it were, by the spirit of community.

Despite the events of the first two years of my life, all of which I will recount and reconstruct in due course, I know nothing of war, and to me this scene does not speak of suffering or danger or devastation. To the contrary almost, I sense here, for I cannot yet think about such things of course, not yet for a long time – I sense that a beginning of some sort is taking place. And, true enough, that *was* a beginning of sorts, indeed a beginning so radical that now it puts me in mind of nothing so much as the Demiurge in the cosmology Plato lays out in the *Timaeus* as he is about to fashion and shape the material world, to make some *thing* out of the existing chaos. Of course, many people preferred to think of that historical situation more as a *return* to something that had been lost, or as a *recovery*, or maybe even a *redemption*, for people tend to hope that such words will talk them into great deeds good and evil. So the atmosphere was heavy then with those conceits. But in fact it all turned out to be nothing more than just an utter beginning, and I was right in my sense of that scene. I was, however, all wrong when I summed it up to my five-and-a-half-year-old self by saying the word "friends" and smiling.

Little boy, I am compelled now to say to that little boy, addressing him as a stranger, for I feel no connection with that time and place and least of all with him – little boy, are you really me? You, a human being still in the bud, yes, a bundle of potentialities maybe, but to all appearances still no more than a handful of clay to be molded by those whose lot it was to be responsible for who and what I would be? But of course that little boy really was me. The few memories I have of those times, and also the portrait of myself with the cherubic smile stretching across the good likeness that Leslie and Rose had had painted from a photograph of me just about then, when in a burst of bourgeois aspirations they also had their own portraits done – those images dispel all my doubts and feelings to the contrary. No, I cannot help but recognize myself in that avatar. Most unmistakably, little boy, I see you observing the action from afar, analyzing collective behavior as you try to understand motives and methods, surrendering to wishes for harmony and mutual benefit, for what all my life I would seek by routinely asking for "just a little peace and quiet." Indeed that was me, and indeed, thanks to personal and historical circumstances, as well as the workings of heredity, in some respects both superficial and profound then already the clay had been molded.

In any case, the scene across the street was definitely not a festival of fraternity. But at so tender an age I did not yet know what Communism was and could not yet recognize that scene as Communist-inspired. I was just an ordinary child, and a moment before I had probably been sitting on some kind of raised chair I would think at my newly-acquired desk, tense with lip-curling concentration as I manipulated a pencil with my right hand, even though the job belonged to my left. Rose knew that that's how I would have to write in school, and she was preparing me, training me ahead of time in order to cancel out the natural disadvantage. And maybe even to put me ahead of others. So I think of my reaction to the event taking place in front of my eyes as something just kind of innate to children, and I say kind of only because I suppose that there are exclusively mean-spirited children too. It was only a few months later, when, not yet six, I entered school, that the direction of my ideas about the world passed to people motivated quite otherwise than Rose, and I was first exposed to ideology. Now, like an open-mouthed chick in the nest, I hungrily swallowed the propaganda-worms, and so quickly learned to value only the common good and to consciously and correctly link to the *Communists* everything socially attractive, including the subject of that recent Sunday-morning two-reeler.

It was still Indian summer when, well, not an order but an instruction was given in school to collect scrap metal. The Communist authorities sounded the on-your-mark through Mrs. Csikász, my teacher and their mouthpiece. "Students! Scour your war-damaged neighborhood for metal debris! Bring the iron and copper, the tin and aluminum to the collection centers set up in schools!" As I listened to Mrs. Csikász's explanation of those words, images of the war-waste across the street from us danced before my eyes. I saw the rusted-out gear-wheels trampled into the dirt, the slabs of greenish-brown pig-iron leaning like forgotten tombstones, the half-buried metal stalks that bigger boys could in a game you might call junkyard pole-vault pull down a bit with the weight of their bodies and then watch vibrate back into place. I already had a plan.

Although I was not permitted to pick things up from the street and especially not to dig things out of the rubble in that intriguing, beckoning empty lot, that Sunday Rose herself crossed the street with me – a very narrow street as I confirm on every trip to Budapest, barely enough for two small cars to get by each other – and she let me loose like a dog off the leash to root about. She followed me up and down the mounds, inspected whatever I sniffed at and scratched, rejected several items that would have required a weight-lifter to lift, but then finally she herself pointed to a length of pipe that Fernand Léger might have imagined during his mechanical period. It was about two feet long and two inches in diameter, pierced by several threaded holes and made of a metal or alloy that apparently did not rust, something I too found acceptable, and something that many, many years later I actually identified as a vehicle's manifold.

We would have passed but a few people on the way to school Monday morning. Under our feet, the pavement was cracked and broken, and tufts of grass sprouted in between the chunks. A truck may have rumbled by, and a horse-drawn wagon probably clattered along the cobble-stones, with the animal heeding nature's steaming, smelly call almost in rhythm with the clip-clop of its metalled hooves. I try now to conjure up before my mind's eye the protagonists of that scene, the no-nonsense woman and the well-fed little boy by her side. I am in short pants, a white shirt and snow-white knee-socks, listing to the right from the waist up, carrying the dirt-caked pipe, with each step knocking it against my bare pudgy thigh and my left sock, tottering from side to side. Rose is not yet 41, a stranger still to hair-dye and wrinkles, a strong, stable figure, solid and straight and confident even as she walks down the street. And how she is walking! She watches me intently. My little boy, she is thinking, is going to school. He is a good little boy. He loves his mother. Something like that. She is wearing a plain cotton dress that falls to just below her knees, beige with a self-effacing pattern and cinched at the waist by a narrow leather strap. Her face is a study in consternation and cunning as she lunges toward me with most every step she takes, hands extended, ready with support if I should stumble. But since she is a vigilant enemy of dirt, the repeated soiling of my sock may actually be her primary concern here. Those hands may actually be reaching out to snatch away my burden rather than to catch my person.

When we entered the class, Mrs. Csikász motioned to me to put the pipe in a corner on top of the metal scraps already contributed. I remember her well, but probably only because Rose included my class photograph from that year with the few things we brought with us to America. She was a tall woman in her forties maybe, with braids coiling about her head like a wreath, stern and careworn but kind. Was she a widow, a woman rendered forever companionless by the war, do I remember that Mrs. correctly? She always wore black – blouse, sweater, skirt, stockings, shoes. In my memory I compare her with some of the eager young instructors who taught me in subsequent years, many of whom I liked very much, and I have no doubt that she would have chosen the *convent*, if possible, rather than the Party when the time came for her to join something. And yet that morning she was full of praise. She complimented Rose, who was actually not yet *again* the laundress, since we still had a maid in those days – she complimented her on how snow-white my socks were not just then but always, and me on my diligence and dutifulness. If only everyone were like Tibor, she said, calling me by my Hungarian given name.

You were sure a good little boy, little boy, I think now. You did as you were told, you played by the rules, you craved approval. And conversely, you were not willful, never had the urge to rebel and never felt oppressed by authority. But, you know, in this case at least you did not have to be such a... well, tool. You didn't have to be so perfect! Or was it a reflex already? An involuntary response? Of course, both your parents, both Rose and Leslie were meticulous in their work, perfectionists of a sort, although definitely in a good way, I hasten to add. So maybe you also took pride in your work already, so to speak, that is quite possible, but still, how can you deny that by such excessive obedience you were also pleasing your pleased-by-excessive-obedience parents? And, of course, he who wants to please will also want to avoid conflict. And he who resents having to please will want to be independent. So it all adds up very nicely, doesn't it? And at such a young age too, little Tibi!

For a year or two after these early-boyhood events I still had no idea what the Party was, and not even an inkling that, on Stalin's orders, it was just at that time it was bringing the newly democratic and multi-party Hungary under its exclusive control. What I did have, however, as you have seen, were very positive impressions of Communism. Impressions, I should add, that have persisted. For even after all the decades, when I now replay the rubble-clearing scene in my mind – following the man in the sun-splashed foreground taking his few steps from right to left, sleeves rolled above his elbows, in one hand a plaster-splattered plank, in the other a brick – I still feel its attraction. And, similarly, when I recall that pile of metal in the corner of the classroom, as I had repeatedly for a few days after the event, when I recall that foot-high jumble of twisted steel rods, rust-encrusted plates and just pieces of plain household hardware, the manifold – ah! the manifold, thrown casually across the top but clearly the most significant contribution of all, it doesn't speak to me of its superiority to the rest but joyfully joins in the chorus of common effort.

You see, for me these episodes became Communist parables of a sort, which elated me then, as they continue to even now. I still like the cooperation among the neighbors, the individual's dedication to the collective, and especially the equality dramatized by the unglamorous tasks, the shared sweat and dirt, the shared carrying of planks and pipes and scrap metal. Or at least the ideas of those things, I like *them* very much. Think of me back then as some kind of diminutive Levin from *Anna Karenina,* joining the village folk not exactly to do the threshing, but rather to sort out the order of the world. From high up on my balcony, I open my arms to them, and I open my heart. I like that we have become friends. That equality and fraternity reign amongst us. Of course, then I didn't yet know that all my life I would also dislike and resist team work.

A few months after the scrap-metal adventure, in another part of town as they say in Batman sagas, Leslie was having a different kind of encounter with the Communists. He was in his office in the shoe factory he and a partner had started with nothing but big ideas right after the war, but which had more than 200 employees by this time. The postwar years were a tricky time to be growing rich in Hungary, for people throughout the country were demanding the dissolution of concentrations of wealth. The old, long-outdated social order, or as much of it as possible, had to go. In June 1946, in a self-righteous confiscatory spirit, the government ordered the nationalization of mines. And then at the end of the year it extended the policy to the largest industrial plants, and in 1947 it was the turn of the banks. Of course, small potatoes like Leslie had nothing to fear from these sentiments and events. But then in early 1948 the Communists began their final push to gain complete control of the country, and that marked a turning point in the economic transformation and also a parting of the ways between official policy and popular sentiment.

The nationalization of all factories with more than 100 workers was now decreed. But fairness and modernization were no longer offered even as pretexts. Openly, this now was the attack on capitalists required by Marxist theory and Communist practice, an attack on a social class and the implementation of a policy to establish state ownership of *all* the means of production. After this measure was put into effect against the 594 enterprises to which it applied, 90% of all workers in mining and heavy industry, and 75% of all workers in light industry had been transferred to the state's employ. All that now remained was just some mopping up, and a law of 1949 took care of that. It mandated nationalization of all workshops having ten or more employees, and that was it. The radical theory could now wash over facts like a tsunami. With damn-the-torpedoes dispatch, a profound social and economic revolution had been effected.

I should add that the attack on private ownership extended to agriculture too. Here the early fairness-driven stage was the enthusiastically greeted land reform of 1945. This was an actual redistribution of land achieved through the breaking up of great estates into a multitude of small peasant holdings, and thus a proliferation of ownership. But then the Communist phase followed again, which here took the form of a forced transfer of ownership *out* of the hands of peasants and *into* so-called collectives, into which the farmers and farm workers themselves were also herded. A countrywide dispossession! And a grim betrayal! For, obviously, collectivization was an undoing of the land reform, and as such the object of a more bitter resistance and an even more profound hate than the wiping out of private ownership in industry.

All that now remains of that shoe factory is a letter dated May 2, 1949, addressed to Leslie, typed on the business's own letterhead and slipped into a now tattered envelope also bearing the concern's name, address and logo. The letterhead is a piece of cream-colored paper about five inches by eight, with the outline of a woman's right-foot summer shoe printed in red in the upper left corner. The company data appear in blue: JU=RO Luxury Shoe Factory (the name was made up of the first syllables of the names of the partners' wives), a Budapest address in the VIIth district (and within the area that had during three months of the German occupation of 1944-45 been the city's Jewish ghetto), Owner: Hajdu László, Export, Import, telephone number and the name of the bank in Pest where regular customers could maintain charge accounts.

In anticipation of routine correspondence, the letterhead had been prepared with an imprint of the presumed writer's signature in the lower right corner: Hajdu László, Master Shoemaker, address, telephone number. The letter reads as follows: "To Mr. Hajdu László, At your request, we are certifying that the Secretary of Industry has appointed a director for the JU-RO shoe factory, which was your own proprietary business, and the factory is undergoing nationalization. This certificate is being issued in connection with tax matters. Respectfully (an illegible signature)."

Seven and a half years passed between May 1949 and the day we slipped through the Austrian border to a world where governments *do* compensate you for your property. I imagine Leslie the evening before, sorting through his papers with shaking hands, unfolding each document, trying to calm his nerves. How, under such circumstances, do you decide what will retain its significance over the years? Why take that letter along? Might it help in regaining what he considered rightfully his own, or was it just a memento of a terrible injustice and a faded dream? That letter would accompany him across the border and across the ocean. It had been a reminder during seven and a half years of domestic exile of who and what he had been, and a reminder it would remain in foreign exile for the rest of his life. It would keep demonstrating that even before we fled Hungary, Leslie was already living in a new world and ruing the loss of the old.

Leslie took with him to the grave the details of that day in the merry month of May when he lost everything. So all I know about the specific events is that on a glorious morning, as the breeze chased flocks of white fluff across the blue sky, some men, including presumably the one who signed the letter, for on the basis of the use of the factory's letterhead, I believe that the letter was prepared on the spot – that some men just walked in through the door and when confronted by Leslie bluntly informed him that he was no longer the proprietor. That brutal intrusion brings to my mind a scene from Visconti's *La Terra Trema*, a film from the late 40s, which I offer you now as just one example of the intimate and irresistible connection I find between Italian neorealist cinema and my childhood. Just one glance at an urban scene from any of those movies, the overcast skies, gray cityscapes, the stucco cracked on old facades, and I am back in short pants on a November afternoon wandering about my neighborhood. In the scene in Visconti, the representatives of a bank enter the protagonist's home, foreclosure judgment in hand, and in an utterly business-like and step-aside way begin to inspect and inventory the house in front of its soon-to-have-been owners. It could just as well have been Leslie and the Communist agents. And just like those Sicilian fishermen, Leslie could not have been taken by surprise. Surely, he had to have been anticipating the Communists' move; the law decreeing the expropriation of owners like him had been on the books for over a year by then. I have to wonder how he managed to evade the expropriating writ even that long.

Ownership and then the loss of that factory shaped our postwar Hungarian lives above all other things. More than the domestic discord, more than being Jewish. For Leslie, it was a question of success or failure in life, a race he would never really think himself qualified to run in the New World. For Rose and Leslie, it was also a staggering financial blow. During the preceding three years or so we had had a comfortable middle-class life; afterwards we were mostly hard up. In the course of a few minutes, the wealth was gone and the plentiful cash-flow of the immediate postwar years dried up to a trickle at best. Overnight a sense of ease and confidence about the world was routed by tightness and worry. And no less importantly, that ownership marked Leslie as a capitalist and not a worker or a peasant, and stigmatized all of us as class aliens. If that makes you think of little green men from Mars, very much a 50s image, then you're getting the idea. For suddenly Leslie was, we all were, monstrous creatures. Outsiders, interlopers, hostile agents from another order, system, realm. Never mind our actual circumstances, we were now branded as members of the bourgeoisie, against which the proletariat was waging a war of, well, yes, annihilation. We had to be killed off or die out or be eliminated in what-ever way possible, so that we couldn't sabotage, as we were assumed subver-sively to be scheming to, the building of a just society. In other words, once more we were in the ditch up to our collective neck.

Rose and Leslie, around 1939

But Leslie's connection with JU-RO, undoubtedly rechristened with a dehumanized, no-pride-in-property name, like Shoe Factory No.6, did not end there. The Communists needed him. He was a valuable man because he knew how to run such an operation and they didn't. So they put him on salary and made him the manager, the man who ran the show as far as production was concerned. In short, they took his business but left him his work. And that was no minor mercy. And since running a factory remained for the rest of his Hungarian days the most valuable thing he had to offer, that became his Hungarian career to the extent they let him have one. In August 1952 he even completed a 10-month training course in technical management required by the Ministry of Light Industries. It's easy to imagine who attended the course with him: a bunch of class aliens. An ingenious measure that was, that requirement. With one blow, it both pilloried its object and reduced him to the condition of an obedient dog. For what *had* to be the actual subject of instruction in that course? What else but ideology.

I can only imagine how demeaning and reality-scrambling it was for Leslie to walk into that factory on May 3rd, the day after the nationalization, and all the days after that. The men and women who had worked for him had now become his bosses. Even though he continued to give orders, or let's say directives, with regard to the work that was being done, he had lost his authority. Worse than that, he had been declared an undesirable and been shamed in front of those whose superior he had been. What he remembered most bitterly were the workers' council's meetings – horrible occasions. Each week Leslie would give a report on production, then he would be dismissed. As a class alien he was not, like each of the workers, an owner of the enterprise, and he had no right to participate in the discussions of those who were. Forty years later he still felt the sting of the humiliation of being told to leave the room. In a hoarse voice he would declare that of all the losses inflicted on him by the Nazis and the Communists, that had been the worst.

It was forty years later, in the middle of 1988, that the run-aground planned economy finally forced the Hungarian government to contemplate the unthinkable, the privatization of some state assets. In other words, finally some nationalizations were to be reversed. But first some heavy political seas had to be navigated. In October 1989 the National Assembly adopted a new democratic constitution, and in the spring of 1990 the first multi-party elections were held. Now, with Communism cashiered and an unadulterated market-economy about to be reinstituted, consideration of the rights of those once dispossessed could no longer be put off. So a fierce debate ignited. Some favored restitution plain and simple. But while this might have been possible with respect to land, it was obviously not practicable for more labile commercial ventures. In the end a compromise emerged giving former owners only partial compensation and even that only in the form of something like shares of stock in recently privatized enterprises.

So Leslie's moment had come, a long-delayed vindication, or so it might have seemed. But he got hardly any satisfaction out of it. It was 1992 and he was in his 80th year. He and Rose had by then finally worked out a tacit accommodation: he was devoted to her alone and utterly, and she valued and appreciated his devotion as he had always wanted her to. She finally loved him, maybe for a while then already, and they each proclaimed their happiness. He had also just recently been diagnosed with prostate cancer. So the factory, a resuscitated ghost, paled in comparison with more this-worldly concerns. And also, the ground rules offended him. He had no use for the shares, he didn't want to own anything in Hungary, he would never live there again, most likely not even visit. Wasn't it twenty years now since he had last returned? They should repay him in dollars. And everything would also have to be done there, so who would take care of it? He knew I would not accept the headache, and, really, having no Hungarian interests then whatsoever, I could not be expected to go to Budapest for *this*.

So we contacted my Cousin Péter in Budapest, Gyuri's brother, and he confirmed that in fact the shares could be sold locally, with a 10-20% discount being usual, I seem to remember. He also said that his wife,

Manyi, would be willing to act as Leslie's agent in the matter, and for that Leslie offered 25% of the award. That promised not to leave much, but still it was worth the work on the application. I did not hesitate and neither did he. We provided the basic facts and offered only the May 2nd letter as proof. We had nothing else. But it was enough. A decision was issued about 18 months later. The records of the Ministry of Light Industries did indeed contain a resolution of nationalization dated June 13, 1949 (after the fact, of course), affecting the JU-RO Shoe Factory, the property of Hajdu László, with 265 employees. At the prescribed rate per employee, the value of the nationalized property came to 6 million forints, or $24,000. Partial compensation, again according to a schedule, was granted in the amount of 860,000 forints, or about $3,400. Manyi got a discount rate of 8%, but with payment of various minor fees and exchange rate fluctuations and heaven knows what else, Leslie was to get only $2,000. A ludicrously small sum.

"Your mother and I," Leslie said one day, speaking to Marika and me in the grave voice that was the all-purpose implement in his melodrama toolbox, "we have decided to give you half the money." To each of us five hundred dollars, and they'll keep a thousand. And actually, he had also decided to send five hundred of it to his youngest sister Bözsi (pro-nounced Beu-dji), the poor widow without children living in Siklós, a small town in southern Hungary. She needed all the help she could get. So I added my five hundred to it and instructed Manyi to transfer only a thousand to Leslie. I was glad to have it over with. I was disgusted with both the procedure and the award. Even if you could manage not to see the amount as an insult, what were you to make of the complete absence of… well, moral context? But Leslie didn't seem to mind. He expected nothing better from that country. And by then I must have been anxious to change the subject too, for I never asked about the husband of JUdit or JUlia. What kind of partner was he anyway?

Had Marika been school-age when the factory was nationalized, Rose would have gone to work I believe. But as things were, she could do no more than turn the maid's room opening off our kitchen into a small household enterprise. Immediately she let go the only maid of ours who ever occupied that walk-in-closet-size chamber, and after that a boarder – or should I say a roomer, since the person did not eat at our table – usually resided in the cramped quarters that barely accommodated a day-bed, a metal wardrobe much like an old-fashioned office-supply-cabinet, a table just large enough for a pair of knees to be squeezed between its legs, and a single chair. I wish I knew more about Rose's business activities and could give you some details, but I was never privy to them. I know only that she would have been tough and strong-willed, and bold in those days too, a ready risk-taker by nature and also by necessity. Obviously, not very much like her son. It's just not in me to be a terror, as you may have guessed by now, like Rose must have been when interviewing prospects. I can just imagine the scene.

Here is Rose, born apparently to give orders and exhale superior airs, there the would-be occupant of the maid's room. Probably, pseudo-mistress and quasi-servant sit on identical kitchen stools, but they might as well be sitting on a throne and a turned-over bucket. Rose fires a question, waits for a response, frowns, then fires another, all the while her eyes fixed in an unblinking scrutiny. The candidate answers meekly, uncomfortable in his or her inferiority, and doubly uncomfortable because the Communists have managed to kick over *every*thing amounting to an accepted form of address. Sir and madam are out, in fact all expressions of respect are suspect, and comrade is plain nauseating. Now Rose frowns again. Then she enumerates the rules, and her tone makes it clear that violation of any one of them would be tantamount to *lèse-majesté*. Of course, in her younger days she too had been, as I've mentioned already... well, not exactly a maid but certainly a household employee who would have lived in servants' quarters, but that had not even dented her *hauteur*. All right, she says finally, unawares how much she herself regrets concluding this rite of exaltation-by-humiliation, we'll give it a try. Of course we will, for despite the shortage of housing in the city, she did not have the luxury of rejecting applicants.

In truth, of course, Rose was a *grande dame* only in her demeanor and her self-estimation. For if I want to see her as a contented woman, I have to recall her at work. But for not being covered with flecks of coal dust or smears of mechanic's grease or the sweat of the tiller of the soil even, she was the ideal Communist worker. Always smiling or even humming, just like the lathe operators I remember from the Hungarian movies of those days, black-and-white and red all over, or Taxi Nancy, the good-natured cabdriver-heroine of a popular song that celebrated the quaint gender-equality of the laboring classes then being so strenuously encouraged. She *loved* to work, to the end of her days. And as snobbish and haughty as she was all her life, the status of the work didn't matter to her at all. Her position with Mrs. Frankel had in fact been her favorite among all her jobs, ever. A high-class maid. Apparently she loved the work of running a large household and loved also Mrs. Frankel. Although what she loved the most, even more than working, was giving orders to others *while* she and they labored together. Under the Communists she did really marginal work, producing marginal goods. But then too she had the last laugh, or smile I should say. For then too she enjoyed what she was doing.

Making ends meet was difficult, especially until Rose went to work, but also after that. Even I could tell that we struggled with daily expenses, and I remember the first time I noticed a pristine rectangle on the wall where until then the two coats of off-white had always been protected by a painting. I gazed up at the spot, uncomprehending, like you might stare at a hole in a wall where a single brick has been removed, for in order for them all to fit, the paintings had been hung left-and-right, up-and-down very close to each other, as you see in pictures of 18th-19th-century European private galleries. I could not guess that the thing had been sold, just as at first I also could not imagine the meaning of the frequent trips Rose made to the state-run pawnshop, bulging bag hidden like a rash on the way out, flattened and in the open on the way back. But I saw or heard nothing to suggest that others had it any easier. For the absence of even necessities *seemed* to affect everyone. Shortages of things like sugar and flour and rice were endemic, and the impoverished condition of society as a whole apparently blocked out, as the light of the sun blocks out the light of the stars, the relative well-being of certain individuals and families.

I should add that my ignorance about money and how to get it was hardly confined to pawning, but was vast rather. I did know of course that people worked for money. I knew that everyone wasn't just a Stakhanovite, the Soviet name given to champion workers, those who competed with each other in exceeding production quotas, like marathoners setting endurance records. There was certainly Rose herself, who worked at home after a while, in the kitchen all day long, feeding the cloth or vinyl under the woodpecker's beak of the sewing machine, slippered feet seesawing the cast-iron pedal. But contented worker though she was, this obviously wasn't just her idea of a good time. I knew that she would have preferred to be practicing Schumann's *Happy Farmer* on the piano and continuing with the lessons she had started the same time as I did, back in our own capitalist twilight. And in addition to all that, I also knew that people generally had less money than they needed. But somehow all to no avail. I seem not to have extrapolated from these basics. Certainly, even at fourteen years of age, I did not yet recognize want as a condition you could attempt to change, a condition that through collective efforts *might* be changed.

How could this be, you ask? Well, I can think of three phenomena that contributed to my seemingly stunted development. Surely my tender years had something to do with it, for in that time and place, unlike in our own world today, even at fourteen you were still "really a boy," as Rózsi remarked in an aside during one of my last visits to her. It took me by surprise, that comment, but it also at once slotted my Hungarian years into an inescapable perspective to which I, most likely because of the emotional/cognitive interference generated by my transplantation, had never before had access. So that if I now compare who and what I was at fourteen with who and what my own stepsons were, each in his own way of course, now I see Rózsi's words confirmed, and now I see that despite the presence of many fourteen-year-olds among the gun-toting, tank-defying, Molotov-cocktail-throwing revolutionaries of 1956, she was right: I, like so many others my age, especially those who might have expected to be continuing their education beyond primary school – I was then not even an adolescent yet or a teenager, but really still only a boy and an innocent.

So that was one contributing factor. Another was the utterly unmaterialistic, anti-materialistic you can even say, education I was receiving in school. It's ironic, I know, that a system founded on a philosophy of history called dialectical materialism should want before all else to inculcate the next generation with a thorough idealism, but so it had to be. For communism was aggressively utopian. It preached a way of life in which money and wealth concerned people only as collective, and not as individual, matters. In which everyone was taken care of, as was only right, and in which everyone pitched in, as was also only right therefore. Of course, in the newsreels the Stakhanovite did live in a nicer than average house, but the desire for real estate was not the prime motivation behind his exalted Stakhanovite acts. Much more than the mansion, he valued his medal. Throughout my own schooling, the world was presented to me as if it knew no greed or acquisitiveness or wanting more than the other guy has. So I had dreams and ambitions, but neither they nor the obstacles to reaching them were financial. And I would have found it at least curious to learn that some people actually devote their lives to amassing riches.

The third contributing factor was the secrecy and circumspection about speaking in front of the children that prevailed in our household regarding the subject of making a living, as it did also regarding most other subjects. Sex and death naturally, but much less obvious things also. With us both family mountains and family molehills were camouflaged and became family secrets, and from my readings I gather that we were not very unusual in this. Indeed, for a Jewish family that had survived the Nazi years we may well have been almost *comme il faut*. So with Rose and Leslie we did not speak of interdicted matters in general, did not ask questions about them, did not pass along information regarding them. Of the nationalization, for example, I was never told on that side of the Atlantic, although on this side it quickly became part of our family mythology, referred to freely, quite unlike the events of the war, which were not mentioned at all, just about ever. We did talk plenty, I don't want you to get the wrong impression, especially with Rose about school. But the conversations, though crackling with tension now and then, were anodyne in their subject matter.

Our actual circumstances, to put all this into a more bread-and-butter context for you – our actual circumstances were such that I never thought of us as either rich or poor. It's true that in terms of our apartment and its furnishings we lived in relative luxury. Most remarkably perhaps, there was the hand-painted band of tots on swings, seesaws and rocking horses running around the children's room frieze-like in a never-ending display of delight. But this unusually refined ornamentation of a sort of child-pastoral, and also the short-wave radio with the dial bearing the strange names of foreign cities made even stranger by my phonetic pronunciation, in fact everything of any beauty, ease or imagination that we had were all just remnants of pre-Communist successes. And I myself had hardly any possessions. Maybe fifteen books. I recall a summer, I might have been ten, hanging out at home for many hours with Marika, playing with a can of grapefruit sections Rose had received as a gift from someone. I can't imagine now what the game was, as I couldn't imagine then what grape-fruit was. Toys we had absolutely none that I recall. Never was I the proud owner of the soccer ball being kicked about by the boys around the block. Leslie and Rose did have quite a sizable and handsome library – a single custom-built bookcase with twelve glass-fronted shelves – which included a twenty-four-volume encyclopedia that I loved especially, and we did have, as I just said, many other fine things too. So my immediate surroundings were not at all impoverished. But the inventory of our permanent house-hold goods never increased, for never did we buy anything except food and a very occasional garment. In brief, we did have more things than some neighbors or the families of some of my friends, but also less than others.

Marika and Tibi, 1950

Finally in 1951, when I was nine and Marika six, Rose went to work. Her first job was in a factory, where she worked on a sewing machine and learned how to do piecework as a garment is assembled component by component by a series of seamstresses. From the few snap-shots of her I still have in my memories from then, I know how much she suffered from being separated from the children. In particular, I can still see her appraising me in the winter coat her earnings had put on my back, a coat that accompanied me from Budapest to America, although not quite as far as the Bronx. At least this should keep you warm, my son, she seemed to be thinking, even if I have to leave you every day. For Rose that had to be a wrenching separation, especially because it was the first since the war and her few days in the hospital giving birth to Marika. Was it so for me too then? I don't think so. Of course, I had already by then suffered many separations, as you will hear soon enough. And even then, I think, I was already independent-minded and unwittingly preparing myself for escape, migration and transplantation, which in a way add up to just a set of variations on the theme of separation. Although as good as I was, and am, at parting, I never allowed myself to feel that I left her. I just tried to keep as much distance between us as I myself needed, as I still do sometimes in my dreams.

With Rose out of the home, a neighbor kept an eye on the children after school, which was not much of a burden since we were reliable, instinctively wagon-circling, and not much in need of supervision. But then after about a year on that job, Rose became an out-worker, and a tremendous victory that was. Indeed, now forces were once more properly realigned and order was reestablished. Rose's own sewing machine was moved to the kitchen right by the door to the maid's room, and that is where she worked. I often stood by that door watching her. She was absorbed in her tasks, and her movements were regular, spare and well-timed, as if to provide demonstrations of ease and efficiency. That was a kind of apprenticeship for me. That's how I myself learned to work in a spirit of smiling and humming.

From her employer's shop Rose would bring home long narrow strips of canvas rolled up into large reels. She and I then unrolled them, a procedure made very unpleasant by their clammy feel and peculiar odor. Half the strips were a very dark gray, the others a dirty white. Rose then sewed the strips together, alternating colors, and then sewed together two panels made of the strips so as to form a gigantic sack. Maybe 15 feet by 6. The sacks were then folded – this Rose and I did together and it was always a struggle – and then delivered back to the company's shop. All in all, it was disgusting work, but, obviously, there was nothing better for her. After all, she didn't have much by way of skills, as a proletarian woman might well have had. But I find it outrageous that nobody ever would tell her how those sacks were to be used or why that was a secret. That, I am convinced, was another form of the humiliation Leslie also had to deal with in his working life, another exquisite form of punishment fitting the crime, another little meanness on the part of the vengeful system intent on breaking the class alien's spirit. In any case, after little more than a year Rose was glad to find other work and have those Treblinka-wear-like things permanently out of the apartment.

But nine months passed before her next employment started. Illness interfered. She had to have a hysterectomy, and that led to nearly fatal complications. Of course the children were told only that she was sick, but for once the secretiveness was appropriate I think. So there was another separation, and this time her place at home was taken by a dullness and lack of sensation that pervaded everything. As if suddenly we were all made of wood. As if the whole familial contraption had run out of gas and irretrievably collapsed into a state of inertia. And this already semi-insensate condition was aggravated by the rule that prohibited children from visiting in hospitals. So our phantasms of tragedy had free rein, I suppose, and could not be corralled at all until she was somewhat better and again able to get on her feet. And even then the best that could be arranged behind the back of the hospital staff was that Marika and I would wait to see her outside the iron fence that enclosed the garden of the Jewish Hospital at a time when inside she would be making a wobbly circuit.

I can still see that scene, as she approached us very slowly down a path in a long white robe that entirely hid her feet and her slippers, but because she was on somewhat higher ground than the boy and girl stand-ing out on the street, as if we were all in a Renaissance painting, with the saintly mother already in heaven blessing the children whose lives still lay ahead of them, and yes, of course, with heaven and earth marked off from each other by a very tall iron fence. A distance of four or five feet still separated us when she stopped, looking impossibly pale and ethereal, so that we could not reach her even as we extended our arms through the iron rods with the rusty spearheads on top. Marika started crying, while I just stared open-mouthed at this apparition. With a parting glance Rose moved along and we withdrew our manna-seeking hands.

In October 1955 Rose resumed her out-worker activities. This time she was employed by an enterprise located in our own district, one of the advantages of which was that I, now thirteen, could be sent to both pick up the materials and deliver the finished product. Another was the prod-uct itself: little booties for infants made of a vinyl-like material, cute, deli-cate objects, pleasant to handle. The apartment came alive again, indeed a happiness of sorts tints all my memories of the tiny pink and baby-blue things. Now Marika also participated in the cottage industry. She and I started the process by fingernailing apart the many layers of vinyl stuck together in a stack just as they came off the cutter's table. It was not easy, but it *was* child's play. Then with criss-crossing lines Rose sewed a lining of some sort into the pre-cut soles and inside and outside uppers, and fi-nally assembled the booties. They were so light as to seem almost weight-less, as if they would take wing like turtle-doves do amid fluttering hearts on drugstore greeting cards when Rose lined them up, pair by pair, for a proud, sharp-eyed, 360-degree last inspection. Still, by the time I finally arrived at the shop lugging two large boxes filled with the little puffs, the strings I was holding them by had almost cut my fingers.

All of this had a lasting impact on me. The communist principles, Rose's attitude to work and my youth and innocence – all these things conspired to make me a person who most of his life valued work but not money. Was there anything wrong with that? Well, not in primary school, when I intended to become an engineer, a chemical engineer probably, and imagined myself wearing a lab coat and peering at a test tube but never gave a thought to the kind of living I would make. And not during the revolution either, when suddenly I aspired to be a journalist and made my new choice the very same way. And then still not when I received a lecturer's salary as a member of the unionized faculty of CUNY, because that was a pretty good salary. But then when I became a lawyer, then it was always a disaster pending, until after years the pain of learning to be a financial being abated, and in the end it all worked out all right.

Leslie's workbook, which I found among his papers right next to Rose's, contains his employment record for the Communist years. It's a maroon booklet with tough cardboard covers and 24 pages for entries, about 5-1/2 inches by 4. It is very much like his somewhat larger personal ID booklet, which I also have, and which Humphrey Bogart might well have handed to one of Claude Raines's men in *Casablanca*. On the front cover of the workbook is the national emblem, a ubiquitous visual companion of my childhood, red star at the top of a circular field of blue framed by a sheaf of wheat on each side, with a golden hammer and ear of wheat crossed at the bottom, and the whole thing resting on a base of pleated ribbon in the national colors of red, white and green.

Here is my translation of the text printed on the inside front cover:

FROM THE CONSTITUTION OF THE HUNGARIAN PEOPLE'S REPUBLIC

Labor is the foundation of the social order of the Hungarian People's Republic. It is the right and responsibility of, and a matter of honor to, every able-bodied citizen to work in accordance with his or her abilities.

By their work, their participation in work competitions, their promotion of labor discipline and their contributions to the perfection of the system of work methods, the workers serve the interests of socialist development.

This, as I see it, is the Communist version of the pursuit of happiness. Or of the duty to be happy, maybe I should say, for this declaration is more about what you must than what you have the right to do. In fact, to me these three sentences reek of coercion. I find the very thought of work competitions and labor discipline revolting. As I do also all the specific forms of thought-control and arm-twisting they bring to mind, which you could be subjected to as encouragement to toe the assembly line or punishment for failing to do so. Yes, indeed, the man with the plank was a beautiful sight and symbol, but only so long as you could imagine him a willing rather than a forced participant.

But then coercion *was* the Communist way. For the Party strained compulsively to maintain its power uncontested, and as one of its most self-destructive acts it created an economic life that was to be totally under its control. That was a critical motive for the nationalizations and the establishment in general of the so-called *command* economy. But if all significant decisions about supply, investment, labor conditions, economic goals and the like, matters that in modern economies are governed by the more or less free movement of prices in the market – if all the decisions are made by a National Planning Office, if an octopus-like central agency sets annual production targets, coordinates the distribution of resources, and fixes the prices at which products are sold, then *ipso facto* people have to be coerced. Without the use of force or its threat you cannot redirect individual initiative, the competitive spirit and the drive for personal gain, and, more to the point yet, you cannot repress them. Of course, under the planned economy you were still permitted to exceed production quotas, but if otherwise you insisted on doing things your own way or not at all, or if you tried to keep a little something on the side for yourself, you better watch out! And never mind that this approach was a disaster. That central planning as it was done under Rákosi, our very own little Stalin during the early 50s, further impoverished the already hard-hit masses, just the group that was supposed to benefit the most from it. For that too you were forced to accept and even to pretend to like.

The organization dedicated to enforcing this system was the dreaded Economic Police, known by its Hungarian initials as the GR. Woe to you if you were suspected or accused of economic crimes or misdemeanors, or of having done just something offensive to the workers and peasants! The GR was always there, ready to arrange for your internment or re-settlement. In 1953 there were about one hundred concentration camps in the country with an inmate population of 44,000, mostly class aliens and almost all men, against whom no specific charges could be brought even under a government that made any law it pleased and applied any law it made any way it wanted to. For most of the men the journey that started in a black sedan in the middle of the night ended in one of these places. There they lived under the harshest possible conditions, break-ing stones, mining copper or coal or doing some other kind of heavy manual labor. They were guarded by a force that did not have to account for its actions, or even for the total number of inmates under its control. Resettlement was not as brutal as this. It meant only forcible relocation, usually of an entire family and usually out of the capital and into a place in the countryside. But in this case too, you had to leave almost all of your belongings and rights and lives behind. *When Father Was Away on Business*, a movie by the Serbian director Emir Kusturica, is a favorite of mine. It is about a boy of nine or so, as I recall, with a father who is a convict in a penal camp and a seamstress mother who could be a double for the youngish Rose. They don't have an easy time of it, but had Leslie been away on business, our situation would have been much more catastrophic even I have to believe than what you see on the screen.

On one occasion in 1952 I myself witnessed the GR in action. It was a small job for them I would think, twenty minutes at the site, tops! but the site was our own apartment, which they had come to search. Unannounced. My memory preserves only four still images and a scrap of dialogue from the incident, but that's enough, for fear still grips me as soon as my imagination sets any of the figures in motion. I think Rose and Leslie were more or less expecting the intrusion, because another apartment in the building had been searched a few days earlier and they had thought that the GR could well have come upstairs right then. As survivors of the war, they knew the modus operandi of the Gestapo, and in fundamentals all secret police forces are alike. Right after that first visit to the building they had warned me about what might happen, so when the two plainclothesmen did actually arrive on our doorstep I already knew about house searches as a phenomenon and, if I remember right, I also knew that this would not be the first one Leslie and Rose had to endure. We were all at home when the bell rang. It was evening. Everyone was terrified.

Shot no.1: Leslie standing with his back against the front door, which he has just swung open to let them in. I see clearly his white shirt with the open collar, but his eyes and his mouth, which might reveal some inner state, I can't bring into focus. His face seems somehow blurred by the menace that is oozing in like poison gas.

Shot no.2: The men standing on the far side of Rose and Leslie's room, hats on heads. They are peering and reaching into the depths of the large wardrobe, a black lacquered Art Deco piece, its doors now turned back seemingly further than hinges can go. As if broken on the wheel of history.

Shot no.3: A hand inside a large drawer extending snake-like from the cuffs of a shirtsleeve, a jacket and then an overcoat, and burrowing under a stack of folded linen. Obviously, this is a mental image I formed soon after the actual event, an image of something I could not have *seen*, that nobody could have. There's no possible vantage point from which to.

Shot no.4: The foyer. Several voices hanging in the air, with one man in the pantry off the foyer, the other one standing a couple of feet from the door, as if he had just walked in, exactly where Leslie would stand four years later, suitcase in hand, on his arrival home on the third evening of the revolution. The second man is engaged in a verbal boxing match with Leslie and Rose. The statements are short and few but they fall with a terrible force.

"You are engaged in unauthorized and anti-socialist commerce, comrade."

"I am not engaged in commerce, comrade," said Leslie in a firm but lifeless voice.

"How many sets of bed linen do you own, she-comrade?"

"Two, comrade," said Rose, her mouth dry.

"Why is one set brand new, she-comrade?"

"It has never been used, comrade."

"Are *you* mocking *me*?"

"We purchased both sets about five years ago, comrade," Leslie stepped in, "and have never used the second one."

"You are engaged in the illegal hoarding of goods!"

"I am not engaged in hoarding, comrade."

Rose had had the bed linen made during better times, intending the second set as the eventual replacement for or supplement to the one in use. I still remember the neatly folded cream-colored damask, a flawless stack with the heft of prosperity. Having a back-up set was of course a common practice, but still the situation was utterly bourgeois, as opposed to proletarian, that is, and could also be seen as evidence of hoarding or even black-marketeering. But the GR left. Apparently they were satisfied, or not planning in any case to take further action. This, comrades, is the first documented transgression, etcetera, etcetera. You had to consider yourself warned. And you had to collapse into a chair after they left. Life was unbearable. They could just as easily have taken Leslie away, not to be seen again for years maybe, or ever.

Of course, that wasn't my own ten-year-old reaction. That this had been coercion, that I could feel. Something like a rape even, I would say, although I was still innocent then about such things. And I *was* scared. Never before had I seen my father and mother gripped by fear, and that itself was enough to sweep me also into the paralyzing embrace. But I understood nothing else. Neither the persecution of class aliens, nor what the fear-sowers intended to reap. Indeed, I understood so little that the brief visitation didn't even dull the shine on my initial view of Communism, and certainly not on the halo that myths of unbounded wisdom and beneficence had made me imagine for some time then already to be arcing about Stalin's head. So that even if I too like everyone else had known that the Man of Steel (for that is what Stalin means) himself willed that economic coercion be a staple in our lives, even then I would not have considered possible a connection between him and those beasts with their reptile-hands in our wardrobes. Had I been older, I might even have shared the view of so many others (with respect to Stalin in the Soviet Union and to his disciple Rákosi at home) that such things were perpetrated by rogue police forces *alone*. Boris Pasternak, the great Russian poet, is recorded to have said about Uncle Joe's own murderous purges of the 30s: "if only somebody would tell Stalin about this." For the admiration and indeed love that Pasternak and I and millions of others too felt for Stalin was a great and abiding force of enslavement: it rendered the unbearable bearable while also scattering abroad false hope of an eventual escape from the ÁVO, that is, the secret police, the GR and the like.

After they nationalized his business, the Communists continued to marginalize Leslie, to force him off the playing field and onto the edges of society, to relegate him to the heap of dispensable, discarded men. Then in mid-1953 Imre Nagy, the prime minister who replaced Rákosi, introduced a reform program called the New Course. By and by I will make sense of all the political developments for you, but for now let me just say that the New Course finally granted Leslie some relief. From his workbook, as supplemented by entries in his ID, you can pretty much reconstruct the ups and downs of his working life from May 1949, when the introduction of new rules of property and a new national economy redefined him *vis-à-vis* everything and everyone, right through to the aftermath of the revolution.

During those seven and a half years Leslie had fourteen jobs, with an average tenure of little more than six months. In each of the first three, which saw him through Stalin's death in 1953 and his own 40th birthday about a week later, he was technical director, that is, manager, of a shoe factory. The last of the three factories, however, was located not in Budapest but in Szeged, a city in southern Hungary to the east of the Danube, which was in those days a good five-six hours from the capital by rail, about the only way you could get there. He was back in Budapest again in April 1953, just as economic conditions were hitting a critical low, employed as a laborer at a factory for making insulating materials, but that job lasted only a single day. After that he was a laborer again in something like a foundry, and then, if I understand the entry correctly, a salesman at a store for samples of goods produced by light industry. But by the end of September 1953, and this is where you see the benefits of the New Course, he was again in charge of production at one shoe factory, then another, and his pay was rising. Although then, towards the end of 1954, came another strange interlude, during which he ran a factory for processing leather cuttings and clippings, not a flagship I bet even of the scrap-economy. Six months as production manager for one section of a handicrafts company followed this, and then five months, ending in November 1955, in an identical position with another such company. And finally, during the same month, his move to Makó, a town not far from Szeged, where he was in charge of production at the local shoe factory for almost a year, that is, right until the revolution. Whew!

Was this so terrible? Well, with his wife's help, he was able to put bread on the table, if not always sausages. And ours was far from a poverty of epic proportions. I was certainly always chubby and managed to be so without the benefit of fast foods – although it takes practically no time to make a lard sandwich, our staple. Obviously, you can see more acute and heartbreaking suffering among the homeless in New York City any winter day, and among people of all stations in the many countries and regions where wars, famine or ethnic hatred rage these days. But the comparative is not the only way to understand human misfortune. Think of the situation this way rather: here was a skilled craftsman and enterprising businessman, a family-man ready to deliver services of value in short supply in that society, but despite all his efforts and abilities, he was not allowed to carry out his basic responsibilities, and he was penalized for having played the game well indeed when a prior set of rules prevailed. Moreover, he had hanging over him the threat of losing what he still did have. And all this by way of persecution for being a capitalist, after having just been persecuted to the very antechamber of death for being a Jew. Beaten down day after day, but allowed, as if with even greater malice, to survive.

Of course at that time I didn't know any of this. I did know that money was scarce, as I've said already, and that things of value were departing from the apartment on a regular basis, never to return. A painting, some porcelain, a carpet, some pieces of lace. But that was all. It was only a year or so before she died, long after all but the personal reasons for secrecy had been eliminated, that Rose even then no more than just hinted at the circumstances that first sent Leslie out of town, and so gave me some indication of just how desperate things had been. It happened in September 1952, during some of the bleakest months of Communist terror, the time of preparations for a great Zionist conspiracy trial in Budapest that was to coincide with and so support Stalin's trial of the Jewish doctors in Moscow. Men, and some women too, from all walks of life were being arrested on charges considered insufficient even by the ÁVO. Petty personal vendettas by the new people in power and their flunkeys could send you to torture and jail for long years. The possession of an apartment or furniture coveted by an up and coming official could seal your fate. The ÁVO would rouse you in the middle of the night and hustle you off into that black sedan, which would then proceed hearse-like down the street, vanishing into the darkness past the yellowish light of the lamppost at the corner.

The house search took place in 1952, and I know from Cousin Pista that that same year Leslie just managed, with the aid of well-tended connections from his hometown, to squirm out of the clutches of the GR. Pista even named several people in very high positions with whom Leslie had been on good terms. And in a conversation about such things I subsequently had with Rose, she also happened to mention that Leslie had known everyone, starting with Rákosi and all the way down. And these connections had been so effective, she added, that even when leather for shoe factories had been difficult to obtain, Leslie had for his own factory more than he could use. These were revelations to me of course. It didn't surprise me that he had been a fighter, only that he could fight so skillfully. This was not the aggressive browbeater, braggart and blusterer I had to keep dodging at home. And this was also not, or not only, the boulevardier. Of course, well before these conversations I had already come to see Leslie somewhat differently than I had during my childhood, but even so, I was surprised to hear that, never mind all his annoying traits and his mastery at alienating people, he had been an impressive figure, and part of what he had to surrender because Rose did not want him near other women was a highly-developed sociability with many benefits not necessarily of the adulterous kind.

In any case, I don't know anything else about the squirming encounter, which may or may not have been related to the house search. Rose would no more than just hint that at that very time the GR had taken an interest in Leslie. Well, it had to be just a matter of time. As you know and as Leslie knew too, he was or had indeed been guilty of what then were considered economic crimes, and he had going for him only the strength of his connections and the value of his technical expertise. How then could he ensure that he'd be able to keep providing for his family and maybe even keep on strolling down the boulevards? Was there anything he could do to protect himself from the sadism, the arbitrariness, the lethal lurches of absolute power? Anything beyond just continuing the daily struggle and hoping? Well, he and Rose decided that he should flee. We hoped, Rose said, that they wouldn't bother with him if he was already in some end-of-the-world village. Like a 17th-century Frenchman who'd run afoul of the law in Paris withdrawing to the Auvergne. I will never discover how much Rose and Leslie knew about the coercion used those days to dispose of essentially innocent people and, very often, grab their possessions. But their scheme shows that they knew enough to pinpoint the one chink in the system through which they might have been able to throw a wrench into the works.

Of course, what the workbook describes as Leslie's transfer from the capital to Szeged, which was no village but Hungary's third largest city, by no means guaranteed his immunity. But think of all the advantages it did offer: First, the punishment it intended to evade may already have seemed imposed on Leslie by himself, and that might have been enough to scramble the terror's slot-machine. The so-called flagellants of the Middle Ages, men and women who whipped themselves and their fellows bloody in the hope of making it superfluous for God Himself to punish them, relied on this logic too. Second, in case the family had to resettle, a foothold outside Budapest might have provided a way out. And third, abasing oneself a little can sometimes appease the bully in power at just the right moment, just as making oneself a little more difficult to reach can also sometimes move the frustrated bureaucrat on to the next case. Leslie and Rose may have had some reservations, but nevertheless they trusted their feeling that any quirk or deviation from the norm could make pursuit of him no longer worth the trouble. They had survived worse, and they were both inclined to take action of however questionable efficacy, rather than just sit and wait. They never forgot that the predator they hoped to elude recognized no rules and could change its methods from one day to the next, but then, they had never known any other kind of predator. In any case, this time it may have worked.

So that was 1952. But what about 1955? Did history, so to speak, repeat itself in 1955? Did Leslie have to run again from persecution, just three years later? I don't think so. I will never know for certain, for those who once knew the facts are now gone, and, in any case, Rose had

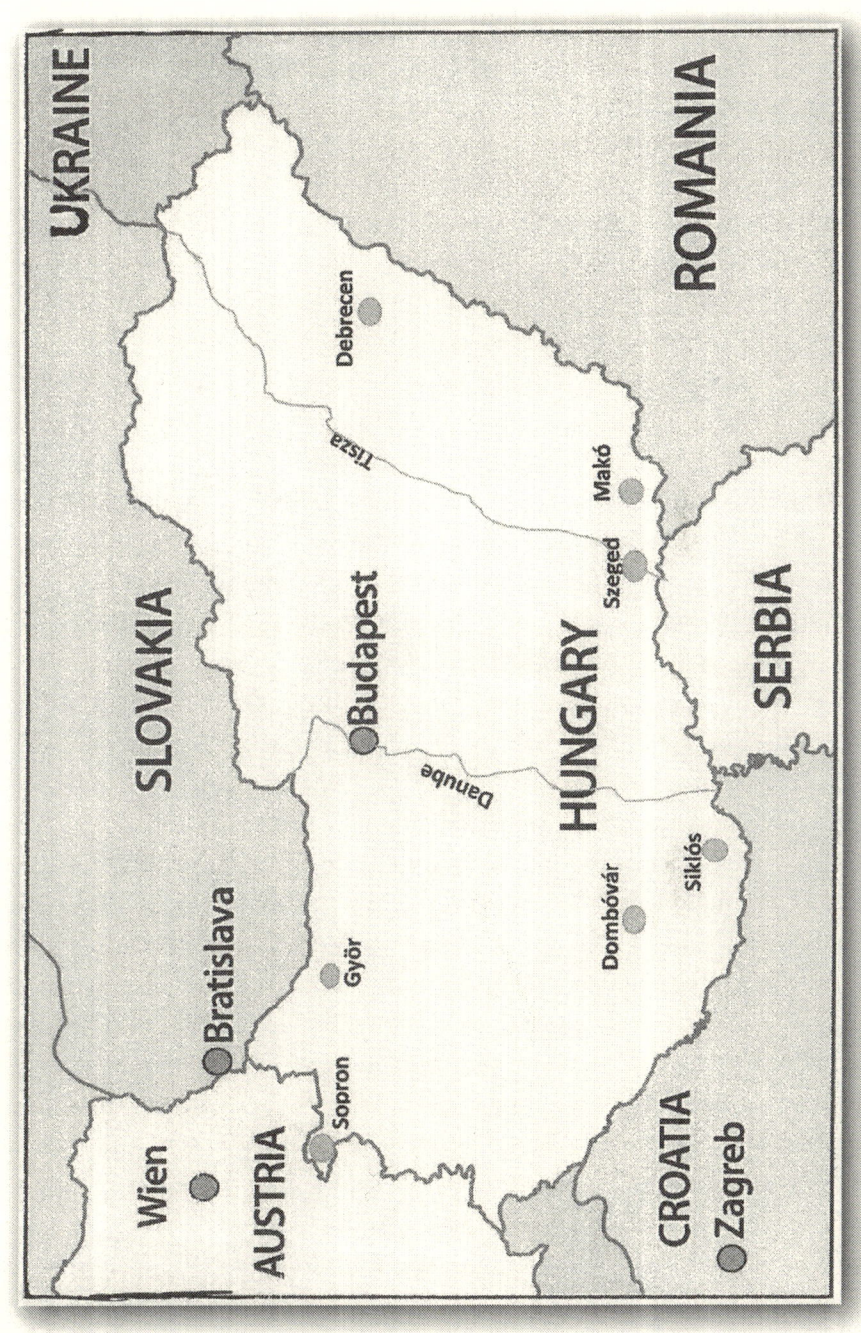

hardly ever been willing to talk or even think about *personally* unpleasant details from those years. Persecution she could be prevailed upon to recount, but not domestic strife. And here I do believe that the historical and the personal diverged. Although Nagy was out in April 1955 and the Stalinists were back in power again, they were no longer interested in essentially insignificant remnants of the old order, the category of persons and things to which Leslie could be deemed to belong. They had lost a good bit of self-confidence during the New Course, and they were focused on the increasingly threatening struggle with the intramural opposition. Certainly, the Stalinist terror of pre-1953 was not reinstituted, although the ÁVO *was*.

So what drove Leslie to the provinces again? Well, this is how I see it. The two positions he held in Budapest in 1955 may not have been exactly his line, and there may well have been money issues too. It's also possible that he had left his last job in the capital because of a run-in with someone, for, as you might well imagine, Leslie also specialized in run-ins. Of the thirteen transfers of employment recorded in the booklet, six occurred on account of *him*. Granted, that can mean many things, but Leslie was Leslie. He had all the bad traits I have attributed to him already, and was also both infinitely thin-skinned and ready to strike back without hesitation for any perceived slight. He was always, until almost the very end, impossible to work with. He dominated as if by instinct, and he did it in the most overbearing way possible. And if that didn't suit you, you had to subdue him. And who could succeed in that? Even Rose managed only after dragging him to America. And Marika and I managed many years later only because in the end, as I said to my own boys many times while that's what they still were – in the end the younger generation always wins. In any case, by late 1955 Leslie may have made himself unemployable in Budapest simply by insulting too many people who expected *not* to be insulted by class aliens. I'm sure he did an intolerable amount of insulting, and thought, to boot, that he was always in the right. I'm only unsure if that alone would have made him unemployable.

But after I consider all the evidence, I have to conclude that more than anything else it was the domestic situation that triggered what actually had to amount to a quasi-separation between them. Do I mean that Rose and Leslie themselves thought of it as such? I don't know. I have no evidence one way or the other. What I imagine is that, as it tends to happen, the conditions imposed on their personal life by objective circumstances sooner or later became an accepted part of that life. The separation of 1952, suffered and endured as a lesser evil (and possibly also the earlier war-time separation, about which more later), was likely by 1955 to have been incorporated into what was understood to be within the range of the norm. So that a job for Leslie far from Budapest, but close actually to Szeged, the place to which he had fled in 1952, could in 1955 have been triggered by either a matrimonial breakdown or something less dire or even much less dire. In other words, separating for economic reasons could function as a safety valve in a marriage that today in America, with our own customs and mores, would have imploded long ago.

In order not to overplay the drama, for that kind of poetic license I don't consider myself to have, I am going to take it as fact that the family's situation in 1955 and '56 was not *specifically* a product of the menace represented by Communism. Our life then already had a different mix of the personal and the historical than it had had three years earlier, which latter mix had itself been different from its predecessor three years before that, and three years before that, and so on. Oh, you really had to hold onto your hat during those years. For then history was a hurricane. An inexhaustible tempest of the kind I have not seen since I managed to wash ashore in this bourgeois democracy, where we expect to be able to keep what is personal to us distinct from what is historical, where we expect to live our own lives the way we want to. But what cheek on our part, this expectation! And what fortuity to realize it even just once in a while! To live in a place and time where the majority of the very large population of a very large country can entertain such expectations! Now *that's* America for you, or certainly that *was* America until some years ago at least, and a good bit of the Western world. And that was surely a historical rarity, if not in fact a singular privilege.

Just think of how addicted we are to this expectation and how reasonable we consider it for all human beings to want to be just like us. All seven billion. For us, the urge to view life as merely a personal affair is very hard to resist for any length of time. And this in the teeth of our sobering collective reality. The human condition is closing in on us as a species, as the white race, as Americans and probably in other equally unforgiving ways also, and yet, mostly we remain focused on our persons and our personal preoccupations. We, each of us and most everyone we know I would think, strive tirelessly to distinguish ourselves from the mob, to stay out of the various human catch-basins that otherwise swallow up the individual. And in this age of extraordinary massification – of mass production, mass consumption, mass movements, mass delusions, mass hysteria, mass migrations, mass deportations, mass executions, and that's hardly the end of it – indeed in part because our age is such, we want more than ever to be self-defined *and* self-destined.

Family myths and memories are silent on the crying habits of my childhood. My boyhood and adolescence, however, I know to have been pretty rigorously dry-eyed. Exceptions were so few that Rose, herself a weep-less woman, noted and remembered them. Then, almost as soon as I began to improvise what was supposed to pass for an adult life, the sorry state of my emotional equipment quickly became apparent, and what was turning out to be a downright inability to cry was one of its manifestations. How I overcame this handicap, or the exact extent to which I did, I can't really say. It just happened in the course of many years of psychotherapy, and a failed marriage and a number of aborted pairings-up too, painful years of many painful days – it just happened that somehow I learned to cry, and to cry always better, although to this day, I confess, I haven't quite overcome the boy in me. Even now things that will reduce most everyone to tears, like a loved one lost or just misplaced, as it were, will not turn on the faucets. What will, on the other hand, is a story of an indomitable underdog, or justice finally won, or the triumph of a great man, like Dante, for example, as attested by the inscription on his statue in front of Santa Croce in Florence, the city that had disowned him in mid-life: "To Dante Alighieri, from Italy." What does *that* say about me, I wonder.

I staged one of my boyhood cries on the morning of March 5, 1953, as I was getting ready for school. When I learned that Stalin had died, I burst out. Who would defend us now from the imperialists' attacks, I shook and sobbed. From the imperialists with their villainous cartoon faces and their cartoon pockets bulging with bombs? Who would inspire the young heroes – all of them named Oleg, as I learned from the volumes of Communist hagiography crammed down our throats in school – to rise unexpectedly from the ranks of the ordinary, to outsmart, out-struggle and out-*sacrifice* the capitalist enemy? Who would, most desperately, guide history on its... well, actually, inevitable course? But I was far from the only one crying. Certainly in the Soviet Union the mourning of all those melancholy Slavs was near-universal and their grief heartfelt and deep. Thousands were crushed to death waiting to see the body lying in state and at the funeral. And in Hungary too I had many to commiserate with I'm sure, many loyal to the Party and the ideals it ostensibly stood for. I don't think I loved the Great Father quite like they did, but I was definitely afraid for my world. After all, this was the Cold War in its most viciously hostile phase, and I a gently brainwashed boy!

My world was the lot across the street. That's where I spent most of my free time hanging out, and that's where my education had started and was continuing. Soon after the clean-up I witnessed, and after the scrap-metal hunt, in other words during the final acts of the Communist power-grab, a crew of groundskeepers had nicely leveled all the unbuilt portions of that lot, sloped the edges down to the sidewalk at 45 degrees, seeded it all with grass, improved it with some benches, swings, a seesaw and a slide, and, presto-changeo! we had what I considered a spacious park and playground. In retrospect it all seems to have happened one-two-three, except for the actual swings themselves – the seats and the chains to suspend them by – for which the crossbars were made to wait, gallows-like, through the take-over. And it all took place right before my astonished eyes as day after day I stood on the balcony gaping. Parallel lines were subduing shapelessness, purpose banishing uselessness, meaning dispelling confusion. The Demiurge was completing his creative task. This was my world. And when Stalin died I imagined enemy forces invading it. Not long before, I had seen *The Battle of Berlin*, a Russian World-War-II epic, in which an underground train packed with passengers is swallowed up by a river crashing through the tunnel's walls, and that became my fright-template for an invasion. Who would protect us now?

Some adults would sit on those playground benches now and then, but in essence the place belonged to us boys. And we belonged to *it*. Even after I was old enough to visit friends ten-twelve blocks away, I still always made time for the *street*, that is, the playground. If you were not an urban child, you will not recognize this phenomenon of a world of your own out in public, I mean not in your own backyard, a world where you can operate unsupervised, in a might-have-been nook of a diorama-sized neighborhood. In that territory enclosed by imaginary childhood horizons I had a life apart from my parents. In what proved actually to be a garden cordoned off from the limitless human wilderness, I had a familiarity and even a proprietary-*ish* feeling. During an infinite procession of afternoons, it is in a garden like this that a city boy used to discover something like his public personality, much about right and wrong, and in time maybe even the opposite sex. Especially magical were the late summer twilights on the playground, my world wrapping itself in a thousand successive shades of farewell, as Rose, no longer visible up on the balcony, called me home: "Tibi! Tibi!" My memory of that garden is forever suffused with a sweetness, like the early morning air in the parking lot behind the bakery here in Mamaroneck.

There were about a dozen boys roughly my age who belonged to that playground the way I did. Our fathers were bookkeepers and janitors, craftsmen and teachers, but we assiduously ignored the evident social distinctions. This we did because we lived in a world of purported equality and also because we had our own hierarchy. We ranked ourselves according to strength, as determined in wrestling bouts won and lost usually right in the playground, with everyone vying for alpha status, or at least for the greatest possible distance from omega. Everyone except the couple of boys, that is, too scared to test their nerve, one of whom, to Leslie's unconcealed chagrin and frustration, was his only son. More than once I happened to be standing around with the guys, when suddenly excitement ricocheted through the air, as if colliding bodies had struck a spark, shouts of encouragement erupted, and we found ourselves forming a ring about two boys grappling on the ground. They panted and snarled and strained like hungry wolf pups, limbs twisted about each other, veins popping out on their necks. We cheered with glee and surprise, and there was a little sadism too, although my own breath usually got stuck in my throat. But then it was over and normal activities resumed, the combatants stanched their bloody noses, and we waited to see if the loser would relinquish his ranking or refuse until after a rematch. Hey, anyone can have a bad day.

In those far from immemorial days, we did not have television or cell phones or things like that, and had to make do without the panoply of entertainment devices that among them parcel out your consciousness today. We spent our afternoons, or whole days during the summer, playing soccer or a no-wall version of handball or a game in which, to Rose's horror, you gained territory by throwing a knife down so that its point stuck in the ground, or card games sitting under a shade tree, or pitching pennies, or watching pennies being pitched as I and all the other penniless boys did, for I very rarely had any money at all, and I mean *any* money – or taunting Totyi, a somewhat deranged and epileptic young man of about twenty, the neighborhood idiot and himself a master of taunting, and then as we got to be about thirteen suddenly inventing new activities the only real purpose of which was to bring us in contact with the girls on the block. But that was it. Even then I knew that brains counted for nothing in that crowd, but also figured out that it wouldn't make sense if the larger world were not otherwise. These boys were not my friends. My friends were my schoolmates. This was my gang.

Then one day this existence and this age of the world ended too. A construction crew arrived as if materializing from the ether, like aliens intent on reorganizing all of earthly life, and soon five four-story buildings rose on what had been *our* playground. All that remained vacant was land enough for one more structure and the rectangle of ground in the center of the block that allowed light and air to reach the rears of all the new buildings. And so, for the second time in a few years, an ontological event unfolded on this central stage of my boyhood life. But this second event, how different it was from the first! Being more mature, I could see immediately that, yes, something was being created here, but more than that, something else was also being destroyed. Immediately I understood that this was a *transformation*. I even knew, and was pleased with myself for knowing, that this thought was an insight. Of course, I did not yet have any idea of the ramifications of the insight, that, for example, the transformation was no longer the work of the Demiurge or of aliens either but of ourselves, or that transforming is what we *humans* do when expressing our Pynchonesque urges, when giving in to the digitalizing compulsions that may best characterize the current post-mythical phase of our career. Or that indeed we are the children of Prometheus, usurpers of prerogatives belonging by right only to the creator-gods.

With that transformation, we were thrown out of the garden. I say only the obvious when I say this and yet I say it hesitantly. For working on a project about your childhood, you learn quickly that, Proust notwithstanding, not everything that's lost is a paradise, and if your childhood happens to include an episode of immigration, then you learn also that neither is everything that's found. Nevertheless, for me the expulsion was heart-rending. Of course, the family hearth across the street continued to be what it had always been, no less and no more, and certainly I was not chased naked into the wilderness with only my hands covering my private parts, like Adam and Eve in that painting by Masaccio. But the day I came home from school and found the construction cranes pivoting about the playground like giant insects, I cried. That was another one of my boyhood cries.

Again it was a spring day, with the acacias in bloom and the afternoon long and bright. I was twelve and I had nowhere to hang out. That is the first time I remember being dispossessed, although that was definitely not my *first dispossession*. Nor my last. For now it seems to me that all the forms of not belonging, not just being dispossessed, have always been, well, something of a specialty of mine. Of all the people you can belong to, your family and circles of friends and professional organizations and churches and the like, and also ethnic groups and nations and even the races of humanity – I have at times *not* belonged to almost all of them. And place and time too, to which you also belong, to your own place or places, and certainly your own times – periodically I have floated free even of the familiar moorings *they* provide. How many times have I detached, decoupled and departed! Withdrawn, withheld and done without! You haven't heard it all yet, not by far! And as I have perpetrated these dispossessions, so I have also suffered them. But despite all *that*, that springtime dispossession was extraordinary. Through all the years and all the partings, *rarely* have I shed the tears of the dispossessed, and hardly ever did I shed them as profusely as when those cranes sank their gap-toothed shovels into the patchy grass of the playground.

But, cheer up! Sorrow was short-lived. After a few days, excitement and a sense of adventure overwhelmed it. I quickly returned to my education. The goings on across the street tremendously intrigued and exhilarated me – the manhandling of the immediate environment, the piling up of the five shoddily-made pastel structures, all the prototypically urbanizing activity. And that was not even all, for we boys, defending our not-even-squatters' rights, also made a constant nuisance of ourselves. So I remember prohibited forays into the construction site, even brush-by encounters with laborers on the job, men and women swaggering in their quilted earth-creature outfits, indulging in words of sexual suggestion, operating according to a rougher social code than I had ever before observed. But most of all maybe I remember ogling the naked display of secret building components before they donned their mantle of brick and stucco for good, and thrilling at the aggressive thrust of the buildings, up and up, day after day, week after week, structure rudely shoving back the nothingness of empty space!

And then the apartments in the new buildings, once they were occupied, they became like so many cans of a new and different demographic stew. The population of our little street – one block long – doubled and grew more complicated, and the gang enlarged and then disintegrated. So now I had both old pals and new, with some who finally, after almost a decade, were able to leave behind whatever ramshackle hovel the devastation of the war had forced them into, and others who had just made a bold move from some periphery towards the center of the capital, some actually small-town folk, like Magdi, the pretty girl with the blonde braids who for hours on end used to lean out one of the ground-floor windows facing the center courtyard and flirt with another boy and me. So I not only lost but also gained something.

Now, in bringing back together the personal and the historical, I can relate the final transformation of that city block to Nagy's New Course, which actually tried to confront the desperate urban housing shortage. Now I can also understand the failure to build out the entire square block, leaving that one structure unbuilt, as it were, flying in the face of both aesthetics and what now, after thirty years as a real estate lawyer, I know of business. In a market economy, with crews and equipment already on the spot and all that pent-up demand, you can be sure that a developer would have found a way to go for the extra profit. But in a command economy, where ideology and political pressures rather than the market determine the allocation of resources as between, say, the production of weapons and the construction of new housing, a city will grow in ways incomprehensible to the uninitiated.

But did I say final transformation of the city block? Well, final as of 1956 is obviously what I meant. For in 2002, on my first post-Communism trip to Hungary, I of course visited the old neighborhood and saw that now the block is fully built. That last empty corner is now stuffed not with one but with *two* additional apartment buildings of maybe 70s vintage. Yes, yes, another dispossession. What a surprise! But no reason for crying.

In 1945, the troops of the Red Army that had just liberated the country from German occupation proceeded, in a not un-German-like manner, to make themselves at home. Ostensibly, the extended visit served the locals as an insurance policy against aggression from the West, but in fact the Soviet presence protected Hungary only the way the Mafia protects the neighborhood. Whether you want the protection or not. For the real beneficiary of the occupation was of course the Soviet Union, which is why in the 50s so many Hungarians, even if they didn't yearn for a restoration of capitalism, would have welcomed an army of Westerners bearing gifts as true liberators.

My disillusionment with Communism began with the gradual recognition when I was nine or ten of the unfairness of the Russians' treatment of their small-country neighbor. My awareness of the Soviet high-handedness was first awakened by the compulsory Russian language instruction for all school-children, which went into effect in 1950. For six years in primary school, and the few months of *gymnasium* too, it was daily Russian classes for me. Whether Mrs. Gaál, my home-room and Hungarian teacher in elementary school, who also taught us Russian as a second specialty – whether she *knew* any Russian, or actually whether her Russian exceeded the most rudimentary, I cannot say. And don't think that's an overly suspicious question. After all, how could Hungary have had a corps of Russian instructors on the ready, hands holding a piece of chalk cocked for Cyrillic action? In any case, however much or little Russian she knew, it was no fault of Mrs. Gaál's that despite all those years of conjugations and declensions I could never put three Russian sentences together.

To me, learning Russian was distasteful from the first. The sound of the language I found pleasant enough, so that wasn't a problem, much more pleasant for example than Hebrew or Arabic, which I'd rather not hear at all, and which then I never had heard, although not actually delightful like Italian and French, which I possibly might have. But then there was the Cyrillic alphabet, which in my mind had a whiff of barbarism, an automatic second-rate-ness about it. Of course this was just cultural snobbery, and I say this as a native Hungarian speaker, much lower than which, I admit, you cannot sink, for extremely strange but not exotic is in the end just plain weird – a snobbery that was just in the air, that I myself had acquired very early on and that was probably founded on nothing more than the thousand or so miles by which Budapest lies west of Moscow. A snobbery rooted maybe in the Magyar memory of the ancestral trek from Central Asia to the Carpathian Basin, or in the case of a Jew to the faux-memory of it, which seems somehow to have conferred on westward an inalienable reputation as the equivalent of forward. But mostly I objected to learning Russian because by the fourth grade already I recognized *it* as the language of our foreign protectors and mentors, and the compulsory instruction therefore an outrage. *Obviously*, common knowledge of Russian could serve only the interests of the Russians, including of course their insatiable appetite for self-aggrandizement and self-glorification.

If I had to rank the Russians' imperialist prerogatives for hatefulness, I would put the compulsory language classes way up high. Up there, for example, with the trade relationship between the two countries, which, as I came to understand sometime after Stalin's death, was that Hungary imported from the Soviet Union unnecessary armaments, and machinery and industrial raw materials too, and paid for these things with much more than even she, an agricultural society, could spare of the grain, sausages, eggs, poultry and other foodstuffs produced at home. Thanks to this quasi-Malthusian arrangement, even in good years Hungarian farmers went hungry, grocery shelves gaped empty, housewives standing on line when something *could* be had nearly scratched each other to death, and we all spread not butter on our daily bread but lard. Up there also with the uranium situation, which developed immediately after deposits of the ore were discovered in Hungary. That's when we all, citizens of a nuclear-armed world, learned what uranium actually is and how, in a routine act of colonialist grand theft, the Soviets were expropriating all that we had of it.

As for Russian self-aggrandizement, it manifested itself everywhere and tarnished everything the Russians and the Communists said or did. Shamelessly, the Russians claimed for themselves many of the great inventions of the 19th century, crediting them to individuals whose names I was taught but promptly forgot and had to look up recently on the Internet. I had learned that an Alexander Lodigin invented the light bulb, Alexander Mozhaisky built the first airplane, a Russian named Cherepanov rather than the Englishman George Stephenson invented the locomotive, Alexander Popov rather than Marconi dreamed up the radio, and so on. Maybe in the Soviet Union, I used to think, these laughable claims are accepted. But not here. So I had to smirk. The brainy boys in school were interested in things like this, and we knew what we knew. And this is just one example of the official elevation of Russian ways and life to the status of models to be aspired to and aped. Our armed forces were also made to adopt the Russian style of uniforms and to wear not a shirt but a much-resented tunic not tucked into your trousers. And we were also supposed to think that only Russian films were truly artistic, Russian athletes unbeatable and Russian history all the way back to the rape of Europa the very hinge of world events. Did we actually believe these things? Not really. They just weren't believable. And although by my last Hungarian years I already knew at least by name the great Russian writers of the 19th century, unlike Edmund Wilson – if you'll excuse the comparison – who in part at least mastered Russian to be able to read Pushkin in the original, I persisted in seeing no justification for having to learn the language.

A feeling of empowerment rushed through me upon each such unmasking of the red pretenders, and especially upon realization that quite openly and deliberately we were being Russified. I also felt, although I had no real basis for thinking this way, that our big brother in the international Communist movement had exposed himself as the phony, hypocrite and liar we had *always suspected* him to be. And a bully, just a bully. So we were not comrades at all – what nonsense! – but his servants. So the great Soviet people and the Glorious October Revolution and maybe even the brotherhood-of-peoples version of the world were just pretexts and lies, and who knows what else? All just a cover-up for imperialism and exploitation, as Communism at home was maybe just an excuse for poverty and ruthlessness and terror. As you see, I was being weaned from my early infatuation.

And the Russification also had its flipside, an equally obnoxious practice. For the Communists were also insistently engineering a rupture with the past, working tirelessly to strip the Magyar people of its own historical identity and remove the Hungarian nation from its established niche in the world. You see, for centuries Hungarians had looked to the West as a civilizational leader and model. In some ways, this was similar to an earlier Russian experience, for just as most members of the Hungarian ruling classes had been either German-speakers living in Vienna or aspiring to be so, so pre-revolutionary upper-class Russians had been French-speakers residing in Paris. It was the Bolsheviks who had first attacked such leanings head-on as soon as they grabbed control, never mind the Western origins of Marxism and communism. They targeted the traditional orientation not only because it had informed the old order, but also because of the immediate and visceral hostility of the Western powers to the October Revolution. But whereas in the Soviet Union the rejection of Western influence amounted to an assertion of cultural independence, the similar reorientation enforced in Hungary during the 50s tended, alas, only to degrade Hungarian identity and thereby benefit the imperial master. And though Hungarians had by then for half a millennium lived with hegemony-minded neighbors and worse, and Hungary, like other small countries in Europe, had indeed only rarely been either willing or able to keep foreign ways out, the new domination from the *east* was hard to swallow.

Of course, neither the re-education provided in the backyards of the internment camps nor any other of the Communists' strenuous efforts seemed able to neutralize pro-Western cultural sentiments, or neutralize them fast enough. For that more time was required, or that is at least the impression I get. A new generation had to come of age before Moscow could reasonably hope to enjoy the level of respect that earlier was only feigned, if that. In any case, Rose, herself a country girl with little schooling, had brought *me* up to look to the West. And though it was not prudent then to learn the languages of the capitalist enemy, she made sure that I could start private German lessons at the age of eight or nine at the latest. She knew – even though neither she nor Leslie nor any of their parents spoke or had spoken German – that that's what proper bourgeois people, Jewish and gentile, did, and she apparently put no faith in the loudly-trumpeted predictions that the old days were gone for good and we would live in a Slavo-tropic world forever. In other words, she arranged my life, or a part of my life at least, so that by the age of eleven or twelve I could experience it as a life lived in defiance of the new system.

My German teacher was a spinster I am tempted to say, although she may well have been a widow. In any case, she was certainly spinsterish or at least governess-like. She lived and received her students in a large room with a floor-to-ceiling tile-stove that hardly ever radiated any heat, in an apartment she shared with others, as was common for people from all backgrounds living in the capital those days, on the ground floor of a soot-blackened building. She taught German, French and English, which I understood at a very early age to be *the* three foreign languages the cultured had at their command, and to that elite, I am glad to say, I was trained by Rose to aspire. I think that despite the expense, which had to strain her already tight budget, Rose had a master plan for me, under which French and English would follow German, once I had made a creditable start in that. But unlike many other bright Hungarian children, we never got that far. After all those childhood years of study, although apparently not study enough, I knew no more German than Russian. Now and then in later years Rose pointed a finger at that withered bloom of a teacher: maybe she had been *nicht gut*. Well, maybe so, but that's really irrelevant. The fault was actually all mine. For despite my very quick, and successful I would say, acquisition of English, I really have no aptitude for languages.

I remember that poor woman vividly, or actually I remember her not at all except for a number of still-vivid details, no more than secondary characteristics, that to me defined her thoroughly even then. There were the lace frills on her cuffs and on her collar and the lilac flowers printed on her apparently only dress, the swish of the fringes on the shawl she wrapped around her shoulders, the nearly transparent skin on her wrinkled hand, her pen and her inkwell. In my memory, but for her lack of literary gifts and youth, she can pass as one of those ever-suffering 19th-century English lady writers, like Elizabeth Barrett Browning. To me she is still the embodiment of everything prewar, which then meant a temporal dislocation of only fifteen years, but in her case seemed like a century. I wonder who she had been in the bourgeois Budapest so reviled during my boyhood. What kind of life had she had before being trampled down into the circle of hell reserved for those considered useless? Had she ever been married? Was she the sole survivor of a decimated Jewish family? Most intriguingly, how did she acquire her command of the major European languages? Might she indeed have been a governess to the children of aristocrats? But that would explain only how she had come to live off those languages not how she had come by them. Or might she have been an aristocrat herself, born into luxury and worldliness, raised in a mansion in Buda and on an estate in the countryside, who, like Nabokov, had herself learned those languages from governesses? After the war, lives like hers were wilting everywhere behind the Iron Curtain.

To me the most remarkable quality of this German teacher, and the thing about her that connected me to the banished past the most immediately, was her handwriting. Even as a boy I recognized that script as both an anachronism and a blatant, unselfconscious, infinitely stylized expression of personality. It was ornate and lyrical, but it also had a surprising strength and self-confidence. Indeed, it was a Chopinesque handwriting. It astounded me that anyone could write with so many grace-notes, as it were, and mannerisms and seemingly unnecessary details, and every time I opened my notebook I admired the beauty of that script and in my mind I heard the nib scrape along the paper. Now that I think back on that notebook and those lessons, the for me defining details of the room where she wrote out those model sentences appear in front of me, and in the lampshades, the tablecloths, the doilies upon doilies, in those lace frills and in the nightcap on her head which I must be imagining, I see everywhere the same precise and time-honored ornamentation that characterized her handwriting. That flowing cursive originated in the execrated past of which she herself was a remnant, a past whose unhistorical pastel softness, so starkly the opposite of the brutalized gray present of the early 50s, was still alive in the quaint curlicues and irrepressible flourishes of her handwriting.

The Communist propaganda machine promoted Russification and de-Westernization as if a single obsession. Everywhere you went, in everything you encountered, most especially in everything in school, the Communist and Russian aspect was highlighted, or thematized, as a literary critic might say. Indeed, Communism and anti-capitalistic animus, together, were the leitmotif of the totality of things. But with me at least, the Communist approach to persuasion, a species of carpet-bombing, you might say, backfired. Indeed, it was the thing that first set me on the road to disillusionment. For whenever something I heard at home or read about in a generally unobjectionable book contradicted a Communist claim or boast, or when surreptitiously I was steered to Western languages rather than to Russian, then all the pretenses were punctured, and the hypocrisy beneath the tirelessly affirmed Soviet-Hungarian friendship stood exposed. In the Soviet Union this would not have happened, for there the authorities exercised much greater control. In 1953, for example, after the fall of Lavrenti Beria, long the chief of the secret police, the editors of the Great Soviet Encyclopedia expunged the entry about him and replaced it with an article on the Bering Straits. By mail, all subscribers to the work were ordered under penalty of law to cut out and destroy the three affected pages and to paste into the mutilated volume the replacements enclosed in the envelope. But in Moscow the system had already been in operation for three decades. In Budapest you couldn't have gotten away with such a bare-faced falsification, at least not yet, and even a pre-teen inclined to skepticism could after a while begin to see things for what they really were.

The narrow-gauge railway in Buda built by the Pioneers in the very early years of Communism is still running. The original cars, or so they look to me, are being drawn by the original Nibelung locomotives, although the operation is still manned by an ever-renewed crew of ever-fresh-faced boys and girls. But in each car a small poster also seeks applicants for the job and the adventure, for it is promised to be both, a recruiting device not needed in my youth, when serving was an honor and a privilege awarded to the most deserving.

In 1953, as a class alien, I was not included among the handful of Pioneers from my school who would spend an unforgettable week choo-chooing through the Buda hills. But that was all right with me, indeed it was a relief. Early on I had been allowed to join the Pioneers, but tying on the red scout-style neckerchief filled me only with indifference. And working on the railroad all the live-long day I found especially unappealing. By then, I had already observed first-hand the life so frequently publicized in dementedly enthusiastic accounts of the camp, the thrills of being a conductor in the company of your worker and peasant peers, collecting tickets, blowing whistles, operating semaphores. On a dappled spring day I had even ridden that shrunk-to-fit line, sitting not far behind the soot-belching knee-high locomotive of a synthetic memory, and I had actually hoped that this fate would never befall me. Literally, the Hungarian word for pioneer means path breaker, which is why the sight of the cream-colored gravel shoring up the rail beds made me shudder as I thought of crushing large boulders into such mineral crumbs. And then, the thought of life in a tent, physical proximity to other boys while performing our daily ablutions, regimentation, the whole semi-military approach to social organization – all that repelled me too.

The message itself that the rejection carried I gave no thought to. Of course, by 1953 I already *knew* that I was different, but I really did not *feel* different. In truth, I didn't really understand social distinctions. It seems that the Communist environment that produced me not only made me hate such things but also blinded me to them. Status, yes, that I understood. I knew that the superintendent in our building stood lower than the tenants, for indeed underneath her barnyard bossiness she was servile. But the idea of social classes or strata was beyond my comprehension. It had been permanently exiled, it was hoped, to that beyond by persistent denial. Basically, I had been taught equality, and I had learned well. As for my own activities, some of which, like German and piano lessons and the bit of stamp-collecting I did and my love of books and bookishness, might have qualified as bourgeois, while others, like hanging out with the gang and playing cards sitting under a tree and playing ball and even standing around making believe I was making time with this girl or that, had to be considered proletarian – my own activities I myself couldn't have dichotomized so. I did not feel like the member of either a socially superior or a socially inferior group.

I don't recall how I was informed of the railroad rebuff, but Mrs. Gaál must have been involved in the episode, as she was in so much else during that ever-closer-to-adolescence life of mine. She was only 28, still quite a young woman from every point of view but a schoolboy's, when already my teacher for three years. I can still see her in my mind's eye, standing with her back to the wall with the big windows, the light coming from behind, a slight shadow veiling her face. Word of her age is just spreading through the classroom like the sea rising into a tidal pool. There were about twenty-five of us boys in the class. We were twelve years old and burning with curiosity about the flesh-and-blood person and private life of this backlit woman, with whom we had daily contact but who was not at all like our mothers. For a while we all had a crush on her, all except the handful, that is – poor inarticulate beasts – who couldn't stop fearing her just because she was a teacher. She was hardly attractive – plumpish, undainty, with a fleshy nose and even a few pock-marks – but we didn't know any better and wouldn't have credited a dispassionate description of her even if it had come with biblical credentials. She taught us Hungarian literature and grammar, as I've said already, and taught us very well, and also Russian language, and she was our homeroom teacher for six years. We spent at least two, and often three, hours with her, six days a week, five years of ten months each. From age eight to age fourteen.

I myself had a full-blown case of that infatuation before I was quite thirteen. Somehow I learned that Mrs. Gaál and her husband, who was rumored to be a cook in a restaurant, or maybe actually a chef and I just didn't yet understand the distinction, having had no experience whatsoever with restaurants – I learned that they lived in a building not unlike ours near my piano teacher's apartment. After the next lesson I rushed out and over to Mrs. Gaál's building, where I peered around the corner before strolling to the front door and quickly locating the husband's name next to one of the buzzers. I tried to picture this unseen-unknown man in the white tunic of his profession and considered what hours he might work, the very thing you would do if you wanted the man's wife all to yourself for a while, which is indeed what I wanted, although to what end I couldn't have said. Through the following months I loitered about that building as often as I could, like Swann skulking outside Odette's house, hoping and fearing to run into her. On my first trip back to Budapest in 2002, I visited the old school and asked about her, but the name wasn't familiar to anyone. I also retraced my route from piano teacher's to homeroom teacher's, but that also could not rekindle any of my memories, and the strip of paper with the name I had once so anxiously scanned the bells for had of course been replaced during the intervening half-century.

As our homeroom teacher, Mrs. Gaál was the keeper of the roll book, the magazine-size flexible-covered repository of vital data and grades for each student in the class. The book stayed in the classroom all day, passing from the hands of one teacher to those of another as they came in to teach a period and left after having done so, but otherwise it was always in her strict care. It was a confidential document, and many precautions were taken not to expose it to student eyes. And yet on two occasions Mrs. Gaál left it open when I was standing by her desk and didn't close it even after she saw my gaze dropping to it and especially to the bottom third of its open pages, where it found my own records.

I saw letters and numbers entered in a grid, but my attention was immediately drawn, as it was clearly meant to be, to the middle of a particularly dense area on the left-hand page where a single oversized capital E occupied a large square. Like a clearing in the forest with a single house standing in it. Our grades were in numbers, not letters, so what could this mean? With a rapid glance, my heart beating fast, I determined that the two classmates with whom I shared those pages each had an oversized capital M near *his* name. So how was I different from them? It was not until after the second occasion, when I confirmed my observations, that somehow I found the solution to that cryptogram for stolen glances.

M, P and E, the three possible entries, stood for *munkás, paraszt* and *egyéb*, the Hungarian words for worker, peasant and other, that is, the social class designations of the students. My classmates were the sons of Workers, I the son of Others. In other words, I was a class alien. And of all things about me, this status spoke with the loudest voice and attracted my teachers' attention first. Unlike the chilly reception from the railroad, which I had handled with a mental shrug, this bothered me. In one part it was the rude labeling itself that rankled; in another it was being so summarily defined. For I was what that E declared me to be, no doubt about it. I was identified for good, and for all to see. Now, mind you, this was not the first tag stuck on me. For years then already I had been a Jewish boy, but somehow that was just my fate. For years also I had been a Hungarian boy, an identity that manifested itself mostly in my ardor for the national soccer team, which happened to be the best in the world for a year or so in 1952-53, and that was something to be proud of only. Indeed, for some time already I had even been a class alien, but until I confronted the objective reality of that E, I did not actually take possession of that shaming-blaming identity. But now, clearly, this was me. Oh, I was dazed and confused when I put this together as much as I could at that age. This was not right. Disillusionment was rising within me as if I'd eaten some spoiled food. And as the gradual recognition of the unfairness of the Soviets to Hungarians had been the first phase of my disillusionment, so the gradual recognition of the inhumanity and brutality of the *whole* system became its second phase.

A year or so after my sneak-peek, when it was already time to plan for life after primary school, Rose and I had a parent-teacher conference with Mrs. Gaál. I of course had very good grades and had nothing to worry about in terms of being admitted to a *gymnasium,* as some others did. For though the Communists had done much, and rightly, to make secondary academic education, as opposed to technical education, less exclusive than it had been before the war, all the *gymnasia* were still highly selective, and only a very small minority of eighth-graders went on to one of these places of *serious* learning. And indeed, Mrs. Gaál said that obviously I should be applying to the well-regarded institution near our home, and Rose had been very pleased. But then Mrs. Gaál went on to voice some concern because the application would be from a son of class aliens, and then Rose was crushed. And I was too.

Now I was truly in the ditch, in the clutches of the historical. For absolutely nothing about this looming injustice was personal. The Communists, or the equivalent, let's say, of the admissions committee at that *gymnasium,* could have had nothing against *me* personally. If anything, I was well disposed to their plans and projects. I was all for a socialist Hungary. But that of course was irrelevant. As they understood things, there was a class war going on. And just because in Hungary the bad guys had already been mostly eliminated or defanged like Leslie, and because you had the ferocious support of the Soviet big brother to the east, you could not relax. For the confrontation was global. As long as there was a single capitalist left on the planet, the proletariat could not rest. What after all was the Cold War if not the world-wide offensive of international imperialists trying to beat back the workers and peasants wherever they had finally claimed their rights? What was it if not a fight to the death between the classes, an effort on one side to hobble the inevitable march of history, and an effort on the other to embody it? Under these circumstances, me and my ilk were a potential fifth column that could not be tolerated. And among the methods used to neutralize us was the dis-affirmative action threatening me.

Back then, at age thirteen, I already understood the uncertainty of my immediate future as a curtailment of my freedom. Yes, I accepted being an outsider, and may even have already felt that I could never be anything else, but I wanted my outsider status and feelings to be *tolerated*. I neither harm anyone nor oppose the ways favored by those on the inside. So if I want to be solitary, let me be so. If I want to be different, call me weird if you must, but let me be so anyway! The insistence on this freedom welled up in me and to this day it doesn't seem to have subsided entirely. That insistence came with me to America, and in fact America seemed so right to me right away exactly because it offered me and most everyone else too just this freedom. It let me be who and what I wanted to be, with the proviso, naturally, that the kind of life you choose, the extent to which you do or do not conform, could exact the very price you were warned about already back when you were making your choice. That was America then, although it is not that anymore, not really. Your heart breaks today just thinking about the daily attacks on tolerance being made in this country.

What would have happened to me had I not been admitted to *gymnasium*? I don't recall the subject ever being discussed. Were Leslie and Rose in a funk, Rose especially? What were they thinking? Maybe I would have been able to attend one of the many technical schools newly established by the Communists, which prepared students for management or desk jobs in industry, unlike the *gymnasia*, which prepared you for the university. Or maybe I would have had to choose a trade or a skill, to learn to bake bread, or to do carpentry or make machine tools. To think that at age fourteen I might have had no other option but to get a factory job would be far-fetched, but even that might have happened. I can't imagine myself in overalls with grease stains, but were it not for America, *that* might indeed have been my future. Now, mind you, these are all honorable occupations. But, obviously, they hardly jibe with what I now know to have been my inclinations and as-it-were talents. And yet, as a historian, I can't even say that any of that would have been a terrible injustice. Choosing one's own path as a working person, rather, that is, than inheriting it, is a modern luxury available only in select parts of the world. Leslie was a shoemaker, and his father had been a shoemaker too. So what right did I have, a class alien no less, to want to be a chemical engineer?

But the possibility of not being admitted to *gymnasium* whipped up a storm of feelings inside me. For reasons that all by themselves would require a complex historical analysis to spell out – for whatever reasons, I expected more. And so, I felt as if I were bound with ropes or in a sort of straightjacket. I felt coerced and restrained. I was being penalized for being an outsider, prevented from being and becoming what I wanted to be. This, more than any other, was the decisive moment of my disillusionment with Communism. For everybody was *not* friends after all, and now I was damning those who desired to hold me down. Damn Comrade Stalin, though that might already have been a *fait accompli*, and damn Comrade Rákosi too! The myth of the Great Leader had burned off like a morning fog, the system stood exposed, the mask of charming ideals – the beauty of fraternity, the justice and comfort of equality – was finally ripped off the hideous face of Communism. Although the ideals themselves survived. To this day they continue to thrive within me, even while they keep searching everywhere for their worldly realization.

Part II

CHAPTER 3

The Revolution Won

YOU MAY NOT REMEMBER THAT much about the Cold War anymore, especially not its early years, not much anyway beyond the permanent battle-readiness that gave it its name, and maybe the infamous Iron Curtain, which descended across the continent in 1946, as Churchill said, and split Europe in two like a watermelon. So let me remind you that on the eastern side of this line of barbed-wire, searchlights, mine-fields and machine-gunners lay a north-south tier of countries, the so-called Soviet satellites, and to *their* east sprawled the Soviet Union itself. The satellites, all of them in the grip of Communism and the Soviet military bear hug, were Poland, East Germany, Czechoslovakia, Hungary, Romania, Yugoslavia, Bulgaria and Albania. On the Iron Curtain's western side lay all of Western Europe. During the 1950s and beyond, the countries to the left and right of this armored frontier formed two hostile camps. Their snarling, tough-guy face-off was the world-historical context of the revolution.

1956 promised to be a momentous year, a great year even for Communism. Stalin had died in 1953, and that allowed the Communist world to take a deep breath and shake off Uncle Joe's spell. In the Soviet Union *de-Stalinization* quickly became semi-official policy and a reform faction even emerged within the leadership. Then in February 1956, in a four-hour rant to a shell-shocked party congress, First Secretary and Premier Nikita Khrushchev, the Soviet leader, famously denounced Stalin and catalogued his misdeeds. Obviously, this was an invitation for the satellites to follow suit, and several of them attempted to. They did so despite the risks that had to come with any loosening of bonds, and despite the obstacles that stood in the way of any lessening of burdens. The time seemed to have arrived for a gentler, kinder Communism.

During the summer, with prodding from a writer's group and the intelligentsia – for in a country without freedom of expression writers can actually be the nation's conscience – liberal elements in the Hungarian leadership were already pushing for a political showdown. Then in early October reformist and anti-Soviet agitation erupted in Poland and quickly managed to wring major concessions from the Kremlin. Emboldened by this example, on October 22nd several thousand students from the Hungarian capital and beyond gathered in the great hall of Budapest Technical University. They came to show their solidarity with the "Polish freedom movement," a legitimate enough cause, the only kind you could hope to get away with of course, and not just a pretext either. But ever since words could travel, resistance to oppression has been contagious, and quickly the feelings of sympathy, support and encouragement for events beyond the country's borders unleashed pent-up emotions about *domestic* matters too.

According to some, Hungary is unique among nations in that its anthem is not the usual hymn of victory but a dirge rather. The claim about Hungarian uniqueness I can't assess, but one hearing is all you need to verify the anthem's reputation. The melody is beautiful but also melancholy and mournful, and the words pray for God's blessing, for abundance and good cheer, and for an end to the historical *misfortunes* of the Magyar people. Amen. Under the Communists, the singing of this anthem and even the flying of the red-white-and-green instead of the red flag of Communism were forbidden. These were considered nationalist acts, and so affronts to the mandatory internationalist spirit that served to whitewash Soviet imperialism. But building from a single plaintive voice to a collective murmur to a defiant chorus, the students in the great hall intoned the anthem anyway, and soon their emotion-soaked words opened the floodgates, and then they were also standing up to be heard and speechifying about taboo subjects, and then they were actually calling out ideas for a set of demands to be presented to the government – what soon became the Sixteen Points – and then even clamoring to have the list of demands broadcast over the state radio station. Momentum was building as each transgression begot the next, as each act of derring-do dwarfed the preceding one, until word of the radio-censors' objections to the broadcast sparked the most audacious idea yet: a demonstration to take place the following day.

The Sixteen Points is a remarkable document. It is ideologically sophisticated, although it is the handiwork of a collective no more conversant with modern political theory than you or I. It anatomizes the oppression that ignited the crisis and itemizes the objectives that plotted its course. It is nothing less than a comprehensive indictment of the regime *and* the revolution's manifesto. In sixteen short paragraphs, which set forth about thirty demands, depending on exactly how you count, the document strips the system's greatest evils of their window-dressing. Reading it, you truly appreciate, as if for the first time since the civil rights movement of the 50s and 60s, our own First-Amendment right to petition the government for a redress of grievances.

The first demand is for "immediate withdrawal of all Soviet troops from Hungary." No pussyfooting for the students in the great hall. Then the Sixteen Points goes on to demand a number of, first, political and then economic reforms. On the political side, there are demands for democracy and for the standard elements of the social contract as it is known in liberal Western societies, including free elections open to *all* parties, release and rehabilitation of political prisoners, and freedom of opinion, speech and the press. There is also, coming at things from a different angle, a demand for Imre Nagy to be appointed, or rather reappointed, prime minister. Nagy, the leader of the reform faction of the Party, had been prime minister from June 1953 (just four months after the Man of Steel was fitted for his not quite sufficiently rust-proof mausoleum) to January 1955. He was an obvious choice for the students, and the demand for *him* emphasizes the moderate mood of these pre-dawn hours of the revolution. Whether he was also a *wise* choice... well, that question was to exercise many cast-members of the upcoming 13-day drama until the very end. But, in any case, there was no one else.

The economic demands are the most intriguing of all because tacitly at least they are socialist. The hammer and sickle still informs them, but only as a social principle now rather than as a war cry. And so, the manifesto mounts a vigorous defense of the economic interests and labor conditions of workers and peasants, but it does so in a spirit of obviously-right egalitarianism, not with the now-it's-our-turn animus that is so natural for Marxist terminology to fall into. Published reminiscences confirm this ideological bent. One insurgent says that the students didn't want to "exchange the communist zoo for the capitalist jungle." Another recalls that "in Hungary in 1956 we wanted to turn the Communist socialist system into a genuinely socialist one." Of course, Martin Luther himself might have said something very much along these lines if asked to summarize his 95 theses, and you know that *they* drove history right off the rails. But never mind that. Luther really was a pious Christian, and the students really were attached to a system under which economic justice is achieved through public ownership of the means of production.

This shouldn't shock you. You know that even today the routine American revulsion to socialism is not shared by many Western Europeans. And back then socialist sentiments were even more powerful, much much more powerful throughout the world than they are now, the vastly multiplied ills and bleaker prospects of contemporary capitalism notwithstanding. In the Soviet bloc itself, the Communists' unrelenting condemnation of private interests, bourgeois values and class distinctions had not been in vain, although so-called progressive ideas would have thrived even without that. In general, the 50s was still a very good time for idealism. Heaven on earth, in one secular guise or another, was widely seen to be drawing near, and schemes of wholesale human improvement attracted millions of followers. To many, socialism was a utopia and a paradise, and who can blame them? Just compare it to the alternatives. And even if the champions of socialism did perceive flaws in actual socialist practice, in their fervor they were firmly convinced of the unassailable virtue and ultimate triumph of their ideals.

Of course, back then the market hadn't yet asserted its dominance over collective life, as it has now, alas, and Communism hadn't yet shown itself a hopelessly foolish investment. In 1956 it was not yet possible to perceive that none of the few ways to set up the basic economic arrangements of society, including ownership of enterprises by their workers, could achieve its own direct goals and also respect the requirements of fairness and justice. In that naïve age, there was not yet, to begin with, enough historical experience regarding the matter, and the planet was also still believed to be an inexhaustible resource for humanity. Innocences now forever lost! So ideological commitment to socialism, as opposed to doubt or total skepticism or even downright hostility, was common back then. This is why the Sixteen Points could continue to embrace socialism and things dear to socialists, why, for example, it could call for economic planning by experts rather than ideologues, instead of just demanding a return to a system of free enterprise.

But socialist or not, all the events of the evening of the 22nd – the assembly in the great hall, the Sixteen Points, the scheduling of the demonstration – were utterly extraordinary. After all, this was a country where the Party absolutely controlled public events and indeed had a stranglehold on public life. Not that Hungary didn't also have a government. It did. But in reality all power was concentrated in the Hungarian Workers' Party, as the Communist command structure and organization of the times called itself, and, more particularly, in the Central Committee of the Party and in that Committee's leaders, in turn organized as the Political Committee, or the Politburo. To their credit, these leaders had no illusions about the situation. They recognized the spontaneous mass action as a crisis, a dangerous crisis even, and a *challenge* to their authority. But even on the question of whether or not to allow the demonstration, the Politburo was divided and deadlocked from the first. The hard-liners, including First Secretary Ernő Gerő, proposed to have the security forces fire on anyone who demonstrated, while the reformers insisted that Nagy *should* be brought back into the government. And Moscow was no help. On this matter, even the Soviet equivalent of the Hungarian Politburo, the Presidium of the Central Committee of the Communist Party of the Soviet Union, could not reach a consensus. So it just sent to Budapest two of its own members, Anastas Mikoyan and Mikhail Suslov, to be its eyes and its ears on site, to advise the local leaders and to direct the response to the flare-up.

October 23, 1956

As a place of human habitation Budapest is quite ancient. It's a natural crossing point just where the right-turning river escapes from the shelter of the hills and rushes into the plain, an inviting spot for a settlement. Already in the 1ˢᵗ century AD the Romans built a fort at Aquincum, in the northern part of present-day Buda, the ruins of which I remember visiting on a field trip one gray day in 3ʳᵈ or 4ᵗʰ grade. But today's Budapest is really a 19ᵗʰ-century city. Its gracious plan, wide avenues and many tree-lined streets go back only that far, including the grand boulevard called the Ring, which girds the oval core of the city with a strip of traffic and trees, and which you might therefore guess to be the paved track of the original city walls. Well, you'd be guessing wrong. The main thorough-fares of the central part of Buda follow the contours of the hills. And in Pest, where most of the 1956 population of nearly a million and a half lived, the urban layout is just geometrical, and very pleasantly so. Six spokes radiate out of the eastern half of the Ring-drawn oval, slicing all of Pest outside the grand boulevard into five sections, like half a pie cut into five slices. The Margit Bridge spans the river at the northern Ring crossing, the Petőfi Bridge at the southern. And in between there are three additional bridges. Altogether, the five bridges strike you as a marvelous thing. As if the city were holding the river in its arms. It is here in the center, in that oval, that the uprising began.

All local universities having been alerted, in the early afternoon of October 23ʳᵈ large numbers of students gathered on the grounds of the

Technical University in Buda and on Petőfi Square in Pest. At 3 o'clock they began to march northward in formation along each side of the river. They had a rendezvous in Buda at the statue of General Bem, a Polish hero, who had fought against the Austrians and the *Russians* in the Magyar War of Independence of 1848-49. So there was a *double* Polish message in the choice of the meeting place, which the Communists, themselves prodigious symbol-mongers, could not possibly miss. The columns of marchers were orderly and silent – remember, back then, before the 60s, even in America public life still benefited and suffered from an old-fashioned formality – expressing their sentiments only on the equally sedate signs they were carrying. LONG LIVE THE SOCIALIST DEMOCRATIC STRUGGLE OF THE POLISH UNIVERSITY YOUTH should give you an idea. But along the way "an ocean of people [first] followed," then joined each group, as a participant recalled, and with that the demonstration began to buzz. "A tormented and humiliated nation was stirring in front of my eyes. People were straightening their backs. They were regaining their self-respect…. It was a good, a proud feeling to be Hungarian that day."

At some point, the marchers on the Buda side observed a woman leaning out of an upstairs window, waving the national flag. It was not the first such sight, for by now onlookers and flags lined the route, but, oh! this flag was different, for this woman had had an ingenious, nigh-poetic idea: she had cut out the Communist emblem from the flag's center, look, look! you could see the ragged edges where the scissors had done their circum-snipping lap, and suddenly there it was, the national colors pregnant with *negative* meaning, perhaps the most widely recognized symbol of the revolution – red, white and green with a hole in the middle. At the sight of this fluttering eloquence a collective cheer went up from the crowd like a thousand-gun salute and then seemed to reverberate in the throats of successive waves of marchers with a self-sustaining echo.

Soon the demonstrators reached Bem Square, but after a brief ceremony there they all crossed the river by the Margit Bridge, and once in Pest, the site of most official buildings and the true focus of national life, they split into three groups. The streams of people were ever swelling, as if always more of the city's secret life-blood were being fed from side streets and capillaries into the arterial system defined by the marchers. Each group had its own destination of course, but I'm sure they were executing something like a master plan, for the tri-vergence was a stroke of mass-mobilizing genius. From here on three concurrent protests were being staged in Pest not only one, three very different but related and beautifully complementary protests. The locations in question were also appropriately and well chosen, not far distant from each other but also not clustering together. And even if the three events managed, even by late evening, to be only variously revolutionary, their concurrence in time gathered in the whole city and indeed the whole day as if under one all-inclusive revolutionary mantle.

The Parliament building in the Vth district in Pest is an immense late-19th-century neo-Gothic fantasy. One glance is enough to tell you that it is an object of great municipal pride and, more than that even, a national treasure. The structure spreads its ample skirts along the riverbank in a central location and confers on Pest a dignity that neither the hills of Buda nor the royal castle that crowns them dares challenge. Behind the crinolined dowager, and completing the rectangular plot of ground on which she sits, is Kossuth Square. The stone- and asphalt-paved portion of the square immediately behind the building is not just space open to the public, as you might say in New York about a so-called vest-pocket park, but space set aside for, indeed consecrated to, great public events and nothing *but* great public events, a national meeting place, a site for festivities, a giant stage for open-air celebrations. It is to Kossuth Square that one burgeoning contingent from Bem Square, now a lively procession, marched. They began arriving at about 5 o'clock, just as it was getting dark, so that two hundred thousand or so of them were assembled there by six. And they were all clamoring for Nagy.

Around the same time, another contingent of similar size arrived in the XIVth district, at a spot beyond the Ring and near City Park. These people were driven there by an idol-smashing urge, for they had come to topple a 25-foot-high statue of Stalin that loomed up alongside a major avenue just a piece down from Heroes' Square, which, by the way, is the other true public space in Budapest, a large, stately, decoratively-paved area, with two crescent-shaped colonnades along one of its sides, where, carved in stone, the larger-than-life figures of the nation's past stand on plinths between pairs of columns. As you can imagine, this crowd was not made up of urban beautification enthusiasts, although such people might also have undertaken the mission. Rather, these were just ordinary men and women ready to exercise self-help, as we lawyers say, in the effort to realize one of the Sixteen Points' demands: "that the statue of Stalin, symbol of Stalinist tyranny and political oppression, be removed as quickly as possible."

I remember that colossus well. There had never been, I would think, another one like it in Hungary. Nothing ever quite so offensively over-sized, and that's no small achievement in a country that had long enjoyed gorging itself on late-19th-century monumental excess. The black metal giant, clad in the usual military tunic, breeches and seven-verst boots, stood on a pedestal of pinkish stone, which itself, in a kind of ziggurat-figuration, rose from a reviewing stand that was wide enough for fifty, sixty dignitaries and was ornamented with brawny workers and peasants in three-quarters relief, which in turn sat atop a base you had to climb by what on a photograph appears to have been twelve steps. The composite structure, erected in 1951, reached an unabashed height of about fifty feet. From his Olympian vantage the Great Leader commanded all that could be seen or imagined. From his solitary eminence, Stalin disdained the residents of Heroes' Square and, like Zeus with his thunderbolts, hurled his favorite Marxist deprecation at them: You are all *history*!

The third group of demonstrators from Bem Square marched to the Radio building, a warren-like building in the VIIIth district just outside the Ring but inside an enclosure that with its walls and heavy front gate kept you at a respectful distance. Their objective, indeed the original objective of the entire demonstration, was to have the Sixteen Points broadcast. But the authorities continued to resist. They were not about to relinquish their monopoly of what today would be called the media, and certainly not for such an armed missile of a purpose. For even if the demands didn't explicitly word-paint the regime as it really was rather than as it claimed and thought itself to be, never mind as it appeared to be or thought itself to appear to be, the demands did make it *impossible* for anyone who heard them to keep ignoring the truth about a lot of Communist practices. So broadcasting the document was out of the question. Except that *not* broadcasting it was also likely to have consequences enough to choke on. In other words, it was another tricky call, quite a lot like allowing the demonstration to proceed or not had been.

But, let's face it, tricky calls it would be repeatedly for the authorities right to the end of the revolution. So it *had* to be by the nature of the situation, by the lopsidedly uneven match. The regime could have just crushed the bastards of course, just about any time, that would have been relatively easy, even if a few square miles of Eastern European urban splendor would also have had to go. But would that have been the right thing to do? And I mean right not in terms of fairness and justice, for this was no mere thought experiment for ethicists, but in terms rather of self-interest, that is, the interest of the Party, of world revolution, of the historical mission of Marxism-Leninism. For even if the vanguard of the proletariat did have a mandate, that mandate had to have limits. Although the groping about by the regime during the preceding twelve hours suggested that nobody had as yet located those limits with any certainty.

Nagy knew that the demonstrators on Kossuth Square were calling for him, but, obedient party-man that he was, he waited for a go-ahead from the leadership before allowing himself to be driven to the Parliament building. So it was about 9 o'clock by the time he finally stepped up to an open 2nd-story window, ready to address the dense crowd. In his hands the text of a short speech he had prepared, which the colleagues in the loyal opposition with him had earlier in the evening condemned as completely unresponsive to the enthusiasm sweeping about the square like a March breeze, maybe the very breeze that, as everyone assembled was likely thinking, had carried to Pest the spirit of revolution on March 15, 1848. "Comrades!" Nagy finally called out, but that word all by itself both discredited the speaker and alienated the listeners. Literally, the Hungarian word for "comrades" means "brothers-in-principle," so it was "we're not *bro*thers-in-principle," "we're not your *bro*thers-in-principle," and other such bitter and disappointed phrases that were fired at him like arrows from the pavement. But Nagy was so impeccably Communist that, undeterred by the reaction, he just went on and quickly demonstrated that he had nothing to offer, nothing, that is, but the dog-eared reforms of his prior premiership.

The crowd's spirit sagged, as if the breeze itself had been trapped. Only a few continued to press the matter. "All of Budapest is here! The nation is here!" single voices only called out now. Maybe it was not yet too late. He *must* rise to the occasion. But Nagy didn't. He couldn't. Those close enough could see that he was bewildered. He could not relate to the citizenry at large engaged in political action and assembled as a crowd no less. Something so familiar to Americans, or to my generation, the Vietnam generation anyway, this statesman and party leader found incomprehensible. It was a force he could not assess or connect with. So he just proceeded with words that died on his lips, urging the demonstrators to be level-headed and maintain a responsible attitude. The crowd was deflated. This was not the leader it had come here to find and claim. Nagy now finished with a few more words, then asked the demonstrators to sing the national anthem and go home. And so they sang and then began to turn around and drift away, confused and, for the moment at least, bereft of purpose. The embers of freedom they were trying to revive had failed to burst into flame. Maybe the authorities had just panicked? Well, just hold on!

For the group by City Park did much better, even though bringing down the metal giant quickly proved to be no easy feat. The approach most readily available was apparently not up to the task. Daredevils sporting coils of rope scaled giraffe-necked ladders propped against the monument, then tried to scale the bronze colossus itself, while

Carpathian cowboys tried to lasso its head. But to no avail. When the trucks to which the ropes were tied engaged their gears, the ropes snapped like so many threads. It took some time before the right men and the proper equipment could be enlisted in the effort, but already before Nagy arrived at the Parliament building someone with a blow-torch had started severing the statue at the top of the boots, and then steel cables and chains took the place of the hapless ropes, and then the trucks did manage first to rip off the huge head and bring it crashing down to the podium – it must have taken at least one small resound-ing bounce – and then to pull down the decapitated body right into the large open space in front of it. Miraculously, the hurtling tons of bronze hurt no one. Sándor Kopácsi, then chief of the city's police and for years after a political prisoner, reports in his memoirs that his men had been instructed not to interfere with this crowd, and they didn't. The work appears to have started at about 6 o'clock and thanks to good old Hungarian know-how was done at 9:37 PM, just about the time Nagy was dismissing the multitude looking up at him. Only the Ozymandias-like boots were left standing.

After toppling the statue, the crowd, on the count of three! pushed the giant head with the heavy chain wound about its base onto a truck, hauled it down Rákoczi Road and dumped it in Lujza Blaha Square, where it could be and was mocked and derided by all. And mockers there were aplenty, for word of the job-well-done quickly spread. Still, here too nothing was ignited, even though much of what was done was incendiary. And, no, strictly speaking this also was not yet a revolution. But the Magyars did proceed vigorously, deriving great satisfaction from de-Stalinizing by defacing. In a contemporary account of the revolution, a British journalist relates that "a youngster found a street sign in a nearby road that was under repair, and tied it round the head. It read, 'Dead End.'" One photograph shows the head disfigured only with the letters WC, and several others with a stop-sign affixed to it. But dead-end sign or stop-sign hardly matters. Either way the thing to notice here is the national sense of humor, which Hungarians are proud of. And well they should be. For if there's any salvation for a small country wedged into a crack between aggressive, hulking neighbors, that is it.

That much-despised figure had stood quite close to the outdoor rink where I loved to ice skate, so I had walked by it many times. And then after the revolution I did one more turn, right along the podium and the pedestal from which nothing towered anymore, not even those giant boots, photographs of which now remind me of Santa's chocolate footwear sold at Christmas. They, or their remains, were prized off and removed on November 16th. On that last occasion I had been drawn to that spot by rumors that in the days following the toppling the public had hacked to pieces the downed statue and all that had remained vertical of it. With crowbars, hammers, acetylene torches, pliers and whatever else worked, the Magyars had reduced it all to souvenir-size bits of metal you could own, sell or just give away, and I had wanted one. An ashtray or a paperweight or maybe a scrap-metal pin, like the one given to New York Congressman Kenneth Keating in 1957, when the American-Hungarian Federation honored him for his work on behalf of refugees. So on hearing of this traffic, I had hustled over to the place I figured most likely to attract it. But the place was deserted, and the bronze carcass, or most of it anyway, had already been carried off by the *ad hoc* metalworkers. I had to return home empty-handed, although not really disappointed. For, in truth, the whole excursion had been only an empty boast, as it were, and even that only to myself. Even if something *had* been on offer, I had had neither the money nor the nerve needed to consummate a transaction.

While the de-Stalinizers were working near City Park, the tension in front of the Radio building kept rising. The director, a tough woman comrade, had first invited in a delegation of students and then seemed not to be allowing them back out to the street. She also tried to fake a broadcast of the Sixteen Points from a mobile unit that had driven up to the front entrance, when in fact the radio was playing only standard Hungarian fiddle-fare. When the hoax was exposed, the demonstrators' frustration grew. Then at 8 o'clock, just about the time the blowtorch surgery got under way in the XIVth district, First Secretary Gerő barked out an angry, name-calling speech on the radio, condemning the students' patriotic fervor as chauvinism and subversion, and threatening reprisals. And that finally did it. Those words were intolerable, and now the crowd exploded!

Bricks and stones flew at the windows of the director's 2nd-floor office, and the hoax-van was repeatedly backed into the sturdy wooden gate. From higher up in the building the ÁVO responded. First it was just volleys of blanks, but then around 9 o'clock came a tear-gas canister that through some freak accident actually killed a student. The situation was becoming desperate. And now the shadows on the roof reloaded with live ammunition, or so you had to figure down below because, bam! bam!, now there were other bodies on the ground too and people were staggering and bleeding and screaming at the murderers above. This could be a massacre, a tragedy, people gasped with rage, they're going to mow us down. And, oh my God! now the gate finally gave way, and young men surged over the splintered boards and like targets in a videogame rushed into the sights of the guns. All caution had vanished. But just at that moment, the killers tried to bring in reinforcements, an ambulance carrying an ÁVO troop dressed as Red Cross personnel, but the crowd saw through the ruse right away – there goes that scum! after them! – chased the new arrivals into the building and swooped down on the vehicle. The doors they practically ripped off the hinges, and inside, stacked high, they found weapons. Weapons and ammunition!!!

And with that, as if with the snap of the finger of some great magician of history, and as if seconded by the clang of the metal head on stone across town, the demonstrators turned into insurgents. Their passion for freedom shot up in flames. Now *they* attacked. Crouching figures scurried between parked cars and trucks, leaping up here and there to blast an upper floor, crawling into position all about the building, firing a round then running a few meters through pale light and shadow, then smashing in a door with the butt of a rifle. Suddenly the enemy was besieged in its stronghold, from which radio operations and personnel had already been evacuated. An army unit with tank support drove up

as further reinforcements, but combat-readiness quickly turned to cama-
raderie, for when the soldiers saw what was happening, they refused to
follow orders and even handed their weapons to the insurgents. Or they
joined them. Workers from a suburban arms factory were also arriving
in trucks full of weapons and ammunition, to supply the insurgents and
to use them themselves. So with both sides well armed, a gun battle ensued. A clash to the death of heroes and villains! There were casualties
on both sides, with uniformed bodies lying about in twisted lumps, and
others too in civilian garb. Here and there blood glistened. But well
after the demonstrators had already scattered from Kossuth Square and
the wild cheers greeting the Man of Steel's crash-dive had subsided, the
people succeeded in wresting the now useless radio premises from the
hands of the secret police. After a slow and resolute struggle of some six
hours, punctuated by stretches of tense quiet, the shots became sporadic
and the last few ÁVO-men escaped through the rear of the shot-up, pock-
marked, ruin-fronted building. At 3 o'clock in the morning the insurgents could finally rest.

So on October 23, 1956, the people rose up against their rulers.
What an epic evening! What an electrifying event! A rhapsody of justice, liberty and brotherhood! From a historical perspective, it was also
the right and proper beginning, indeed the necessary beginning for
a revolution. Never mind the Scientific Revolution or the Industrial
Revolution or even that blessed unbuttoning, the sexual revolution of
the 1960s. Phenomena like that claim the name only metaphorically,
and only by exaggerating their actual likeness to the real thing, which is
what *this* was. And even that is not all, for taken together the events at
the three revolutionary sites were also the right beginning for a war of
independence, which has not been an uncommon sequel to uprisings.
Hungarians had played that little prelude and fugue in 1848-49, as had
the settlers of the thirteen colonies during the late 18th century. So,
indisputably, it was history happening in Budapest, as everybody was beginning to realize, the hard-liners, the reformers and the incredulously
adrenalin-addled insurgents.

October 24, 1956

The moment battle was joined at the Radio building, Gerő understood the situation clearly and had a vocabulary sclerotic with dogma to express it. And so the demonstrators he identified as a mob, its members he called fascists, the demand for withdrawal of Soviet forces he derided as chauvinism, and the whole of what could well have been a democratic movement he condemned as *counterrevolution*. For him, this is what all these phenomena *had* to be because they threatened the Communists' position and policies, and because only such forces under such circumstances could present such a threat.

The Central Committee met in emergency session at 11:00 PM and sat until dawn. But it did not accomplish much. Nagy was elected prime minister and also a member of the Politburo and of the Central Committee itself, but this was hardly a concession to the revolutionary agenda. After all, Gerő, the "soulless, Stalinist technocrat," was staying on as first secretary, and, in any case, with regard to the crisis the two men saw eye to eye. They both subscribed to the fascist counterrevolution interpretation and concurred that things had to be handled in the firmest possible way. Even before the meeting, Gerő and Khrushchev had spoken on the telephone. Initially, they had misgivings about armed Soviet intervention, but as the disturbances intensified, the need for it became always clearer to them both. Finally, Khrushchev gave the authorization, but he acted more on his own assessment of the crisis than in response to the Mayday from Budapest.

Two mechanized divisions were stationed at Székesfehérvár, in those days no more than four hours from Budapest as the tank flies. They were promptly dispatched and reached Buda at 3:00 AM the morning of the 24th. And soon thousands of additional forces from mechanized divisions in Romania and Soviet Ukraine were also deployed to the capital, to a few other Hungarian cities and along the Austrian border. All in all, 31,500 troops, mostly infantrymen armed with AK-47s for the first test in actual battle of the famed Kalashnikov, the best assault rifle of them all, and also more than eleven hundred tanks, many other mobile armored weapons and about 300 fighter planes and bombers. Typical Red Army overkill, for sure, but of course this was an invasion, and as an invasion it was received. As soon as the tanks reached the capital, and especially after they crossed the river by the Margit Bridge, just like the demonstrators had less than twelve hours earlier, they came under intermittent gunfire. And then it didn't take long before the insurgents got their hands on some of those AK-47s too.

The students and workers had already set about arming themselves when the fighting broke out at the Radio building. They had rushed into police stations, army barracks and the arms factory on Csepel Island on the southern edge of the city, and they had demanded access to stores of machine guns, grenades, rifles, pistols and other munitions. Whatever larger weapons, such as anti-tank guns, they managed to get, like the AK-47s too, they had to wrest from the Russian soldiers suddenly all about, some in skirmishes, others by luring the Russians into narrow streets and then outwitting them. They also secured trucks and sources of fuel, and occupied strategic locations, like the Eastern Railroad Station. Then, by whatever means presented themselves, they barricaded squares and intersections, and built obstacles that would force the enemy to detour into traps.

Early in the morning the insurgents began in earnest to fight the Joseph Stalins, as the mechanized monsters were known! You can see one of those 1956-vintage Soviet death-machines up close anytime you want to, right inside a post-Communist museum in Budapest called the House of Terror. It's on the ground floor. Parked on the parquet. Almost as a reflex, you want to jump back even just imagining a thing like that bearing down on you. But not the insurgents. They were guys toughened by life and convinced that for once the country's interests and their own jibed. And by instinct they turned out to be urban guerilla fighters. They looked on these evil contraptions as no more than a rolling force that with the use of hit-and-run tactics and their knowledge of local conditions they could confront, outmaneuver and incapacitate. And so they did. They attacked from several angles and let the Molotov cocktails fly. They covered a portion of a road with silk, poured soapy water over it, and so caused the grinding behemoths to slip and slide and crash into each other. They placed bricks across a road with planks over them, and when a steel hulk pulled up short before one of these fake landmines and a soldier opened the hatch, from upper-story windows they dropped grenades and Molotov cocktails into it.

So for the time being at least the insurgents frustrated even this all-out attempt to restore order. The tanks did rumble through the city, but resistance sprang up all around them. Here, there, from behind trees, from the depths of courtyards, the fighters popped out for a flash and let their rifles and submachine-guns blaze, and every so often a torch-like object hurtled through the air. The monsters responded and left wreckage everywhere in their wake: electric lines dangling from poles, overturned streetcars, ripped-up tracks, burned out cars, cobblestones prized loose, gutted newspaper kiosks, the shattered masonry of once elegant buildings.

Imagine the insurgents! Yesterday you were a student or a factory worker, today you are sneaking up on enemy tanks. Yesterday you were lighting Bunsen burners in your chemistry class or forging farm implements at an open furnace, today you are lighting strips of cloth in Molotov cocktails. And that's because you started something you couldn't even have contemplated a day earlier. You have no organization, no ideology, and no plan beyond the moment's defense or offence. You are only a loose collection of daring young men and some women who think you have nothing to lose and everything to gain, and who share with each other only your enemy and the fields of your battles. You may not even have considered the chances of success or made an assessment of your own strengths and weaknesses, or of the organization of the enemy's forces, and much less yet of the all-important international situation. But momentum seems to be on your side, and you intend to keep the struggle alive. One of the Soviet generals present estimated that 3,000 freedom fighters opposed his forces on the 24th, of whom 80 died and 450 were wounded. Wounded maybe but not daunted. No one was willing to quit, to forgo this euphoria, these heady moments of Magyar self-love and self-respect, and the heroics-inducing conviction that soon your numbers would be in the millions and finally you would triumph.

Photographs suggest, and eye-witness accounts and actual fighters' reports declare, that the insurgents believed themselves to represent the whole nation. Certainly, they believed that all those proud to be Hungarian were and would be with them, and they had good reasons for that. It was indeed a very acute strain of patriotism rampaging through the capital that day like an epidemic of madness. And surely, the two hundred thousand in Kossuth Square and the other two by City Park also spoke for thousands more. And everywhere in the country other students must have shared the bottled-up rage of those already fighting, although not all students of course and not everywhere either, and the same must have been true of factory workers. But what did all that mean? What *could* all that amount to, with no more than an evening's prepara-tions behind it in both organization and the formulation of a program, with the events of the 23rd themselves pretty much unpremeditated, if not altogether spontaneous?

On the 24th, broad popular support for the anti-regime efforts also became quickly apparent, and so the impromptu resistance flash-ripened into a full-blown revolution. In the capital, factory workers began to or-ganize by forming their own workers' councils, while "dismissing" exist-ing, party-controlled predecessors. Other groups proceeded similarly by forming revolutionary councils. And all this seems to have been done perfectly democratically and correctly, with apparently no arm-twisting, with open discussions, nominations and group-wide election of officers and delegates. The very opposite of the usual Communist procedures. How exciting that must have been!

In the morning the industrial workers of the capital declared a gen-eral strike. This form of resistance also had layers of meaning, for the Communists identified the worker at a state-owned enterprise, the only kind, as both employer and employee, and with that vicious twisting of ideas and words turned an attack on bosses into an attack on Communism itself. But the revolutionary elements scoffed at that sophistry, for they knew well what strikes really were, if not otherwise, then certainly from the Communist propaganda that made all it could of such events when they occurred in the West. For, as I recall, hardly anything pleased our leaders more than one of those dig-in-your-heels labor stand-offs the French left used to be so good at. As if, *ipso facto*, the Marxist kingdom of heaven were about to dawn on the banks of the Seine! So the Sixteen Points demanded the right to strike, and on the 24th the call for action, or rather inaction, went out to all trades and enterprises in the name of the workers. And this now actually *was* subversion. For it was a clear repudiation of the base attempt by the Party, the original purveyor of class consciousness, to try now to talk the working class out of just that!

The work-stoppage completely paralyzed production, but since, in a sense, work is one of the things that communism is all about, it did much more than that too. More generally, it cast a vote of no confidence in the Communist economy, and spoke loudly of the hostility to the regime borne by the very class whose interests it supposedly represented. More narrowly, it amounted to a rejection of the on-site chapters and leaders in industrial plants through which and whom the Party had organized the proletariat, and that of course was a rejection of the Party itself. And more loudly, it declared wide popular support for the insurgents and for a view of the uprising as a national democratic movement.

Support also came from the police and from the armed forces. Kopácsi, by this time already soured on Communism, or at least its only available brand, had informed the party leadership even before the marchers had set off from the Technical University on the 23rd that his men would not open fire on unarmed protestors, and he remained steadfast to the end. When the revolution was put down, he was tried with Nagy and got life. In 1963 he was released under a general amnesty and in 1975 allowed to emigrate. As for the army, the incident at the Radio building already demonstrated that the regime could not rely on it either. Then the many turncoats of the 24th reinforced the message. Among them was Colonel Pál Maléter, who joined the revolutionary cause when he saw that the counterrevolutionary agents he was sent to eliminate were mostly teenagers, and when he heard that his men were doing likewise. His new loyalties suited him and allowed him to realize his true potential. In a few days he became *the* military leader of the revolution, arguably its most distinguished hero, and in time, alas, another one of its martyrs.

The revolutionary spirit and activity also spread through the country on the 24th. As news of the events in Budapest traveled, everywhere people grabbed the opportunity to vent their hostility against their rulers. From far and wide, or at least as far and wide as you can be from Budapest and still in Hungary, people rushed to the insurgents' aid, young men coming to the capital to fight, and patriots sending arms, ammunition and supplies. At the same time, local wrongs were also being righted. Party functionaries were stripped of their power, old scores settled with ÁVO-men, some agricultural cooperatives even de-cooperated. In many places, local insurgents assumed the powers of government. They established workers' and revolutionary councils, and as such undertook the welcome task of turning out ruling cliques. By the end of the day, the insurgents could truthfully claim that it was a national movement for democracy and independence that the spark of their ideas and daring had ignited, and there was much cause for both jubilation and fear. Making history, you know, is not for the faint of heart.

Early on this second day, the authorities began to communicate and manipulate. The initial contacts with the public came in a series of broadcasts over Radio Kossuth beginning at 4:30 in the morning. The first announcement prohibited public assemblies, meetings and demonstrations, but it was only at 8:45 AM that the declaration of martial law by Nagy, the newly-installed prime minister, was announced, including summary execution of all those caught committing acts of public disorder, and finally at 9 o'clock the government offered the fuller explanation it apparently felt necessary of why Soviet tanks were running amok in the city. Again, the blame was laid on the overnight attack of counterrevolutionary gangs, with a reference also to the Warsaw Pact, the Communist counterpart of NATO and a mutual defense and aid treaty among the Soviet Union and her satellites.

Quickly on this day the revolution also became an international issue, an episode in the all-consuming drama of the Cold War, and the reaction to it became a bone of contention in the domestic power struggles of the main Cold-War opponents. On October 23rd the presidential campaign in the United States was approaching its climax. It was the Republican Eisenhower against the Democrat Adlai Stevenson, and Election Day was only two weeks away. The challenger was running on the policy of containment formulated during the Truman years, which required only that Communism be prevented from spreading until the weight of its own internal contradictions brought about its much-anticipated collapse. The incumbent, and especially John Foster Dulles, his pious and moralistic Secretary of State, aggressively advocated a policy of "rolling back" Communism from the territories it had recently conquered, like the Eastern European satellites. On the 24th already, an Eisenhower supporter in Congress boasted that the resistance behind the Iron Curtain demonstrated the success of Republican policies, a claim Stevenson rejected the next day. But that was only the beginning, because what Cold-War steps had been taken by the Eisenhower administration, what steps should have been taken instead, and what steps should be taken in the future – all that came now to be discussed in the context of the startlingly dramatic, real-life, hot-war context of Hungarian events.

In the Soviet Union too at this time a power struggle was in progress, although it was conducted quite otherwise than in America. Since the Man of Steel had neither named an heir nor allowed any of his subordinates to establish himself with the Party and the bureaucracy as one, upon his death all his most important lieutenants together picked up the reins of power. But then almost immediately these men began to plot against each other, and after three and a half years their contest for individual supremacy was still a daily affair. Indisputably, Khrushchev was the most powerful man in the CPSU, but his position was not yet secure and he still had to face opposition in the Presidium. His inclination, as clearly indicated by his spearheading of de-Stalinization and his handling of the Polish situation, was to ease tensions. He was promoting a policy of international détente. But always he had to watch his back and not leave himself open to hard-liner sniping. They should not be able to charge that his conciliatory approach allowed the Soviet Union to appear weak to the imperialist enemy, to rival Communist powers like China and the insubordinate Yugoslavia, or to satellite countries that were restless under the quasi-colonialist boot. We'll never know how things would have turned out had Khrushchev been an unchallenged autocrat at the time of the revolution.

In any case, the outcome of the Eastern-European disturbance was to be determined not in Budapest, but in Moscow and Washington. The Russians calculated the Cold-War advantage or disadvantage to be had from yielding to the uprising or suppressing it, and the same could also be said with regard to any possible American course of action. That advantage or disadvantage could be starkly obvious, like the value of a buffer against Western aggression for the Russians, or more or less imponderable, like the destabilizing effect in other satellites of an American signal of an intention to intervene. You see, the lot of small countries is cruel, and was especially so before nuclear proliferation. On the chessboard of nations, the kings and queens used to push the pawns around however it pleased them.

October 25, 1956

Anxious to be liberated from their curfewed confinement and assured by radio broadcasts that order was just about restored, in the morning the people of Budapest poured out to the streets. Nobody seemed to pay much attention to cautionary words or to the martial law still in effect. But once outside, with almost a single glance they could see that the latest official announcements had very little to do with reality. For one, the fighting had not ended and the city was not under Soviet control. In fact, both the Soviet tanks and their li'l-David-was-small-but-oh-my opponents were still about. In several districts streets were patrolled by joint student/police units, and the rebels also occupied local party and police offices. For another, the agents of disorder were *not* looters and hooligans. Look, these are just college students and working people, everybody could see. And look there, behind that broken shop window the merchandise was undisturbed, as was the money, I mean cash, naked cash, in the unguarded collection boxes set up for the families of the fallen. So this was no fascist uprising, you had to conclude almost immediately, obviously no *counter*revolution.

But then what was it? Well, if you had been able to tour the inner districts of the capital, you would have seen insurgents coalesced into small groups, each of which claimed as its turf only a city block or an intersection or a public building. Photographs and film clips reveal them to be mostly young people, including many fourteen-year-olds, although in retrospect their average age has been estimated as 25. But those young people, maybe 15,000 altogether from beginning to end, don't look much like the students who had marched on October 23rd, and the differences go beyond the scars of battle, the weapons they carry or have tucked into some kind of a holster or garment, and the outfits devised for many cold hours outdoors behind the barricades. Mostly, these were young workers in industry rather than future holders of white-collar jobs. It was they who fought the revolution, and not because they were the most pure-minded and idealistic socialists, but because they were the ones who in the last analysis had the least to lose.

But if this is indeed not a counterrevolution, the strollers and starers asked that Thursday morning, then why all the shooting and the armored posturing? Is all that really necessary, or is it just a misunderstanding? Shouldn't we just clear this up with the Soviet troops sprouting everywhere in the city like weeds? During the previous night already, some students had proposed reasoning with the enemy and had printed the following Russian-language flyer: "Russian friends. Do not shoot! They have tricked you. You are not fighting counterrevolutionaries. We Hungarians want an independent, democratic Hungary.

You are not shooting at fascists but at workers, peasants and university students." Now students climbed up on Soviet tanks, handed the flyers to their occupants and started speaking to them amicably, as was only proper among comrades. And it worked. In a few cases at least first heads and then torsos emerged from below, and the soldiers returned the locals' congenial socialist greetings. Then, with hostile feelings out of the way and the all-important ideological connections made, the revolution's flag was hoisted on a few tanks and local children were even invited up on the now tame monsters. And then, amazingly, the new friends proceeded to rumble and march to Kossuth Square, the very place where everything had begun, and where a crowd that would quickly swell to an estimated 20-30,000 had already been assembling from all directions since the early morning, and especially since news of the newly born brotherly love between the people and the Red Army had spread through the city. Now with this miraculous new escort, the crowd felt confident and invincible.

We will never know how the shooting started. All the subsequent, even post-Communist-era inquiries have concluded only that maybe somehow the semi-carnivalesque civilian/military happening on Kossuth Square, so unexpected and so inexplicable, unnerved some of the forces deployed around the Parliament. In other words, they concluded nothing. In any case, the first shots seem to have come from members of the Hungarian Border Guard posted on a roof across the square, shots that threw everyone on the square into a panic. The soldiers in the tanks thought that they'd been led into a trap, so they started shooting too, both at the Border Guard, who fired back, and at the civilian demonstrators, who did not of course. In the confusion, a Hungarian unit guarding party headquarters was even firing at a Soviet unit assigned to the same duty. It was mayhem. And a tragedy. Parents saw their children falling down dead, friends witnessed friends mowed down, screaming people were running into side streets, casting away banners splattered with blood. Before it all ended, one hundred people had been massacred, with another 300 wounded.

News of the slaughter flashed through the city and the country, and reaction to it was instantaneous. The anti-regime elements blamed the ÁVO for the atrocity and demanded its immediate elimination. Demonstrations multiplied everywhere, and fighting flared up in new places and intensified in the old. The insurgents became still more implacable, more determined even than before to see things through to victory or death. Crowds collected in Budapest in front of the American and British Embassies and shouted and chanted for help from abroad. All the good will demonstrated on the way to Kossuth Square evaporated of course, and the mutual hatred hardened like cement. The scene from the evening of the 23rd had been replayed, but this time the regime assaulted the people as if it were an enemy to be wiped out.

The hard-liners were now totally discredited. Clearly, they had no viable plan. Mikoyan blamed Gerő for calling in the tanks and Moscow ordered his resignation as first secretary. His place was taken by János Kádár, until then secretary of the Party's Central Committee, who was neither a Stalinist nor a reformer in Nagy's group and so seemed the right man for the job. Unlike Gerő, Kádár was a home-grown rather than a Moscow-bred Hungarian Communist, meaning that he had spent the ruthlessly right-wing 1930s at home rather than in the safety of Soviet exile. He had joined the movement and the Party as a young man and rose to prominence through years of imprisonment and clandestine operations. In 1949, he was appointed Minister of the Interior, but the following year he became one of the Stalinist regime's highly-placed victims. He was arrested on false charges of spying for the pre-war secret police, beaten, tortured and sentenced to life behind bars. For three years he languished in solitary and regained his freedom only in 1954 when Nagy, as prime minister, freed many political prisoners. Some might have been disillusioned by such injustice and cruelty, but Kádár's faith was unshaken. After his release, his political life continued where it had left off. By October 1956 he was near the top again, and as of the 25th the leader of the Party.

Nagy remained prime minister of course. In the afternoon Kádár and he made back-to-back speeches on the radio, but even after the massacre they did not concede much. Kádár called for reestablishment of order and promised to deal immediately with pressing problems and with Soviet-Hungarian relations soon thereafter. Nagy, a bit more specific, offered assurances that Soviet forces would withdraw from the capital, promised a new government, that is, a new roster of ministers, formed through "the cooperation of a broad range of national democratic forces," and acknowledged that people were justly bitter. What did all this accomplish? Not much. The reformers in the leadership did gain in strength this day, but they also seemed unable to come up with a sensible plan or even just the next step. So at the end of the third day of an always more bitter and bloody revolution, the two factions in the leadership found themselves in a standoff of equal perplexities, or actually in a mutual paralysis. Caught in the headlights! An astounding situation. And even the Kremlin couldn't help.

From the United States there was no immediate reaction to the massacre. In light of the possible catastrophic consequences, the Eisenhower administration had already decided not to trump one invasion with another. So for the moment at least, the tough talk about "rolling back" ceased. Nevertheless, America was in the air everywhere, courtesy of Radio Free Europe. This Cold War fixture headquartered in Munich was an oracle to the disaffected citizens of the satellites and so an arch-weapon in the psychological war the CIA was waging behind the Iron Curtain. It was manned by Communist-hating émigrés, who, amongst them, native-spoke all the Eastern European languages. Their broadcasts ran on tracks laid down by their American masters, but at times careered off onto the wilderness terrain of their own crusading passions. RFE didn't like Nagy. It scorned his early-afternoon speech and suspected him of having brought the Soviet forces into the fray. It found him to be lacking in resoluteness and called him a Communist, and with that you certainly couldn't argue. As for the insurgents, the broadcasters counseled them to resist all compromise. An emotionally appealing stance, for sure. But you have to wonder what kind of an outcome to the uprising those men in Munich themselves envisioned.

I myself of course had nothing to do with any of this. On the morning of October 24th I had no reason to consider the day, a Wednesday, different from all other weekdays, and so, as always, I arrived at school punctually but not too early. The silence and the Sunday-feeling surprised me, but still I ran up the couple of flights of stairs to my first class as usual. But then I stopped! The building was deserted. The corridors and class-rooms empty. How could this be? Finally I looked into one of the men's rooms, and there I nearly tripped over the gray kneeling mass of a wom-an janitor just as she was assiduously affirming her membership in the working class. "Go home," expressionless she looked up and waved me away with the scrubbing brush in her hand, "there's a revolution going on." Although I was exceedingly well-schooled in the idea of revolution, especially the glorious October kind, I don't recall what exactly I under-stood those words to mean. But I also knew better than to ask for a news briefing. Obviously enough, I was not supposed to be where I was. And even more obviously, everybody else knew that a curfew was in effect and didn't show up to begin with. Some of my classmates, none of whom I remember, not a single one of the boys with whom I shared the thirteen or fourteen weeks of that very brief secondary-school experience – some of them may even have been among the insurgents. Now I first wonder how I,… how *we* could have been so deaf and blind to that which everyone else apparently knew. Would things have been different had Leslie been around? Maybe so.

In any case, he wasn't. He was in Makó, the small town in southeast-ern Hungary where, if you recall, he had been working and living since February. I think we had last seen each other a couple of months earlier, a long time by our reckoning then, when Rose, Marika and I had visited there. I remember vividly that adventure from mid-August 1956, my last Hungarian summer, especially the night when the three of us traveled south by truck, a kind of vehicle common back then and there, a very rudimentary conveyance with a narrow rounded cab and a flatbed sort of thing behind it, nothing more really than a series of planks with some guardrails that you could hinge over like the sides of an old-fashioned hospital bed. Rose and Marika had squeezed in next to the driver, but I had to make do lying in the back on some canvas bags smelling of livestock, under the cloudless sky, covered with a rough blanket to ward off the surprisingly cool night air. For me the experience turned out to be indelible. We were on our summer vacation. We were going to Makó because it was in the countryside, or out of the city at least, because Leslie was living there apart from the rest of us, and because neither the transportation nor the sojourn itself was going to cost the family very much. We were trying to make something out of nothing, as you had to so often those days.

We had left Budapest after sunset, soon after the hour when even prying eyes could be counted on to have retired for the night. As we bounced past the last of the city lights and onto the open highway, the sparkle of a million stars suddenly turned the moonless sky into a crystalline sphere. It was my first ever night of staying up. I was lying on my back, gazing at the mysterious expanse above. Never before had I kept company with the wind. Never before had I rushed through the elements with such speed, or been so exhilarated, so by myself and for so many hours. I felt suspended between the rotating planet and the unbounded firmament, and for long minutes I stopped thinking and just allowed myself to vibrate with the speeding, bumping machine and the grinding of the tires against the pavement. Now and then a wedge of light from a vehicle traveling in the opposite direction swept through the space beneath me, as if to lift my magic flatbed and catapult me aloft, like Dante and Beatrice were whisked upward through the heavens. We arrived early in the morning. We walked through a gate into a courtyard enclosed by several houses, including the one in which Leslie had a room. Rose was to share that with him, and Marika and I were to share a room in one of the other houses.

Early the next morning Rose shook us awake, her face a stone-slab of determination. She already had her bag with her and was just packing ours. We were leaving as soon as possible. Back to Budapest. We traveled up north by train, one of my very few boyhood train rides. It was a stifling-hot day, with no room whatsoever along the bench-like wooden seats. We had to ride in the front vestibule, half-sitting on suitcases too flimsy to support even a child, swallowing the soot the steam locomotive blew through the open window into our faces every time the tracks curved or the wind shifted. Not a word was uttered, and I didn't dare ask Rose what was going on. I just assumed that she had again been confronted with one of Leslie's misdeeds, which by then I understood to involve other women. Between that aborted vacation and his sudden arrival on the evening of October 25th he may have been home one or even two weekends, although I don't remember anything like that.

We lived a very short distance from the *gymnasium*, just the width of a major thoroughfare and the length of a short block. So I was still on the run when I reached home, two-staired it to the 5th floor, unlatched the front door by reaching in to the armpit through the bars of the narrow window in its center, and I called out to Rose: "Anyu, give me money! I'm going to buy bread! There's a revolution going on!" Even without the subliminal memories of the then-recent war, which might have been playing blind-man's-bluff in my psyche for all I know, I would have known to be on my toes about things like this. Already experience had taught me that the more incomprehensible the news, the greater the likelihood that necessities would become unavailabilities and utilities would be disrupted. And I could never be nonchalant about skipping a meal. So I had refined running down to the bakery to a Pavlovian reflex.

As I slammed the door behind me, Rose turned on the radio. She would have tuned in either Radio Kossuth or Radio Petőfi, the only two stations, and I'm not even sure that the latter broadcast during the revolution. In any case, from either the one or the other she would have received only the disinformation the regime was disseminating about attacks staged by counterrevolutionaries. So she learned what was *not* happening and remained ignorant of what was. But didn't she have any other sources of news? Well, she was on good terms with the two direct neighbors we had and also on okay terms with some others. But friends she and Leslie did not have, although acquaintances aplenty, especially Leslie, who, as you know, had been a businessman and was always a tireless busybody. And we also had a telephone, which was still something of a luxury and a privilege. But I doubt that she would have inquired with anyone. Most likely, the radio was enough for her, and whatever news I brought back with the bread or without. I don't remember which.

You see, that apartment I grew up in was a desert isle, and why it was so is hardly a mystery. First of all, there was the Holocaust. Many of Rose and Leslie's relatives and friends had perished in the catastrophe, although not all of them, as happened to many Hungarian Jews. Then, there was also, and probably as decisively, Rose and Leslie's marriage and relationship in general. True, Rose was very charming in a sort of Central-European way, but friendship between the two of them and other couples was almost unthinkable because she was chronically *ashamed* of him. And indeed, Leslie was a boastful, loud, tactless man, easily offended and not shy about hitting back either, but he was not exactly unpresentable and certainly not as rough-hewn as you might think. The real problem here was actually their own interaction, or rather the mutually repelling high-and-low charges about them, the trigger-fingers atwitch, the discontent ever at flood level. And then, finally, there was Rose's own self-isolation. And, of course, if you build the walls around you thick enough and high enough, you'll find getting out no easier than getting in. Being all will and no tell, Rose had no use for friends, and consequently had none. No wonder we knew so little about revolutionary developments, either that day or the several to follow.

By the way, I was right to think of bread as soon as I heard about the revolution, for the fight for freedom immediately disrupted daily life. Obviously, food deliveries could not be made to the capital. So bread was foremost on everyone's mind, although the bread situation would not be critical as long as bakers could get to bakeries and their supplies lasted.

Throughout the revolution I remained the family bread-buyer, and enjoyed the tacit right to break off and wolf down the corner of the freshly baked two-kilogram loaf on the way home. Milk was not a concern for us because we didn't drink milk, or coffee or soft drinks for that matter, and only the occasional cup of tea. As for fresh fruit and vegetables, which would have been pretty scarce back then by October anyway, we could do without them for a few days. We might have had a few potatoes and onions in the usual bin, and the flour and sugar canisters may also have had a dusting or even more at the bottom. Meat we would have quickly missed had circumstances not forced us years earlier already into a mostly meat-free diet. Out on the terrace of our apartment, a tall old-fashioned milk can of enameled metal was filled with lard, as-needed portions of which Rose ordered me to bring inside year-round simply by pressing a large spoon into my hand. We had a very simple diet! Nourishment more like that of the Hungarian peasant through the ages than what I partake of today or not.

But we did also have a treasure trove of winter reserves in our pantry, a separate room off the foyer not much more spacious than two tall telephone booths would be. All summer, Rose had brought home basketfuls of fruits, which she and the children then peeled and pitted, stewed for a whole day in a vat, until at sundown she poured or spooned or stuffed the jam or juice into bottles and jars of several kinds. In retrospect now, those days seem like an idyll to me, Rose walking around barefoot in the sweltering heat, wearing just a halter top and a pair of blue shorts, directing life in her own Arcadia. I remember especially well the elegant narrow bottles of tomato juice, which were tightly sealed and then packed into a large laundry basket lined with featherbeds for a two-day heat-treatment that would protect them from mold. As for eating, I was partial to the apricots, which have been a Hungarian national food since occupation of the country during the 16th and 17th centuries by the Turks, themselves the greatest apricot producers in the world, and which is also the source of a national drink, apricot brandy. Delicious fire-water. In the final step of the processing of the apricots, Marika and I even let the heap of pits on the terrace dry and then carefully cracked but not smashed them open with a stone to extract the almond-like kernels. In most Octobers our little pantry, something very much like the one where I imagine Tom Sawyer's Aunt Polly to have kept her jars of jam too, for the raiding of which Tom had to famously white-wash the fence of the feared and flouted lady's house – in the fall our pantry gave a false impression of abundance. It had floor-to-ceiling shelves running all around, with the bottles and jars deployed all along them, grouped by shape and color it seemed, like regiments on a Napoleonic battlefield. So starvation was not yet knocking on the door.

As I've said, it was on October 25th that Leslie arrived home. Unexpectedly. I was in the dining room when a key rasped into the lock on the front door, and I stopped in my tracks and just listened. I heard a series of clicks as the tumblers repositioned, like the sound of branches breaking before the grizzly bursts into the clearing, and then the door opened and closed. The person making those sounds could only have been Apu. I took the half-dozen steps to the foyer and saw him standing there by the pantry, expectant but ill at ease, as if uncertain of the welcome he would get, as if trying to bring his own inner sound into harmony with the prevailing vibes. His hand still gripped his valise, his hat still sat on his head. I myself was caught red-handed feeling my feelings.

By the standards of those days he was a big man, six feet tall, a good 180 pounds. I've already told you about his temper, his pugilistic youth and the air of ferocity about him, to which details you should now add his boxer's walk with the toes turned inside a bit. His nose, broken in the ring more than once, was long and drooped a little, but he was a handsome man, dashing and imposing even. Not at all the flightless creature he became on this side of the Atlantic. But even then his hairline had already receded, although he always retained a thin thatch on top, so that you never thought of him as a bald man. Or I never did anyway. Rather, you noticed his green eyes and his serious and even brooding cast of countenance, and quickly figured out that when he was not smoldering, then he was preparing to. Back then he tended to dress in dark suits and

gray or white shirts, very much the working man who had risen to a management position, although he also wore ties, which for the Communists
was an unmistakable sign of bourgeois tendencies. I can't imagine how
he developed his taste for the awful, loud clothes he favored in his last
decades, as if one of Fellini's aging grotesques had been cast to play him
in his dotage. But maybe it was just the desire to look younger. I guess I
better watch out.

Now that I keep rerunning that arrival-scene in my mind, and maybe
just because a few frames of it are still especially vivid, I am struck not
just by how little I remember of what my father was like back then, but
also by how complete a stranger he was to me throughout my boyhood. I
can't even say that he was a mystery, for I don't recall ever wondering what
he really was like. The truth is that neither my imagination nor my five
senses, nor indeed what you would think of as the in-born filial feelings
I should have had – none of these things had the power to perceive anything but the fearsome in him. Although that is far from all there was, as
now I know very well. But that didn't matter, and I *remember* nothing else.
Of course, the years themselves, my own years, that is, may have erased
youthful impressions, and his own aging process may have done so too, as
well as the experience of immigration, which for him was violently transformative. But at the most all that must have been just so much contribu-
tory negligence, as we lawyers say. For those youthful impressions could
never have amounted to more than distant glimpses. The truth is that
my early years were marked by a thorough and now regrettable failure to
make emotional, physical or even intellectual contact with him.

On that Thursday evening three steps separated us, maybe two and
a half. I could have taken them, but I didn't. His stance and air stopped
the natural impulse in me, not, for sure, of the son running to greet his
father, but just of the one at home welcoming the one who has just arrived. He also didn't take those steps, for he performed his role in the
Freudian family romance no less well than I performed mine. Rose was
in the kitchen to his left, so that inadvertently he had inserted himself
between mother and son and so upset the natural order of things at home

according to which *Rose* was the fulcrum between him and *me*. Finally he turned towards her, ready or not! The three of us without him, Rose, Marika and I, had always seemed family enough for me. If as a child and a boy I had any happy family times, it was with mother or sister or both. Now of course I know that this probably was not any more his fault than hers, and maybe even less, although Leslie did spoil good times almost routinely. But for the moment at least, whew! she seemed glad to have him home.

But still, let's be realistic: this was no reunion, only something like a reassembling. A re-establishment of normalcy, if you wish, but only in the sense of the usual. I remember that scene well, and now it strikes me as a moment from a play by Pinter (*The Homecoming* itself or another), strangers well-known to each other on the stage, people collected in a room but kept apart by fear and suspicion and an indefinable menace. The suitcase in Leslie's hand and the hat on his head were perfect. A man trapped as if by himself, but at least semi-intentionally. Sitting, as it were, in the audience, I watch now and inside I tremble a little. I am reminded of two other family images conjured up in my mind at one time or another. The first one came to me when an acquaintance illustrated how delightful it had been for her to raise children by recalling that the family's – father, mother, two teenage sons' – customary expression of good feelings had been a group-hug, a kind of love-huddle. Well, we were not like that. The second one was triggered by a psychotherapist's comment that in any family the dynamics work as if each person were tied to each of the others by strings around their waists, so that a change in position by any one must produce a change in everyone. Well, if you now imagine those strings replaced by sticks, each of which is manipulated at each of its two ends so as to always maintain a certain distance between the manipulators, then indeed you're seeing the Hajdus. Or seeing them anyway as they were back then.

Leslie had not been in my thoughts during the preceding days, I would think, and maybe not even the preceding weeks. Among a good many other things, that also shows how little urgency I felt on account of the revolution. I don't recall actually thinking so, but I must have believed that the upheaval would pass in a few days, leaving everything, I mean in my own life, essentially unchanged. By then I had already embarked on my long career of denying the force of history on individual lives, and could not think of the revolution as having even a potential impact on me. I had just assumed that Leslie would return in good time, that this was not a crisis, and for me that was that. Fortunately, proper *paterfamilias* that he was, Leslie understood the situation more clearly than I, and when the shooting started he apparently felt the need to be at our side, even if he was not sure of the reception he would get. So somehow he returned home – in a motorcycle's sidecar, in a horse-drawn cart hauling produce, on the back of a sputtering truck, all of the above? – and he and Rose seemed to be cautious-to-cordial with each other. Unlike the revolutionary opponents, they were enjoying a cease-fire, although for how long you couldn't predict, for back then it always blew hot and cold, or rather lukewarm and cold, between them. But through the seven weeks that still remained of our lives in that country, Leslie resided at home.

October 26-28, 1956

So how exactly did things stand on the morning of the 26th? For the authorities not well at all. In addition to everything else, now they were also branded tyrants and mass murderers for all the world to see. And they could no longer even *try* to justify the tank-implemented urban renewal of the capital because, clearly, the marines were not about to land on the shores of the Danube. In a campaign speech Dulles even reassured the Soviets by declaring that "we do not look upon [the satellites] as potential military allies." But if the military action was turning out to be ruinous for its perpetrators, the revolution was thriving. The loose network of armed resistance had for three days already proved itself immune to both blandishments and threats, equal to every force the authorities dared launch against it, and able to survive on nothing more than bravado and the nation's support. Although as a political movement the revolution was still disorganized and fragmented, and hardly prepared for the give-and-take of the peaceful exercise of power. And it still also lacked a leader, having failed so far to win over its chosen one.

It was the authorities that had to make a move now, and so they did. At a meeting of the Politburo on the morning of the 26th, Ferenc Donáth, a reformer, startled his colleagues by speaking of the revolution as a "mass movement," and proposed that the leadership enter into discussions with participants and "respond to and satisfy their rightful demands. The party," he declared, "should not position itself against but should stand at the head of the mass movement that wants to use democratic instruments to build socialism." Rightful demands, eh? And building socialism? Well, this was startling indeed: a radical reinterpretation of events, an axis-tiltingly alternative view, maybe even an admission that the counterrevolution theory was downright wrong. Maybe it was the prior day's massacre that did it, or it was just a reformer's less doctrinaire reassessment of the whole situation, or maybe both, but in any case this was an argument in favor of attempting a *political* rather than a military solution to the conflict.

In the plain meaning of the words, the revolution had of course become a mass movement already on the 24th. But when Donáth referred to the mass movement, he went well beyond plain meaning and factual description. In communist theory a mass movement is the popular base the party needs for support and as the justification for its very existence. Without a mass movement behind it, the party is only a clique of hollow-eyed men with tobacco-stained fingers conspiring in cheap cafés, but with it, it is an awesome political force. It is therefore the party's mission to build a mass movement, as actual parties did usually try to do. And as actual parties, if ever they managed to come to power, invariably *claimed* to have done, whether or not they actually had. But the Hungarian situation was different from all that. For here you had a real mass movement, no doubt about it. The uprising was unquestionably the act and deed of the masses, something ready-made for being led and even socialist! So maybe the revolution was actually an opportunity? Maybe this was actually communist heaven? That remained to be seen. For now, let's just say that starting on the morning of the 26th, individual members and bodies within the Hungarian Communist leadership set out to gain control of the mass movement that was the revolution. And they hoped to do so with concessions and also with a not too blatantly compromising definition of rightful demands. But not so fast! This was not going to be easy. For the mass movement of October 1956 really had no reason to bargain. Yes, a change of attitude was nice, but it was going to be even nicer when solidly anchored in a change of conditions.

As for Nagy, the reinterpretation split open the ground under his feet and left him in a scary straddle. For, uncomfortable though it was, now he had to start acknowledging that each side had a claim on him, and that, reciprocally, his sentiments and experiences bound him to both sides. Indeed, Nagy occupied a pivotal position. The Party wanted him to assume leadership of the movement because a movement with a leader is more susceptible to being tamed than one without, especially if the leader happens to be an infiltrator. The movement also wanted him as its leader for the reasons I already mentioned, and also because a disillusioned insider at the helm would have been tremendously affirming. And, obviously, in terms of the existing power structure, Nagy was better placed than anyone else to do right by either the Party or the revolution. So each side tried to secure his loyalty and to influence him every way it could. The mass movement kept on trying to seduce him, the Party tried not to lose him.

The diversity of views within the leadership notwithstanding, the Party began to make concessions right away. An afternoon broadcast declared, first, that the government to be formed by Nagy "will completely rectify the mistakes and sins of the past, and with the support of the entire nation guide the people's rightful demands to their solutions." (Yes, guidance to be provided by those who themselves needed it the most!) Then, almost as if cribbing from the Sixteen Points, it went on to approve the organization of workers' councils and the demand for higher wages, and promised a new relationship with the Soviet Union based on independence, equality and non-interference in each other's internal affairs, and changes in the economy, in agricultural policy and in the governance of the Party. And then, in a semi-heart-felt, semi-jargon-choked closing, it called for fraternal peace, an end to the nation's terrible trials, life without fear, the well-being that comes from productive work, and an independent, democratic, socialist Hungary! A little bit of everything: startling promises, reminders of basic principles, appealing but in the given context empty words.

At a meeting on the 26th the Central Committee also appointed a so-called Directory, joining Nagy and Kádár and four others from across the Party's political spectrum in a plenipotentiary authority. And on the morning of the 27th, Radio Kossuth announced the formation of the new government and ballyhooed it as the broadening of the national leadership first promised in Nagy's post-massacre speech. And indeed, the dyed-in-the-wool Stalinists had been cashiered and replaced by four ministers who were definitely not representatives of, but at least closely associated with, long-banned parties, what the Communists derisively referred to as "democratic" political organizations. But, self-defeatingly, *the* Party did not release its grip on political life enough to make a real difference, and then at just about the time of the announcement the hard-liners instigated a furious Soviet attack against a rebel stronghold, as they say in samurai movies, and that sabotaged everything. So much for all the gestures of compromise and all the assertions of trustworthiness. They might as well have all been just lies and tricks. All the concessions now seemed reneged, the public mood remained as hostile as ever, and the fighting was not any closer to an end either. To boot, the less numerous and less well equipped insurgent defenders survived the furious attack and through sheer pluck won this encounter too.

During the 26th and all day the 27th, Nagy was inexplicably and "annoyingly passive," but then finally at the evening meeting of the Directory he put forward some proposals and insisted that they be accepted. If not, he threatened to quit. And needing him as they did, the authorities made more concessions. The Directory resolved that: (1) neither Hungarian nor Soviet forces would initiate an engagement with the insurgents, in other words, a cease-fire was in effect, (2) the Party and the government would accept some of the revolutionary demands, and (3) the events of the last few days were not a counterrevolution. Yes, Nagy was being openly disloyal now, and the day was not over yet. Soon after this meeting, Nagy and Kádár met with the Soviet emissaries and got them too to approve the resolutions, the cease-fire included, in other words, to join them in suing for peace. For that in truth is what they were doing, although they were being sincere, I believe, when they named their new position a "change of course." They could not admit even to themselves, much less trumpet to the whole world, just how thoroughly they had by now knuckled under to the people's will and how irresistibly the mass movement itself had seized control.

The next morning, the 28th, the Directory briefed the entire Politburo on the change of course. It too calmly accepted the *faits accomplis*. Here too the initial outrage and subsequent bungling had led not to standing at the head of anything, but to a tail-wagging friendliness rather. But then the suggestion that the public should be informed of the latest developments by the government rather than by the Party, now that was too much. The hard-liners came out swinging. But again Nagy handled the situation. He responded decisively, firmly and on the offensive, and that silenced these guns too. And this now was an unequivocally anti-Party stance. Indeed the prime minister and the government had just sidelined the Party, the vanguard of the proletariat, the Goliath of power that had long been arrogating center stage for itself. Only two days earlier Kádár could still argue that re-establishment of order required nothing more than separating the masses from the counterrevolution, like you separate a fool from his money, and bringing them into the *Party*'s camp. In other words, the Party simply had to reinstate its own theoretically correct relationship to the masses. But now, in what was a sharp blow to the laws of history – now the Party had lost whatever mandate it had ever had, and in the realignment of political forces only the government could be seen to be offering the kind of self-effacing leadership the mass movement seemed to be demanding.

In the Kremlin, the Hungarian situation was raising ever deeper concerns. There too the military intervention was considered a failure. True, at 1:20 PM Radio Kossuth announced an immediate general cease-fire and much of the fighting did actually stop, but these results had been achieved through repeated setbacks rather than successes by the Soviet troops. Suslov had been called home for the day, and his report in the late afternoon did much to convince the Presidium that its only options now were support for Nagy or military occupation, the latter of which, said the chairman of the Council of Ministers, would be a "dubious venture." There really was no other choice. By way of final word Khrushchev said: "We will declare a cease-fire. But we must foster no illusions. We are [only] saving face."

While the Soviet potentates were still deliberating, Nagy went on the radio to deliver the government's declaration. He began with the re-interpretation, referring to the recent days' events as "a great national democratic movement that had developed with an elemental force and now embraces and unifies all our people." Then he went on to enumerate many revolutionary demands that would be met, praised the "new organs of democratic self-government that have sprung up at the people's initiative," announced the formation of a new National Guard to be made up of "units of the army and the police, and [of] the armed squads of the working people and the youth," that is, the insurgents, promised the immediate withdrawal of Soviet troops from the capital and their negotiated withdrawal from the whole country, and also promised to dissolve the ÁVO once order was restored. In other words, he officially *adopted* the revolution's program.

So how exactly did things stand now, two days later, on the evening of the 28th? Well, the leadership's efforts to control the mass movement had failed thoroughly, while the revolution had gained steadily. But even aside from Nagy's only touch-me-not embrace, achievements were still significantly incomplete. Concessions on two critical issues were still required: the country's political system, that is, the demands for a multi-party democracy and free elections, and the price that must be paid by those responsible for past atrocities, a problem Nagy was not trying to ignore. And in the reigning spirit of loud opposition, many people still continued to voice their dissatisfaction with the existing state of affairs. And on top of that, still Washington provided no support for Nagy, however incidental or vague, and especially from this day on Radio Free Europe, contemptuous of the prime minister's wanting it both ways, repeatedly branded him a party-hack and trotted out every anti-imperialist comment he ever made, however incidental or routine. But despite all that, and this too cannot be denied, a political solution had actually emerged by the end of the day and a great great victory had been won. After all, the authorities had truly and formally accepted the reinterpretation first proposed two days earlier, and they had acceded to most of the revolution's program. And, visibly, the system had been shaken to its roots. Armed rebellion had fought the oppressors to a draw. Protests had been recognized as rightful, mistakes acknowledged, demands granted. The people's judgment had been rendered and heard. The usual power relationship between the ruling personnel and the masses had been emphatically reversed. And there was no turning back,... well, unless there was.

October 29-30, 1956

The October 28th victory elated the nation as only a great historical achievement attained against all odds can. On the 29th, a sense of communal pride burst forth from the mass of ordinary citizens, the joy of breaking out of shackles, a celebratory delight in this vindication too long delayed, this validation of nationhood long pursued and repeatedly frustrated. Eyewitnesses speak of euphoria and ecstasy throughout the country, while *The Monday Newsletter,* an independent newspaper, exulted in the international recognition of Magyar dedication to freedom and heroism. One and all paid homage to the freedom-fighting youth of the country, the true architects of the victory. Even the mean-spirited Communist press joined in the cheerleading.

Everywhere in the capital good will reigned. Newly formed district councils assessed the destruction, announced the resumption of work and mobilized volunteers to cart off the rubble. For its part, the government took well-publicized steps to restore public transportation, telephone and postal service, to repair the damage caused by the fighting and, above all, to assure that the food supply remained adequate. From the countryside farmers drove horse-drawn carts and trucks loaded with food into the city. They had come in their Sunday best or their dung-caked boots to affirm the real and *true* solidarity of workers and peasants. They proudly delivered to the freedom fighters the sustenance they had brought, offering it as their own contribution to the national cause.

The Monday also reported about events and conditions throughout the country. Everywhere, you can fairly say, the revolution had triumphed. Revolutionary bodies, democratically and often spontaneously chosen, had seized control, throwing out the old party leaders and disarming ÁVO troops. In some places blood had been shed, in others not. Expressions of support for the new government came from localities east and west. The larger towns had even sent delegations to the capital to call upon somebody high in the government and transmit local views and demands, very much like French communes had after the defeat of the *ancien régime*, empowering *ad hoc* representatives to speak with revolutionary leaders like Jean-Paul Marat, who was itching in his bathtub and penning vitriolic denunciations of "enemies of the people," a favorite epithet of the Communist authorities that Marat himself had coined.

But jubilation shared the national stage with solemnity. On October 29th the nation also attended to its dead. Many of the fallen heroes were buried with honors. But many bodies also remained unidentified on the urban battlefields, often covered with flags that parents, brothers and friends lifted, one after the other, as they searched for missing dear ones. The sense of destruction all around could easily sober you up.

International commentators also hurried to greet the popular victory and gloat. A chorus of voices began to rise about the apparent cracks opening up in the monolith of Soviet power. On the 27th already American experts were interpreting the revolution as a sign of the waning of Soviet influence. On the 29th they saw it as the worst *political* defeat yet suffered by the USSR in the postwar era, and in a campaign speech Vice President Nixon even declared it to be a turning point in the Cold War. On the 30th Msgr. Béla Varga, a hero of the Hungarian resistance during the war, subsequently speaker of the parliament and now an exile in the West, went so far as to characterize events as the *Red Army's* greatest defeat.

On the air, these up-beat pronouncements were coupled with calls to maintain the commitment to freedom, and the much-repeated message made a strong impression on me. I even remember chatting about it with Leslie and Rose, the first Bolshevik-bashing *conversation* I probably ever had. But this was indeed a rare opportunity, and we had all the time in the world. There we were, a family entangled in a network of emotional fault-lines, recently reunited, alone together and stripped down to existence without routines. Only Rose continued some of her accustomed daily activities. She even worked a little bit now and then, and her primly paralelized feet may even have been pedaling the sewing machine when Leslie walked in. That she could to some extent at least carry on her usual life even during those days stranded behind our threshold eased the domestic tension a little. And we were all thankful for any respite from what later I came to understand as Rose and Leslie's private negotiations, the constant thrust and parry that in the end turned into a revolution of their own.

I myself went out every other day or so, down to the bakery to join the long line waiting for the scent of the loaves just out of the ovens to waft reassuringly down the street, or hotfooting it to the state-run grocery store whenever news climbed up through the stairwell that something or other was available. I also ventured out once or twice beyond our immediate vicinity just to look around, but trained by Rose to be fearful, I always stayed in familiar precincts and kept a careful distance from danger. So actually I saw nothing out of the ordinary. In any case, but for the occasional thunder of tanks rolling along the main thoroughfare, and the single incident of a half-hour's intermittent firing at each other by one gunman in the attic of our building and another in a fenced-in lot across the street, our neighborhood remained very quiet, more quiet even than usual. At home, I had my books and my solitaire deck, and I kept busy by myself or hung out with Marika. She of course did the same, playing inside, as they say, amusing herself the best she could.

How Leslie occupied himself I can't recall or imagine. Sitting quietly was never his forte. Did he go out of the house? Was he constrained by the curfew that stayed in place until the 28th? Did he look up friends or acquaintances, or mosey around to possible places of employment? Certainly many workers were back in their factories, and management too. Would he go back to Makó? Did he want to? Did Rose want him to? These are questions I can't answer. But I do know that it had to be very trying to stay home all day marinating in the marital tension. I have always had a tendency to hit the streets, or the road as the case may be, after an especially heated exchange. Although that hasn't happened for years, thank God. I never could see any benefit to anyone from staying around, suffocating in the silence. Although some people are of another mind, like Barbara for example. Leslie himself liked to go I think. So where would he have gone under the circumstances? Could he have gotten a meal someplace? In a restaurant or somebody's home?

By this time, finally, even I was aware of the daily events of the revolution. Finally, even we considered it indispensable to listen to the radio, for even we were completely caught up in the excitement and counting down to victory and the end of that hated regime. By then we had also become addicted to Radio Free Europe. As far as I know, never before had Rose and Leslie tuned in the forbidden frequency, but now there was little risk involved in doing so. The beleaguered Communists could hardly worry about you and your radio. And now through Radio Free Europe suddenly America became a part of our daily life, which, despite my two aunts in the Bronx and my grandmother too, America had until then never been. Indeed, this was also the time when emigration first barged into discussions of what domestic arrangements would be going forward, or so I can safely conclude from the few comments about our transplantation dropped by Rose soon after we arrived in the New World, mostly referring to how she had argued and pushed for it and how Leslie had resisted. Emigration to America, the oh so fabled land of freedom and wealth and ease, the promise and dream of three generations of Eastern European Jews and the road-ready and road-weary of other parts of the world too.

Refugees made by the revolution first started trickling across the border into Austria on the 25th or the 26th, and as early as the 27th the Austrian government granted asylum to everyone, regardless of their reason for flight. The Austrian frontier, all 160 miles of it, stood reportedly unguarded. On the 29th, even with railroad service disrupted and private vehicles other than the horse-drawn kind practically non-existent, about 100 people passed through the shreds of the Iron Curtain, and charities in Vienna got busy raising emergency aid for refugees sleeping on straw pallets in border-village school gymnasiums. When Rose learned of this on RFE, her ideas about the future must have exploded like a Roman candle. So you *can escape from this life by escaping from this country*! And that, apparently, can be arranged. Given our confinement and the difficulties of communication, she is not likely to have discussed these things with her sister Erzsi, the only one remaining in Budapest, who had a close relationship with my Aunt Anci – one of my two aunts in the Bronx, the other one being my Aunt Pearl – but she knew that Erzsi had been wanting to emigrate for years. And indeed, Erzsi and her daughter Ági were among the *early* refugees. But in any case, by the 29th Rose might already have been interested in news of America as only a would-be immigrant can be. And Leslie? Ach! He could not bear even the idea. So that even if by then America *had* revealed itself to Rose as her best chance of victory on the home front, she may not yet have played that card.

Although there was indeed not much risk left in listening to RFE, it still seemed prudent to lock all doors and windows, lower blinds, draw curtains, shut off all the lights and start talking in whispers before we gathered around the set and watched the cat's eye on the console until the familiar sounds issued, when at once we all brought our ears closer to the speaker, as if dangled on the same string. If somebody were to ring or knock, we intended not to answer. At opportune moments Leslie would tiptoe to the front door... well, as close anyway as he could ever come to tiptoeing. He would hug the wall so that his shadow should not be visible through the door's glass panel, then press his ear against the thick slab of wood, as if he might actually hear someone or something out in the hallway. He too must have been speculating, but in a more focused way than I just was, about the implications of the possible outcomes of the crisis for *himself*, what would happen if things went as the Americans seemed to want them to, what if not quite that way but still victoriously for the insurgents, might there be hope for compensation of some sort, for other opportunities maybe, to be somebody again – ah! there were so many possibilities. And all of that must have had further implications for how many roofs we as a family would have over our heads in the future and where it or they would be. Had he too been thinking about America already, then the prospect of a better life in Hungary, or an even *much* better one, would have made the New World still darker to him by a shade or two. And also improved his chances of getting his way. Oh, his head must have been spinning! So much was always at stake, his life always teetering on some precipice!

Throughout the day, Nagy and the government did all they could to disarm civilians and get them back to work. Assurances that Soviet troops would be leaving multiplied, as did pleas and arguments for surrendering weapons and restoring order. The formation of the new National Guard presented great organizational difficulties, but some progress was made even in that. At 5 o'clock came the announcement that the Minister of the Interior had dissolved the ÁVO. That elicited further jubilation, but it also raised the specter of popular violence against the men in gray, and indeed the following day a clash between insurgents and still-armed remnants of the murderous troops did lead to lynchings, to what the new revolutionary press quickly condemned as "lamppost justice." Throughout the city, there were still pockets of resistance too. Many insurgents did not want to lay down their arms until *all* of their demands had been met. But much of the fighting was now replaced by negotiations. In a very un-Stalinist spirit, there were talks at the Parliament, at the Defense Ministry, at police headquarters. Rebels, rebels, everywhere!

It was on October 30th finally, after half a night of anxious solitary deliberating, that Nagy acceded to the mass movement's last major demand. When one of the non-Communist members of the government brought up the possibility of further reorganizing the cabinet to make it more like it had been at the time of the postwar coalition, Nagy just simply admitted that, yes, that may be a necessity. And so it was indeed, because by then the one-party arrangement had become pretty much impossible. To continue to insist on a monopoly of power for the Hungarian Workers' Party was suddenly absurd because that Party had largely disintegrated. Pooff! So it was better to *reculer pour mieux sauter* as the French say, to temporarily retreat as a way of salvaging what remained, to revert to a multi-party system as the only chance of survival for the Communist Party, which might otherwise have been kicked down a one-way road to irrelevance. The laws of history embarrassingly notwithstanding.

And so at 2:28 PM on October 30th, Nagy again addressed the nation over the radio, but this time, finally, he spoke not of a change of course but of the *revolution*. Three times in a very short speech he used that word, starting off this way: "The revolution that continues to unfold throughout the country, this mighty movement of democratic forces, has brought us to a fork in the road.... And so the government, *acting in concord with the Party's Politburo,* has in the interest of further democratization of national life terminated the one-party system and reestablished itself on the basis of the democratic cooperation that had prevailed among the coalition parties reborn in 1945." Then he announced that to this end an executive cabinet had been formed within the government, seven individuals representing four parties, including the Communists, and finally he urged his "Magyar brethren, patriots, our country's loyal citizens [to] safeguard the revolution's achievements." No special pleading for the Party here!

But even these revolutionary words were *still* not quite everything. First, the free, multi-party elections demanded by the various manifestoes, starting with the Sixteen Points – such elections were not even promised. And, second, the democratic cooperation of the political parties, just what did Nagy mean by that? Was he, head of the government and a Communist I mean, and still quite possibly a fence-sitter – was he actually willing, if so it should come to pass, to let go of the left-leaning political direction adopted in 1945 and more or less accepted since? Or was he still committed to maintaining a society hostile to both the pre-war system and Western-style democracy? Who can say? But even with these questions open and these issues unresolved, this speech of his of the 30th was generally understood to be the death-knell of Communism in the country, the slinking away of a defeated wreck, the demise of a system overwhelmingly not wanted. Good riddance!

During these hours Joseph Cardinal Mindszenty, a prominent name on the roster of Eastern-European Cold-War resisters, was also liberated. As Roman Catholic primate of Hungary, the cardinal had always been an outspoken opponent of the religion-hating Communists. In 1949 they arrested him on trumped up charges, drugged him and tortured him. He was tried and sentenced to death, then his sentence was commuted to life imprisonment, and he spent most of eight years in solitary confinement. Finally, in1956 he was released from prison and put under house arrest in a castle near Budapest. But on October 30th an army unit working with the insurgents learned that the ÁVO planned to move the Cardinal to a different location. Seizing the opportunity, at once two tanks and an armored car set out for the castle. Around the same time, a large group of local villagers armed with pitchforks, spades and other farm implements also assembled on the grounds and called for Mindszenty's release. At first, the ÁVO-men in charge panicked, but then, having a sudden change of heart, their senior officer approached his prisoner "with humility and respect," declared that he and his men had formed – just listen to this!

– a revolutionary council and that the Cardinal was free to go. Just then the army unit arrived and disarmed the ÁVO-men without a single shot being fired. And as if in the final scene of a Hollywood production by a Hungarian Grant Wood, when Mindszenty climbed into the armored car waiting to take him to his archiepiscopal palace in Buda, the villagers cheered him and the joint victory, and waved their pitchforks.

Also this afternoon, during Nagy's address actually it seems, Soviet troops started withdrawing from Budapest. The forces of darkness driven out by the light of the good and the right! And to the muffled drumbeat of what you could easily mistake for a retreat, the Presidium in Moscow was also adopting a new policy regarding the satellites, spelled out in a "Declaration by the Government of the USSR on the Principles of Development and Further Strengthening of Friendship and Cooperation between the Soviet Union and Other Socialist States." The Declaration re-examined the relationship between the dominant power and its tethered neighbors, and arrived at conclusions that were precedent-shatteringly radical and utterly unexpected. It stated in part that:

> The countries of the great commonwealth of socialist nations can build their mutual relations only on the principles of complete equality, of respect for territorial integrity, state independence and sovereignty, and of noninterference in one another's internal affairs.

> The Soviet government is prepared to enter into appropriate negotiations with the government of the Hungarian People's Republic and other members of the Warsaw Treaty on the question of the presence of Soviet troops on the territory of Hungary.

"A miracle," that's how Allen Dulles, brother of John Foster and Director of the CIA, greeted the Declaration. And a miracle it was indeed. For the Presidium had just put its imprimatur on the revolution's victory, had just vindicated reform- and independence-sentiments in the satellite countries, and more. Truly, it was a turning point in the Cold War and the dawn of a better Communism. It was also a cause for stunned joy, and the crowning achievement of and the triumphant conclusion to the revolution.

And so, on October 30th, after eight days of demonstrations, strikes and massacres, after battles that left thousands dead throughout the country and reduced parts of the capital to war-waste, once more a normal life in a free Hungary seemed possible. Soviet troops were completing their withdrawal from Budapest, while the government labored to satisfy the people's demands, continued to negotiate with the armed insurgents about their inclusion in the National Guard and proceeded to release remaining political prisoners. And the foreign oppressor too had come to its senses. Breaking a 40-year historical habit and contrary to all the doomsday scenarios of the Cold War, the Communist leviathan had relented and chosen the peaceful path to dealing with a brave but insignificant neighbor. The revolution had been won. Tyranny was shaken off. Freedom, personal and national, was finally a Hungarian reality.

What? The revolution won? I can imagine your uncomprehending protestations. Isn't it common knowledge that the revolution ended in bitter defeat? Haven't I myself made that clear already? Yes, of course, the revolution was famously lost. I might not be here had it been otherwise, Nagy wouldn't have been martyred, Kádár wouldn't have ruled the country for the subsequent thirty-plus years, and so on. But before it was lost, the revolution was actually won. For the reinterpretation was only a beginning, indeed only the first step in the process of the authorities' adoption of the revolution's program, a process that continued and gained speed and assurance and indeed was quickly completed, and so resulted in the resounding victory of the democratic movement of the Hungarian people.

Obviously, I haven't yet reached the end of the story, but I imagine that you're already puzzled: this is exciting, kind of, but what does it all amount to? Once things calmed down, what did all this really mean beyond Hungary's borders? And beyond Hungary's history? Well, you're right to be asking these questions. We have to be sensible about this. Fifty or sixty years after it happened, when even the last generation of those to whom it mattered in the happening is dying – at such a point a historical episode should be able to justify its claim to a place in the store of knowledge of the at-all historically inclined person. And if it can't, then it's time for it to go, to withdraw to a back-lot property room, a place maintained by specialists just for their own enjoyment.

There are two ways to see the Hungarian revolution in this regard. You can, for one, see it as the last in the series of violent popular movements of political liberation that began in North America in the 1770s, which of course makes the events of '56 the final iteration of a major historical phenomenon with a long and distinguished past. Or you can see it sort of an opposite way, which identifies those events not as the last in that series but as in fact the first in another. For if you emphasize the non-violent *popular challenge to the order of things* the Hungarian revolution represented, then it emerges as the precursor to what has been called the wave of successful democratic movements that started in 1974 with the overthrow of the Greek junta and of autocracy in Portugal, and continued in subsequent years with similar transformations in Spain, then Argentina, Brazil, the Philippines, South Korea, the collapse of the Soviet Union and the change of system in its satellites, South Africa, Georgia, Ukraine in 2005, and perhaps others too that I'm forgetting. Each view is valid and meaningful of course, and neither means to exclude the other. So you can, if you want to, think finally of the Hungarian revolution as a transitional episode, and that positioning adds still more historical meaning to it.

But the forward-looking view of the events, the preview of a by now achieved future, reveals, as the one that faces backward doesn't, both meaning and significance. Promptly after its occurrence, Hannah

Arendt jubilantly credited the revolution with having offered the first ever demonstration that totalitarianism *can actually be resisted from the inside* and may even be defeated so. What impressed Arendt so deeply, and in the aftermath of Nazism and during the darkest days of the Cold War even gave her hope for a better future, was of course the resistance I just labeled a popular challenge. And indeed, the great achievement of the revolution was its demonstration of a spontaneous and self-sustaining power in the people themselves. That, and that alone, is what made it a world-historical event and a precursor of liberations to come, or, I'll venture to say, what conferred a lasting significance on it. So then is it time for the revolution to be banished to the back-lot property room of specialists or not? Well, I'll let you make that decision for yourself, historically inclined reader.

CHAPTER 4

A Brief History of the Jews in Hungary

PREHISTORY

As I'm sure you know, the term "prehistory" refers to times before the invention of writing. Since no records could be created or kept until then, it was the introduction of that particular communications technology that in any given place served as history's starting gun. Today this definition is considered a bit old-fashioned, I know, but it's still useful and I don't really have an argument with it. However, in compiling this history of the Jews in Hungary, I have encountered what strikes me as a different kind of and entirely unrelated prehistorical phenomenon. There is evidence, you see, of Jewish presence amongst Magyars from the 13th century right through the end of the Middle Ages, but then during the 16th and 17th centuries the local Jews readily discarded their relationship with the Magyars for a relationship with the occupying Turks, and then during the country's reconquest the Jewish population was pretty much destroyed. Consequently, at the beginning of the 18th century, Jews first migrating into Hungary had to establish new communities. So the Hungarian Jews of the 18th century, together with later immigrants the ancestors of all Hungarian Jews ever since, were not the descendants of the Hungarian Jews of the 17th century or of *their* ancestors. Rather, their lives, individual and collective, constitute the beginning of a new history and make all that came before a kind of prehistory, or actually a kind of Jewish prehistory.

The earliest evidence of Jewish presence in the Carpathian Basin is from the 3rd century, a time by which already the Jews had no more than a memory and a promise for a homeland. But this presence, a sort of pre-prehistory, seems to have come to an end with disintegration of the Western Roman Empire. During the Dark Ages, which oxymoronically dawned in the 5th century, the Basin was only sparsely populated by tribes that sort of just moved on or merged into newly arriving groups or were wiped out by them, until the Magyars arrived at the end of the 9th century and settled permanently. The Jews themselves returned only sometime later, when the juices of commerce were finally starting again to trickle at least. In his Charter of Freedom of 1251, King Béla IV of Hungary granted Jews the right to live in his kingdom under *his* special protection and according to *their* own laws. The Jews were permitted to practice their religion, choose their rabbis and judges, and build their synagogues. Béla knew that "keeping" Jews, as you might a particular species of domesticated animal, was financially advantageous, for the Jews of course paid a tax for the privilege of being kept. And the Jews could also perform services that others could not perform or be trusted with. For example, during the 13th century, they operated the royal mint in Buda, striking coins that bore Hebrew letters. They also managed to have Béla's charter renewed by each successive Hungarian monarch right through 1526.

Harrying Jews was routine in medieval Europe. They were always outsiders and indeed objects of religious hatred whom Christian society often could not or would not tolerate even to live with side by side. Everywhere they were segregated in terms of where they could live and what they could do. The authorities never tired of decreeing their forcible mass conversion or mandating church attendance by them. In many places they were required to wear distinguishing signs, such as a cone-shaped hat or a yellow badge. And often they were accused and convicted of ritual murder, the so-called blood libel, that is, the killing of Christians and the use of their blood in making the Passover matzo, which many

Christians believed to be a Jewish practice. When disaster struck or religious enthusiasm ran amok, Jews were often massacred by the hundreds and thousands. And of course periodically they were actually thrown out of towns, provinces and countries. At various times they had to quit Paris, Strasbourg, Brittany, Gascony and Anjou. In 1290 they were expelled from England, in 1305 from France, in 1492 from Spain, in 1496 from Portugal. In 1349, upon outbreak of the plague, they were expelled even from Hungary, although they were readmitted in 1364, as they were sometimes in other places too.

So you might say that back then already the so-called Jewish question confronted Europeans: what to do with or about this strange people who were related to Christians and indeed to the history of humanity itself in a way unique and ultimately beyond sorting out. And as you see, the solutions implemented at one time or another – keep them separate, un-Jew them, boot them out, kill them off by the most up-to-date ways and means – might already have formed the basis of a required course in a school for inquisitors. But maybe in Hungary, in the less densely populated eastern part of the continent, this problem was not so urgent. Maybe Hungary was a little bit like the large Kingdom of Poland, the so-called *paradises Iudaeorum,* to which Jews expelled from Western Europe migrated in significant numbers, there to become the collective ancestors of the great Ashkenazi branch of Jewry. Certainly, during the Middle Ages it seemed that way.

But then in 1526, the Turk came to Hungary, as Cervantes would have said, using the singular of the word in the collective sense it apparently had then, and for the Jews that changed everything. Having just swallowed the last morsels of the Byzantine Empire and then gobbled up the rest of the Balkan Peninsula, the Ottoman Turks made a quick meal of Hungary's forces at the Battle of Mohács, just to the west of the Danube before the great river enters Serbia as borders lie today. Suddenly, the country was a civilizational frontier, and there was nothing anymore to stop the invaders until they reached Buda and beyond. In 1529 and again in 1531 they besieged although did not take Vienna, and in 1547 Ferdinand I, the Habsburg ruler, King of the Romans, future Holy Roman Emperor and among many other things also King of Hungary by inheritance since 1526, simply had to concede Turkish rule over the central and eastern part of the country, including the cities of Buda and Pest. In effect, the kingdom had been dismembered, that is, had its first experience of the territorial surgery so often performed on very much unetherized Eastern European realms. The country was now split into three about-equal parts: the occupied lands, a western-northern strip under royal control, and Transylvania, which was ruled by a semi-independent prince beholden to the infidel. The occupiers were not dislodged and the territorial tatters not stitched back together for more than 150 years. Buda fell to the forces of the so-called Holy League, a coalition led by the Habsburgs, in 1686. The Turk gave up its claim to all portions of the kingdom only in 1699 by the Treaty of Karlowitz.

Under Turkish rule the Jews fared better than the Christians. In 1526 Sultan Suleiman the Magnificent took the Jews of Buda with him when he left the conquered city – as Nebuchadnezzar had done in the Book of Chronicles with the craftsmen of Jerusalem – and he put them under his protection and granted them trading privileges throughout his empire. He also imposed a tax on them, but nothing more than what they were immemorially accustomed to and expected to pay anyway until the end of time. Then soon Jews from nearby towns and also from other parts of the Ottoman Empire started moving back to the old capital, and promptly they even had their own neighborhood. They also cooperated with the Turks, whom they preferred as lords and neighbors to the Magyars, and enjoyed all the benefits of such cooperation. And why not? Under those circumstances, wouldn't you also choose the host who is tolerant and lose the one who persecutes you? Even if you're a masochist, as often Jews are reputed and would indeed have good reason to be. In any case, by the end of the occupation, the Jews of Buda numbered six-seven thousand and constituted the largest Jewish community in all of Hungary. Compare, I'd like now to say, the situation in Buda to that in Debrecen, a city located on the Great Hungarian Plain between the Tisza

River (the Theiss in English) and the Transylvanian border, and even then probably the second largest urban center in the country. But that I can't say. Because there, at the meeting point of the three 17th-century Hungarian fragments, where none of the three governments actually had a secure hold, there were no Jews at all. Because in Debrecen Jews were *not allowed*. Is it any wonder that in 1686, during the reconquest, the Jews fought on the side of the occupiers?

The Jewish population got pretty much crushed as the two civilizations ground against each other like giant millstones. Upon taking Buda, the Habsburg army slaughtered a portion of the town's Jews and held the others for ransom. It took some years for Samuel Oppenheimer, the Viennese financier, official supplier of the emperor's armies and Jew *extraordinaire*, to rescue the last of them. Then, as the Habsburg forces advanced through the occupied region, the Jews ran before them. But they were always caught, and either killed or imprisoned. By 1699 only a few Jewish communities remained in the country, and they were all located near the western border, eking out a living on the estates of a few great aristocrats. You can think of this collateral-damage destruction as the decisive event that rendered all that preceded it a Jewish prehistory.

ARRIVAL AND RECEPTION

After the reconquest, a number of anti-Habsburg uprisings broke out, but even with encouragement for the rebels from Louis XIV of France, all to no avail. By 1711 the country was under complete Austrian domination. The Habsburgs were Holy Roman emperors, and after 1806, when Napoleon finally dissolved the by then anachronistic empire, they were emperors of Austria, sovereigns of a congeries of kingdoms, principalities and duchies. They were also kings of Hungary of course, which they began to treat as just another, although major, component of their vast and varied domains. For the Hungarian nobles, who spoke German and did not understand the Magyar spoken by their inferiors, Vienna now became the place to live and rococo Viennese ways the style in which to do it. No less importantly, the many Saxons, Flemings and Rhinelanders who had been settling in the country since the 12th century and would continue to settle there after the reconquest dominated guilds and commercial life in general, and they contributed greatly to making German the linguistic currency in cities and towns. So at the beginning of the 18th century Hungary and particularly its Magyar population found themselves in something like a colonial status both politically and culturally. And things were about to get worse.

You see, many people had died in the Turkish wars and in the frequent outbreaks of the plague during the 17th century, and even more had fled the violence and devastation. And then the rebellions of the first decade of the 18th century only added to the losses. So the population thinned out and the economy lost its momentum. The Danube ceased to be a major commercial route, and Debrecen, which had grown nicely during the preceding two centuries, was again reduced to agrarian isolation, to no more than a dusty time-forsaken city as might be imagined by a Hungarian Garcia Marquez. Right after the calming of the disturbances, the royal authorities and also the great aristocratic landowners sent emissaries to neighboring lands to attract prospective settlers and so repopulate the country. Significant numbers of Germans, Serbs, Croats and other Slavs from the multi-ethnic Habsburg empire responded to these calls and thus imposed a crazy-quilt ethnic pattern on the already much-Germanized country. So Hungary, at the time a major realm three and a half times the Hungary of today – so Hungary then remained until it was again dismembered in 1920 by the post-World-War-I Treaty of Trianon, a dismemberment undertaken to undo that very pattern. In historical hindsight the demographic collapse of the late 17th century came to be known as "the withering of the Magyars," although if you just shush your poetic Hungarian soul for a minute, you can also think of it as no more than the historical circumstance that first allowed the ethnic Magyars' absolute majority to be reduced to a mere plurality. But a portentous turn of events it was any way you look at it.

The history of the Jews in Hungary begins anew with the 18th century. The repopulation signaled their return, but not in a straightforward
come-and-make-yourself-at-home way. For one, Jews were excluded from
so-called royal free cities, that is, cities under the direct and exclusive lord-
ship of the king and therefore enjoying a high degree of self-government.
Unfortunately, this is exactly where the Jews wanted to live, although not
just out of perversity. For these cities were the most vigorous and prosperous, and this is where the Jewish peddlers and craftsmen might actually
have found the most customers and where other commercial ventures too
were likely to present themselves. But these places of opportunity were
open to them only for limited visits, a restriction intended among other
things to give local German merchants and craftsman guild-members
the advantage of insider trading in a very literal sense. Of course, the
city fathers had the power to relax the restriction, but would *you* take in
a boarder of questionable reputation who, you also knew, intended to
steal your kids' affections? Well, they didn't either. For another, Cardinal
Kollonich, archbishop of Esztergom and chief pooh-bah of the court's
repopulation effort, did not like Jews and wanted to keep them out.
Instead, he wanted German and Austrian settlers, and with enticements
of land, tax exemptions and gifts of farming implements got them by the
wagonful.

These were powerful disincentives, but the Jews overcame them because they had to. Because they were confronted by a proto-genocidal
menace, if you'll excuse the anachronism. For just at this time, Emperor
Charles VI wanted to curb the growth of the Jewish population in the
crown territories of Bohemia and Moravia, the provinces that today constitute most of the Czech Republic. A fitting predecessor to a long line of
Eastern European social engineers and a sovereign with his very own ingenious solution to the Jewish question, Charles attempted to achieve this
objective by means of a decree limiting each Jewish family to marrying
off only one son. The others had to remain celibate, or wifeless at least.
Of course, the Jews were bound by the divine command to be fruitful
and multiply, so they found this intolerable, as would most anybody else

too I think, Torah-toter or not. But how could they resist other than by moving on? And so they did, for as if with a scourge, the emperor's brutal prohibition now drove them in pulses and waves to neighboring Hungary. They were indeed orphans in the storm, and they had to and did make their way despite the locked gates of the royal free cities and in the teeth of Kollonich's preferences.

The Jews who entered Hungary could settle only on the estates of the nobility or the Church. Of course, these estates were not negligible tracts, and in the case of the aristocrats, the relative handful of leading noble families, they were of princely size. In any event, this was good enough for the Jews as an initial base of operations, as what I am tempted to call a *home* base. Nobles had the right to welcome the Jews – unhitch your beasts, unload your carts – and did so because they were looking to increase their revenues and found value in commercially gifted im- migrants ready to pay a hefty tolerance tax for a place to live and make a living. Suppressing then the wave of nausea frequently brought on by the new settlers' outrageous beliefs and outlandish customs, the nobles allowed them to set up their prayer-rooms, ritual baths, slaughterhouses and cemeteries, the four institutional cornerstones of any Jewish commu- nity, and even granted them the degree of administrative and judicial au- tonomy their religion required. This is what happened in Óbuda, that is, Old Buda, the town north of the capital city that in 1873 was united with Pest and Buda to form Budapest. A Jewish community had flourished in the town already in the 14th century, and a new one was established after the reconquest on the estates of Count Zichy, the head of one of the country's great aristocratic families. By 1720 the Jews were supplying this lord's castles with almonds, oil, sugar, tropical fruits, horseshoes and barrels, and their community, with a proper synagogue first built in 1732- 33, was by then accepted as an integral element of the town's makeup. Óbuda quickly became the major Jewish settlement in the country.

The migration from the north had begun in the late 17th century. Altogether it continued for about a hundred years and in the end ac- counted for the new, or at least much renewed, Jewish presence in all of

Hungary west of the Danube. A 1735 countrywide census of the Jews demonstrates that although by then the court too saw the potential here for significant revenue, from a purely demographic point of view the movement still did not amount to much. If you adjust the tally to reflect the aristocrats' brazen habit of hiding their most valued Jewish tenants from the royal head-counter, you have to figure about 2,500 Jewish families in the country at the time and a total Jewish population of about 12,200. Of the 2,500 families 42% were immigrants from Bohemia, Moravia and other imperial territories, and another 13% from Poland. That leaves about 5,500 Jews who were either native-born or possibly transplants from still other places, which makes 3-4,000, or less than 0.1% of the estimated 4 million total population of the country in 1700, seem reasonable as in turn an estimate of the number of Hungarian Jews at that earlier date. And if you continue to play around with these numbers and boldly ignore all the footnote-qualifications that are surely in order but hardly relevant to rough approximations, you'll find that during the first third of the 18th century those pulses and waves from the north averaged maybe forty families per year. Yes, a drop in the bucket, that's all that the Jews were in Hungary at this time, but a drop of what? A drop of poison perhaps that contaminates the whole concoction and so must be purged, or a drop of an enzyme, a yeast-like liquid or growth hormone rather that will enrich and enliven the more inert main constituent and so should be welcome?

In the places where the Jews did find tolerance at a price and did settle, they plied their trade as tailors, cobblers, brandy distillers, furriers, goldsmiths, silversmiths and bookbinders, and from such places they made their wholesaler's import-export journeys and their much more typical peddler-circuits. Unlike their Christian neighbors of course, they could not own and did not till the land. But here already, even at the very beginning of their history in the country, they were not an unstratified mass. They had something like an upper class of their own, in part hereditary and indeed tribal, and in part reached through individual merit, a traditional and informal nobility of learned men, rabbis and leaders of communities, people who tended to be better off than the rest. Mostly though, the Jew was poor and lived a hard and fearful life. Even the most downtrodden peasant, still bound hand and foot by the vestiges of a typically Eastern-European, post-medieval serfdom, despised and looked down on the Jewish peddler, whom the census identified as a merchant, but who in fact was a dusty-footed creature of crooked by-ways, tramping hunched over from village to village, his bundle of wares of hare-skin, leather, scrap iron and shells for making buttons tied about his shoulders with a frayed rope. A beast of burden, to all appearances without a home, his few coins hidden from bigots, brigands and thirty-percent-men somewhere in his Jew-garments, a stepchild of fate, a wanderer in the desert of his eternal exile. A Jew!

Dr. Miklós Hajdu was an uncle of Leslie's, a lawyer, a private scholar of Jewish history and a prominent member of the Budapest Jewish community. In 1939 he published a little book called *Shavuot in Szenicze: From the History of the Hónig-Hőnig and Bock Families*, Shavuot being of course a Jewish holiday in the spring and Szenicze (today Senica in Slovakia) having before Trianon been a small town in Hungary. Leslie owned a copy of the book – it's not likely that more copies were printed than the number of living members of those families in that still antediluvian year – and I inherited it from him. The centerpiece of Dr. Miklós's study is an account of an incident in 1739 involving a certain Rabbi Jacob Moses, a forefather of Leslie's and indeed my own grandfather to the fifth power, that is, going back seven generations, as demonstrated by one of the two genealogical tables of the Rabbi's descendants that Dr. Miklós pieced together and appended to his text. When I undertook this project, I was counting on making the most of the many historically illuminating facts about my ancestors I thought that text to contain. Unfortunately, it contains rather few. Nevertheless, I am very thankful to Dr. Miklós for having preserved what he still could. And when I read that he had for reasons never explained put off writing this particular book throughout a writing career spanning forty years, I am especially glad to have found an ancestor in whose footsteps I can walk even if only briefly. For despite the cousinage I now feel for Dr. Miklós, I cannot for a minute ignore how different we are, he, the pre-Holocaust, God-loving, Zionist, observant, tradition- and ancestry-bound Jew, and I,… well, a Jew pretty much only in name.

By 1660 already a Jewish toll-collector had set up his toll-house in Szenicze, for this evidently was one of the locales where the continuity of Jewish presence stretched across the entire Turkish occupation like a cat-walk. Eighty years later, at the time of the incident, a Jewish community of about fifty families comprised of over 220 persons, including a teacher and two chirurgeons, flourished in the town, with a hand in every sort of local business, cash, credit and in kind. The Jews lived as tenants of the local nobility, recognized their landlords or their landlords' lord as the public authority maintaining the peace, and on occasion also had access to the imperial-royal officials who themselves had authority if not always real power over the local grandees. The incident related by Dr. Miklós reveals a great deal about the Jews' situation in Hungary during the first half of the 18th century.

On the night of May 10, 1739, someone stole a monstrance and an-other ritual vessel from the tabernacle of Szenicze's Catholic church. Immediately, suspicion fell on one George Petrassek, a Christian, who was brought before the local seigneurial court and duly charged. At once Petrassek confessed to several thefts, whereupon, according to the frontier-justice ways of those days, he was condemned to death and taken to the scaffold. But then the court, always a step ahead or at least not too many steps behind malefactors, and in the hope of perhaps discover-ing other criminal acts too, postponed the execution and ordered that Petrassek be put to the torture. The condemned man had of course noth-ing to lose at this point, so under 2nd degree torture already he owned up to, yes, having taken the ritual objects, and as even more pain was inflicted on him, also identified his accomplices. They were another Christian named Irlyna, the Jews Samuel Löb and his son, and also Rabbi Moses, the magistrate and leader of the Jewish community, a relatively substantial and privileged person according to the 1735 census, the own-er of ten cows and a still for distilling brandy, and a tenant of the Baron Miksa Horeczky, to whom he paid a high annual tax. The four men were immediately made to confront their accuser and respond to his accusation, but even in the face of emphatic denials Petrassek stuck to his story. Back to the scaffold he went then and got his due.

Now the court turned to deal with the alleged accomplices and by way of facilitating their confessions, subjected them also to every legally permitted means of torture, an enumeration of which might quickly convince you that maybe justice is not blind but just can't bear to look. The younger Löb and Rabbi Moses continued for a while to insist on their innocence, but the senior Löb, an elderly man, succumbed under the 4th degree and Irlyna under the 12th. They both admitted that they had had a part in the theft and also implicated the two holdouts. Then after further turns of the screw, as it were, the younger Löb also confessed and even offered details of a planning session attended by all the culprits and of the paternal pressure to participate brought to bear on him. Only Rabbi Moses, apparently an uncompromising literalist with regard to the commandments, could not and would not falsely swear to having done something he actually had not.

The judges had promised the accused Jews that if they confessed and converted they would not be harmed, and it was it seems with this promise in mind that both Löbs did confess, and after being jailed, or thrown into some kind of dungeon I would guess, also converted. Nevertheless, after Irlyna confessed too, all four accused men were sentenced to death. The court considered first cutting off Irlyna's and the Löbs' hands, but then, in a sudden fit of due-process remorse, decided against doing so since it had not been proved that those hands had indeed touched the ritual vessels. They also did show some mercy to the Löbs for having converted and ordered that they be punished no more than having their necks broken. Irlyna and Rabbi Moses, on the other hand, although I'm not sure of the exact significance of the distinction, were to be hanged, and upon death all four bodies were to be burned on a pyre. Hanging and burning were to be the lot also of a certain Benjamin Wolff, a Jewish tobacco merchant from out of town also convicted of the crime, even though important people from Nikolsburg, a sizable town in Moravia, and others too swore by affidavit that Wolff had not even been in Szenicze on the night in question, and Wolff maintained his innocence even under torture.

The Jews of Nyitra County, where Szenicze was then located, outraged by the injustice visited on the innocent men, did the only thing they could, which was to promptly petition King Charles III (the aforementioned Emperor Charles VI) to suspend execution of the sentences and have the hasty acts of the seigneurial court and the documents generated in the legal process reviewed in Vienna. In response, on June 22nd, the royal chancery did order as the petitioners had requested, but by then it was too late. On June 13th, the senior Löb had been beheaded, and Rabbi Moses, Benjamin Wolff and Irlyna had been hanged from a tree, after which all four bodies had been burned. The younger Löb had been given the opportunity to learn the tenets of the Catholic faith and pay restitution to the despoiled church in Szenicze, and was eventually let go.

Dr. Miklós describes the local noble, a certain Count Nyári, whose court condemned and executed Rabbi Moses as "personally cruel and capricious towards Jews as well as his peasants," and reports that the community in Szenicze had preserved the belief that even for a man of such high rank the 1739 miscarriage of justice was so egregious that the king stripped the count's court once and for all of the power of life and death. As both an addendum to and an amendment of the official record, he also recounts a version of the fateful incident he had heard from his own master as a historian of Hungarian Jewry, who himself had heard it in his own childhood from a very famous old rabbi, who in turn had heard it from his own grandfather, who had been present at the proceedings. An excellent example of the oral tradition at work that is, I must note, performing flawlessly in the printed 200th-anniversary commemoration and in the process even providing its own bonafides.

According to that grandfather, the cause of the noble's vengeance, for that's what it was, had been a certain *Schöndel Schossburg*, that is, the Schossburg Beauty, a Jewish woman originally from Schossburg in Moravia (apparently the home of poor innocent Benjamin Wolff too) who had married a man from Szenicze. One day a servant of the count "allowed himself a gesture or movement of some sort that had insulted the *Schöndel*'s womanly honor," says Dr. Miklós, whereupon she slapped the servant's face. The count, sitting in his court, fined her a ducat for this, but at the same time he also touched her disrespectfully. The *Schöndel* then asked him jokingly: "And what kind of fine is payable for slapping a nobleman's face?" "Ten ducats," replied the count. Defiantly, the *Schöndel* threw the money on the table and gave Nyári a ringing slap. The count, already a laughing-stock, thought it not seemly to have a score to settle with a woman, but swore to settle it all right with her fellow Jews. So around noon after the thief Petrassek was taken into custody, he was escorted to outside the synagogue and told to point to some of the exiting worshipers by way of identifying his accomplices. And so Rabbi Moses met his fate.

Oh, yes, the grandfather had also added that before their execution Rabbi Moses and Benjamin Wolff, not wanting to risk reciting their dying prayers bareheaded, had asked that their skullcaps be *nailed* to their heads. And so on the second day of the Jewish festival of Shavuot in the year 5499, each man was adorned with that bespoke crown of thorns, then the noose was slipped over his innocent head and the sentences were duly carried out. Since the victims' co-religionists considered them martyrs who had died for their faith, they adopted the practice of saying a special prayer for their souls in the Szenicze synagogue on each anniversary of the tragedy, as calculated according to the Jewish calendar of course. In line with the tradition-governed ways of Judaism, this practice was still observed 200 years later. In fact, Dr. Miklós even includes in his book a separate insert with the text of that prayer, which, he advises, the reader, like myself for example, may conveniently place in his own prayer book and the prayer itself recite wherever he may be performing his religious observances on the day in question. The prayer, printed in both the original Hebrew and a Hungarian translation, says that the martyrs "surrendered their souls to hard and bitter torture and surrendered their bodies like sacrificial sheep." It then goes on to ask God to let "their souls wing their way to the realm of eternal life." Rabbi Moses is identified by his full name, Moshe Ben Jaakov, that is, Moses, son of Jacob. Following his death, his first son came to be known as Jacob Bak (Bock in English), B-k being an acronym for the Hebrew Ben Kadoshim, that is, the son of martyrs. His second son was Joseph Hőnig, my direct ancestor.

But just exactly how was Rabbi Moses a martyr? Well, he was obviously so because his life would have been spared had he converted, because he died rather than deny his God. In other words, because he was killed for *being a Jew* and for no other reason. But if that is all there is to it, then isn't everyone ever killed just for being a Jew also a martyr, even if that makes for an awful lot of martyrs over the years? For the career of the Jews in martyrdom started very early. It's hard to say just exactly how early, but certainly the struggle of the Maccabees in the 160s BC was already in response not to conquest or marauding or being carried off as slaves, but rather to Seleucid efforts to suppress Jewish religious practices. Then around the year 40 AD an even more definitive episode of martyrdom was triggered by the Jews' refusal to worship the Emperor Caligula as a god, a collective act of faith that set the stage for the First Jewish-Roman War and the destruction of the Second Temple in 70 AD. And not much later, with the rise of Christianity, the martyr-tendency took permanent possession of center court in Jewish history as the Jews rejected baptism and committed themselves for good rather to remain different from Christians, to hold on to their differentness as a group, insistently and incorrigibly even in the face of extreme pressure to do otherwise, while also demanding to be allowed to live, to *live as Jews*, in a Christian world. Of course, the Jews have not been alone in preferring to die rather than submitting to another religion, culture or worldview. They have been no different in this respect from all the Catholic and Protestant casualties of the European wars of much of the 16th and 17th centuries, or from the Kurds, the Catalans and the various peoples of the Caucasus, for example, who have been and are still today ready to give their lives for national independence. But the Jews outdid all these peoples and others like them too in that after 70 AD they were not sacrificing in an effort to either acquire or defend a homeland.

In any case, by and large it was the readiness to die for his faith and lack of a country that accounted for the Hungarian Jew's situation during the first half of the 18ᵗʰ century, which I can summarize as follows. The Jew lived with his bags packed, for his arrangements were always impermanent and his tomorrow always uncertain. The Schossburg Beauty could banter with the count, but you could insult her at will; Rabbi Moses could live in relative comfort, but you could murder him with impunity. So I understand, and you do too probably, why his family could not keep living its traumatized Jewish life in Szenicze, why it had to move on. Not because the Jew was a wanderer, never mind the figure of medieval legend and many works of art, for he was obviously a properly domesticated human being with the need to be rooted in some given location, but he wandered plenty nevertheless, had no country to call his own, and perhaps most importantly had no connection to *land* or *the land*, or to any piece or parcel or portion of mother earth. The Jew could not stand; the Jew could only run. And the Jew could never be content with this lot in life. So he was ever in search of a domicile of just the kind that seemed nowhere available to him: a place where he could make a secure living by the standards of the times and was accepted and safe, where he could be in the midst of the Christian world and allowed to be a Jew.

But wasn't a home like that just a Jewish wish-fantasy? What reason was there to think that the Jew, first and foremost an outcast, a being who derived all meaning in life from his beloved faith, from the religion that in any world other than one of tolerance would always have to make him exactly what he was then – what reason to think that he would ever find such a home? Under what conditions, if you can think of any, would he be able to make his own what now belonged to others, others who hated him and were revolted by him and indeed found it against their own most cherished principles and deepest interests to feel otherwise? Where would or could such a place ever be? Could you possibly imagine or hope that that place would turn out to be Hungary?

A MORE OR LESS GRUDGING ACCOMMODATION

Maria Theresa, Holy Roman Empress and Queen of Hungary from 1740 to 1780, was no Jew-lover. During 1744-45 she even expelled the Jews from Prague, the last European monarch to resort to that particular form of persecution. An old story has it that when she had to receive a rich Jew for a private audience, she retreated behind the mock-fortifications of a linen screen, as if to ward off some kind of physical or spiritual contamination. Nevertheless, conditions and opportunities for Hungary's Jews improved somewhat during her reign, and for the by-now usual economic reasons. You see, Maria Theresa overhauled the empire's administration, and the corps of officials newly installed in all the provinces of her vast sovereignties governed with full awareness of the economic value that could accrue to the country and indeed to their mistress from activities the Jews could be counted on to undertake. And so the officials began actively to side with the Jews in their cat-and-mouse games with the royal free cities. For example, they issued warnings to the Pest city council when it was trying to prevent Jews not only from settling in town but also from staying there overnight. And they seem even to have achieved some results with this, for Jewish merchants did start doing steady business in Pest from the 1750s on, even though they had to be content with residing across the river in Óbuda. Unfortunately, in other cities they made no progress. In and around Debrecen, for example, it was only towards the end of the century that Jews appeared at all.

The first *significant* improvement in the Jews' lot came in 1783. Three years earlier, Joseph II, Maria Theresa's son and her co-ruler for some time already, the emperor sort of associated with Mozart, got sole possession of the throne, and he was an enlightened man and a reformer. He believed in religious tolerance and in making all human resources available to society at large, including resources that had until then been stifled by feudalistic rules or arrogated for private benefit. True, Joseph was despotic by temperament, but ironically that meant, among other things, that he was not averse to using force to foster freedom, that is, compelling his subjects also to be tolerant. And so, in 1783 he issued an am-I-the-emperor-or-what decree granting Jews the right to settle in royal free cities throughout Hungary.

The decree did not exactly put the keys to the city gates in the Jews' hands, but it did inject a radically new attitude into the overall state-and-religion relationship. Royal agents and the city fathers of Pest still had to lock horns over the issue of *where* in the city the Jews could reside, and certain neighborhoods continued to remain off limits to them, but nevertheless by the end of the century Jewish migrants were coming to Pest not only from Óbuda but also from throughout the country and even from neighboring kingdoms. The community now numbered more than one thousand, was established in one of the newer districts, shopped in its own market, ate out in a handful of restaurants serving kosher food, worshiped in a legal prayer-house with its own rabbi (although the Torah scroll still had to be rented from Óbuda) and encouraged its descendants to honor their forebears in its own cemetery. A modern historian summarizes the business activities of the Jews of Pest at this time as follows: "they typically traded in grain and cattle, tanned and sold leather, fur, wool, linen and other textiles. Most frequently they dealt in leather, for tanneries were not organized in guilds and did not require the permission of any guild, a trade license was enough." And Pest was not the only place of greatly enlarged opportunities; albeit still slowly, expanded Jewish settlement now proceeded in many parts of the country.

The Jewish population grew steadily, as did its economic importance. In 1787 there were 83,000 Jews in Hungary, an almost fivefold increase in the half-century since 1735. And in 1784 the Jews made the wagons groan by delivering an aggregate tolerance tax of 80,000 forints to the imperial treasury, while all the royal free cities together paid only 15,600. No wonder they called them free. Of course, a good deal of the demographic surge resulted from immigration. Jews from Bohemia and Moravia were still heading south, although that influx was already slowing down. However, in the First Partition of Poland in 1772, another one of those Eastern-European territorial surgeries, the Habsburgs grabbed the province of Galicia, which had an unusually large Jewish population, and that acquisition triggered a 100-year-long movement south that eventually created a Jewish presence in the eastern, and especially north-eastern part of the Kingdom of Hungary, just as the earlier mass migration had created one in the western part. But the two contingents of newcomers were so different from each other that from here on you have to think twice before speaking collectively of Hungarian Jews. For the Jews settling west of the Danube tended to be progressive economically and otherwise, whereas those seeking a new home in the northeast were very poor and thoroughly traditional. But as these things work out frequently, the new arrivals from either point of departure fit in well with the Jewish communities already existing at their respective destinations.

Altogether there were several Josephinian decrees that bestowed or imposed new rights on the Jews, including even extension of compulsory military service to them. But these decrees were opposed by the Christian population, although not to the last letter and not to a man. Not surprisingly then, upon Joseph's death in 1790 the Jewish gains were challenged. The cities of Pest and Nagyszombat, for example, wanted to expel the Jews newly settled within their territories and would actually have done so had they not been prevented by local agents of the royal government. Seeing how things were going, in the same year Jewish representatives, whom I would guess to have been the leaders of the Pest community, petitioned the Diet, the country's bicameral representative body, to sort of confirm the decrees by ordering their enforcement, which the Diet did graciously do, but only after it diluted the most radical measures. The *right* to settle in royal free cities itself was watered down like institutional soup to apply only to Jews who had already established themselves in such locations at an earlier date. But maybe as a gesture of good faith, or actually a sop, the Diet also condemned the blood libel, not actually outlawing it, but just calling it a "medieval superstition" and likening its legal recognition to witch trials in days of old. Heh, heh, kill 'em with kindness!

Developments in Debrecen neatly sum up the not entirely negative reaction of the *cities* to these early, and quite logical I think, initiatives for inclusion of the Jews. Since no Jew had managed to settle in Debrecen prior to 1790, none had to be allowed to do so now either. And the town council made sure that none did. But the number of Jewish peddlers at the local fairs did keep increasing, and some of them, like the seeds of a non-dominant species, even planted roots just outside the large dry ditch that surrounded the town in lieu of a wall, although they were still prevented from spending even one night inside. The council also liked the commercial benefits of the Jewish presence and did permit first establishment of a Jewish inn outside the moat, and then in 1791 the building of a synagogue, which the city even financed, near the inn. So at this date the Jews were still accepting even the crumbs brushed off the table for them, like the right to butt up against but not to settle *in* the city, although in hindsight these very ungenerous concessions did signal an improvement in their situation and, yes, a veritable foot in the door.

The last decades of the 18ᵗʰ century were also the time when in another part of the country Joseph Hőnig, Rabbi Moses's younger son, pioneered Jewish settlement. Dr. Miklós reports that after the terrible events the family cleared out of Szenicze. Sometime later, the Church made Joseph the manager of its benefice in Buda – most likely by way of compensation of sorts, our family reporter conjectures, seeing here perhaps some principle of collective responsibility in action, since the Church itself had not harmed Rabbi Moses – and then about thirty years after that, around 1770, that is, as a promotion of sorts perhaps Joseph was given the lease of the Church's estate at Mágocs in Baranya County, in the southern section of today's Hungary, west of the Danube and not far from the town of Dombóvár, where Leslie himself was born much later of course. So Joseph and his three sons moved to Mágocs at a time when Jews were not yet living in the county. Venturing into the unknown, where he himself would be a stranger. As his ancestors had done so often, and his successors too, say I, would occasionally.

Joseph's wife is not mentioned by Dr. Miklós, and Joseph may indeed have been a widower, but having more than a casual interest in your-life-is-what-you-carry relocations, I have not been able just to fall into line with the family chronicler's silence. Instead I have named the woman Gietle, a name I know to have been used in Leslie's family, and imagined that she, a woman with a nervous constitution who never got over the Szenicze tragedy and lived her years in Buda compulsively cloistered in her estate-manager's home – that she too did start out on the long journey with the family, two priests and three feral-looking servants. But the first afternoon, hardly a dozen miles south of the capital and with the October sun already low, the convoy of three wagons had to sidle over to let pass a heavy carriage drawn by a gleaming team of six. The countess inside, on her way back to the city, stopped to let one of the priests kiss her gloved hand and then even had her footman help her down. She was splendid in a tall crested hat and a red riding habit. Upon being told of Joseph's services to the Church, she demanded to see the man's wife so she could give her a coin. The priest got Joseph to climb down from the bench and very reluctantly Gietle also emerged from the Jewish privacy of the wagon, her kerchief knocked askew by a canvas flap and covering her left eye. She curtsied awkwardly. The noblewoman looked at her with an insolently insistent gaze, reached out her hand, said "here," and when Gietle failed to extend her own hand, dropped the proffered coin into the dust. After that encounter Gietle crawled out from the wagon no more. Three days later, with still many leagues to Mágocs, her body gave out and she died with a long gurgling sigh. Joseph blessed the Lord in his infinite wisdom.

In 1939, there still existed in the family's possession a German-language contract of purchase from 1791 between the Town of Mágocs and *Jozseph Hőnig Jude*, pursuant to which the latter, apparently retired from his service to the Church but wanting to stay on in the town, bought a house on a lot of about an acre and a half. The contract stipulates that this forefather of mine was not to sell the property to another foreign Jew, but that he and his descendants themselves were to live on it. This is how Joseph became the founder of the Honig/Hónig/Hőnig (the name was spelled variously) and then also the Magyarized-in-name Hajdu and Hajnal families, members of which made their home over the years in numerous towns and villages of Baranya, and then also in Budapest and Vienna and obviously even beyond those European capitals. Joseph, son of the martyr Rabbi Moses, as his gravestone notes, died in 1795 and, according to instructions in his will, was buried on a plot he himself had also purchased, which later was expanded to become the town's Jewish cemetery. So he founded not only Leslie's family but also a Jewish community that thrived for a century and a half. Not a long time as these things go, but a noteworthy fact even so.

Joseph II and his devotion to tolerance were products of the Enlightenment, which in turn was, among many other things, a time of ferment for ideas about Jews and their role and position in society, a recasting of pretty much all European thinking on the subject. During the second half of the 18th century, men of ideas in both Germany and France debated whether or not Jews were foreigners, whether or not they could be enfolded into Christian society, whether or not they, all of them together, that is, were a nation, as had long been accepted, and if not a nation then what. Through the beneficent agency of reason, which was the Enlightenment successor to the faith of earlier ages, in the course of the discussions the Jewish question decomplicated itself, as it were, like the magician's string when he loosens all the knots with a flick of the wrist, into a matter of *religion* and no more. So that finally the Jew could be perceived as not so different from the Christian after all, except of course in his religious affiliation. Gotthold Ephraim Lessing, the great 18th-century German philosopher and dramatist, even wrote a play provocatively suggesting that a Jew could be admirable. In other words, to the Enlightenment generations the human being began to emerge from behind the visage, the attire and the customs of the Jew, and suddenly he was recognized, in both senses of the word, as not *essentially* different. In 1791, during the Revolution, the new understanding even manifested itself in the emancipation of, that is, the granting of full legal rights to, the Jews of France. Now that really was liberty, equality *and* fraternity!

No less significant than the appearance and spread of these ideas was the eagerness with which the Jews themselves received them, and indeed staged an enlightenment, the Jewish Enlightenment, or *Haskalah*, of their own. The most notable product of this Jewish intellectual and cultural movement was the German Moses Mendelssohn, a remarkable thinker who once, in the younger days of both men, beat out Immanuel Kant himself in a philosophical essay contest, and also a close friend of Lessing and indeed something of a model for the hero of the latter's play *Nathan the Wise*. But many Jews well short of genius also wanted to blunt the actual differences and dispel the apparent ones setting them apart from Christians. Like men just recovering from a long illness, they too wanted to breathe the bracing air of the new ideas and grabbed the opportunity to bolt from the nursing home of immemorial beliefs, rituals and customs. Indeed, they set out to do what until recently had been unthinkable: *reform Judaism*. Some argued for a more or less radical streamlining of tradition that was to proceed in tandem with their efforts on behalf of specific secular phenomena, such as the much-publicized scholarly effort to purify the German language by cleansing it of corrupt dialects like Yiddish, for example. Others were taking advantage of sectarian cracks within Judaism itself, which allowed them to think for the first time that *choices* could actually be made. And still others just could not resist applying the principles and methods of liberalizing and democratizing movements, once they became aware of them, to their own circumstances. In any case, enough Jews turned out to be sufficiently secular-minded to assure the rapid emergence of new forms of Judaism that both permitted and demanded a new relationship to the Christian world.

For the Jew, at issue here was his identity. Who was he now, and how was he to present himself to this modern world of Christians who no longer thought of him as had the goyim of old? In the past, he had been the non-Jew's idea of the Jew, although that identification had been a purely practical arrangement, with implications aplenty for his safety and livelihood but not for his sense of self. Obviously, Christians had never been able to understand what made him tick. And derision, legal constraints and even persecutions had not been able to dent his self-esteem, given the security of his special ethnic connection with God and his pride in a culture and a history of 3,000 years, which he incorrectly believed already to have passed the 5,000-year mark. But all that was likely to have little significance, now that he had been standardized as just another person albeit with a different religion, now that he had been invited into a world that demanded deeper *individual* character, as Saul Bellow once observed, now that he was to measure himself against people willing to accept him and work with him and even compete with him. Now he had to be someone and something that was appropriate for and recognizable in this world, and he had to be so genuinely and openly. No faking anymore or remaining private or hiding behind a beard. Lucky for him that the businessman was a leading player in this modern world. For he was, or many Jews were at least, as familiar and comfortable with that identity and as good in that role as any European. So he had reason to be confident that he would manage his identity-puzzles just fine.

By the turn of the 19th century, the new ideas and modernizing attitudes were reaching even Hungary. Already they are startlingly present in the preamble to a petition submitted to the Diet of 1790, which lays the foundation for the Jews' requests in these words: "Throughout the wide world, we have no homeland other than Hungary, no father other than the king,… no brothers other than those in whose society we live and die,… no refuge other than the duties all human beings have to each other without exception." This of course is a surprising avowal, given that only two years earlier, in 1788, the first reaction of Hungarian rabbis to the extension of military service to Jewish young men was an opposition born of the dread that, God forbid! Jew might have to fight Jew. Could it be that the French Revolution, which started to remake the world in the interim, and in the course of which Enlightenment ideas were so-to-speak put into practice and found, even insofar as they purported to be universal, a national formulation – could it be that the revolutionary events had also remade the leaders of the Pest Jewish community, so that by the time they were plying the quill they were enthusiastic Hungarian patriots? Not very likely. I have of course no way to know what these men thought or how they felt, but I believe that the preamble is not an altogether sincere statement. It is a self-serving although entirely forgivable exaggeration rather. But what matters here is that the Jews put those words on paper at all. That they themselves were familiar enough with Enlightenment trends just to write what they did. For that familiarity, because what it was soon to lead to, was both the most promising and, if you will, the most ominous element in the condition of Hungary's Jews at the turn of the 19th century.

But even if Hungarian nationalism was not yet really on the Jewish agenda, reform and modernization were. During the first decade of the new century a prominent rabbi from southern Hungary began promoting reforms such as preaching in German rather than Yiddish, a modified sabbath ritual and even organ music during observances. Of course, traditionalists angrily rejected his ideas, especially the scandalous claim that a certain fish, a kind of sturgeon, was kosher. But he also found many supporters. In Pest, the first Jewish preacher, as distinguished from the congregation's rabbi, was appointed around this time, and he addressed his flock in German. And the third prayer-house in the city, built in 1820, was from the start the temple of the reformists. Soon after its consecration, the congregation hired a cantor, who added a boys' choir to the service, which indeed made it remarkably like *Christian* worship. So the opposition between the two approaches was becoming more clearly defined. This Cantor Denhof was what then already you might have called a modern Jew. He was well read in secular subjects, wore fashionable clothes and shaved his beard. Sometimes he even accepted invitations to entertain at charity events in aristocratic salons. A story has it that on one occasion he gave a magnificent rendition of the aria "Rachel, quand du Seigneur," a 19th-century favorite from Halévy's then new opera *La Juive*. At this performance he appeared so worldly and so un-Jewish that someone from the audience complimented him afterwards: "Sir, you played the Jew real well." Now by way of contrast consider the epitaph of the cantor of one of the traditional synagogues in Pest: "He was able to express all the sufferings of the Jewish people in one sound." These two men led prayers during the same years in the same city almost within earshot of each other, but being Jewish meant very different things to them.

Cantor Denhof puts me in mind of Al Jolson's Jack Robin in *The Jazz Singer,* and indeed of Asa Yoelson himself, and for me the Hollywood version of the sectarian identity crisis underscores how little we really know about what had above all to be personal experiences. But who back then would have created a record of such a transformation, and a record no less available to me today? He who abandoned tradition is not likely to have, and neither is he who cleaved to it. It seems accurate, however, as suggested by the movie and readily seconded by common sense, that the most wrenching bouts of temptation and doubt and anguish would have been fought in the context of just that kind of inter-generational, father-and-son dramas, and knowing how thoroughly fanatical deeply religious people can be, at least in the three great theistic faiths anyway, many such clashes of urges and convictions could well have ended in ruptures and rendings and *shiva* sittings. Surely the Yom Kippur reconciliation on the screen was not always the denouement. And mind you, we're not talking about conversion here. In any case, the conflict could continue until the older generation died, although then the whole affair was probably over. Some sibling relationships had then to have been patched up maybe, but whether they were or not, the wounds healed, the memories faded, and for the sake of his own mental health the rebellious son let life itself confirm him in his choice. And then there was nothing anymore to prevent him from wriggling out once and for all from his hair shirt of quasi-apostasy.

Leo Castelli was the quintessential New York art dealer of his day who made art stars of Andy Warhol, Jasper Johns and many others. He was born in 1907, the same year as Rose, the son of a Hungarian banker living in Trieste and his Italian wife, both of them Jewish. Throughout Castelli's youth, his father Ernesto's maternal ancestors, the Weiszes (spelled the Hungarian way of course), gazed down on the grand family dining room from two photographs. One picture showed Ernesto's great-grandparents in the attire of traditional Jews and Mr. Weisz sporting sidelocks.

The other presented Ernesto's grandparents wearing a modern suit and dress, and appearing to be the prosperous landowners they had actually been. Tradition, I figure, was broken apart from the inside around 1840. And the diptych on the wall was probably the final manifestation of the identity crisis. For Ernesto, the living tissue of any memory, direct or mediated, of the third generation going back had long ago shriveled up and left behind only the skeleton of lineage, and the elder Weiszes had by then been reduced to little more than illustrations fit for a textbook of Jewish history. At the most, I suspect, the photographs themselves vouch-safed Ernesto only the kind of reminiscences I myself am indulging in right here and now regarding my own ancestors. They no longer evoked any gripping emotions. Some sadness only, I would think, still attending those ancestors in Trieste, and also a feeling of wonder and a bit of confusion, a ghost of the assurance a steadying force can impart to you, and a sensation of inner rippling, as it were, as when a stone drops into a still lake and sinks and sinks. For as Thomas Mann says: "Deep is the well of the past. Should we not call it bottomless?"

The Napoleonic wars were good for Hungary's agrarian economy and also gave Jewish merchants the opportunity to begin modernizing trade. The Jewish community of Pest thrived especially, with the Jewish quarter growing crowded, expanding and acquiring a previously unknown importance in the life of the city. At the most central intersection along the quarter's boundary stood a complex of buildings known as the Orczy House, the second largest building in the entire city, a multi-functional structure, almost like a town all by itself, with many apartments, storerooms, a wine-cellar suitable for long-distance merchants, restaurants and cafes. From the 1820s, when the Jewish presence in the country first reached a sort of critical mass, the occupants of the Orczy House became always more predominantly and then exclusively Jewish, and soon the premises itself came to accommodate the Jewish essentials of a prayer-house, baths, a rabbi's home and office, congregational offices and a slaughterhouse. It also happened to be next to the Jewish market and could quickly become therefore the center of Jewish commercial life in the city. The Orczy Café, which first opened its doors in 1825 and was during the earliest decades of its long existence a form of mercantile exchange for traders not only from Pest and Buda but also from most of Europe, included a strictly kosher kitchen and had Jewish newspapers on the tables. The synagogue built in 1820 was in one of the courtyards of the Orczy House. After its rabbi instituted a system of representation for the building's tenants, the men so elected became de facto representatives of the entire Pest Jewish community, and when in 1833 royal agents acknowledged that role, the community itself acquired a quasi-official standing.

Years earlier already, the failure of the Josephinian initiatives had demonstrated to the progressive elements within the community that if they wanted Hungarians to be more accepting of Jews, if they wanted the legal constraints and burdens encumbering them to be lightened and citizenship and complete equality under the law to be granted, then they themselves would have to wrest these improvements in their condition from their own neighbors rather than wait for imperial decrees to do the job. Now in the 1820s the time for this seemed to have arrived. But how were they to do this? Indeed, you have to ask, how does a minority group excluded from mainstream society ever win inclusion? What can a hated group do to be embraced, welcomed and loved? More to the point maybe, how does weakness convince strength to share its privileges? Of course, there have been many excluded groups throughout history, peoples kept out usually on account of their race, color or creed, Native Americans, for example, or the various other native peoples of all of the Americas, the Gypsies of Europe, the Irish *in* Great Britain and others too, but their experiences do not help in assessing the task that was then ahead of the Jews of Hungary. For few of those groups ever, if any, had the opportunity or the nerve or even just the hope necessary to try so to change their circumstances. Only in the case of the Jews and of African-Americans later on in the civil rights era, as far as I can tell, did the specific historical circumstances of the exclusion permit the launching of concerted inclusion efforts.

When the campaign for these improvements got started, the Jews of Hungary were already not entirely outside the wall of exclusion. An earlier breach in that wall from which they benefited greatly was made in Western Europe by the Enlightenment and the *Haskalah*, and the consequent movement for Jewish emancipation. For the pioneering French example was promptly exported by Napoleon to all the lands he conquered, and though the conservative reaction after 1815 did undo pro-Jewish decrees in many places, it could not turn back or even halt Jewish aspirations. The ideology of human dignity elaborated by the Enlightenment was not about to disappear and was ever at hand to shame Christians into accepting Jews as equals. And so in Western Europe Jewish artists and intellectuals like Heinrich Heine began promoting greater Jewish rights by working in their homelands for the cause of national awakening and the extension of political freedom in general, and their Hungarian counterparts followed their example. And much was achieved. A number of the larger states in Germany, including Prussia, emancipated Jews during the first two decades of the 19th century, with Belgium and Greece following in 1830 and the Netherlands in 1834. Unfortunately, emancipation also spawned new forms of non-legal discrimination, as the emancipation of slaves in the United States was to also by begetting its bastard, Jim Crow, but that of course was no argument against it.

And then, as views about religious and ethnic differences evolved with the Enlightenment and the *Haskalah*, the Jews of Hungary also began to find the freedom and the will to assimilate. In other words, they began to transform themselves into people more and more like members of mainstream society and thus further breached the wall of exclusion. And, as it turned out, assimilation was relatively easy. For one, given the timing, the intention generally required was not to become more Magyar but rather the less radical and less offensive one to become more modern. Indeed, the assimilating Jew and his Hungarian neighbors were actually sharing the experience of leaving behind their respective age-old customs and ways, and embracing the modern world. For another, aside from religion, the differences between Jews and Christians were fairly superficial and susceptible to quickly scarring over. So like Cantor Denhof, many Jews were now adopting modern attire, Western political and intellectual views and a generally acceptable appearance and personal habits. Even language posed little problem, because Jews spoke Yiddish, which of course is nothing other than a German dialect, and in Hungarian cities and towns German was the most commonly spoken language. Finally, assimilation was relatively easy, because nobody was trying to obstruct it. It seems that no one thought actually to take the trouble to *keep* Jews visibly distinct from Christians. The medieval badges of Jewish identity had been long ago abandoned as apparently unnecessary, and the time had not yet arrived for their genocidal 20th-century reintroduction.

The wall of exclusion was further breached when the Jews forged a special relationship with the politically active classes in the country, that is, with the aristocracy and the landed gentry, and so acquired powerful sponsors. You see, the Jews, on the one hand, and these classes, on the other, had begun already by the turn of the 19th century to work themselves into a twofold mutual reliance. First, although perched at the top of the agrarian food-chain, the owners of estates great and small *depended* on established merchants with international connections to get their products to what were no longer local or even domestic markets. And in this still-not-ready-for-capitalism country that could mean only the Jews. Without the wheelers-dealers of the Orczy House, who, all in the hope of a nice return of course, bought it from the barons of the Great Hungarian Plain and sold it to further middlemen or local distributors in Vienna, most of the grain grown in the country would have feasted only mice. Second, it was also Jews, like Joseph Hőnig for example, who began providing professional estate-management services to the landowning classes and so liberated the latter from responsibilities they were not in any case qualified to discharge. In that role, the Jews found their own financial security and also made it possible for their suddenly well-revenued masters to live a *Sachertorte* life *mit schlag* in Pest or Vienna.

These symbiotic entanglements had first developed at the turn of the 19th century and then just kept increasing in importance as Western Europe industrialized and challenged agricultural Hungary to integrate itself always more thoroughly and profitably into the continental supply-and-demand networks.

And in the 1820s an even more compelling identity of interests came to solidify this co-dependence and actually made the Jews indispensable to society's dominant group. Within the Hungarian nobility a liberal faction came into being at this time, a political party of sorts dedicated to the country's modernization, the sparking of Magyar nationalism and the ousting of German in favor of the *native* tongue as the country's official language. There was also of course a liberal faction within Hungarian Jewry, the reformers and the thousands of ordinary believers who already worshiped according to modern ideas and considered themselves members of the modern world. Neither one of these factions was strong enough to carry the day against its particular opponents. But between them there was a fit. If the Jews, who were in any case in the midst of shaping their own modern identity, became Magyar in speech, sentiment and *ethnic* membership, then they would increase the Magyar proportion in the country's population from a nice enough but heart-breaking plurality to near a chest-thumping absolute majority, and so they would make a critical contribution to the nationalist goals. In exchange for that the liberal nationalists would support the Jews' improbable hopes and wishes to belong to Hungary as their country and national home, as the Jews had already made believe they were a generation earlier in their 1790 petition. And so both parties did. It was a perfect alliance, a reciprocal back-scratching so all-around satisfying that it was bound long to prosper.

But there was also opposition to the Jews and their undertaking, and it came mainly from two sources. The commercial classes, that is, old-time merchants and members of crafts guilds, patrician town fathers and city-dwellers in general, were the most determinedly opposed to granting Jews equal rights under the law. In the eyes of such people, Jews were still just customer-stealers and business-spoilers in what seemed like mostly zero-sum games. Of course, they saw only a small part of reality, but what they did see, you have to admit, they saw clearly. The Jews were indeed competitors, and tough ones at that. So frequently even in Pest they still had to suffer humiliations when trying to obtain a license to settle. But there at least sometimes the victimized Jew could get support from the royal government; elsewhere he could be unhesitatingly rebuffed. In Debrecen, for example, the city council discussed the issue of Jewish rights and how liberal voices throughout the country were speaking up in its favor, but then it just continued adamantly with its exclusionist position. In 1829 the country's established commercial classes even tried to form a united front in face of the common enemy, and to that end towns sent representatives to Pest to formulate a petition to well-disposed members of the Diet. But then these particular efforts just fizzled out.

As you would expect, very stiff opposition was also generated by prejudice, by a variety of mostly irrational but deeply ingrained, traditional, indeed folklorish anti-Jewish sentiments. Some Christians just plain hated Jews. But to many others less vehement, and under the law too, the Jews were still just Jews, the grain merchant still a peddler with only a gold watch fob across his vest in place of the frayed rope of old. And so they were still treated with contempt or at least disdain. Sarcastically, Christians called the Orczy House the Orczy Palace, as if a Jew could ever possibly live in an aristocratic residence. After all, everybody knew what the Jewish quarter of Pest was like, with its street vendors, gabbling unwashed crowds and strange smells, more like a Middle Eastern *suk* than a proper European neighborhood. And the many Jewish boys who attended a Catholic or Protestant school rather than the Jewish school established in Pest in 1814 had to sit at back-of-the-bus desks and politely tolerate pointed slurs on their faith and their customs. At a minimum, people just considered the Jews' trying to barge into the country's life like this, like it belonged to them, a national affront. Would such prejudices ever disappear? Well, many Jews were actually confident that they would, that more strenuous assimilation, continued pro-Magyar enthusiasms and the passage of time would finally win them not only full rights but also a general acceptance. But what else could they have done?

Beginning in the 1820s the Jews began openly to promote their agenda, relentlessly petitioning the state, the counties and the towns for improvements in their status. At first they focused on abolition of the humiliating tolerance tax, but their pleas fell on deaf ears. The treasury was loath to give up the lucrative tax, and the aristocracy too wanted to hold on to this protection-money in respectable guise. And in general too their requests for the loosening of restrictions were stonewalled. In a proposed publication submitted to the censor in 1834, a disappointed Jewish writer could still list, as if drawing up a balance-sheet, the following as the Jews' remaining chief complaints: absence of civil rights, ineligibility for official positions, prohibition from buying or renting real estate from members of the nobility, being limited to commerce alone as a way to make a living and to medicine as a profession, and exclusion from mining towns and from many royal free cities. Meaning to insult no doubt, the censor noted on the submission that actually Jews could also make a living by leasing manufactories, rights to distill liquor and slaughterhouses.

Under the constitutional system prevailing in the country, known without even a tinge of irony as enlightened despotism, law-making required the participation of both the king and the Diet. First, the king, that is, the emperor in Vienna, had to convoke the two-house representative body, which he did only irregularly and as the government deemed financially necessary, as had also been the practice of the kings of England with regard to Parliament through the 17th century and the kings of France with regard to the Estates-General through the 18th, until revolutions put an end to such prerogatives. The Diet then took up matters it considered important or proposed to it by the king, and whatever laws it passed were then sent to Vienna for final royal approval. The Jews of course understood these legislative arrangements and knew that the fate of their campaign was in the hands of the Diet. In any case, it was only action by the Diet, though by today's standards even that was highly undemocratic, that could possibly be considered an expression of the views of the Hungarian people. So the Jews concentrated their efforts on the representative assemblies meeting in Pozsony (today's Bratislava) from time to time.

In 1825, after a 13-year hiatus during which the country was governed by imperial decree, the king convoked the Diet once more. It was a historically significant assembly that came to be known as the first of two Reform Diets, and already the Jews entertained high hopes that among the reforms it considered would be a favorable response to their much-petitioned grievances. But it was not to be. The commentators say only that more pressing matters seemed to take precedence. The next Diet, which convened in 1832, also produced no results, but the second Reform Diet, convoked in 1839, did in its second year. This latter Diet was to pass the law making Magyar the country's official language, so it was led by forces allied with the Jews and sympathetic to their quest, and was expected *finally* to grant the full equality under law many felt by then to be long overdue. And sure enough, emancipation did pass the lower house, but then, frustratingly, failed in the upper. Enacted instead was a much more limited law with almost-empty provisions, most notably the right for Jews to own land and reside in any city, town or village, excepting only mining towns. But of course this was not much more than affirmation of the status quo, since the new rights extended only to pursuit of such businesses and professions *as the Jews had been* pursuing and to acquisition of land for building their homes *where they had* acquired land before already. A grave disappointment! Maybe even a slap in the face.

There were two Diets during the 1840s, but they also failed to advance the cause of the Jews. One reason for this was a reaction to the law of 1840 that brewed up throughout the country, in particular because it was seen, as insubstantial as it was, to have opened even more the taps of the Galician influx. Another was the passing of the leadership of the liberal movement to Lajos Kossuth, or Louis Kossuth as he is known to English-speakers. Although Kossuth believed strongly in emancipation, and is in fact often considered *the* emancipator, he viewed the Jewish quest in the context of overall national politics and deemed it advisable to proceed at a more measured pace than his predecessors had. So whatever progress there had been was now pretty much stalled.

Obviously, the Jews had to try to sway public opinion in their favor. And so, from the 1830s on, their liberal allies were assiduous in calling public attention to the injustice of the oppression, the baselessness of anti-Jewish prejudice and the benefits that emancipation and assimilation, including above all the enlargement of the Magyar nationality within the country, would confer on the nation. In particular, the writer and statesman Baron Joseph Eötvös presented the case for the Jews in especially forceful and convincing terms. And wherever the opportunity presented itself, the Jews themselves confirmed the claims made on their behalf by their own public-spirited and patriotic acts. In 1838, for example, a devastating flood of the Danube provided the Jews of Óbuda with a newsworthy opportunity to demonstrate their fellowship with Christians. As ice-floes carried by the ice-cold waters of the raging river swept over Pest, the Jews on the other side showed extraordinary courage, kindness and concern for all people and livestock in danger, helping to rescue them from bobbing, buffeted boats and sheltering them in their synagogue, which you could enter after all without being struck dead on the spot. And then in 1840-41 the Jews further promoted their own cause when, with Eötvös's encouragement, a Jewish linguist completed his years of labor and published a Hebrew-Hungarian bilingual edition of the Torah. Now even that which had never been much of a mystery could be considered demystified!

These efforts did help the cause, as did also the political maneuverings, but all in all the three decades of Jewish campaigning for acceptance and equality produced meager results. If you compare Joseph II's decree of 1783 with the 1840 law, the Diet's most liberal response to Jewish demands, you have to rub your eyes and wonder if time had stopped. For 57 years later it's pretty much the same rights that are being granted the Jews all over again, and once more without a real rewriting of the attendant rules. For a law is only as good as its enforcement, and in this case prejudice-free enforcement was far from countrywide. Kassa (today

Kosice in Slovakia) immediately sought designation as a mining town, Győr issued licenses to settle only on very difficult terms, and Pozsony was going to allow Jews to live only within its old ghetto. As for the Debrecen authorities, they still operated under the influence of the guilds and so allowed still only relatively few Jews to settle, and even those who gained the privilege still faced a hostile and rigid town council that treated them as disgusting pollutants and obstructed them in all their endeavors every way it could. So quickly it became apparent that without significant ancillary rights, as it were, the privilege to live in cities re-granted in 1840 did not amount to much.

It is notable, though, that even while their legal gambits were being deflected or blocked, the Jews were gaining ground in other ways. For one, during these decades the Jewish population continued to grow. By 1840 there were 239,000 Jews in Hungary. And the growth was more than proportional, with the percentage of the country's Jews increasing from the 1.3% of 1787 to 2.6%. For another, they were also moving to the cities in significant numbers, as well as dispersing into small towns and villages everywhere, including of course Baranya County. A census conducted there in 1846 records the presence of 476 Jewish families, not including those of Pécs, the major city of the county, ten of whom were descendants of Joseph Hőnig. The tabulated names include a Salamon Honig, who was Joseph's grandson and my own great-great-grandfather, another empty frame hanging in the family picture gallery. Or almost empty, I should say, for I do know that he was a "substantial tenant farmer" (as were also six other of the ten Honig families), even though his annual income just covered his own and his dependents' (wife, two sons, a daughter and a Christian servant) expenses, with nothing left over for the profit column. But the details of Salamon's life that I'd really like to know about were of no concern to the census-taker and have therefore not been recorded. Was he a reform-minded Jew or a traditionalist? Certainly, only 80 years later, his own grandson brought up Leslie as a Hungarian-speaker and an aggressive man with a fork when there was pork on the table. Was he already in 1846 a Hungarian patriot, as his descendants were to be right through the 1920s and 30s? And, what I am the most curious about, did he consider his situation to be one of security and stability built on a half-century of half-hearted acceptance, or were his bags still permanently packed, figuratively speaking, and his own great-grandfather's martyrdom still a frequent reminder of what it might truly mean to be a Jew in Hungary?

During the 1840s there were also the following additional signs of progress in the Jewish struggle. Now the Jewish elite of Pest began joining even the social and cultural activities of the nobility. In other words, the cantor himself was now sitting in the audience. And now there were also more opportunities than ever for economic success. And, just as importantly, the belief also further strengthened *on both sides* that the Jew could indeed assimilate to a degree where really only his religion, but not his lifestyle or behavior or even the scope of his life, so to speak, would have to differentiate him from his Christian neighbors. In 1847 the chief rabbi of Szeged published a sort of declaration of assimilation, the first two points of which read as follows: "(1) The duties we owe to our fellow men we owe not only to Jews but also to non-Jews." And "(2) Acknowledging that Hungary is our real and only homeland, we will try to inject a few drops of love for her and of patriotic zeal into the hearts of all our brethren." This second point was apparently intended as an apology for the still many unreconstructed Jews in the country, some of whom at least, disaffected with the direction things were taking, began even to question how assimilation and this Hungarian patriotism thing really differed from conversion itself.

But now the Jewish campaign entered a dramatically new phase in which everything changed. In 1848 came the revolution and then the War of Independence, armed attacks on absolutism and Austrian domination, tumultuous events for the Jews, as for all Hungarians of course, although not entirely in the same way. The Jews immediately supported the revolutions that ignited on March 13th in Vienna and on March 15th in Pest, and that support may, ironically, have contributed to the *pogroms* that quickly followed in Pozsony and Kassa and Pécs – well, near-pogroms since they stopped just short of killing. The looters, arsonists and wield-ers of sticks and clubs were mostly *German*-speaking guild-members, who thought that now for sure the Jews will demand equality, and also saw the political disturbances as an opportunity to hurt and avenge themselves on their more successful capitalist rivals. At demonstrations signs read-ing "Long Live Liberty!" alternated with others reading "Out with the Jews!" Even in Pest County, the newly appointed authority, controlled by *German* patricians, at once ordered the expulsion from the city of all Jews who had settled there after 1840. The vehemence of these senti-ments surprised Kossuth, now the revolution's leader, and convinced him that sticking up for the Jews just then would have been an affront to the fervor of the masses. So a Jewish petition of grievances submitted to the revolutionary parliament provoked irritation and was impatiently re-jected. Always thinking only of themselves! But what *in fact* were the Jews thinking? Well, after an as-it-were momentary shock, they swallowed hard, dismissed the troubles as nothing more than "isolated incidents" and whole-heartedly devoted themselves to the national, and so also anti-*German*, cause. Although a few of them at least also must have muttered: if only the Germans were alone in all this.

Then in September the War of Independence against Austria broke out, and at once anti-Jewish sentiments vanished. Now the Jews who came to enlist were welcome. And they came in numbers indeed from all over the country, even surreptitiously I suppose from regions inhabited by the nationalities that were now fighting on the side of the Austrians against the Magyars. Kossuth estimated 20,000 Jews in the National Guard, seven times the number that would have actually reflected their proportion in the population, a higher multiple than the Magyars them-selves. In other words, of all the nationalities they were the most heav-ily represented. Overachievers, of course! And on top of that, the Jews fought bravely, and also offered financial aid and other services to the cause. Now suddenly they were seen in a different light. There was a re-versal, indeed a flipping, of public opinion, the kind of thing that would happen if a couple of studies showed that eating, let's say, bacon was *not* bad for you. Jewish loyalty and sacrifices were even duly acknowledged in late July 1849, when at its last session the parliament emancipated all Jews born in Hungary. The bill was introduced by the prime minister, who asked the body how it could not grant equal rights to those who even without having them are shedding their blood for the nation's liberty? It passed without opposition. So the campaign had indeed succeeded, the nation had embraced the Jews as brothers. A few months later, Francis Joseph, the young emperor-king who ascended the throne during the hostilities, nullified the emancipation, as he nullified *all* the acts of the revolutionary authorities.

Nevertheless, 1848-49 was a transformational time for Hungary's Jews. This was the point where, it seems suddenly, although preparations had been underway already for half a century and the liberal alliance too was already a mature thing of decades – the point where the stream of Hungarian Jewish history ceased to be, or rather, submerged itself in the larger stream of *Hungarian* history. Just think what an utterly radical remaking of mentality this had to be for a people whose God had always communicated with them through history itself, for perhaps the most historical people the world has ever known. Living by that now long dammed up history, with its own calendar of religio-historical feasts, its own eras and ages arranged into their own sequences, its own count of past years even, had always been a major element of being Jewish and certainly of understanding what such an existence could ever mean in a larger worldly context. That history had long stood the Jews in good stead, had rallied them reliably for more than two millennia, through the unendingly recurring times like Rabbi Moses's, when life was a workaday martyrdom and the fanaticism that makes having your yarmulke nailed to your head an ingenious idea. True, that history, as had always been widely known, was more and grander than just a national narrative, it was rather a history that at least at its beginnings embraces the whole world and all of humanity, and only after a conveniently ignored proliferation of humans does it narrow down to a not too atypically megalomaniacal and divinity-riddled national narrative of the kind the Jews themselves invented by the telling of that very story. But whatever else that history had been to others, to the Jews it had always been *Jewish* history.

But then in 1848-49 something extraordinary happened. On the very downbeat of Hungarian history's most glorious and tragic two years, at the very moment when the Magyars themselves finally acquired a national consciousness and for the very first time told themselves their own national narrative – right then the Jews entered the life of the nation. For some time already they had been wishing and struggling to do this, but until then they had not been ready for it. At the conception of the nation in the 1820s they had still been hardly more than half-attentive bystanders. But now at its inception, at a time when it must have seemed instinctive and well-nigh irresistible to do so, they could and did choose to be fully-engaged participants and so they too actually started living *Hungarian* history. And they of course rejoiced in their newly-acquired heritage, and they made the transition to it so avidly and fully and faultlessly that they might have, like I just did, claimed it as their own already from further and further back in the past, from the years of the Reform Diets, the awakening of Hungarian nationalism, Metternich, the Napoleonic Wars and Josephinism. But, really, it was only in 1848-49 that the claim of a homeland boldly made in the petition of 1790 was finally and for the first time truly validated. Then the Jews finally got the homeland that until then had always remained only a misconceived and misdirected wish.

Of course, this homeland cost them dearly. And indeed, they all acknowledged and mourned the bodies left on the battlefield. But that just made it all the easier to ignore the less obvious but no less grievous loss, the loss of Jewish history, of something that had always been of the essence of Jewish identity. For what remained of *that* now but the Passover Seder?

EMANCIPATION AND ITS DISCONTENTS

After 1848-49 there was a price to pay. The victors imposed a huge fine on the Jewish community, but the Jews, then as always kings of cash, got a nice discount for immediate payment in full, and so ended their special punishment. And then things even improved. In Hungary the 1850s was a Janus-faced decade of, on the one hand, Austrian repression and, on the other, innovation and development sponsored by the oppressor, with newly-built railroads and capitalistic projects of all sorts transforming the economy. The Jews stoked the engines of growth however they could, until they were covered not with soot but with gold, and even speckled with glory. At the same time, the government also pampered them, trying to make sure that despite the nullification, they neither felt less than equal nor were disadvantaged by actually being so.

And so, these were good years for the Jews of Hungary. Everywhere throughout the country their communities flourished. They were breaking down barriers, enjoying new freedoms, swimming ever closer to the mainstream. By 1857 the Jewish population had increased to 407,800, with an always larger percentage living in cities. The Pest community, 40,000 strong by mid-century, needed a synagogue more capacious than any it already had, and its prosperous members wanted something grand. So they bought land in Dohány Street, pursued and eventually obtained the necessary license, held a well-publicized competition for the architectural commission, and had an imposing structure erected in what's identified as the Oriental-Byzantine style, although I'm not convinced that such a thing really exists. Upon its consecration in 1859, it became *the largest synagogue in the world.* In size even today it is exceeded only by Temple Emanu-El in New York. Brazen, you think? Ambitious? Confident in the future? Disgustingly ostentatious? All of the above? Well, I don't know how to think of it. Or actually I do know, and I have even let on to my answer already. Brash and American!

But the 1850s also saw the differences *within* the Jewish community sharpen and grow more formal. The progressives now came to be known as the Neologs. Although with regard to most of their positions they were comparable to Conservative Jews in the United States today, and so seem quite moderate now, their insistence on a general secularization and modernization was unacceptable to the traditionalists, who were not yet but would soon be labeled the Orthodox. This latter faction included

some who unbendingly set themselves against just about any kind of reform and stood in favor of strictly maintaining the old ways, but also many
others who did know how to straddle the identity-divide when necessary.
As the number of Jews in the country grew, and with their number their
wealth and influence, the two approaches to the faith continued to become respectively more malleable and more rigid, until one group could
no longer stand to worship under the same roof with the other. Well, everybody just wanted to connect with God the right way. Isn't that what it's
all about? The Pest Jews managed to solve this problem while still maintaining a functioning umbrella organization. It was in a spirit of cooperation that the Dohány Street synagogue was realized, and realized as a
Neolog bastion. It could hardly have been anything else of course, given
its two towers, which made it look very much like a church and earned it
the byname of the "Israelite cathedral." The Orthodox went along with
all this, but only on the condition that soon they too would get an appropriate new synagogue, which the community did indeed erect for them
during the late 1860s. Unfortunately, not everywhere in the country did
the two factions find it in their hearts to be so accommodating.

During these years the Austrians courted the Jews, seeing in them
a potential ally in blocking the Hungarian drive for independence.
But the Jews were not to be had. Despite their continued second-class
status, despite even the strong resistance they could still encounter in
Debrecen, for example, when trying to acquire houses or land, they
were devotedly Magyar. They stood firmly with the liberals. And the
liberals of course had their own ideas about the nation. Soon the Jews'
sentimental stalwartness proved to be a smart bet as well. For, starting
in the early 1860s, Francis Joseph loosened controls, invited the rebel
nobility back into the political fold and began once more to convene
the Hungarian governing bodies. Now it seemed that, hooray!, the very
last piece even was in place for realization of the most cherished goal
of the Jews of Hungary. But though enactment of emancipation by the
restored Diet seemed inevitable, in both 1861 and 1866 the Jews still
got only promises. Then finally in 1867 Francis Joseph and the liberals

made a deal known as the Compromise, a constitutional restructuring that created the Dual Monarchy of separate Austrian and Hungarian lands and governments under one crowned head of state. And now this win-win solution, trumpets!, this alchemical compounding of Habsburg rights and Hungarian national aspirations, ushered in an era of peace and prosperity for the Magyars and, fanfare!, *emancipation*, finally, and what in retrospect came to be known as a golden age for the Jews. May it last until the end of time!

At its first session, the new Hungarian Diet again emancipated the Jews. And this time it stuck. Finally they were truly invited to join the nation. But there was a *quid pro quo*, although it was one already given by some in part, and now gladly given by most in full measure: the Jews and Judaism had to accommodate themselves to the nation. Quite explicitly and officially now the Jew was expected to assimilate, that is, to become in his language, values, national sentiments, self-identification, mode of dress, family name, relations with the wider world and with modernity itself just like the Magyars, or rather just like the Magyars who lived according to the liberal ideas and practices of the reinstalled ruling class. Obviously, it couldn't have been otherwise. Just imagine the traditional Jew in his polymorphously peculiar headgear and caftan, his ways in part antiquated, in part pseudo-exotic, his Yiddish a mealy-mouthed mumbling to the Christian ear, everything about him an incitement to prejudice. No, that wouldn't have worked. The Neologs understood this and promptly set about becoming or further affirming that already they had become proud, patriotic, Magyar-speaking Jewish Hungarians. And by then even many of the Orthodox spoke only Hungarian, dressed and groomed themselves in the accepted manner, cooked the typical Hungarian-Jewish way and overflowed with love and enthusiasm for the fatherland. But, as I just said, others among them were not flexible. They would rather have given up emancipation than assimilated and forsaken tradition.

As part of the reform that Judaism itself was to undergo now, the Hungarian leadership expected, and very reasonably too from their point of view, for they were trying to run a country after all – they expected the Jews to clear their heads of their two-thousand-year-old Diaspora as of a bad dream and to organize themselves like other religions do, into something authority-friendly like a church, into something like the centralized networks that Christians had inherited still before the Middle Ages from the Roman Empire. To this end, under the aegis of Baron Eötvös, now Minister of Religious and Educational Affairs, the leadership of the ever-modernizing Jewish community of Pest proposed a General Jewish Congress. And so one was organized. On December 10, 1868, 220 deputies from throughout the country assembled in the auditorium of the Pest County Hall. 132 progressives sat on the right side of the hall, 88 traditionalists on the left, dividing the body into, as it were, two parties, although not in the same proportion for sure as their respective percentages within the entire Jewish population. Indeed, the Neologs were *grossly* overrepresented. Eötvös opened the Congress with a speech that included these words:

> The state now offers you the opportunity to rule independently in all of your religious matters and to determine according to your own ideas and principles how you wish to organize and govern your communities, something no other country has ever offered your co-religionists. I have great confidence and trust that freedom, which affects favorably all noble human endeavors, will soon bring its fruits to your community too, and that your institutions as well as your spiritual and intellectual life will develop rapidly. Since the blessings of freedom must be even dearer to a people who have been oppressed for the last two thousand years, it is my conviction that the very freedom granted by the constitution of Hungary will bind the Israelite citizens of our country to the fatherland in all circumstances.

Long, enthusiastic applause followed, more than a few tears I suspect, and shouts of "Long live the fatherland!"

But things did not go well. The Orthodox deputies, evidently hard-liners, had arrived with inflexible positions already formulated, rejecting practices that were already widely accepted, including the Magyarizing of names and the use of Christian dates on letters, and extending to every-thing that turned rabbis from something like the magistrates of the con-gregation into something like Christian preachers. Quickly it became evident that at the County Hall there would be no compromise. And sure enough, long before the Congress concluded its work ten weeks later, the Orthodox deputies had walked out. Leaving but a rump parliament of Neologs to set up a national organization. Then in 1870 the Orthodox reconvened in their own congress, and now they themselves willingly donned the administrative straightjacket, stipulating only that it not be a special model designed for Siamese twins. So the national organiza-tion, together with local districts, now split into two, and having finally recognized itself to be a compound entity, indeed something not unlike the Dual Monarchy itself, Hungarian Jewry officially divided into two de-nominations. As if the Diaspora were not punishment enough! Although there were actually three persuasions, with the third one, the self-styled Statusquo, usually being on good terms with each of the other two. The Statusquo were Jews and congregations of Jews who, either because they prized unity above all or because they could not see themselves fitting into either of the two denominations, came to the conclusion that stick-ing with what they knew was best, and so continued to function in a state of comfortable compromise.

The split may have been defined in terms of religious dogma and practices, but it also corresponded to and accentuated existing so-cial differences within the community. The progressives had all along tended to be urban folk, live a generally bourgeois, individualistic life mostly in western Hungary and feel an affinity with Jews from Bohemia, Moravia, Austria and especially Germany. In contrast, the traditionalists lived mostly a rural *shtetl*-like communal life in the northeastern part of the country and felt an affinity with Jews from Poland and Lithuania. Liberated as they were by the split too, liberated from all the baggage of a past best left behind and from those who insisted on still lugging it along, the Neologs could now assimilate even more rapidly and completely, and they could prosper all the more unrestrainedly. In contrast, being uncoupled from the Christian-aping, assimilating renegades, the Orthodox could now withdraw into an always greater isolation from the modern world. They even took their children out of Jewish schools, for it was better to attend public schools than be exposed to noxious Neolog influences. They also became always more susceptible to Hasidism, including various radical versions of it that continue to this day to thrive in Brooklyn, New York. For some communities the disunion actually meant an unending upheaval. The Jews of Debrecen, for example, first opted for the Statusquo persuasion, then lost one part of their membership, and the wealthiest part at that, to a Neolog splinter group and then another part to an Orthodox group. And all along, the community leaders labored futilely to maintain or restore unity. In any case, the nationwide split could never after be healed, and it had ramifications far into the 20th century, utterly catastrophic as you'll see for the Orthodox, but less so although still greatly tragic for the Neolog.

In addition to Debrecen's importance as (by Hungarian standards) a major urban agglomeration, I also keep returning to conditions and developments there because it was Rose's hometown. Her father, Samuel Ferencz, died there, as you may recall, in 1935. Rose didn't remember where he had been born, so I know only that he had moved about all his life from this village to that country town to another village, all of them near the regionally dominant city and in Hajdú County. My grandfather did his military service in the cavalry of the Empress Elizabeth, Francis Joseph's consort, and now in my imagination he is a faceless figure riding a spirited stallion, although he is just as likely to have spent the requisite number of years crawling around the stables with a muck-bucket in his hand. Later in life he was a mechanic who worked on agricultural machinery and for some years before the Great Depression ruined him even owned or leased a mill that he operated in conjunction with his smithy. Rose herself was born in 1907 in a tiny village where she herself, her parents and an older sister, my Aunt Pearl, resided only for a short time. Three years later, when her mother died in childbirth with a younger sister, Samuel, a man from Debrecen now in his early thirties, found himself alone with three daughters, the oldest of them five. A matchmaker probably made a quick buck then because Samuel remarried at once to the widowed mother of a young boy, the only woman I ever knew as a grandmother. They went on to have five more children. Her family was from Nagyvárad (today Oradea in Romania), a city not much east of Debrecen but actually in Transylvania. She probably took him sight unseen, calloused hands and all, but there must have been some negotiations before Samuel counted out the matchmaker's fee. For Pearl was sent to live with a less overburdered relative in a neighboring village, and the groom eased sectarian concerns by promising henceforward to be a good Jew, that is, to observe the kosher laws and keep the Sabbath too. And I believe that so he was for the rest of his life.

All I know about Rose's biological mother and her family is a name: Karolina Grosz. And that's a dead end. But the meager facts I just laid out for the Ferencz family have sort of pushed me into extrapolating something like an imaginary history for *that* lineage too. As I've said already, Galician Jews immigrated into eastern Hungary in great numbers during the first three quarters of the 19th century and especially after the 1840 liberalization of the residence rules. Samuel's family, I imagine, was among those migrants, your typical Galician Jews living the traditional life, what may fairly be described as Orthodox. Specifically who may have been the original migrant from the *shtetl* I cannot guess. Since Samuel was born in 1877, I figure that his father must have come into this world around 1850, and *his* father in 1825 or so. They, or maybe an uncle from either of those generations, are the likely candidates. But even though I can't identify which of these faces lost in the straggling crowd perpetrated this particular you-own-only-what-you-carry relocation, the relocation itself arouses a welter of old emotions in me about my own experiences of 1956. And no wonder. For as you will see in due time, the two moves do fall easily into a theme-and-variations kind of pattern, since once on the road neither Leslie nor this great or great-great maternal ancestor of mine possessed anything but what he so to speak carried on his back and the more than few doubts that he will *ever* arrive exactly where he was intending to go.

I'll call him Jacob, this ancestor, who I imagine had saved five crowns and a bit of inventory during the previous two years, starting to scrape it all together as soon as he first decided to chance the 200-mile, three-week journey to Hungary, where life was said to be less miserable, and where many of his neighbors had already gone too, although only the Almighty knew which of them had made it and which had not. You needed more money to leave of course than to stay, that was the catch obviously, but this was surely his time, what with Yitzhak leaving now too and, who knows, in a year's time the mule might also be too old. So before daybreak on a misty summer Sunday he arranged all his belongings on the two-wheeled handcart he had extended in the back and mongrelized by jerry-rigging a shaft to in the front, the bed, the chest of drawers with the winter clothes and his materials, for he was a hat maker, the table and the three stools, the trunk with his tools and dummy heads, the blankets, the two pots and the kettle and the pail, the two sets of tin plates (one set for Passover) and the tin basin, the tarpaulin to protect them from the rain, and the smaller trunk with the prayer-books and a few other religious things and household things – he loaded it all onto the cart so as to leave room enough back there for the children and Liesl to while away the time, for surely they couldn't walk the whole day. He also stowed about a dozen hats of various kinds, that was his inventory, for they had provisions only for a few days, after which he would have to sell things in the villages they passed, or barter them for food, for even if you were not a peddler at home, you had to be one while on a journey like this.

I picture the highway as a barely passable pitted track at first, but the mountains loomed up very soon after they got going in earnest, and then they started climbing along rocky paths, up to almost 3,500 feet, where only a mule could pull that wobbly cart without breaking a fetlock, and at times Jacob and Yitzhak and even Liesl had to push and maneuver, and now and then also run around the cart to tighten the ropes about the dangerously yawing chest of drawers, their rickety mainmast while sailing these uncaring seas of fate. During the day bears stared you into the immobility of terror, at night you cringed as the wolves wove the forest cover into a net of barks and howls about you. And then downhill on the other side turned out to be even worse, with shoes worn out now on all feet, bottoms tied to uppers with pieces of string. But just when Jacob thought he could bear this heaving and stumbling no more, light scattered the forest and disclosed the plains ahead of him lazing in the sun, bless the Lord!, although now you kept getting stuck in the *sand*. Ah! to be a poor man! But at least they were well in the kingdom by now, leaving Polish behind for a clownish mixture of some other Slavic tongue and the gibberish rolling off those greasy moustaches, and now they just had to find, if only their strength would hold out, a livable place someone was willing to let them have on terms they could maybe meet.

And all the way to Transylvania, perils for the migrants lurked everywhere you turned, or the fear of them anyway even when there was actually none. But they all made it, I suppose. Jacob bade farewell to Yitzhak Berkowitz in a village long forsaken by luck from the looks of it, although hopefully not by the good Lord. The place had no hat maker, but the necessary heads, yes, they all had that, so this then was it, for better and for worse, like a marriage of sorts, true enough. Then after some years I figure, and in any case only after the middle of the century, for Jews settled around Debrecen in numbers only that late, he or a descendant of his, no more laden with possessions I would think than before, continued or just literally married or wandered into Hajdú County, while still maintaining opportunistic contact with Nagyvárad, which later on may have facilitated Samuel's union with my grandmother. Most likely, Samuel was born in Hajdú County, where the family was already known in Jewish communities, including the ones he later joined and quit. And although village Jews in eastern Hungary tended to retain the old ways, he or maybe his father could not resist the siren-song of the more secular life not just open to but actually urged upon them after 1867. So they strayed from the traditional path, to which later even the good-Jew Samuel returned only with one foot.

But that's all. All, alas, that is known or that I can reasonably imagine of my ancestry on my mother's side. I'm certain that the couple of Ferencz cousins I still have could add nothing, and even if I took up haunting whatever Jewish cemeteries may still exist in Hajdú County, I would at the most be able, I think, to fill in a few blanks, and even them only in a tentative and unilluminating way. Rose herself already had nothing from or regarding the pre-war past except for a single book, which I of course inherited. On the cover that book calls itself *A Century of Debrecen Jews* and on the spine *The Memorial Book of Debrecen Jews*, and indeed it is both a history of what was a century-long era of Jewish life in Debrecen and vicinity and a commemorative list of the names of the local Jews who perished in the Holocaust. Two columns of names inside an inky frame on each page. It was published (in both Hungarian and Hebrew, conveniently starting at opposite ends of the volume) on the basis of subscriptions I would guess in Tel Aviv in an unspecified year that I would also guess to have been during the 1970s. It's the source of my information about the Jews of Debrecen. It lists two of Rose's brothers, who died in the forced labor service on the Ukrainian steppes, and two names are no defense against the feeling of insignificance that stole over me like an icy shadow when, reading that book on a winter evening, I again owned up to how brief earthly afterlife is if you're an ordinary person, how quickly your history vanishes even aside from the Holocaust if you did not live a public life. Although, I have to admit, with the recording technology available today being what it is and always improving, like it or not, this may actually no longer be our fate or the fate of our progeny.

But indeed, memory is short and *history* itself has only a feeble hold on us modern folk. Consider, for example, the Jews of Hungary after emancipation, who were assimilating now more than ever, in greater numbers and always more completely, with many of them pursuing worldly success and all that it entitles you to as if they had simply forgotten history. Or rather, as if they had convinced themselves, as many of them must have, that belonging and acceptance and even power were truly what they had always wanted, and that in achieving those things they were actually *honoring* their history. Or, indeed, as if they, true proponents and products of modernity, were simply blind to the Sebaldian vision of the present as perforce generated by collective pasts. In any case, throughout the land and from all classes, the Jews now set out to feed, blend and homogenize their lives and culture into the dominant but still backward, provincial and even semi-feudal life and culture of the *Magyar* Christian population. And their progress during the half-century from the Compromise to World War I was remarkable even when compared to Jews upon their emancipation in other European countries. Indeed, the Jews of Hungary turned these years into an era of modernizing gains of all sorts, a *golden age* in many respects (which I will now enumerate) of very gratifying solutions to the myriad-faceted problem of just who and what these newly-minted Magyars of Israelite faith would be and how exactly they would fit in.

The assimilation is considered to have been completed by the turn of the century. By then a higher percentage of Jews than of any other minority were claiming Magyar as its mother tongue, conversing in that language at home, reading newspapers in it, and reading *Hungarian* literature rather than any other. Many Jews had also Magyarized their family name, like all of my grandfather Miksa's cousins, including of course Dr. Miklós, abandoning Hónig for Hajdu or Hajnal, and many now also spurned traditional Jewish given names for their children. So Jacob, Moses and Aaron, and all the other patriarchs, matriarchs and prophets too, major and minor, now yielded to Hungarian or pseudo-Hungarian arch-ancestors like Árpád, Attila, Géza and Béla. There were always more and more mixed marriages too. In 1895, the year Judaism was added to the Christian denominations on the list of the official religions of the realm, they were finally legalized too, so that now for the first time a Jew could give in to his secret lust for a *shiksa* and assimilate even without having to convert. Although there were a fair number of baptisms too, a fair number of Jews who went all the way, as it were. But that too was widely accepted, for at least the leaders of Christianity and Judaism now recognized each other as equals. The chief rabbi of Debrecen was good friends with the local bishops, Catholic and Lutheran. On national holidays, crowds of Christians even came to hear his sermon. During the 1880s the Debrecen Jewish women's union held charity events for the benefit of Christians, and it was not unusual for rich Jewish landowners to leave part of their estate to the Protestant Collegium.

Some historians consider the fragmenting of the Jewish "nation" in Europe during the late-18ᵗʰ and 19ᵗʰ centuries, and even more crucially the reduction of Jewishness in many cases to no more than a religion, to have been acts of a regrettable Jewish self-denial. And, obviously, self-denial there surely was here. After assimilation Hungarian Jews were not just differently Jewish but also *less* Jewish. But by the same token, they were also more Magyar, so that for the Jews Magyarization indeed made this half-century, firstly and above all, into a golden age of national identity. And think of it what you will, it's easy for us in our allegedly post-nation-state world to be cynical, but back then *every* modern European man desired and was often willing to die for a national identity. So for the Jews this was also a tremendous enrichment of the spirit. To be a modern European man or woman, to stroll through the recently opened City Park of Budapest on a spring Sunday morning – much like Madame Swann strolled through the Bois de Boulogne – to stop to say hello to a friend and exchange a word or two maybe about the soprano in the new *La Traviata* at the opera! And best of all, for this actually was a *net* gain, to be still Jewish too! For so you were still. I mean isn't that how it worked for Christians? They were also both patriots and God-fearing men.

And that, by the way, was also the official position. As an emblem of the Jews' transmutation, after emancipation Hungary's Jews were designated *Magyars of the Israelite faith*. In fact, the words "Jews" and "Jewish" actually disappeared from official usage and were replaced by the somewhat antiseptic "Israelite." The ethnic relabeling, a simple trick of stage-lighting, as it were, that commonly accompanies the passage from the night of prejudice to the dawning of tolerance, made a lot of sense. It suggested that the Jews had sort of been reborn, that they were no longer the Jews of old, that you should not mistake them for those unspeakable people. And rightly so, for indeed they *were* no longer that people, the Jews, the subjects of that seemingly unavoidable question. Now they were Magyars instead, an identity highly esteemed and thoroughly honorable, an identity they affirmed and reaffirmed whenever possible by standing in granite-like solidarity with their countrymen. From pariahs to patriots. And still they were also of the Israelite faith, of course.

During these decades, the Jews rendered many great services to their passionately loved country, but none greater than their economic contributions. You see, as late as the middle of the 19th century, there was no capitalist class in Hungary. Many in the upper classes, gazing west through the windows of the casino at the end of a day of decadent leisure, did wish for the country finally to be yanked out of its Eastern European backwardness and its creaky semi-feudal economy finally to be modernized, but they themselves were not up to doing the capitalists' job, or at least not with the necessary energy and efficiency. But the Jews were. For unlike Christian Hungarians, liberal *and* conservative, the Jews already operated according to capitalistic values. Whereas they already thrived on risk-taking, the market and capital itself, non-Jews were still accustomed to and felt comfortable only with economic relationships founded on status and on the social hierarchy. Indeed, non-Jews sought security and had confidence only in official regulation and in landownership. For them the rational handling of money, acknowledgement of the laws of the market, perception of an advantage of some sort as a thing of economic value, and the spirit of competition and risk-taking remained strange, Jewish traits.

So in effect there was a vacant economic slot, an empty seat very near and maybe even at the head actually of the table, which the Jews elbowed their way to as soon as they could. Everywhere in Western Europe, after emancipation the Jews had played a significant role in economic modernization, but in Hungary they did more than that, much more. But isn't that exactly what had been necessary and what they had been encouraged and expected to do? Please, the Jews had heard clearly the tacit entreaty, go ahead, industrialize the country and modernize it, and as the country profits, you should too. So with what appear to have been open, honest and entirely respectable intentions, the Jews pretty much took control of the economy. And since generally these were times of strong economic expansion, they also enriched themselves, or at least much improved their circumstances. So that indeed, for them this was, secondly, a golden age of prosperity.

There were about 150 families of Jewish great-capitalists, and they held all the key economic decision-making positions. And while all Jews did not command what a contemporary expression called "Jewish capital," that is, great wealth, the largest fortunes did belong almost exclusively to Jews, and the largest risks too were taken almost exclusively by them. Above all, the Jews financed the entry of the Hungarian economy into the industrial age, and so if it made any sense at all – economic, national, social – to speak of modern Hungary, you would have to put them very high up among its founding fathers. A good deal of the capital for this forward surge came from the Hungarian Commerce Bank of Pest, a Jewish enterprise that was established in 1841 but became the major financial institution of the country only around the time of the Compromise. The Commerce Bank bankrolled the development of railroads, a telephone network, the capital's system of trams, suburban railways, and in 1867 the festivities of the coronation itself. But in addition, Jewish capital also controlled many industrial enterprises, and it even entered agriculture. In Debrecen, where there was no mining venture or industry to establish or whip into shape, Jews became large landowners. They were notably active at auctions where the holdings of nobles who could not keep up with the destructive tremors of modernization went up on the block. In fact, there was no branch of the economy where the investment of capital did not pay off for both the investor and sooner or later the general public, and the Jews were involved in it all.

Thirdly, for Hungary's Jews this was a golden age of prominence. For one thing, there was the demographic reality. In 1869 the Jewish population was 545,000, in 1890 710,000, in 1910 910,000. A hefty increase, two-thirds over a 40-year period, an increase that raised the Jewish percentage of the total population from 4 to 5. Immigration did account for some of it of course, it had to since the better to do Jews no longer even had large families, but that also created a presence of sorts, even if in some cases a negative one. But the Jews' prominence was founded not so much on aggregate demographic figures as on their numbers in positions of power, status and visibility. And just listen to these numbers! According to the last pre-World War I census, Jews made up one-fifth of all owners of estates of more than 1,500 acres, and almost half of all the tenants of estates larger than 150 acres. So outside the cities, the once pitiable peddlers suddenly became lords and even princely lords. As for the cities themselves, I can demonstrate the increased urban prominence of Jews only indirectly because that's all that the statistics at my disposal allow, but there can be no question of it. In 1869, 30% of Jews were urban, in 1910, 50%. Of non-Jews, 14% in 1869, 18.77% in 1910. More convincingly, though, the proportion of Jews among merchants, industrialists, bankers and professionals ranged between 40 and 60%, and those were of course the front-page urban pursuits *par excellence*. But what do you expect? It was the Jews who during these very years actually modernized these pursuits in Hungary.

But what is even more vividly telling about the new everywhereness of the Jews and also about the impact of their massed numbers, is an account, however brief, of their activities in Budapest, where 25% of them resided. Budapest was a vibrant, avant-garde, sophisticated, world-class city during these years, which you can even compare if you get carried away to the contemporaneous Vienna of Musil, Mahler and the Secession. And it was the city of its Jews. In 1910, when the Jewish population of the Austrian capital was 11%, Budapest's was 23%. Karl Lueger, mayor of Vienna at the turn of the century and an unabashed antisemite, memorably dubbed the place Judapest. And, of course, you could only smile proudly. Jews were simply everywhere, especially in Pest, and enjoyed, very much in many cases, extraordinarily high visibility. They put their mark on the city in a thousand ways. Some of them not only moved to neighborhoods that had never seen a Jew before at all, but also built mansions there. A good example of their prominence, you can almost say their predominance, is offered by Andrássy Road, to this day the most exclusive and elegant boulevard in Pest. The avenue, first envisioned in 1841 by Kossuth himself as a masterstroke of urban beautification and improvement, was built during the 1870-80s. In its early years, *three-fifths* of the houses standing on it were owned by Jews, who were in addition notable among the bankers financing the construction and also contributed three of the leading architects to the undertaking. On the basis of this kind of Jewish presence in the capital and the ideal assimilated life the Jews lived there, historians have compared late-19th-century Budapest to New York City itself as it has been since the end of World War II.

The modernization of the country in which the Jews played such a key role effected profound changes in the conditions of society too. In a word, Hungarian society underwent an *embourgeoisement*. In one part, this occurred through the development of a new urban middle class, which, naturally, was formed by the Jews, who were in any case looking about for a place appropriate and fitting for themselves. In another part, it occurred through the general spread of the bourgeois values that the Jews themselves tended already to embody. Among these values were the recognition of earning a buck, to be downright American about it, as honorable, acceptance of moneyed wealth as no less a basis for status than land, and an appreciation in general of a society of looser, more flexible, less permanent ties. A society with one ramp going conveniently up and another one, the one with the soundtrack of screeching brakes, going down. These values were not themselves economic phenomena, but, directly or indirectly, they were all related to getting and having. Which of course meant that when the Jews were stirring the best-when-boiling capitalistic brew, they were creating not only an economy but also a society responsive to their own needs. Being, as they were, the most active force in a status-scrambling social configuration, for them these years became a golden age of self-interested social restructuring. Nice work if you can get it, like the song says.

Here then is what, after all this, Hungarian society came to look like at the turn of the 20th century. The old aristocracy is still what you first see at the top of the pyramid, but by now its members have some company and even would-be company. For the approximately 150 families I just mentioned, the great-capitalists, and also some Jews with very large land-ed estates, all of them arrivistes of course who are continuing to operate in business strictly in the counting-house bourgeois manner – these fami-lies are actively aspiring to the premier echelon and assiduously living its lifestyle. They are marrying into the aristocracy, building mansions in the capital and acquiring estates and palaces. They are also enjoying a glittering social life, hunting, being lavishly hospitable, and in some cases even joining aristocratic social clubs. Many of them can even sup-port their claim to such loftiness by recently granted patents of nobility. Between 1863 and 1900 almost a hundred Hungarian Jews were elevated to the rank of baron – yes, your Excellency, almost one hundred – usually in recognition of their economic contributions to the fatherland.

If now you descend to mid-slope, there you will encounter first of all the gentry. They are families of a quite numerous landed nobility, tradi-tionally and still the political elite, but now mostly a gentlemanly middle class, still imbued with the old values, some of them sliding into impov-erishment, but others living more comfortably than at any time within memory on the steady income of estates leased to or under the manage-ment of Jews. Mostly, these are good times for them. But next to the gentry, at mid-slope you will also encounter the new modern bourgeois class, which includes many many Jews, about 20,000 of them according to the last pre-World War I census, made up of middling entrepreneurs, cunning, striving men, and also self-employed Jewish doctors (49% of all doctors), lawyers (45% of all lawyers), journalists, engineers, architects, academics and teachers. To this class also belong the Jewish tenant-owners and managers of sizable estates, found by the census to number about 2,000, who emulate the lifestyle of the gentry but are hard-nosed,

capitalistically-thinking businessmen during the week, anything but gen-
teel. Unlike the aristocracy and the gentry, by and large closed-entry
systems, this class is open and readily expandable. With enough talent,
effort and luck, you *can* make a place in it for yourself, as almost all its
existing members around 1900 had done recently at one time or another.

Carried downward still by gravity, you now come first to what in continental Europe is usually described as the petit bourgeoisie, and in the
English-speaking world as the lower middle class: shopkeepers, trades-
men and semi-professionals. Their ranks include about 150,000 Jews,
most of them engaged in small-time commerce or industry, a fair number
in independent white-collar work, and a few landowners with a hundred
acres or so. And finally, you see the peasantry and the working class,
including the Jewish masses, which tend to live in villages. I suspect that
my grandparents' families, both the Hónigs (although not all branches of
them) and the Ferenczes, belonged to this last, by-the-sweat-of-thy-brow
group. But of course the pyramid has to have a base, as the laws of geom-
etry require, and the laws of human relations apparently no less.

Altogether, these turn-of-the-20th-century social arrangements, very
European but also uniquely Hungarian, represented a great accomplishment for the Jews. For this is just how they might have hoped things
would be if ever they were to find themselves living in the modern world.
Well, that hope had actually been realized through their more or less
steady rise in status as individuals and families during the preceding half-
century. Certainly, in just a few *decades* the Jewish masses had reached a
social position they would not have dared dream of prior to emancipation, and more enterprising individuals among them had done a whole
lot better than that. And a little advancement up the social ladder only
fed the desire for more. For upward mobility can be addictive, especially
if you're an immigrant or an outsider first allowed to catch a glimpse of
the treasures inside piled up high and higher. And so even Jews who enjoyed only modest success tried every way they could to have their newly
acquired economic position recognized by society. And the Jewish haut-
bourgeois, whose grandfather, or in some cases his father, had been a

door-to-door peddler, expected society to do as he himself and other Jews too did, and consider the improvement in living conditions achieved by his own hard work an assimilative and patriotic coup too. He was a good, devoted, fatherland-loving Hungarian, and for that he desired universal approbation.

In terms of cultural life too, the growth of Jewish participation was simply astonishing. Of course, the assimilated Jews largely abandoned Jewish culture, and also firmly rejected any clever suggestion to develop what you might have called Jewish-Hungarian culture. Instead, with remarkable zeal they threw themselves into the making of the bourgeois culture necessarily implied by a bourgeois society, so that for them these decades became, fifthly, a golden age of culture-making, indeed the age of the making of a *great* bourgeois Hungarian culture. First of all, they swarmed into the universities. In the mid-1860s they constituted 10% of all students, in the mid-1880s 28%, in 1913 29%. They were also numerous and prominent in academic and scientific endeavors, crowding research libraries and laboratories, and contributing a good many members to the Hungarian Academy of Sciences. They also got involved in every kind of cultural undertaking, and they were in the forefront of everything that was culturally new. They made critical contributions to the development of the modern Hungarian press, to the newspapers and magazines that first went beyond political reporting during these years. They took the lead in the creation of a Hungarian theater, in part by importing Western European dramas. They established theaters, cabarets, dance halls, concert halls and movie theaters. Often more Magyar than goulash, they also played a leading role in the development of the modern Hungarian language as spoken above all in Pest. They were active in the translation of the great works of Western literature into Hungarian. And they also painted, sculpted, composed and versified professionally, justifying the common impression that modernism was an overwhelmingly Jewish phenomenon. Themselves bourgeois in origin, these artists loved nothing more than to *épater les bourgeois*.

And for those Hungarians who lived too pedestrian a life to know anything of these myriad achievements of their new countrymen and of the many contributions they made to national life – even they were likely to know of the great sporting triumphs of Hungarians of the Israelite faith, for whom this was also, sixthly, a golden age of champions. An unexpected gain maybe for a tribe of Talmudic scholars, but why not? Sports became a public passion in the 1880s, and from the starting gun Jews were vying for and achieving athletic prominence. Of the 11 gold medals won by Hungarians in the five pre-World War I Olympics, five went to Jews and two more to fencing teams made up mostly of Jews. And again why not? Isn't wielding the epée, the foil and the saber the *Hungarian* national sport *par excellence*?

And, finally, the Jews also entered public life. In Hungarian, the arrival of the Magyars in the Carpathian Basin in 896 and the subsequent conquest of the country are called the *honfoglalás*. Literally, and admirably concisely you might add, the word means *the taking possession of the fatherland*. In 1896 countrywide celebrations marked the millennial anniversary of this foundational event. The historical moment was a zenith for the nation, and its newest full-fledged citizens felt themselves entitled to share in it in full. And rightly so. For by this time Hungary indeed was their home, the nigh-miraculously conjured, nay, the hard-earned and well-deserved, fatherland of a people who had expected to have such a thing again only at the end of time. But here they were nevertheless, brimming with pride and wiping away the tear that always accompanies that dirge-like but irresistible national anthem. By this time they were participating even in political life, and doing so to the typically excessive degree they were evidently used to. In 1883 there were no more than ten men of Jewish descent in officialdom, while in 1914 such men constituted more than 5% of the civil service, and by then a Jew had also served as mayor of Budapest and a few others as ministers of state. Even in Debrecen, after the turn of the century Jews began to fill both appointed and elected positions in the city administration. As for membership in the Diet, altogether five men of Jewish descent sat in the two houses in 1883, but a jaw-dropping 25%, or 102, in the House of Deputies alone in 1905. Indeed, in 1896, while sharing the national joy, the Jews were also celebrating their own greatest gain: the taking possession of a fatherland, which for them made these golden years, finally, the age of their very own triumphant *honfoglalás*.

But it also turned out that, alas, some Hungarians were just simply not willing to accept their newly-minted compatriots of the Israelite faith. A Jew is a Jew and always will be! Győző Istóczy, a deputy in the lower house, began his antisemitic agitations in 1875 already with a parliamentary speech given in the ranting hysterical style that later became *de rigueur* for those of his ilk. He was most severely exercised by Jewish equality under the law and the proposal to legalize mixed marriages. This was, obviously, just eight years after emancipation and indeed in response to it, and it was also, and I say this with rue not with pride, earlier than similar denunciations of Jews even in Germany. But it failed. Liberal elements in the government were repelled by the dark ecstasy and rejected the retrograde views, sticking to what has been described as the "assimilationist contract," nor did the Diet have any interest in the hate-mongering. So for the time being no antisemitic movement developed in Hungary, as it would soon in Germany, Austria and France. But Istóczy did not fail *entirely*. He did inflame the ever-festering disease of the soul that anti-Jewish sentiments have sometimes been called, and seems even to have provided encouragement for some incidents, like the rampaging attack on their Jewish fellows by Christian students at the university in Pest in 1881 and their demand that the numbers of Jews be reduced.

But then in 1882 a *cause célèbre*, known as the Tiszaeszlár Affair, revealed just how thoroughly the country was in fact infected. On April 1st of that year, just three days before Passover, Eszter Solymosi, a 14-year-old Christian servant-girl from Tiszaeszlár, a village about 35 miles northeast of Debrecen, was sent by her mistress to do the shopping, an errand from which she never returned. The village, in one of the poorest and most backward areas of the country, was home to Slovak peasants and some Hungarian ones too, and also to some Orthodox, mostly Yiddish-speaking Jews, recent immigrants from Galicia who, even with their horns hidden under tall hats, remained an alien species within the Christian population. General distrust of the Jews was widespread in the region, and soon someone, now suspected to have been a local landowner, parliamentary deputy and close friend of Istóczy's, whispered in Eszter's mother's ear, like the serpent in Eve's, that the disappearance may have been the devilish work of the Jews. Indeed, it now seems likely, although we'll never know for sure, that the whole affair was masterminded by people already prepared to take radical steps to deal with the Jewish question.

The county court then either made a mistake or committed a deliberate act of prejudice. It ordered an inquest and appointed as the investigative magistrate a young notary who from the outset was convinced that a ritual murder had taken place and did not change his mind even after a jury completely exonerated the accused. The findings he soon sent back to the court relied pretty much exclusively on the information provided by Móric, 13-year-old son of József Scharf, the synagogue's sexton. Apparently, Móric had seen everything. First his father had charmed Eszter into the Scharf house on the pretext of being needed to blow out the candles, it being the Sabbath, you see, and then – this Móric observed through a keyhole – his father and some other literally blood-thirsty congregants threw the girl to the ground and the slaughterer cut her throat. Slash!

Even before an official report of the inquiry was made public, the capital's antisemitic press, for already such a thing existed, got hold of the news and in its usual sensationalistic way launched an attack on all of Hungarian Jewry. Then on May 23rd Istóczy's friend brought the matter before the Diet. Istóczy himself also spoke up, duly reminding the body of the Damascus Affair, an 1840 antisemitic eruption in which Syrian Jews were charged with (and then completely exonerated of) murdering a Capuchin friar and his servant for the usual Passover-season reason. Without delay the French antisemitic press also reported the Tiszaeszlár events and did not fail to warn that if it could happen in Syria, which of course it had *not*, then it could happen in Hungary too. Back in Pest the liberal government condemned all these attacks. But that was not enough to bring down the antisemitic fever rising in the capital and beyond, with the leading provocateurs continuing to insist that *all* the Jews of the country were implicated. Anti-Jewish disturbances soon followed. Evidently, the Jew-bashers perceived this as an opportunity finally to get even for the emancipation, which in their estimation amounted to national suicide. As if the whole country had gone mad with bigotry!

These were times when the national Jewish organization in Budapest tended to have little or no contact with Orthodox immigrants, and may even have thought itself too grand to care about the circumstances of people they were in any case too well manicured to shake hands with. At first in this instance too the leaders were just stunned by the outburst of violence and hatred. They just continued chatting politely in their plush cafes, completely refusing to acknowledge that the shark, babe, has such teeth, dear. But then their proper instincts returned, they sized up the situation more realistically and retained Károly Eötvös, a distinguished jurist and parliamentary deputy (although no relation to the by then late Baron Joseph), as counsel for the defense. The organization also received support from Kossuth, who from exile thundered his defense of the principle of equal rights. Regardless of race, religion or language! Fortunately, Eötvös turned out to be not just another hired gun, but a very able man of conscience and principle. After minimal investigation it became clear to him that the allegations had absolutely no foundation. Young Scharf had obviously been brainwashed, as you would say today, as if he had been a captive of terrorists. Soon Eötvös was utterly committed not only to having the charges dismissed but also to demonstrating their absurdity and exposing them as an affront to the legal system.

Meanwhile, three men in a rowboat pulled a somewhat decomposed body from the Tisza River. Doctors determined it to be a girl of Eszter's age who had not been harmed or violated. So the death was an accident or a suicide, most likely the latter. The body was wrapped in Eszter's garments and identified by several people as Eszter's, but her mother, I imagine her shaking and shrieking in protest, approaching the body as if despite herself – well, somehow she could not be certain. And her equivocation was all the excuse the notary needed. He now closely questioned the boatmen and by the use of methods that were legal but also amounted to torture, as if nothing had changed since 1739, extracted from them a confession that first had to have been spoonfed into the mouths of the uncomprehending, squirming peasants, namely, that they had been bribed by the Jews to exhume a body, throw it in the river and then pull it out. Sooner or later this kind of thing always happens. After a while stories like this just tend to teeter off the edge of plausibility and crash. In Tiszaeszlár it was an assistant of Eötvös's who contacted the boatmen and actually managed to learn from them the truth about the confession.

The trial opened on June 19, 1883, and ended on August 3rd. Seven weeks. By July Tiszaeszlár's Jews had to be relocated to neighboring villages for their own safety. The synagogue was abandoned and soon vandalized. And Tiszaeszlár itself became a tourist attraction. The proceedings were highly dramatic, I mean dramatic even beyond the usual cinematic way trials have about them, especially the confrontation between Móric and his father, who had not seen each other since the authorities had grabbed the boy and made him believe that Jews are Satan's creatures. On the witness-stand Móric maintained his story despite his father's pleas. You see, just like the Löbs at Rabbi Moses's trial, again and again fathers and sons. But in a seven-hour grand finale, Eötvös dissected the testimony and established that it was all lies upon lies, lies born of base prejudice and an atavistic hatred. And justice did triumph. The fifteen defendants were acquitted and released. So something of the greatest significance had changed after all. Although the poor defendants were of course not compensated for the long months in a lock-up and their ruined lives, and the torturers and their ideological tool of a chief, the young notary, were not held accountable.

Reactions came in pretty much where you would expect them, keeping in mind that this was only the 1880s. In an official pronouncement, very properly, the Vatican affirmed that the blood libel itself is absurd, and unhesitatingly Western European bishops concurred. Their Hungarian colleagues, however, either too sensitive to local sentiments or too insensitive to common sense, did no better than remain silent. The French antisemitic press claimed that Jewish money had again carried the day, and the domestic Jew-haters, who were unwilling to accept the outcome, concurred. Of course Istóczy himself could not admit defeat.

The verdict was greeted with demonstrations. In Budapest there was also looting. In Pozsony, where hatred of the Jews had never really abated, military action was required, but it was only on August 11th that the Minister of the Interior declared a state of emergency and authorized the police and the army to use their weapons. As the demonstrations and looting spread to the south and the northeast, a few people were even lynched, and here and there the police openly defied orders from above. The anti-Jewish crowds were made up mostly of lower-middle-class and working-class people, but the instigators tended to be members of the gentry and the local clergy, journalists and lower civil servants. The madness just kept intensifying, the country was sinking deeper into violence, but at the same time you also couldn't help feeling that it was all actually a true popular movement, some sort of spontaneous national purification rite, a healthy catharsis, you might even say. But what could you think of this if you were a Jew, especially an assimilated Jew? The intensity of the hatred threw you back like a fire too hot. But wasn't this your country too? The government itself got serious about the situation only when the disturbances began to target not only Jewish but also Christian landowners and tenant-owners and so to take on the guise of an agrarian revolution. Then finally the highest-energy antisemitic flare-ups were quashed, although at best the Jewish question could be said to have been driven into remission. And as quickly as possible the authorities went back to emulating the Hungarian bishops. They looked away. They just wanted to close the file.

In October Istóczy founded the National Antisemitic Party. Its program included "the breaking of Jewish power and the countering of Jewish influence in the political, social and economic spheres, namely, in the press, in finance and credit, in commerce and transportation, in industry and landownership." The party also demanded first a restriction and then the outright abolition of the civil rights conferred through emancipation, withdrawal of the still pending bill to legalize intermarriage between Christians and Jews, and the denial of liquor licenses to Jewish applicants. But this now was too much even for the government. After all, the Jews were not, or *still* were not, so much leeches as the collective goose that laid the golden egg. The country needed them desperately if it were to enjoy continued economic growth, win freedom from Austria and appeal to foreign capital as a place safe for investment. So the authorities took a firm position against the attempt to institutionalize the hatred. And despite broad popular support for the demonstrations, the party itself failed. But the year had just about come to a close before order finally prevailed throughout the land. And altogether thousands had been arrested. Ah!! It was best just to move on.

During the next two decades Hungarian capitalism matured and a *non*-Jewish entrepreneurial bourgeoisie came into being. And so, the earlier need for the Jewish contribution diminished greatly. Now the Jews were no longer so much filling a void as denying a place to true Hungarians in all the interesting races being run. And now the longer-term consequences of Jewish modernization and Magyarization were becoming evident to everyone. Indeed, it was not only a few Jews who had grown rich. It wasn't a question of just a handful of upstarts. And the abominable money-grubbers had not only commandeered the economy, but now also wanted to rise above their abominable place in society. And whereas maybe a few rich Jews could have been tolerated, a competitive, presumptuous, take-charge, more clever by half and highly visible Jewish minority could not. But, still, the liberals in power did not waver. They remained vigilant about antisemitism. The lid stayed on, and I have found no further references to violent incidents before the outbreak of

World War I, even if antisemitic political groups did continue to form, and a widespread resentment of Jews did prevail just about everywhere. In Hajdúnánás, for example, a town of about 20,000 halfway between Debrecen and Tiszaeszlár, twice in just 1911 the hue and cry went up about the blood libel. In each case a boy went missing, whereupon immediately the townspeople accused the Jews and a Hasidic shopkeeper in particular of having ritually killed him, a threatening crowd gathered, and when the police came, instead of protecting the Jews, the officers began an investigation. In each case the missing boy turned up in a few hours.

But then with the very first battles lost in World War I, antisemitism swept the country like a flash epidemic. And it happened *as if automatically*. Now the Jews were being denounced and reviled for everything but treason itself: not serving in the armed forces, or not like Christians anyway, managing to avoid the greatest sacrifices at the front, profiting as suppliers of the troops, profiteering generally and hoarding goods during shortages. Parasites! In fact, none of this was so. Jews served like everybody else and died like everybody else, although since many of them had finished secondary school, they did tend to serve as officers. In any case, by 1916, when the initial wartime united front was already in tatters, one of the most avidly received political alternatives urged on the rudderless nation included militantly anti-liberal and avowedly antisemitic provisions.

Francis Joseph died in 1916, and though there was a Habsburg heir, at the end of the war the Austro-Hungarian monarchy was on the verge of collapse. Worse yet, at the Paris Peace Conference its fate was to be determined by its enemies, whose mantra now was *national self-determination*. Woe then to the preposterously multi-ethnic Kingdom of Hungary! *Good-Bye to All That*. In Budapest events began to move with dizzying speed. In October 1918, the liberal elements in several parties and among the country's intellectuals formed the Hungarian National Council, which managed to assume power and with minimal bloodshed in the capital and only a little more outside it to put in place what amounted to a bourgeois democratic revolution. Not surprisingly, given the liberal program, 40-50% of the representatives to the Council were Jews. Almost overnight, a republic was set up, the suffrage extended, a land reform forced through, and the so-called nationalities problem gropingly pushed towards a federalist solution. But opposition from monarchist, clericalist, nationalistic and generally conservative elements remained so fierce that the threat of civil war now loomed over the country. In March 1919, an impasse among the factions allowed the Communists, a party founded only four months earlier and still in diapers, to grab power in a sort of accidental putsch and so, following the Russian model in lock-step, establish a regime of frantic and relentless terror and the short-lived Federal Socialist Soviet Republic of Hungary. Of course, Jews were also numerous and prominent in *this* bloody no-holds-barred venture.

133 days later, on August 1st, the Soviet Republic collapsed. Conservative elements took control of the country and set up a counterrevolutionary government, and with the Trianon debacle intensifying Magyar desperation and canceling any benefit the Jews had to offer, unleashed the brutal revanchist white terror of 1920-21. Now antisemitism knew no restraint or constraint. Jews were robbed and killed on impulse, subjected to get-even investigations and tortures, prosecuted on trumped up charges, beaten if they belonged to athletic clubs that dared to win matches against Christian teams and interned in camps where they worked under very hard conditions, got little food and were disposed of with impunity. And all this happened in the open: with the apparent leave of the authorities, and under the frenzied leadership of avowedly antisemitic organizations that mockingly boasted of their racist policies and practices. You had to go far back in the country's history to find persecutions of equal virulence.

But then of course the terror ended, as if to prove right all those Jews who maintained that antisemitism was just a passing phenomenon, just part of the soon-to-be-exhausted toxic runoff from the war. Alas, the violent means were only replaced by legal ones. History was in run-away gear, and you couldn't possibly put it into reverse. The Parliament of

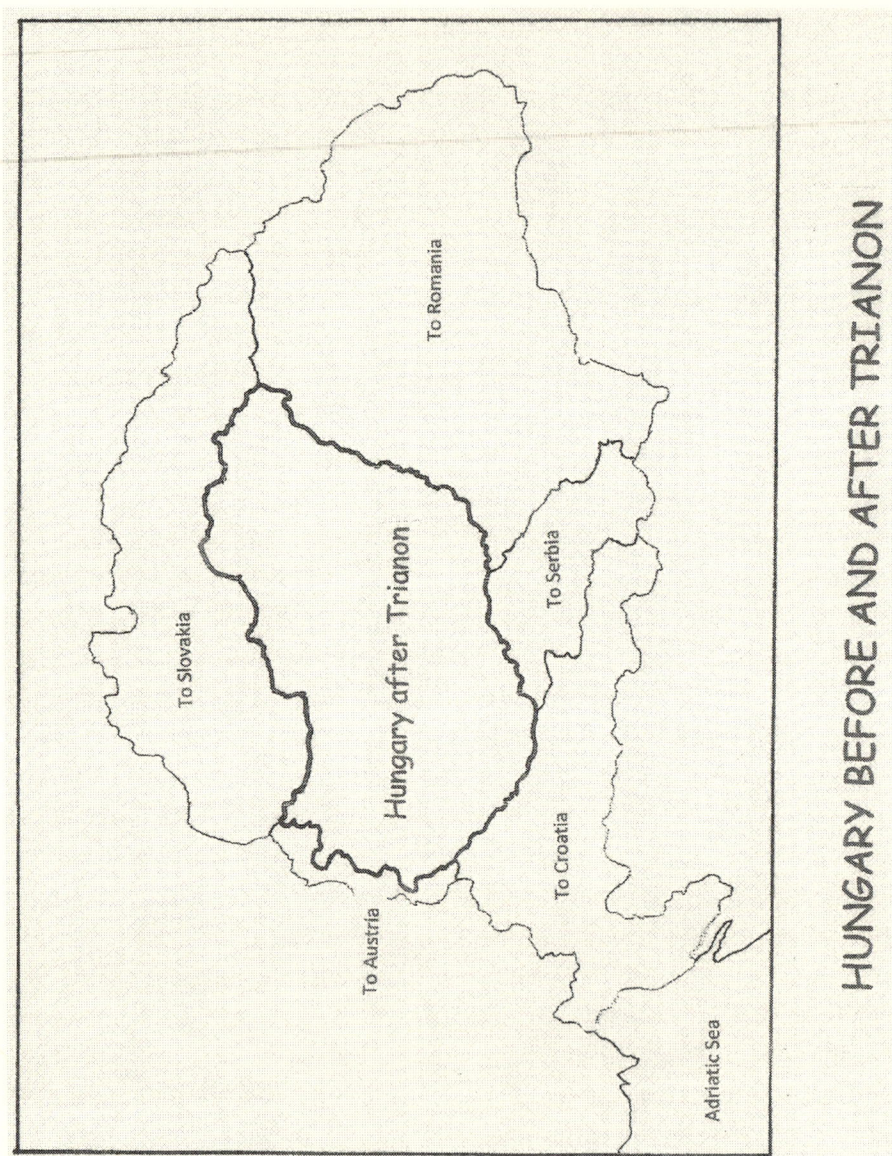

1920, in a state of shock from the game of draw-your-own-Europe played on it at Trianon, devoted most of its discussions to the Jewish question. Hoping to appease the far right and thereby moderate the antisemitism raging in the country, in September it enacted the notorious *Numerus Clausus* law, which restricted the number of Jewish students admitted to universities to a proportion no greater than that of Jews in the entire population. It was the first disability imposed by law in what at first slowly and then feverishly became a dismantling of emancipation. It was the first time since collective expulsions went out of fashion that Jews were *stripped* of rights.

So, yes, the Jewish question was once again on the public agenda. And indeed at the top of it. And now, after assimilation and the Jewish achievements of the golden age, it was more resistant to a solution than it had ever been. I mean, you could not turn the Jews back into peddlers, you could not declare cities off limits to them, by now you could no longer even tell who really was a Jew or mostly a Jew or maybe not anymore but still quite recently a Jew. Sure, the *Numerus Clausus* was an ingenious attempt at a solution, but clearly not enough. Something more thorough, more drastic, more ruthlessly effective had surely to be figured out. But what exactly could or would that be?

So there you have it. A brief history of the Jews in Hungary. A sad tale it seems to me, even without the mid-20th-century descent into inhumanity, which I will relate next. For in the *broader* 300-year context the golden age of Francis Joseph is no longer a triumph at the end of a long struggle, but rather an aberration, and maybe not even that, maybe just a misnomer, or indeed just an illusion. Could it be that the Zionists were right after all, at least from a European perspective, for in the New World the usual rich ethnic mixture of societies seems to provide the Jews with enough cover not to have to live either with blinkers or in constant fear of the worst?

Well, I hope not, because the last I looked Israel hadn't yet exactly solved the Jewish question either.

In 1896, at the time of the millennial celebrations and soon after Judaism was recognized as one of the official religions of Hungary, the President of the Israelite Magyar Literary Society, a rabbi and historian, made this declaration:

> During these vicissitudinous thousand years, Magyar Israelites exulted, wept and bled together with the Magyar nation and learned to love this sacred land, which sustained them and received their fathers' remains. They had learned to love her as their mother, even before she accepted them as her children. As we now rejoice that this nation has acknowledged the legality of our religion, we not only feel, but *know* that we are Magyars.

With the benefit of clearer hindsight, you have to reject this vicissitudinous thousand-year fantasy – a thousand years indeed. The truth about Jewish integration in the so-called golden age is more accurately and soberly conveyed by a recent historian's words about the Dreyfus Affair, which so profoundly convulsed France during the final years of the 19th century: "Assimilation... turned out to have been a myth, since overnight one Jew [Dreyfus] had gone – in Hannah Arendt's terms – from being a parvenu to a pariah. In this context the worst offence of the Jew was [to] no longer embody... the world of money to which his talents and history had [long] consigned him.... If the Jew's crime was [to have been] a foreigner, a far worse sin was to think he might cease to be one."

CHAPTER 5

The Holocaust-War

THE HOLOCAUST IS A STAPLE of today's cultural diet. You can order it according to taste, seasoned with adventure or history or moral edification, as you like. In novels, reportage, historical accounts, movies and personal recollections, survivors tell of the deported, of those in hiding, of the righteous ones who provided succor, of those who evaded the agents and institutions of the extermination regime, of little children sent alone into safety, of villains who paid the price of their evil deeds and repented and those who did not, of lives broken or fundamentally transformed or even reclaimed phoenix-like from death. And there are also the stories told by professionals of one sort or another. All in all, an inexhaustible feast. But it hasn't always been this way. In Hungary after the war Jews submitted to a self-imposed prohibition against speaking of their own trials and of the Holocaust in general. They may of course have asked each other in whispers, whom did you lose and how did you survive, those may have been necessary or unavoidable debriefings, but in mixed company, as it were, they rarely referred to their persecutions or indeed their Jewish background, and public figures among them observed this practice absolutely unfailingly, as if it were actually a taboo.

To the survivor, the Holocaust had been a nightmarish ordeal of humiliation, powerlessness and being dehumanized. You could hardly admit even to yourself how you had been degraded. And in any case, you found it impossible to comprehend your experiences, to cobble together the episodes of persecution, the suffering and the recurring threats of death into a coherent cause-and-effect story. Nor did you know the actual history of events, the general trajectory of the genocidal scheme, its practical management, the evil that in many ways was also just war by demographic fine-tuning. So how then could you have talked about what had happened to you, even if you had wanted to? But back there, in that world governed by reserve and decorum, informed by the bright line distinguishing the public and the private, and strictly compartmentalized in Hungarian not only by the formal and informal modes of verbal address, but also by the requirement for most everyone to speak to an older person or one in a position of authority, like your mother for example, through a construction that best translates into English as "would it please my mother to tell me" – in that world you would have recoiled anyway from confessing your shame and debasement. How humiliating it would have been to recount humiliation! How foolish to double down. You might not even be believed. But surely you would be stigmatized.

And then in addition to all this, there were also objective reasons for the silence, for hiding your feelings about the losses and injustices just suffered. There was, for one, the persistence of antisemitism, as demonstrated by the view of many Hungarians that the Jews had actually deserved everything they got. And demonstrated in some towns even by pogroms, as if to get in one more good punch even after the bell, during the immediate postwar years. But that shouldn't surprise you. After all, it wasn't the Jew-haters who had been exterminated. For another, there were those who did not count themselves among the antisemites but who had profited anyway from the expropriations and expulsions, and these people also did not want to hear about crimes perpetrated against Jews, for that kind of talk can lead only to wild stories about who used to own this thing or that, and the Jews, you'll see, they'll try to fast-talk back into their own name what their forefathers had undoubtedly stolen from good people to begin with. So it was best not to complain or seek sympathy, never mind a crazy idea like having justice done. And, face it, you also knew that if you got yourself in trouble, the authorities would not stick up for you. For that was not part of the Communist agenda. Instead the reds just harped on the uniqueness of Russian losses and routinely downplayed the atrocities committed against others. So what could you do then if you were a Jew and had decided not to emigrate but to stay in Hungary, as had Leslie and Rose, for example, and many others too who expected a better or easier life there than in some distant foreign land like Palestine or America – what could you possibly do but keep your mouth shut?

Well, that's exactly what Rose and Leslie did, and they had their own reasons for it too. Above all, in the family at least and outside it too I suspect, they were, as I've said, given to secrecy. Indeed, they loved secrecy. It was one of the most effective weapons in their interactive arsenal. On one occasion, and for all I know there may have been others too, Rose even managed to use it reflexively, that is, by turning known facts into a secret to be kept from *herself.* It was only after Leslie's death and after setting out on this project of mine that I first had the excuse and the nerve to give Rose an opportunity to say something about the marital difficulties in Hungary and the motives for our transplantation. I was hoping for something sincere, but any comment would have done, or just a nod of some sort, or even just a raised eyebrow, but all I got was a startling resistance to acknowledging those matters at all. Of course, they had been painful things, the kind you forget readily, but Rose was definitely not acting like someone who didn't remember. When you get to be my age, you too will know only too well what it is like to really lose a memory. For instead of simply declaring that she had no recollection of these things, or that she didn't want to talk about them or, miracle of miracles, that all the issues had been subsequently resolved, she just refused to venture even a glance behind the curtain of time separating the present from that past. That's why I have to say that she had secreted that knowledge away from her own self by means of some kind of sublimated but as-it-were deliberate excision from memory or some other similar but unidentifiable sleight of mind. For her these previously well-known things had just ceased to exist. But she had not forgotten them. Oh, no! Rather, she remembered, but only not to remember.

So given the kind of people they were, Rose and Leslie were not likely to have felt stifled by a self-imposed silence about what I will call the Holocaust-war, compounding that term because separately neither of its two components is adequate as an overall signifier for all that they went through as part of the war itself and of the mostly concurrent deadly persecution of the Jews. And the fact that they themselves were not noticeably damaged as survivors, and, as you'll see in a minute, that otherwise too their sufferings and fate had been quite far from the worst – that did not for them in any way weaken any of the arguments for saying nothing. But had someone dared to question their silence at home, there would have been no need at all even to refer to their natural secretiveness, for two specific circumstances could also have been offered by way of a pretty incontrovertible justification. First, the Holocaust-war was considered an inappropriate subject for children because most any comment about it would have had to be something like a casual visit with death, if you can imagine that, and children had to be protected from such encounters. Second, Leslie's parents had perished in Auschwitz and two of Rose's brothers, including her favorite, on the eastern front, and obviously the survivors were entitled to any reaction to that they wished or needed to have, each his or her own, and certainly, not talking about it and especially not with your children, and more especially even since silence on the subject was very widespread – no, you definitely had the right to do that and not be reproached for it. But, consequently, I started this project knowing only the barest details of my parents' lives during those years, and but for this project I might well now be dragging my heels towards the grave with that ignorance still intact, and intact for good.

However, the reasons for the silence at home as-it-were expired after some years. Soon Marika and I were no longer children, the pain of personal loss must also have dulled, and we know that public attitudes also shifted in the direction of openness. But all that made no difference to Leslie and Rose. Nor to me. My own resistance to approaching the subject persisted through the decades. In this respect at least, if perhaps not in others, I have been truly a member of the Second

Generation, as the children of survivors are known collectively. On the rare occasions when I thought about that resistance, I attributed it to my complete lack of interest in those times, I saw it as just part of my reluctance to learn also about the related historical events. Of course, with the rubble-strewn vacant lot across the street and the propaganda-apparatus a perpetual-motion machine all about me, I became aware very early that there had been a war, indeed a world war, but I have only the haziest memories of when I first started to comprehend that the Jews as a race had also been murderously persecuted and in Europe in large measure exterminated, nor can I remember how I came to have that information or who supplied it or what it was exactly even. Yes, it may have been my parents or just Rose, and so it actually was I believe, except that the thing said, whatever it may have been, was not said to me but only within my hearing, or if it was said to me after all, then it amounted to nothing more than just an allusion or a reference to the Holocaust-war in such general and hurried terms and in any case in such a way that I knew better than to ask for any detail or clarification or indeed to ask at all. If I hadn't before already, then with that incident I got the idea: this was not something to talk about. And so I didn't. Nevertheless, when finally, in America, I was confronted with the enormity of genocide, with the word, the idea and the gas chambers, I was shocked, but not as if all that was entirely unexpected.

I did not ask about personal details of those terrible times until recently, indeed until it was almost too late, and even when I did ask I did not ask systematically or outright. Until quite recently I never even wondered why I was not asking, although now I can set a whole phalanx of subsidiary reasons next to that finger placed across my lips during childhood. There were my absolutely-no-thanks attitude to Hungarian history, my avid Americanization, my lack of any Jewish identity, the desire I harbored for a long time to be my own man rather than a product of Rose and Leslie, fear of what I might find out about the first two years of my own life, and fear even that I might have to try even if just for a few minutes to crawl into the skin of my *own* infant self. All of these things contributed to the situation, and other still more peripheral things too I'm sure that I can't nail down right now. But that finger, so to speak, *that* more than anything else was responsible for my non-action. If I wanted to be kind, I'd say that that prohibition was something like the taboo common amongst primitive peoples against naming the dead, but that would be just egg-headed speculation. Closer to the truth, and what I really feel when I let myself sink into imagining such an encounter, is that disregarding that prohibition would have been a violation of the rules of intimacy that I at least felt to prevail in the family. Or more precisely, the rules of intimacy I felt to have been established by Rose. Stay away! Keep your distance! And not just with respect to the Holocaust-war but in general. And stay away not just physically but emotionally too. That was the message she must have had a million occasions to deliver. So I was scared off as a child and I learned early to get by without much of what she didn't offer and didn't want to get. Although, mercifully, in recent decades I've had at least a little success overcoming even that particular maternal legacy.

The prohibition was finally broken only in early 2002, again after Leslie had died and after I had already embarked upon this project, which as you know is intended among other things to shine as much light as possible on even the most time-barnacled family secrets. Leslie's death, you see, had been a great liberation for Rose, not because he had ever compelled her to keep her feelings in check – no, no, Leslie himself had always been a very emotional person – but because her grief was too much of a hurricane even for her own defenses. Indeed, you just had to look at her to see that she was defenseless against the grief. And that pitiful experience damaged her fortifications for good, for all of her remaining two years. Obviously, they were now beyond restoration or rebuilding. Did the loss pull the scabs off the long-buried losses of her childhood and early adult years too? Mother, brother, father? Did it maybe allow her to finally grieve for them too? Yes, possibly. In any case, the solvent of grief poured all over her apparently permafrost emotions had its effect.

Need I say that for me too Leslie's death was an emotional liberation of sorts? The fact that I set out on this project in response, as it were, itself demonstrates that much. And then of course the project liberated me further by allowing me to approach the taboo subject in the guise of a professional. Hey, I'm just doing research. This is *not* intimacy. This is a scholarly investigation rather, not scientific of course but at least social-scientific! That was a great help, for clearly I was then and still am now better at submitting to the emotions appropriate for a historian on the *qui vive* than for a son hearing the details of his own parents' persecutions. Not a bad way to keep your distance, eh? Well, not bad, but also not good enough. For the fact is that even with the benefit of my professional persona, when finally I did bring up the Holocaust-war with Rose, I didn't really. Actually on the first occasion it was she who did that, as even determinedly silent survivors may do in their waning years. I wish it had been me, but obviously at the time I was still struggling with the family prohibition and under a spell of the kind that falls so commonly on members of the Second Generation, still fully complicit in the unnecessarily much too prolonged and just-short-of-a-lifetime ignorance. I myself asked only after she had spoken first. Can I say then that in the end it turned out to be a joint effort? The historian and his mother?

So some information was salvaged after all, and I also finally cut short my self-denial, or at least did not allow it to die a natural death. For refusing all those years to claim, or should I say reclaim, my childhood was exactly that, self-denial. Here then is what I have managed to corral, almost despite myself, of the details of those years, what I finally know of the family events of the Holocaust-war. It's really not very much, and I'm not likely ever to learn much more, but what I know is, first, the few brief stories told by Rose on two or three occasions and the playing-hide-and-seek-with-herself comments she dropped at other times too. Second, what Rózsi and Anci, my two aunts still alive during the first few years of my working on this project, related to me about their own experiences and also their recollections of what Rose and Leslie had gone through, all of which in Rózsi's case anyway I have tried to pass through an imaginary sieve fine enough to filter out sibling distortions. And, third, what I have read in the English-language literature and some of the Hungarian too about Jewish life in Budapest from the outbreak of hostilities through liberation by the Red Army in January and February 1945, and Jewish life in the forced labor service, where Leslie served it seems for more than three of those years. The book learning helped me put some flesh on the bones of Rose's comments and also gave me a frame for an account a good bit more coherent than her scattered episodes. Still, as you'll soon see, the story is riddled with holes and has question marks going in more directions than a Spanish marketing survey. I wish I knew more, damn it, I do. But when the course of events finally lifted that spell, then with its customary irony it also eliminated my last *significant* source. When finally I could have asked, there was no one anymore to reply.

A FAMILY AT WAR I

The animosity between the right and the left in Europe, and especially between the powerful and in many places power-wielding extremists on both sides, had been growing more bitter and violent throughout the 30s. Admiral Miklós Horthy, head of state as Regent of the Kingdom of Hungary, and his successive governments were careful to maintain neutrality, but Hitler's ever more expansive bear-hug was getting more and more difficult to elude. For one, public opinion was increasingly pro-German and overwhelmingly anti-Bolshevik. The memory of the short-lived Hungarian Soviet Republic of 1919 and the red terror that accompanied it was still fresh. And of course the country had long and close associations with the German-speaking world. Very quickly, Hungarians also recognized Hitler as the power-broker, or indeed continent-carver, who could arrange for them to regain some of the territory they had lost after World War I, as he actually did in 1938, when in the process of dismembering Czechoslovakia he returned to Hungary the southern strip of Slovakia and also Slovakia's easternmost province, Transcarpathia, also known as

Carpatho-Ruthenia. For another, Hitler himself also promoted the connection every way he could. Openly he tried to acquire Hungary as an ally, or better yet a client state. Before invading Poland on September 1, 1939, and so starting the war, he had even requested Hungary's assistance and had in exchange offered her still more of the Slovak carcass. But the Hungarian government stuck to its independence-minded policy, though the *quid pro quo* offered, which would have been more balm yet on the national wound, was sure tempting.

Nevertheless, by the end of the 30s the country had shifted drastically to the right and the stance I just described as pro-German had become actually largely pro-Nazi, or fascist, as it was called in Hungarian. In 1937 a domestic National Socialist Party proudly came into being, and in January 1939 the government announced the country's intention to quit the League of Nations and, disgustingly, join the pact established in 1935 between Germany and Japan. So in November 1939, the time Rose and Leslie first locked themselves into the marital embrace the first two decades of which reminds me of nothing so much as a performance-art work from the 1980s in which a man and a woman lived together for a year, tied to each other at the waist by an 8-foot rope but never touching – in November 1939 Hungary itself was not yet at war, but all around her war was breaking out. For promptly upon the invasion of Poland, France and Britain declared war on Germany, and a few weeks later the Soviet Union launched an attack on Poland from the east, and then occupied the Baltic States and moved troops and ships against Finland. Was this going to be,… could this possibly be another world war?

Despite the beginning of armed hostilities, in Hungary it was still possible to lead a private life. The historical hadn't yet completely swallowed up the personal. And, as I've just said, Rose and Leslie got married in November 1939. Marika has two or three photographs of the event, most notably a picture of what I take to be the entire wedding party, the bride in a beautiful white gown, the groom in formal dress, top hat and all. But the fancy outfits notwithstanding, it seems to have been a simple, small affair. Rose's sister Pearl and her husband Hugo and two young children are there, and also Rose's stepmother. Leslie's father, my grandfather Miksa, is there too, Rózsi is there, and also a few other figures unknown to me and probably erased a few years later by the German-Hungarian killing consortium. But most close relatives, not being Budapest residents, are absent. And judging by the assembled countenances, joy, the state of being, that is, not a sister or cousin with what in that place and time would have been a preposterous and presumptuous name, seems to have been absent too.

Hugo and Leslie had known each other from the shoe trade for a while already, and so boy and girl met earlier that year and quickly married. He was 26, she 32. She had had many suitors and several offers by then, but had not loved any of them I believe. She certainly did not love Leslie either, and may have yielded even to him only as a last refuge from spinsterhood. But convinced that soon she *would* love him, he had persisted. If you could see the two pictures I have of his mother, my grandmother Gizella, you'd understand why. Here surely is a woman whose children had to win her love anew each day. But at the nuptials itself, Leslie was no longer suffused with optimism. In a rare, if not unique even, reference to those years, Rose told me after she was already a widow, and as if telling a story only about the dear departed, that as they left the premises of the civil official he exploded with rage. "You're just like a woman! Already lying!" he hissed at her. He had been infuriated by her affirmative response to the official's question of do you love this man. You should see the it's-going-to-be-a-long-siege look on his face in the wedding picture.

But all these developments, both the international and the domestic, had their antisemitic components too, or their antisemitic implications at least. The Hungarian Parliament enacted the First Anti-Jewish Law in May 1938. It was not an unexpected blow and, as you know, despite its name not the first discriminatory legislation of its kind either. In fact, it only gave another tug to the ropes already strangling Jewish employment in retail and other businesses too, and further constricted the number of

Jewish professionals in law, medicine, engineering and journalism. On Leslie it had a direct impact. He was a master shoemaker recently arrived in Budapest with dreams of not sitting in his glue-stained apron behind a nowhere workbench all his life. But since a Jew could no longer get a license for the kind of enterprise he contemplated, the best he could do now was to work out something with his already-licensed friend Hugo. Unfortunately, those two were an incendiary combination. For the rest of his days, Leslie railed against his swindler of a brother-in-law for having cheated him when he was at his mercy. Unfortunately, I could never learn just what had happened. The Second Anti-Jewish Law, enacted in May 1939, carried on where the First one had left off. It reduced even further the Jewish quota in a variety of lines of work and professions, and, in a baldly racist stroke, defined Jewishness as having one parent or two grandparents born into the faith. "These two laws," a historian of 20th-century Hungary has observed, "against which very few dissenting voices were raised, accomplished the cruel reality of excluding virtually all Hungarians of Jewish descent from the rest of Hungarian society." This then was the public world of the newlyweds.

But they carried on of course, as people tend to. They found a place to live near Pearl, in the VIIth district, the traditionally Jewish quarter of the city and at the time actually the largest Jewish settlement in the world. Leslie continued to work with/for Hugo. All I know about Rose is that she was no longer with Mrs. Frankel. I would think that neither the war nor the metastasizing antisemitism accounts for their rush into the aim-to-maim emotional combat that was their marriage, for *au fond*, it seems to me, it always comes down to whether it is alone or with another that you want to go through *whatever* awaits you. If it is with another, then you've got a partner for better and for worse. That anyway is how I think Rose must have thought about it, because she was so clear for so long about *never* loving him that hastily marrying this man had actually to have been a much-deliberated act. He, of course, was just in love. In any case, after the exchange of only the opening shots in their conjugal warfare, he was called up, as they must have expected he would be.

He had been discharged as an artillery-gunner from his regular military service in 1935 and was therefore top-grade cannon-fodder at a time of inevitable armed conflict.

So Leslie was in the army, an army that suddenly had its hands full. Of course, preparing for war can by itself take up your whole day, but this army was doing more than just that. It was also marching into territories lopped off from Hungary by the Treaty of Trianon, "traditionally Hungarian" territories that the cruelly dispossessed homeland was now triumphantly re-annexing. In August 1940, thanks to further generosity from Hitler, the northern half of Transylvania was snatched back from Romania; in April 1941 it was a part of Serbia. By the way, in November 1940, between these two revanchist aggressions, Hungary finally dispensed with all semblance of neutrality and became the first country to join the original three of Germany, Italy and Japan as the Axis powers. In part it did this because, like the kid brother tagging along with the big boys in the gang, its citizens wanted to feel internationally important again, in another part because, like the small-time investor having the opportunity to go in with the high rollers, they wanted to reap the outsized profits being expected, but most of all because they shared the far-right Axis ideology. Whether or not this had a direct impact on Leslie, and if so what kind, I cannot say. He too may have been among those marching east or south or just training to fight the war on the side of the Nazis, or he may not. But if he was, that would have been a little bit like having to dig your own grave, which more than one Jew was in fact doing already in Eastern Europe. And, mind you, they were mass graves.

I don't know if or when Leslie was next discharged from the army. It's even possible that he was bounced directly, rather than with a cooling-off period at home in between, that is, from the frying pan of the army into the fire of the compulsory labor service. But even if that was so, then for a good while still he was granted fairly regular weekend furloughs, like the one during which I imagine them, as if to defiantly assert that as late as February 1942 some fragments of personal life even amongst Jews still managed to escape the clutch of history – during which I imagine them to have conceived me. In any case, the direct or indirect move from the one service to the other was for them the first concrete manifestation of the *combined* historical situation I'm calling the Holocaust-war. For some years already, as you have seen, they had been confronting an anti-semitism more categorical, unrelenting and vicious than any ever experienced in Hungary, and they had been suffering and warding off its blows the best they could. But now upon them were thrust also the burdens of a war already raging through the continent and beyond. Strictly speaking, this war had two avowed objectives: territorial expansion and the elimination of hated enemies. But the people promoting this war were by and large also advocates of antisemitism, and that rapidly transformed the war into the Holocaust-war. So for the first time Rose and Leslie had to confront the full array of hostile forces, although not yet in their full battle fury.

Forced labor for "unreliables" in lieu of military service was a uniquely Hungarian institution. First introduced in 1919 by the counterrevolutionary forces, it insured that subversives would not escape the risks of the military, and having already cheated the country of their loyalty, would not now also deprive her of their service. Not an entirely unfair approach I guess, once you get past the initial division of men into knights and knaves. In any case, in July 1939 labor service of three-months' duration, a modification of sorts of the earlier practice, became compulsory for all men of military age "not fit to bear arms," with those words not yet appropriated for the bigots' codebook. At this time the lot of the inductees in the two kinds of service was still quite similar: both wore uniforms, were grouped into squads, platoons and companies, had the same pay, received the same rations, used the same forms of address, observed the same rigorous discipline, and if the labor servicemen did not carry weapons, well, give each man the tools of his trade: guns for killers, shovels and pickaxes for those doing road construction, airfield maintenance and the unloading of supply trains. At this early stage, labor service was also still quite tolerable. If the location of their duties allowed, servicemen were permitted even to eat and sleep in their own homes.

The exploitation of the anti-Jewish potential of the system began in 1941. All Jews now became subject to *two years'* compulsory labor service, and at the same time the institution was stripped of its military-like attributes and degraded into an overtly racist slave-labor-like operation. So hatred now poisoned the earlier ostensibly practical arrangement. Now labor servicemen were no longer issued uniforms, had to subsist on reduced rations, had no right to receive packages, to buy food or even *accept* food, had their mail censored, were not eligible for furloughs and had to wear yellow armbands that readily identified them as Jews and as targets for abuse by sadistic officers and guards. The methods of conscription also changed at this time to include the calling up of servicemen on an individual basis rather than by age group. This practice, something almost in the nature of a bill of attainder if you think about it, allowed the authorities to single out prominent and wealthy Jews of *any* age, community leaders, well-known professionals and those who had been denounced, as many were out of envy, bigotry or hatred for *you* specifically. Because persecution was, you see, not only categorical now but also personal. And finally, labor servicemen too in significant numbers, not just the regular military forces, were sent to the front.

In June 1941, as you might recall, Hitler invaded Russia. Hungary soon joined the attack with a limited force. But at the end of the year, when the Red Army managed to halt the invaders near Moscow, Hitler pressed hard for more assistance. Hungary had to dispatch 200,000 additional troops, nearly one-third of its total forces, accompanied by 50,000 labor servicemen, altogether a poorly equipped army that by late summer 1942 was defending a 100-mile-long front along the River Don deep in Russia. The lot of these labor servicemen was inhuman. In addition to sinking tank traps, building bunkers and unloading munitions, back-breaking but necessary tasks, they also had to undertake the impossible and the reliably lethal, like digging fortifications in the frozen ground, propelling supply trains that horses could no longer move along muddy roads, clearing minefields by marching over them. Quite openly, many of the officers supervising these work details intended for the Jews not to survive. In January 1943, after the onset of an especially brutal winter, Soviet forces broke through the front at the city of Voronezh and routed the Hungarians. Nearly 80,000 soldiers were killed or wounded, and 60,000 captured. The labor servicemen, including two of Rose's brothers, fared even worse, many of them starving, freezing to death or succumbing to typhoid as they staggered west – as had Napoleon's forces in 1812 – retreating across the continent in complete disarray, leaving wounded, crippled, diseased comrades behind. Not more than 6-7,000 managed to reach their homeland.

Evidently, Leslie escaped the worst of this. He was indeed in the labor service, if not right from the end of his post-honeymoonal military stint, then from the time of the general call-up in 1941 at the latest, I believe. In any case, for some time he was stationed in Budapest and seems to have served under relatively decent conditions. I know that in November 1942, the time of my birth, he was garrisoned at some barracks not far from the apartment in the XIIIth district Rose and Leslie had moved into during the preceding two years, which itself was not far from the neighborhood where I was to spend my childhood. Several times I heard Rose tell the story of how when she went into labor, the taxi rushing her to the Jewish Hospital careened by those barracks, where some servicemen were passing the time outside, and the friend and neighbor who accompanied her leaned out the window – when I go in for a close-up I imagine her eyes narrowed against the wind and her kerchief wildly flapping – and called out to the men: "Tell Hónig his wife is on the way to the hospital!" And soon after she got there, Leslie showed up by her side, and with him his agitation, like Dr. Jekyll escorted willy-nilly by Mr. Hyde. But I myself did not arrive until the following day, when he couldn't again take the liberty, and that is how on account of the labor service, he was right with my opening squeal relegated to a subordinate position in my life. Did days pass then before he could see and hold me? Did weeks? I don't know. I know only that a separation, a distance, a being kept out-of-reach by both personal and historical conflicts undermined the father-son relationship right from the start.

So all the labor servicemen did not suffer the fate of those on the killing fields of Voronezh. Some possessed skills more useful than being a trigger for a landmine, and I believe that for a while Leslie himself was spared the front on account of what he could offer as a craftsman. Rose did say once that he was in the labor service in Budapest for two years, all the time cutting-pasting-sewing-nailing boots for the brass I would think. Most likely, it was only in late 1943, around my first birthday, that he too was ordered east somewhere to the Soviet Socialist Republic of No Return. Now we were really separated, he and I, he and Rose, and indefinitely so, for we didn't know, indeed nobody back in Hungary could have known, anything about his whereabouts or his fate. You had to worry if he was still alive. As millions had to worry about millions of others too in and out of uniform and of the compulsory service, and until they showed up to dispel the worst fears or a luckier comrade confirmed them, millions had to live with the uncertainty. The Holocaust-war indeed continued gobbling up more and more of personal life. So then did a constant anxiety about her husband possess Rose through the rest of the war? I don't think so. More immediately pressing matters, crises more of the moment, tended to commandeer her attention, as they must have commandeered most everyone's. "You should never have just one worry" is a Hungarian saying Rose was very fond of all her life, and I am too, even though it doesn't do well in translation. Well, then she certainly had worries by the bushel.

There was no fighting on Hungarian soil during 1941-1943, but still these were years of war. Similarly, the Holocaust, already raging in Germany and many other parts of Europe too, flared up domestically only in two brief and minor killing episodes, but of course the tentacles of persecution were already wrapped around all of the country's Jews, constricting them and choking them. The hardships besetting everyone affected them yet more severely. Certainly, now the world didn't let them forget even for a minute that they were Jews, not even while they were living what little still remained of a personal life. A woman of great resourcefulness, Rose had to make a life for herself and her infant all alone. For the time being at least, and who then could say anything about the future, she was deprived of family. Husband enslaved to the labor service, siblings but for Pearl scattered throughout the country and abroad, husband's family apparently unapproachable or just unapproached. And I suspect that the contacts with Pearl also didn't offer her much. All those frail bonds connecting brittle people, you could not possibly rely on them under circumstances enough to test your average saint. So Rose had to look elsewhere. In exchange I imagine for sustenance, care and whatever else could become necessary, that friend and neighbor in the taxi, a sweet diminutive lady who lived alone, middle aged or even getting on in years already, someone Rose mentioned sometimes later in life but whose then role I first understand only now – at some point she became my nanny. And Rose seems to have made do with that and nothing else, except of course exclusive possession of me. Rarely did she recall anything from those times, and even then only how enormously gratifying the first year and more of motherhood had been with an infant as marvelous as myself. You know, the usual proud-mother routine, notable only because coming from someone who almost never seemed overcome with love.

To say that a state of emergency prevailed during these years would be an exaggeration. Instead, imagine only a world where all arrangements at all times were understood to be contingent, where not only your deeds but also your sense of life encompassed only the very day, where the future looked nothing so much as a series of randomized fright-images. A world now completely without normalcy. In order to reduce the instability and avert even worse, the government established controls and, among other things, introduced rationing not just of essentials but of everything you might need, like bread and milk and meat and soap and light bulbs, for example, and maybe that helped some. But still the standard of living was beginning to approximate the standard of dying, inflation turned your cash to confetti, and the war effort and an overbearing ally claimed all resources. Rose did I'm sure whatever she could to provide for us, but all I know of her efforts is that for a while she earned a pittance laundering the white smocks of the eight employees of a dry goods store. And she was lucky to have even that work, because for Jews the chances of employment were now close to nil. Don't forget, in that society discriminatory behavior was considered a virtue, restrictions on Jews were multiplying, steam and ash were already escaping from the volcano of antisemitism. The Third Anti-Jewish Law of 1941, a paroxysm of racist revulsion, prohibited marriage and sexual intercourse between Jews and non-Jews; the Fourth of 1942 outlawed ownership of land by Jews. Rose had her resoluteness and unhesitating determination and the joy brought to her by baby yours truly, but otherwise misery hobnailed with fear was trampling her life.

And soon things got worse. At the end of 1942, once Germany lost her aura of invincibility, an opposition to the war coalesced in Hungary. Soon even feelers about a separate peace were put out to America and Great Britain, although the only result they produced was about a year's worth of what-if-we and what-if-you discussions. But what could the Hungarians have been thinking? Any peace they might have bargained for would have depended on American and British forces reaching Hungary before the Red Army did, and that became less likely with each passing day. Obviously, the panhandlers should have approached Stalin, but for *that* they didn't have the stomach. In any case, the German intelligence services were on the job as usual, and in September 1943, when he learned of the Hungarians' double-dealing, coming on top of what he considered their general wishy-washiness, the Führer had prompt plans drawn up for occupation of the now strategically indispensable country. Then, with the invasion scheduled for March 19, 1944, Hitler summoned Horthy to a meeting on the preceding day and there demanded a promise of no resistance. At first the Regent sputtered, but then he acquiesced. He accepted the bully's laughable-lie of a pledge to withdraw the *Wehrmacht* as soon as a proper pro-German regime could be installed in Budapest, for what else could he do? Order those Hungarian peasant boys to bushwhack their Aryan big brothers? You might as well just promote them all to commissars. So the following day the German troops were generally well received, even though the occupation was sure to plunge the country and especially its Jews into the worst horrors of the war yet.

THE HOLOCAUST IN HUNGARY

I will try to recount the events of the Hungarian Holocaust from the point of view of the perpetrators, even though that compels me to make *them* into historical figures, describe *their* deeds, imagine *their* words and thoughts, focus on what I must call their, achh! *accomplishments.* Even though I have to, briefly at least, make them my heroes, the way Milton had to make Satan the real protagonist of *Paradise Lost.* Of course, that is exactly how the perpetrators of the Final Solution, Aryan and Magyar, saw themselves, aside from the fallen angel bit, that is. In their own eyes they loomed titanic indeed, the doers of great deeds to be enshrined in the national memory, men who were devising and executing a breathtakingly ambitious plan, a herculean task, a historically significant refashioning of the nation, an undertaking self-consciously mythical.

So here is what one of the officers of the so-called *Eichmann-Sonderkommando,* or Eichmann Special Unit, a 150-200-men force of seasoned operatives, might have written about the dejewification program in Hungary in an imaginary August 1944 letter to his father, a high-ranking Nazi, back home. The Unit was named after Lieutenant Colonel Adolf Eichmann, who from 1934 was in the Jewish Department of the SS Security Service, in 1938 in charge of the failed effort to force the emigration of the Jews of Austria, and from 1939 until the end of the war in charge of the concentration of Eastern European Jews in ghettoes and their transportation to the death camps. After the war Eichmann escaped from the camp for SS men where the Americans were holding him and eventually made his way to Argentina, where he lived under a false identity until 1960, when he was abducted by Israeli agents. In 1961 Hannah Arendt went to Jerusalem to attend his war-crimes trial and report on it for *The New Yorker.* Her controversial book, *Eichmann in Jerusalem: A Report on the Banality of Evil,* appeared in 1963. My information about Eichmann is based mostly on his own testimony at the trial, as given from the bullet-proof glass booth in which he was confined while in the courtroom and as reported and interpreted by Arendt, and the more recent work of a few other commentators.

"The chief," the letter begins after an affectionate salutation, "as the six of us, the collective second in command, now refer to Colonel Eichmann, had advance notice that the Wehrmacht was going to occupy Hungary, so we had time to prepare. The task ahead of us, the deportation of maybe a million people, was daunting, but the chief was certain we could manage it. After all, we had already organized the transport of 3.5 million prisoners. We have been extremely effective, Papa, wherever the Unit has operated. We are very proud of our work, all of us. Still, Hungary presented unique problems: the job had to be done with the greatest possible speed and under ever more persistent attacks by the enemy. And a million is still a million!

"Starting on March 10th, the chief held a three-day planning session for us officers at Mauthausen in Upper Austria. I know you've been there, so you know it's a beautiful place. And then at least the camp was well run. We all looked splendid, our gray uniforms neatly pressed, but nobody had any illusions about the challenge facing us. We studied the country's geography, the railroads, administrative districts and the ethnic distribution in the various counties. We also received detailed reports on how our troops would deploy throughout the country, the status of domestic forces and developments along the eastern front. Then on the 19th we entered the country with the occupying forces, with the chief following three days later.

"We went to work at once. Before all else, we ordered the establishment of governing councils in all the Jewish communities. This is the chief's usual opening gambit, as you know, and there are good reasons for it. Only a Jewish council can provide an exhaustive list of the Jews in a given community, and only they can locate the individuals identified without spooking them and then even convince them of the wisdom of absolute docility. Which is what we must have! And almost the best part, as the chief has said more than once, is how ridiculously easy it is to work with the councils. The least bit of kindness, like a personal or family exemption – only temporary of course! – from some anti-Jewish measure, can turn these men into eager helpmates. The chief is very good at dealing with the councils. He even enjoys dealing with them. He calls the councils "the very cornerstone" of our operations.

"The first days of the mission were critical, as they always are. That's when you have to lay the groundwork, and *every*thing afterwards depends on that. So immediately we dismissed from positions of power all Hungarians who are not fully committed to us. We purged the government, the police, the gendarmerie – that's a national law-enforcement and military organization here – the local administrative and executive personnel, the leadership of trade unions, social organizations, even schools. You have to be thorough in such things. We did not spare the half-hearted, nor the independent-minded who might think their own judgment defines their duty. We are a military force, and we intend always to run as military an operation as possible. At the same time, we also appointed right-thinking people to key positions. They were not difficult to find. The Hungarians are good people.

"When we arrived, we already had partners in the Hungarian state administration waiting for us. Working with them, we immediately launched direct attacks on the Jews. The idea was to take them by surprise and to hit them hard. So we went out and just arrested some prominent people. That always puts them all in their place. Then we prohibited them from traveling, from owning cars or radios, using public baths or swimming pools, entering restaurants, bars or cafes. We also dismissed them from civil service jobs and excluded them from the press and public performances of all sorts. That isolated them. Then we requisitioned most everything they owned: houses, apartments, business equipment like printing presses, personal possessions of value like art objects, musical instruments and silverware, even household goods like mattresses and blankets. That pauperized them. We also had safe-deposit boxes in the names of Jews blocked, Jewish commercial and industrial establishments closed, and required Jews to go promptly to state financial offices and declare the value of all their property. The last preparatory step was a decree requiring Jews to wear the yellow star as of April 15th.

"One contingent of the Unit also spearheaded a drive to eliminate all Jewish influence from the social and cultural life of the nation. We were rewriting history, scrubbing the collective memory clean of all traces of the soon-to-be-former Jewish presence. Our own experience in these matters was particularly helpful to the locals. We ordered schools and libraries to remove all books by Jewish authors, domestic and foreign, prohibited publishers from printing or selling such books, and scheduled book destruction festivities in cities throughout the country, including one in Budapest on June 16th, at which 447,627 items are reported to have been sent up in flames. The most exciting fireworks I've ever seen!

"The Hungarians were in awe of our cool efficiency. The chief is right in saying that there is no substitute for careful planning. We ordered all these measures and had them executed and enforced promptly, on schedule and without a hitch, just as everything had been penciled in on the calendar at Mauthausen. It is a pleasure to be a cog in such a smoothly running machine, as they say. The dejewification was in high gear before you knew it. All cylinders were firing. In just a couple of weeks or so, in what is hardly more than a tick-tock on history's clock, our tireless and systematic efforts completely dismantled Jewish life in the country, and even began to erase the memory of what it had been. It's always startling how short memory can be, especially during wartime. All that remained now were the Jews themselves.

"Papa, you remember the six-step program for the Final Solution I described to you last year? At the special dinner you and I had during my last leave? Well, all that I just told you adds up to the first two of those steps as taken in Hungary, that is, expropriation of the Jews and their isolation. Implementation of the remaining four – roundup, ghettoization, deportation and elimination – we began with a meeting in Budapest on April 4th, just 17 days into the operation. It was at that meeting that we drew up the master plan. The meeting was attended by the chief of course, us officers of the Unit, and the Hungarians in charge, most notably László Baky and László Endre, the heads of two departments at the Ministry of the Interior. It was an exciting day. It even had a touch of the festive about it. The Hungarians really admire the Reich! Even now! Many of them also speak good German and even know a little Goethe.

"We again studied a map of the country and assessed the resources available to us – and, remember, this is not just the truncated remnant, the so-called Trianon Hungary, that existed before the Führer took up their cause, but the much larger territory that also includes re-annexed areas – then the decision was made to streamline the dejewification process by grouping the ten gendarmerie districts of the country into six Military Operational Zones. Then we proceeded to identify the people who would be in charge of the roundups and ghettoization in each of the Zones, and we formulated general guidelines for local officials. A wonderfully productive day! The chief was in rare form!

"By the way, the chief lived deservedly well in Budapest during the entire operation, and he was upbeat. He had been worried about possible complications with the local authorities, but as it turned out, he made good contacts with no trouble at all. He and Endre became close friends – Endre is a fine man – and especially after a few crocuses poked their heads up in the run-down parks, the chief enjoyed the still considerable charms of this city on the Danube, a lady friend or two included. He also had the necessary local assistance I believe on all levels, people were eager to help and very competent too, most of them anyway, reliable and efficient."

Let me interrupt here while my fictitious letter-writer refills his pen in order to urge you to try to think of these dreadful things in the context of the enormously complex undertaking that the Final Solution was. Imagine the administrative and logistical demands of an operation carried out mostly on foreign soil, during an all-out war you were at first winning and then losing, during years of desperate fighting on two fronts. Try to think of all that had to be done. You had to, under these straining-with-every-muscle circumstances, manage millions of people who could panic or riot at any moment, manipulate the reaction of your own compatriots, never take for granted the acquiescence of the citizens of any occupied country. A job so formidable required a very accomplished bureaucracy and a bureaucratic culture that could shape both conditions and relevant attitudes, and penetrate not only officialdom but all of society.

Bureaucratic apparatuses, including of course local functionaries both within the Reich and without, played a decisive role right from the start. The very idea of extermination emerged in 1940-41 not as a flash of inspiration vouchsafed to some evil genius, but as the bureaucratic solution to the problem of what to do with the Jews who had been penned up in the ghettoes of Poland in order to make room for the large numbers of *Lebensraum*-seeking German settlers, a solution arrived at by typical feasibility-analysis methods. And then, from coming up with the idea, these apparatuses, civil and military, went on to direct the whole operation every step along the way. So first it was the bureaucracy that gave concrete you-will-live-and-you-will-not meaning to the Führer's order of genocide, defining who exactly came and did not come within its purview. And then it was also obviously the bureaucracy that organized the taking of each of the six steps, choreographing them with precision, making decisions at all levels of government, formulating procedures and establishing schedules and routes, bobbing and weaving to stay out of deteriorating circumstances, finessing the constraints of limited human, social and material resources. In other words, the bureaucracy, the many thousands who *facilitated* the actual mass murders, did everything, and it did everything that could be done.

But in addition to *doing* everything, bureaucracy as a modern phenomenon also contributed to the Holocaust through its methods and values, and specifically through its commitment to rationality. Bureaucratic culture acquired this particular component during the Enlightenment, the intellectual movement that designated strictly rational science as the proper methodology through which to encounter all phenomena to be studied and even coined the term "amoral" to describe the proper approach of the scientist to his subject. It is because bureaucratic apparatuses pursue scientific amorality and shun the value-laden ways of religion that they tend to describe but not prescribe, to explain but not preach or guide. That they are devoted to solving problems without morally evaluating them, to judging only performance and contribution to the achievement of some ultimate goal, not the goal itself. Eichmann himself was no bureaucrat but a true SS man rather. As the voluminous recollections he committed to paper and magnetic-tape in Argentina reveal, he had been the enterprising, cagey, self-promoting leader of a low-profile but top-priority operation. But in Jerusalem he *played the bureaucrat.* That was the role he assumed, seeming to believe that it was the most congruous with his claim of being a just-following-orders man. Look at him, there he sits in his glass box! – a perfect bad-will ambassador of the bureaucratic culture that contributed so much to what Arendt calls Germany's "moral collapse."

Bureaucratic culture achieves amorality by treating moral problems as if they were no more than bureaucratic difficulties. Call it a category mistake or a re-contextualization or the dry-rot of humanity, whatever the intellectual process, it is epitomized by the habit of reducing everything to numbers, as when the bureaucratically-minded counts individuals in order that later he should be able to account for them, when he crunches them into statistics and graphs the better to calibrate his own operation's progress, and when in the case of the Holocaust he actually *numbers* them on their skin-and-bone forearms, that is, dehumanizes and numerically re-identifies them after having just destroyed their you-would-have-thought-inalienable civil identity. The man imbued with bureaucratic culture, however highly or lowly placed, does all this because he knows that the world is more easily grasped when rendered abstract in this Platonic manner and men more effectively acted upon when thus made uniform. And he does it because dealing with numbers, quantified values and mathematical relationships increases the efficiency of his operation, and that is really the paramount thing that any good bureaucrat concerns himself with. No wonder from the very beginning the problem for the perpetrators was not whether it was humanly permissible to murder millions but whether they had the organizational means and skills to do so. Well, they made sure that they did.

"After the Budapest meeting," the letter home now continues, "the pace picked up. The first item on the master plan was registration of the Jews. Specifically, we ordered that Jewish communities prepare and submit complete lists of all their members, men, women and children. In a tactical move designed to produce exhaustive results – for if here and there you overlook a Jew, you've defeated the whole operation – the demand for the lists was made by two different government offices, one of which, the Ministry of Supply, claimed to need them in connection with the proper allocation of food. Then, according to the plan, on the basis of the lists the gendarmes were going to round up the Jews, with the operation proceeding Zone by Zone. As a precaution, no gendarme was to work in his home county, for, like they say, everybody has a favorite Jew. In rural communities and smaller towns, the Jews were to be assembled in synagogues or community buildings. There, they were going to be separated from all the valuables they carried and subjected to some sharp questioning about other valuables they might have stashed away or given to neighbors for safekeeping. Then, they were going to be transferred to the ghetto of the nearest city, a restricted area that had the rail facilities necessary for quick and efficient entrainment of the ghettoed population. The ghettoes were to have been designated, set up and under guard by then, for the Jews of the larger towns and cities were to be rounded up into them directly.

"During the month of April, we had Baky and Endre issue a number of decrees and a number of secret directives, including things local authorities had to know about their own roles in the Final Solution. But, on our advice, the Hungarians also knocked together some stage-scenery for the operation, inserting in the decrees provisions that legalized each anti-Jewish step and justified it by a tailor-made policy statement, and also promoting the use of appropriate language for what was going on. So, for example, there were oft-repeated statements that ghettoization is really just part of the effort to establish a healthier national housing situation by allotting to the Jewish minority no more than its fair share, that the removal of Jews from villages to larger towns is just a response to the demands of national security, and that deportation is just, as we used to say in Germany too, the first act of *resettlement.* These were not brilliant inventions, but that's not what matters, as you know, Papa. In any case, given the public mood, the uncertainty of all arrangements and the widespread willingness to grasp at any imaginary straw, they did the job.

"On April 7th, with time pressure even more intense now than before, pretty much the same people who had attended the earlier master plan meeting also attended a further conference. By now we worked together very well. Confidence and enthusiasm were running high, the momentum of early success was palpable in the room, and we were ready to further refine plans. Preparations were almost complete now. Among other things, we settled the geographical order of operations, although on this matter there was a divergence of views initially. And here, unfortunately, we badly miscalculated. It was our one and only *major* error. Let's deal with the capital first, Endre proposed at the conference, and get rid of the filthy Jews with all the *influence.* No, no, the vermin in the countryside have to go first, most of the others, myself included, responded. It seemed to make sense to get rid of the Galician rabble first, the lice-ridden Yiddish-speaking hordes in the re-annexed territories. And that move would also prevent the Jews of Budapest from fleeing to and hiding in the countryside, we figured. The discussion was pretty heated. In the end the matter was settled by the chief's orders directly from Berlin, which specified combing the country from "east to west." So there was nothing more to argue about. We agreed to start in Gendarmerie District VIII, or Zone I, that is, Carpatho-Ruthenia and northeastern Hungary, and move west from there. The command group of German and Hungarian experts was to set up its headquarters in the city of Munkács [today Munkachevo in Ukraine], distinguished by being the only large Hungarian urban center with a Jewish majority. Special executive committees were to direct operations in the three other large towns of the Zone. I still maintain that it was a good plan, although soon enough events proved Endre to have been dead on in his instincts.

"By April 12th registration of the Jews was complete, and on that day Endre held a meeting in Munkács itself. I was there as the German advisor in charge. City and county level officials – civilian, police, gendarmerie – had by this time already received directives relating to the Final Solution, and they were prepared to work out local plans. Then it was the turn of lower-level police chiefs and gendarmerie commanders, and mayors and deputy prefects. Cooperation was remarkable all the way down the line. The air crackled with efficiency even in that provincial nowhere, with good people at all levels doing what they could to promote the Aryan objective. We were proud of ourselves, Papa, and we Germans especially received many tokens of respect. So we now addressed the specific locations for the ghettoes, the roster of personnel to be involved in the roundups and also in the subsequent stripping of the Jews of their wealth, and the timing and coordination of all the other steps that would have to be taken before all the Jews of Zone I had finally been corralled into the new concentration centers. For a few days after the last of these preparations, the troops and other participants just stood ready, impatient and waiting for the starting gun finally to sound."

Actual operations, which my fictitious *sonderkommando* chronicler did not witness, began at the crack of dawn on Sunday, April 16th, just 29 days after arrival of the Special Unit, after only four weeks of preparations, and, for a touch of poetic justice, on the first day of Passover. The gendarmes were ready! They roused the Jews in the hamlets and villages of Zone I, gave them just a few minutes to pack a few things and took them to local synagogues. All the time, the rifle butts that had just struck doors remained raised, but actually there was no resistance. In the synagogues jewels and cash and valuables were taken from the Jews, with force if they were being stupid, while their homes were officially sealed, although nobody thought that would stop anyone wanting to settle accounts as advantageously as possible. Then during the next few days the gendarmes rounded up the urban Jews too and marched them to the ghettoes of the thirteen larger towns of the Zone, which were mostly just a-few-square-block areas in Jewish quarters or abandoned or idle factories, empty warehouses or brickyards, or even just fenced-in lots. Then they marched the rural Jews from the various synagogues to these ghettoes too. Again, everyone was pathetically compliant. Randolph Braham, the preeminent historian of the Hungarian Holocaust whose scholarship forms the indispensable foundation for my account here – Braham puts the aggregate Jewish population of the Zone at about 180,000 individuals, mostly Orthodox and Hasidic. They were all quickly concentrated in sixteen ghettoes. The operation was swift, efficient and by-the-book. The gendarmerie performed with despicable distinction.

On April 24th, Eichmann, Endre and some other German and Hungarian officials, including my chronicler I imagine, undertook a tour of the ghettoes of Zone I. In the city of Kassa, in Slovakia, local leaders joined them. Ostensibly the event was an official duty, and the group did inspect the new concentration centers and refine various procedures, but Braham does not hesitate to call it a triumphal tour. And indeed these men, when they saw with their own eyes the Jews so penned up and so manageable, as it were, despite their very large numbers – these men had reason to feel satisfied with their efforts and justified in their chests-thrown-out self-confidence. Endre promptly submitted a calculatedly clever and false report to the Minister of the Interior, stating that "the provincial ghettoes have a veritably sanatorium-like character. The Jews are finally getting fresh air and have changed their old lifestyle for a healthier one." The Minister forwarded the report to Horthy, who accepted it at face value. So everything was proceeding very well, and better than that even. "Like a dream" is how Eichmann repeatedly described this stage of the operation in his testimony. He was clearly pleased. Pleased to be so expert and effective in this, the crowning achievement of his career.

On May 6th or so, Endre and an entourage of central and local dejewification leaders made a further tour of inspection. This one covered

Zone II, or Northern Transylvania, where the roundup and ghettoization had begun just a few days earlier. Here too, after thorough if somewhat rushed preparations, the operation was moving ahead splendidly. On the evening of May 2nd instructions had been issued to all local communities and publicly posted. Again, the Jews had been roused at dawn, marched to local synagogues, divested of everything of value, and so on as was already routine. Here too, no resistance, as if everything were running on auto-pilot. Success begot success. The Jewish hordes followed orders like cattle, or like sheep, as if not capable of imagining, as if too prosaic and pedestrian in their thinking to imagine, the end that Aryan genius had devised for them. Most of them still believed they were being resettled. And the Magyars remained passive or, better yet, cooperated. The ghettoization of the Zone was pretty much completed in a week, allowing Eichmann and his men to turn to the deportation phase for Zones I and II. They resumed the roundups in the other Zones only on June 5th, when Zones I and II were already almost completely dejewified.

But don't let the smooth-clicking-of-gears ease of the operation, up to this point and all the way through to its bestial conclusion in Auschwitz – don't let it obscure the difficulties the planners and perpetrators encountered in all the places where the Holocaust raged. Most importantly, don't forget the psychological obstacles to killing thousands and indeed millions of people. Arendt identifies one such obstacle when she speaks of the need to overcome "the animal pity by which all normal men are affected in the presence of physical suffering." I take it that by the words "animal pity" she means the seemingly automatic pity even an animal will feel for a creature in that situation. But even if she doesn't mean exactly that, her point is obvious, and so is the phenomenon in question. Even Eichmann, whom you tend to think of as an embodiment of cold-blooded, eager slaughter – even Eichmann on his visit to Treblinka in 1941 to familiarize himself with an extermination camp and its operations, even he was unnerved to the point of collapsing when forced directly to witness the last minutes or some of the last minutes of lives about to be extinguished. So it was essential that in the perpetration of the Holocaust, especially in the carrying out of the tasks of the *hands-on* mass murderers, animal pity should not be aroused.

Another psychological obstacle was the unconscionable immorality of the killings. For the basic sense of morality, which may be relative to the society you are part of but seems pretty much an absolute component of social existence – that sense was bound to render unbearable the psychic demands of killing millions of people. Maybe it would even unhinge the perpetrators. And, contrary to what you might think, Nazi ideology was not all by itself a sufficient bulwark against the psychological assault. Undoubtedly, the top leaders and organizers, Eichmann very much included, had under the influence of the ideology achieved a state of racist fanaticism that could preserve their sanity. But there were also some even highly-placed party-members who – usually, I believe, to their own chagrin – found the ideology inadequate. Even gussied up as it was in its black-shirted, goose-stepping, Nuremberg-Rally ferocity. These men could be very much troubled in their consciences, and often their feelings of guilt manifested themselves even physically. As for the garden-variety racist, whether someone in the middle echelons and or just a Holocaust *worker-bee*, there were among these groups too men and women well served by the ideology, as well as men and women with qualms uncalmed or calmed but not enough.

The Nazis handled the problem by developing and relying on psychologically neutralizing conditions and measures. The most important of these was the war itself. I say most important because the war not only affected everything but affected everything and everyone to the physical and emotional core. As Thucydides made clear almost 2,500 years ago, war can utterly transform social life and rob men of the already limited rationality they possess. Indeed, it is fair to say that only in wartime, and only under conditions of such all-out, years-long war could the Holocaust have been accomplished. For war entails, and especially the total war of Holocaust-time entailed, much killing, constant violence, ready brutality and the necessary, and if necessary then complete, triumph of expediency over scruples. People quickly got used to not questioning orders, to being reduced to dispensable instruments in the pursuit of overwhelming ends. Daily news reports all related to the war, work of all sorts was reconfigured by the war, family life was permeated by the triumphs and sacrifices of the war. Under such conditions, you could hardly afford to be delicate about your own, well, yes, *patriotic* contribution to the Holocaust. In the face of such sweeping consensus in the affirmative, you could not possibly argue that the Jews were *not* the enemy. Of course they were! And so, you hated them and were proud to organize their dispossession and deportation and proud to kill them. In any case, war turned the killing and all the complex facets of the evil enterprise into routines, and always the initial killing itself made subsequent killings easier.

In a sense, the Holocaust was an immense industrial project, a superbly engineered project with psychologically neutralizing procedures of chilling efficacy built into its very design. Like this: <u>Procedure</u>: a hierarchical division of labor separated planners and doers, those who conceived the operation and those who executed it. <u>Result</u>: no one involved had *both* to think about the atrocities and actually dirty his hands committing them. So some killed only in the abstract, while others just carried out orders. <u>Procedure</u>: the process of mass murder was broken down into separate successive tasks, each to be performed by different personnel. In other words, there was also a functional division of labor. <u>Result</u>: almost all participants became intermediate links who performed *tasks innocuous in themselves* at a greater or lesser distance from, and unawares if you so wished of, the final unsettling outcome. Consequently, most consciences were not pricked. <u>Procedure</u>: the armies of participants were made constantly aware that the complex technical standards governing their own discrete tasks were required by and were in the service of a sophisticated and tightly coordinated overall effort. <u>Result</u>: the co-perpetrators focused on their individual portion of the technical and abstract *group* responsibility, rather than on their own individual moral responsibility. And finally, <u>procedure</u>: the assembly-line-like organization of the extermination sites allowed many tasks to be handled by Jews themselves operating in squads of inmates from labor camps rather than by guards or other Aryans. <u>Result</u>: since the inmates were both dispensable and mostly in a survival mode that knows no morality, there was much less of an opportunity for animal pity to arise and gum up the works. At first glance these procedures seem to be ingenious responses to the psychological burdens of routine killing, but if you think about it – by and large these are just modern organizational techniques.

Also very helpful in neutralizing consciences was what Arendt calls the "systematic mendacity" of life under the Nazis, referring to the widespread official practice of not calling things by their rightful names. And so, deportation was known as resettlement, and killing as special treatment. As for the cover-up constituted by the euphemism "the Final Solution," towards the end of 1941, when Eichmann was first told that "the Führer had ordered the physical extermination of the Jews," he was also entrusted with another vital piece of information: that very code name for the operation. This form of lying was so prevalent that sometimes when Eichmann was to meet other officials for the first time, he might even be issued "language rules," which were not a set of propositions by Wittgenstein but a list of words rather that intentionally misdescribed the things they labeled. But Orwellian vocabularies are pernicious things. And indeed, after a while the whole German nation was seeing reality through false lenses. Or so you have to conclude from the belief held by ordinary people that the gassing in the extermination camps was nothing more than "the humane way" of killing "by granting a mercy death," just as the so-called euthanasia campaign of 1939 for "incurably sick persons" implemented throughout the Reich in carbon-monoxide vans had been. Reassured by these habits of linguistic falsification, perpetrators did not even feel the need to hide what they were doing, because they themselves and others too who knew what that actually was *believed* it to be really something else. No opportunity then here for animal pity, nor any use for a moral instinct.

Right around May 14th, at the very point where I interrupted my account of the Hungarian Holocaust, Endre was interviewed by a Nazi-oriented newspaper and so was given the opportunity to indulge in some fine displays of Hungarian mendacity. He was not boasting, but he was pleased to remind readers of the historic importance of his department's work, the "ridding [of the country] of the Jewish poison, a[n act of] self-defense that will end Jewish predominance." Decent man that he was, Endre also emphasized that the "ghettoization was carried out humanely and with the avoidance of all rough conduct. Really, no harm is befalling [the Jews]. They can live among themselves in one group within the borders of the ghetto in accordance with their own folk and racial laws." Masterfully loathsome! Always just a grain of truth mixed in with the distortions and lies, just enough to make the whole thing go down if you're so inclined without even swallowing hard.

One way to think of Eichmann's testimony at the trial, to think of the whole false personality that he inhabited so perfectly, is as a bravura demonstration of the use of language rules. Eichmann presented himself, his relationships with Jews and his war-time activities through a set of euphemisms and sanitized formulations that did not generally contradict the facts but definitely falsified everything. In effect, his testimony was a pack of lies. But the lies fooled Arendt. She accepted Eichmann's words about his intentions and attitudes as accurate accounts of the past, which they weren't at all, and she accepted his self-characterization as no more than just an average foot-soldier of Nazism, which he emphatically had not been. The Argentina documents and the memoir he wrote in captivity, to which, you should note, Arendt did not have access, his eager post-July-8th efforts to deport just a few more trainloads of Hungarian Jews, which I'll come to shortly, and this proud boast, which he made frequently after the war: "I will leap into my grave laughing, because the feeling that I have five million human beings on my conscience is for me a source of extraordinary satisfaction" – all these things and others too confirm that all his life Eichmann was guided by the perverted Nazi moral code, understood history as a relentless racial struggle, and had in his dealings with Jews been motivated by a murderous hatred. A man of deep and abiding evil he was. A man proud of his extraordinary accomplishment and a stranger to doubt or remorse. And then he even fooled Arendt. But as embarrassing as Arendt's gullibility in this regard may be, it is not of much consequence. For it does not in any way undermine the validity or significance of her summary observation about the banality of Nazi evil, that is, about its *all-too-human, non-demonic everydayness.*

The final act of the Final Solution in Hungary began in the middle of May. The effort to line up rolling stock for transportation of the Jews out of the country had begun earlier of course in April. But it was only on May 4th-6th that representatives of German Railways, the Hungarian gendarmerie and the Special Unit could convene in Vienna to finally conclude arrangements. "We agreed," the imaginary letter-writer continues with a report of this event, "that of the various possible routes the most secure for the secret movement of the repulsive cargo would be the one running north and then northwest across eastern Slovakia and up to Upper Silesia, skirting the highest mountains but still offering much natural beauty that the vermin of course would not see, haha, with control of the trains transferred to the Germans at Kassa, and then on to Auschwitz. The freight cars would be provided by us, and even with the Red Army approaching the Carpathians, Berlin assured the chief, as you may know, Papa, that for *this* mission the necessary equipment would be made available. The entrainments and deportations would follow the east-to-west scheme of the ghettoizations, begin on May 15th and proceed in an orderly manner but on an extremely tight schedule of four trains a day. It was a very ambitious plan, but so it had to be. And when you're up to the task, you enjoy a challenge. So nobody balked. The details, including the departure schedule of the trains from the several ghetto entrainment points, we discussed with local leaders on May 8th-9th at a meeting in Munkács. Everything had remained calm of course after the ghettoes had filled up, these people reported, but they were on tenterhooks anyway. You could not delay a minute! It was left to the locals to organize absolutely everything on the ground, like even who, for example, would provide the chalk needed to mark the number of Jews inside each wagon after the doors had been slammed shut and locked.

"The deportations from Zone I began on schedule on May 15th, just a mere 58 days after the occupation began and only 29 days after the roundups started. The air at headquarters in Budapest crackled with excitement. Each train carried a human freight of about three thousand crammed 70-90 per car, each car equipped with two buckets, one with water, the other for excrement. The Jews were herded to the entrainment platforms, once more completely searched for valuables, usually deprived of their personal documents and thus their identities as legal persons, and shoved, squeezed and forced into the cars, which were then chained and padlocked. The men in charge were instructed to be very business-like, and so they were I understand in all respects except maybe some-what rough in handling the freight, but what do you expect? We required a careful tally of the numbers of deportees and daily reports moved up through the chain of command. The totals mounted rapidly, like some kind of lottery. May 19: 62,644, May 23: 110,556, May 25: 138,870... June 3: 253,389, June 8: 289,357. That was the final total for Zones I and II. A truly amazing operation! After that the roundups, ghettoizations and deportations moved west Zone by Zone. As you must know from official sources, the last trains for Auschwitz left on July 8th carrying Jews from the suburbs of the capital. Everything well-nigh flawless. Well-nigh per-fect! Sure there were a few mix-ups, with a few cars arriving at the wrong destination, to the good or bad fortune of its occupants, an unneces-sary reprieve here, an end a bit accelerated there, but all in all, it was remarkable. Although the job isn't finished yet, already the air is easier to breathe. And I say this with a heavy heart, Papa, since fate is not being kind to the Führer and to the great German people, but to me the success of the operation feels actually like a victory."

The grand total of deported Jews, and the plan as it had been in-tended was never fully realized because, for reasons I'll come to presently, Horthy ordered a stop to the deportations on July 7th – still the total came to 437,402 persons hauled away in an operation lasting only 96 days, that is, less than 14 weeks. The thorough cleansing of the entire country ex-cept the capital. An achievement long to be remembered and celebrated!

That number of people, concentrated in 55 ghettoes, had required 147 trains to transport them out of the country over 38 working days. As more than one especially bureaucratic official undoubtedly calculated, that represented an average of 2,975 persons per train and an average of 11,510 per day. *Exactly* as planned.

In Auschwitz, preparations for the mass arrival of maybe as many as a million Jews from Hungary had begun early in the year. A new train disembarkation platform, or ramp, as it was actually called, was planned and constructed. Like most everyone involved in realization of the Final Solution, the camp personnel took pride in its work and strove to improve procedures. This adjustment to the extermination routine, made to accommodate the expected influx, allowed the prisoners to be detrained closer to, and *within walking distance* of, the crematoria, and so eliminated a 2-kilometer-long connecting truck-ride, by then the only real inefficiency in,… well, the death machinery.

It just so happens that the only photographs of Auschwitz in operation are from May 1944 and show crowds of Hungarian Jews disembarking along the new ramp and approaching German doctors who were there to separate the few strong enough to be sent to the labor camp next door from the vast majority, the 80-90% to be sent immediately to some bungalows to disrobe in preparation for what they were told would be delousing showers and from there directly, and with hardly an hour or two I would guess having passed since their arrival, into the gas chambers. The photographs also show squads of prisoners from the work camp sorting the items found in the luggage left on the trains by the people whose lives and bodies were at the very same time being annihilated, after which the squads proceeded to disinfect the freight-cars and remove all traces of their recent human cargo, watch the train pull out and then clean up the ramp as well, so that everything was ready for arrival of the next group still in the grip of the resettlement myth. The camp personnel, equipment and procedures also functioned flawlessly, a fitting finish to all of Eichmann's efforts and the hard work of the Special Unit and the Hungarian dejewifiers. Close to half-a-million people were "processed" in Auschwitz in less than eight weeks, and as many again could also have been, I'm sure, but for the very irritating order to halt the deportations.

The events of March 19ᵗʰ through July 7ᵗʰ, 1944, or so, the events I just related, do not constitute all of the Hungarian Holocaust, although they do represent the Eichmann team's major local achievement. Antisemitism also took the lives of numerous Hungarian Jews both before those weeks and after. Braham has assembled the evidence and his figures are likely to be final. All in all, partially restored Hungary's Jewish community of 825,000 lost 570,000 persons, or about 70%. Had Horthy not stepped in as he did, the country would really have been transformed. As it was, the fundamental demographic shift occurred only in the countryside. And since most of the Jews of the capital survived, *and Communism quickly followed,* there was no cultural shift of the kind intended, namely, the cultural dejewification that had been desired since the 1920s and strenuously implemented since at least 1938. But despite the unfinished business, those active in the Hungarian Holocaust were right to be triumphant about their work. Aside from the evil, the horror and the seemingly incomprehensible depravity of it, that is.

A Family at War II

As you have seen, rather late but, alas, not yet out of time, the Holocaust arrived in Hungary, and like a tornado it ripped devastation through the land. For the Jews, at once it became all of life. As residents of the capital, Rose and I were safe from the extermination regime that operated through early July, but that did not exempt us from all hardship and suffering. To begin with, the initial step that then led pretty much directly to destruction was imposed on all the Jews. As of April 5ᵗʰ, all of us over the age of six were required to wear a 4-by-4-inch canary-yellow six-pointed star sewed on the upper left side of our outer garments. From then on the fate of the Jews of the capital did follow its own course, but that also had its horrors. Certainly, a general outline of what was happening in the provinces was *known* in Budapest, so the capital's Jews still had plenty to *fear* and they also could not help interpreting every event as either a sign that they too were about to be deported to their deaths or that they would be saved after all. And the relentless anxiety itself was also often trumped by actual attacks on your life.

As I've said, a few days after marching into the city, the SS and the Gestapo units began arresting random groups of Jews and stripping all Jews of their property. Then from the middle of June, Budapest Jews were confined in two ways: in space restricted to living in about 2,000 so-called yellow-star buildings, and soon also required to stay indoors except between 11 AM and 5 PM, and even then allowed to go out only for medical reasons, official business or to do their food shopping. So you lived however you could, without thinking about what tomorrow might bring. Then on June 30th, the authorities ordered and the gendarmerie began to herd the Jews of the city's *suburbs* into two brickyards, surely for transportation to someplace or other, and between July 6th and 8th packed them onto trains. The pall of mass killing now darkened the horizon all around Budapest and the winds were not favorable. You lived in a panic, and the fear could paralyze you. When would it be the turn of the Jewish population of the capital itself?

But July 7th brought a reprieve. Horthy, still head of state, banned further deportations. He was no Jew-lover, and right after the occupation he even gave the first puppet-government free rein over the Jewish question. And he also was not moved by the staggering enormity of the evil, as were by this time many even among those revolted and repelled by Jews. It seems rather that Horthy was responding to sudden international pressure, which itself was prompted by the detailed and precise eyewitness account of *genocidal* operations at Auschwitz given by Rudolf Vrba and Alfred Wetzler, two Slovak Jews who had escaped from the camp on April 7th. Their report appeared in the Swiss press in June, and that finally made it impossible for whatever semblance of a public conscience still existed in the West to continue mostly to ignore the highly clandestine but not unknown *genocide* in progress for two years already. Now the murderers' pretense that the cattle-cars were transporting the Jews from Hungary only as a labor force could no longer be maintained, and official protests from Sweden, Switzerland, the Vatican and even the United States, as well as domestic concerns about the country's reputation, had to be acknowledged. Finally on July 7th, declaring that "I shall not permit the deportations to bring further shame on Hungarians," words both revealing and damning, Horthy sought to put an end to the national dishonor.

For the time being then, the Jews of Budapest were saved, and they were euphoric. But the Germans and their eager Hungarian partners were not to be put off so easily. The Red Army was approaching, as was the Third Reich's defeat, but the dejewifiers were hell-bent on completing their evil task. They knew, as did their intended victims, that killing and survival were each now engaged in a race against time. The day after the stop-order, the ever-efficient and now gangsterish Eichmann managed to smuggle out one more train and also devised a plan for another group of 1,200 to be deported on July 19th, many of them from Budapest. Meanwhile, the ethnic cleansers were also exerting pressure on the government to lift the deportation ban and even set August 15th as the target date for resumption of their operations, and when they missed their own deadline, they reset it first for August 25th and then for September 18th. The persecuted observed the preparations in a gravely despairing mood and, as the calendar drew closer to each appointed date, felt themselves being dragged over and over to the edge of the abyss. It was also during these days that the authorities were working on a plan to move persons holding Swiss and Swedish "protective passes" into special yellow-star buildings, the so-called "protected houses," and move out of those buildings Jewish residents not so privileged, and of all the blows of misfortune it was this proposed exchange that ignited the wildest panic amongst the capital's Jews. For surely those who were to be displaced would be deported actually. And then in short order the job would be finished.

I try to imagine how Rose and her infant lived during these months of the German occupation. I know that we moved into a yellow-star building, in mid-June I would think, a building almost directly across the street from the old apartment. So from a place that had a bed-sitting room, a kitchen and a bath, Rose had to hustle into a single room and had no choice but to leave behind even the few pieces of furniture we had, including the sofa-bed sometimes she referred to as her trousseau. Of course, even if she had had room, how would she have made the move? Wasn't it hard enough just with my things and me on her hip or in her arms? *Nobody* of course had a young husband to help with somebody else's fatherless baby, and the old men had no more strength than she did. So in the new place she must have straightened my little cap, given me a smile of terror and reassurance and handed me to the nanny, who may herself have just been moving into those same rooms, and then run out to carry and drag her own and the nanny's things across the street, the mattresses maybe but not the beds. Into the new building and up the stairs and along corridors clogged with others also driven to this high-ground by the antisemitic flood, finally arriving winded, stunned by the coercion, the curfew and all the other new restrictions, and grimly deter-mined to keep protecting me. But she knew that night was falling and the net drawing ever tighter.

For even as penned in as the Jews were, and their contacts with the rest of the world reduced to the clandestine and the incidental – even so, every rumor-wracked resident of the yellow-star houses had to know what was going on, certainly the broad strokes in which I just presented it and undoubtedly in more detail too depending on both the house and the knower. So Rose, I assume, knew about the protective passes and the deportation target dates and was already scheming with all the power of her wits and charm and energies to evade the lethal peril. To *escape*. Yes, I have to believe that already right then she was thinking about escapes, escapes that were probably not even among the several that in the end she actually perpetrated. For escaping was still possible. The trap hadn't yet snapped shut. But where to? I wonder if her mind was racing and her feelings roller-coasting, as they well might have been. Maybe the coun-tryside? Better the Russkies than the Nazis! But how? She could leave right after midday, many people did, that long kerchief to tie up the arm he's in... find someone to hide them and feed them as long as necessary, but who, or if she could pass as a Christian woman, but the little boy *was* circumcised and easily exposed... to manage, maybe with false papers or someone vouching for them, but how did you get false papers, although you heard about people who had them, and there were good people all around, lots of people hated the Nazis and the fascists and were willing to help, if only she could find someone who actually could. Or maybe she was just cool and efficient and controlled even in her thoughts. Or maybe her iron-willed lucidity was being interrupted by more or less frequent and even more trying but still suppressed rages. In any case, during the summer, though always on the lookout, she stumbled upon no opportunity, nor did she have better luck during the early weeks of the autumn, when the Germans were so preoccupied with the advancing Soviets that the government could even look away as the International Red Cross and neutral states tried to ease the Jews' plight just a little.

But that bit of decency was short-lived. You see, by the end of the summer, Horthy and the men in the government loyal to *him* rather than to the occupiers finally owned up to the fact that if Hungary did not want to host a clash of titans, then quickly an armistice had to be arranged with Stalin. But the Germans were ready with a counter-move to this about-face too. And so on October 15th, when Horthy announced Hungary's withdrawal from the war, and the Jews, almost giddy, tore off their yellow stars and emerged from their yellow-star buildings celebrating, the Hungarian armed forces and dejewifiers retorted by reaffirming their commitment to the struggle against Bolshevism and recognizing a government dominated by the Arrow Cross, the political and paramilitary organization of the domestic Nazi movement, and its leader Ferenc Szálasi, who just then was seizing power. So there would be no armistice here. And never mind that by this time the Germans had clearly lost the war; that didn't stop the combatants from continuing to wage it relentlessly. Indeed, each side was ready to commit its all to keep or capture Budapest. For Hitler, Hungary suddenly assumed the dramatic guise of a last chance, while the Soviets could not leave *behind* the front lines a major city defended by plenty of men, arms and armor. So the Soviets set about encircling the city, and once that was effectively accomplished, Hitler forbade his troops to break out, which actually suited them just fine, preferring as they did a quick battlefield death to surrender to an enemy that had learned butchery and savagery from Genghis Khan and a slow annihilation in a Siberian camp if you were lucky. The struggle for the city went on until February 1945, with conditions rapidly deteriorating even from the critical already reached by October.

Since the war could no longer be won, elimination of the remnants of Hungary's Jewish population now became the main objective of the local authorities. So the night of something like a Hobbesian state of nature, in which life is characterized by "continual fear, and danger of violent death," had arrived. Gangs of rabid Arrow Cross killers – jobless, aimless hooligans and violence-besotted Jew-haters wearing armbands bearing the despised and feared cross with an arrowhead tipping each of its arms – now terrorized the city. During the three-month period between Szálasi's coup and the liberation of Pest by the Red Army on January 18, 1945, the Jews of the city, whether inside houses marked to *attract* the minions of death or out on the street, whether obeying all the crushing restrictions or flouting the rules wherever possible, whether in possession of protective passes or just the hoi polloi of the cursed and ill-fated minority – the Jews were at the mercy of roving bands that, under pretext of levying penalties on violators of the law, were free to rampage wherever they pleased, robbing and beating Jews, forcing their way into yellow-star houses and later the ghetto, and hauling away and murdering the inhabitants. Many in these bands were working-class youths no more than 15- or 16-years old. Too young to join the armed forces, but old enough to wield machine-guns and carry grenades, to round up starving, unarmed and cowed Jewish men and women, drag them to party offices and kick and torture them or march them down to the Danube embankment, make them strip naked and shoot them dead into the icy river. More Jewish corpses for impromptu disposal.

Soon after grabbing power, the Arrow Cross government mobilized all able-bodied Jews for public works projects. Eichmann had advised and encouraged this as a way to both fortify the city against the coming Soviet assault and move the country closer to being completely cleansed. By October 26th, about 35,000 Jews, about a third of them women, had been sent to the eastern edges of Budapest to dig trenches for long hours with practically no nourishment, to sleep under the open sky, to be herded about, brutalized and tortured by Arrow Cross guards who gleefully shot stragglers and the exhausted. Yet these laborers still fared better than those "to be lent to the Germans [pursuant to an October 18th agreement made with Eichmann] for work in behalf of Hungary." These latter, also men and women, were force-marched in groups of about two thousand and daily stages of about 30 kilometers along the so-called "death road" from Budapest to the Austrian border. The victims were called up on November 2nd and 3rd, and the "death marches" themselves, what in Argentina Eichmann blithely referred to as "Jew-treks," began on November 8th. Of course, many of the unfed, unsheltered, abused and mercilessly culled marchers did not make it to the end of the approximately 250-kilometer, or little more than 150-mile long, ordeal, where the survivors were handed over to the Germans, who sooner or later undoubtedly murdered them all. For months, devastated bodies and discarded belongings littered the death road throughout its length. Jewish corpses not even worthy of disposal.

At least one of Rose's escapes was from a death march, and maybe more than one. What exactly happened I'll never find out, although now I do know a little more about that particular trial than I could gather from the terse aside-ish statement I heard maybe three times through the years, namely, that three times altogether she "had been taken away" and three times she had managed to extricate herself from death's clutches. Of course I never asked for details, that's right, nor did anyone else either, and once at least I believe I was not the lone listener. I never even dared to think about probing the darkness. Those words and the thought of my mother overpowered or suffering or dead must at first have horrified me; later on they only unnerved me. So for decades I remained in an insensate state of ignorance, an ignorance so complete that when friends or politely curious acquaintances inquired how that was, how did the Hónigs survive the war, those Hónigs, that is, who did survive, I could never even imagine how Rose could have conquered her challenges, like having to break or slip out of a sealed cattle-car, which is what I thought she had done for how else can they take you away – I could never even imagine that, for I had never ever heard of any Houdini, a Hungarian Jew by the way, who had. I don't recall how I ever responded to the friends and acquaintances, because the whole idea would always throw me into a state of confusion, prompting me most likely to engage in some kind of all-around awkward diversion and to think quickly about something else. And never think back.

It was only during her last years, that time in early 2002, that utterly unexpectedly Rose once said a few words to me about one of those incidents. On the way, she recalled as if to herself, she and another woman had said to each other, "At Dorog, that's where we'll have our chance!" Dorog was and is a town about 40 kilometers northwest of Budapest, with a population of miners who had had at that time a reputation for hating the fascists and had thereby inspired hope in my unsinkable Jewish mother. And sure enough, she went on, when they had reached the place – and in my head I could hear the imaginary train crawling to a halt with a whine – a local man had walked by and had urged them to run off to a nearby cemetery and hide there until dark. And so they had indeed managed to do, to sneak away, literally running for their lives, and later the man had come to get them, had taken them to his home and had helped them get back to Budapest. My God! I gulped down Rose's words and nearly choked on the situation itself, her saying it just like that I mean, in a half-dozen sentences or so after a lifetime of silence. My mind went blank, and I was speechless. I couldn't bring myself to ask, "But, Mom, how did you escape from the train itself?" Again I couldn't. But like never before, this time I was aware of the distance that separated us and of my reluctance to cross it. I was actually aware of recoiling from the possible intimacy. Poor helpless fool that I am. And of course that was alright with her. But how could it have been otherwise? It was she herself who had once upon a time established that distance, and then proceeded through the decades to maintain it uncrossed.

But soon after that I did regain my wits and even arranged a couple of occasions for the two of us to talk about those times. And then she did tell me other things too, although nothing else ever about Dorog or that train. I can say honestly that I peppered her with questions, although not with the panache of a paprika-sprinkling Hungarian, and also not with questions very specific or very direct either. And I was such a jackass that I even complimented myself on the skill with which I had kept her talking, allowing her visibly to recollect and speak freely, and how I *managed* not to scare her off. In any case, there I was, having become privy to various long-held secrets, including the Dorog vignette that unexpectedly elaborated the repeated original statement, but now nothing made sense at all. Only months or even years later, after much reading and getting my bearings about 1944-45 Hungary, did I one day suddenly see her with my mind's eye as she *really* might have been: escaping to the shelter of the departed not from a death *transport* but from a death *march*. But of course! I of all people should know that you can't understand the past unless you know your history.

But I will never learn any other details of her ordeal. Like how much time passed between reporting for duty, so to speak, and arriving back at the place that was her, I mean our home. After all, for several days before they were ordered out on their deadly journey, many of the marchers were held in the yard or open shed of a brickworks in Buda. And what about the day and a half or so of slogging along in that condemned company under the murderous menace of the machine-guns? And how exactly did she get back from Dorog to Budapest? Hidden on what means of conveyance? With her yellow star still in place or without? I can imagine her, 37-years-old and in her prime, alert but trembling with fear, fierce determination and animal cunning, but that's all. And I also would like to know about her other scrapes and escapes. Was she pressed into other death marches too? Did she tumble into a ditch and slip away from a labor battalion? Had she been caught in a net cast by an Arrow Cross gang and then managed to escape intact in all the shooting, bludgeoning and confusion that ensued? I'll never know. But now I can think of her in those straits a little more concretely, and now more than ever I see her as a hunted animal, a hollow-cheeked creature slinking in the shadows, on the run and always looking for food and drink and maybe shelter, and ready to do *anything* that could save her life. And so save mine.

For there is also the question of where *I* was during these death-tempting/death-defying episodes. I had my nanny of course, but for Rose to leave me with her would have required a highly personalized view of a patently historical peril, and Rose was not about to make that mistake. The nanny was no safer from persecution than she herself. Fortunately for us, in August the International Red Cross had set up about 35 orphanages for Jewish children in the city, some safer than others I assume and any one of them the safest or least safe on any given day. In at least one emergency, and maybe more than one, it was in one of these establishments that Rose dropped me off. Like a bag at the baggage check! She undoubtedly expected an imminent threat to our existence, and so she rushed along under the November sky, holding me tightly in her tense arm, a nametag sewed into my jacket, panic and hope and a life-and-death anxiety driving her on, counting her steps and the blocks remaining before she could duck into the building she had often made a mental note of before, if only other mothers and infants and toddlers were not already pushing to get in through the always inadequately guarded and only half-open doors. This was my only chance. She could not have responded to the call-up with a child in her arms and expected him to survive. And even this was unthinkably risky. The day after she again felt sufficiently safe to pick me up, an Arrow Cross gang burst into the place, seized all the little ones and flung them into the Danube. Tiny Jewish corpses easily disposed of.

I was two years old. I wanted to run around and get in trouble, but not this kind. Talk about the terrible twos! Clasped in her arms, our hearts racing to the same beat, I must have been near gagging with the fear that enveloped us, afraid to whimper even. Very early on, if I am to believe her, and she wasn't one to exaggerate, she had trained me to perform incredible feats of physical self-control, and I'm not talking just about toilet-training, taught me skills that have both plagued me and stood me in good stead much of my life. How often had she by then compelled me not to make a sound and remain still despite the urge, the life-affirming, life-preserving instinct, to cry out? To squirm or flail about? Well, I believe I lived up to her demands that day too. For finally we did enter the orphanage, or so I imagine, and with all the sisters and volunteers wishing they had four hands, Rose was just motioned to a room, to put me down there on a mattress and leave me, maybe the last time ever to see me. And so she did.

Throughout my thirties and forties, although not before I think and definitely not after, I was subject to a recurrent dream, a frightening dream although not a nightmare, a dream that would not wake me but would remain a weight on me throughout the day. I am an infant lying in the crib, while a woman leans over me, extends her arms and bends down to pick me up, but then, in a myth-of-Tantalus re-enactment almost to the letter, draws away before having even touched me. The face performing these abrupt reversals is a primitive mask of metal or some other kind of polished material frozen into a single grossly-stylized grimace that expresses no emotion I could ever identify. Asleep or awake. Over the years I related that dream to two psychotherapists, neither of whom ushered Rose into my speculations about what it might be saying to me. I myself tried in vain to pin something or other, now I really can't remember or even imagine what, on the woman in my life at the time of each reporting. Convoluted dead-ends, those attempts were! Then the dreams just stopped, and only years later, when somehow it occurred to me that the as-it-were plot of the phantasmagorical scene was actually a frequent experience of mine as a two-year-old – only then did Rose finally take her obviously rightful place in what cannot in all fairness be called a *heavily* disguised memory. For, as you will soon see, that scene or a significant part of it was enacted not just once but quite regularly. She, who would rather have done anything else, was repeatedly forced to leave me, and to do so without making or even allowing *me* to make any fuss about her withdrawal. Good luck to me! And to her too!

But then soon escaping became even more difficult, because when the fugitive returned she no longer had a place even relatively safe to go and to take me to. You see, around the end of November, the government ordered a further concentration of the Budapest Jews – the easier to swoop down on them all at once – into two ghettoes newly established in Pest: the so-called international ghetto and the large ghetto. The former, consisting of a group of "protected" houses near the river in the XIIIth district, was restricted to Jews carrying international safe-conducts and remained in existence only briefly. By early December, Arrow Cross gangs had made life too dangerous for its inhabitants and so scared them also into the larger holding pen. This latter ghetto, an area in the VIIth district enclosed with a wooden stockade that the Jews themselves had hastily to throw up, included about 300 buildings. Initially, all the Jews not assigned to the little ghetto had to relocate to this wretched warren, which no Christian was allowed to enter and no Jew to leave, and where food and water and heating fuel were barely sufficient to maintain life. By December 2nd about 170,000 of the city's 200,000 Jews had crowded in there. Some of them found comfort in numbers, but others, like Rose, defiantly stayed outside, believing themselves safer hiding behind a false identity or out of sight.

One evening in November, with the typically overcast day fading at an early hour and the minimal street lighting unreliable, Rose sat on a park bench, her arms wrapped tightly about herself to ward off the cold, looking haggard but not unkempt, *never* unkempt, her coat shapeless over three sweaters and without its yellow star, for that was a risk she had to take, and less of a risk anyway than wearing the thing, that she had already settled in her mind. She had, I imagine, just managed to snatch from some grave the foot she already had in it and had then sidled back, as it were, into the city, but what was she to do now, she was at her wit's end. Would she have to spend the night on that bench? How do people have the strength to go on? Would she make it until daybreak? Maybe she heard some sounds then as if people were approaching, for she scurried off, slackening her pace only when passing through better-lit spots, trying not to arouse suspicion or pique the interest of a potential predator. After a while she came to a grocery store a couple of steps down from the sidewalk, the only open place about. She went inside. She looked at the anorexic heaps of grains in open bins, the three red jars on an eye-level shelf, the other shelves mostly empty, and then she looked around again. (These kinds of details are my own invention of course.) Finally the woman behind the counter broke the silence, and soon Rose, on the lookout every minute for a miracle, was telling her how she had fled the countryside before the advancing Russians and now had nothing and was homeless in the city and without papers. They commiserated. Then before Rose walked back out into the cold, still alone, hungry and scared, the woman pulled out a ration book tucked in next to the cash register and pressed it into her hand. A customer, our guardian angel in disguise apparently, had left it behind a few days earlier.

The next day Rose, or now Erzsi according to the ration book, went to the war-time equivalent of a placement agency. Yes, such things still existed, but only for true Hungarians of course. So again she told her story, and the gracious ladyship behind the desk assured her that your papers are fine, dear, and referred her as a live-in maid to a family named Lénárt, a couple and their grown son, an officer. On the first evening on the job, as Rose told the story, she found the officer's boots outside his bedroom door, and demeaning though she considered it, she shined them. But the next day, when she set the table and served the first meal she had prepared, at once the city-slickers were shocked into the recognition, as people often are in war stories, that their new maid was not at all the country girl she had claimed to be, and Mr. Lénárt even apologized if he had spoken inappropriately to her, to be followed by the son, who apologized specifically for the boots. And the day after that Rose already began to play offense. She confessed to Mrs. Lénárt that she was actually an unwed mother who had had to leave home because of a falling out with her father, and now before it was too late she had to retrieve her child from an orphanage. Mrs. Lénárt said she'd have to discuss the matter with her husband, but at once Rose started to talk about leaving, whereupon Mrs. Lénárt said, look, why don't you get him now? What could be the harm? And so Rose ran and got me from the Swedish "protected house" where she had managed still to shelter me at least, and so I too, a disoriented tyke, passed routinely from one less or more caring hand to another, maybe numb to all feelings already as I've been a little all my life – so I also took up residence at the Lénárts'.

And now finally a daily routine, something every child needs, imposed itself on my life. But what a routine it was. During the four or five weeks until Pest was liberated, Rose worked for the Lénárts and I was locked in her room by myself all day, and at this point in the telling Rose patted the pocket of her dress to indicate that the keys were safely with her all the time. So there I was, obviously less imperiled than before, but again bereft and abandoned. Or, more to the point, there I was, charged with an alternating current of very tight togetherness with my mother and its opposite. She left, and I was left alone, to be silent and still I assume, to find peace of mind on my own, to suffer her withdrawal without complaint or tantrums or banging on the door with my tiny two-year-old fists, likely feeling that I was unworthy of her love and that maybe this time she and her love would actually not return, until the day drew to a close, or until she herself could no longer bear the separation and had to tear herself from her chores, until she, a fairy-mother with a feather-duster, unlocked the door and filled that dingy back room with her everything's-all-right presence, until she again pressed me to her bosom. Ohh! One consequence of the intermittent reinforcement, as B.F. Skinner might have called this cruel though necessary game and my occasional stints in the orphanages too – one consequence I now think was an attachment to her even more indissoluble than if she had been near me in a way not heartbreaking for either one of us. In any case, for this reason I'm sure and others too as you are probably beginning to see, I was indeed attached to her for the rest of her very long life, with an attachment very strong, although not very warm I think even in my childhood.

But on further consideration of that daily routine, I must now assign to it an even broader influence. For when I conjure up my toddler self during those forlorn hours and days, thrown back on my own meager resources, compelled to find emotional sustenance in myself alone, stifled in my fits of rage and my urge never to let go, then I see my whole life laid out in front of me. For all my life I have been unattached and self-sufficient, not absolutely of course since I do have friends and *am* married and have two *step*sons and a daughter-in-law whom I love as if they were my own in every sense possible, but quite extremely nevertheless. All my life I have found it very easy, like a bionic creature snapping off prosthetic limbs, to break attachments or not allow them to form at all, and when I think back on all I may have deprived myself of in doing so, I find that only rarely did those lacks and losses hurt me even just a little, but amounted rather to a reward of more of the solitude and self-sufficiency that have always felt necessary and right to me. In other words, I usually broke attachments or let them break precisely because I *preferred* to be without them. Of course, there were reproaches and cover-ups and convoluted excuses without end, but, I must confess, very few regrets. For early on by way of compensation I became addicted to what psychologists call a *flow* experience, my favored and longed-for cognitive state, and now I can only hope that the addiction will last all my life.

Of course, even a quick glance at my life reveals many events each of which alone seems sufficient to account for all the detaching – from girlfriends, one wife, numerous friends, acquaintances and, preposterous though it may be, I will add, etcetera. There was obviously the transplantation, a break with everybody except the immediate family, a break with everything Hungarian as complete as only a much more than metaphorical iron curtain could make it. Then the assimilation in America, involving several attempts to fit into and then pluck myself out of one or another personal/social/intellectual environment until finally I hit upon the one I felt most comfortable in. And then the semi-voluntary withdrawal from the academic world and the reluctant and never-quite-done-with-the-squirming acceptance of a life in the practice of law. And I could go on, for I haven't even mentioned a mother who did not like physical contact, the probably complete absence of playmates during my wartime early years and a broken marriage. Undoubtedly, all these formative-at-any-age experiences did tend to make me extraordinarily predisposed to solitariness, but all these things, I think, pale in comparison to the hours and days of that two-year-old. It was back there, I'm now convinced, that I first learned to appreciate certain kinds of deprivation as the well-worth-it price of survival, and back there also that I developed the habits that have richly compensated me for those deprivations. It is those hours and days, I believe, that I have not shed as I shed baby-fat, that I have not been able to live down or even really *wanted* to live down after a certain point.

So for the time being Rose and I were safe at the Lénárts', but ahead of us still we had the dangers of the liberation. On December 9th heavy artillery began to bombard the northeastern section of Pest, and on December 24th the saturation-bombing attack was extended to the entire city, which the Red Army had just encircled. Although it was precisely these developments that many, including the Jews of course, had been waiting for, now we were all living and dying on the battlefield itself. From December 30th through New Year's Day 1945, it was three days of non-stop bombing and artillery shelling, 7-10 hours a day, after which the city center was no more than so many mounds of smoldering rubble. And it was only then that the Soviets launched a general assault and weeks of savage building-to-building combat. Death and transfiguration. All in all, the siege and the battle proved so intense, bloody and long that even while the carnage was still raging both sides already referred to Budapest as a "second Stalingrad." Pest was liberated on January 18th, Buda on February 11th.

Once the bombardment started, the only relatively safe place in Pest was a cellar. So people had to live underground for several weeks. Desperation and restlessness did drive them up into the open air now and then, but mostly to no avail. For you hardly dared move about and rarely could buy anything. By November already the regular supply of provisions to the capital was severely disrupted. By late December the death rate from starvation had climbed so high that even the Arrow Cross government was alarmed, although Szálasi still refused Red Cross offers of food aid rather than have to meet the condition of sharing it with the ghetto population. On Christmas day all public transportation ceased, and on December 30th the already very intermittent electricity and gas service failed completely. Mountains of refuse piled up throughout the city. Toilets didn't work. Methodically, war had dismantled civilization and demonstrated once more that as peace creates wealth, not so much in the sense of riches but of well-being, generalized armed conflict creates illth, to use a term coined by John Ruskin. And even as all about uniformed men were sacrificing their lives for one system of laws or another, lawless gangs freely pillaged, raped and killed.

There was jubilation in the ghetto when the Red Army finally established control, but conditions did not improve immediately. For now you had to live in fear of the liberators. At the conclusion of the siege, the Soviet command granted its troops three days of "free looting" throughout the entire city, with no constraints. This barbarity carries my imagination back to Visigoths armed with swords and arrows sacking Rome in 410 or the crusaders looting Constantinople in 1204, and even more to the Protestant city of Magdeburg so conscientiously destroyed and depopulated by Catholic troops during the Thirty Years War as to give rise to a German verb that translates into English as to *magdeburgize* and means to annihilate utterly. And, as you would expect, looting included the raping of women. For indeed the Soviet conquerors, juiced up on victory and their Genghis-genes, practiced mass rape as their right and also as some kind of collective recompense for the losses and privations the enemy had inflicted on *them*. When the Yugoslav Communists protested to Stalin about such a fate being visited upon their own people, the Man of Steel brushed off the complaint, saying, "Doesn't Djilas [the Yugoslav emissary] understand that a soldier who has marched thousands of kilometers through pools of blood and through fire and water will want to have a little fun with a wench or steal a trifle?" And the wilier of these conquerors could rape even without overt violence. They could easily suborn the act with "a little bread, a little flour, a little lard, a tiny little bit of sugar," as a joke of the times had it. You see, food supplies to the capital began to normalize only in June.

Wearing the conquerors' uniform, Leslie entered Budapest with the Red Army. By then he had picked up enough Russian to serve as an interpreter, although strictly speaking he was a regimental shoemaker. How this came about I learned from Rose. As I've said already, I don't know when or how or why the compulsory labor conscript was dispatched east or even how far east. Maybe to the Ukrainian or even the Russian plains, and they comprise a vast territory, and I also remember his mentioning Siberia several times throughout the years, but Leslie was a compulsive self-aggrandizer, and in any case that would contradict the unmistakable geographical progress of the war. But wherever he may actually have been, he was definitely captured by the Soviets and thrown into a prisoner-of-war camp. There he was put to work as a shoemaker for a Soviet regiment, a not unimportant job if you consider that an army may march on its stomach, but it has to wear shoes, or boots rather, to march at all. Then one day, so the story goes, out of cunning or pride or just the love of his humble calling, Leslie made a pair of boots for a colonel so excellent that the good man, not wanting to leave to chance the continued enjoyment of this craftsman's services when the front advanced to the west, transformed the prisoner into a private. A click of the heels, a wave of the wand. And so Leslie cobbled his way home, one pair of army boots at a time.

During the siege, while Leslie was undoubtedly plying his trade just outside the capital, Rose and I and about 40 others were crammed into a cellar. It was another desperate situation. I imagine that initially a few dim bulbs may have illuminated the ugly space strewn with mattresses and blankets and the occasional wobbly chair, but once the power failed we had only kerosene lamps and candles, and they didn't last forever.

Day and night, the cold stiffened you into a sack-like lump, with only your limbs sticking out and twitching in response to the thunder-beat of exploding bombs. And you lived in constant fear of the end. A direct hit was likely to send down beams and bricks that could crush you, or it could just cut you off permanently from what passed those days for life, liberty and the pursuit of happiness. I myself must have been screaming as the shockwaves crashed about us. And then of course you also had to eat and drink. And if you still had a few morsels, or could even get more, consuming them in front of those without even that much forced you into a shameful dilemma. How could you share? But how could you not? It was not easy to swallow your meager mouthful with all those eyes staring at you out of skin-and-bones skulls.

As soon as the frequent bombings started, the Lénárts had gone off to the greater safety of their weekend house in Buda. The cellar to which Rose had decamped was part of the building in Pest where her employers both lived in an upstairs apartment and had their street-level gourmet store, what in German, and hence in Hungarian too, is called a *delicatessen*. At some point during our confinement, when sneaking off to scavenge something for just the two of us became too impractical or when the situation first manifested itself to her as a threat to the common good, she made a move. With smudges of dirt-like chocolate icing on her face and plaster-dust like confectioner's sugar on the hair sticking out from under her kerchief, she stood tall and revealed to the company that she had not just a personal stash but something more like sustenance for all. Making reference to the *delicatessen* upstairs, she again patted her pocket to indicate that she had the keys to it, two pats when she actually made the revelations and two more almost sixty years later when she told me about making them. Then with equal portions of courage and caution she led her fellows upstairs. For all of us, Jews and gentiles alike, it was liver pâté for the rest of our burrow-bound days.

After liberation, Rose and I went back to the former yellow-star house across the street from the old apartment, for that was still the closest thing we had to a home. And that is also where Leslie went to look for his family, coming from Soviet headquarters, to which he was now assigned. I picture him striding along in a state of great anxiety, strong and solid, just a bit gaunt but actually well-fed enough, a thoroughly lean and toned human machine. He was going to start at the apartment of course, but who knows what could have happened to her? And Tibike? If he didn't find *her*, he'd go look for Rózsi. He walked around a wide and deep bomb crater, glaring at people who looked back at him with suspicion and curiosity and then quickly stepped aside. They're afraid, he thought. They don't know he's a Hungarian in Russian uniform. That he's Jewish. He stumbled. Goddam it! You can break your neck! Mama and Papa, he thought, the stories you hear. And the girls? He skirted some mounds of smashed-up masonry to get to the far side of the Ring boulevard. A few more blocks then, and he started to encounter buildings with their walls still intact, even glass in some windows, although not many. Destruction still all about, but more and more signs also of continuing life. He didn't know if Rose and I were still alive, or his parents or any of his three sisters. He didn't know anything about anybody he had ever known, the slaughter, especially amongst us Jews, having been so extensive and indiscriminate. He was 32, full of energy, with even a taste of the Soviet victory in his mouth. But he had no idea what kind of life he had come back to. Although it would have to be better than what had just sort of ended.

Once he reached the old neighborhood, it must have been easy for him to figure out which doors to inquire behind, and Rose did promptly receive the message he left for her. After getting Leslie's message, Rose left me with the superintendent in the former yellow-star house, "a decent man and trustworthy," and went to leave *him* a message. So finally then we were reunited. Right away Rose and Leslie – he in a Russian uniform, pistol in holster on his hip – and the three Russian soldiers who were accompanying him went across the street and up to the old apartment. Leslie banged on the door until a man opened it. It could not have been a pleasant surprise then or ever to see four Russian soldiers on your doorstep. Leslie pushed the man aside and strode by him into the foyer. He looked about deliberately, item by item, then pushed by a half-cringing, half-outraged woman into the large room, the vague look of which I myself still remember. Rose was right behind him. They surveyed that room's contents too.

"This is mine!" Leslie declared accusingly, pointing a finger at a day-bed and confronting the man and the woman two breathless steps behind. Through a window to his right, I imagine, the low sun of a winter morning casting a shaft of light between the two couples.

"This is my apartment!" Leslie continued in an aggressive tone. "And the bed and the chest of drawers and the day-bed and the armoire are mine too! And the crib!!" he cried out, pointing to my crib, which had only some pillows piled high in it. "That's my crib!"

Hearing one of the Russians speak Hungarian restored some confidence in his hosts.

"It's not yours! It's ours!" the woman shot back defiantly. "What makes it yours anyway? Who are you?"

And indeed, why would we believe this Russian soldier, we have never seen him before, nor this woman, the new occupants protested angrily. They had just been the lucky ones who grabbed the apartment and the furniture and the other belongings Rose had had to leave behind in June. But Leslie knew himself to be right. Hadn't he and his family lived there for four or five years? And wasn't that day-bed with the paisley upholstery Rose's trousseau?

"This was my apartment before those fascist scoundrels put you in here. And it's mine again!" And with that he stepped into the shaft of light and with one smooth motion unsnapped the holster, drew the pistol and pointed it at the man. "Mine, you hear!"

Well, that ended the argument. They got back what still remained of what had been theirs. How? Did Leslie and his comrades just simply throw the new occupants out? Or did he give them some time to pack a few of their *own* things and find other accommodations? It was the dead of winter after all and the city in ruins. But such a thing was best not postponed. And what did his victims think? The Jew, and a Bolshevik of course, reclaiming his ill-gotten gains. Of course. It *would* have been better to get rid of them all. They deserved everything they got, and more.

So it was over. Well, the war was at least, and the official persecutions, but you couldn't be sure about much else. Certainly, the world did not return to its condition as of 1939 – not that you had been longing for that – nor to its condition at any time prior to that. It was a new world rather, a world mostly of hunger and rubble. And your own life no less was also in a history-induced shambles and badly in need of reconstruction. But how were you going to do that? How would and did Leslie liberate himself from that uniform? How did Rose deal with neighbors who just weeks earlier had been hunting Jews? How, indeed, could you put back together your personal life, or what was left of it after all the killing and suffering?

"Your father's here," Rose had said to me after receiving that message, "but of course," she added decades later, "you didn't know what a father was." That's right, I didn't. For how could I have? Even if I had learned before he had departed to recognize him for what he was to me, for sure I would no longer have remembered him when he returned. So maybe that's not all that Rose meant by that better-late-than-never addendum? Maybe a hidden meaning was lurking behind those words? Maybe her comment actually offered a glimpse of a family reunion that had been filled with as much rejection as rejoicing?

If I try now to imagine the occasion, I see at once that conflict threatened from all sides, indeed a good all-around melee. Undoubtedly, Rose's love immediately became an object of competition, with all the usual Oedipal complications, with Leslie's outraged and impotent jealousy entirely appropriate, but not so my own perception of him as a dangerous challenger. For I was sitting pretty. And maybe there was also a rivalry for my own affections. Rose herself must have been fiercely possessive, given that I was the only person alive she loved and had come through the months and indeed years of survival to love even more. Certainly never in her life did she give away any part of me without a fight, least of all until much much later to Leslie. But maybe she had nothing to worry about either, for by then I may actually have been too exclusively hers ever to allow myself to be shared. By then I may even have been not only unaware of fathers but also unwilling to learn about them. So Rose, as usual, was holding all the cards, but I can't imagine how she played the hand. I could try to construct the scene that was played out by those three characters, with an age-appropriate part for myself, something quite accurately Leslie-ish for the man in the uniform, for I saw him play such parts often enough, but Rose.... Well, there is no Rose in my memory adequate for this job. The emotional demands of the role are simply too great, and I certainly can't take a chance on her playing it with a heart as cold as that apartment itself was. I don't want Leslie, surely a savior sent when most needed, to be subjected again to the feeling that even then nobody really wanted him. Even if that is exactly how it was.

For I myself had nothing to offer him, the father I did not know until the beginning of the 27th month of my life. Although that did not *have* to be fatal to the father-son relationship then embarked upon. You can, I would think, start such a relationship even later and make a resounding success of it. Yes, I'm sure you can, I know you can, although not if you also have to contend with Rose's feelings about Leslie, which were actually my birthright, feelings that had bubbled up already I'm sure in my amniotic bath. Leslie never had a chance. And neither did I. From the moment I became sentient, there she was, my mother, the sum-total of my object-world, the length and breadth of my consciousness – there she was with her severely limited ability to love, even if she did love *me* exceedingly. And there were also the near-fatally aggravating circumstances: the persecutions in which we got caught together, the terrible months on our own that I survived only because repeatedly she saved my life as she saved her own, and managed, to her credit, to do it at a cost to me no greater than my psychic well-being. If I let myself, I can piece together a little of how I must have felt during those Holocaust-war times, a precious endangered life held close and entrusted to her care for every minute of the day and night, a small threatened existence dependent on being under her constant and complete control, a frightened being ever obedient to her commanding and all-inclusive presence, her creature, her property, her purpose. The father-son misadventure of many years was only part of the lifelong tribute I paid her. For in addition there were also my many neuroses and the miseries consequent upon them, as well, to be fair, as the accompanying compensations that have bestowed much happiness upon me.

So Leslie and Rose were reunited. After, let's say, two years of separation, innumerable horrors and adventures, and experiences you'd call life-changing today. They must have had a lot to talk about, a lot to tell each other. So what do you think? An evening sometime after that unimaginable reunion, he knew where to get a bottle of wine and maybe even some sausages, although that would have been more difficult, she had a couple of candles, I was already bundled in a sheepskin jacket and asleep, so do you think they sat down with hands in Red-Army-issue gloves at a much-stained table to exchange their stories?

Well, think again. For what stories could they actually tell? They were not, either of them, storytellers. Of course he was a braggart, a slayer exclusively of very large dragons, but how far can you push that, especially with a matter-of-fact wife? And even with due allowance for the passage of time and the vagaries of memory, if I can judge by everything she finally told me, I have to say that she, like most everyone else too I would think until tales of the Holocaust became fashionable – that she had always thought of it all as just a handful of highlights and episodes, a few still-unsubmerged islands in the ocean of death, and ultimately as many slip-throughs as close calls. After all, they had only a haphazard knowledge of the course of the war and of the atrocities maybe even less. And then there was also the question of how much and what you actually want to put into words, something you had probably not done before. Do you want to relive those emotionally wrenching, desperate and revealing things even with your spouse? Especially if you're as defensively ensconced and reflexively secretive a person as Rose was? Indeed, how much do you even tell yourself? So the more I think about it, the more convinced I am that nothing like that evening ever happened, that mostly each of them just opportunistically picked up snippets of information about the other, and otherwise a curtain of silence woven by discretion, shame, hurt and different ways of presenting yourself to the world shut each of them off from these experiences too of the other.

But maybe that was actually okay. Maybe the Holocaust-war was not as wounding an experience for them as I have tried to make it. Maybe I have actually put too much emphasis on it and expected too much from it. For without quite admitting it to myself, I had definitely hoped that this reconstitution and recounting of those months and years of persecution would somehow afford me an epiphany or two and even justify my shifting from Rose to the really bad guys the brunt of the responsibility for the damages *I* suffered. As I've said already, at the time I conceived my project I was already glowing with an eternal-flame enthusiasm for Sebald's novels, especially his tragic and lyrical masterpiece about Jacques Austerlitz, a child of the Holocaust who succumbs to a compulsion to make his own back-trek and in the process manages to reconstruct the coming to grief of his early life. And though I have neither Sebald's poetic powers nor Austerlitz's serendipitous informants, I had hoped for something like the revelatory discoveries that for good and for bad awaited that poor fictional character. Well, I had hoped in vain. For, obviously, there is no shocking Holocaust-war secret in my own past to expose, no traceless but all-transforming trauma that made me what I have been and am. For sure, I understand my past better now than ever before, but there is nothing here like an epiphany, no solution to a puzzle, indeed no puzzle even. What I have brought to light cannot be, as it were, figured out, and it doesn't even amount, I now see, to much of a Holocaust-war recollection. And so, while Rose does get all the credit for assuring my survival, she also stands accused. I'm just glad that extenuating circumstances do provide her with at least a partial defense.

One day, after I had already reflected on these matters at some length, I remarked to Cousin Gyuri that surely the war and the Holocaust had shaped the lives of all the Hónig children. "Yes, their lives," he responded, "but not their characters." And he was right, for so it was indeed, just so, at least with regard to Leslie and Rose. For their lives, unlike the lives

of so many others, other survivors, that is, were *not* radically and fundamentally transformed by the Holocaust-war. Indeed, Rose and Leslie do
not seem to have been traumatized. Quite likely – for knowing only what
I know, I cannot speak with certainty – they had not been humiliated and
shamed and victimized to the nth degree. They had not been stripped of
all the powers that are usually subsumed within a sense of self. Their wills
had not been crushed. They had indeed been marked for death, as had
so many others, that's clear, but at each turn they had either outwitted
their nemeses or had had luck on their side. Although they did participate in the subsequent years of Jewish silence about the ordeals, at moments they had known even success and triumph. Moreover, events from
just a few years later also suggest that their earlier sufferings, as great and
multifarious as they may have been, did not leave permanent scars. For
during the late 40's, when persecutions of another kind began, promptly
Rose and Leslie's perspective shifted. More than once I heard him say
that he could forgive the fascists but not the Communists, as if tacitly he
understood that the former were only thugs, while the latter represented,
alas, a general approach to the modern world. His statements to that
effect I now take as confirmation of Gyuri's assessment of the Holocaust-
war's impact on them. And as an argument too against ascribing their
shortcomings as parents, indeed their failures, to the persecutions.

But, still, I can't be absolutely sure. In *After Such Knowledge*, her
thought-provoking book about the memory of the Holocaust and the
Second Generation, Eva Hoffman makes the cautionary point that often trauma doesn't show, that often it manifests itself as nothing more
notable than a mode of behavior or just a personal peculiarity. So I have
to wonder if after all maybe Rose *was* emotionally crushed. Now, that of
course is possible, but no more than that. For even if something *like* that
did happen, it did not happen with the devastating force the words suggest. At the most, the trauma of the Holocaust-war served as a contribu-
tory factor, as it had in the formation of my own psyche, a factor clearly
secondary to what I might call pre-existing conditions, that is, the pre-
Holocaust-war traits that have somehow to account for all those spurned

offers of marriage as well as the terms attached to the one finally accepted. And then lived. Indeed, the general pattern is undeniable. After the war Leslie and Rose were not suddenly different people embarking on essentially new lives. Rather, they resumed the earlier lives built upon their only-ever personalities, that is, their characters, and resumed them with a vengeance. Almost as if the details of the terrible interruption had been forgotten rather than just locked away in a secret compartment of memory. Judging by his postwar behavior, his endeavors and successes, he quickly rebounded to his frustrated and forever uncalm pre-war self. And she, I would say, was still emotionally distant yet commanding as ever in all respects.

And of course my parents' good fortune in escaping the Holocaust-war relatively unscathed also spared me, and Marika as well, the usual fate of the children of survivors. In my boyhood, I indeed tried for some months or years to ascertain if I did really love Rose and Leslie by speculating on whether or not I would offer to step into their shoes if they were about to be pushed off a roof by some unspecified evil-doer. In other words, whether I would rescue them even if in the process I myself would have to perish. For what it's worth, I could never come to a conclusion. This test of my own feelings, I now realize, and note that in this context I put an equal emotional value on the lives of the two people looking at me from up on the roof – this test may have been a Second-Generation game, although probably not, but anyway, aside from this, I don't believe I indulged in any of the neuroses typical of members of that cohort. Or rather, to the extent I did indulge in neuroses, and I did so quite self-indulgently, I did not do so because of what Rose and Leslie had suffered during the Holocaust-war. That is, it was not as a member of the Second Generation that I was overly attached to them, that I had and sort of have trouble forming relationships, that I tend to repress emotions. I am convinced that to the extent you can point to outside agency in such matters, the obvious and true *personal* cause of these neuroses of mine was Rose herself and Leslie to a lesser extent and not their wartime experiences, and the as-it-were *historical* reason for the neuroses was the emigration rather than the Holocaust-war. And mostly of course, and after a certain age entirely, my craziness in all its manifestations was simply mine.

Sometime after that reunion Leslie and Rose tried to put the Holocaust-war still further behind them by a visit to the Lénárts. We, the three of us, wanted to express our gratitude and maybe also correct any wrong impression about who was or had been what. That kind of thing must have been downright restorative after the debasement that had had such a big part in the persecutions. Rose remembered a lovely encounter. Most importantly, our hosts, officer son included, had sworn that from the first they had set eyes on Rose they knew that she was not a maid. Well, maybe they had been telling the truth then, and maybe not, but obviously from the first about that they hadn't been right. For whatever *else* she may have been, always Rose willingly remained Mrs. Frankel's maid.

As for the miner from Dorog, he never again took the stage as far as I know. So here I offer him long-overdue thanks and my undoubtedly too-belated wishes that his good deed be repaid many times and in many ways during a long and righteous life.

REMEMBRANCE

In 2009, a few weeks before a visit to Hungary, Cousin Gyuri forwarded an email to me without any comment of his own. The communication consisted of a link to a website and a short message. I understood the words of course, but the precise sense of the text, obviously just a fragment from a larger back-and-forth, I could not grasp. I could just gather that in mid-April a Holocaust commemoration was to be held in some unspecified place in Hungary. The organizer of this event, someone at the Center for Holocaust Remembrance, was anxious that it be attended by descendants of the victims, including those from Magyarmecske, a village not much west of the Danube right by the Serbian border, a village I never heard Leslie himself mention but that did have, as I had come to understand from Rózsi, a connection to the Hónig family. It seemed that Gyuri himself, as such a descendant, was being invited, and with a click he had extended the invitation to me too.

Barbara and I were not going to arrive in Budapest until early May, so there was no possibility of attending the commemoration. But would I have wanted to, I wondered, even if the dates *had* worked out? My Cousin Pista, also a paternal relative, who had been in the camp in Buchenwald, indeed in the same barracks as Imre Kertész, the Hungarian writer who won the Nobel Prize for Literature in 2002 and is the author of *Fateless,* a novel about that very place of horrors – a few years earlier Pista had described such events to me. He had been attending them in the town from which he himself had been carried off, where they are now an annual rite. Usually, the few remaining survivors show up, he had said, for there were only a few survivors to begin with, and by now even Pista, one of the youngest of the deportees, was turning 80 – so a couple of survivors may be present and also the descendants of both victims and survivors. I imagined what it would be like to congregate with a bunch of Jews to focus on our Jewishness and on the persecutions it can occasion, and the prospect did not thrill me. I didn't think I'd want to be there, Second Generation or not.

Then I clicked on the link in Gyuri's email. The website had the word "mecske" in its address and contained five files with about 200 photographs altogether. Immediately you could see that they were photographs from the 1920s and 30s, a few of them showing an interesting detail or two of life from those long-ago times, but mostly they were just strangers' family pictures, looking at which can reduce you to a vegetative state in no time. I went through the files rapidly, looking at a horse here, a building façade there, and most everywhere a handsome blond man with Harold-Lloyd-style round glasses and sensuous lips. And then, in a group shot of two 16-, 17-year-old guys, six girls the right age for them and four younger kids – in that group, leftmost in the front row, prone on the ground but propped on his elbows, I saw *Leslie.* He was one of the youths. The blond guy was the other.

After a few days Gyuri responded to an email from me in which I conveyed my disappointment at missing the commemoration and my desire to hear all about it. Could we all go down to Mecske, as it is usually called for short, during the upcoming visit, he wanted to know. But for very few commitments, I told him, Rózsi having recently passed away, we were at his disposal. I didn't say that at first I had found the collective Jewish clothes-rending unappealing and needed the photograph to transform the prospective journey down south for me into a research adventure for my project. It was enough for him to know that now I was avid and intrigued. And so, early one cool May morning, Gyuri, Barbara and I got into his van, a vehicle manufactured apparently before the invention of shock-absorbers, and set out on the three-hour ride to Mecske. While still in the city, we picked up a woman named Jutka, the original recipient of the email that had catapulted me into this adventure and the daughter of the blond man in the photographs, himself named László Ney, or Laci.

Jutka promptly explained that we had been invited to Mecske by a man named Péter, a former teacher there and now a civil rights lawyer. Mecske has a large Gypsy population, and Péter, as part of his work with the Roma children, had organized something like an oral history project to find out what had happened to those children's forebears during the Holocaust. But soon after the project got under way it became apparent that, for reasons I tried to but couldn't get clarified, the information forthcoming related mostly to the local *Jews*, and at that point the project was refocused on them. The upshot of all this was the eventual installation in the village of a plaque commemorating the persecution of the Jews, including a sister of Ney Laci, and an exhibition of some sort in Budapest, which in turn resulted in a prize for Péter and then some publicity. When Jutka learned from a newspaper article of the respect paid to her family, she immediately contacted Péter. He, no less devoted to his own project than I am to mine, had been looking for relatives and descendants of the persecuted all along and was excited to make her acquaintance and post her father's family photographs on the project's website. He also asked if she knew or knew of any other members of the handful of Jewish families formerly of Mecske, and that is what prompted her to get in touch with Gyuri, a childhood acquaintance. You see, Laci Ney had become friends with Gyuri's father in the forced labor service and had, after the war, actually introduced him to his future wife, my Aunt Klári, Leslie's middle sister and a girl from Magyarmecske.

It was a day of brilliant sunlight. About us as we arrived was a world not so much conjured up from the past as persisting in a shrug-of-the-shoulders timelessness. Although the village nestles among the gently rolling hills of lovely, low-key countryside, when you look down its one straight and level street, not treeless but with trees so meager as to be almost shadeless, you see an apparently unbounded phenomenon, as if you were on the very ancestral steppes of the Magyars. You hear the punctuated sounds of children playing in the schoolyard, in the flat distance here and there you make out a few figures moving slowly in front of houses that squat behind high fences next to pigsties, chicken coops and goat-pens, but you feel that nothing ever happens here, only summer squalls and winter frost and other things known collectively as the weather. I looked up at the few wispy clouds inching their way very high across the sky and then turned my face into the wind skipping across this margin of the great Eurasian grasslands.

Péter welcomed us. A terrific guy, about 40, full of enthusiasm, intelligent and very well informed, with the words tumbling out of his mouth like eager acrobats, each one grabbing by the ankles the one ahead. He is an activist who seems to be tireless in doing what he can to make the world a better place. After introductions, he apologized for the simple lunch of soup-sausages-potatoes we were about to share with the children in the school dining hall, which demonstrated that even in Hungary, where the cooking is unfailingly tasty and delicious, institutional food verges on the inedible. After lunch we dropped in on the principal to learn about the teaching of the Romanian dialect spoken by the local Roma, chatted briefly and posed for pictures with some of the children especially involved in Péter's project – the Second Generation on display as visiting dignitaries – and then went out again into the all-illuminating sunlight to look at the plaque recently affixed to the wall of the main school building.

The plaque is a foot by foot-and-a-half or so slice of dark-gray marble that identifies itself as **MEMORIAL TABLET** and declares: "Through the decades, **Magyarmecske**'s Jewish residents prayed here, in Samuel Lederer's former home. **On April 26, 1944**, the gendarmes carried off **13** women, men and children from the village. Eleven of them never returned from the death camp at Auschwitz and other Nazi concentration camps." Then follow ten names in boldface in two columns side by side, with one more centered below them. Then the text continues: "Erected by Magyarmecske's local government, the district's public school and the community's residents. 2008." The fourth name on the left is Hónig Miksáné. My grandmother. Leslie's mother.

I myself have two photographs of my grandmother and I have seen maybe two or three other photographs of her too. So even then for many years already Gizella – Hónig Miksáné means only Hónig Miksa's missus – had existed for me more concretely than *just* a necessary kinship slot, but not by much. Well, at that moment all that changed. As I gazed at that name, read again the words introducing it, and then gazed some more, unexpectedly and startlingly, almost as if taking me by my reaching-up grandchildish hand, the woman assumed an additional, and indeed a constitutive, concreteness in my mind – if you allow, that is, that mental states can be concrete at all. In the time it takes for a thought to form, she became a person! There she was! Gizella! Right in front of my mind, and I don't mean my mind's eye! Who would have thought such a thing possible? Lost for all those years and then found, as it were.

Now that I recall that scene, I see that circumstances were just perfect for that discovery *d'outre-tombe*. Barbara, Gyuri, Jutka and Péter – their reading her name the same time that I was too, or about the same time, that by itself was a powerful stimulus, one puff at least of the breath of life that infused, and so gave a virtual reality in that shadowless light to, my grandmother. Our location was another, my being in *her* habitual surroundings, the village where she had dwelt most of her 52 years, and even the specific details of the place, which to me at least looked as if they had changed only minimally from what they had been back then. A third was the plaque itself, her name carved in stone, permanence itself as the figure of speech has it. And, finally, my emotional, as it were, availability must also have contributed. For, suddenly Gizella was immortal for me, back from the dead, or a little less rhapsodically, no longer *just* dead.

"My father spent some time here too," I remarked as we walked away, speaking to myself or to all, living and dead, who could hear, asking you might have thought rather than stating. "I even saw him in one of the pictures on the website," I said a few steps further on, still a little dazed but unmistakably now addressing Péter. He, in response, drew a large white envelope from his shoulder-bag and handed it to me, and said that in fact Hónig Laci was to be found in *three* photographs. He had printed all three of them on one sheet of glossy photographic stock, which I pulled out from the envelope as I thanked him. Both of the pictures I had not caught before were contemporaneous with the one I had. The blond youth, the owner of the camera I would guess from the case hanging by a strap from his neck, was in both, they must have been taken during the same summer, for clearly it was summer, young people at leisure, the two teenage boys with various members of the same cast of twelve mostly, probably the same day even. The year was about 1930, and Leslie must have been just a brief visitor in this poor-man's Combray. For by then his summers were not idle anymore, if ever they had been, except maybe for the week or two's absence allowed him from his father's shoemaker shop about fifty miles away in Dombóvár, where he was an apprentice.

In one of the new pictures, behind some of the usual kids and some new ones too, there is a third row of swarthy figures, a young man in a garrison cap holding a dog, a woman in her 20s with a child in her arms and a girl of about eight or nine standing in front of her, and most remarkably a tall man in the fullness of life, his shapeless trousers and shirt festooned with large patches, two heavy rings on his fingers, and one hand holding close to his mouth a pipe with a thin stem more than a foot long. Clearly, these people were Gypsies. And just as clearly,

Leslie and Laci Ney and also some at least of the other most likely Jewish kids in the pictures had been on friendly terms with them, or maybe with the local Gypsies in general, including Zsiga, their much-respected and still-remembered headman, as Péter identified the pipe-smoker for me.

Later, when I had the chance to study the picture closely and at length, I found my imagination winging through dappled sunlight and around some Roma caravans strung along the edge of the forest. The Jewish kids from the village are loitering about a cluster of three of them, with one of the boys, Leslie to judge by his posture, sitting on a stool talking to a Roma boy who is grooming two horses. As if in a dream, the visitors are whiling away the summer day, hanging around, being worldly in the company of the slightly disreputable, exotic and forbidden, maybe even sharing a sense of being outsiders with them. Typical behavior for teenage boys. I heard insects buzzing, but I didn't even try to make out the boys' words. Words might have spoiled the magic.

Right next to Mecske is Gilvánfa, a village inhabited *exclusively* by Roma. Péter shepherded us there now for introductions to some of the people who had been involved in his project. Sanyi, the man of the first house we visited, is the person who actually remembered seeing, as a boy, the horse-drawn wagon pulling out of town late that April evening in 1944, with the thirteen Jews in the back, wearing their yellow stars. (Yes, it was in the evening rather than at dawn, and in April rather than in June, in other words, not in line with the dejewification master plan because of special security concerns of the authorities, given the proximity of the Mecske area to the Serbian border.) Sanyi asked us to come in, and we did so for a minute, but the house and the rooms were really too small, we seemed to be almost stuck to the very place where we happened to come to a stop. Later I realized that *all* the houses in the village were small, as if memories of the low ceilings and tight confines of the cara-vans still gripped the local imagination. Certainly, all the Roma we saw or met were people of a certain appealing delicacy and of small stature, as if poorly nourished during their early years.

Quickly we stepped outside and into a farmyard napping in the afternoon sun, followed by Sanyi, his wife and a granddaughter of about 20, a fair-skinned, dark-haired beauty, her eyes flashing at you sideways with a seductiveness and brazenness that made me think of Carmen, the cigarette girl from Seville. In the yard, Sanyi stoked the fire in an earthen oven for baking bread, a patted together contraption that looked something like a crudely-made medium-sized dog house, with smoke drifting out an opening at its rear end. The oven consumes itself every two or three months, he explained with a smile that rearranged the complex network of wrinkles on his friendly face like the turning of a kaleidoscope and went on leisurely poking at the fire with a stick hardly thicker than the stem of that pipe in the photograph. That strange temporariness made an impression on me. Of course, until recently these congenial people were nomads of a sort, I thought as we climbed back into the van and moved on to our next appointment. Their lives had always been a series of resettlements, literally of course, an eternity of wandering in the desert, more transient even than my ancestors had been at any time since they had first arrived in the Promised Land.

Back in Mecske, we stopped in front of an ordinary small house no more than ten doors down from the school, the house that until 1944 had belonged to the Spierers, that is, Gizella's family. The present owners were a couple in their forties, the man maybe fifty but so nut-brown and weathered that I had a hard time guessing, with two daughters in their early twenties, as I soon found out, one of them married and both of them working and living in a nearby city, but the younger one planning soon to move back home, buy a car and commute to work to save money. I smiled and chatted politely while the wife gave me a tour of the house, but all the time an anxiety not to trample on anything not seen or even mentioned preoccupied me. From the yard we had walked into a small kitchen, from which the couple's small bedroom opened to the left, and to the left of that the larger room the daughter was to occupy, straight ahead a tiny bathroom and a toilet cabinet tucked in next to it, and finally to the right some kind of a chamber, maybe a pantry. I looked about that time-capsule, secretly listening for long-muffled voices audible only to me, expecting ghosts to project themselves out of the walls, gliding on air. I shivered in my mind, as it were, trying not so much to shake off these un-expected new attachments as to steel myself to accept them. At the first opportunity I escaped outside, still careful not to touch anything I didn't have to lest it vanish. Barbara and I then visited the pigs and goats in their enclosures, observed the rooster on patrol in the barnyard, thanked our hosts and said goodbye. Péter rode with us to the edge of the village. It is uplifting to be with someone like him.

The next day I put together all the information I had already had about my grandmother with what I had acquired on that little excursion. She had been born in 1892 probably in Mecske. I don't know how long her own parents, my great-grandparents, had been living there by then, only that her mother died before her father did, and he himself died not long before the onset of the atrocities. The Spierers had had a dry-goods store, the only one in the village of course, located in the larger room in the house, which then had a direct entrance from the street. In addition, my great-grandfather had also had an egg business that involved picking up eggs produced by local farmers for delivery to a wholesaler. I don't know if my grandmother had had any siblings, although I do remember Spierer relatives in Budapest whom we had visited regularly during my childhood. Around 1912 Gizella married Hónig Miksa of Dombóvár. In the mid-1920s, according to Rose, who brought the family skeleton out of the closet only when I was about forty already, the couple divorced because my grandfather, otherwise a saint of course, drank and gambled and womanized, and must have done so to extremes I would think to trig-ger consequences so extraordinary for that time and place. Then Gizella, with her four children, the oldest of whom, Leslie, would have been around 12, moved back to the parental household, dry-goods store and egg depot in Mecske, into the house I had just visited, minus electricity and indoor plumbing. And they proceeded to live there in great poverty, Rózsi had once told me, she herself having moved to Budapest during the early 30s, to be followed by Leslie in 1938 I believe and then also by

Klári probably sometime during the early 40s, leaving Gizella with only Bözsi, her youngest daughter. They were two of the 13 people deported from the village in 1944, just a few weeks before Miksa was deported to his death from Dombóvár. What a life, or so it seems. Although you can never tell. Well, almost never.

The fate of those who perished is of course self-evident; of those who survived can be mired in ambiguity. Bözsi, for example. Over the years I had pieced together bits of information about her returning from Auschwitz aged only about twenty but her health and nerves wrecked, and living her post-1945 life in the small town of Siklós not far from Mecske. She was married to my Uncle Pista, another Holocaust survivor, or maybe a survivor of the forced labor service, a man who from the late 60s on worked his own vineyards under the scorching summer sun, uttered few words and worshiped his wife. Bözsi herself was not so lavish with her affections. The story is told that she refused to visit him in the hospital during his last illness and he died alone. Several years later, she hanged herself from a horizontal gas-pipe, a gruesome Central-European death worthy of the novels of the Austrian writer Thomas Bernhard. I would like to think that her Holocaust ordeal had ruined her life, but then I'm reminded of Gyuri's comment about character and I'm not so sure. And I'm also reminded of *Cousin* Pista, who is actually a nephew of Leslie's and a shining counter-example. During the bombing accompanying liberation of Buchenwald he lost a leg and by then was also close to death from some kind of disease and from life in general. He spent the next year-and-a-half in a German hospital, where he was nursed back to health, perfected his German and made peace with his persecutors, although not yet with God, as he once said to me. Awaiting him then still were other personal tragedies, but he is married, has a family and had a successful career in the Hungarian newsreel industry. He is an active, humorous, lovable old man, and even when he talks about his misfortunes he knows no vindictiveness or self-pity.

When I think back to that little house, a not particularly attractive dark green, I feel that it's connected to my own house in Mamaroneck, and so to my own self, with a thread or a tendril or a line of some sort, with what I will call a root because I *must,* cliché though it be. The transposition of the concept from the world of plants to the experience and practices of human legacy succeeds much too well for me to spurn it. Even though, to be entirely and insistently clear, never before did I have or claim such a thing. I have always been an immigrant with no roots, and before I was an immigrant, I was a native with no roots. Of course, no roots can only mean severed roots, for we all come from somewhere, even those of us who have lost all connection to predecessors. Even those who cannot possibly find traces of their roots, like foundlings can't in 18th-century novels, at first anyway. At times my lack of interest in blood descent, as opposed to the cultural baggage I carry as a historian and a product of Western civilization – at times I have blamed my rejection of ancestors on the external circumstances of my life, which often enough were indeed acts of severing. But if those circumstances had made me reluctant to connect or even to inquire, so had they or others essentially like them made others downright eager to. So there must be more to it than just my many experiences of cutting off, although I myself cannot even speculate what. In any case, rootless *is* what I have always been. Although finally, as you have just seen, I managed, as it were, to liberate myself a little from myself and set out to find my roots or something like that, and now I am astounded that at so late a date and so long after it had already become utterly unlikely I actually did it.

At this moment Gizella is in front of my mind's *eye,* even more real for my having walked right in her footsteps, she is out in the back slopping some slop before the pigs, and I see Laci too coming through the gate, wearing the same clothes as in the photographs. He is in a rotten mood for some reason but hunkers over to his mother nevertheless and respectfully kisses her on the cheek. She hardly responds. She knows he's hungry. He's always hungry, and look at how gaunt he is! At least his face isn't all cut up, as it is so often. They are just beyond my reach, both of them, I would have to take only two steps to touch not only my grandmother but my father too, the other obvious beneficiary of this re-grafting act of mine.

I have to wonder, the way the whole thing came upon me right after his death, if I didn't undertake this whole project with just the hidden intention to confer upon *him* whatever it is that my being rooted can on him confer. Could I actually be performing a filial duty? It would make sense, you know, if I were. For now it seems to me that being attached to your roots is one of the more basic ways to honor thy mother and thy father. And so to honor yourself, to give your own life some kind of meaning, even if not all the meaning you might want, but meaning nevertheless, and just who do you think you are to just cavalierly forego something like that? Although you have to, if you possibly can, go back even further than your own parents. After all, Leslie all by himself cannot account for every point and way-stop from Mecske to Mamaroneck, or at least from Mecske to the Bronx, even if he does account for most of the journey.

CHAPTER 6

The Revolution Lost

IN HUNGARY THE REVOLUTIONARY FEVER of 1848 took the form of a nationalist movement. By then, as you know, the German prince and sort of
many-headed hydra who wore the Austrian imperial crown and ruled
from Vienna had been for three and a half centuries also wearing the
Hungarian royal crown. Under the Habsburgs, the German minority living throughout the kingdom had grown and the Magyars themselves had
been increasingly Teutonified. But during the first half of the 19th century a reaction had set in, the yearning for the recovery of a Hungarian
identity became a collective ache, and the ethnic urge was approaching
birthright grade. Then on March 15th, with recitations and proclama-
tions Sándor Petőfi and other poets and writers inspired the nobility and
middle classes of Buda and Pest to join the liberal political opposition,
and all of them together to formulate a program of reforms. Promptly
then, appointed representatives of these groups produced the Twelve
Points, which, in essence, demanded national independence, a limited
democracy and bourgeois liberalism. Then, because the aristocracy also
supported this program, and because the revolution raging at the same
time in Vienna frightened the imperial authorities, the reforms quickly
became law. The Diet enacted them, and its Viennese masters signed off.
And so, in just a few weeks, the modern, nationalist, liberal revolution
achieved its goals: Hungary had a new government accountable to a new
National Assembly.

During the early 1830s, when Louis Kossuth first emerged as a journalist and a public figure, he was already committed to the cause of Hungarian national identity and self-determination. As a subversive, he did a few years behind bars at the end of that decade but then just continued his tireless agitation, flashing his extraordinary genius for oratory at every turn and soon becoming the spokesman of the reform movement. In 1847 he was elected to the Diet as the deputy from Pest, and there quickly assumed the leadership. And then, after the March-15th call to revolution in Pest and the rapid granting of the reformers' demands by the emperor-king, Kossuth became a member of the new government, and then in the whirlwind of changing international circumstances and the storm of reaction whipped up by the quick victory, he took the helm as the *national* leader.

By August the revolutionary fires had been put out in other parts of Europe, and surely, they said in Vienna, it was now time to deal with the Magyars. So first the Austrians goaded the large Croatian minority living within Hungary to demand its *own* independence. When the Magyars refused, being no less fond of ethnic lording-over than the Austrians, the Croatians attacked with a large army. And then the Austrians *themselves* attacked. You wouldn't have put your money on the Magyars, but for almost a year they held their own in this War of Independence against the greatly superior enemy forces. When things were not going well, and right to the very end, they believed that foreign powers would provide the necessary aid. After all, their cause was receiving wide sympathy in the West. But, in fact, foreign aid went only to the foreign bully. Franz Joseph, the young Habsburg emperor-king requested the aid of Czar Nicholas I, an archconservative and his cousin and partner in imperialist high-handedness, and in August 1849, it was a Russian army of 300,000 that invaded Hungary, put down the revolution and occupied the country.

With the outbreak of hostilities the already legendary Kossuth began his extraordinary career as both head of state and head of government. His energy and devotion to the cause were unbounded. In the effort to raise a Hungarian national army, he criss-crossed the country, going from village to dusty village, addressing and rousing groups of peasants. And promptly his listeners joined up, for they identified him with the nation, with the freeing of the serfs, with liberty itself. After the defeat, Kossuth went into exile and then for decades, and even after the stay-at-homes had hammered out the Compromise of 1867 and embraced Franz Joseph, whose subsequent reign is still remembered as a half-century of peace, prosperity and national dignity – for decades he continued to promote his lost cause in Western Europe and the United States, and to spellbind audiences in the English and French he had learned from books during his imprisonment. He now became a myth, the myth of unrelenting struggle against tyranny, the myth of the unsinkable 19th-century patriot-spirit that leads, cajoles and shames his countrymen into the fight for their freedom as a nation. This myth contributed greatly to my powerful childhood memory of 1848, a memory not of defeat and failure, which in fact is what it had been, but rather of a time of magnificent deeds, virtuosic linguistic feats by Petőfi and Kossuth, and the revolutionary fervor that only death can extinguish.

In my own Hungarian years this myth was still alive and well. In 1956, already during the summer students frequenting opposition circles had declared that if it was indeed the spirit of 1848 that imbued them, then Imre Nagy was *their* Louis Kossuth. And on October 23rd, the demonstrators expected the mythopoetic 19th-century champion to be addressing them in the square named after him, or expected Nagy at least to try to live up to his great predecessor. So for Nagy the role was inescapable, although it was also unsought and utterly unsuitable. And unfortunate too, I would say, for on the balance inheritances like that tend only to *burden* their recipients. For a while even Shakespeare felt himself to be in Christopher Marlowe's shadow, but poets and painters can at least make it their anxiety-laden business to overcome the influence of their predecessors, while statesmen usually have their hands full just dealing with actual circumstances. The fact is that between Nagy and Kossuth there really was no question of footstep-following or even of any resonance. For Nagy simply was *not* like Kossuth. Attribute for attribute, the two personas strike you as a mismatch. Nagy did not have Kossuth's genius or imagination, and he was not a firebrand. On the contrary, he was all caution and reluctance. Kossuth's proclivities and gifts allowed him to become the single-minded, unconditionally devoted revolutionary that he was; Nagy's called for a lot of on-the-one-hand and on-the-other temporizing. Kossuth evoked admiration and discipleship; Nagy made you scratch your head and raise your eyebrow.

But even aside from the only wished-for Kossuth-Nagy filiation, some connections and indeed similarities between 1848-49 and 1956 should be obvious to you already. In both cases, the Magyars pounded their collective chest and rose up against imperial oppression by a neighbor. Certainly, the eager student scribes on the stage of the great hall of the Technical University aimed for a parallelism between the Twelve Points of 1848 and the Sixteen of 1956. And echoes of 1848-49, then the focal point of Hungarian history and national memory, also reverberated with the demonstrators throughout the initial hours of the uprising. The commemoration on Bem Square, with the location already 1848-inspired, included a recitation of the incendiary Petőfi poem the author himself had first declaimed on March 15, 1848, which exhorts Magyars to rise and answer the call of their country, and has this oath as its refrain: "By the God of the Magyars we vow that slaves we will no longer be." A few hours later on Kossuth Square, as paper-torches illumined the night with a flickering 19th-century glow, the crowd followed the national anthem with a singing of another old favorite, Louis Kossuth's Recruiting Song, which I can sing for you still today. And this was just the beginning. Other similarities became apparent too as events unfolded, most especially the final heart-rending one, the one between the overall course of the two revolutions. For the earlier scenario – a victory quickly won and then a crushing defeat soon administered by Russian armies – was also repeated a hundred years later.

The complex international and domestic endgame, which I am presenting to you here as a historical episode of nine moves, began on October 31st. For indeed October 30th was not the revolution's victory, nor a turning point in the Cold War, and certainly no break with the brutal past and with what was to remain the crushing inhumanity of the 20th century.

1st Move. On October 31st, while Hungarians were savoring the good news announced in *Pravda*, the Soviet Presidium was reconsidering its decision. And now things looked quite different, in Hungary and out of it. Suddenly the revolution found itself in a traffic jam on the highway of history, and as a vehicle it was breaking down. Khrushchev presented his views this way:

> We should reexamine our assessment and should not withdraw our troops from Hungary and Budapest. We should take the initiative in restoring order in Hungary. If we depart from Hungary, it will give a great boost to the Americans, English, and French – the imperialists. They will perceive it as weakness on our part and will go onto the offensive. We would then be exposing the weakness of our positions. Our party will not accept it if we do this. To Egypt they will then add Hungary. We have no other choice.

Apparently, overnight Khrushchev had overcome his concerns about an occupation. Or, in any case, he now found an overriding need to uphold the Soviet empire's prestige, and also anticipated that pulling out of Hungary would become a domestic political liability for the brutes-in-suits in the Kremlin. By Egypt, he was referring to the Suez Crisis, which had erupted a couple of days earlier and was a failure for the Soviets. To it he did not now dare add an apparent defeat in Eastern Europe. So the Hungarian situation had to be brought under control.

I don't want to go easy on the Soviets, especially not when they are about to crush the revolution like a bag of trash in a garbage truck, but in its own way the Suez Crisis was indeed a companion-piece to the Eastern European drama unfolding on the world stage. Although it had started in the late 19th century, British imperialism in Egypt, with many features not unlike the Soviet stranglehold on the satellites, was by the 1950s reduced to no more than operating rights over the absolutely crucial transportation artery of the Suez Canal, which Britain refused to cede to its rightful territorial owners. In the years running up to the crisis, Egypt was ruled by the caricature-friendly King Farouk, a corpulent, spendthrift, dissolute figure. The king paid scant attention to his subjects, steadily ignoring the humiliation they felt on account of both the loss of the 1948 war with Israel and the continued mocking semi-colonialist presence of the British. In 1952 a bloodless revolution ignited by Arab nationalism and the deplorable living conditions of the masses convulsed the country, sent Farouk packing and brought Gamal Abdel Nasser to power. Promptly, Nasser set about building up Egypt's military might for a rematch with Israel, but quickly his negotiations for arms with the United States floundered. It was at this point, in October 1955, that Khrushchev approached Nasser with an arms deal on excellent terms. Nasser jumped at the offer. And so Egypt, until recently a country ruled by a monarch addicted to imitation Louis-Quinze furniture known to this day as Louis-Farouk, ornate details, over-gilding and all, was now drawn into the Soviet orbit.

The actual crisis erupted on July 26, 1956. In a move that made him a hero to the many peoples then still chafing under the Western colonialist yoke, Nasser nationalized the Suez Canal Company and threw out the British. With two-thirds of Western European oil passing through the canal, Egypt suddenly had a stranglehold on the continent's economies. There was only one way to deal with this, and that of course was war. And so Britain began immediate secret preparations to attack, and soon France joined her, mostly because of the adverse effect Nasser's sloughing off of the chains was having on France's position in Algeria. Willy-nilly, they were in this together now, the two colonialists. Given Nasser's ties to the Soviets, the United States also found the Egyptian self-assertion troublesome, but actually thought twice about supporting the proposed war, which would be plainly illegal and contrary to the United Nations Charter. That was a surprisingly upright course of action, I have to say, especially because it was adopted in the midst of what amounted to a tour de force of cynicism. And the best was yet to come.

Skittish about the risks of open aggression, Britain and France cast about for a more palatable way to proceed. They first appealed to the Security Council for assurance that the canal would remain open to international traffic, but clearly that accomplished nothing. It was then that the French devised a trick, a hypocritical charade designed to hide the imperialists' true intentions. Let Israel attack Egypt and drive toward the canal, and so create a threat to shipping operations. Then Britain and France will have the legal right, or what should appear to be the legal right, to step in as policemen, demand mutual withdrawal and themselves occupy the waterway. A brilliant plan, you say, sure to work as long as you can also put the rest of the world into a coma. But Israel liked it. What could be better than a Western-sponsored attack on an Arab neighbor made progressively stronger by Soviet arms? And in October the British government also signed on. Exactly what you would have expected from them, given the long British history of hare-brained imperialist schemes, embarrassments and debacles. So the three participants began now in earnest to work out details and, ever wary each of them of both confederates and inveterate enemies, to provide the others with the many assurances and cross-assurances necessary for such complex and critical skullduggery. The United States, not as directly affected and so likely to oppose the whole conspiracy, was kept in the dark.

On October 28th already, Khrushchev perceived an instructive parallel between Suez and the situation in Hungary. Right after the Presidium decided to support Nagy's new government, he remarked that "the English and French are in a real mess in Egypt. We shouldn't get caught in the same company." Imperialists, he evidently thought, are always at risk of being booted out. Then on October 29th, while international diplomatic circles were very much preoccupied with Hungary, Israel launched its attack. When Britain and France demanded that the parties withdraw from the canal, the Soviets, unwilling to risk armed confrontation with the Western powers, quickly pulled out their advisors and heavy weapons. It was this Cold-War setback, this loss of the Middle East influence that he had so brilliantly established only a year earlier, that Khrushchev was referring to at the October 31ˢᵗ meeting of the Presidium when he said that in case the Soviets quit Hungary, the Communist leadership's domestic constituency – essentially the Soviet armed forces, the domestic power-structure and the state security organizations – could add Hungary to Egypt. These men were not invulnerable like Stalin had been. Two withdrawals in two days might have made things uncomfortable for them at home.

News of the Israeli attack, coming before both the mirage of victory and the reality of the Kremlin's about-face, struck Hungarians with the force of sudden despair. Upon receiving it, they immediately foresaw a trade-off and considered themselves betrayed by the West. The Soviets had to believe, they figured in Budapest, that their restraint in Egypt, their forbearance in an area of long-established Western influence, would be reciprocated by their adversaries in Hungary. Well, as you well know but the freedom fighters didn't, Dulles had already on October 26ᵗʰ tripped all over himself signaling to the Soviets that the most prominent candidate for savior-in-chief had in fact abandoned all thoughts of armed intervention. Still, the Egyptian developments seriously damaged the revolutionary cause. Most importantly, the world diplomatic situation was now thrown into greater complexity and confusion. In a sense, the entire Cold War, the as-it-were generative context of the revolution, was finding itself redefined and reconfigured once more. All eyes now turned to the Middle East, and even at the United Nations Hungary no longer commanded first priority or undivided attention. It should hardly surprise you that in an age of *world* wars, *international* governing bodies and ideologies aspiring to *global* domination, Hungary again faced the prospect of being reduced to a side show. Even in her moment of glory, the small country could not long escape her small-country fate: maybe not a stepchild, but very much a younger sibling in the family of nations.

In addition, the Suez Crisis also encouraged all-around bad behavior by sovereign powers. Certainly, the Soviets had always acted without compunction in foreign affairs, ignoring all international legal standards when dealing with the weak, and by their actions, although not their sanctimonious words, proclaiming that only might makes right. Still, they were not entirely insensitive to the moral judgment of the rest of the world. Easier for them though than changing their own practices was to point to equally gangsterish behavior by the Western democracies. And on October 29th that's exactly what they had the luxury of doing. Now Britain and France seemed every bit as domineering as the empire in the East, and world opinion did indeed condemn them as aggressors. In Britain the unprincipled adventurism even cost Anthony Eden's Tory government the support of the electorate. So the reprehensible invasion of Egypt and the shameless pretext offered for the subsequent British and French intervention, which fooled only those who wanted to be fooled, provided the Soviets with a kind of carte blanche. And on October 31st, when the Presidium decided to stamp out the revolution as if it were no more than a scout troop's campfire, its members had the satisfaction of knowing that their behavior was no more unscrupulous than the behavior of their Western enemies, and that the rest of the world knew that too.

2nd Move. So, obviously, Suez was reason enough for the Presidium to reconsider its position. But if Mikoyan, or anyone else, had any lingering doubts, he was surely relieved of them by news of the October 30th massacre of Communists in Budapest in front of party headquarters, and the threat of a complete Communist collapse implied by the "lamp-post justice" perpetrated in the course of it. The Presidium learned of the bloody incident on October 31st, but the first references to it and to the general situation are to be found only in the comments made on November 2nd by János Kádár, who had been summoned to Moscow meanwhile. Subsequently, the massacre proved invaluable to the oppressors, for they could identify it as all by itself a legitimate reason for invasion and press it into service as an inexhaustible source of propaganda. Just think about it: for the Communists the headquarters incident triggered the inalienable right to act in *self-defense*. Never mind that the massacre was promptly condemned by every revolutionary organization. And never mind either that it was just a very unfortunate episode, a stain, alas, on the reputation of the whole revolution, but in no way a cause or even a symptom of the disintegration of the Party. For decades there would be no one to rebut the Communist self-justifications that vilified it as the work of a "Horthyist-Fascist mob... that wanted to overthrow the most glorious achievement of the twentieth century: the people's democracy."

What actually happened at party headquarters was this: For some days already, rumors had been circulating that hundreds or even thousands of revolutionaries and other victims of the ÁVO were languishing in the building in underground prisons. On the morning of the 30th, insurgents rushed inside, determined to find and liberate the captives and unaware that 47 ÁVO-men were holed up in there. Shooting started immediately, forcing the insurgents to retreat outside to Köztársaság Square. Soon reinforcements joined them, which allowed another assault, and when it became obvious that a storming of the premises was imminent, three of the local party leaders exited the building waving a white sheet tied to a stick. The three were greeted by merciless machine-gun fire. Then the ÁVO-men emerged, and they were mowed down too. Then the crowd hanged two of the bodies by their feet, kicked them around and set them on fire. Altogether, 23 men died at the rebels' hands. Following the slaughter, the insurgents frantically turned to the task of finding the underground prisons, but without any success. With sounding machines and excavator cranes and with the aid of the city's engineers, the search went on for three days and was abandoned only when the Soviet tanks entered the city. Evidence from recently opened archives suggests that the cells and torture chambers may in fact have existed, but we're likely never to know for sure.

3rd Move. So the Presidium resolved to invade Hungary and had the resolution promptly implemented. Early morning on November 1st, Nagy was informed by his own sources in the northeastern part of the country that the direction of Red Army movements had changed. Instead of leaving, the familiar ranks of mechanized armor and personnel carriers were now entering. In addition, Soviet troops already in the country were sealing off airfields. However reluctantly, Nagy had to conclude that the Soviets had, after all, opted for a military solution, and that he now had to make a possibly irreversible life-and-death decision. Would he capitulate or fight? Would he collaborate with the occupiers and so have a chance to stay in power, or act as the head of an independent state and resist however he could and at whatever price? Would he kowtow to Moscow as usual, yes comrade, or stick with what he knew was right in Budapest? He quickly made up his mind to fight. Obviously, he had found here something worth more to him than life itself. You have to wonder what *exactly* that was. The new multi-party cabinet, solidly behind the prime minister, met and received reports on the readiness of the armed forces and the new National Guard, and discussed what steps might be taken under the circumstances. But before all else, the suave and arrogant Soviet ambassador Yuri Andropov was summoned once more to explain the westward movement of forces. At an afternoon meeting he offered only a transparent pretext.

4th *Move.* That same day – bravely, defiantly, desperately – the government declared the country's neutrality, withdrew from the Warsaw Pact and called for support from the permanent members of the UN Security Council. Fine sounding words, those! But in the end the Hungarians' hopes that the UN would be both able and willing to enforce the principles enshrined in its charter proved unrealistically high. For even in 1956, only eleven years into the UN's career, it was already quite clear that the organization itself was never more committed to the rule of law than its most powerful members. Did nobody care then about fairness and liberty and heroism anymore? Well, some people surely did still, and the lessons you learned by reading Conrad still applied. People and nations still admired high ideals, they did still have the best intentions, but just then they happened to be preoccupied with even more important things, or maybe less important ones. Given the overall international situation, the Western powers could no longer indulge in a singular focus on Hungarian events. And so, in diplomatic proceedings the two pressing affairs got thoroughly entangled, all to the benefit of the Soviets and to the detriment of their rebellious satellite. The British and French maneuvered to have the UN consider the two issues in tandem in order to dilute the negative reaction to their own machinations in Egypt. And the United States, although it had no unrelated motives, abandoned the Hungarian cause because of its fully justified unwillingness to stand up to the Soviets on account of it, and because of its eagerness to have the Middle East crisis resolved. And in any case, what kind of support could the so-called free world have given?

5ᵗʰ Move. Meanwhile, the Presidium proceeded to develop a political agenda to complement the military activity already underway. Clearly, a government had to be formed to replace Nagy and impose itself on the country. It was to be labeled a "provisional revolutionary government," with the perplexing revolutionary qualifier being offered, I suppose, as a sort of back-formation from the counterrevolution idea. Kádár and Ferenc Münnich, another Communist considered reliable, were discussed as possible leaders, with Kádár appearing to have the lead. But how was the Kremlin intending to effect Kádár's conversion? Well, the Soviets were certainly expert at twisting arms and otherwise facilitating things on the road to Damascus, but surely this was not an occasion for forcibly recruiting a candidate. The job was much too critical for that. Better an unproved but committed newcomer than a seasoned but half-hearted veteran. It's well known of course that Kádár turned out to be the Kremlin's man and then during the second half of the 20ᵗʰ century the central figure in the country's public life. It's also no secret that in 1956 he betrayed his as-it-were comrades. But Kádár never unburdened himself as to what exactly transpired, and even if he had, you would not be able to take him at his word, as you would not be able to take anyone else either in that situation. You'd have to worry not so much about a conscious effort to cover up as about the mental tricks the teller of the tale might be playing on himself. In any case, here is the story as it was pieced together after the deaths of both Kádár and Communism.

On November 1st, the Presidium instructed Andropov to summon Münnich, his regular contact in the Hungarian party leadership, and through him Kádár to the Soviet embassy in Budapest. Münnich told Kádár that the purpose of the meeting was clarification of Soviet troop movements, so the latter readily accepted the invitation and left the Parliament building in a car belonging to the Ministry of the Interior. But then before the two men actually entered the embassy and without any explanation, the Soviets requested that they get into an armored vehicle for the next leg of an unexpected journey. Kádár seemed reluctant but complied. The armored vehicle proceeded to an airport outside the city, where Andropov finally informed Kádár that the highest Soviet authorities wished to discuss the Hungarian situation with him, and wished to do so in secret and as soon as possible. Was that intended as a reassurance, or was he being abducted? Who could say? In the late 1990s, when a Hungarian historian was preparing a definitive biography of the late Party's late general secretary, a Russian diplomat who had been present at the airport for the hush-hush departure could not say if Kádár had objected to boarding the plane or, accepting the situation as it was, did so willingly. Indeed, nothing is known of noble Brutus's thoughts or feelings as he climbed the stairs for the flight into the center of the storm.

The plane landed in the Ukrainian city of Munkachevo. From there the two Hungarians were taken to the nearby city of Uzhgorod, where Leonid Brezhnev, the dashing young Soviet official whom Khrushchev had ordered to organize the whole excursion and succeed with it if he "did not want to lose his head" – where Brezhnev awaited them, and where they boarded *separate* air force planes to fly to Moscow. As the biographer learned from the same Russian diplomat, in 1972 at a meeting outside Moscow Brezhnev, by then the party boss, severely criticized economic developments in Hungary, but then attempted to cheer Kádár up with the following words: "We've been in a tougher situation already than this, you and I. Do you remember the 2:00 AM flight on November

2, 1956? You were sitting alone, collapsed into yourself, not knowing what fate awaited you." And so it had been indeed. Unexpectedly, and certainly unintendedly, Kádár's life had reached a turning point. He was on some kind of a brink. He had with him only the clothes he was wearing. He was going to be humiliated, arriving in Moscow like that, like a drifter between seasonal jobs in a B-picture, but undoubtedly things were meant to be this way. Surely he sensed that he was now either a prisoner or, if he accepted the terms that would be dictated, the leader of his country.

While this was happening, and as further preparation for the invasion, Khrushchev and Georgii Malenkov, another Presidium member, flew to Warsaw to inform the Polish government of the Soviet plans, and then on to Bucharest, to Sofia, Bulgaria, and on November 2nd to Yugoslavia to make certain of Tito's support. The Czechoslovak leadership was also informed. It's best while you're whipping one of your dogs to pet the others. Of course, no one objected, although the Poles, just a few weeks ago themselves in the now Hungarian position, were not enthusiastic. Tito, on the other hand, thought the Soviet approach correct and Kádár the right choice as head of the government to be installed.

Right after arriving in Moscow, the Hungarians attended a session of the Presidium. Kádár, called on to present a status report and answer some questions, was in a tight spot and had no idea where exactly the Soviet leadership stood on things. I mean why hustle him here like this, like a gagged hostage in a sack flung over a strongman's shoulder, why whisk them away like this, together but apart? Was the October 30th declaration but a moment's dream? He had at least to *suspect* a continued pro- and anti-Stalinist tension in the room. And there was of course the question of his own future too. Could he be candid? How much should he skew his assessment to the expectations of his listeners, how much did he have to be concerned for his own skin, his own hopes, his wishes for his country? The notes made of his comments are fairly extensive but far from unambiguous. Historians disagree on whether he was driven by savvy and cunning or just robbed of focus by the complexity of the revolutionary events. To me, his report seems mostly fair and accurate.

He did not pull his punches and spoke like a true Communist. Certainly, his primary aim was the propping up of the Communist organization in Hungary and resuscitation of Communist ideas and indeed ideology. He didn't pander much to his audience or put himself in a falsely favorable light, as one in his position would surely be tempted to.

"These were workers; the leaders of the group;" he is noted to have said, "they arrived at the coalition government; they're seeking the ouster of the Rákosi clique. They fought for the withdrawal of troops and for the order of the people's democracy." With real insight: "we classified it as a counterrevolution and with this turned [the people] against us – they did not feel themselves to be counterrevolutionaries." And then repeatedly: "I have to say that everyone demanded the withdrawal of Soviet troops...." But then Kádár's words began to suggest a modified counterrevolution interpretation, that is, a narrative of a genuine popular movement over-whelmed by reactionary elements. He stated, not entirely inaccurately if you consider any pro-democracy shift a counterrevolution, that "Nagy's policy has counterrev. aspects to it.... Hour by hour the situation is mov-ing rightward.... The Austrians support a fascist organization (in West Germany – a Hungarian organization) 35 thous. people (Horthyites)." Then a blunt comment about the political confusion in which "the weak link is the [Communist party]; it has ceased to exist," and finally another suggestion, namely, that Soviet forces be used only to *support* a Hungarian government. "The [direct] use of military force [to put down the upris-ing] will be destructive and lead to bloodshed. What will happen then? The morale [maybe the translator should have rendered this as moral standing or reputation] of the Communists will be reduced to zero. The socialist countries will suffer losses. Is there a guarantee that such cir-cumstances will not arise in other countries?" A brave and mostly honor-able performance.

The next day, with Khrushchev back in Moscow, and with Kádár, Münnich and a third Hungarian also attending the Presidium's meet-ing, the remaining details of the post-revolution political situation were settled. Kádár was not about to take the lead, but Khrushchev at once took on the job of convincing him. And he was masterful. In a wily piece of gap-toothed Communist self-criticism, he admitted prior mistakes by the Soviet leadership and recognized that not all of the insurgents were enemies. Then he reassured Kádár that Rákosi would have no role in the new government, would not in fact be allowed even to return to Hungary, and finally insisted that military intervention and replacement of the Nagy government was the only possible course. Then he yielded to Kádár. Generously, he gave the Hungarian all the time he wanted to criticize former Soviet relations, especially the ability of Rákosi and a handful of his men to monopolize contacts with Moscow, and to complain about some policies, like the naming of streets and cities after Soviet leaders, as offensive to national sentiments. And now, after this stroking and manipulation by the ham-fisted Russian, Kádár was indeed ready and willing to take his turn with the knife. *Et tu, Brute?*

But what actually did it? After suffering through the near-abduction and then staying pretty much true to himself while confronting the masters of half the world in their own lair, what *exactly* made Kádár betray his comrades on November 3rd? If I can presume to have read his heart and his mind, it was, first, the conviction, which Khrushchev managed to instill in him by exploiting some Leninist fears ever-festering deep inside him, that because of Nagy's shortcomings the counterrevolution had during the last two days gained the upper hand. "They're killing Communists," Kádár himself is reported to have remarked in an allusion to the massacre undoubtedly, "and premier Nagy provides a cover. The government lacks the forces to put an end to it. What must be done? Surrendering a socialist country to counterrev. is impossible. I agree with you. The correct course of action is to form a rev. government." And second, it was the realization Kádár came to while listening to Khrushchev that the Soviets were determined in any case, with or without him, to forge ahead, and that if he himself did not accept the leadership, then Rákosi and Gerő would or someone else of their ilk. And that, he knew, would be a disaster. A disaster for Communism, for the people of Hungary and for himself as well. For then he would surely have to pay for his own deeds during the preceding week and a half, and pay probably with his life. So in the end it was a no-brainer, as they say. Perhaps to salve his conscience, or more likely to honor and even preserve something of the truth and glory of the revolution, this was then his final policy comment to the Presidium: But the new "government must not be puppet-like, there must be a base for its activities and support among workers. There must be an answer to the question of what sort of relationship we must have with the USSR."

6th Move. During these days life in Hungary was getting back to normal. Maybe things would work out, you could think. Neutrality was declared two days ago, and still they haven't shipped us all to Siberia. In fact, they're still negotiating about withdrawal of their troops. Feigning business as usual, Nagy reshuffled his cabinet to include more non-Communists and thus to make it more representative. Among other changes, Pál Maléter was promoted to major general and appointed Minister of Defense. In Budapest shops reopened and people tried to have uneventful days. Some workers even returned to their jobs and many workers' councils voted to reinstitute a regular work schedule on Monday, November 5th. But normalization also had its fearful counterpoint, for the Red Army was already blocking off cities and roads, and a huge contingent of 20,000 men advanced close to the Austrian frontier as a precaution against any Western reaction to what was about to happen. In response, the new National Guard and the army made defensive preparations, medical stations were hastily set up, mobilization was ordered in several places, and Soviet troop movements were being monitored.

7h Move. Then on November 4th it began. Suddenly before sunrise armor pulsed with life, and at 4:45 AM Soviet troops crossing the border from Romania launched a general attack. Five divisions of mostly Mongol and Kirghiz personnel moved on Budapest. They were sure to be unfamiliar with European developments, the strategic geniuses in the Kremlin figured, unable to communicate with the locals and unlikely to forget why they were armed and so far from home. Tanks, artillery and troops entered the capital from several directions, including along the main artery, rrrrr, running behind our own building. I have no recollection of the pre-dawn disturbance, grrrrrr, that must have woken me, probably because I was no stranger to such sounds. Undoubtedly, I remained lying in bed, watching only with my mind's eye as the relentless monsters, GrrrGrrrrGrrrr... stole the scene from dawn, tracks grinding over the cobblestones, engines roaring, ungainly bodies lurching, turrets and guns swiveling with the blind motions of a robot. The images would have come to me readily, for tanks had been the stars of the military parades of my boyhood, long columns of armor and troops that marked the various national holidays instituted or just rechristened by the Communists, who in this case at least liked to pour new wine into old bottles. But this was not a parade but an invasion. These were death-machines that arrived, unmanned to all appearances, but shattering human senses and ready to destroy everything in their path.

At 6:00 AM Kádár broadcast an announcement from just over the Ukrainian border, proclaiming formation of the Hungarian Revolutionary Workers' and Peasants' Government and declaring that the presence of subversive fascist elements justified the intervention by Soviet troops. In his own statement, delivered about an hour later, Nagy announced that "Soviet troops launched an attack against our capital city with the obvious intention of overthrowing the lawful, democratic Hungarian Government.... I inform the people of the country and world public opinion of this." The army was ordered not to engage the Soviets since resistance would have served no purpose. Nevertheless, as the Red Army advanced through the country, both sides suffered heavy casualties. By 8:00 AM, the Soviet troops had occupied the Ministries of Interior and Defense and surrounded the Parliament building. After the invading forces passed through our neighborhood, I probably fell back to sleep. As close as we were to the city center, for the time being at least, things seemed normal all around. The tanks seemed to have come and gone.

At first the insurgents resisted, as did people in general. They had seen this before. Many also believed that help from the UN or from the Western powers would arrive momentarily, and many others simply found themselves unwilling or unable to give up. So-called freedom radios using portable transmitters broadcast desperate appeals for help to the West; defiant posters appeared on the walls of buildings; small groups of fighters ambushed the enemy at strategic locations, often eliminating a half dozen armored vehicles before moving on to the next spot. Hey, is this a revolution or what? But this time the Soviets were merciless. Any edifice from which a shot was fired they leveled with shells from their tanks. A UN Special Report prepared subsequently noted that "Soviet tanks … move[d] along the main boulevards [of Budapest], firing indiscriminately into houses to strike fear into the people." In the battle for the last rebel stronghold, in the XXIst district, in addition to the usual artillery and land forces the invaders also used squadrons of fighter planes that maintained a steady bombardment. A reminder of the winter of 1945. In short order large sections of the capital lay in ruin. Another reminder. Bodies littered the streets, faces covered only with a handkerchief or a piece of paper. Within three days armed resistance was broken in Budapest.

8th Move. But what about Nagy? Wasn't he, after all, an old soldier, a weakling rather than a quisling even by the Presidium's lights, and a player sure to be useful in the tricky transition? Of course he was, which is exactly why Khrushchev and Tito agreed in advance that he and his entourage would receive an offer of Yugoslav asylum. And so he did, and the Hungarians accepted the offer, but everything happened so quickly that even before the Soviet assault had reached its full intensity, already Nagy and his close advisers and associates, and many members of their families, 42 people in all, were inside the Yugoslav Embassy. But just a minute! This is not how things had been intended to work out and not the outcome the two leaders had expected. The asylum was to be offered, to quote Khrushchev's frustrated words from what Tito called a "shrill letter," only after Nagy had declared "his government's inability to deal with the forces of reaction," and only after he had resigned and "thus [made] it easier to establish the new Hungarian Revolutionary Workers' and Peasants' Government." But who knows what went wrong, you know how easily this kind of thing can happen in the real world. In any case, events outpaced the maybe too-finely-tuned plans and in the end Nagy both refused to concede anything and got asylum. And, yes, the big comrades did look like a couple of all-thumbers from *Big Deal on Madonna Street*. And Nagy wasn't even trying to get the better of them, and had no control of the situation anyway.

But even if Nagy gets no credit for the snafu, he does emerge from the incident looking very good and strong. Suddenly he turns out to be his own man. Since his early years in the Communist movement, Nagy had had a tendency for desertion, for losing self-confidence and retreating into silence, for falling prey to colliding motives and agonizing moral dilemmas. His failure to provide adequate leadership is considered one of the main reasons the revolution was lost. Had he tried to curb the extremists and steer the revolution towards a position more like the Polish compromise or maybe even a national Communism along the Yugoslav model, had he offered a program combining more modest Hungarian goals and a lesser threat to Soviet security, the Presidium might have put its money on him. But Nagy had done none of these things and had not been the leader the revolution needed. Only *after* the Soviets reversed course on October 31st did he finally rise to the occasion. As if being disowned by his masters set him free and allowed him to shine forth as a man principled and pure. From now until his trial and execution in mid-1958 Nagy stood firm for the more or less social democratic ideals of reform Communism. And henceforward he was sure of himself, and showed himself not to be weak at all, just helpless, literally helpless. He died not only a martyr but also a hero. He never resigned as prime minister and never compromised just to make things easier for himself or for Kádár.

9th Move. Worldwide, reaction to the Soviet invasion and all-out war-waging, to the apparently decisive blow, was mostly predictable. Communist regimes supported the course of action adopted by the Presidium and echoed the modified counterrevolution cover story. India, and Burma, Ceylon and Indonesia, the rest of the so-called four Colombo powers, equivocated for a while, but eventually Nehru at least condemned the USSR. In general, Arab countries did not get involved. But in the West, governments and people were unrestrained in their expressions of outrage. In the days and weeks after November 4th, protests and demonstrations were held in front of Soviet embassies in many capitals, and many countries refused to recognize the Kádár government. It was a very big deal! As it tends to work with stereotypes, the Western nations reacted each in character. That is, obligingly they confirmed the ideas already had of them by charter-flight American tourists, who first started descending on the continent just about that time: Italians attended masses honoring the dead freedom fighters, the Swiss barred USSR entrants from ski competitions, and the British cancelled a royal variety show as unfitting in a time of mourning.

In the United States, Hungarian-Americans came out in force to protest and pray, and strong emotions ignited throughout the country. New York State and New York City designated a Help Hungary Day; the residents of Connecticut protested with three minutes of silence; Cincinnati announced a day of sorrow for the trampled nation. Workers and labor unions expressed their solidarity with their Hungarian brothers, with George Meany, president of the AFL-CIO and an outspoken anti-communist, calling for a free-world boycott of the USSR, and New York longshoremen refusing to unload automobiles arriving for the use of Soviet embassy personnel for over a month. And official action fit the public sentiments like a key fits its lock. The White House protested to the Kremlin; members of Congress urged a tough stand; the government suspended the cultural exchange program with the USSR.

But the most notable and lasting reaction to the crushing of the revolution was that of left-wing groups in the so-called free world. Some leaders and organizations, like the Italian Communist chief Palmiro Togliatti and the Communist Party USA, subscribed to the Moscow line. But socialists in Asia and Norman Thomas in the United States condemned it. And more importantly, the Soviet invasion triggered a crisis for *Communist* parties in the West. In Italy, Great Britain and the

United States (with its insignificant communist movement) party members in numbers turned in their cards. In France, Jean-Paul Sartre broke with the party and joined other leftist writers in challenging Soviet colleagues to debate the "Hungarian drama," while in a defensive move the party had actually to *expel* those critical of the USSR. In addition, French workers also refused to support the invasion, and the Italian labor movement actually went into a decline as a consequence of it. You would not be wrong in seeing here a sort of secondary cresting of the tidal wave of Communist disillusionment that followed Khrushchev's secret speech about ten months earlier. Even if your faith in Communism managed to survive exposure of Stalin's monstrous inhumanity, this brutal confirmation coming so quickly on its heels that Stalinism was still alive and well, this was likely to break it.

Today the revolution is usually seen as a 13-day affair, October 23rd to November 4th, but during the weeks following the invasion a different perspective tended to prevail. So, for example, a November 24th report in *The New York Times* summed up the situation with this headline: "HUNGARY'S REVOLT ENTERS 2D MONTH: Strike, Disorder and Exodus Continue." And indeed, the revolution continued, and in terms of its haphazard organization and splintered action, and therefore its fundamentally *popular* character, it remained very much like it had been all along. A people's movement to the last dregs. But in its bitterness and desperation, this last phase was different from all that had come before. For though at one point it did seem almost ready to burst into flame once more, mostly it was just smoldering discontent and a corresponding series of please-and-punish efforts to extinguish it.

Right after the first lethal Soviet assault, the Communist authorities instituted some punitive measures, but at this early stage the emphasis was on *connecting* with the people. Among the new government's first acts were abolition of the anniversary of the Bolshevik Revolution as a holiday, elimination of required Russian language instruction in schools and confirmation of the disbanding of the ÁVO. At the same time, factory workers, miners and teachers received pay raises of 18% on the average, and the system of compulsory delivery of farm produce was scrapped. Favorable measures were also put in place with regard to individuals in the professions, shopkeepers and craftsmen. But the people would not be mollified. They rejected all of the government's well-targeted efforts at a rapprochement. A general strike went into effect on November 11th, with the Budapest Central Workers' Council assuming something like a leadership role. The Council issued manifestos listing the conditions on which workers would resume the capital's clean-up and return to work, and its representatives negotiated with Kádár. But with no results. Since the workers still understood themselves to be fighting the revolution, their demands actually aimed to reproduce the Sixteen Points and were not amenable to being trimmed back into some kind of compromise. So the strike went on, and with railroads idle and miners foremost among the resisters, the shortage of food and coal for heating made the capital a miserable place. Although I don't remember suffering any of this.

Many people fled the country. As I've said, already during the last days of October some Hungarians crossed the unguarded Austrian border and presented themselves – here we are, we're your headache now – as asylum-seekers and refugees. But from November 4th, the early travel-in-luxury migrants were followed by thousands more who had to slip through the Iron Curtain however they could. For a few days the precautionary Soviet buildup near the frontier remained in place, but then the troops pulled back somewhat, almost as if to let the bad apples voluntarily cull themselves from the bunch otherwise unblemished. And escape routes were not tightened up for about two weeks. Most days 3,000 people managed to cross, but occasionally as many as 6,000. Some left because they feared prosecution on account of their revolutionary activities; others because they could no longer stomach the system they had lived under for eight years, even aside from its recent unconscionable brutality; still others because they had just simply lost faith and had, as it were, to bolt from the church. And finally, there were those, quite the majority I would guess, including the Hajdus, for whom the post-revolutionary confusion just presented an opportunity to leave, and who left for reasons that had little or nothing directly to do with the historical events that had just taken place.

While trying to stay alive, the forces of resistance were also gazing across the ocean. Support from the United Nations was more crucial now than ever, although actually no more likely. On November 4th the General Assembly passed a resolution calling on the USSR to stop the armed attack and withdraw its forces, and on Hungary and the USSR to permit observers to enter the country, and also requesting Secretary General Hammarskjold to investigate events and conditions, and to assess Hungarian need for aid and call on all nations to give it. Although hardly more than a wish-list, this resolution pretty well defined the nature and extent of the UN's involvement in the revolution from here on. It was these issues and how best to nudge them from the optative to the indicative that occupied the Assembly whenever the Hungarian crisis came before it during the next fifteen months, and it came before it regularly. But not much was accomplished. Indeed, hardly anything. Mostly, the august body just kept busy with procedural wrangling about priorities on the agenda during those Suez-preoccupied days, the credentials of the Hungarian delegation, and special sessions. The United Nations had 76 members at the time. Anti-Soviet resolutions regarding Hungary tended to command 50 votes plus, with about ten against, and the rest abstaining. Blocks of nations formed briefly to push one approach to the problem or another, one tactic against the opposition or another. But to the chagrin of even some of the delegates, all this was to not much avail.

Meanwhile, Nagy and company remained sequestered in the Yugoslav Embassy because nobody knew exactly what to do about them. The three parties, the Hungarians, the Soviets and the Yugoslavs, all of them cautious but thoroughly unprincipled, continued to negotiate. The asylum-givers wanted to be rid of the group but, according to international custom, could not just throw it to the wolves. For their part, the wolves wanted the wool before devouring the sheep. Tito insisted that the Kádár government guarantee safe passage, but that the Kádár government was not willing to do until Nagy endorsed and so legitimized it, and Nagy continued stubbornly to refuse. Finally, the Soviets decided to force the issue with this crude scheme: Kádár would give the requested guarantee, the Nagy group would then leave the Embassy, immediately they would be arrested, a statement admitting their mistakes and a promise not to take hostile action against the new government would be extracted from them, and then they would be sent to Romania, whose Communist leader had agreed to hold them in custody. And that is indeed what happened on November 22nd, or something like it anyway. For a while events followed the script, right until the Soviet secret police arrested the group riding in the bus and drove them to an undisclosed location. But then Nagy refused. He still wouldn't sign a statement of support for the new government. Let them do to him what they might! Just imagine the big comrades' apoplectic fits! Again foiled, the Soviets finally transported the group to Romania and held them all *incommunicado*. For months. In other words, they kidnapped them.

In early December the government changed tack and launched a program of reprisals against participants in the revolution. From then until the end of 1959, 35,000 individuals were charged in connection with revolutionary activities, brought before so-called people's tribunals and summarily convicted. An additional 13,000 were interned, and many others were banned from their homes or dismissed from their jobs. About 350 people were executed. It's been estimated that all in all more than 100,000 individuals and their families were punished. It was a thorough house-cleaning meant to disinfect the whole country, and scrub out and sweep out the following three groups, all the bacteria, garbage and dirt: the actual freedom-fighters, usually individuals in their twenties and thirties; people who were respected in their communities or workplaces and could be considered leaders; and those who held national office during the revolution and were *unwilling* to recognize the legitimacy of the new government. This new wave of terror stifled all opposition and rendered society mostly apolitical. It also cast a shroud of silence over the revolution that was not to be lifted until a new generation came of age.

But first the reprisals provoked a new surge of resistance and violent clashes. The first notable event occurred on December 4th, one month after the invasion, when despite a ban on demonstrations 30,000 women dressed in black converged on Heroes' Square to honor the rebel dead and sing the national anthem. During the following two weeks, street fights and bloody clashes with the police erupted throughout the country, Soviet tanks and the Hungarian police were kept busy dispersing demonstrations, and at times it seemed that a new armed revolt was even taking shape, like thunderstorms piling up into a hurricane. Strikes were multiplying, in many places thousands of workers showed up at factories but refused to work, and then the Central Workers' Council announced a general strike intended to be only the first stage of a "creeping paralysis" that would soon, it was hoped, bring down the government. Indeed, rumors had the government on the verge of resignation already. The situation seemed to be drifting, public discontent was dangerously high and the economy was crippled. And the authorities? Well, they were just locking up everyone critical of the repression and locking down all resistance organizations. There was no one left even to try to negotiate with.

But soon Kádár made more concessions. Easter Monday and the second day of Christmas were restored as public holidays. Miners received another ten percent raise. The government even relaxed its official hostility to Christmas and lifted the curfew, with the result that worshipers jammed the churches for the holiday as never before under Communism. Obviously, the people wanted their opium and got it. At the same time, the first signs of something like resistance-fatigue also appeared. On December 17th *The New York Times* reported that "actually workers had been drifting back to their jobs during the last two days, apparently with the idea of earning some money for the Christmas holidays." Also on December 17th the Central Workers' Council officially terminated the strike movement. It's hard to say if the concessions bought some good will or if moving on had just become the most urgent imperative all around.

In any case, the revolution did not end with the year. You still continue to hear of sporadic clashes during the early weeks of 1957, but mid-January is probably as good a cut-off point, if not a complete terminus, as any. The repression still maintained its grip, but something like a new status quo had been achieved, and domestically at least the revolution seemed settled. Without a doubt, it was lost.

Only the diplomats were not yet exhausted and at the UN the sparring continued. After all, the Cold War was still raging, and nobody in this arena cared that the revolution could no longer be revived or even resurrected. Was anything accomplished? Well, the international organization did manage to have Red Cross personnel and medical and other emergency relief admitted to Hungary, but otherwise it was futility upon futility. UN observers were kept out of the country with one excuse or another. On December 12th, the General Assembly passed another resolution, this one hailed by Henry Cabot Lodge, Jr., the US ambassador, as the "high-water mark" of the session, "condemn[ing] the violation of the UN Charter by the government of the Union of Soviet Socialist Republics in depriving Hungary of its liberty and independence and the Hungarian people of the exercise of their fundamental rights." But this achievement too was followed by disappointment because it had no more impact than anything that preceded it. Another rap on the red knuckle, that's all. Then early in January, the Assembly voted to create a five-nation commission to hold hearings on the Hungarian situation and obtain testimony from refugees. The commission's report, presented at the end of June, indicted the USSR for crushing a spontaneous revolt and held the Kádár regime responsible for "strong repressive measures." But this too was no more than just a Cold-War exercise. In September, the Assembly once more condemned the USSR and appointed a Thai diplomat to try to win compliance with the resolutions. But the Hungarians rebuffed the Thai, and the year ended without further developments. So in the UN too things just fizzled out.

Of course the problem of Nagy and his group was still in search of a solution. The idea of actually putting the kidnapped men on trial may have originated with Kádár himself or maybe with a few members of the party leadership. In any case, the prime minister, back in Budapest in early April after a visit to Moscow, reported to his Provisional Executive Committee that "the comrades think it proper that we call [Nagy] to account with suitable severity. It is impossible," he added, "to imagine the whole country's political situation without us establishing suitable order in this matter." Clearly, he was anxious to be haunted only by ghosts and urged the Committee to proceed with all due speed. So promptly Nagy and his colleagues were transferred back to Budapest and proceedings were initiated. Nagy and Maléter and Kopácsi and several others were indicted. They were charged with organizing a plot beginning in 1955 "to overthrow the people's democratic regime," and with then carrying out the plot in October 1956. Most of the allegations were based on the defendants' actual acts, which were now for the first time characterized as criminal. The defendants pleaded not guilty, but in order not to compromise the proceedings the government did not resort to torture. The leadership and its lawyers had over-painted the events of the revolution in a new Caravaggesque color-scheme, and, overcome by a preposterous delicacy, they did not want to sully their work with a tainted trial. Although in solitary confinement throughout, the defendants did not confess. Nagy remained especially defiant. Consequently, the trial, though perfect for a show, could not be conducted in public.

A series of problems required a fourteen-month delay between the return of the defendants to Hungary and conclusion of the matter. Since the trial was bound to attract widespread attention, its international implications had to be considered. Its timing could not be allowed to interfere with, that is, render the Soviet leadership sitting ducks at, a special session of the UN or an upcoming CPSU summit and certainly not the great power summit Khrushchev was hoping for. It also took time to convince all the Eastern European Communist leaders of the modified counterrevolution interpretation and of Nagy's involvement in the alleged plot. In May 1957 Khrushchev retorted thus to Polish objections to the proposed proceedings: "Was [Nagy] an [imperialist] agent in the legal sense? Did he take money? This is not material. But he did the enemies' work…. [O]ur friends will understand that his role was treacherous." And if they don't? Then they're not really friends? All along the main impetus was provided by Kádár. He opposed the delays whenever possible, and squashed suggestions that the sentences, once imposed, be reduced or even followed by a pardon. In the end, all the defendants were of course convicted as charged. Nagy, Maléter and a third person were executed on June 16th, 1958. Kopácsi received a life sentence, but was released in 1963. Ferenc Donáth received twelve years but was amnestied in 1960. This all may have been political necessity or vengeance, but it surely wasn't justice.

As you've seen, from the beginning Kádárism was sticks-and-carrots, and so it continued for a while. The repression lasted until the end of the decade, but despite that the conditions of life under the new party boss kept improving. The areas of difficulty remaining after early 1957 were eliminated during the next five years. Soon the regime also reconciled with writers and intellectuals, with both sides giving some. Even the collectivization of agriculture was finally achieved; what could not be done with force was done with persuasion, like the pensions offered in agricultural cooperatives, a previously unimaginable benefit for peasants. In 1957, the range of goods in shops also increased significantly, tourism abroad, unheard of in my boyhood, became a possibility, and even the category of "social background" was removed from university applications. And then by late 1962 the regime was also gaining international recognition. Early the following year, the UN accredited its representatives, and Kádár instituted a general amnesty for political prisoners. At the Seventh Party Congress in November of that year, he invited everyone to cooperate in the construction of a socialist society, those in the party and out, supporters of the regime and *je m'en foutists*, materialists and those of a religious disposition. "Anyone who is not against us is with us," was the well-known live-and-let-live slogan he put into use.

By Eastern European standards, life was good in Hungary for the remaining years of Kádárism. Yes, the one-party system continued to prevail and Soviet troops remained garrisoned in the country, but the arbitrariness with which the Stalinists had exercised power disappeared. You could breathe. Personal freedoms expanded greatly, so you could attend church and listen to Western radio stations and even belong to private associations not controlled by the police. The party was no longer a ubiquitous ideological loudspeaker. After 1968 even the standard of living improved significantly. A Polish visitor to Hungary in the 1960s wrote that "[a]lmost everything is incomparably better than it is with us, let alone the astonishing popularity enjoyed by Kádár as opposed to Gomulka. We won in October 1956, but in the long run we have lost. The Hungarians lost at the time, but in the end they have won." A well-known Hungarian journalist has remarked that "[i]n a strange transformation over the years and decades the hated 'Gauleiter from Moscow' became the 'father of the nation,' respected even by some of his erstwhile victims, and the universally despised stooge of a superpower became an internationally respected statesman." Kádár remained in power until 1988. But as Gorbachev was transforming the socialist world with his policy of *perestroika,* Kádár, the former champion of reform, proved too old and sclerotic to keep up with the new possibilities. At a party congress in May of that year he was politically outmaneuvered and relegated to a ceremonial position. He died the following year, just as the whole Communist venture in Eastern Europe was going through its death throes.

How then are we to see Kádár as a moral agent, to assess his conduct during the 50s? In the balance, was he a good man or was he less than that? To me his virtues exceed his vices. I am struck, first of all, by his abandonment of the reprisals in 1962, the prompt extension of the olive branch to almost everyone and the relatively comfortable and free life he engineered for the country for the next quarter-century. Why did he do these things, and why, as it were, at the earliest possible moment? Only one answer to those questions seems adequate: because they were the right and decent things to do. And then there is also the indisputable argument that by accepting henchman duties in 1956, Kádár blocked the ambitions of much more vicious candidates. As for the reprisals and

Nagy's execution, he cannot possibly live them down. But at least he continued the terror only as long as the Soviets seemed to demand it, and his early conversion to a more human form of communism was so well timed that it even survived Khrushchev's ouster from power in 1964. But still, he must be charged with having offered himself as the instrument of Soviet oppression in 1956. Another man might have turned away in revulsion. Wouldn't that have been the morally right thing to do? Yes, it would have. But that other man would have served only his conscience and not his country. Hungarians seem to concur with my assessment. In a poll conducted by several media organizations in 1999, Kádár came in third, after Saint Stephen, the country's first king, and István Széchenyi, the indispensable 19th-century modernizing reformer, as the greatest Hungarian of all times. An afterlife far better, I'd say, than what Brutus found according to Dante, sharing the 9th circle of hell with Judas Iscariot, being chewed in Satan's mouth for eternity.

It may have pretty much faded for the rest of the world, but in Hungary the memory of the revolution was still thriving on its 50th anniversary. Indeed, the occasion was commemorated with much noise, many retrospective assessments and a myriad displays of emotion both right-on and misdirected. Barbara and I were among the thousands participating in the public events, although we almost missed the occasion. What happened is that by 2006, the year in question, we had a tacit understanding that we'd spend at least one week in Budapest every year, with only the most desirable week having to be designated each time. And only after we had already considered all our other commitments and the climate of the various places we wanted to visit, and had already narrowed the choice down to either the lilacs' bloom or what the French call the *vendange* – only then, suddenly one day while not even thinking about far-away places, did the special significance of the year present itself to me, as the weight of his own body floating in the bathwater had taken the form of a thought in the mind of Archimedes. But that changed everything. Now we quickly reshuffled all our plans the best we could, for, obviously, given this project of mine, I had to be in Budapest on October 23rd.

On the big day Gyuri and Juci (pronounced You-tsi), his lady partner of many years, joined us in attending the main commemoration in Pest for that two-week first-cheers-then-tears entr'acte in the late great historical production known as Hungarian Communism. They were somewhat puzzled by my enthusiasm, and the halting revelation of the hopes I harbored, as I still did then, that finally in the fervent affirmations of the ideals, events and aspirations of the participating patriots I would find, like grains of gold in the mud, the basic ingredients of a Hungarian identity of my own – *that* sheepish confession did nothing to unconfuse them. But they humored me and my apparently uncut umbilical cord as we drove across the Erzsébet Bridge, parked as close as we could to the ragged edges of the multitude clogging the city's arteries and then as-it-were oozed further and further into the thickening human mass. And they continued to humor me even when, suddenly, with a shudder and in the grip of a suffocating revulsion, I turned around and, spastically grabbing for Barbara's hand so as not to lose her, staged what under the circumstances amounted to a frantic retreat. You see, in that pulsing human aggregation, in the amplified harangues and the overheated sentiments spelled out all about in the threatening letters and symbols of placards, I found my identity not as a Hungarian but as a Hungarian *Jew*. And I finally admitted to myself that never the former but only the latter of those identities would I ever manage to bring forth.

How did this happen to me, later I wondered. For as I've stated many times already, I never had a Jewish identity. In Hungary, being Jewish had meant very little to me. Never finding myself in a true locker-room situation, I had hardly paid attention to being circumcised, and early on I had imbibed the Enlightenment notion that we are all essentially equal. And thanks to the ground-rules set by the Communists, and this was crucial, I never had to confront the intolerant racist inequality that had been so common a reaction to that notion. Then came New York, ah! New York.

Here of course circumstances were entirely different, but *plus ça change....* For here, where so many things and people are Jewish, and the world can easily seem like an invitation writ large to jump into the deep end of Jewishness with both feet, here you can also *reject* Jewish habits. And that is exactly what I did as much as I possibly could, getting involved in no Jewish practices whatsoever beyond bagels and lox. So again my religion did not even infiltrate my identity, never mind dominate it. Still, in 2006, the Hungarian-Jewish identity did not exactly ambush me, as it had ambushed many complacent Hungarian Jews only after the Germans occupied the country in March of 1944. Rather, it had started even before my first trip to the old country in 2002 – it had started cozying up to me, inviting and enticing me, extending its arms to me in a welcoming-the-prodigal embrace. Indeed, it had become a sort of shadow-companion to me a couple of years earlier. In hindsight, its appearance, indeed its act of *honfoglalás*, its claiming of a home within me, had been anything but stealthy, even though I had long refused to recognize it for what it was and had continued therefore whenever the need arose to declare it to be something I had none of.

As I've also said, my recollection is that I started reading Sebald in 2000, although it may in fact have been 1999. I had come upon *The Emigrants* while browsing the fiction shelves in the fondly-remembered Coliseum Bookshop on West 57th Street, and with almost the first words and the first photograph it had gripped me like few other books ever have. The emigration-Holocaust theme I found immediately riveting, although I had never been susceptible to such stories. At once I realized that, with its penetrating sense of the brutal impact of historical forces on our private being, this book was offering me a key that could unlock secret truths even in my own life. Next I read *The Rings of Saturn*, which has no Jewish theme at all, but which also astounded and enthralled me. Here is a writer, I thought, with magnificent and extraordinary powers. I want to read everything that he's written and learn about him all I can. Finally, in 2001, *Austerlitz* appeared. *Its* Jewish theme was more prominent than even the most fully worked out narrative in *The Emigrants*, and for weeks, literally, Austerlitz's lost early-childhood memories of the Holocaust, their long-unrecognized impact on his life and his attempt to track them down and piece them back together had me, a non-crier, if you'll remember please, in tears. Now I was aware that something strangely Jewish was happening inside me. My immersion in that book and in the *Goldberg Variations* saw me through the upheaval of Leslie's death in October of that year, which then found its faint, aestheticized echo in Sebald's untimely and to me soul-impoverishing death in December.

Leslie's death was a turning point in this respect too. Unexpectedly so many things changed, among them notably the connection between generations, which I had failed to understand at all until then. To be sure, in my scholarly work as a historian I had usually made the most of a genealogical approach to evidence. How and to whom things were handed down – property, values, titles, skills – could tell you a lot about the long-ago worlds I studied. So I had pored over well-established genealogies and pieced together others not yet compiled as far as I knew, I had analyzed them for patterns and tried to test rules of law against the actual practices they revealed. But, ironically, a personal attachment to lineage and genealogy, when I encountered it in real life, I had always dismissed as just snobbery and being puffed up with status, a worthless, distasteful, un-American class thing. And, not disdaining to just even hear about Rabbi Moses, who was he to me anyway? – I had always rejected the possibility that my own name too could appear within such a system of trunk-and-branch lines. But then the words "my father" were transmuted for me from just a verbal designation to a tiny ritual that evokes something venerated and then lays it back to rest, as the Torah scrolls are removed from the ark at the beginning of the service and replaced there at the end – and then shortly before my first trip to Hungary, when I took Rose to visit Leslie's grave and there reluctantly looked about for a couple of pebbles to place on his headstone, as is the Jewish custom, then finally I realized, as if the mirror of life I'd been looking into for many years had just for the first time been wiped clean, that now I too was actually accepting an inter-generational as opposed to just a historical past, if not exactly claiming an inheritance, then at least owning up to one. And although I was not explicitly aware of its being so, in its form and mode of transmission, and perforce in its content, that inheritance was *Jewish*.

At the time of that visit to the cemetery, I was also already researching the history of Jews in Hungary, and an article about the common Hungarian sentiment in 1945-46 that the Jews had gotten exactly what they deserved was like a squirt of growth hormone on my stripling H-J identity. How could any Jew have wanted to stay in that just-more-of-the-same country, I kept asking myself, living next door to those who had just yesterday been so efficient in dispatching his kind to the gas chambers? In other words, like a child squeaking open the door to a forbidden room of knowledge, I tried to think of us the Hajdus as above all Jews, indeed as objects of persecution, and then immediately upon my arrival in Budapest in 2002 I was at once rudely pushed into that room. The guy from whom I was renting an apartment met me at the airport, drove me into the city, showed me around the premises and then asked to see my passport. After jotting down some relevant information from it, he handed it back and by way of goodbye said: "we're both *nyilasok*," *nyilas*, that is, archer, being the word by which members of the Arrow Cross had been known. I sort of shriveled as a little Jew popped up beside me in that room and wailed in dismay like a figure by Munch: what is this guy saying? That we are both Jews or Jew-killers? It felt suffocating for a stranger to suggest that I was either, and especially for no apparent reason. So I mumbled something and slammed the door behind the guy. Disgusting creature! It was a while before my breathing slowed and I realized that, seeing the date of my birth, he had just made a casual comment declaring us both Sagittariuses, which I actually am almost but not quite.

The day after I arrived, Rózsi promptly began her usual manipulating. She told me that as part of my visit Gyuri will want to take me to Siklós to visit the Hónig family gravesite where Bözsi had been buried not much before Leslie himself had departed, and then told Gyuri on the phone, with me in earshot, that *I* wanted him to take me there. To think that she was engaging in this miscellaneous puppeteering for my own benefit makes no sense, nor that she was doing it for Gyuri's, so the visit had I believe to satisfy her own needs or her own ideas of what is right, or, as it usually turns out, the former conceived as the latter. In any case, a couple of days later we went. Gyuri did it apparently in the belief that I wanted to go, and not for lack of my protestations beyond any misunderstanding that I did not. And indeed I didn't. I didn't see any reason to. Hadn't I just gone to visit *Leslie's* grave? Not even quite three months ago? But then not going seemed, what? It seemed uncaring, indecent, a sneer at family ties – hell, it seemed disrespectful of your own dead. For, obviously, these people were my family. I could not argue with that. So we went for the three-and-a-half hour ride and the even longer return trip along a route more scenic and interesting. And indeed the countryside we drove through on the way back to Budapest was beautiful and we had dinner in Villány, a memorable evening amidst hills with very fine vineyards and I was in the company of someone I really love.

It was about two on a cool and sunny summer afternoon when we reached Siklós. We pulled up before the cottage across the road from the Catholic cemetery, next to which you find the much smaller establishment for the Jewish dead, together with its gatehouse. The cottager, named Erzsi, who is the gatekeeper and also a florist running her business from the gatehouse, I immediately dubbed Eliza Doolittle of Siklós. She and Gyuri know each other well, for she apparently had been maintaining the family gravesite for some time, and they doused their greetings so liberally with the syrup of routine Hungarian over-politeness that I enjoyed the encounter as I might have an extra helping of dessert. She handed him the key to the gatehouse, promised us an espresso when our business was done, and sent us off to the little classical structure with walls bearing the stains of what before they were washed off or painted over had to have been Jew-baiting graffiti. But for the pick and shovel and rake in a corner and some stacks of plastic pots for plants the place was empty. Gyuri lifted the key to the gate itself from off a hook, pointed in passing to the gas-pipe running just below the low ceiling as the one from which Bözsi had hanged herself, I shivered at the thought of her dead-already-before-dying choice, and then we walked back out into the sunshine. I was a tourist, a historian doing research, a visiting member of the family. The choice of roles available to me was wide, but not a single one of them did I feel comfortable inhabiting at the moment.

The cemetery itself was a rectangular enclosure having a width of six graves end-to-end, a length of about thirty graves lying closely packed alongside one another, and very narrow passageways in between every-where. Here and there along those passageways, and confounding rows and columns, scraggly shrubbery tinseled with cobwebs gleamed in the sunlight. With a buzz hardly more audible than if coming from a distant star, insects landed on and took off from their *pieds-à-terre* on the gos-samered leaves. They had to be the only regular visitors to that nether-worldly outpost. Upon closing the gate behind us, Gyuri headed straight for the family gravesite, where not only Bözsi, but also her husband Pista, who died in 1991, and Klári, the third sister and Gyuri's mother of course, who died in 1984, had found their final resting places. I wandered along the passageways, trying to take in the ranks of ghost-burrows, in my mind correcting the geometrical sins late arrivals had committed against the apparent ground-plan, but I was stubbornly unsure which way to turn or even look, how to visit or inspect, who or what to be in this realm of the dead. I actually felt no more of a connection or the possibility of one with the departed Hónigs than with any of the other Jews long returned to dust under the stone slabs. To me, the personal and the historical seemed finally to have merged within the no-longer-even-patched walls of the cemetery, a field of ditches where all individual lives and deaths had been both reduced and elevated to the fate of all people, Jewish and gentile. Amen.

I kept turning left and right along the paths, trying all the while to organize my thoughts, collect the facts displayed and implied all about, decipher the meanings inherent in that necropolis. But actually I was so focused on the events of 1944 that I completely failed until it was too late to think of using the dates on the gravestones as evidence of the approxi-mate date of origin of the town's Jewish community. Later on I settled on the general impression that the as-it-were followers of Joseph Hőnig first reached this margin of Baranya County and were first interred in this cemetery during the 1860s. From those times on, the Jewish community seemed stable, steadily replenishing itself and likely even growing in numbers, right until 1944, when the natural succession of generations, as was demonstrated here too, was perversely cut off, never again to be restored. From after that date there is only the monument set up by a Weisz family for the father who died in the 1970s and the memory of the ten-year-old daughter who perished in the Holocaust, three memorial tablets with the names of a few people murdered in Auschwitz, and, finally, the Hőnig gravesite, a large horizontal slab of black granite rising above the remains of the two sisters and the husband, and in anticipation also bearing Rózsi's name. (An anticipation she proceeded to frustrate in 2008 by being buried in Budapest.) Two half-Jews still remained in Siklós after Bözsi's death, but for certain she herself was the last person ever to be put in the ground of that quasi-archeological site. The last member of a once thriving community less notable for its beginnings than for its end, the last local witness to a failed dream of home.

Gyuri cleared some dead petals off the grave and generally tidied up the site, and then we let ourselves out of the cemetery enclosure, replaced the key in the gatehouse with the gas-pipe and knocked on Eliza's door once again. She had the espresso ready in a minute, and we settled around a small table with a green-and-white checkered oilcloth and munched on homemade cookies as Eliza told, or retold I should say, the true story of Bözsi's last days. There had been, it seems, an official story – official in the sense I would guess that it was broadcast about town and also considered sufficient for the transatlantic brother – according to which Bözsi had put an end to her own life on account of her broken down physical condition and the sufferings attendant on her many illnesses. But that is not really what had happened, once more Eliza felt compelled to confide. Bözsi had not been seriously ill, as even the autopsy had shown. There had indeed been times during recent years when she would have the doctor call on her five times a day – and she put up a hand with fingers outspread – but it had all been only theater, as Gyuri put it, only a performance. In truth, the suffering was all emotional, an extreme loneliness, an irremediable, existential sense of being alone. And Eliza, her faithful amanuensis in taking care of the family gravesite, which had been Bözsi's primary occupation and preoccupation during the last decade of her life, and the person who had probably had more contact with her during those years than anyone else and had herself been the one to discover the gruesome denouement – Eliza was certain that Bözsi had not intended to kill herself. She had meant rather to bungle the whole affair and just create some commotion, but had then bungled the bungling. Or so said Eliza Doolittle of Siklós, but maybe she was being too subtle I thought, drawing in this case too fine a distinction between intention and act.

Near the end of *The Emigrants*, Sebald's unnamed but mesmerizingly Sebald-like narrator travels to Bad Kissingen, the spa town in Germany where Max Ferber, one of his emigrant protagonists, was born. Ferber gave the narrator the epistolary memoirs his mother had written and mailed to him in England prior to November 1941, when both of his parents were deported from that town to their deaths. In 1991, with the memoirs "very much on [his] mind," the narrator journeys to the German town to search for Ferber's Jewish past. And a decade later, in the midst of slowly acknowledging my H-J identity, I journeyed to Hungary in order to search for my own Jewish past. In Kissingen, searching for any trace of the Ferbers, the narrator is quickly reduced to going to the Jewish cemetery, although "what I saw there," he says, "had little to do with cemeteries as one thinks of them; instead, before me lay a wilderness of graves, neglected for years, crumbling and gradually sinking into the ground amidst tall grass and wild flowers under the shade of trees [that] trembled in the slight movement of the air." Leaving Siklós, I thought it uncanny that my path too should have led, and almost as if against my will, to a Jewish cemetery. But then at once I saw through the coincidence. At once I understood Sebald to be saying that, actually, in the lands of the Holocaust, if so I may label them, the cemetery is an inevitable destination. Where synagogues and kosher restaurants and ritual baths have long ago been pulled down or converted to more *goyishe* uses, the only Jewish institution with visible vestiges will be the burial grounds. Where hatred could not uproot even the dead, and time will have to wreak the final destruction.

For a few days after the trip to Siklós, the thought of Bözsi as the last to be buried in that cemetery, as the last of her kind in terms of her generations-spanning community, had me in its grip. Rózsi had no patience for my gloom. "What does that matter, that Bözsi is the last one," she snapped when I launched into my lugubrious ruminations. But the little Jew inside me would not let go, and I could not make him. After all, Hungary *is* his turf. You have some responsibility for this state of affairs too, he reminded me. For in a sense wasn't 1956, or didn't it quite unintentionally become, a tying up of some of the loose ends of the Holocaust? In 1941 Nazism set to work expelling the Jews from Hungary or at least engineering their exodus. And Nazism made a hell of a job of it. For many even of the Hungarian Jews who survived the camps, many of that few, did not return to Hungary. Finally they had learned their lesson. Still, after the dust could be said to have settled and the ashes, as it were, drifted down and turned the Danube gray, there were still some Jews in the country, maybe 275,000, maybe fewer. From that time on, estimates of the number of Jews in the country vary widely, but certainly there was then some attrition, and then in 1956 some more Jews, including the Hajdus of course, had the chance to get out and did. Maybe 16,500 of them, reported *The New York Times*, a number it translated as 13% of all the Jews in Hungary at the time, which thus would have been about 110,000. That was the contribution of the revolution's refugees to the Nazis' efforts, one small step that brought Hungary even closer to being a place in which Bözsi was driven by loneliness to become, and as soon as possible, the last Jew ever buried in that cemetery.

I too escaped then of course, escaped from Hungary, the land of the little Jew, who I believe was then not yet inside me. I wonder if he might have left me alone altogether had I remained there through the many more years of Communism and even beyond, right up to 2002. Might

I have turned out then to be like Gyuri and Éva, the second wife he has not lived with for years now but whom Barbara and I also know very well? They are about ten years younger than I, so they have been forged in a different historical crucible, and that may be decisive here, but they have no H-J identities whatsoever. Of course, their fathers had both been Communists, and they themselves did not learn of their own Jewish roots until their twenties. They know that antisemitism is alive and well in Hungary, but that knowledge seems not to affect them and neither does the antisemitism itself, except in very incidental ways. I'm astounded by their attitude – I who belong to nothing but my own little circle – although I don't think there's anything wrong with it, and now I am rather convinced that under no circumstances could I have become their kind of non-Jew. But you never know.

In any case, I have to keep Gyuri and Éva in mind when I ask myself, as I did so many times after leaving the Siklós cemetery and as I do each time I feel paranoid in Budapest about being identified as a Jew – how is it possible to be a Jew in Hungary these days? I can't deny that many people are indeed well-disposed to Jews or at least neutral to them. There is a lot of peaceful, enlightened, even fraternal coexistence. There are also affirmative developments, like the Raoul Wallenberg monument, which is in Szent István Park, one of the most beautiful spots in Pest, along the riverbank and actually quite close to where I grew up. The low pedestal with the statue of a modernist figure slaying a modernist dragon on it was erected soon after the war but overturned in 1949 by the Communists, the new dragons in town. For they recognized no war heroes or saviors other than their own. The base disappeared for good, but the statue, without a plaque not in any way a reference to the Swedish diplomat who sacrificed his life to save Hungarian Jews, turned up in Debrecen at some later time. And then in 1998, after both heroes and dragons had been cut down to size, the mayor of the capital appointed a Wallenberg Statue Committee, and on the 50th anniversary of its demise, the monument was reconstituted and re-erected. This is certainly one aspect of Jewish life in Hungary today, but only one.

If you had asked Rózsi how Jews can live in Budapest today, she might have said something like the following, although maybe not as neatly packaged as it is coming out of my own mouth: For a long time there was a common life between Magyar and Jew in Hungary, and indeed Jews considered themselves and were accepted as Magyars. Then the brain-fever of nationalism infected the country, and then came Trianon and European antisemitism and finally the Holocaust, although even that was orchestrated only at the last minute and only by a minority, and then some terrible times followed, but even then the Jews received some unusual and significant protections. And the Holocaust, those scoundrels have to admit, did not succeed, as it were, even if the Jews were decimated. For there are still Jews in Hungary! And the common life continues. But you know that it's never been easy to be a Jew. We have always been envied and hated. – That's what Rózsi might have said, and I might very well have replied to her this way, although not so much out of disagreement but just to not let the other point of view, which you already know, go unstated: That's all true. But at the same time, what right did we *ever* have to even think that we Jews would be allowed to remain in this country and claim it in any part as our own? Is not the whole idea of the Diaspora that no place can be such a place? That's why, in large part, it's never been easy to be a Jew. Yes, that's how I would have felt compelled to respond. Summarily. And had Gyuri or Éva been sitting with us on Rózsi's terrace during this exchange of views, he would have been fiddling with his cellphone and she staring bored into the distance.

On my Hungarian trip of 2003, one afternoon at Rózsi's I met Zsuzsa, a widow a few years older than myself and one of the people Rózsi relied on in her retirement. After clearing off lunch, Zsuzsa got up, reached for a plastic bag and handed it to me, saying "I got this from my stepfather when he died and haven't been able to figure out what should happen to it when I go. So I want you to have it." In the bag was a book, a Hungarian translation of Flavius Josephus's *History of the Jews*. I was, well, taken aback, but did a good job I think of looking pleased and touched and thankful, and the ladies were satisfied. But to be once more the recipient of a legacy, I sputtered inside, and a Jewish legacy and Jewish identity-object at that! Yes, of course, I am a historian and a reader, and of course I am Jewish, but at the same time hardly the next generation after Zsuzsa and, in my own mind at least, hardly a willing bearer of a Jewish tradition or identity. But obviously that's not how Zsuzsa saw me. For her I was apparently part of a vigorous and vital Jewish life, a representative of the America she herself had not been lucky enough to grab, but to which she aspired and through which she could feel her stepfather, and maybe even Hungarian Jewry, continuing to live on. Well, was the joke on her or was it on me?

On arriving home in Mamaroneck, I dipped into the Magyarized Josephus. Not bad. And then, reading about the Jewish War sent me to my old Encyclopedia Britannica, where I knew I'd find a good summary of how exactly the Jews dispersed after the destruction of the Second Temple in 70 AD and what course Jewish history took through the subsequent centuries. So I got comfortable and read the whole lengthy story and was actually gripped by it and by a new and tenacious feeling that it was my *own* story I was reading. The story of how a person like me became a historical possibility. All the passion with which I had so often read about classical Greece, and various aspects of the Middle Ages, and the Renaissance in Italy and the North, and France in the 16th century and the 17th and the 18th and in the Belle Époque, and even Lévi-Strauss's travel-writings about South America, which have a lot in common with history, and other things too – all that had been different from that new feeling, and in some ways inferior to it. For the new feeling was not only as it were narrower and more exclusivist but also included an involuntary, incontrovertible, indeed unavoidable sense of belonging. And what I belonged to was Hungarian Jewry. Already then I knew that Hungarian Jews were different from the rest, and having then just recently visited the National Museum in Budapest, I also knew that willy-nilly Hungarian Jews were also different from the Magyars. Indeed, Hungarian Jewry, I felt, yes, *felt*, was and is pretty much a distinct historical phenomenon, to which I myself belong. And as if to confirm all this, the next day finally I began reading Dr. Miklós's book.

So I arrived at the 2006 commemoration with a still mostly unwanted but nevertheless well-developed H-J identity, but without any expectation that it might be relevant to the situation, or any clear understanding that it is an identity active mostly if not exclusively when I am in Hungary. Still, what had that identity to do with the half-century-old revolution? Well, as it turned out, it had a lot to do with it. I failed to see that connection in advance only because I was ignorant of the revolution's post-1956 history. You see, while I did study the causes and events of the revolution, as any good historian would, I foolishly assumed, as no historian ever *should*, that now with Communism cashiered the revolution to be commemorated would be the as-it-were objectively true historians' revolution. But how unhistorian-like that was of me! As if I did not know that even *professional* historians are not all alike, and that always there will be some ready to write the proverbial *victor's* history. Who, after all, had air-brushed Communist history for Stalin to render it Trotsky-less, who had for the Whigs' sake made the history of early modern England into the first two acts of the epic drama the last act of which was their own triumph, who but the historian apostles and historian church fathers had baptized the Hebrew Bible the Old Testament so they could bring it to its proper conclusion with their own Christian scriptures, and I could go on? But now I have seen the error of my ways and have read *Retroactive Justice: Prehistory of Post-Communism*, a fascinating book by István Rév, a historian and Academic Director of the Open Society Archives at the Central European University in Budapest, and now I understand only too well the connection between the revolutionary commemoration and Hungarian sentiments about Jews.

After the November 4th invasion, Kádár and his forces, I will call them the Communists, although I don't intend by that to imply anything at all about the political convictions of Nagy and his group – the Communists knew that their legitimacy depended on public acceptance of the "true" version of the revolution, and as a group that maintained its monopoly of power against the people's wishes, they never stopped worrying about legitimacy. So they turned the writing of the history of recent events into a decades-long propaganda campaign, waged by a corps of creative idea-men, that is, historians, and a battalion of party-hack spin-doctors. The four main offensive moves in this campaign were the following:

1. The modified counterrevolution interpretation was promptly elevated to the status of official history, with the unfortunate but unique October 30th massacre being blown up into an emblematic anti-Communist bloodbath. This history took the logically compelling form of crime (October 30th) rightfully followed by punishment (November 4th), and so it also explained how that latter day demanded and deserved its newly instituted annual celebration.

2. A cult of the *martyrs* of 1956 was established. For its temple, in 1959 they built the Pantheon of the Working-Class Movement, locating it in Kerepesi Cemetery, a sort of national cemetery founded in 1847 and long known as the Père Lachaise of Budapest. Inside the temple were buried, indeed reburied, many Hungarian heroes of the Movement, starting with 19th-century socialists, moving on to leaders of the 1919 Soviet Republic, fighters in the Spanish Civil War, etcetera, and culminating with the military and secret-police officers killed in the revolution. In Hollywood, when a sequel is tacked onto a movie that had never expected one, they describe the relationship as retroactive continuity. Well, that's exactly what was being engineered inside that Pantheon.

3. Concurrently with establishment of the Pantheon, a historical narrative about counterrevolutionary forces was also constructed. These forces, the story went its merry retroactively continuous way, first appeared as the perpetrators of the white terror following defeat of the 1919 Soviet Republic, went underground until they could return as the Hungarian fascists of 1944, some of whom remained in the country after the war as saboteurs

and then launched their final attack in 1956. Around 1960 two Communist historians wrote a thriller called *The Spearmen*, chronicling the exploits of a right-wing paramilitary organization that played exactly these historical roles. It was hugely popular for decades. Fiction imitating fiction, you might say.

4. In 1967 the Revolutionary Youth Days was instituted. This name was given to an annual series of spring commemorations of the events that made up the so-called Communist revolutionary tradition. And these events,... well, some of them had a good claim to qualify for inclusion, like the birth of the Red Army for example, but others were sheer nonsense, like the anniversary of Yuri Gagarin's space flight. But that hardly mattered. For the real purpose of the Youth Days' elaborate conception was the breaking of the popular connection between March 15th and October 23rd, the latter of which could hardly be celebrated in the spring and so might be consigned, they hoped, to obscurity.

As you can see, it was an aggressive, shamelessly untruthful, mind-bending campaign, and it was not waged in vain. Over the years, the Communists captured more than a few minds.

In a poll taken in 1988, more than 55% of Hungarians agreed that Nagy had been a counterrevolutionary. You have to wonder, if Communism had lasted just a little longer than it did, might the mendacious historical rewriting have achieved its *full* purpose? A sobering thought, that! But practically speaking, it was probably only the revolutionary generation and its children that had to be hoodwinked. In any case, in 1988 there was still, obviously, the other 45%, which testifies to the continued existence of the so-called democratic opposition, those on the side of the revolution and against its violent repression, and also to the continued vitality, despite all the retroactive razzmatazz, of the view that the revolution had actually been the last hope for a true socialist utopia. That its goal had actually been not counterrevolution but reform of the system. During these years, Nagy also remained the symbol of 1956, a symbol the Communists could contend with only by denying both *its* existence and the brutally abbreviated life of its embodiment. Most notable along these lines was Kádár's refusal at all times from the day of Nagy's execution to the day of his own death to mention the revolution's prime minister by name. When he had to refer to his predecessor, he would say only either "the dead man" or "the one who is dead" or some other locution like that. And with good reason. For even while Kádárism was conferring its benefits and winning its converts, any reference to Nagy, any reminder, however innocent, of the actual events of the revolution threatened to expose the tectonic fault-line beneath post-1956 political arrangements that the Communists were forever denying.

Then, of course, in 1989 came the general disintegration of Communist rule in the Soviet Union and throughout Eastern Europe. In Hungary, 1956 continued to occupy the center of national self-awareness to such an extent that the revolution may be said to have functioned as the fulcrum on which the balance tipped from one system to the other. Nagy's remains, together with the remains of those executed with him, had been interred in a secret unmarked plot in Kerepesi Cemetery. During the early '80s, rumors had begun to circulate about the number of the burial plot, and on successive Octobers 23rds crowds would have gathered there had they been allowed to. But then, in 1988, as the Communist regime was beginning to take on water and the *Antigone*-like situation was about to enter its fourth decade, suddenly permission was granted to the families to privately rebury the bodies. This of course was a crack in the *foundations*. Then in the spring of 1989 a new poll startlingly confirmed the foundering of the regime: 90% *dis*agreed with the labeling of Nagy as a counterrevolutionary. Now the regime relented even more and actually gave the green light for nonofficial *state* funerals. And in the end, on June 16, 1989, on the 31st anniversary of the execution and only three days after the beginning of discussions on the transfer of power, the massive reburial ceremony at Heroes' Square was attended even by the prime minister. No greater honor could have been bestowed on a Hungarian than what Nagy received that day. He was elevated to the company of Grand Prince Árpád, the leader of the Magyars when they first occupied the Carpathian Basin, and of Louis Kossuth himself.

The transition from Communism to democracy was a completely peaceful process, with the ceremony on Heroes' Square its single most memorable event. And the significance of the revolution for the change of system and regime was officially defined at the first opportunity, that is, in the introductory words to the first law enacted by the first post-Communist legislative body just minutes after resignation of the last Communist government:

> The freely elected new parliament considers it its urgent task – one that cannot be postponed – to enshrine in a bill the historical significance of the revolution and freedom fight of the fall of 1956. This glorious event of modern Hungarian history can only be compared to the revolution and freedom fight of 1848. The Hungarian revolution of the fall of 1956 created a foundation for the hope that a democratic social order can be created, that no sacrifice for the independence of the fatherland is in vain.

Like I said, no greater honor, nor greater glory. And that wasn't even all. For there was still another act of retroactive historical continuity that could now be and was committed, and an ingenious one at that. After the funeral, the democratic, and hence anti-Communist, opposition that had brought about the reburial came into power. And at least a little bit justifiably, it did not hesitate to declare itself the heir of the revolution, for we are, after all, the heirs of those we bury, as if 1989 were nothing less than the immediate morrow of 1956 and the last of the national revolutionary triad of 1848-1956-1989. This now was the revolution's heyday! And finally its true victory.

But this victory too was short-lived. At the first post-Communist elections conservatives and socialists, the latter the leading faction of the new left and a self-denying descendant of the Communists, confronted each other. The conservatives won and immediately set about dismantling the transition's understanding of 1956. In order to appropriate it as *their* own, they actually affirmed the Communists' charges that, yes, the revolution was indeed a reaction to socialism, and argued that the goal of that reaction was a return to the conditions they themselves wished to recreate, namely, the conditions that prevailed before the German occupation of March 1944. That of course was pretty much a fantasy. Nagy himself they also claimed by remastering his anti-Stalinist image to make him an anti-Communist altogether, and by finding him to have personified the proposition that democracy and Communism are incompatible. In response, the socialists presented themselves as actually the heirs of the *national social democracy* element of the revolution and claimed filiation with Nagy as he was in his later reform-Communist phase, which they identified as a predecessor of the Czech Alexander Dubcek's 1968 "socialism with a human face," itself a predecessor of the Velvet Revolution of Vaclav Havel, which only the blind could fail to see as an older brother to the politics of the newly-minted Hungarian socialists themselves. Well, that at least is a *possible* reading of the facts. In any case, the victory of the revolution affirmed during the transition was quickly shattered. In the open political climate the revisionist fury knew no bounds, and the left-right struggle for possession of the revolution became a permanent theme of the country's political life.

The two ideological foes seemed able to agree on only one representation of 1956, namely, the monument to Nagy erected in a prominent location near the Parliament. It is a life-size statue of the prime minister standing at the top of the arc of a footbridge over a pool of water. In essence, suspended between the two anchored ends, neither here not there. Finally an interpretation that doesn't invite argument.

Initially the major players in the new post-transition multi-party system were the Hungarian Socialist Party, its junior coalition partner, the Hungarian Liberal Party, and Fidesz, the Hungarian Civic Union, a center-right organization. National elections took place every four years starting with 1990. The Socialist coalition won in 1994, 2002 and 2006, Fidesz in 1998. But soon an ultra-nationalist, *antisemitic* far-right movement also emerged, all fired up to play the serpent in the garden of democracy. Jobbik, which stands for Movement for a Better Hungary, was the more important of the two extremist parties. And like every other faction, the far-right also immediately grabbed the revolution and claimed it as its own. One of the leading figures at the 2003 meeting where Jobbik assumed its current organizational form was Gergely Pongrátz, the graying leader of a memorable group of fighters in 1956. In a widely publicized speech, he lamented his own generation's advanced age and called on the party's members to pick up the revolutionary torch. A senior moment, as they say, or what? For what justification could Pongrátz have had for identifying the far-right as the true heirs of 1956? As I see it, and there really is no room for debate here, if 1956 has any true heirs at all, they are the Socialists, with Fidesz being only opportunists and Jobbik nothing more than self-deluded pretenders or liars.

The stage for the 50th anniversary commemorations was set a month in advance. On September 17, 2006, an audio recording of a behind-closed-doors speech made several months earlier by Ferenc Gyurcsány, the Socialist prime minister, was somehow made public. Among other things, Gyurcsány reminded his audience that during the past four years he and they had utterly mismanaged the country and that in order to get re-elected had thoroughly lied to the public. A deep wound that leak turned out to be, and maybe a self-inflicted one! By the evening, large crowds demonstrated in the capital and in other cities, clamoring for Gyurcsány's and the government's resignation. The next three days brought more demonstrations and riots and arson, and also riot-police and brutality. At one point protestors estimated to number 40,000 gathered on Kossuth Square, fighting broke out in several key locations in Pest, barricades confronted the mounted police in many cities, and the authorities had to use armored vehicles, tear gas and water cannon to disperse the crowds. In other words, nationwide civil unrest. You could read about the daily events in *The New York Times* and the international press in general. One episode involved an attack on the building of Hungarian Television, which succeeded only briefly and accomplished nothing, but put you immediately in mind of the Radio building in 1956. Another featured a mob of ragtag vandals who, when attacked by the police, proudly likened themselves to freedom fighters. But by the fourth day order returned. Of course, the exchange of charges and counter-charges continued, together with the international coverage, and peaceful demonstrations too sporadically in many places and daily in Budapest until October 23rd.

On the anniversary itself the capital surrendered early to the vagaries of multi-crowd dynamics. The official ceremonies were planned for Kossuth Square, but first the site had to be forcibly cleared of the anti-government demonstrators congregating there for weeks by then. Protesters collected near the offices of the official Hungarian News Agency and at Saint Stephen's Basilica not far from the Parliament. Fidesz was trying to hold its own celebrations at the Astoria Hotel, with the very large crowd nearby overflowing in all directions from a broad bend in the Erzsébet Ring. It is this last giant assemblage we were stopping-and-going into, Gyuri, Juci, Barbara and I, as I've said, very slowly after a while because bodies were densely packed. I was a little put off by the herds of humanity, but in contrast to all those compulsory November 7th celebrations and May Day parades of my boyhood, I was expecting a genuinely joyful outpouring of national memory. Well, that's not how things turned out.

It was a crowd of ordinary locals, everybody dressed half-skier-half-shopper for the October urban outdoors. At a good distance from us but well within sight, people were listening to the speeches being made from a high platform below several banners, and all the while waves of energy pulsed through the multitude like tremors trying to coalesce into an earthquake. Then a rumor passed by like a gust of wind, from Gyuri to me to Barbara, that not far from the platform a demonstrator, a 65-year-old veteran of the revolution we learned later, had climbed up into a 1956-vintage tank, one of the Joseph Stalins parked on islands in the boulevard as part of the commemoration, managed to get it into gear and to lurch through the streets for a hundred yards or so, scattering about shards of pavement and curb, dispersing protestors like a wolf coming down on the fold, propelling the police into action, giving the entire event a carnival-turned-horror-movie feeling. Explosions of crowd-noise provided a cadence-crushing bass-line to the increasingly feverish phrases of the speakers.

And then I heard it over the loudspeakers, the sinister words of who? an extremist interloper, a pandering politician, an embittered loser? – sinister words that seemed to boom over all the rest and for me summarized both the prevailing mood and the underlying emotions: *Hungary for true Hungarians.* Suddenly I felt threatened and persecuted. The thousands about me, all those who had come to hear these speakers, they didn't look or act hostile, they didn't wear Arrow-Cross armbands, they were not subjecting Jewish-looking men to the trousers-down test. But I did not want to wait to see whether or not they would. For I knew very well that "true Hungarians" was nothing but code for *non-Jews*, and having learned by then all I had about the last century of Jewish life in Hungary, any suggestion of persecution was enough to turn me into a grandson of the grandparents who had not been allowed to live long enough for me to know them. The little Jew inside me jumped up from what he had from the first identified as the hot seat, and I grabbed Barbara's hand and bolted. Only the commemorative sardine-can environment slowed me down enough not to have to explain to Gyuri and Juci why suddenly I was flooring the pedal in reverse.

Until that moment I had participated in the commemoration only as a curious historian. Indeed, right from our arrival in Budapest, my emotional distance from all that was going on by way of preparations for the anniversary – the celebratory signs and displays everywhere in the city, the rallies and other crowd-events being organized by each of the political parties, the giant banners strung along the Danube embankment on the Buda side with artists' images of things I could not identify, an exhibition of commemorative art in the Pavilion of the Arts and an another one in the offices of the XIIIth-district historical society, the dozens of new and reissued books on bookstore shelves – my emotional distance from all that readying repeatedly declared that I had no Hungarian identity. Although I *was* really interested in everything. And I do have a very deep connection with the Hungarian language and also with Hungarian history and with many of the Hungarian things I came to know on my visits. But aside from the language, which still bubbles up in my soul, although not in my dreams, these are but passions of the mind. Not *just* passions. And the fellow-feeling appropriate for an ethnic or national community of memory, which would have been the genuine article, has always eluded me. But the reference to true Hungarians changed all that. Instantly, I was transformed from historian to Hungarian Jew, a very accessible identity by then, still well nourished, I would guess, by the fears of late-1944 buried deep in my subconscious.

Soon after my retreat from the commemoration crowd, all hell broke loose around the Astoria, to quote the next day's edition of a local tabloid. What exactly happened I cannot say, for I am not savvy enough about the Hungarian media to sense which reporter or news source has an axe to grind or a hatchet job to do. To boot, there was indeed a lot of confusion, with forces operating behind the scenes for sure. But nobody is denying that each of the political factions was angling for an advantage, both by making itself look good and by making the others look bad, so you can lay the blame at anyone's door you wish. It's plausible that the far-right extremist human mass wanted to attach itself to the Fidesz celebration at the Astoria in order to gain some additional legitimacy, and also that Fidesz was resisting such a move by the extremist human mass for fear of being tainted. It's also plausible that the police were just trying to keep order, but also that their tactics were designed to actually press the extremist human mass into the midst of the governing Socialists' opponents. What is certain is that at one point the mounted police charged, clubs swinging, tear gas canisters exploding, water cannon cannonading, rubber bullets flying into the crowd we had just flailed our way out of. Immediately, there were accusations of police brutality and counter-assertions of the patience and restraint used by the authorities to deal with an unruly and provocative mob. But videos leave no doubt that the police used force indiscriminately. Aside from everything else, I'm glad not to have been an eyewitness.

A few evenings later – stupidly or maybe out of the residual panic I was still in the grip of I failed to include the exact date in my notes – Barbara and I were wandering in the area of Kossuth Square, stopping now and then to look at the wares of the street vendors who were hoping to sell just a few more scarves, souvenirs or bottles of soft drink before it was time to quit. The crowd, including those who, judging by their used-merchandise appearance and the sleeping-bags and blankets drawn about their shoulders, must have been spending the nights right there in the open – the crowd was peaceful. Without any introduction, a thin, tired-of-life man stepped up to a lectern festooned with the so-called Árpád stripes, eight horizontal bands of alternating red and silver, the heraldic symbol of the Árpád dynasty, which had in subsequent centuries been routinely used as part of the country's coat of arms, but had recently been adopted by Jobbik and so remind many of nothing so much as the very similar Arrow Cross flag. After a brief speech about the fatherland and, yes, about true Hungarians, scratchy music started, whereupon the sparse crowd stood at attention and intoned the anthem of the ethnic Hungarians living in Transylvania, whom both Fidesz and the far-right, but not anyone who values sanity above rage or power, want to reunite with the ancestral homeland. Wondering if this was still intended to be part of the commemoration, I also stood silently, just like those who want-ed to deny my Magyar-ness, and worse. At least this second time I did not escape in a panic from the nest of vipers.

In memory of the victims of the Soviet invasion and as a protest against the police brutality of October 23rd, Fidesz announced a candle-light march across Budapest for November 4th. But the response was neg-ligible. In fact, soon the entire episode of riots and demonstrations came to an end. Political life returned to its by-then-accustomed ugliness, and as far as I can tell, no one took the trouble to bemoan the hijacking and trashing of the revolution, indeed its being rendered simply irrelevant. But maybe that just confirmed that the revolution's fate could hardly have been different. Given the post-1989 political fragmentation, which had in a sense been made possible by the revolution's ultimate victory, what else was possible? For that victory did not open up new paths so much as sent the country right back to the 1920s, to its yearnings for the West, on the one hand, and the nursing of its Trianon wounds, on the other. The victory over an initially terroristic and then basically dissimulating system quickly yielded to an angry, directionless, every-man-for-himself malaise, which the revolution could serve only as a serially abused byword.

Still, in the end, the revolution defeated Communism. So what if it took 33 years, and assists from... well, you can make your own list. But when Communism was gone, and the Soviet bully with it, then the revolution also was again lost. For the revolution had success only in destroying things. It wanted to create things too of course, but actually too many things, and incompatible things at that. If you had for some reason to put its creative goals into one word, a word that would summarize them as Stalinism summarizes all that it had wanted to destroy, the best you could say would be pluralism. In other words, the revolution may be said to have aimed at creating a society in its own image, that is, a pluralist society. And so it did. But then this pluralist society, this democracy, for that's exactly what it is, wasted no time destroying the revolution itself by destroying its memory. So, in essence, when Communism died, so did the revolution. After half a century, in a bitter historical joke, victor and victim turned out to be but opposite sides of the same coin.

CHAPTER 7

Faith and Fear

IN HIS MEMOIRS, CHURCHILL RECALLS the so-called percentage deal he made
with Stalin in October 1944 at the fourth Moscow Conference of the leaders of the Allies. I imagine the two men to have been sitting opposite
each other rather than the usual photographic side by side, as Churchill
scribbled the words Romania, Greece, Yugoslavia, Hungary and Bulgaria
on a slip of paper, and next to each the respective shares of influence the
Soviets and British were to have in that country. Hungary was 50%-50%.
Churchill then passed the paper to Stalin, who checked off each item
and then passed the paper back. "Might it not be thought rather cynical," Churchill then said, "if it seemed we had disposed of these issues so
fateful to millions of people in such an offhand manner? Let us burn the
paper." "No," replied Stalin, "you keep it."

And why not? Uncle Joe never considered this an actual deal, and I
would think that Churchill didn't either. And indeed it was no deal. It
was just opening moves. Sure enough, already the next day the British
and Soviet representatives revised the numbers to give the Russkies an
80% say in Hungary, and in 1945 Stalin himself summarized his own
unequivocal view on the spoils of war this way: "This war is not as in
the past; whoever occupies a territory also imposes on it his own social
system. Everyone imposes his own system as far as his army can reach.
It cannot be otherwise." Of course, Stalin made sure that events proved
him right.

A few months later, in the wake of the Red Army and its devastations, political life in Hungary once more burst into bloom. Spring was on the way. Four parties invisible during the right-wing ascendancy of the 1930s and the war years came out of hibernation and by the summer of 1945 again constituted active organizations. They were the Smallholders, that is, peasants with modest landed property, with the largest membership at 900,000, the Social Democratic Party with 350,000, the National Peasant Party with 200,000, and the Bourgeois Democratic Party with around 50,000. But there was also the Hungarian Communist Party, an upstart with overweening ambitions and the incomparable advantage of Soviet sponsorship. In 1942, before the big round-up of undesirables, there had been 400-450 active Communists in the country. At the end of 1944, at the time of the Red Army's siege of Budapest, there were about 3,000, but the Party was already poised for explosive growth. Surviving Jews were inevitably drawn to the Communists as the only political group that had *not* failed to stand by them in 1944, and with their support and other recruits too the ranks swelled to 30,000 registered members by February 1945, to 150,000 by May and to half a million by October!

These five parties immediately set about building a new state and a new society. If you could forget about all the killing and destruction that produced it, you could consider this an extraordinary opportunity. And in any case it was exhilarating to be free, to have your country back after so many years of suffering and despair. All the players professed to hold democratic values, although the Communists and Social Democrats also advocated collective ownership of the means of production. Representatives of the parties convened as early as December 1944 and formed the Hungarian National Independence Front, which committed itself to ending all irredentist policies, forging good relations with the Soviet Union and other neighboring countries, disbanding right-wing organizations, repealing anti-democratic laws, punishing war criminals, encouraging private enterprise, but also bringing about land reform, better working conditions, nationalization of coal mines and state supervision of large banks. In other words, liberal democracy garnished with socialism. The Allies promptly endorsed the Front and its program, and still before the beginning of the last year of the war a provisional legislative body made up of representatives of the parties convened in Debrecen. There was no strictly numerical or electoral reason for it, but the Communists held 39% of the seats in this Provisional National Assembly. During the next summer, after delegates from the rest of the now entirely liberated country also joined the body, the Communists allowed their portion of the seats to decline to 36%.

The Assembly established a provisional government, which began at once to put the program into effect and to repair, insofar, alas, as that was possible, the damage of the fascist years. The first order of business was declaring war on the Third Reich and signing an armistice with the Allies. The armistice, with its terms dictated by the Soviets, provided for Hungarian withdrawal to Trianon-drawn frontiers, payment of war reparations and supervision by the Inter-Allied Control Commission, which in practice meant them of course. Then the provisional government turned its attention to domestic matters. On March 17, 1945, it promulgated the historical land distribution decree, which immediately reduced the percentage of peasants either landless or owning less than one acre from 46% to 17%. Given obvious personnel constraints, bureaucrats could not be retired wholesale, but politically reliable people were put in charge at least of all institutions. Twenty-five right-wing parties and organizations were proscribed, anti-Jewish laws were repealed, a list of war criminals was put into circulation, and summary proceedings against those caught were initiated in the so-called people's courts staffed by appointees of the coalition parties. So far, so good.

The word is not often used, but all this added up to quite a revolution. A very significant equalization of all sorts occurred, and the whole country was also dragged, presumably not stillborn, from a condition of putrefying feudalism into some semblance of modernity. On the one hand, the upper classes were dispossessed and disabled. The gentry, that is, the lower nobility, had long been the leading social group in Hungarian politics and society, with its position resting on its ownership of land and on the labor and rents of the peasants on its estates. Well, the land reform pretty much eliminated *them* as a class. At the same time, many other members of the power hierarchy also lost their positions on account of their connections with discredited regimes and policies or even personal involvement in what now were considered grave crimes. On the other hand, for the first time the lower classes began to share power with their so-called betters. For not only did the land reform turn landless peasants into a new propertied class, not only did two of the five political parties in the coalition espouse the democratic and economic rights of working people, but 32% of the delegates to the Provisional National Assembly as originally constituted were actually smallholders and agricultural workers, and 23% were industrial workers. Several months later, when representation in the Assembly was extended to the entire country, these numbers adjusted to a still almost world-turned-upside-down 23% and 27%.

Few people argued with these changes. Nor could any of them be justly put on the Communists' and socialists' tab, for all the changes had true popular support. Indeed, they were long overdue and they were progressive social adjustments, if not always administered in the least punishing manner. In the aftermath of the war there was general enthusiasm almost everywhere in Europe for left-wing programs, and even for movement upward from the bottom of society to the extent that could be achieved by reforms in the educational system. But in part at least, this *was* radical stuff. Men with dirt under their fingernails in Parliament? Ancestral estates taken without compensation? Granted that a war to the nth degree had just shattered the country, and there would never be a better time for serious reform, still, no country in Western Europe had ever done such things or remade itself so. So the new arrangements were radical, but also so fair that, unless you were one of the dispossessed, you just couldn't help being enthusiastic about them. In addition, this was also not an attempt to approximate some ideal, to be repeated whenever the strong fancied a repetition, but a one-shot practical move rather, a necessary and opportune fix, something like what financial pundits call a correction in the stock market. In other words, this was not an attack on the rules that made the world go round or the givens of human nature, but a therapeutic effort merely to adjust society in ways that would in the future allow those well-known rules and those givens to operate more smoothly.

Despite these measures, though, you could not deny that life in Hungary after the war was a nigh-hopeless struggle. Still, there were those, for once Leslie and Rose among them, for whom what turned out to be three years of quasi-democracy quickly became a gone-before-you-can-grab-it golden age. When Leslie returned to Budapest in his Red Army uniform, he had nothing but the sidearm in its holster, his claim to a few sticks of furniture and his ambitions. He had first come to the capital in 1938, if you recall, with the intention of turning his shoemaker's skills into some kind of business. That's what enterprising shoemakers did in that time and place, and that's what his own father had done already some years before in a provincial city, setting up a small workshop fronted by a room where customers could sit down and stick out their unshod feet, taking in apprentices and making shoes and boots for local retail at a time when production in that trade for wholesale was probably still unknown. Of course, all by itself going up to Budapest showed that Leslie had bigger dreams, or it showed that he was at least willing to chance being trampled down into the urban proletariat. In any case, antisemitism and the war had kept his ambitions in check for a while. But then he returned a survivor and a victor to a country where soon his legal disabilities would be lifted, and now he also had important connections.

As I've said, once more the family moved into the modest apartment the couple had occupied from before the time Leslie had been called up. And then as soon as the arts of war surrendered the stage to the battles of peace, he began, I would think, to see about starting a business. I don't know how small he opened or how rapidly he expanded, and I don't know when he first realized that it was a whole factory from nothing he was conjuring up and running and owning. I can only imagine him rushing about town in a state of determined excitement, large feet taking giant strides, fingers wagging at people as he hectored them and brought them around with energy where others might have used charm. Where did the capital come from, what licenses did he have to buy with what favors owed him, how did he find a suitable premises in that down-to-the-bones city, who were his suppliers, who would be his customers? I don't know. But however he did it, everything worked. The business boomed. He was a success and we prospered. Marika arrived in 1946, Rose was a full-time mother and housewife, and in 1948 we moved to the larger, more modern, more centrally located cooperative apartment with the maid's room where I grew up and where I acquired my first memories. The Jewish shoemaker from the country-town was moving up in the world. Just as he had set out to do, for being a businessman and competing for and winning at money and status, and having a family of course, had been pretty much all he had ever wanted from life.

But I'm getting ahead of my story here, the realization of Stalin's war-consequences dictum, that is. The Communists' leader throughout these years was Mátyás Rákosi, by 1945 a veteran of several decades of subversive activity. In 1919, at age 27, Rákosi was already enough of a figure in the Hungarian movement to become a member of the governing body of the revolutionary Soviet Republic and upon its liquidation to be interned with the other leaders. Released in 1920, he was ordered by Béla Kun, the Party's leader, to travel to Moscow under a false identity and report to Lenin. So, already as a young man, the Hungarian Jew managed to reach the very nerve-center of the Communist world-colossus, where he fit in perfectly. At once he became embroiled in the factionalism splitting the exiled Hungarian comrades and also began working for the Comintern, the organization formed by Lenin to direct the forces of the international movement. He went on clandestine missions to Western Europe, succeeding in some, failing in others, but reliably ruthless in all. Then in late 1924, just when his young reputation and support in Moscow were at a low point, he arranged to be sent back home to build the party there. As you can see, he was very ambitious and always gave a hundred percent.

Still, his ascent to the top, very much like Stalin's at the very same time, was not a foregone conclusion.

In Budapest, the authorities watched Rákosi for eight months then picked him up. Under interrogation, he let his ego get the better of him. Not even out of fear but just to show how much of an insider he was, he betrayed some secrets. This blabber-mouth performance was bound to have consequences, and indeed the Comintern secretary in Moscow soon recommended his expulsion from the Bolshevik Party. But Kun took his side, and then for a while his fate was actually up in the air, until finally Stalin stepped in. And the Man of Steel not only let Rákosi off without any disciplinary action, but even rewarded him, as it were, by casting him in a starring role in a grand Communist production that was to play on the world stage. The Hungarian authorities were about to prosecute fifty or so Communists for the red terror of 1919, and Stalin designated Rákosi as the defendants' leader and chief spokesman. This was not only an honor but also an opportunity, and Rákosi had the nerve and the brains to make the most of it. He played his part extremely well. In his memoirs he boasts that he and his comrades turned the courtroom into a "party tribunal." He got eight-and-a-half years.

By 1934, Rákosi had served his sentence. But before he was released, new charges were brought. There is reason to believe that the Comintern itself provoked the new trial, itching as it must have been to stage another international Communist show, but the evidence is not conclusive. In any case, Rákosi is reported to have turned ashen when a newly-arrived prisoner revealed the supposed plans to him, but then he quickly recovered and declared himself ready for the further sacrifice. And in court he performed even more brilliantly than the first time. Of course, the prosecution demanded the death penalty, but he got off with life behind bars. And now he was a hero and a champion! His supporters organized international protests. His reputation soared. He was elected to the Comintern's Executive Committee, the first man behind bars to receive that honor. If ever he would be free, he would surely play a leading role in the Hungarian movement.

But don't feel sorry for Rákosi. During the late 30s, jail at home was a haven for a Hungarian Communist. In Moscow and Leningrad and at the outposts of the Gulag, as the system of penal colonies and forced labor camps came to be known after the acronym for the name of the agency administering it, with a gulag being a specific unit of the system – throughout the Soviet Union, now under Stalin's personal rule, many of Rákosi's comrades, including Kun, perished in the two years of merciless purges known as the Great Terror. But of course, Rákosi himself did not see things that way. And he wondered why he was not among the prisoners being exchanged from time to time. Finally, and again, it was Stalin who came to his rescue. In 1849, in General Bem's time, when the czarist forces vanquished the Hungarian army, they also captured 58 regimental flags. Ever after, the Magyars yearned to recover these national symbols and to cleanse the nation's much-defiled honor of at least this one expugnable stain. Having now all of the Russian past to do with as he would, in 1940 Stalin arranged an exchange: Rákosi for the flags. And by then it was again safe for a loyal Communist to be in Moscow.

So this was the man who in late 1944 returned from Moscow. The task ahead of him was to be lengthy. He and the other Hungarian exiles in Moscow had intended to grab the reins in Budapest at once, as their predecessors had done in 1919, but Stalin had decreed a period of transition, to last maybe as long as 10-15 years. To him it seemed ill-advised to foist this mostly Jewish group of Communists on a nation so deeply antisemitic. Why confirm everyone's most obvious prejudice against the Bolsheviks? In addition, the task ahead was also delicate, for Rákosi had to slip the totalitarian straitjacket on the country nice and gentle, without arousing undue resistance, doing it so that the Hungarian people will have seemed to have walked into it voluntarily, with arms willingly extended, so that as many people as possible at home and abroad would believe that here indeed democracy had triumphed. The Communists were not concerned about a civil war here, not with the Red Army presence that was sure to become a structural element of national life. But an official narrative of righteous and justified advance to power and total control was essential. In other words, Rákosi had to get himself and the Communists *elected* into office. And that was going to be a trick worthy of a great illusionist, a kind of reverse Houdini, donning handcuffs and leg-irons, climbing *into* sealed caskets and all. Surely, this was going to be the most demanding and remarkable of all his performances.

But certain things couldn't wait. Already at the time of formation of the provisional government, the Communists made sure that public agencies of force would be under their control. This meant the Ministries of the Interior and of Defense, and no less importantly the ÁVO, the new secret police. Formation of this last actually commenced in Debrecen during the last days of 1944 and was the work of the Communists alone, without in this case participation by or consultation with any of the other parties. So the ÁVO was modeled strictly on the NKVD, as the Soviet secret police was known in those days, operated according to the procedures and methods of the prototype organization, and reported throughout its existence not to Interior or any other branch of the government but only to the Party itself. The Communists also did not delay in introducing their strategy of choice for culling their rivals and enemies: you identify them as fascists and fascist sympathizers, then hunt them down and eliminate them. Of course that sounds all right, and even sensible and smart, and so it was in some instances. But from the first the Communists used the damning words in an Orwellian manner, and so they accused even people who had been engaged in wartime resistance to the Germans, independent-minded clergymen, and members of pre-war and wartime youth organizations of all political persuasions. Such people were usually arrested on trumped-up charges, then tortured, and then convicted of fascist conspiracies on the basis of manufactured evidence. During 1945 and '46 alone as many as perhaps 200,000 such people and others similarly innocent were deported to labor camps in the Soviet Union. In a less brutal application of the strategy, in 1946 László Rajk, Minister of the Interior, also accused 1,500 civic associations of harboring fascists and therefore banned them, associations like sports clubs, Christian trade unions and professional organizations and guilds. So the Communist terror came to Hungary right in the tracks of the Russian tanks.

It was in the prevailing spirit of forced delay and false pretenses that the Communists prepared for the elections of 1945, their first trial at the polls. Their chances actually looked good, very good. After all, the land reform they claimed for their own, the franchise had just been extended to everyone over the age of 20, men and women, with no property or educational qualifications, and at their own insistence voting was to be by party slates rather than individual candidates. This last advantage, the product of a little unfair maneuvering, was obviously not textbook democracy, but Rákosi couldn't deny himself that much leeway. Hey, if you want power, you have to fight for it. The turnout in November was a remarkably high 92%, but even so for the Communists the results were disastrous. In contrast to their paltry 17%, the Smallholders got 57% of the votes and could obviously have formed a government all by themselves. Luckily, the Soviets, experts since Menshevik days in making the most of minority positions, were there to rescue their comrades by calling for a "grand coalition," which Zoltán Tildy, the Smallholders' leader, reluctantly seconded. A little delay was okay, Tildy decided. Soon a peace settlement would supersede the armistice, and then the Red Army would be sent packing and the people's will would finally prevail. So despite the clear message of the balloting, the new government included the unloved Social Democrats and Communists, with the latter retaining control of the institutions of force. The Assembly elected Tildy president, and the position of prime minister went to the Smallholders' number-two man, Ferenc Nagy.

It was at this disappointing and embarrassing juncture that Rákosi instituted his "salami tactics," as he referred later on, when no longer compelled to dissemble, to the process of defeating the non-Communist parties by "cutting them off like slices of salami." The technique, utterly disingenuous although not outside the bounds of legitimacy, was a political refinement of the strategy of choice and worked like this: by portraying a rival party as a safe haven for fascists (or at least sympathetic to fascists), the Communists were able to get it to slice off its right wing, then after further accusations of reactionary tendencies to disown its centrists and so on. In the first application of this stratagem, the Communists combined with the Social Democrats and the Peasant Party to form the Left-Wing Bloc and immediately called on the Smallholders and the other coalition partners to be more vigilant and militant about fascist remnants in their midst. Not wanting openly to confront a group supported by the Soviet Union, the Smallholders complied, expelling some of their own members from the Assembly for being "reactionary" and dismissing about 60,000 administrative personnel on the same grounds. That was a good slice, or maybe a good two slices. Attracting more voters is one way to win an election. Hobbling the opposition before the voting even begins, crippling, maiming and generally decimating them is another, as Rákosi was going to demonstrate.

It was not easy back then and there to follow political developments, but whatever you did hear tended to raise alarms. All this violence and threats and maneuverings! You know what the Bolsheviks are like! And let's not forget that the Soviets want to rule the whole world! But what can a poor conquered nation do? How can it defend itself? Liberal elements now began to voice serious concerns: repeatedly the Communists are making a mockery of pluralism, everything is moving in an anti-democratic direction, a new era of occupation is upon us. May it last no longer than the 150-year visit by the Ottomans! And all this was more worrisome yet because of the hardships of daily life. During 1945-46 hundreds of thousands of people were starving, freezing and hiding from looting Soviet troops. The country's war reparations obligations were astronomical, the economy was a burned-out wreck, agricultural production had practically ceased, and the hyperinflation of 1946, triggered mostly by the reparations payments, the newly-floating currency and the threat of the nationalization of industrial property, was the worst ever recorded in the history of the world. Yes, the world. Just look at this ruin of a country! It's a breeding-ground for extremism, that's what it is!

Later in the year and in early 1947, in response to a dangerous development Rákosi had to get more aggressive. Briefly he even had to drop the pretense of fair play. There was a new number-three man in the Smallholders Party, a member of parliament who did not hold national office like Tildy and Ferenc Nagy did, but who did want to stand up to the Communists. The sooner, he believed, the better. Seeing that things could get out of hand if this were allowed to continue, Rákosi struck first, and he struck hard. The Communists accused the man of participation in an "anti-republican conspiracy," offering as evidence a pack of lies gathered by beatings and blackmail. The man responded by asserting legislative immunity. The Communists then moved to waive the immunity, but the Assembly balked. For a moment it was open conflict. But the Communists quickly defused the situation and ate their cake too by having the Soviets arrest the man on charges of anti-Soviet treason and ship him to the Soviet Union. In protest, about fifty Smallholder delegates quit the party and formed a separate organization. So the bare-faced aggression paid off handsomely. Now they themselves are slicing the salami, Rákosi must have chuckled.

In February 1947, finally, Hungary signed the Paris Peace Treaty. But for those who had hoped for relief from the Communists' trashing of the rules of a pluralist society, it was a huge disappointment. For the treaty just affirmed the terms of the armistice. Borders were pushed back to the 1938 lines, so once again it was the bitterness of Trianon, although now people seemed more ready to accept even that. The country's relationship with the Allies was also formally defined and full sovereignty regained, so on paper at least the nation was released from parole. But not in fact. The Soviet garrison of many tens of thousands of troops stayed put and showed no intention of ever departing. The Soviets claimed to need a land-link with Austria, you see, which was in part under their postwar control, and there was no one to deny it to them. In effect, Hungary seemed to have become a vassal state, going right back to jail, and this time on an apparent life sentence. The liberation and the daring democratic hopes had turned into another national catastrophe, not just the end of the war but also the dawn of a new national servitude, tinted blood-red by the bright future ahead for the Communists. So could Rákosi abandon subterfuge now? No, not yet. Maintaining a semblance at least of legitimacy and courting popularity by means, for example, of antisemitic and anti-black-market, that is, anti-private-business, diatribes would remain part of his mission as long as he ruled.

Nevertheless, by mid-1947 the Communists' intentions could really not be mistaken. Now they were proceeding on several fronts. Political pressures reminiscent of the early Nazi days continued as Rákosi's veiled threats against Ferenc Nagy's family forced him to emigrate at the end of May. The state, that is, the Communist, takeover of intellectual life began around this time too, although it achieved its goals only a couple of years later. Non-Communist newspapers, magazines and publishing houses were closed down or taken over by the reds. And it was an ill wind that blew from the East. The Sovietization of education had started already in 1946 with new left-leaning school syllabuses. The Church objected to this and then to other innovations too, especially the new textbooks and the nationalization of the publishing companies that printed them, but it just could not beat back the Communist incursions into its immemorial sphere of influence. The drift left towards totalitarianism could not be denied anymore. But again, what could you possibly do?

Rákosi now forced another election. Obviously, he had to keep testing the waters, that is, the voters, but I wonder if he really wanted to. In any case, the date was set for late August 1947. In preparation, the Communists did what they dared to improve their chances, and by then they dared a lot. First, they compelled the Assembly to disfranchise about 10% of the electorate on pretexts like being of German descent or having held an official position under Horthy. And then they forced through the legalization of an absentee-ballots procedure that prepared the stage for the electoral fraud they were plotting. But still, they were again disappointed and embarrassed. They received 22% of the votes, more indeed than the 17% of two years earlier, but even together with the Social Democrats and the Peasant Party their share was still only 45%. What really hurt, though, was that the sliced-way-down Smallholders and its successor parties still received 52%. And had there been no fraud, that number would probably have been as high as 60%. The much-repeated claim to be representing the masses and the popular will was sounding ever more hollow. How could someone as smart as Rákosi so miscalculate? Twice now in two years, a preponderant majority of Hungarians had cast its ballots in favor of private property and a multi-party democracy, that is, against the Communist program. Obviously, the terror still had much to accomplish.

Sometime during these unsettled years Leslie also joined the Party. I learned of this only a decade later, in Vienna around New Year's 1957, while we were waiting for visas to immigrate to the United States. On a few occasions, as he was sitting glum and defeated in a frayed armchair in our refugee hotel room, I heard him mutter his concern about the American authorities finding out that he had been a party member. I even remember that among the personal documents he had carried across the frontier was his canceled membership book, with the word CAPITALIST stamped in black across his photo and name, I used to imagine, as it must have been not a minute after he was so designated in May 1949. A strange document to take along, don't you think? Maybe he slipped it into a pocket as just another easily portable piece of the life he was about to leave, but more likely as something that might have helped us if the whole escapade failed. In any case, that membership book, far though it had gone already, never reached America. Somewhere along the transcontinental trek he must have ditched it, double-edged badge of shame that it was. At some point he must have come to his senses.

Had the American authorities in Vienna known, whether by his own admission or otherwise, and in the unlikely event that things had gone that far nevertheless, the immigration agent might well have asked him why he had joined. Well, just trying to be a good businessman. Somebody had put the idea in his head, and that's also where his friends were, the Jews, that is, although there were also many Jews who in fact did not support the Communists and voted for Smallholder candidates. But didn't

he know that the Communists were against the private ownership of factories? How could he not? The propaganda war against such things had
started promptly in 1945. So then he had to be in a state of denial, as
they say? No, not in denial, I would say, for Leslie understood his own
predicament very well I think. He understood that the thing that mattered to him the most in life, that is, his success, his new status, his factory – sooner or later that thing would also make him a marked man. For
the Communists were bound to take control, and then sooner or later he
would be expropriated and persecuted. But however he understood the
historical situation, he was trapped, for walking away from the factory was
something he could not do. He would not choose his own ruination just
to forestall the Communists' bringing it down on him. Rather, he would
just carry on and hope to salvage something when the inevitable became
fact. And I ask you, could anyone have done otherwise? Escape from
likely misery by jumping into the actual thing with both feet? No, no one.

As for joining the Party, that, depending on its timing, may have been
either insurance, what you might call takeover coverage, or an act of desperation. Yes, Leslie was just an opportunist, one of those people you
find at every change of regime or system who accommodate and start
out at least just paying lip service, hoping it will be mistaken for paying
obeisance. And then later on we'll see, some might also think, although
it's obvious that for Leslie conversion was not a possibility at any point
down the road. For never could he have come to believe in the principles of communism, in dialectical materialism, the class struggle, etcetera. He would always believe only in Elohim and in business. Always a
crypto-capitalist at least. So becoming a card-carrying member, to use
an American term of emphasis, was actually absurd, exactly the kind of
absurd you find a lot of in the fiction written in the satellites. In any case,
he signed on, for this was his way of dealing with Communism, and like
most of the Jews in Germany and points east in the 30s, he took comfort
in a hundred reasons why things were in fact going to be all right, a hundred scenarios more optimistic than the most dire and the most likely.
I think that from the perspective of those times what he did and what

Rose did, for I assume she went along with the Communist sham, made good enough sense. And when the time came, they would just have to improvise, to fake it, to get by somehow. After all, it had worked with the fascists, who had first taught them about persecution. They were going to try to avoid the fate of the system's enemies without actually becoming the system's friends.

Fortunately for Rákosi, 1947 was also the year when the Cold War first began to grip the world in earnest. Truman finally recognized the accuracy of Churchill's Iron Curtain figure of speech of March 1946, accepted the diagnosis of international relations underlying George Kennan's containment doctrine, and in March put a new foreign policy in place. He terminated American treatment of the Soviet Union as an ally, announced American preparedness to assist any nation threatened by external aggression and instituted the Marshall Plan. Of course, Stalin saw this as a threat to Soviet domination in Eastern Europe and responded in kind. Never mind the oil-and-water reaction he anticipated from the gentile Magyars to the Jewish Communists. Among other counter-measures, at a September conference of European Communist parties held in Poland, delegates from the countries occupied by the Red Army were ordered to speed up and promptly complete Communist takeovers at home.

So finally Rákosi was liberated from one constraint at least. That must have been a relief, since impersonating a democratically-minded statesman did not come to him naturally. But though he had been ordered to act boldly, forcefully and expeditiously, his performance was not yet over. As I've said, it never would be, for until the end the Communists had to keep on trying to convince the masses that Communist rule rested on a real majority. What did come naturally to Rákosi was making people do by force what they would not willingly. And so on the economic front he now put both industry and agriculture on a Communist crash-course. I've already told you about the nationalizations of industrial property that began in 1946, progressed through the next two years and reached a bitter culmination in 1948 and '49. The plan to fully collectivize agriculture was also made public in February 1948. These now were unpopular policies. But Rákosi did not hesitate, indeed, could not have even if he had wanted to. So unashamedly he put ideology above electoral senti-ment here. Although it's hard to resist the impression that always his most fundamental motivation proceeded from his insatiable will to power.

In June 1948, a new political consolidation began. A storm of violence and scheming and whatever else could throw the greatest fear into your rivals. As the first step, and following the traditional order in such mat-ters, the Communists launched a savage assault on the Social Democrats. They started by eliminating their left-wing rival's leaders, throwing some key figures in prison, intimidating and ousting others, and convincing still others to emigrate. Then they easily forced the remaining higher-ups, now all appropriately terrified, to merge their organization into the Communist Party, with Rákosi as first secretary. As window dressing they even adopted a new name, the Hungarian Workers' Party. The new par-ty's manifesto proclaimed a Marxist-Leninist ideology and the goals of rapidly building a socialist system and removing all remaining reaction-ary elements. Without doubt, if there was to be socialism in Hungary, and there surely was, it would be on Communist terms, which for the time being at least meant Stalinist. As for the other parties in the coalition, the Communists neutralized or eliminated all of them too, liquidated was the word they preferred, by the end of the year. One party was sum-marily banned by the Communist Minister of the Interior. After this, another one simply withdrew. When their turn came, the Smallholders had to accept a new leader who was easily manipulated, and then Tildy was disposed of by house arrest and false charges of espionage brought against his son-in-law. A coalition was still in place of course and the gov-ernment was still pluralist, but now only in name. In reality, 1948 was the decisive year of change, and it ended without any resistance and with the Communists in unhampered control.

Winning an election had now become an entirely different proposi-tion. Rákosi was now free to falsify appearances however he wished, and surely no one was going to object. If you have no actual opponents, you can legitimize any offense or absurdity. So it was time to legalize the new situation. To begin with, in February 1949 the Communists formed the Hungarian Independence Popular Front, which united whatever political factions remained under their leadership. Then in the spring, in anticipation of the voting scheduled to take place in May for what would actually be a one-party Assembly, Popular Front committees were set up throughout the country to publicize and demonstrate the *voluntary* unity overarching the multi-party political arrangement. You have to wonder what people really thought about all this. At the polling places, the voters were presented with a single slate of Popular Front candidates, who were all, every single one of them, nominated by the Communists. You could vote for the slate or not. There was no other choice. According to the official reports, 96.04% of those eligible turned out, and 96.27% of those who cast ballots voted for the slate. Maybe so, maybe not. The government subsequently formed was all Communists but for a few Popular Front fellow travelers.

In August the Assembly took the last step required to formalize the new arrangement by approving a new constitution modeled on the one promulgated in the USSR in 1936. The document created the People's Republic of Hungary, which it proudly declared to be "a state of the proletariat and working peasants," a state in which "all power belongs to the working people," a state in which "the working people progressively drives out the capitalist elements and systematically builds a socialist economy," a state that "under the leadership of our working class, steeled by decades of struggle, fortified by the experiences of the socialist revolution of 1919, [and] with the support of the Soviet Union... is advancing towards socialism along the path of popular democracy." The pictures of the founding fathers, Marx, Engels, Lenin, Stalin, now appeared everywhere, and next to them Rákosi, short, fat and bald, a little torpedo of a man, with a face rendered inexpressive by jowls and heavy features. He was a constant presence in my childhood, for he aspired to be the personal embodiment of the nation and made sure that by dint of the metonymy of his picture he presided in every public place and over every public occasion. At all times, that image reminded us of the class struggle and the dedication to prevailing in it that gave meaning to our lives, that united us, or in the case of the Hajdus stigmatized us as aliens.

It was a great victory for the Communists, a fulfillment of the laws of history, a source of powerful national myths, a singular achievement for Hungarian workers and peasants. Long live totalitarianism!? Well, that is at least how they marketed it to the public, friendly and hostile, domestic and foreign. So did Rákosi accomplish what he had set out to do? Certainly, even if here and there a few arms had to be twisted, there had been and was nothing you can characterize as resistance. And of course Stalin had been proven right in his reading of postwar arrangements. As he had made sure he would be. Percentage deals were for suckers. But the credit for the Communist success goes not so much to Rákosi and his displays of political illusionism, but to the massive Red Army garrison in the country, the secret police rampaging and spreading fear, the flow of information to the public valved off always more effectively. Still, it had all been damn clever and most of the procedures had been made to look proper, even if, nauseatingly, the stink of coercion pervaded everything. Communists and the few other admirers of Stalin swallowed the official story, but everyone else choked on it. In other words, Rákosi's charade fooled very few who were not fooled already before he ever stepped out on the stage, while unfriendly eyes saw here only a long-expected bloodless coup, a grab by the Soviets and the Communists, and a major historical tragedy for the country and its people.

Communism is usually considered an enemy of religions, but it is more illuminating to think of it as actually a religion itself and a rival to all other religions. The secular position of religious institutions, their economic and political power, accounts for a good bit of the rivalry. But that was not all. There was a struggle also for your mind and your soul as an individual, for your unquestioning allegiance. So wherever they could, at the earliest date the Communists launched their attack on other religions and also began aggressively to promote their own ideology, inspire *faith* in it and win converts to it.

In Hungary the Communists established control of almost all schools in 1949 and quickly demoted religious instruction from a compulsory subject to an optional one. But they knew better than just to padlock the churches and outlaw traditional worship. Rather, they set out first to weaken the institutions and destroy the personnel that had long been the dispensers of the opium of the masses. And so, they scrapped some religious holidays and re-characterized others, turning Christmas Eve into the Pine Tree Festival and the saint's day of Stephen, the first Christian king of the Magyars, into Constitution Day. They abolished some monastic orders and demanded that the Catholic and Lutheran episcopate swear oaths of loyalty to the new constitution. Some of those who refused, including Cardinal Mindszenty, they imprisoned on trumped-up charges, which convinced many others to knuckle under. Finally, they established a State Office for Ecclesiastical Affairs to be the *overseer* of all religious activities. For a lot of people, all this added up to more than enough discouragement even with regard to something as central to identity as religious beliefs. In 1951 43% of students in primary schools still opted for religious instruction, but the next year that number dropped to only 26%. In secondary schools, with a more select and ambitious student body, the proportion was only 10.5% already in 1951. There are no figures I know of for church or synagogue attendance, but that declined too I'm sure.

I myself received religious instruction in school only in the first grade in 1948-49. I don't recall anything at all I might have learned, with only the feeling of exclusion remaining with me as the rabbi led the other Jewish boy and myself to an empty classroom, and the gnawing curiosity about what secrets revealed to my Christian classmates by a priest were being kept from *me*. I don't know whether or not Leslie went to Friday evening services prior to the takeover, but he certainly did not afterwards. Only his daily evening prayers, twenty minutes or so every day, twenty-five on Fridays, standing in a corner, prayer book in hand, unaware of the world about him – with only that did he continue. And during the Communist years, if the doorbell rang while he was at it, he just, as it were, finished the sentence, then snatched the yarmulke off his head and jumped to put the worn leather-bound book in a drawer, spoiling his dignified inner focus with a scrambled fury.

As I passed from age six to age seven and eight and so on, I watched our celebrations of the main Jewish holidays gutter out. First the Passover Seder was an elaborate affair, although never of the inordinate length, complexity and apparent pedantry, and also what the devout characterize as joyousness, that I was to suffer through later at the home of an otherwise fondly-remembered Orthodox uncle in the Bronx. But then the Seder was stripped down, and finally scrapped entirely. Chanukah candles disappeared in 1949, the year after I had asked for and received a box of colored pencils as my only ever Chanukah present, a precious possession I used sparingly and lovingly throughout the lower grades when copying maps into my notebook as part of my geography homework. I also remember being on stage in the traditional Purim play of Esther and Mordecai, but only once at a very tender age. And by age ten I was even excused from attending synagogue on the major fall holidays, the only occasion when Leslie and Rose would don the last remnants of their now-never-worn bourgeois finest, all other articles of the kind having already been sold, and, with prayer books tucked under their arms, try to pass through the neighborhood unnoticed in the early twilight.

And then one day, without the subject ever having been broached, I was told that I would have to start preparations for my Bar Mitzvah. In 1955, after the New Course dialed down a bit the risks of religious practice, you actually dared to do this. Although for Rose and Leslie the traditional celebration was still a nearly unmanageable rite of passage. True, the necessary institutions still existed and the Hajdus were not strangers to them either. But there were daunting financial demands – the rabbi's fee, a special outfit for the celebrant (Rose herself could probably make an old dress into a new one for Marika), the coffee that had at the least to be offered the guests after the service, maybe even a donation to the synagogue itself. And personal problems were also dogging the *joint* undertaking. So many details to be discussed, such a complicated affair, your only son, your firstborn's Bar Mitzvah! And with Leslie just about to relocate to Makó! But if they could not do this together, then how? So some kind of division of labor with a veto always a possibility had to be worked out, although in effect even then, as theoretically at least I stood on the threshold of manhood, he must have surrendered me to my *mater*. But despite all that, the show went on. It had to. After all, it pretty much came down to being Jewish or not. And *that* we definitely were.

After the high holy days in September, I began my lessons with the rabbi. He resided in a parsonage of sorts, a three-room house next to the synagogue, which was no more than a twenty-minute walk from home. The synagogue building was intact, miraculously I think, just the way it is today, as I saw on a recent visit to Budapest. It stands now just as it had back then, with the large stars of David still providing the masonry inner framework for the circular stained-glass windows, although after an ultra-Hungarian transformation it now serves as a fencing hall for members of the armed forces. I wonder if it was ever deconsecrated or, to spare a syllable, just simply desecrated. The rabbi gave lessons in one of the parsonage rooms, which was furnished with a large table and chairs, heavy blue tomes stamped with the reverse-runes of Hebrew, and daylight-damping drapes. In retrospect I can't even estimate his age, but I suspect that he was getting on in years. He was the first person I ever met who had the to me unappealing habit common to religious Jewish men I believe, kind of an equivalent to clearing your throat or absent-mindedly cracking your knuckles, of briefly pushing back your black hat on your skull, scratching your stubbled scalp, in his case graying and stubbled, and then pushing the hat forward again into place. In the tense monotony of the lessons I used to wait for this gesture, but though I wanted to, I could not spare enough attention to keep count of its recurrences.

This man and I had no rapport whatsoever, largely because he wanted none I believe. He must always have had Bar-Mitzvah students, by which I mean Jewish boys with no religious education, only the need to be taught in one gulp, as it were, just enough to get through the big morning's ritual, and he may always have had a distaste for the type. Although in pre-war Budapest Jews like that were surely not bad customers, and even if they didn't know the difference between the Torah and the Talmud, they still had respect for a man of God who reminded them of their grandfathers and didn't eat *treyf*. But after the devastations of the Holocaust and the Communists' programmatic sallies against religion? As I draw near the man in my memories, the curse of the survivor upon him, I feel for him and imagine his bitter musings about me. Just look at him! There he sits across the table, twice a week, dutiful like a child born into servitude but swaddled in ignorance and apathy. Just another omen, the future, or perhaps non-future, of all that really matters. What, oh, Lord, have we done to deserve *this* punishment?

At our first meeting (arrangements having been made, I went by myself), he explained my crossing-the-desert-in-a-rowboat task to me. I had to learn to read out loud a passage from the Haftarah, which is a series of selections from the Hebrew Bible. Memorizing such a text was neither permitted nor practicable. So I had to acquire a low-level proficiency in reading Hebrew characters and learn to utter the passage with reasonable fluency. As with Leslie's praying, an understanding of the words was not required. For understanding is nothing without a feeling inside, although, I ask you, how can you get the feeling without some understanding? In any case, the rabbi must have known from experience that I would not have been able to keep my focus without the aid of a translation and without some idea of what I was saying, so as we went along, and then repeatedly as I practiced, he supplemented his own Hebrew utterances with their Hungarian equivalent. Frankly, that didn't help much. But I can still remember enough of the passage to locate it now in the King James Version. It was all or some of the middle portion of chapter 6 of the First Book of Kings, definitely verses 11-22. It describes the building of the house of the Lord on the orders of King Solomon, the First Temple, that is, and more particularly, the materials – cedar and fir – of which the temple was constructed, the size of the structure and its parts, and how the whole house was "overlaid" with gold. Behold, the sanctuary of my ancestors, which meant absolutely nothing to me!

But when I started going to school, and even before Judaism was as it were taken away from me, another religion also demanded my attention. And when I call communism a religion, I am not just speaking metaphorically, for a religion is what that system of ideas and beliefs was understood to be from the very beginning. In 1847, when in London Engels was elected to the Communist League, that organization was looking for a pedagogical text for its members and recruits, something in the question-and-answer format commonly used in the Catholic Church to inculcate the articles of faith, something that can be regurgitated by rote. The task of preparing such a catechism was assigned to Engels, who promptly produced what he called a *Draft of a Communist Confession of Faith*. Obviously, the religious terminology seemed more appropriate than any other to the author. It was eliminated from the text only the next year, after Marx reworked Engels's second draft, incorporated his own theoretical ideas into it, and heeding a suggestion from Engels himself dropped the catechism format in favor of a manifesto. So that's how the religion connection began, and despite Engels's secularizing afterthought the religious appeal of the ideology never disappeared. It is probably no coincidence that Stalin and Mikoyan had been seminarists as young men, and other old Bolsheviks too came from devoutly religious backgrounds. And it was definitely not hyperbole for Nadezhda Mandelstam, a Russian writer, to recall in her memoirs that "[i]n the Twenties, a good many people drew a parallel [between communism and] the victory of Christianity and thought this new religion would last a thousand years."

Engels's foundational draft, as revised, appeared in 1848 as *The Communist Manifesto*, the joint work of Marx and Engels. Its first chapter begins with the biblical-sounding assertion that "the history of all hitherto existing societies is the history of class struggle," and then the pamphlet proceeds to review the actual struggles between pairs of contending classes witnessed by the centuries, right up to the authors' present, that is, 19th-century Europe, which it declares to be the setting for the final, Armageddon-like struggle, that between the bourgeoisie and the proletariat. Marx and Engels offer a compellingly accurate description of modern industrial society and a persuasive account of its origins too, all of which soon Marxists began to construe as a revelation of the laws of history, that is, of the way the world is by *necessity*, of the scheme of human fate, of the true God-less providence. To be fair, Marx himself always rejected this over-interpretation of his "historical sketch of the genesis of capitalism in Western Europe [into] a historic-philosophic theory," always objected to the religion-like element his followers saw there writ large. After his death, Engels recalled that on account of this divergence of views his mentor and co-patriarch had during the 1870s been in the habit of commenting that "all I know is that I am not a Marxist," which to me sounds very much like that other oft-made church-betrays-prophet observation that Christ was not a Christian. But then Marx died and his institution-building apostles prevailed, as apostles always do. And despite its founder's sentiments, communism became a secular religion, with sacred texts, articles of faith, high priests and acolytes, and all the usual trimmings.

The new religion's most fundamental principle was materialism. Marx derived it from something incontrovertible, as befits a fundamental principle, from what he considered the basic reality of the human condition, namely, that in order to survive human beings must secure for themselves the *material* requirements of their existence. So, as Adam and Eve found out, work is unavoidable, and in many places where men work a division of labor also quickly becomes a necessity. Such a division eventually creates classes, that is, it groups together individuals who in the process of production fill similar roles as each other and different roles than members of other groups. More specifically, to the process some individuals contribute the means of production they own, be it land, tools or special know-how, while others contribute nothing more than the sweat of their brow. And as the members of a class share with each other their economic roles, so quickly they also come to share their ways of dress and habits of thought and personal conduct and approach to life. In other words, workers will think alike and behave alike and see the world alike, as will landlords and peasants and the clergy, etcetera. In other words, you can recognize a slum-dweller in or out of a slum. This primacy and decisive influence of economic acts and relations makes them the basis of society, indeed the base on which human beings build a superstructure of "legal, political, religious, artistic [and] philosophic" conceptual systems. Or as Marx put it: "It is not men's consciousness that determines their existence, but, on the contrary, their existence in society that determines their consciousness." This understanding of human existence is materialism.

Of course, Marx did not invent materialism. In the Western world, the roots of that philosophy go back to the ancient Greek thinkers Democritus and Epicurus, who, surely not coincidentally, were the subjects of young Karl's own doctoral dissertation. But Marx did first bring the idea of the primacy of matter to the attention of non-intellectuals, and did also first display materialism in the marketplace of ideas as part of a worldview ready to slug it out with established religious beliefs. To many people the most upsetting thing about this upstart was of course its sidelining of God. Within the Marxian scheme of base and superstructure, God and gods ingloriously lumped together are but elements of an ideology and thus no more than mental constructs rising out of the material foundations. And Marx's attack on the supernatural did not proceed, as such attacks tend to, from the skepticism of the rationalist or the rebelliousness of the disgruntled. Marx did not question the validity of proofs of God's existence or reproach Him for this vale of tears. Rather, he just put God into the actuality of the world as he saw it. So now, just when Darwin was throwing his coming-out party for your simian relatives, which Marx applauded as a materialist bash, you had another reason too to forget about being made in the Creator's image and about the soul, your very own spark of immortality. You had to trade in those flattering illusions for the reality of a creature governed by physical needs and mired in self-aggrandizing fantasies. Materialism was strong medicine. If that had been all that communism offered, there would have been no Cold War, and maybe no World War II either. But that was just a beginning.

Judaism and Christianity, two of the old faiths from which communism, the new faith, had to charm away believers, are proudly historical religions. It is through history itself that the relationship between the Lord and the children of Israel becomes manifest, and it is after a historical genesis that Christianity passes through historical time, through all that preceded the present, and on to what is usually understood to be a historical fulfillment. And the third leading European faith of the 19th century, the secular faith of progress, which instead of ethnic or personal salvation could fill you only with the satisfaction that comes from participation in a universal destiny – progress was also intensely historical. Indeed it was nothing more than a one-directional superhighway urban-renewed right through the tangled paths and roads of history. So if communism were to thrive at least side by side with these rivals, it had to compete with them specifically, and again of course only in a secular way, by its take on the passing of time. Well, communism did what it had to. It outperformed both the grand narrative of Christianity and the idea of progress by offering, first, an account of the past rendered more compelling by details and, second, something its rivals couldn't, namely, a mechanism of change other than miracles. But, obviously, in all this of course communism enjoyed a great advantage, for it started out by claiming exclusive rights to the very *laws* of history.

Marx accomplished these feats by nothing less than a rewriting of the history of arguably all of humankind, by rethinking that history as a set of variations on the theme of materialism. The general scheme of Western history as that is understood today – antiquity, the Middle Ages and the modern world – was already in circulation by Marx's days. But back then that scheme was still just a patchwork, a rickety narrative undermined by immature conceptualization and shoddy construction. True, its messiness was in line with the inevitable messiness of human life itself, but in the 19th century that was not yet appreciated as a virtue. In any case, system-builders, and they were and are to be found everywhere, were now uneasy with that scheme as it was. To them it was an egregious case of apples-and-oranges to maintain that the ancient world was done in by the barbarian hordes, but the Middle Ages ended thanks to the revival of classical learning by Petrarch and an elite cast of Renaissance manuscript-hounds. But then along came Marx. And armed as he was with both Hegel's idea that history has a built-in logic and his own materialist philosophy, he could take the three eras of Western history, differentiate them from each other on the basis of their predominant modes of production and productive relations, and so wind up with a unified narrative of dramatic sweep. Now it all made sense, as you always knew it had to.

It all started, as Marx laid it out, with hunter-gatherers, who were still innocent of the institution of private property and of any form of authority too other than the family and the family-like, men and women whose mode of production he and Engels named primitive communism. After some time, with the adoption of agriculture, the settling down of people in villages and even cities and the appearance of a division of labor, this stage ended and ancient society came into being. Now for the first time material conditions were *forcing* humans into relations of production they would not have entered freely. In this particular case, the new kind of productive relationship was that of master and slave. Then at some later point, significant changes in the size of populations, the density of their settlements, the so-to-speak user-friendliness of their environments and their own productive and technological abilities once again created a new productive relationship, that of lord and serf, and provided the foundation for the political and social system Marx labeled feudalism. And finally, scientific and technological advances, an increase in trade and the accumulation of capital, and industrialization and urbanization brought into being yet one more productive relationship, that of capitalist and wage-earning worker. Of course, this latest re-shaping and reorganization of the economic base promptly remade society again, including political forms and practices, and remade it from top to bottom. The resulting world, Marx and Engels's own, they called capitalism. And then they rested. For that was it! History from soup to nuts!

But that was not all. For in addition to the overall scheme, Marxism also revealed the dialectical process through which one economic system and society metamorphoses into another. Dialectics, a method for resolving philosophical conflicts, was originated by the ancient Greek thinker Heraclitus, whose surviving writings most notably include the following two statements: "ever-newer waters flow on those who step into the same river" and "the paths up and down are one and the same." Through the centuries these words have been understood to mean, first, that everything is always in flux and, second, that the flux arises because everything is always rife with internal contradictions. During the early years of the 19th century, Hegel put these two ideas together and came up with his own dialectics and a view of existence as not eternal stability or just some kind of oscillation, but continual development rather. It now seems hard to believe that just two hundred years ago our ancestors did not think of the world as an aggregation of forever developing component parts, but they did not indeed until they encountered Hegel's process-based view. But then very quickly there was a profound shift in the way people saw the world. In retrospect, Engels described it this way: "The great basic thought that the world is not to be comprehended as a complex of ready-made things, but a complex of processes in which the things... go through an uninterrupted change of coming into being and passing away... has... so thoroughly permeated ordinary consciousness that, in its generality, it is now scarcely ever contradicted." Marx and Engels then took Hegelian dialectics, adapted it to their own materialist philosophy, and went on to formulate what they considered to be the general laws of processes in both the external world and in human thought. And then they used these laws to unconceal the workings of history in general, and of the succession of the societies created by the various modes of production in particular.

The basic unit of Marxian dialectics is thesis-antithesis-synthesis. This abstract formula fits, among many other things, the series of events in which an economic system (the thesis) matures to the point of its maximum efficiency, but in the process develops internal contradictions and resistances (the antithesis), causing the pro-and-con elements now to re-pel, now to clash, until finally they resolve into a new system (the syn-thesis). The transition from feudalism to capitalism provides a specific instance of this general pattern of change. Just when the feudal econom-ic system (the thesis) reached its most perfect state, the aristocratic class of lords found itself beset by two forces (the antithesis) that the system's success had itself created. On the one hand you had the serfs, who now demanded their freedom of movement, and on the other the rising com-mercial interests, which demanded a share of political power and social status. The lords resisted, but at some point they found that their antago-nists' economic power had already created a new system. For by then (the time of the synthesis), the formerly agrarian economy was turning into a more industrial one, serfs were becoming artisans and factory-workers, the nouveaux riches were infiltrating the political class and intermarry-ing with the aristocracy, laws designed to protect only landowners were giving way to those protecting the owners of other forms of capital too, and new political and social ideas about the sources of power, the place of the individual in society and other such things were replacing the old. In other words, the thesis and the antithesis had merged into a new and other thing. And the ultimate agent of transformation here was indeed the class struggle, as Marx and Engels had identified it in *The Communist Manifesto*.

This was all very important and interesting of course, but Communism's prophet and assistant prophet seemed instinctively aware that since a secular religion could not promise heaven, it had in order to succeed to promise heaven on earth. So after painting a Dickensian picture of the life of wage slaves under the capitalist system, and offering a compelling and profound explanation of the economic realities of the modern West, Marx and Engels, with the key to the future, that is, the laws of history, in hand, provided a communist version of the second coming. A triumphant conclusion! *Paradise regained.* They predicted that as an always greater portion of economic activity became mechanized or otherwise industri-alized, as the capitalists' power kept increasing, and as the workers' class consciousness kept sharpening, the class struggle would intensify. Then the revolution would burst upon the world, with the proletariat seizing control of the state and beginning to abolish private and institute common ownership of the means of production. Classes would disappear, and the class struggle with them, the producer and the consumer would become one, there would be an end to exploitation, laws and institutions as enforcers of the interests of the powerful would become unnecessary, and slowly the state would wither away. To paraphrase Bob Dylan, "there [would be] no kings inside the gates of Eden." The primitive communism of old will have returned in a more sophisticated and durable form, and as the resolution of age-old antagonisms and the dialectical synthesis of a millennia-long process of development. So would humanity be redeemed, promised the prophets of the communist faith, all the while urging you to prepare for this future and, for your own benefit and the benefit of all mankind, do all in your power to hasten its arrival.

Childhood is a good time, if not indeed the best time, to acquire religion. Saul Bellow has remarked that he had been a Jew committed to a serious practice of his faith already in his first consciousness, that is, his earliest childhood awareness of himself. Well, you already know about *my* first consciousness, and now also that as a boy I was exposed to two religions and rejected them both. In each case there were obvious reasons of course. Judaism was devalued in my eyes by the Communists attitude to it, and it was also not appropriately pressed upon me by my parents, who were prevented from doing so I suppose by the marital conflicts raging in the home, by their own ambivalence and more generally by post-Holocaust feelings and circumstances. Communism did appeal to me by preaching justice and equality, but then the actual behavior of Communists quickly spoiled the idyllic prospect and left me disillusioned. But these in a sense were hardly more than excuses, for in each case the rejection also had a more fundamental cause. The Jewish faith seemed too obscurely foreign and implausible to me, and as for communism… well, I could never believe that history operates according to laws, that the future can be a *predictable* outcome of the present. So more to the point was that in fact I have always lacked all religious urges and been deaf to the lure of the mystical, that I could never let belief in any faith nor the keeping of any kind of religious tradition define me. Even now that I do finally have my Hungarian Jewish identity, even now I have not changed in this respect. And so, I still have no faith and honor no tradition. Even with the benevolent influence of my whole family, for Barbara and my boys and daughter-in-law are all deeply spiritual people, I have been able to do no better than just abandon dogmatic materialism and admit the possible existence of a universal spirit of some sort.

But something *has* changed. When in preparation for the Bar Mitzvah I was studying my portion of the Haftarah, already then I knew of course what gold was, but cedar and fir meant nothing to me even in Hungarian, nor did the measurements, expressed as they were in units as strange as cubits. And actually, the whole passage I found not only puzzling but also inexpressibly boring and pointless. It touched nothing in me either mystical or musical, and those I think are the tendencies of a language most likely to appeal to a non-speaker, especially in case of a repeated uttering of syllables, which can turn even the most enchanting of sounds into barks of sheer nonsense. But now, when I read those words of First Kings in English, now my sense of wonder *is* set free, almost like it is when I read, as I never tire of doing, about the arts and crafts of Chartres or Amiens. As if those words had been chosen just for me. And, in particular, when the Lord says, "And I will dwell among the children of Israel, and will not forsake my people Israel," I am struck by a sense of majesty. Although even now I am not apprehending the divine, or feeling it to be hovering near. I am not humbled or rendered submissive or brought into the fold, baa, baa. It's just a flush of the aesthetic, that's all it is for me, no more than just the first fine careless rapture of poetry.

Stalin was Rákosi's senior by only thirteen years, but the two men were like father and son to each other. Or more like God and the Biblical patriarch actually, since routinely Stalin's acolytes called him a divine being, yes, the god Stalin. In addition to being at times Rákosi's savior, Stalin was also, right to the moment of his own death and beyond, Rákosi's mentor and sponsor, his ideal and idol. And Rákosi was Stalin's ardent disciple, eager to walk in his great teacher's footsteps, to *think* like Stalin and to *act* like Stalin. Stalin-fever infected Rákosi already during the 30s, but it was only in 1945 and especially after 1948 that he could begin actually to live out his enthusiasms. And to do so to his heart's content. With the takeover, new forms of emulation suddenly became possible, and Rákosi was ready to take advantage of them, to become the apostle of Stalinism to the Magyars. Stalin had many obedient pupils during the postwar years, but Rákosi was proud to be known as "Stalin's best pupil." And indeed, of all the leaders of the satellite countries, Rákosi became the most like the Soviet dictator, emulating him indiscriminately, without regard to whether or not emulation was sensible even from a Communist point of view. So in trying to understand Rákosi and appreciate his policies and leadership and governing style, it is indispensable to be familiar with the relevant aspects of his master's terrible career.

Stalinism may be said to have been an abhorrent method of government instituted by the Man of Steel and condemned ever after its eponym's death by all but a handful of like-minded murderers, like Saddam Hussein, for example. One of its elements was the so-called personality cult, which is what the Communists called the phenomenon of a leader making his own *self* rather than socialist progress the focus of political life. Although Stalin condemned this practice, he also showed himself its undisputed master. By a variety of means he induced his underlings to see him as "the incarnation of the very idea and dream of the new society," to quote Milovan Djilas, a Yugoslav Communist and imprisoned critic of the system, "as someone infallible and sinless,... as the victorious battle of today and the brotherhood of [the] man of tomorrow." Stalin's own somewhat more modest estimate of his own position as of 1935 at least is revealed by this brief exchange with his mother: "Joseph, what exactly are you now?" she asked him. "Do you remember the czar?" he replied.

"Well, I'm something like the czar." Another element of Stalinism was the gang-leader aura that Stalin enjoyed among his own retinue, among the luminaries of the CPSU and the government, the henchmen and hit-men who spread his terror, the whole goulish, Brechtian crew that called him the *Vozhd*, that is, the Boss, underworld connotations and all. But these elements were hardly more than tools of the trade for the man who was one of the great mass terrorists of history.

Stalin's career as *terroriste extraordinaire* began in 1928, a year of good harvests but a catastrophic drop nevertheless in deliveries of agricultural products to the state, that is, in the food supplies the central planners could make available to people in the cities. This could not be allowed to happen again. Stalin, already the leading voice in the Politburo, the Presidium of those days, decided that the state had to take control of agricultural production, that indeed it was time to scrap in its entirety the relatively unregulated economic system of the preceding few years and replace it with the unequivocally Communist practices of state ownership of enterprises, collectivized agriculture, central planning and rapid industrialization. Of course, not everybody in the Politburo agreed with the proposed shift, and despite his preeminence, Stalin was still expected to deal with the objections in executive-committee fashion, that is, with discussion, persuasion and maybe even compromise. But sharing power was not his way. Instead, he assessed his support in both the Kremlin and among local party and labor union leaders, and bulldozed ahead. By the beginning of 1929 he managed to outmaneuver the opposition, and within a few years succeeded in imposing the vise-like grip of a new economic system on the country.

Stalin's methods were drastic it seems to me beyond comparison with any predecessors, and with most successors too. In agriculture, he instituted three programs of mass coercion: a highly stepped-up system of grain-requisitioning, liquidation of the social class of the kulaks, the wealthiest stratum of landowners remaining after the post-revolutionary elimination of the nobility, and forced collectivization of peasant holdings. More specifically, between 1929 and 1931, he had 1.8 million persons, kulaks and their families, or so they were labeled when fingered for their fate, deported from their homes and taken to the ante-rooms of death, that is, the gulags in Siberia and north of the Arctic Circle. At the same time, he also had *all* agricultural products forcibly collected from the peasants in Ukraine, the Northern Caucasus and a big fertile region of southern Russia known as the Black Earth territories, leaving these peasants with literally nothing – no food to eat or seed to plant. The resulting famine of 1932-33 killed *six million* people. In addition, he had the mostly nomadic population of Kazakhstan forcibly settled on the land in a collectivized arrangement. This government action annihilated 80% of the region's livestock, which in turn compelled half a million Kazakhs to migrate to Central Asia and another million and a half to China. To break peasant resistance, 25,000 tough young volunteers from factories and the militias were told that the kulaks were planning a grain-strike against the urban population, and were then sent out to the countryside to enforce the collectivization program. And so they did.

In industry, Stalin decreed a society-transforming expansion, the so-called First Five-Year Plan of 1928-32, and ordered production quotas hiked to punishing levels. How else could a labor force projected, that is, permitted and required, to increase by only 32% during the five years realize a projected, that is, permitted and required, increase in productivity of 110%? The pace on the factory floor was sure to break everyone except the biology-defying Stakhanovites, workers who scaled like hillocks the quotas that others found to be mountains reaching to the clouds. And all the while living conditions kept deteriorating. Cheap replacement labor was always available as peasants fled from the devastation of the country-side, so the wages of industrial workers were being actually reduced. In cities and towns food rationing had to be put into effect. But Stalin was undeterred. He declared in 1931: "To lower tempos means to lag behind. And laggards are beaten. We don't want to be beaten. No, we don't!" And in the end he was pleased. The Plan achieved its goals almost a year early, and even by the skeptical estimates of outsiders industrial production increased between 1928 and '41 at the rate of 10% per annum. In a remarkably rapid forced transformation, the Soviet Union was indeed becoming an industrialized country. And Stalin certainly didn't care about the human price.

By 1932 Stalin had achieved his general objective, of which collectivization and the First Five-Year Plan were only the major components: control of society by the state. All the major aspects of the lives of 150 million people were now regulated. This was the way he liked things, and a good many of his subordinates, from the central government down to petty local officials, liked things this way too. And that was exactly as Stalin wanted it, because he needed the full cooperation and more of these underlings in implementation of his policies. His *modus operandi* was always to provide only central direction and leave ample room for local initiative. In addition to producing excellent results, this method had the advantage of turning local officials into his willing accomplices and the advantage also of inducing them to vie for his approval through overzealousness. So regimentation to a previously unimaginable degree had been achieved, with everyone following orders and more than a few also giving them. But, said the Stalinists, this was the only way to build socialism, indeed this itself was already an indispensable *part* of socialism. After all, wasn't a socialist economy by definition a planned, that is, a controlled economy? And were you not completely justified in extending that argument from the economy, the material base, to all aspects of collective existence?

But in getting his way, Stalin also aroused new opposition. Whatever there was of it among the people themselves he crushed promptly, while the opposition within the Communist establishment itself he dealt with between 1936 and '38. The liquidation during these years of those who disagreed with him or had disagreed with him earlier or *might* disagree with him later was the Great Terror. Almost 700,000 party officials, officers in the armed forces, artists, intellectuals and "socially dangerous elements" were executed, and a like number sent to prison camps. A million and a half people! This was the heyday of the show trial, a practice going back at least to the case of Joan of Arc but made into a regular instrument of political oppression only by Stalin at the time of the First Five-Year Plan. As its name suggests, this was a trial conducted only to provide a show, with guilt having been determined beforehand. An old comrade, a veteran of the Revolution, a greatly respected public figure, or even a former member of the *Vozhd*'s inner circle would be arrested in a surprise nighttime visit on trumped-up charges. He would then be interrogated and, with Stalin's express permission, worked over by the torturer. Phony evidence of espionage, conspiracy to assassinate Stalin and restore capitalism or some other anti-socialist activity on his part would be assembled, sooner or later he would sign a confession and a trial would ensue. During these years there were three great show trials in Moscow, with 16, 17 and 21 defendants, respectively. On the stand, each man confessed and broke down. Then he was sentenced and handed over to the executioner or the warden. Penal camps had been in existence in Russia for a while by then, but now new ones were also being built to accommodate the influx, like the camp at Vorkuta inside the Arctic Circle, the main road of which the Humorist of Steel had had designed in the shape of a skull. It is estimated that altogether seven million people entered the Gulag between 1934 and 1941.

Some of the victims of the purges had indeed opposed Stalin at one time or another, but most had just managed to arouse his suspicion. In any event, it's fair to say that none of these men or women was guilty of anything alleged against him or her. But Stalin felt justified in all this nevertheless, there is no sign of any doubt or soul-searching on his part, he was even proud to fully inhabit his historical role as a successor to great slaughterers of men like Genghis Khan and Ivan the Terrible. He also maintained his habit of implicating in the Terror as many subordinates as possible. For example, under his guidance, the NKVD merely set arrest quotas for the various administrative districts of the realm. It was local officials who had to devise the rules and methods for identifying and proceeding against a sufficient number of victims, although they did have to apply for permission from above to exceed the quota, a way of currying favor appreciated at the top. When finally public life threatened to collapse on account of the loss of so many important and experienced people, the Terror had to end. But by then Stalin had gained control of the Party and the government. By then he had completed the consolidation begun in earnest between 1928 and '32, so that now power was concentrated in *his* hands alone. He was no longer accountable to the Party or to anyone in fact. He had become a personal despot. Now *everybody* feared him, and feared his minions too, until fear gripped the whole country.

And still the terrorist was not ready to rest. Throughout the war and after he continued his depredations. In 1945 there were 5.5 million people in places called "special resettlement" camps, forced-labor colonies, and filtration prisons. In 1953, the gulags held 2.75 million prisoners and controlled the lives of an equal number of "specially displaced people." But enough of this catalogue-aria of horrors! Instead, I'll address the question you really want to ask, namely, what exactly can be understood to have motivated these inhuman brutalities? A couple of great Latin American novelists, and others too I'm sure, have tried to fathom the mind of the tyrant. I've enjoyed the very considerable fruit of their imaginations, but I find the concrete historical reality of Stalin more overwhelming yet. And with regard to some of *his* evil deeds, what we today would call national security was offered as the official justification. But that was bogus of course, unless you take the term to refer to Stalin's own *political* security. Slave labor, or what amounted to it, might have been a more real reason, for the inmates of the Gulag made invaluable contributions to the country's economy by the railways, canals and industrial plants they built, and the mines and factories they worked. In addition, Stalin also had his own personal needs, in particular the need to allay his raging suspicions about possible rivals or challengers and those with too much knowledge of prior atrocities. Once Khrushchev actually overheard him mutter, "I trust nobody, not even myself." But underneath all these motives, for finally even the historian has to psychologize a little, you see the urge to reorganize society, to bring it into line with ideologically prescribed models, to eliminate all men and women who do not correspond to preconceived types, to mold human nature, to expand the power of socialism and checkmate its enemies, to steer history. In other words, you see the megalomania of an evil would-be god, paranoia and a will to dominate all.

If now you examine Rákosi's rule from 1948 until at least the beginning of the New Course, you will find striking similarities. Upon coming to power, he immediately set out to create for himself a personality cult worthy of his satellite-Stalin magnificence. At once he promoted himself into the Communist pantheon of Marx, Engels, Lenin, Stalin – no "and" – and, as I've said, had his omnipresent image displayed not alone but next to those of the *true* divinities. He strongly encouraged people to jump to their feet in the middle of all sorts of speeches, as if they themselves were no more than punctuation marks, to applaud and rhythmically chant: "Long live Rákosi! Long live Rákosi!" In 1952, on the occasion of the nationwide celebrations of his 60th birthday, he graciously consented to the publication of a volume of tribute from Hungarian writers entitled *Hungarian Writers on Mátyás Rákosi*, to the public exhibition of a replica of his jail cell from the 1930s, to the delivery of a disquisition by the president of the Hungarian Academy of Sciences entitled "Mátyás Rákosi and Hungarian Science," and so on. The festivities culminated with a gala in his honor at the Opera House in Budapest. And whereas Stalin considered himself the successor of the Romanovs, Rákosi became a kind of Admiral Horthy, by, for example, taking over some of Horthy's estates and keeping on as his own chief game warden the man who had filled that post under his predecessor.

Like Stalin, Rákosi also force-fed his economic policies to his people. For Rákosi too, it was nothing ever but *forced* industrialization and *forced* collectivization. His own grandiose First Five-Year Plan, covering the years 1950-54, had one un-compromisable objective: to turn Hungary into a country of iron and steel. That neither iron ore nor coal, the two things you need to make steel, was produced domestically, it ignored. In the course of preparing to be self-sufficient for the coming great war with the imperialist West, in some years Rákosi poured almost one-third of the national income into heavy industry, driving workers like a slave master and publicly destroying falsely accused saboteurs. And while all of his people were enduring the resulting misery, the terrorist-in-chief was also cramming collectivization down the peasants' throats, compelling them by the harshest means to contribute their precious smallholdings to widely detested, state-owned, bureaucracy-breeding farm-cooperatives. The collectivization led first to a disastrous decrease in production, then to rationing and shortages, and finally, after Stalin's death, to a very unpleasant trip to Moscow by the leadership.

The prototypical Stalinist episode of the Rákosi years was the Rajk affair of 1949. Rajk was a homegrown Hungarian Communist. A charismatic and popular man and a leading figure in the movement from 1943, he had been a member of the Politburo, Minister of the Interior – which under a regime engaged in eliminating rivals was not, as you can imagine, a job for the finicky or overly scrupulous – and then Minister of Foreign Affairs. In other words, one of the top public figures in the country. In June 1949, very soon after the Communist takeover, Rajk was arrested. He was charged with spying for the imperialists and maintaining connections with the Yugoslavs. All nonsense, of course. At first Rajk just denied the charges. But after a while his friends convinced him that to achieve its purpose, the planned show trial had to climax in a confession. They also assured him that his death sentence would under no circumstances be carried out and his name would be cleared. So Rajk finally agreed. He confessed to everything, as the accused in show trials always did. He was promptly hanged, together with fourteen alleged associates. He parted from life with his faith intact and the words "long live Stalin!" on his lips, as had so many of the Soviet dictator's own victims through the years.

I know it sounds preposterous, but the Rajk affair was intended primarily to demonstrate Hungary's solidarity with Stalin's anti-Tito policy, and was a demonstration made by other satellite countries too. But this case was only the most blatant of many and can hardly be understood on its own. What then could have accounted for Rákosi's acts of terrorism?

Could it have been the Cold War, given that these were some of its most brutal years, productive of extraordinary mass craziness in America too? Or can Rákosi's beastliness be attributed to the exigencies of consolidating power on the fraught morrow of a coup? Yes, maybe, although neither one of these things can really explain Rajk's fate. Well, then, maybe it was the benefits it brought Rákosi personally, the very same domestic benefits the Man of Steel was used to deriving from his *own* show trials? Eliminating a rival, or revving up his engine for a run of purges, internments and resettlements? Sure, in some cases this too had to have a part. But more important than any of this, it seems to me, more important as his motivation for terror was the desire to emulate his master, to serve by imitation, to pay homage by obeying unspoken and even just imagined orders. In a word, to *be* like Stalin. And *that* he certainly was, even if his copy-cat dictatorship never reached Soviet proportions. But of course it had neither the time needed to accomplish that nor the stage on which to do it.

But don't doubt it: the intention was there, as was the readiness to act, and that allows me to float the idea that maybe Baby Monster should after all be considered a villain as great as Papa Monster. I know that goes against the prevailing victim-count approach to judgments of this kind, an approach I recognize to be just about indispensable given the absence of alternate criteria. And I do of course also feel, and feel with a certainty, that the two men are really *not* commensurable, if you know what I mean, although I'd rather not have to spell out how or why. Only Dante could devise a joint suffering for their shades, which is what the damned are in hell, that would duplicate for eternity all the sociopathic complexities of their relationship as mortals. And yet, as a historian I must insist on the slightly inconsistent corollary to all this that just for *wanting* to be like Stalin in so many respects including the loosing of a plague of terror on his country, Rákosi is as culpable as Stalin. Think about it.

On my 2002 trip to Budapest, in the course of tracking down traces of my childhood, I visited the two official remnants of those dark Rákosi years. One of them was Statue Park, a repository tucked away near the edge of the city for decommissioned working-class figures still considered to have a nostalgic value beyond the scrap metal they represent. Corralled like that, the over-muscled heroes and heroines make you think of nothing so much as a species driven to extinction by a more graceful rival with a larger brain. The other remnant was a museum named the House of Terror, a place dedicated to preserving a memory of, or maybe just satisfying an ephemeral curiosity about, the brutalities of Hungarian public life during the 1940s and 50s, the evil deeds committed by the Germans and the Soviets and of course by the Hungarians themselves. The museum is a grizzly attraction, as it must be given its intent and content, equal parts show business and self-definition as confected by the children of those two cursed decades. The exhibition fills an 1880s neo-Renaissance mansion on Andrássy Road in Pest, the very building that served from 1937 to '45 as the headquarters of the Arrow Cross Party and from 1946 to '56 as the headquarters of the ÁVO. A house of terror indeed! A crowd waiting to be admitted seemed to linger permanently outside its doors, like the sickening-looking pool of liquid under the suspect's chair in an interrogation room. I waited in line patiently and wondered what might have brought my fellows to the place. The pursuit of a frisson, historical inquisitiveness, or a desire maybe, like mine, to reconnect with their past? Finally it was my turn to enter.

Inside, you immediately start to climb two flights of stairs. Niches are let into the walls along the way, and you keep stopping to examine the busts of Nazi and Communist leaders displayed in them, a grotesque series interrupted now and then by block-like objects that apparently claim to be works of art, even though they aim only to command stalwartness or proclaim the grit and glory of the movement. You walk through reconstructed party offices, committee rooms and courts of law, and the stench of absolute power rises about you and slowly overspreads the network of chambers. In one room you see clever illustrations of how at the end of the war Arrow Cross militiamen just exchanged their bile-green outfits for the gray uniforms of the ÁVO. In another hall somber filmed testimonials of survivors run in loops on half a dozen screens, and somehow you sense the collective dread that had gripped the country during those times. You pass glass cases holding the few disintegrating possessions of victims herded into camps – photographs, prayer books, letters, belt buckles – and you shudder as the walls lined from floor to ceiling with dossiers stuffed into hundreds of boxes begin to press in on you. Even the unrelieved black and red, the respective colors of the two systems, even they assault you with the fearsomeness of the irrational. An unease settles upon you as you realize that they were all sadists, those who used to people these rooms and corridors.

At the end of the tour you enter a glass elevator that has ascended empty and been waiting in its glass shaft for passengers going down to the basement. There, as you already know, have been reconstructed the cells and chambers where the torturers and killers had carried out their most bestial procedures. You face the doors and stand inside the glass enclosure, and by the time it starts its slow and fateful downward grind, you're already clammy with claustrophobia. As you sink below ground level, a voice from behind your back identifies itself as belonging to the man who formerly had the job of cleaning the execution chamber. Then the voice begins to recount the routine of an official killing.

Death row. The prisoner's last letter to loved ones that's soon torn up and thrown away. At dawn the walk to the gallows. Then the noose is slipped on from behind. The legs are bound together, the step-stool kicked out from under the feet, the crack of the spine as the executioner wrenches the head to the side. The step-stool is restored to its original position. The doctor climbs up to confirm, stethoscope in hand. *Death.*

As the last words die, you come to a stop with a slight bump and exit into a world of gray cement. It is a twilight of some sort, the regularly spaced bulbs in little wire cages notwithstanding. You walk around, if you dare. You inspect the regular cells, an iron bed and toilet in each. Then the punishment cells: the one so narrow in all directions the prisoner can only stand, the one so low that at all times the prisoner must *crouch*, the one with an inch of water all across the cement bottom, the one that's hardly more than a recess in the wall, to shove the prisoner into and slam the bars on him. The victims of the Arrow Cross and the ÁVO look at you from photographs from other eras hanging on the walls. You go into the torture chambers, with the electric prod lying on a rude table, a pair of pliers next to it. A coil of rope and some rubber truncheons on a low shelf. Everything rudimentary, even the few devices you can't quite identify.

In a larger open area at the end of the central corridor is the execution chamber. You're not allowed to enter. You can only step up onto the low straight-backed chair standing outside against the wall, your shoe falling onto its flat seat like a stone. You peer down through a little square window. Officials did this when the place still served its original function. Sand on the ground. The gallows is just a heavy wooden post bolted into the concrete, without a crosspiece, with the end of the noose hooked onto a short sturdy dowel sticking up from its top. A three-stepped stand at its foot, a ladder behind. You are looking down into death's domain.

Let's say that the new faith arrived in Hungary in 1945. Very quickly then it began to gather believers of one sort or another, and, as you know, by October of that year it had a half-million of them, counting only card-carrying members. Still, many people in the country did not welcome the newcomer. The outcome of subsequent elections leaves no doubt about that. There were many reasons to dislike Communism, and you needed no more than a smattering of information about the new faith's tenets and how they had been implemented during the past 25 years in the Soviet Union to be able to list them. Some people did not even hesitate but just packed up and left.

In *The Captive Mind*, a book published in 1953, the Nobel-prize-winner Czeslaw Milosz tells of his encounter with the new faith. That happened in Poland of course, but it could have happened just like that in Hungary too. Milosz was 34 at the end of the war and already a recognized poet. Immediately the Communists started wooing him and pressuring him, trying to convince him of the inevitable correctness of their own approach to building a better world. The Communists treated writers, musicians, film directors, intellectuals and academics this way, in essence trying to convert them. For with their background, reputation and position in society, such men, and they were pretty much all men, were sure to *enhance* the new faith's credibility. The high esteem and influence such men enjoyed in European societies of those times is confirmed by a 1956 comment of Khrushchev's that "if ten or so Hungarian writers had been shot at the right moment, the revolution would never have happened," and also by the number of artists and intellectuals who through the years figured as prominent dissenters. But despite the supposed ideological superiority of Communism and also the promise of fame, many of these men resisted, offended as they were in particular by the way the new faith was already curtailing their professional freedoms. For them this was also a matter of conscience, and conscience was, you see, *their* capital. Unfortunately for them, the resistance itself could transform the wooing into threats and so push the resister ahead on the road to emigration.

Milosz did join the Polish diplomatic corps in 1946 and was soon posted to the Polish embassy in Paris as cultural attaché. Although aware that his attachment to his homeland and the home-culture was the wellspring of his creativity, in 1951 he went into exile, briefly in France and then in the United States, to return to Poland part-time only after the fall of Communism. *The Captive Mind* is his account of how Communism was clamping prison bars about the thinking of its adherents. It includes the variously tragic stories of four not-named but easily identifiable fellow Polish writers, each of whom was converted postwar to what "in the people's democracies the communists speak of [as] the New Faith, compar[ing] its growth to that of Christianity in the Roman Empire." Here and there incidentally, Milosz also reveals his own temptations to join the Communists, which he managed in the end to withstand only by becoming "a poet who has no longer a language of his own."

Milosz resisted the pressures because for the privilege of playing a part in the building of a new social order the new faith demanded nothing less than your mind and your soul. This price was to be paid in two ways. First of all, you had to learn to see the world anew, had to learn to operate in a dual reality, as it has been called. On the one hand, you like everyone else would have the lived experience itself, but on the other you would also have the revolutionary ideology. And the latter would be so powerful that whenever a discrepancy arose between the two, you would automatically resolve it in favor of the latter, that is, reflexively interpret actual events and conditions as demanded by the dogma. Here is how Arthur Koestler, a Hungarian Jew and a writer living in Western Europe and a Communist from 1931 through 1938, when finally he managed to pry off the shackles of faith binding him – here in his own words is how he entered into the dual reality: "Gradually I learned to distrust my mechanistic [as the Communists put it] preoccupation with facts and to regard the world around me in the light of dialectic interpretation. It was a satisfactory and indeed blissful state; once you had assimilated the technique you were no longer disturbed by facts; they automatically took on the proper color and fell into their proper place." And so, in the early 30s the German Communists betrayed the Social Democrats, their leftist brothers, to the Nazis, but they told themselves that they were justified in doing so because the Social Democrats were betraying the proletariat – just listen to this! – by holding themselves forth as an alternative to the Communists. Well, this obviously was the shabbiest kind of sophistry imaginable, and Milosz's stomach revolted at the mental discipline it would have required to be convinced by it.

Secondly, you would pay the price by acceding to the Communist demand, first made during the 1920s, to remake yourself into something like the "new Soviet man," a new synthetic human strain, a selfless individual who valued the public good above his own interest and felt at home "in the East," where, as Milosz says, "there is no boundary between man and society." Many of course acceded to this demand. To a remarkable extent, and not only among believers but all those too who were not determined to resist, the officially articulated collective vision did succeed in absorbing the individual perspective, even so far as the almost universal phenomenon of private property was concerned. It's depressing but so it happened. The masses fell into step as social existence became something like a science-fiction extravaganza. And so during the 30s Soviet citizens by the thousands were convinced to publicly burn their diaries, the keeping of which, with the private reflective details they were presumed to contain, was considered individualistic and therefore anti-social behavior. You were expected to participate in ritual expressions of collectivism, and you had to provide the authorities with a brief autobiography to be made part of your file. All of this served to increase the pressure on you to focus on society rather than the individual, and to adopt a way of thinking that assessed official measures on the basis of their imagined impact on all of mankind rather than on their actual impact on individual men and women. This forced transformation too Milosz could not and would not stomach.

But abandoning old beliefs and allowing new ones to take possession of you often amounted to a spiritual crisis. It was like being reborn. It was, to put it into rather bloodless words, a shift of your philosophical and moral devotion from the well-known, richly contextualizing, always fervently embraced past to a glorious future yet to be built, a shift from a life nourished by rootedness and tradition to a life of struggle for a better world that surely will come. For those whose encounter with Communism was an interplay of hesitation and resistance, on the one hand, and blandishments and demonstrations of no-alternatives, on the other, as it was for Milosz's anti-heroes, the process could be agonizing. At the last minute Milosz *himself* had the strength to stand his ground. Or rather, "the growing influence of the [New Faith] on my way of thinking [finally] came up against the resistance of my whole nature." He simply could not forsake "[looking] at the world from his own independent viewpoint,... tell[ing] the truth as he [saw] it." But many he knew succumbed. Their crises brought on great nervous anxiety and often actual illness. The candidate knew that he had now to progress from just criticizing capitalism, which was not very difficult, to *approving* the new articles of faith and the efforts being made on their behalf, which was. He had to abandon his lifelong beliefs and submit to an "enslavement of his consciousness." And he had to endure and indeed suppress the shame of knowing that he will be championing evil under the guise of the good. But after long hours of solitary anguish, suddenly the skeptic found himself convinced that indeed "there is no other way.... No other salvation on the face of the world." The crisis was over. He was now a new man. Or she was now a new woman.

But artists and intellectuals were mostly an exception. And ordinary people, as I've already suggested, dealt with the coming of the new faith by more or less accepting it. The details of the relationship of the Soviet people to Communism are the most revealing in this respect. During the 20s, following elimination of the truly counterrevolutionary elements in the long civil war, the Bolshevik leaders sort of just fumbled around with Lenin's legacy, and it was only in 1928, as you have seen, that Stalin began to establish what quickly became the system. In terms of popular support, the Man of Steel achieved mixed results, which itself was a remarkable success. A great many people were quite enthusiastic about Communism and were ready even to sacrifice for it. Surely, the Stakhanovites did not ruin their health or make enemies of their fellow workers just for the few extra rubles or even for the glory. Rather, they believed in Communist goals and wanted nothing more than to contribute to their realization. And that's not hard to understand. After all, they and many other workers and peasants too did derive actual benefits and much hope from being members of this new and apparently vibrant society, which was catapulting you into the modern world, introducing and even inventing new industrial technology, bringing literacy to all of its citizens, laying railroads across continents, providing schools and teachers and places of recreation for ordinary people, unearthing vast treasures of natural resources, building great cities. These men and women were proud to believe in the new system and its promises, to endure the hardships of building this society, to claim as their very own the vast fruits of their collective labor.

Although there was a lot of grumbling and dissatisfaction too. For life *was* very difficult. The rapid transformations of all sorts caused wholesale suffering. Collectivization was destroying village life and sending peasants to the new cities in droves to join the industrial proletariat. In every way possible, religion was being wrung out of the social environment, with the regime letting it be known that the law did not frown on even physical attacks on clergymen of *any* persuasion. In order to become Soviet, you were also being pressed to abandon whatever ethnic identity you might have. So all about traditions were being wiped out, identities sent to the rubbish heap, and your world, the only world you ever knew without even imagining that there could be another, was collapsing. As for Stalin's terror, for the peasant and the industrial worker it did not manifest itself as a distant mass murder but as the specific instances rather of his own children starving to death because of the catastrophic grain-collections or of his own fellow lathe-operators being carried off to the Gulag without any credible reason. Ultimately, the coercion and the fear it inspired deformed every psyche. Even life in Nazi Germany pales in comparison with Soviet conditions during the 30s, 40s and 50s. Jews and Roma and Bolsheviks did indeed have to fear for their lives in the Third Reich, but others at least, the great majority, could go about undisturbed as long as they observed the rules. In contrast, in the Soviet Union *everybody* lived in fear, although that must in itself have made a new belief system seem necessary.

And indeed it's hardly an exaggeration to say that the new faith was the Communists' primary tool of governance. Citizens who believed trusted the Party and didn't question or criticize the government or its ideologically inspired policies and measures. Of course, believers were not well-schooled like Koestler or Milosz and could not understand dialectical materialism or the other fine philosophical tropes of the dogma. But like those medieval Christians who could not fathom the Trinity but adored the accessible and maternal Virgin Mary all the more, they had faith, an inner certainty that silenced all their possible misgivings about the many specific ways in which, despite the sinew-straining and mind-numbing assurances to the contrary, the actual world was routinely falling short of the promised one. And, as a rule, that faith was unshakable. For communist theory had been designed, as predictive schemes tend to be, to repel arguments formulated to discredit its claims, deny evidence marshaled against its validity, and reward the believer for believing the unbelievable, or the unprovable at least. On the basis of their faith alone, most believers had no difficulty accepting "the necessary lie," as Koestler says, "the necessary slander; the necessary intimidation of the masses to preserve them from shortsighted errors; the necessary liquidation of oppositional groups and hostile classes; the necessary sacrifice of a whole generation in the interest of the next."

It was thanks to faith that the ordinary Soviet man and woman could, as I've said, internalize the goals of the new-Soviet-man campaign. Convictions that the Party was infallible, Stalin was in effect a god, and the Communist way represented the inevitable working out of history greatly eased a task that would without them have seemed impossible and even repugnant. Of course, the rule-makers in the Kremlin, themselves already enlightened new men, also did what they could to help. And so efforts that could aid you in achieving this transformation were institutionalized. You could, indeed you had to, purify yourself of recidivist thinking and residual anti-social tendencies by self-criticism at your workplace and within party cells, while admonitory examples of how the determination of even the most devoted can slacken were provided by the show trials. But as the surviving diaries of Soviet citizens indicate, much of the work of self-purification was performed in private. The diarists labored diligently to cleanse their own thoughts of the inappropriate, ascribing their doubts about the system or about this or that prohibition or hardship to their own shortcomings, and, trusting their faith, tried to find a sense of fulfillment in rote conformity to the ideal of the new Soviet man. Just look around! Brainwashing agrees with fundamentalists of all sorts.

Most importantly, the faith was strong enough to confront and withstand the potentially disillusioning impact of the terror and each of its manifestations. To believers, the proscenium at the show trials became invisible and they readily mistook theater for the real. Ever firm in their conviction that the maltreatment or even murder of individuals and classes of people was only advancing the inevitable progress of humankind, they did not consider such acts unjust. Their faith prevailed even as they acknowledged the terror, and enabled them to go about their daily lives in a world pervaded by fear even when they themselves were the victims. Recall Rajk's last words! Or consider the following story. In 1949 the three arguably most important men in the Soviet Union, aside from the Man of Steel, that is, were Molotov, head of the government, Kalinin, president of the Supreme Soviet, and Poskrebyshev, Stalin's secretary. These men saw their superior daily on business. Almost invariably, they also participated in the revelry of his nightly dinner gatherings, which tended to stretch into the wee hours. They ate, they drank, they laughed with him, but all the time their wives, yes, the wives of each of the three, were either in prison or in a gulag. And deservedly so, the men and their wives probably even thought, for they too, like all the terrified millions around them, bowed to the wisdom of their great leader, whom they perceived by then not as the actual flesh-and-blood, smallish and shrunken Stalin, but as a being so superior as to be beyond the purview of ordinary human judgment. It is even documented that Polina Zhemchuzhina Molotova not only adored Uncle Joe but actually could not tolerate anyone being critical of him. Such it was to be a keeper and a captive of the new faith.

But with respect to the terror, Communist faith was not only a shield but also a sword. Not only did it ward off disillusionment on account of the atrocities, it actually commanded their perpetration. And there was nothing unusual in this. How often throughout history has faith required the persecution and destruction of the infidel! Since the earliest historical times men have waged wars under the sign of their tribal gods and reduced their foes to mountains of corpses for those gods' greater glory. But the Communist situation was somewhat different. In no way was Rajk an infidel, nor was Nicolai Bukharin, at various times chairman of Comintern and editor of *Pravda* and then a casualty of the Great Terror, a spy or a traitor or an enemy of the people. Nor Zinoviev nor

Marshal Tukhachevsky nor Solzhenitsyn. Indeed, it's likely that none of Stalin's notable victims, in addition to being innocent of the alleged crimes, ever even betrayed the faith. And, yes, you can make the argument that the peasants who resisted collectivization were the infidel, but even in orthodox Communist circles many rational people saw things otherwise. Nevertheless, you were convinced of the sacred obligation to defend the faith at all cost and believed much of the ambient evil to be the doing of just that. Thank goodness that you were not called upon personally to swing the cudgel, although if you had been, well…. But, no, for providing an ever-guiding example of unwavering lifelong commitment to the struggle, for that's what it was, a lifelong struggle and a great responsibility to the cause and to us all – for that example and for swinging the cudgel too, you had to be grateful to the Great Father.

But then Stalin's death changed everything, and changed it so fundamentally that you have to consider revising your ideas even about the power of faith. The demise of the Man of Steel did not completely remove terror from the Communist political curriculum, but something like a revulsion did sweep over the Eastern bloc, a revulsion that to me seems like the emotional component, what today might be called the soul, of de-Stalinization. That process, scrubbing the world clean of Stalin's taint, or at least some of that taint, began right after his death on March 5, 1953, and soon "de-Stalinize" entered the dictionary as "to counteract the excesses of Stalinism or the influence of Stalin, as by reversing or amending his policies, removing monuments to him, and renaming places named in his honor." This finally was the reaction to a monster who had imposed his *personality* on a large part of humankind and had managed, without really much by way of ideas or beliefs notably his own, but only with the aid of a god-scorning faith and a soul-crippling, scruple-scuttling fear, not only to bring death to some twenty million people but also to make them die with words of praise for him on their lips. So that after this man's own death, his much-mourned death, his mortal imprint had painstakingly to be removed from the world.

Right after the tyrant's death, all the Presidium members agreed, tacitly at least, that some of Stalin's atrocities had to be undone. The criminal files especially of the many tens of thousands of political prisoners had to be reexamined, many of those banished to the *Archipelag Gulag*, as Solzhenitsyn named it, had to be released, and Stalin's role in the abusive system had to be documented and maybe even made public. Why? Clearly, the new leaders, all of them lieutenants of the late great Communist colossus, and none of them blameless in the systemic terror-mongering – they were reacting mostly to the especially outrageous cruelty and insane paranoia of Stalin's last years, worrying about their own skin and reputation, and trying each to outmaneuver the others in the suddenly uncharted seas of Soviet power. But it seems that in addition to all of that they were also motivated by an innate sense of justice and a suddenly discovered commitment to a world where a "moral minimum" at least, as Vaclav Havel once labeled it, was maintained. The urge to right wrongs took possession even of Lavrenti Beria, Stalin's secret police chief and First Deputy Premier at the time, and other than his late boss the most vicious and sadistic of all the red terrorists. It was Beria, for a few months the most likely successor to the Man of Steel, who finally and promptly sprang Polina Zhemchuzhina from her years in a labor camp.

De-Stalinization reached its climax in Moscow on February 25, 1956, at a famous closed-door session of the 20th Congress of the CPSU. By this time Beria had been eliminated and Khrushchev was fairly securely in charge. It was his decision to make what has come to be known as the secret speech, the four-hour-long barrage, which I've mentioned already and which enumerated and catalogued Stalin's crimes and misdeeds for the benefit of the more than one thousand delegates, who were asked to keep the revelations to themselves. Recently exonerated ex-gulagers had urged Khrushchev to destroy the tyrant's myth and had confirmed him in the belief that given the dark stories now circulating in Moscow, such an airing would cleanse and strengthen Communism. But Khrushchev had the support of even the hardliners in the Presidium. To a man, the new leaders had come to recognize the Man of Steel as a mass murderer and also realized that *not* unmasking him at this first Stalin-less Congress might later expose them all to a charge of having been accomplices in what they now saw as his *abuses* of power. As the reasoning behind the speech required, in subsequent weeks copies of the secret text bound as a red-covered booklet were distributed to party higher-ups, to be read to up to seven million party members and 18 million members of Komsomol, the youth division of the Party.

The speech did not go as far as it might have, but even so it was devastating. During Stalin's reign, said Khrushchev, "mass arrests and [the] deportation of thousands and thousands of people, and executions without trial or normal investigation, [had] created insecurity, fear and even desperation." Stalin had been personally responsible for "physical methods of pressure, torture [that reduced the innocent] to unconsciousness, depriv[ed] them of judgment, [took] away their dignity." Stalin, who on his last birthday had been celebrated by his whole empire as the Greatest Genius of All Times and Nations, had actually been a cowardly and incompetent wartime leader, the mastermind behind the "monstrous" deportation of whole Caucasian peoples, the destroyer of the country's agriculture. Those present at the secret speech – picture an amphitheatrical phalanx of cheap suits and ill-fitting uniforms – could not have been delicate creatures. And yet, the public desecration of the divinity, the first assault on the myth, shattered their world and sent some of them fainting. "The shock had been indescribably severe," one high-ranking Soviet party functionary recalled subsequently, "especially since this was the first time we'd been told officially of Stalin's crimes.... I was crushed.... I sensed that Khrushchev was telling the truth, but it was a truth I was afraid of."

The word itself, de-Stalinization, appeared in English only after the official de-deification. In the September 1957 issue of *The Economist*, the British weekly, it was coupled with a reference to, of all things, the failed Hungarian revolution. "The echoes of destalinization and Hungary have reverberated among the Apennines," the reporter stated. Among those echoes you could make out the death-knell of Italian Neorealism. In 1957 Visconti made *The White Nights,* a marvelous movie from an early story by Dostoyevsky with Mastroianni and Maria Schell. This romantic work signaled an abandonment of the dominant school of Italian film-making, of the black-and-white working-people's tragedies often played by non-professional casts, which preserved such an unparalleled visual record of postwar Italian life and, as I've said, unintentionally and to me irresistibly of life also in Budapest during the first half of the 50s. As if an era had ended, the ideological approach, already suspect to Italians beginning to rediscover a sense of national optimism and enjoying a slowly rising standard of living, was now, in response to these Communist debacles, replaced by the new *novo-intimismo* as it were brought to life by its remarkable and luminous stars.

If faith allowed Stalin to succeed while he was alive, and by succeed I mean allowed him to be a world-class terrorist and *still* not tarnish Communism, then why you might ask did it fail him once he died? Shouldn't faith have insured that the terrorist's passing will be an enthronement high above rather than a swift kick down to hell? But these are not the right questions to ask. For Stalin's death did not change the faith. What it did was bring a release from fear. Or, even more to the point, it revealed that the pervasive fear that faith appeared to have mastered had in fact been the true instrument of Stalin's success all along. Only in the process of its own riddance was that fear finally exposed to be what it really had been: faith's manipulator. And a force therefore mightier even than the faith. For as the fear was lifted, suddenly terror became no longer acceptable and certainly not something to be praised. And while I have found no evidence that in post-Stalin times people refused to perpetrate terror, it's obvious to me that some at least would have done so if put to the test. In any case, once faith was, as it were, set free, it showed itself strong enough not only to have endured the terror, but, almost as if immune to the base schemes of earthlings, also to have outlived the shame of letting itself be used for evil. After all, in the end it was not Stalin's inhumanity that defeated Communism but just the eventually lethal dose of historical wear and tear. As for the terror and the fear, they were defeated and perhaps could only have been defeated by death.

De-Stalinization was a turning point in Communism's history, or in its European history at least. Although at all times since the beginnings of the movement disillusionment had claimed the occasional comrade or fellow traveler, wholesale disaffection had never been a problem, and strenuous justification of fundamental motives for the benefit of believers had never been necessary. But all that changed in 1956. For many believers *this* now was a crisis, something very much like the reverse of a religious conversion, the reverse of a process in which a person becomes imbued with new beliefs, embraces new ritual practices and maybe even adopts a new way of life. Indeed, revelation of the terror and its workings, of the decades of routine and brutal repression on false pretenses, finally made you question what had until then been not only a code of guiding principles for life but also an attitude of blind trust. And a set of comfortable assumptions, to boot, about right and wrong and personal responsibility. But it seems that more often than not the instinct of self-preservation compelled Soviet believers to distinguish between Stalinism and Communism. So maybe you didn't have to question *all* the things that had allowed you to live your daily life of faith. Despite your delusions about Stalin and the horrors that are finally behind us, I mean, aren't they? – maybe despite all that you really didn't have to jettison all those long-cherished thoughts and feelings, maybe you *were* after all a morally superior person, one of the righteous, one of those who really do know and understand the world and its history. So, with inertia mostly triumphant, as it usually is, the faith of many believers was shaken but in the end managed to survive this most painful but salutary purge.

In Hungary, de-Stalinization began promptly. That very unpleasant Moscow meeting where Rákosi was at least half-disgraced took place in June 1953. Now a reformer, even if just a reformer in sheep's clothing, Beria turned on Stalin's best pupil, shouting: "How could it be acceptable that in Hungary, a country with nine-and-a-half million inhabitants, a million and a half were persecuted?... A person who's beaten will make the kind of confession that interrogating agents want.... We will never know the truth this way. This way innocent people may be sentenced. There is law, and everyone must respect it." So Nagy got the premiership and steered onto the New Course, which kept Stalinism in check for a while. But in April 1955, when the fortunes of the reformers in the Presidium seemed to wane, a resurgent Rákosi made a move against Nagy and threatened to beat back Hungarian de-Stalinization altogether. And then came the secret speech. Khrushchev had not consulted with the satellite leaders before decimating the party congress, and it's easy to guess why. The Polish leader, at the time in the Kremlin hospital with pneumonia – when he read the text of the speech, he was struck by a heart attack and died the next day. His successor said that the speech "was like being hit over the head with a hammer." And later Khrushchev himself admitted that the speech was "especially painfully received in Poland and Hungary," referring undoubtedly to the October disturbances in both countries.

In Hungary, Khrushchev's revelations greatly emboldened the reformers. A late June meeting of the recently formed writers' and intellectuals' organization known as the Petőfi Circle loudly condemned Stalinism. Of course, these people seem to have been mostly practical rather than ideological adherents, a common type in the satellites, where Communism was still a recent phenomenon, faith in the new system apparently not widespread, and fear not yet a national addiction. Although there were true insiders too, like Kopácsi, who lost their faith pretty quickly upon learning the truth about Rákosi's terror. All these men and women were not satisfied with just ending the abuses and now joined the always more open effort to reform the movement. So instead of trying to salve their consciences with thoughts of historical destiny, they devoted themselves to reshaping the power struggle within the Party, strengthening socialism and generally working to clean up a system that was "psychically unbearable," as Milosz put it. This development was clearly reflected, first, in the successes of the New Course, and, second, in the revolution itself, which, as you know, had Soviet domination and the oppression by the Hungarian Communists and not socialism itself as its target. And the ultimate outcome you also know already: when finally the Soviet Union felt assured of Hungary's Cold-War loyalty and the Communists felt securely in control at home, Stalinism was abandoned quickly and for good, ideological crusading subsided, and political life finally lapsed into a sane secularism no one could have even hoped for only a few years earlier.

In the Soviet Union too, from the 60s on the beacon of faith was being progressively dimmed by reality and the here and now. Many things swelled the incoming tide of skepticism and cynicism. The economic and human costs of choking off contact with the West were becoming prohibitive and so forcing the authorities to ease up on the reins, even if in many cases that reduced their mass-communications monopoly to not much more than a nuisance. And sure enough, acquisition of more realistic knowledge of capitalist societies confirmed the dismal failure of the command economy and brought Communist dogma under greater and greater pressure, until the faith had to go on the defensive and even retreat. At the same time, the *nomenklatura,* the bureaucratic-managerial corps that actually exploited the working class and was dubbed the "new class" by Djilas already in the 50s – the *nomenklatura* was ever enlarging its prerogatives and becoming downright hereditary, until the country was being run not by idealists but by not very competent careerist bureaucrats, and nothing it seems could put society back on the track of true communist ideals. No wonder everything collapsed before the end of the century, and the men and women in charge didn't even resist.

Communism flourished for seventy years before reality did it in, as George Kennan had said back at the very beginning of the Cold War that it would. That's not a very good run, not for a world-historical ideology in any case. Of course in the old days the collapse would not have come so early or summarily. The Soviet Union would have been a rotting empire for some time, another sick man of Europe, or actually the world. But nowadays lingering no longer seems possible. As if there is no time for that kind of thing anymore, as if challengers, secret or otherwise, are ever in the wings of every regime, ready to drive home the consequences of ideological bankruptcy, and do it as injuriously as possible. Not so long ago you could still argue that the Russian Revolution was the most momentous event of the 20th century, but more recently even Eric Hobsbawm, the great British historian who was one of Marxism's few remaining apologists, called the system that century's "greatest fantasy."

Part III

CHAPTER 8

December 13, 1956

THERE MUST HAVE BEEN HABITUAL night-owls in some parts of Budapest, toilers on the graveyard shift, artists and students taking advantage of the quiet and magic of the dark, those robbed of peace of mind by a guilty conscience, revelers and mopers in their cups, and of course those stricken with the ordinary misfortune of insomnia. But as a boy I knew nothing of that. My ignorance I attribute first of all to Leslie and Rose, who did not have a so-called social life, and secondly to a world not yet ensnared in a global net of electronic signals, in which the rhythm of life, especially for children, tended to be much closer to nature's schedule than it is today. In any case, Marika and I used to go to bed early and, aside from the magic-flatbed ride, I knew nothing of the night.

But that Thursday all that changed. The previous evening, soon after I came up from the street, Rose informed the children that "tomorrow we're going to America." Well, that certainly explained the presence of the stranger in the apartment, a faceless person in my memory as people often become after decades, and faceless also as was somehow everyone we encountered in the course of blasting ourselves out of one life and belly-flopping into another. I later learned that the stranger was a farmer, peasant was the actual Hungarian word, from near the Austrian border. He was going to sleep in the maid's room that night and on the morrow assist us in sneaking up on the Iron Curtain and finding a crack in it to sidle through. I don't remember how I felt upon hearing Rose's words, but given the kind of person I am and was even more back then, I would guess that a heightened but feelingless state of alertness probably describes it pretty well. I understood that a new life was about to start, a NEW LIFE, but could not in any detail imagine what it was going to be like or what I would have to abandon completely and leave behind in order to begin it. For whatever meaning the word "America" already had for me then had been instantaneously trashed by the summary announcement that soon it would be our home.

The best they could, I believe, Rose and Leslie had already thought through what awaited us on the journey. They had considered its unpredictable length, indeterminate itinerary and entirely wish-fulfillment destination, and must especially have already decided what exactly we could and would take along. I figure that in their individual and collective deliberations they had foreshadowed something like three different futures. There was ahead of us first of all the escape itself, the immediate future. That was a simple enough affair, though dangerous too, a train ride and a walk in the country, which required only provisions for one day, breakfast, lunch and dinner, all easily quantified I suppose as a certain number of lard sandwiches. That presumed of course that everything would go according to schedule, which, alas, the forces of one small country and one superpower seemed determined to prevent. But you could hardly anticipate the problems that could pop up, never mind solving them with greased-up slices of bread. Then came the days or weeks, maybe even months, that would pass between departure and arrival, an intermediate future maybe just as iffy as the immediate but not in the same way. Leslie and Rose knew from listening to Radio Free Europe that refugee organizations were in full operational mode, companies of eager guardian angels hovering all about, but what exact resources they had at their disposal and how exactly they would take care of us remained matters of anxious conjecture. Food, clothing, shelter – would they all be provided all along in minimally sufficient quantities and qualities? But whether or not they would, either way you were not relieved of having to decide how many pairs of socks, for example, had to be packed for everyone. And then finally there was the new life, the future constituted by forever after. What of the old life would survive in it? What did you need to take along to meet long-term practical needs and the who-knew-how-intense yearning to keep alive the unforgettable and too easily forgotten past? So the task at hand was simply this: stuffing those three futures into two suitcases neither too big nor too heavy.

We rose very early our last Hungarian morning. It was well before dawn when Rose flipped the switch for the ceiling lights, allowing me to see for one last time the figures of children on swings, seesaws and rocking horses painted in pastel hues of blue, orange and green on the four small lampshades, just like on the frieze-like band running high up on the walls all around the room. Few words were uttered, for everyone knew what had to be done. We dressed quickly, cast a last glance back into the apartment or not, and then walked down the stairs from the 5th floor. An automatic elevator was available, but the five of us, and our two suitcases and two bags, all we had, would not have fit into that beautiful little cabin of caramel-brown lacquered wood, by far the most elegant feature of our unpretentious modern building. But even aside from that, we could not have chanced someone being woken by the hum of the mechanism, which pianissimoed into two of the three apartments on each floor. And so that even our footsteps should not resound, we added what now seems a comic touch by wrapping our booted feet in rags and descending silently, carefully high-stepping as later I often saw gangs of cartoon burglars do.

The superintendent, a small, wiry woman ever bustling about in a housedress and a kerchief tied at the back of her head, losing her temper and charging about squawking like a bantam cock – she knew of our plans. She had been alerted and appropriately suborned. So she got up at four o'clock, shuffled out in her slippers and quilted robe and opened the tall narrow entrance door to the building, using the single key with the overlong shaft she had been holding aloft, the sight of which had always put me in mind of the seemingly one-legged storks popular in Hungarian folklore. She whispered a hurried goodbye. The adults shook hands and we departed. If crossing the Rubicon is an apt figure of speech here, then this was it. We walked out into the to-me-unknown urban night, having taken the decisive step and succeeded in uprooting ourselves from our immediate surroundings at least. And having done so with the knowledge of those only who were sure to benefit from our flight, and so could be counted on not to try to thwart it.

Rose and Leslie had prepared as well as possible. I don't know if it had been the work of a few days or a few weeks, and it's hard to judge from the timing. Certainly, we came late to the game. 130,000 refugees had already preceded us to Austria. Without doubt Rose and Leslie had been aware of the illegal exodus pretty much from its beginnings, and aware also of its intensification after the crushing of the revolution. For it was impossible to keep something like that quiet, and would have been even if national life had not been by then for months flung repeatedly from tempest to storm. News of escapes could easily be had over the RFE, and the country was rife with rumors anyway about the departure of people you knew distantly or had at least heard of. Don't forget that a myth of its own times was being played out here, or a chapter at least of the myth of the Iron Curtain, which had with its remarkable metaphorical prowess held the imagination of mankind in its grip during those days. As I've said already, we definitely knew about my Aunt Erzsi's flight, and I suspect that Rose had started considering our options, or actually her options, maybe even before the second Soviet invasion. After all, isn't that what you do when you realize that *opportunity* is knocking?

Of course, Rose and Leslie knew that the undertaking was dangerous, and that it had been getting more and more so. The Soviets had again sealed the border on November 5th, but 16,000 people had escaped during the first week after the invasion anyway, a good many of them young men with more than enough reason to fear for their lives. On the 13th *The New York Times* reported that the borders were being unevenly patrolled – in some places by troops on foot with police dogs, in others by soldiers willing to help the fugitives, in still others by no one at all – and the illegal crossings continued. But a week later already the Russians were tightening the escape routes, in particular around the marshy area a few hundred yards from the border near a lake shared by the two countries where one group of would-be refugees lying pressed to the frozen ground saw a Soviet tank roll up and keep firing at the bridge that was to have taken them to freedom, as it had taken so many others already, until the structure collapsed. Then Hungarian soldiers under Russian command combed the area, shouting threats to shoot anyone who did not surrender. Two days later the Russians completed demolition of the bridge and rounded up an estimated 3,000 people wandering in its vicinity. Nevertheless, the influx into Austria did not appreciably slacken, with crossings by boat continuing at night where the bridge had been. People who were lucky merely had to stroll a short distance to the border, while others were cowed for hours as flares burst overhead and machine-gun fire rattled through the sleepless hours. During the last days of November twenty bodies were left unburied as a warning along a popular route, a first and then a second belt of minefields was laid about a mile inside the country, and patrolling soldiers and tanks became ever more difficult to elude. And yet, by December 1st altogether 100,000 people had crossed to freedom.

But then quickly the risks of the whole venture became more widely known, failed attempts began to be punished rather than just blocked, and the numbers started declining. The daily count, which could go as high as 9,000 during the second half of November, was reduced to 3,000 and even less in early December. The tighter circumstances and the narrower choice of possible routes caused an "underground railway" of sorts to spring up and introduced business relationships where previously only solidarity and good-will, and maybe an occasional bribe, had been needed to secure the necessary assistance. Although heroic gestures by locals and railroad workers still did enliven refugees' accounts of their adventures. On December 10th, three days before we set out, the *Times* reported that "flight by auto has become virtually impossible. There are not enough minor roads on which to elude the growing number of highway patrols.... All the refugees who [crossed that night had] left Budapest by train.... By [then] most of the guides had been arrested, and the prices of those still in business were rising steeply. Townspeople and peasants sheltered the refugees overnight, but a house to house search was said to have led to the arrest of almost half.... Yesterday's order forbidding all travel in western Hungary appears to have been a signal for a final drive to end the flow of refugees." What timing!

It would be an exaggeration to say that we went at the last minute, since the daily refugee count did not dip below 100 until January 25th, and did not cease to be reported altogether until mid-February, but we went when it was already difficult to make it rather than easy, and we did so because Leslie resisted. As I've mentioned already, occasionally through the years Rose let it be known that at one point she had been prepared to depart with the children, whether he came along or not. Clearly, she saw the revolution as an extraordinary opportunity to emigrate, whereas he had no real desire to go, and indeed did not want to go. Exactly when America had first appeared on the horizon of *her* aspirations, now I mean just as a fantasy rather than an actual possibility – that she would never say, and I don't know. Throughout my formative years America had always been in the background of the family consciousness. It was put there and kept there by the letters we received from Aunt Pearl, with black-and-white photographs often slipping out of the envelope, glossy rectangles gleaming as if a thousand flashlights had all popped simultaneously in order to immortalize those modest citizens of the Bronx and their *automobile*. And there were also the occasional packages of used clothing from Pearl, with preposterously colorful products of a fledgling consumer culture bursting forth from their eagerly opened tops like a rainbow of silk scarves from a magician's hat. Through all those years America meant such things to us and much else too. It was a country of freedom, the letters actually said, and of dreams of course, the glittering mirage beyond the grim Hungarian facts. But how had all that seemed to Rose in particular? Did she now and then mentally test-drive herself as a Bronxite? Did she ever wish to emigrate, if only we could? Well, if she did, she never let it be known. But at some point during late October-November 1956, she gave Leslie an ultimatum of sorts. If he wanted to keep her and his children, he would go to America; if he didn't care – or if he wanted to lose them, I bet that's how she put it to him – then he would not.

For his part, Leslie had to see the ultimatum as a demand that he sacrifice everything for wife and kids. And that of course is what it was, even if it was other things too. I certainly would have seen it that way had I been in his shoes. Although it's also hard to say what exactly the everything consisted of once you subtracted wife and kids. The fact is that in his heart he already knew that for him Rose was both indispensable and insufficient. He couldn't live without her, but he also couldn't live, given the way she was, with her alone. He was in a bind. But in the bitter balance he must have found the loss of her yet more terrifying than the loss of everything else that her continued presence obviously entailed. So after a while, and I don't mean just a few days, for my guess is that being a practical person and a mother she had brought up the idea sooner rather than later – after a while, when already it seemed that the opportunity could vanish any day, they *both* packed their bags. They would live life together after all, and she had to be glad for that, for he was indeed a damn good worker and a resourceful man. Of course, of course, there were also the children, let's not forget them, for certainly I don't want to downplay Leslie's feelings for Marika and myself. But in truth, Rose had so thoroughly appropriated us by then, had so completely enrolled us as her troops in the battle with him, that for him wife and kids was clearly just one thing.

But you should not let the hesitation and the delay obscure the boldness of the decision. By December 13th they were risking everything, for by then would-be emigrants were being shot. But they had always had nerve and determination. I imagine them, sometimes together but mostly apart, lying in bed in the dark of night with eyes wide open, thinking back over and over on how life had been, all along and especially recently, evaluating the present situation in light of their own wishes and interests, then speculating on how things might or might not change. And their temples were throbbing. What fateful decisions! They reviewed the ups and downs making a living had been since before the war, and the antisemitism of those years and the ones that followed, and the almost insuperable difficulties of their marriage, and the daily struggles and joys of raising two children, and they imagined how all these things would be different in America for better and for worse, and their jaws tightened imperceptibly and suddenly his face flushed as he heard the barking dogs that might be straining on the leash sniffing for our scent as we neared the border, and they let their thoughts dart from how much cash they could get if they tried to sell all their possessions in a few days, and the possibly unimaginable obstacles of setting up a new life, and the few members of Leslie's family who remained in Hungary and from whom he would now have to part maybe forever, and they considered many other things too.

The detailed plans and actual logistics they could not have worked out before early December. Conditions were too volatile for that. But when the time came, first of all they turned whatever possessions they had into cash. They disposed of pretty much everything, most of it for pickup after our disappearance, some of it for nothing more than smiles and good will and promises of heaven knows what. A few things they deposited for safe-keeping with Rózsi or Klári, things they could not part with outright, and a permanent loan seemed to be the easiest lie you could tell yourself and swallow. At the same time they also reduced their personal belongings to a bare minimum. Back there you never got rid of anything except actual waste, and I can't even imagine what had to be done with unwanted things. They also scoped out the available means of getting out of the city, settled on what seemed best and did everything possible to assure success. When you hear how we actually proceeded, you'll think that they too must have read the December-10th piece in the *Times* that I just quoted from, because they made our plans as if armed with the information *it* conveys, and also because the unanticipated events and their responses to them also followed the details recited there.

Once we were on our way, the moment required every watt of your attention. But during the days or weeks of preparation there must have been time for a few thoughts at least about the ending being so carefully planned. For it was very much an ending too. Much of what they were arranging had to do with winding up affairs in the old country, tying up loose ends, terminating existing arrangements. As you've seen, Leslie and Rose had lives that had often been derailed and frequently restarted. Still, they were now in their forties and about to undertake a dismantling and building up anew perhaps more thorough-going than any before. And a voluntary one at that. Those particular circumstances, and also the long period of anticipation, must have made this ending very difficult to deal with, especially for him. For he not only did not want to go but also did not know how to repress his feelings. In any case, supremely unaware as I was of what went on in their heart of hearts, I can try to evoke their pangs of the impending midlife ending only this way: in just a few desperate, anxious days or weeks Rose and Leslie divested themselves of all belongings, of all they had managed to erect about themselves as protection from the environment and from enemies; they divested themselves of shelter, comfort, all their arrangements for making a living, of language, accumulated wealth if they had any, personal belongings, nationality, citizenship, relatives, familiarity with surroundings and places of memory; they divested themselves of the past and the present. They held fast only to the future, although that is never really yours to hold at all.

And so at 4:00 AM, the night of Thursday morning, December 13, 1956, we were on our way. We were transplanting ourselves, which may sound like and was indeed a life-changing event but is nevertheless and has always been a common enough thing to do. Human migrations began right at the beginning, with the movement of homo sapiens out of East Africa into other parts of that continent, and then into Eurasia and to all of the world. But those early wanderings don't really count, because hunter-gatherers belonged no place to begin with and, I imagine, only drifted to satisfy their needs and only explored to satisfy their curiosity. Those practices changed only with the invention of agriculture. Now suddenly human beings were sedentary, domesticated creatures, that is, men and women living in fixed abodes. And the condition of being settled, together with the society of greater complexities that entailed, seemed to bring with it, now and then and actually in a dialectical manner, the needs and opportunities to unsettle, that is, to migrate. In fact, even pastoral people, who live in moveable homes, even they have at times felt compelled not just to move to the summer pastures but to migrate. Certainly, that is what the Magyar tribes did during the centuries when in what seem like trial-and-error stages they relocated from Central Asia to the Carpathian Basin. So, farmer or herder, any time you could be transplanting yourself, as most likely your neighbors were doing too, and doing so for one or more of what have always been and are still today the handful of usual reasons: to escape climate change or natural disasters, to gain more *Lebensraum*, to flee from an enemy or an encroaching neighbor, to rob what belongs to others, to conquer distant lands and extend your dominion, to spread the faith, to leave persecution behind, or just to have a more comfortable and secure life. From this list of reasons you can see that some transplantations have been voluntary while others have been forced, or rather willingness and external compulsion have been mixed in various proportions in most cases.

Still, it seems, for you cannot ever quantify something like this, that since the late 18th century, the explosive growth of the world population, improvements in transportation and the totalization of war have *forced* more and more people to seek their livelihood or safety away from their homes. And for some time now, the transit from the old abode to the new one, whether familial, communal or tribal, has for many been probably more perilous than ever. You carried your life in your hands, as it were, and tried to lavish on it the meticulous care demanded by an organ rescued from a car-crash victim. Even if you were not a refugee and did not have to escape, risks and dangers waited to mug you around every corner. But lest I create false suspense and then disappoint you, I will state right here that we were among the lucky ones. For we pretty much just slipped through the Iron Curtain, as if we had Superman's powers, and then found ourselves in a welcoming and benign place, from which we proceeded to our new home expeditiously. Despite the misapprehensions that must have been nagging at Leslie and Rose, our transit was *not* fraught with the many hardships, dangers and even horrors you see and hear about on the evening news. We experienced nothing like the life of refugees in camps in many parts of the world today, or the Vietnamese boat-people of the 1970s at sea in flimsy barks sometimes for many months, or the millions of displaced persons in Europe after World War II, or Americans crossing all or a portion of the continent as they migrated west, and again I could go on. True, we did have to cope with uncertainty and anxiety, and we did have to put up with statelessness and homelessness and rely entirely on the kindness of strangers. But those things were as if momentary, and they were very soon forgotten too in the both pleasure- and panic-inducing Alice-in-Wonderland aftermath.

In the pre-dawn darkness then of that December day we set out on our mostly silent march to the Western Railway Station, a landmark on the Ring Boulevard at a distance of about forty minutes from where we lived if you're walking in the company of an eleven-year-old and two suitcases. Yes, we were stealing away, dispossessing that self-righteous and hold-onto-its-own world of our presence. The scene comes back to me now that I am focusing on it, a couple of flashes of memory, I can see us and sense us in the unfamiliarity of the insensate night, although what I actually felt and thought are lost, and what anybody else may have felt and thought were never articulated or communicated in any way. Given his cauldron-like temperament, Leslie would have liked it otherwise I think, he would have liked the world to end in fire not ice, but Rose froze him out. I can only guess the anxiety, fear, sorrow, determination and excitement that must have been gripping them, having cast off as they had into vast and unknown waters, with the far shore at an immeasurable distance and survival there, despite all the opulence guaranteed by legend, a risky business. Now that I have passed through middle age, raised children and provided for a family, although all during the most favorable of times and in the most sheltered of worlds, I can only cringe and gasp when

I consider their situation: having nothing in the world, fleeing towards what at best will be a new life, another new life, in which they will be naked, just-born, defenseless babes, and speechless too, with seemingly not much of a feel even, despite Leslie's wartime adventures, for what a foreign language can be.

In the station, a typical 19th-century glass-roofed structure, the lighting was dim, the shabby-looking trains with their dark windows looked as if asleep, and the people, a surprising number of them given the hour, made no sound that could disturb the peace smothering the city. In my recent researches I came across an article in the *Times* dated December 13th, which explains the count of less than a thousand for the day with these words: "The smaller influx of refugees, however, was little tribute to the occupying Soviet forces. It only underscored the effectiveness of the Hungarian workers' general strike and the complete tie-up of railroads, the chief means of escape from Budapest." On reading this, something like a wave of retroactive anxiety swept through me. Had Leslie and Rose known about the strike? Had our farmer-guide? Had this particular interplay of the personal and the historical entered their calculations? Or was this an additional and maybe insurmountable obstacle? But then I calmed myself. I recalled the fundamental reality of the day, namely, that at that time and with regard especially to the venture on which we had launched ourselves, you could count on nothing. Not on the men needed to run the trains, not on the coal needed for the trains to run, and not on anything else either. There was no such thing those days as normal, regular or even usual. Life went on, but it was only a game of chance, with all the safety equipment disconnected and the emergency personnel too busy with their own problems to respond to your alarms. So you needed more nerve than usual just to formulate your schemes and more strength maybe than you'd ever had. As you see, there was the possibility that we'd be foiled even before the sun rose and at any time after that too. And although we were well prepared, in the end we managed to reach Austria only because our luck in avoiding and dealing with the unexpected held up in general and also specifically in four instances.

Immediately, Leslie started rushing about the station and the farmer too looked left and right and behind, although in an apparently more deliberate fashion. After a while a few of the trains began to awaken, clanking and hissing as if clearing their throat in the morning. But was an invisible drama also building up a head of steam here in the film-noir shadows under the sightless rectangles of the grimy glass canopy, a drama of railroad personnel not present? Soon we all started walking up and down platforms, lifting the suitcases for a few steps then putting them down, glancing at the rust-edged destination-boards on the cars, watching people climbing up the steep steps to the vestibules, looking over nearby doers and idlers. Here and there, I suspected, people were doing business. Leslie stopped a man and then a woman to ask a hurried question, his eyes darting about even as he leaned in the better to emphasize his words. Then he went off to buy tickets at a ticket window, trying to carry on as if his intentions were innocent and the usual order of things still prevailed, and maybe he got them or maybe he bought them only on the train, I don't remember. On and off, he was also consulting the farmer in anxious *sotto voce*, pointing at the front of the train and then at the rear, and maybe also confirming our cover story of going to Sopron, the farmer's hometown, to visit family members with names and at addresses memorized through drills of repetition, which we hoped not to have to recite, in part because the story was feeble, and in part because any encounter at all with public authority was likely to be fatal to our efforts. You had to be circumspect about your every move, as I'm sure Leslie was being, for despite his worrying and anxieties and hot-headedness, he was very sure of himself and skillful at getting what he needed under even the most parlous of circumstances, with which both he and Rose had already contended often enough.

Finally, the farmer pointed to one of the dingy cars of one of the superannuated trains, a public conveyance amounting all by itself to a spoof of the regime's command-economy priorities. We climbed in, handed up the suitcases, with our bodies laid claim to two empty high-backed benches facing each other near one end and settled in. Rose gave everyone something to eat, and we ate and waited. Anxiety gripped us. I myself had been on trains on only two or three previous occasions but was just too possessed by our situation to be curious. Although acutely aware that arrival at our destination was not assured, I did not even try to imagine how life might be if we had to turn around and trudge back to the still warm but already no-longer-ours homestead, our momentum stalled, our courage mocked. After a while the car filled up with faceless human specimens aggregated in small groups. They sent furtive glances all about, some declaring rectitude, others conspiratorial solidarity, still others nothing at all. They were to be our companions for some portion of this westward expedition. Surely everyone there had a story and some passengers, like us, must have had more than one. But not everyone was embarking on a surreptitious undertaking or a journey you might want to recall sixty years later.

Then the train began to move – and that I consider our first specific stroke of luck – one lurch, then another, and then a slow glide into the outdoor darkness, carrying us away from home and into the future. I sat by a window and despite my quasi-anesthetized condition I felt a twinge of the pleasure such movement can impart. I watched as the trackside lights approached and then revealed nothing as they reached us. At first the train made frequent stops, some at stations with names that meant nothing to me, others at just apparently random places. Did fear grip the adults each time, maybe now the railwaymen are actually walking off the job? Well, Leslie at least was as tense throughout the whole ride, if not the whole day, as Fontaine, the jail-breaking Resistance fighter and hero of Robert Bresson's *A Man Escaped,* and you can't be more tense than that. He was also functioning at his best, the adrenaline pumping all the time, senses heightened, muscles of his jaw taut. After Esztergom the day dawned gray, the color of the piles and patches of snow all around, as also of our mechanical caravan and of the river flowing back towards where we had started out, downstreaming in an impersonal, presumably timeless process occasional glimpses of which seemed to reassure me, although I know not of what.

For me the transplantation meant many things of course. Right here I want to mention just two of my beliefs about the whole episode, which had already taken hold of me as I was staring out that window and then kept their grip for a long time. First, there was my tacit but absolutely un-equivocal understanding that leaving was forever. That like most immi-grants to the New World before steamships began to ply the vast waters, I would never be able to return. Not for a visit or a nostalgic tour of the old places, not to a bungalow in the Buda hills or on Lake Balaton in the autumn of a life of satisfactions and growing fat in America, and not to continue the fight for the homeland, for which the freedom fighters long remained ready. After all, we were escaping, and as escapees, we would be violating the law and becoming criminals with prices on our heads, our pictures in my imagination at least tacked to the walls of guardhouses at every point of entry into the country, like wanted posters in the post office. Indeed, we ourselves were now confirming our class alienage and sealing forever our fate as *personae non gratae*. For me, this was an essen-tial element of the whole affair, a drastic consequence that seemed more than anything else to stamp the day with a finality I had never thought possible. But did Rose and Leslie see a forever thing here too? I have al-ways assumed that they had, but now that I have raised the question I see that I really can't answer it. I of course was too young and naïve to know that conditions always change and even world-historical phenomena like the Cold War pass or thaw a little at least with time, but they were not. On the other hand, they could have been just too stunned by the one-two punch of fascism and Communism to believe that the horrors would ever end or even just recede. To imagine even just that fences could be mended, as they were indeed to this extent at least not many years later.

The other belief was that I was not an exile, and indeed nothing that day or during the entire transplantation could fill me with a sense of loss or rob me of the cautious excitement that easily withstood the few anx-ious individual moments. Even the utter break with everything except the immediate family did not seem a particularly frightening prospect. Indeed, while I have after arriving in America always felt thoroughly like an immigrant, and after some time here also quite a bit the native, I have never felt like an emigrant. What I left behind never meant much to me, except maybe during the first few months in the Bronx, while I did indeed slip into fits of homesickness. For Dr. Selwyn and Ferber, two of the major characters in Sebald's *The Emigrants*, and for Austerlitz too, emigrants all of them from the continent and immigrants to England, the transplantation is an utter break by which life and its very meaning are permanently impaired, a break that assumes increasing importance in their later years and comes eventually to dominate their stories. For their lives in England turn out to be just so many years in exile, years of banishment from the earlier *normal* life, where feelings freely flowed, optimism reigned and you were intimately connected to people and to the past. Well, for me the transplantation was nothing like that! Nor a loss of paradise, as it might have been had Proust lived it. If anything, for me the emigration was a fitting sequel to an already long career of abandoning and being abandoned and breaking deep connections with little regret. You know how much I enjoy visiting Hungary and faking being Hungarian, but even while there the only Hungarian past I see overwhelming my present, other than the Jewish thing of course, is my still quite serviceable expertise in leaving. No, I never feel or felt like an emigrant.

I didn't feel like an emigrant even as I sat on that train, which came next to Komárom, and then an hour or so later to Győr, the location in the country's circulatory system where the branch railway and roads separate from the main arteries connecting Budapest and Vienna, still about fifty miles distant from Sopron. Győr is one of the country's largest cities, but large only by Hungarian standards. Under Communist rule, unauthorized travel beyond it was forbidden, as it was also around Siklós on account of *its* proximity to the *Yugoslav* frontier. Then I didn't know, but revolutionary fervor had been high around Győr all along and resistance there had persisted almost as long as in the capital and was re-erupting in its final gasps those very days. These were all good reasons to keep up your guard at all times and watch for the railwaymen, who were still at their posts and could generally be depended on to express their own displeasure with the regime by spreading news of the presence of uniformed personnel and so alerting would-be fugitives. And sure enough, a minute or two after the train came to a halt in Győr station word percolated to us that soldiers were boarding to check identification cards and other relevant papers. Leslie and the farmer exchanged ears-pricked-up glances and acted immediately. This confrontation must be avoided! Valises and bags now flew off luggage racks and out the window. Rose and the children clambered down to the platform. Up and down the length of the train passengers were disembarking in an orderly and quiet manner, as if testing with their toes the temperature in the pool of repression and fear. Unhurriedly so as not to attract attention, and according to the by-then established allocation of burdens, we picked up our luggage, Leslie took Marika's hand, and we made our way safely out to the streets. That warning was our second specific stroke of luck.

But what now? How indeed does an emigrant emigrate even when there is a railroad strike, as there was for us now in effect? The best way he can, of course. If he has at least a destination, then he just looks for a road leading toward it. If not, then he just sets out in a desirable direction. In either case, transportation he hopes to secure somehow only once he is on his way. And if the emigrant is also a fugitive, then he does all of that while also feeling as if festooned with targets of concentric circles front and back. And so for a while we walked through the city, hoping to dodge the law and evade despair, in the direction of Sopron the farmer kept assuring us, which is a notch below Győr in size and status, the second-ranking urban center of the northwest section of the country. We had already discussed the possibility of stalling in the farmer's home for a day and crossing only the following evening if we got there too late, or too tired, to try for the border that night. But other than that we had no plan, nothing but our objective to get to Sopron without being discovered. And discovery was not just a remote possibility but an ever-present danger, for just about anyone laying eyes on us could have at once recognized the refugee family being shepherded by its hired-hand border-jumper. Just picture us. A man, a woman, a boy, a girl and two suitcases. Obviously, a family adrift but becalmed, dressed in the unfashionable layers of the homeless, carrying all its meager belongings, in pursuit of a dream beyond reach, a dream susceptible to turning like milk, to souring into a nightmare. Picture us as roadside-dwellers a Gypsy would have pitied, victims of circumstances and history, reluctant migrants afraid of sinking into vagabondage. Looking like this we tramped along. It may have been around the noon hour as we proceeded down a street parallel to the highway running through the city. That seemed less risky than the main road, but it also offered no signs of life at all. For already we were in the shadow of the Iron Curtain. Already we had entered the forbidden zone.

After a while a truck rattled along from behind us and to my surprise the farmer just stepped into the middle of the street and calmly flagged it down. He chatted with one of the men in the cab, then stepped back. The truck moved on. Soon another truck came up, with a dark gray cab and gray canvas stretched around a frame affixed to the bed. A motorized descendant of the prairie schooner, I would now say. This time we were in luck, indeed this was our third specific stroke of luck. The truck too was going to Sopron; it had a cargo of maybe a dozen crates that filled only the front half of the cargo area; and for a negotiated sum the truckers were willing to have the farmer ride in the cab with them and let us wedge ourselves between the front of the truck and the crates. An obvious enough hiding place, and one used regularly, to judge by the reports of other refugees, but how many other hiding places could there have been on any means of transportation then plying that route? So obvious or not, it was a godsend, and suddenly we could consider ourselves back on track or something like that.

At that time, the largest denomination of Hungarian currency was the 100-forint note, a faintly pinkish rectangle of paper embossed in a dark pink. I had seen some over the years but had never *had* one of course. It would have been a lot of money for a kid. The average worker's pay at that time was 800 forints a month, as I just learned recently, and while neither Leslie nor Rose had been an average worker in most any sense of the word, it was only during the New Course that *he* made more than the average. And Rose must always have made less than the average because she worked at home. In any case, 100-forint notes were not common in our household. All the greater my astonishment then on seeing Leslie, after a sum was apparently agreed upon with the truckers, reach into his pocket and produce a very large wad of paper money, pink from the outermost to the inner, although I did not fail to note to myself that there was room for a lot of doubt about what exactly was stuffed in-between. That two-inch-thick stack of bills was, I suppose, what they had managed to get from selling things. That was all our worldly means at the time, aside possibly from some jewels in the suitcases or on Rose, and certainly there was Leslie's watch, which had repeatedly been identified for me as a valuable Swiss-made object, and that it would surely have been if sold new in a store. There was also a Leica camera, and maybe the lace that Rose treasured but could have converted to hardly more than a meal or two. Nothing else. Leslie now peeled off the right number of bills and returned the wad to his pocket. The two men climbed onto the truck and began to move the crates about. Leslie and Rose were anxious for all of us would-be emigrants to be hidden and on our way. Everybody hurried.

While the truckers completed their work, we stood about, casting nervous glances ahead and behind, and stamping our feet not so much on account of the cold but just to underscore those moments of stand-still in that day of compulsive and compulsory forward movement. Then upon a beckoning signal we handed up our valises, scrambled up onto the boards after them and crawled in front of the crates. We perched on our luggage, four abreast and snug, whereupon the two men pushed the crates together and against our backs. The engine sputtered to life. On to Sopron rolled the truck, smuggling its human cargo, the three enter-prising locals in the cab working for the extra buck, putting private needs ahead of the interests of their class – for surely they belonged to the great historical alliance of workers and peasants – the regime, the system, the ideology. Did they have any feelings about us or our venture? Did they detest the defectors, revile the rootless Jews, sneer at the city-dwellers? No one ever asked or even hazarded a searching look. It would have been foolish to, as well as beside the point. After all, despite the undoubted solicitousness even at this late date of denizens of the frontier areas for Austria-bound fugitives, and despite the continued pockets of resistance too, the revolutionary fervor had already much dissipated. What I witnessed was pretty much just a business transaction, just what the reporting in the *Times* would have made me expect had I then already been a raised-on-freedom, sitting-pretty-in-New-York reader of the *Times*.

The truck was advancing into territory that was off-limits to some of us and turned the others into accomplices in a criminal act. I would think that we all, except maybe Marika on account of her tender years, were increasingly aware of our proximity to the mythic Iron Curtain. I myself understood nothing more about the thing than its two basic purposes, for its mystique of brutal malevolence and world-historical significance had until sometime later remained incomprehensible to me. The first of those purposes was of course to prevent people and things from leaving the country. Everyone in Hungary those days knew that going abroad was impossible, except of course to another country to which it *was* possible, but to which for reasons very much related to that possibility you wanted *not* to go. The path to everywhere else was blocked. That was just part of the tyranny of the day, as I saw the situation. As was also the years my grandmother, a woman in her 70s, had to wait for an exit visa, to come to New York to live with her daughter Anci. As indeed was also the very need for us to be escaping rather than simply having the right to go. The second purpose was to prevent people and things from entering the country. In his initial iron-curtain references, made even before his famous March 1946 iron-curtain speech, Churchill was already emphasizing that "we do not know what is going on behind" it. The isolation of the East from the West, the shutting out of Western influence both intentional and incidental, the hiding from prying eyes even, was immediately perceived as a primary Soviet objective in erecting the barrier. For yet another part of the tyranny of the day, and an essential part, was to seal workers and peasants off from the outside world, to keep them imprisoned in their ignorance of it and in their force-fed false opinions about it.

Migrants undermined this never-the-twain-shall-meet arrangement. By leaving, they disturbed the order of things and seemed to proclaim that the Communist paradise was good only for leaving behind. By leaving illegally, they also compelled the authorities either to cover up the departures or to strenuously vilify the departed ones. And then upon resettling, the migrants promptly became participants in so many cross-border linkages. Two of Rose's sisters, Pearl and Anci, had been postwar emigrants and had maintained an exchange of letters with Rose and with Erzsi, respectively, Erzsi being the daughter with whom my grandmother lived in Budapest. True, the Communists monitored your mail, as everyone knew, but they did not dare on a long-term basis anyway to make the Iron Curtain completely impenetrable even to correspondence, that is, to literally break the connections. I guess that would have been a piece of tyranny much too blatant even for them. Nor could they contrive threats sufficient in effect to render the communications ideologically harmless. Certainly, the facts and ideas about America I picked up from those letters and packages did not make me any fonder of Hungarian ways. And then specifically in the aftermath of the revolution, the Communists even had to compromise a little. It was probably best to lower the barrier for a short time it seemed, whatever the consequences. But, as a result, if you then became a fugitive, you couldn't even know what or where exactly the Iron Curtain was. I mean, once past Győr, weren't we already at least on Iron-Curtain territory, as it were? Well, in any case, we trusted our farmer-guide to be initiated into the mysteries, and we ourselves were also edgily on our guard. There was no way to know when the barrier-masters and their minions would tire of compromising and go back to devising extra punishments for your kind.

But I myself, as the truck rolled along, I forgot all about the dangers of the road, for I actually had other worries. As a boy I was subject to motion sickness. Buses, trains, metros, streetcars – there was no mode of transportation through the doors of which I did not have a history of stumbling out as waves of nausea swept over me, through the windows of which I had not projected out streams of vomit. And now, being jarred, jostled and jolted, I was nervously monitoring my alimentary organs for the first signs of nausea. And sure enough, they came upon me soon, in the beginning just a few fleeting sensations, but enough to throw me into a panic, into what would have been a frantic search for escape had I not known that there was no escape in the midst of escaping. So I just sat rigidly, focused on the rising tide of signs and feelings that was soon to turn into a literally rising tide, sweat pouring down my face, gripped by equal portions of fear and disgust at the prospect of the wrenching convulsions and of spewing vomit all over myself. At the last minute, reaching across Marika, Rose pressed Leslie's fedora into my hands and nodded vigorously. Sick as I was, I was more incredulous yet. After all, it was Leslie's *hat*. But again Rose pressed the hat into my hands and indicated beyond the possibility of any misunderstanding that she meant for me to throw up into it. I don't know if she had sought or received Leslie's concurrence to this sacrifice or not. She may have just snatched the thing off his head with such an air of determination that he had not dared to object even while he could have. But that's a mother for you. So I vomited into it, and it was disposed of, though I don't remember how. Obviously, the scene could have been played as comedy, but at the moment nobody was in a laughing mood. And then I was all right.

As we rode along, I was staring through the slats of the truck's frontboards and at the gray backside of its cab. The world was passing by unseen and unheard too, for the strained laboring of the engine and the tires' grind against the road deafened me to all other sounds. And we ourselves uttered not a word. Nothing needed to be said, and the unnecessary would have been unwelcome. Then the truck came to a halt. The men in the cab seemed to be exchanging words with other men, the faceless confronting the faceless, and from the general sounds I took the language to be Russian. Then the engine was cut, the doors of the cab opened and slammed shut, and heavy boots pounded alongside me and towards the back of the vehicle. There was no more doubt now, the words of command were Russian, as were the few syllables of the truckers, muttered timidly by men deprived of their native skills of communication and subject to a superior force. A glimmer of backlight then made me feel exposed as the rear flaps of the canvas were lifted. I froze with fear. I imagined the Soviets to be two soldiers in their bilious khakis, with submachine guns slung around a shoulder, one hand resting casually on a barrel whose angle of elevation, for the moment minimal, menaced all of us like a crouching beast, ready to spring up, leap and attack with deadly claws and vicious growls. More words and syllables were then uttered, some emitted from a closer range than others, as if heads were being poked into the truck's enclosure, or bodies leaning into it even. Then a quiet moment during which the soldiers seemed to consult with each other, then the backlight was extinguished, the boots stomped away, the cab doors opened and slammed, and slammed again, engine, gears engaging, the initial lurch, and we rolled on. Phew!

Only after we arrived in Sopron, emerged from our hiding place and entered the farmer's home did I learn the actual details of that encounter. We had indeed been stopped by two Soviet soldiers, boys maybe not yet out of their teens, with the Asiatic looks of the far reaches of the mighty empire, conducting a routine check, demanding identification papers, casting rapid glances inside vehicles. All had gone well until the canvas flaps were thrown aside to reveal two freshly-killed hares lying at the back of the truck. I had never seen dead rabbits or any dead animal at all, with the exception of a squealing fatted pig running about a courtyard in always smaller circles, blood spurting from beside the knife stuck into its throat, just killed but not yet prepared for pot or pan, which I saw at the age of seven when Leslie and I had traveled by train to a pig-killing in early winter, an affair with long knives, bonfires and monstrous shadows, which I tend maybe not too romantically to remember as a kind of saturnalia. In any case, I could not imagine what those lifeless furry shapes might have looked like or how even in my haste I could have not noticed them when climbing aboard, but there they were obviously when the soldiers demanded to know if the truckers had weapons and if not, then how had they managed to kill the animals. Here linguistic skills gave out. One soldier stood to the side and aimed his gun at the darkness under the canvas while the other pushed his gun up on his back and readied to swing himself up onto the truck's platform. It was at this point that one of the truckers grabbed the hares by their limp ears and wordlessly offered the animals to the soldiers. It worked. The gun was lowered and muscles relaxed. We were free to proceed. And that was our fourth and final specific stroke of luck.

Now we were really approaching the border, inserting our very selves into the international context, and now the reality of the Soviet occupation confronted us as I don't recall it ever doing in Budapest. The dangers were multiplying, that you had to take for granted. Given the requirement for a special permit to be where we were, at all times we had to be expecting the kind of identity check we had just gone through. How would we deal with the next patrol? If challenged, we could have responded only with some money, which the occupiers would have had no use for. Or maybe the Leica? Ahh! But no one troubled us again. The truck stopped somewhere in Sopron and disgorged us onto cobbled streets under a sky darkened by clouds and the early evening of a northern winter. I remember nothing of that town or of the way to the farmer's home on its outskirts. I remember only the gloom that pervaded the house, maybe some bunk beds in the shallow depths of a brusquely foreshortened interior, and a man and a woman sitting by the stove when we arrived, each of them around thirty I would guess, faceless and thrown together only by the adventure in which they were to join us. We idled there indoors until an unvaried darkness allowed our group to set out for the crossing itself.

Of our under-age personal belongings, Marika and I had each been permitted to take along two items, to be included in the Hungarian world we had enclosed in our two suitcases, as they might have been in two boxes by Joseph Cornell. Of course, the objects had to meet stringent size and weight restrictions, so I cannot identify them as in fact our favorite possessions, although I also can't recall anything else to which I myself was more attached. If Barbara and I had to make a run for it when the kids were growing up, I ask myself – and even the thought is horrifying – would I have considered the kids' feelings about their belongings and treated those feelings as no less legitimate than my own and as insistent on and worthy of being satisfied? I'm sure I would have, now that I think about it. Isn't it utterly natural to do so? So I shouldn't give undue credit to Leslie and Rose for their thoughtfulness in this respect. Rather, I will just take the two-object allowance as a comment on the essential connection we have with our belongings, and on how naked are those who migrate or, worse yet, flee or are driven from their accustomed abode. And I am not thinking here of necessities, which constitute a problem of an entirely different kind. But other things, objects you do not need to live but only to be someone, an individuated person, the one whom you believe yourself to be, objects that you cling to even as a child, in one part to satisfy an urge to possess and thus in a sense to extend yourself in space, and in another to reassure yourself of your own continuity and thus to extend yourself in time.

But once you leave and swallow the bitterness of letting go, the loss you feel on account of the things left behind may quickly dissipate. Indeed, while you are actually migrating, those objects are likely not to matter at all. We, for example, were more utterly dispossessed with our suitcases than the Joads even of *The Grapes of Wrath* with their little truck piled high with rough-hewn belongings, but so what? We were going to America, and they had been going to California, which for them during the 1930s was something very much like *America's* America, and at that moment that overshadowed everything else. We all had destinations, and more than that, destinations of the most desirable kind. Neither we nor they were anything like the thousands of Parisians fleeing their city in June 1940, clogging roads, driving, leading carthorses, riding bicycles or on foot, carrying whatever they could. They were hoping to return, so what they salvaged was going to have an impact and maybe even a decisive effect on whether or not they would be able to resume their old lives. But for us and the Joads life on the road was nothing but a future, in blind reliance on which we all believed that our respective you-have-only-what-you-carry conditions would be quite temporary. The objects Marika and I took along, and even most of the things packed by Rose and Leslie, were supposed to be a means of sustenance only during the hopefully brief submersion into an abject homelessness, during a temporary withdrawal from what I will call a low-density object world in anticipation of entry into a high-density one. A brief objectless deprivation that soon would yield not just to a mere restoration of how it had been, but, for us as well as for the Joads, to yippie-yi-yo-ki-yay. Although after you find a new home and get involved with objects once more, the feeling of loss and the bitter taste can return periodically.

In June 1938, three months after annexation of Austria by Nazi Germany, when after much hesitation and many difficulties Sigmund Freud, 82-years-old at the time, finally left Vienna to seek refuge in London, he was already assured that all the contents of his consulting room, including the famous couch, were also being moved there. As it is often put, the great man had to pay a *ransom* to be allowed to leave, and a flight tax was also imposed on the export of his belongings, in particular his personal collection of Egyptian, Greek and Roman antiquities, which formed part of the furnishings of that room and included more than *2,000* small objects. Although Freud had to turn to his student Princess Marie Bonaparte for the necessary funds, without the collection he was not willing to leave. For he was a man properly if not indeed too well attached to objects and, by the way, a collector otherwise too, of case histories, dreams and jokes. I, on the other hand, if you'll pardon the comparison, I care little about objects now nor did I care anymore for them back then. I do admire beautiful things, works of art, antiques I see in museums or in the houses of wealthy friends, festive garments, fine things made of precious metals, first editions of books I love and I could go on – but I don't have the desire to own them. I've tried it now and then, but always the chase turned out to be more satisfying than the catch. But since I am attached to the historical past in so many ways, I do wonder if maybe I could have been at least a little bit like Freud, if having had the means to do so I too could over a lifetime have assembled a collection like his, or something like it, appropriately scaled down to my humble self of course. But no, I can't imagine doing that. However, if a single object, a Greek terracotta sphinx, let's say, or an Egyptian coffin mask, had somehow come into my possession, I can see myself treasuring it and appreciating it as an embodiment of the past, of the place and times in which it was made and of the spirit, skills and intentions of its maker, himself a representative of a way of life and thinking that has long fascinated me. So maybe even I could have loved the right object after all.

In 1956 I chose the first of my two take-alongs without a moment's hesitation: my Swiss army knife. Or, to be precise, not *my* Swiss army knife, but a friend's. I had swapped my stamp collection for it, actually a few loose pages in a folder, swapped it temporarily at least, for he wouldn't have given up something as fabulous as that marvelously engineered instrument for my ordinary, haphazard collection, and I wouldn't have either had I been in his shoes. To me that knife, which had been made with beauty and utility in mind, and which I wanted more for the beauty than the utility, or rather more for the beauty of its appearance and its manifold usefulness than for its utility – to me that knife represented perfection. I can't recall any other occasion in my life when an object of my own so captivated me. Not a camera, not a garment, not a statuette or piece of pottery, not a car and certainly not electronic equipment. To me that knife was nothing short of the various exquisite pre-industrially produced things you can run across in Europe, like, say, the 17th-18th-century mosaic table tops of semi-precious stones you see in the Palazzo Pitti. Okay, so it wasn't mine, but under the circumstances I had to take it. Leaving it in a drawer with some puffs of lint and a couple of loose thumb tacks would have accomplished nothing. And I was glad of that. Although in America I never knew what to do with the knife. I never used it or even looked at it, but kept it, yes, in a drawer with a magnifying lens and some foreign coins until Ari, my older stepson, then a teenager, borrowed it and lost it. And then I replaced it with another Swiss army knife not quite as perfect, which I also never look at, handle or use.

Then, well... what about the second object? At first I suffered a moment of embarrassment, as if I had just failed something like introductory object-attachment, but then I picked something that was a repository of memories. I had two songbooks for voice and easy piano, "The Best Songs of 1955" and "The Best Songs of 1956." They were cheap, light, thin paperback volumes, sheet-music size, printed on coarse paper, one bound in blue, the other in forest green, with red branch-and-leaves-and-flowers motifs taken, quite incongruously given the contemporary self-image of the music, from typical Hungarian folk-embroidery patterns sinuously underlining the simple white lettering on each cover. I chose the 1956 songbook as the second object to take along, but only as a means of conveyance for elements of my then identity and of an about-to-be-abandoned culture and not at all for itself. I chose it because my early-teen feelings were deeply embedded in its songs, almost as if I had been living in a movie romance, although of an unusually prim kind. But the preservation scheme did not work. A single week was all the Bronx needed to rob those tunes of all their soul. A cheap pink AM radio was one of our first American purchases, and the insinuating melodies and rock-a-billy rhythms emanating from that small plastic box, even with words that were incomprehensible, silenced all other music for me. Which I did not mind at all. After all, I did have an intense desire to assimilate, and even aside from that, this was the very music young people longed for even *in Hungary.* Everybody wanted Elvis for king. I revisited that songbook only once many years later, right before I trashed it. And all the songs I forgot utterly, except for one that did unexpectedly come back to haunt me after fifty years.

In terms of the function the take-alongs were expected to perform, Marika's choices seem to have mirrored mine, as mine mirrored hers. The fountain pen she had recently received as a gift I see as very much analogous to the Swiss army knife, and the pair of diminutive porcelain figurines, a ballerina and her partner, I see as an expression of the desire to preserve an element of one's fantasy life, of one's underage imagination, and so as analogous to the songbook. And Marika's objects too,

434

like mine, were molded into stories, although quickly everyone forgot the fate of the former, while remembering well that the latter never made it to America. You see, in Sopron, while anxiously the adults waited for the darkness of another night to descend, Marika got to playing with our host's daughter and even showed off the figurines, which must have been in her pockets. The little girl admired the delicate and diminutive dancers, painted I now imagine in the pale pastel colors typical of Hungarian porcelain, and Marika promptly gave them to her. Just like that. Why did she do that? What was the connection that sprang up between the two little girls, so irresistibly, so briefly? Is this in part at least how Marika emigrated? Was she the most realistic of us all? Well, you can only speculate about her motives. The decades themselves have dimmed the details, but even right then I think, even then it would have been difficult to sort out the reasons, given the circumstances, the personalities, their backgrounds, and given all the tangled meanings, as anthropologists tell us, that can lurk beneath the surface of a gift transaction.

It must have been in Sopron also, during our few hours there in the farmer's house, that Leslie replaced the hat. He absolutely needed another one because we had the whole winter ahead of us, and also because back then a man without a hat was still less than completely dressed. Over the years the motion-sickness incident came up in family conversations a couple of times, but the matter of the replacement never did. Leslie was just fine ending up as the person who sacrifices for his family, although I'm not sure that's the way he had felt during the upchuck itself. But I don't mean by that doubt to suggest that he was ever less than the dutiful father and after some time the dutiful husband too, and much more than that even. As the one who sacrifices, that's how Leslie always cast himself, that's how he felt the most comfortable. Rose also sacrificed readily for the children, but for Leslie never prior to their last years together, when they were already so mutually dependent that any sacrifice for the other was also an act of self-preservation. Their biggest sacrifice for the children had of course been coming to America. Yes, a sacrifice, because Rose and Leslie, speaking with one voice or two, always professed to have undertaken the risks and rigors of transplantation "for the children." They wanted the children to have a better life. But for the children, they at least suggested, they would not have ventured. After everything they had been through by then, and in their forties already, Rose actually 49, and not knowing a word of English? No! Emigration was a sacrifice, and they had sacrificed for the children.

Now, to be sure, this was not something often repeated, and never just volunteered. They trotted out those words only when asked directly why, but that could and did happen just about any time. Why had they taken to the road? Well, for the children. Why had they grabbed the unexpected opportunity? To promote the children's welfare. I myself always accepted that at face value and so did Marika I dare say. Or let's just say that we never discussed the matter with each other, which is what we would have done had we thought there was anything to think about, to find peculiar, to be suspicious of. But we never did. Then, many years later when Barbara and I took up with each other, it was she, with her unfailing nose for emotional secrets, who quickly pointed out that it all didn't add up. If the reason had been a better life for *all of us*, then why didn't they say so, that would have been a completely respectable and or-dinary reason. But "for the children" – wasn't that obviously a cover-up for something, and not a good cover-up either because it actually drew attention to the realities of Leslie and Rose's then situation by the mere fact of trying to find motives independent of it? At first I couldn't admit it, but then I had to: she was onto something. But where did that get us? Were we looking for something general or something specific? An event of those days or a chronic condition, as it were? Maybe the pretext had been discredited, but that revealed nothing about the actual facts that we hadn't known already. Barbara came back to the subject now and then, but I put it out of my mind as another mystery never to be solved and therefore an idle thought. And also, as you know, until after Leslie died I didn't ask questions.

So for many years I had at least tacitly accepted that we had fled Hungary and come to America not actually to escape from Communist persecution, or because we wanted to put antisemitism behind us, or on account of the desire for an easier life here, or for the children's future either. In other words, for many years I did not know and could not have said with any conviction why we had fled. But then in the summer of 2004, Barbara and I were visiting in Budapest and on a Sunday afternoon we went with Gyuri and his daughter Eszter to Rózsi's summer cottage in Buda to celebrate her 90th birthday. And there, *à propos* of nothing and in an even tone even as she was lobbing a hand-grenade into the lazy conversation, Rózsi said that I should know that Leslie had had a woman friend in Makó and had even fathered a child with her. A half-brother of mine who arrived in this world bearing a price-tag, because the mother took Leslie to court, where he had to admit paternity and was ordered to pay child-support. A half-brother of whom nothing further was ever heard. Well, the grenade turned out to be a dud. I immediately translated for Barbara and called the news to everybody else's attention too, but the birds just continued their chirp-conferences in the trees and the insects their insect-business. I could not think of anything appropriate to say to Rózsi. A half-brother, really?

That evening at Gyuri's we hashed it all out, the four of us and Juci. You see, in that intimate crowd Rózsi was well known for considering herself the smartest, the best informed and always a step ahead of you, and, frankly, she did not have much credibility. After all, there was the old story that her blindness resulted from a wartime injury, which is what Leslie and Rose had always been told by her and believed, but which was conclusively contradicted by the subsequently confirmed fact that macular degeneration had struck her early in life. There was also the never-before-aired claim, first heard by Gyuri just a few years earlier but then heard frequently by others too, that in the war she had lost not only a husband but also a daughter. And, last but not least, there were the conflicting stories she had told me about Bözsi's wartime sufferings, stating in one version that Bözsi had indeed been put on the cattlecar but had then escaped and spent the six months or so until liberation protected by a Nazi soldier, and stating in the other that in Auschwitz Bözsi had had the job of carting the bodies out of the gas chambers and into the crematoria, and among those bodies were her own parents, my grandparents Miksa and Gizella. How then could you know what was true and what false? And even when she told you of Bözsi in a post-Holocaust hospital ward saying to a doctor that she had seen too many corpses already to mind the body of an old woman that had not been removed from the cot next to her for a disturbingly long time – even then, I ask you, what could you believe or dare disbelieve? But, at the same time, what kind of twisted mind could make up a story like the half-brother?

On our next trip to Hungary, Gyuri referred me to a lawyer, who told me that the records of the paternity suit from just about a half-century ago should still exist in the relevant county offices. So I hired him to investigate the matter, gave him all the facts and mulled over what I would do if he found some traces and could give me the new relative's name. I thought the most sensible move would be to then hire a private detective and let him locate the person in question and find out something about him. *Then* I would decide whether or not and how to pursue the matter. I certainly did not want to be mistaken for a long-lost American half-brother anxious to make up for the disadvantages the bastard had to suffer just so Leslie could provide more lavishly for me. I also foresaw a punch in the nose as a possible gesture of welcome and wanted no part of that either. For good or for bad, however, the lawyer found nothing, not at least in the records of the county where Makó is located. So we'll never know. I was disappointed, but Rózsi found the outcome satisfactory. For some reason you can only surmise, she hadn't been that keen on my hiring the lawyer to begin with.

But the matter was not yet closed, for at some point I suddenly realized how neatly the half-brother story dovetails with the aborted family vacation in Makó during the summer of '56, the night-ride in the back of the truck and Rose's stony look as she rushed us out of there the next morning. Rózsi's revelation at the Buda cottage about fifty years later suddenly illuminated that bizarre incident. Finally, I could formulate a convincing set of circumstances capable of triggering Rose's violent reaction. Could it have happened just like that? Did she, the one day we were there, have to confront not only Leslie's latest paramour, but also acknowledge that the woman was carrying his love-child, in her belly or in her arms? Either way, this transgression was not just more of the same. How then was she to deal with *this* shame and *this* betrayal? And then soon enough on top of that came the outrageous waste of money they didn't have. For by the time Leslie returned to Budapest on the third day of the revolution, the paternity suit had to have been concluded and the right of the woman to money for many years to come had to have been determined. And that now had to have been the last straw! Maybe Rose was already used to Leslie's flings and had found a way to live with them. Or maybe she hadn't. But this! That food should be taken out of the mouths of her own children to nourish his bastard! That her own hard work had to make up for what was lost by dint of his filthy philandering! This nobody could tolerate.

Had it not been for the revolution, who knows what she might have done. She might even have ended the relationship, or more likely just kicked him out without divorcing him. But as things turned out, and I hate to say this because I want you to make up your own unbiased mind about her actions, she came up with a rather elegant alternative. She grabbed hold of the emigration scenario or maybe just let ripen what had been germinating in her mind for a long time already, and decided to flee with the children. And his own decision was his own business. He could stay with his whore and his bastard or come along. Now that is not only elegant but also makes sense! She must have believed, or may even have been convinced, that in the New World he would be as if dis-armed against her. Or maybe she thought that they'd be, each of them, more compelled to stay together, and so live a life indeed better "for the children." Or maybe she was just frantically looking for some way short of a complete break to end the untenable existing arrangement, ready to seize any future, however fraught with risk, as long as it sufficiently unsettled the present. For that is certainly how the future worked out. No wonder neither one of them ever addressed the subject openly. They preferred to keep his transgression a secret from the children, and her retribution too.

So that's how it all happened I think: the need to solve a sordid personal problem made us plunge into the stream of history and hope to be swept to a safer shore. But the matter deserves another formulation too, one arrived at by a more conventional historical analysis. Do you recall learning in school that the causes of World War I are best understood if set forth under two headings: immediate causes and underlying causes? Well, so it is too with our emigration. The bastard half-brother was the immediate cause, without whom and which we would have stayed put. The underlying causes you know already: the hardships and hopelessness of everyday life under Communism, the well-known and often reminded-of attractions of America and the still unsettled position of Jews living among Magyars, all of them powerful even when counterbalanced as they were by the expected difficulties of starting over. These underlying causes were no less essential than the immediate one, and we are not likely to have fled without the impetus provided by them either. But immediate or underlying, by itself neither was sufficient. So this is the full explanation, which could not be assembled as long as any component part was missing. But then out of spite or revenge or to have the final victory, or maybe just in the service of truth – she was capable of thinking that way too, and it *was*, let's not forget, her 90th birthday – Rózsi revealed that hidden component. Or she fabricated it. In any case, I am now satisfied, though I must at the same time stipulate that in the end we will never know for sure why exactly we found ourselves in Sopron on that winter evening, facing the unknown, reaching out for the rescuer's hand *d'outremer.*

For the last installment of our flight our party of seven set out from the farmer's after two or three hours of waiting. The moon was hidden from sight, but through the shifting breaks in the clouds a milkish gray light seeped down and silhouetted all of creation. We slogged across open fields, here and there small islands of dirty snow, passing by clumps of bushes and trees left and right, shoes sinking into the plowed soil whether you walked on the ridges or in the depths of the furrows.

Approaching the limits of the known world, as it were, in the dark on the seemingly uninhabited land, our squishy footfalls might have been leaving their traces on a never-to-be-discovered planet. The farmer estimated that the mud-walk would be about ten kilometers, which was more than could be expected of Marika. So after a while Leslie carried her, putting her down only in the few places where the tricky footing required him to, skinny legs like a bird's stretch-kicking to a landing. We were, all of us, together in that we advanced and intended to advance as a group, yet we were all separate too, each of us but Marika responsible for him- or herself. Encouraging words, and helpful gestures too, passed from one person to another, but first of all you attended to your own progress. I had expected this terrain to be bristling with landmines and was not entirely assured by the farmer's obviously accurate claim that in his company we had nothing to worry about. I can no longer remember how I then imagined the encounter of landmine and human being, Monty Python's antics having long ago monopolized my thoughts on the subject, but I know that the fear of triggering some sort of catastrophic explosion ebbed and flowed within me.

After a while, it may have been one hour, it may have been two, but definitely not more than three, a row of trees appeared athwart our cross-country direction, made visible by a sudden diffuse glow to the right. Human presence obviously, maybe even human activity, quite near, or maybe not quite. I was unsure. We proceeded, our path unchanged, our pace unslackened. For the first time that night, the skeletal winter countenance of the landscape impressed itself upon me. The few trees here and there between us and the source of the light were nothing so much as a desultory network of black lines rising above the muddy footing, momentary entanglements shooting out into ever-fainter lines of escape, which in turn soon vanished in the seemingly upward-shining light, a replica of a system of nerves maybe, each strand of which rushed first to the very limits of sensation and then disappeared into the absence of it. I no longer recall if opinions were actually exchanged on who or what accounted for the light and how, or if I merely had a speculative conversation in my head. In either case, no conclusion was reached. Then as we neared the row of trees and appeared also to have drawn somewhat closer to the source of the light, a small rise in the ground confronted us, a berm running both to left and to right, from which the trees themselves actually rose. At a signal from the farmer, we formed a single line and one after the other, Marika even walking, took the two or three steps up the rise and then passed between two trees and down the other side. "We are in Austria," said the farmer after he too, the last among us, crossed that elevation hardly higher than a makeshift grave.

Exhilaration, the casting off of shackles, a sense of triumph? No, not at all. For us there was nothing like the kneeling-to-kiss-the-wet-earth effusions reported about earlier refugees. In fact, no notable demonstrations of any kind of love of or gratitude for freedom on the arrival side. What about the departure side then? *Before* we crossed, had there been any expressions of loss, resignation or the pathetic mental rending of the fabric of habits, connections and sentiments? Any resistance put up by the animal sense of territoriality? No, not that either. Farewells, if any there were said or sent, I did not hear them, and if a tear had collected in an eye, darkness would have concealed it. But a lingering backward glance, a palm laid on the ground for a final touch, or arms thrown open for a symbolic embrace – these things I would have noticed if they had taken place. Was there no feeling then for the fatherland? For it's not impossible, you know, to love your country even while you're fleeing it. On the contrary. In part at least Louis Kossuth's fame derives from the patriotic, sacrificial fervor of his years in exile. But maybe the Hajdus *never* loved Hungary. They certainly had reason enough not to love a good number of Magyars. In any case, after they left I never heard any words of affection from them for the old country.

But what about the Iron Curtain? Where was it, I had to wonder. Indeed, *what* really was it? I already knew that in Hungary all theaters had an actual iron curtain that could confine fires to the stage, and I certainly did not expect anything so literal to mark the borderline between East and West. I did understand that *the* Iron Curtain was, first of all, a metaphor. But I had also assumed it to have some kind of objective correlative, to be something more than a rhetorical masterstroke by Churchill, more like something analogous to the stone that Dr. Johnson kicked in order to refute Bishop Berkeley's philosophical claim that our ideas alone are real. And indeed the prohibition to enter the frontier zone was itself part of the actual Iron Curtain, and undoubtedly it had other parts too, such as landmines and fences and double fences and strips of no-man's-land and military installations with watchtowers and searchlights and canine patrols. But whatever the Iron Curtain may have added up to altogether, quite obviously its physical reality was nothing like the uninterrupted, unbreachable, Berlin-Wall-like barrier *suggested* by the metaphor, certainly not the night we crossed it and probably ever. Although I know of no apparent reason why it wouldn't have been. In any case, it's obvious that our farmer-guide could run his day-trips business precisely because he knew of one or more spots at least where the metaphor was just that, just words.

But even if you overlook these Iron-Curtain-ly shortcomings, shouldn't there have been flags on the berm, or barbed wire, or some unmistakable border-markings at least? Or maybe just one of those gates found at railroad crossings, the red-and-white upright pole with the mesh skirt hanging down from it that swings slowly to the horizontal when a train draws near, with a bell clanging or some other kind of warning sounding all the time? Of course not. For God's sake, that's exactly what we were trying to avoid! I mean weren't we escaping and keeping as far from official crossing points as possible? Still, we were not in the marches of Hungary, as the realm's borderlands might have been called until a few centuries ago, where semi-independent marchlords were the last to submit to the central authority and thrived on contesting indefinite frontiers with neighboring princes. So I was disappointed by reality, as Proust is when he finally reaches Balbec, for example, or much later Venice. All in all, actuality was less imposing than the heavy lines that snake through maps where borders lie, in some cases doubled or even tripled, in others multicolored, in others yet accompanied by a series of fine black lines trailing in parallel, a kind of shadow that appears to be cast by something monumental. Yes, actuality was unremarkable and ridiculously mundane. Just think about it, that row of trees and that berm were all the border there was, all the border that was to be had by way of physical reality. And perhaps most disappointingly, one side of the border line seemed in no way different from the other.

In any case, whatever that border was and was not, we were on the far side of it. There we were in Austria, still before midnight I would think, having escaped from the Communist evil in less than 24 hours, having eluded the many imaginary and real tentacles extended by fear and peril and curling invisibly about our throats. We had just become emigrants. And with the fear lifted, we could pay attention to more everyday concerns. First of all, as emigrants, we were in need of a bed for the night. We had eaten not so long ago at the farmer's, and must have drunk something there too, but it still felt like nourishment had been unduly forgotten for too long, especially in light of the unusual exertions and anxieties of the day. But all of the necessities, I could sense, would now be provided. The tension seemed to have ebbed. It was a short walk to the nearest village. Quite suddenly we stepped into the light emanating from a local military building that had been converted to a reception center for refugees, where immediately that status was bestowed on us. It felt good to be recognized as *something*. A tin mug with bullion and a big wedge of American cheese were also pressed into our hands. I had never seen either a tin mug or such cheese, but I liked them both. Straw pallets lined up against the wall awaited us. We joined the few earlier arrivals. The light above the desk with registration papers on it and welcome volunteers behind it burned all night.

So that's what happened on December 13, 1956. Leslie and Rose took advantage of unsettled conditions, defied the authorities and illegally crossed an infamous international boundary. They had prepared for the venture, accepted the risks, and exposed themselves and their children, however temporarily, to the fate of public enemies and criminals. They put aside all pro-and-con thoughts, personal sentiments and *longue-durée* considerations, as French historians might put it, and for one day lived like animals, aware only of safety and basic physical requirements, the things Abraham Maslow put on the lowest level of his pyramid of human needs. And they succeeded easily enough. Although their timing was less than prudent, they had calculated well, and the daring getaway was mostly uneventful. There was little need for improvisation. The potential dangers did not materialize. In fact, the escape turned out to be sort of routine, as if they had not been imprisoned very securely after all, although they really had. By the end of the day they had left the country of their birth, forsaken the security of what after all had been a decent home and stood ready to face the unfamiliar and the unknown. May the world treat them kindly from here on, may the enemies of their outwitted prison guards remain committed to their cause, may the do-gooders not tire for a while yet of helping the helpless!

But any proper summary of the day's events must also note that Rose had gotten her way, or surely now was going to get it. Ahead of my parents there was indeed America and a new life awaiting, and for her the real possibility of a much better domestic existence. The old ways had been left behind, and in any case they had already been proven no longer serviceable in the last round of marital combat, which now, as I keep mulling over immediate and underlying causes and their relationship to each other, I realize to have begun even earlier than I've already suggested. Oh, I am still convinced that the half-brother was the trigger, but now I suspect that the situation was already critical even before that midnight ride to Makó, and had been so at least as early as my Bar Mitzvah on November 19, 1955. And here is the actually *negative* evidence that fuels my suspicions.

I've already told you about the preparations for the big day, and don't have much to add about the event itself. I have practically no memory of it, nothing in fact except that I wore my first pair of long trousers and so, according to a common expression at least, became a man. Of the social function, I certainly can't call it a party or a reception, nor can I say how much it corresponded to local standards of the time – of these things again nothing comes back to me except a vague sense of feeling insignificant in a room full of dark-suited people (indeed, despite Auschwitz, in my unreliable memory the selfsame people I see in photographs of Rose and Leslie's wedding, and wearing the selfsame outfits), a room so plain as to be almost barracks-like, and a hefty dog-eared book of jokes, puzzles, riddles, optical illusions and the like, a used and probably treasured item, which I received from someone as a present. Undoubtedly, Rose and Leslie were present, and Marika too, for I assume I would remember if it had been otherwise. But that's it! Nothing else.

The absence of memories is remarkable. I might accuse myself of having so disliked induction into a secret society in which I felt a stranger that subsequently I made a business of forgetting the whole thing, or of having had some other reason for expunging all traces of it, but that would be off the mark. For the absence of memories is, or was, not just mine. More remarkable yet than my own oblivion is that neither Rose nor Leslie ever mentioned the event. Never! Almost half a century was still ahead of them, almost fifty years of reminiscences, but during it all never a word about what after all had been a unique event. Never a word from Rose about a milestone in the life of her son, the person she loved the most. And never a word from Leslie, a religious man, about a pivotal religious celebration in the family. As if it had never happened. That's what I call negative evidence, and that's what I will now use to support a positive proposition.

The backward extension to the Bar Mitzvah of the striking selective amnesia that also wiped away all traces of the disastrous trip the following August and everything else too right through to the resolution of sorts reached in December and our departure – I take that reaching further back as a sign that the last chapter of Rose and Leslie's old life had already begun by then. What initially had set things off, assuming it was not the marriage itself, I don't know of course, but as I continue my retro-flipping of the calendar pages, I come to Rose's hysterectomy and long illness in early 1955, and that I realize may well have represented a hormonal upheaval with foundation-shaking consequences. But there's no real evidence to support such speculation. The entries in Leslie's workbook indicate a strange series of jobs starting in late 1954 and then his own termination of the last employment in Budapest on November 25, 1955, a week after the Bar Mitzvah, as if he had just been waiting for that event to occur, and his ID booklet testifies that his domicile in Makó, and presumably his employment there too, began only on February 1, 1956. Why the strange jobs and the final quitting I also don't know. He had had the last position for only five months, and from that you can draw any conclusion you want. Where he was, where indeed, or what work he did in December and January also cannot be established, although these too may be relevant facts. In any case, I'm willing to assume that the marital relationship was already well beyond the usual over-the-counter remedies throughout 1955, and then it just kept deteriorating, and under the circumstances – and here I mean all circumstances, family, financial, even official – there seemed to be no way out. Until the revolution, that is. Until one day Rose recognized the opportunity that history and good luck were handing her, decided to embrace it, and so set in motion the train of events that after some threats and hesitation, after some anxiety and despondency, made December 13, 1956, the day we escaped from Hungary and set out for America and a new life.

Although I never knew exactly why we became emigrants, I always did know that we had volunteered for the position. That we didn't *have* to go and did only because we wanted to. So I have always known that I also have what I see as an alternative life: a life lived as a Hungarian in Hungary. An alternative life that is not at all implausible, for it might well have happened.

But it was only recently, on one of my early trips back to Hungary, that I became aware of a second alternative life. It happened in 2003, quite unexpectedly and actually in connection with my researches into the revolution and the other things I have been writing about. That was still a trip without Barbara, the second of two occasions in two years for me to fill myself up with Hungarian memories, culture, thoughts and feelings. Looking through a magazine devoted to the week's events in the capital, I noticed a limited run for a documentary film called *Anya*, that is, *Mother*, made by Miklós Gimes, a child émigré to Switzerland in 1956 and the son of a father with the same name, a father who was executed with Imre Nagy and so was one of the martyrs of the revolution. How perfect, I thought, and carried by anticipation and unaware of the ending of daylight saving time, for it was the end of October, I showed up at the movie theater an hour earlier than I should have.

The movie was playing at the Urania, formally known as the Urania National Filmtheater, a Budapest landmark and something of a national treasure that on the first visit became one of my favorite places in the city. The building was erected during the 1890s, during the capital's golden age, just a moment after it had reached its zenith, which somewhat arbitrarily I date to the1880s, the decade when two major works by Brahms premiered there. The theater opened in 1899 as a venue for live dramatic performances, but started also to screen movies in 1900 and has been exclusively a movie theater since 1916. The façade of the building is in the Venetian style, but the interior is a beautiful specimen of Moorish Revival architecture, a style supposedly harkening back to Moorish Spain, the golden age of Diaspora Jewry, which explains why it has been so popular in synagogue construction too. For example, the Dohány Street synagogue, although labeled Oriental-Byzantine in style, is itself Moorish at least in part, and Moorish Revival is also the style of the Central Synagogue in Manhattan, as it was in part also of the old Temple Emanu-El at Fifth Avenue and 43rd Street, demolished during the early 20th century. Everything about the Urania building, interior and exterior, is exotic and opulent, but at the same time also delicate and unostentatious, a charming expression of naïve make-believe, almost as if the word "revival" were meant to be taken literally. The building was restored in 2002, and since then shows off to the greatest advantage both the grace of its exterior and all the beauty of its interior details. And the main auditorium seats only 700. It's not a convention center, like so many American Moorish Revival movie theaters, which I could never warm up to.

Being so early, I looked around. From various vantage points I admired the exterior, appreciating in particular the indirect red and green lights installed on extruding architectural bands and shining up the façade. Even the chilly autumn wind couldn't destroy the tropical-nights ambience they cast about the building. I stepped inside, bought my ticket, and then strolled around and admired the large foyer, the scalloped archways and the ornately carved wall mountings above mantels and in upper corners. The paneling all around is of a richly-grained brown wood, with capitals and other architectural highlights proudly gilded. The marble floor is inlaid with simple geometrical shapes. I went upstairs to one of the two cafes in the building, which also houses the College of Theater and Film, and, as intended, was immediately drawn to an oculus of sorts, a large circular opening in the middle of the *floor* cordoned off by a filigreed iron railing. I stood by that hole and looked down into the entrance hall with the box office, and felt as you might in an inner court-yard of an Alhambra of the North. Hanging down flat from the outer side of the railing into the entrance hall was a very large battle-scarred Hungarian flag with a surprisingly large circular hole cut into its middle with jagged lines. It was the only display I saw anywhere about town in commemoration of the revolution's anniversary. A few people were passing the time at the dozen or so tables, bathed in the warm light reflected back from the polished boards of the floor. I sat down.

As the waiter set down my espresso in front of me, a group of about twenty women and men began to assemble in one corner of the upstairs hall. They were dressed casually but for two of the women who wore cocktail dresses over leotards. Then the tango music started, and I realized that under the Moorish arches I happened to be witnessing a class in that Argentine dance. For a while I watched the tentative steps and accordioning embraces of the dancers, then went downstairs to look around the crypt-like basement with the Indian café that fits very well into the international chaos of the building and the activities it attracts. Having set aside the Hungarian Jewish reality as if it were a joker, all day I had been shuffling like a black-jack dealer thoughts about my own ethnic identity, what it is and what it is not, and now I marveled at how easily and casually cultural elements from all over the world mixed in that theater. I also reminded myself that, of course, sophisticated people have always loved a pinch of the foreign and a touch of the exotic, adopting now elements of attire typical of this country, now bits of the folklore of that. So why, I then asked myself, was I pursuing an exclusivist analysis of a kind that ethnicity may actually not demand? And never mind that people I find myself with, especially in Hungary, also tend to wonder out loud whether I *am* Hungarian or not. What is it, after all, that makes you, or can make you, Hungarian? And what makes you American? And just as important-ly, are the answers to these two questions analogous? Or are the rules for a country of immigrants different from the rules for one of emigrants? Then, at a loss for decent answers to such questions, I slowly proceeded back upstairs and into the auditorium.

Anya got only one star from local reviewers, but I think it deserves more. It's a fine work actually, even if by now its subject does seem a little threadbare to Hungarians, what with the change of system, the concur-rent rehabilitation of the revolution, and their proper due, so to speak, having been paid to the hero-victims long ago. The filmmaker, I'll call him Miklós and his father I'll call Gimes, was born in 1950, emigrated with his *anya*, Lucy, to Switzerland to settle near Zurich in 1956, and was eight therefore when he learned that his father had been executed. As its title suggests, the film is about Lucy, and she is on the screen at least half the time, a lovely, intelligent, disarming woman, a wild beauty in her youth, and in my faltering, exaggeration-prone memory looking now ever more like a moviestar. She speaks German with ease, as do apparently all the Hungarian émigrés in her Swiss-German circle, Central-European minds and spirits, mostly artists, intellectuals and individuals devoted to causes.

Lucy and Gimes were born Jews, he in 1917, she in 1921, making her 35 in 1956. (They were just a few years younger than Rose and Leslie, but despite the obvious parallels any kind of comparison of the two couples seems completely unapt.) They met at the end of the war, when already living in the capital, and quickly became devoted Communists. He was one of the leading journalists in the country, writing for *Szabad Nép* (Free People), the Party's official newspaper, and so a respected and influential person. In looking back, Lucy relates that it was the Party that actually educated her, and says that in fact the Party was involved in all aspects of their lives, which during the early years they did not resent. But after Nagy was toppled from power in 1955 Gimes lost faith, joined Nagy's circle of opposition, and then on a journalist's professional visit to Paris considered staying there in the company of a pre-Lucy lover, but returned after all, only to take up with an actress named Aliz Halda, who is still remembered today. And then soon he broke with Lucy and Miklós, and broke with them so conclusively that in 1989, when the martyred revolutionaries were ceremonially reburied, with Lucy and Miklós present for the occasion, most people considered not her but Aliz the revolutionary's widow.

Miklós, in addition to being a respected Swiss journalist and filmmaker, seems to have remained Hungarian too. Certainly, when he is in Hungary, he is treated as a real Hungarian. Also, his command of the language, as demonstrated in a fluent voice-over throughout, is unquestionable, and that says a lot about someone who was only eight when he stopped living in a Magyar-speaking society. How different all this is from my own situation! For one, in Hungary rarely ever does anyone mistake me for a native. For another, although my Hungarian is very good, as I've said already, I recall how on that particular trip especially I was mired in a linguistic muddle, wanting to speak Hungarian but too often coming up with the right word only in English, or thinking in my normal English but ever tripping over the Hungarian words popping up in my mind like ghosts during a midnight reverie. But it didn't *have* to be this way, I felt and thought repeatedly while watching the movie and often since. I too might have lived Miklós's life. I also might have allowed myself to have Hungarian friends, or more than the only one I ever did have in high school, might have kept the language alive within me, might even have married a Hungarian girl, celebrated the old holidays and cultivated the indispensable national fatalism. I saw very quickly that the people on the screen had a hyphenated identity, Hungarian-Swiss, or two half-identities, or two identities existing side-by-side in rough parity. And in one or another of those too-finely-tuned-by-half characterological arrangements I saw my second alternative life.

I tried to understand why I *didn't* choose that life. It wouldn't have been difficult to pull off. It's not as if I had gone native, to use the label made for the identity-adventures of some Europeans who starting in the 17th century abandoned their own civilization and adopted the mentality and ways of a non-Western culture. Like the Englishmen who went to India as colonialists and then for whatever reason made themselves or allowed themselves to be made into Indians. Or better yet, like the woman who was the prototype for Natalie Wood, the niece in John Ford's *The Searchers*, abducted by Comanches as a child and then five years later almost murdered by John Wayne, who would have rather seen her dead than let her remain with her captors as she would have preferred. By choice or perforce, these people all crossed the dividing line between mutually hostile civilizations, and, worse than that, left the conqueror and took up with the victim, and put the modern behind themselves for the sake of the more primitive. But what I was doing, becoming American, was nothing like that. To be both Hungarian and American would not have required a joining of incompatible things. On the contrary, in a society infinitely inventive in the field of ethnic design and famously tolerant as these things go of half-and-half and even more fractional hybrids, I would have been fitting together elastic and plastic parts, each one ready to accommodate the other and susceptible in the process to most any adjustment. So why then did I not become a Hungarian-American, or a Hungarian-Jewish-American if you insist?

Was it, I asked myself, my mistaken belief that the parting was forever? That probably had something to do with it, although forever can be an argument for keeping the Hungarian identity as much as for chucking it. Was I maybe ashamed of Hungary then and just didn't want to seem country-bumpkinish for coming from such a small-time place? Possibly, except that always I was proud of the revolution, as who wouldn't be, and specifically of great Hungarians like Bartók for example and what I remembered of the *mitteleuropäische* charms of Budapest and the superb cuisine and Magyar poetry and many other things too. Well, then, maybe, like any teenager, I just wanted to be like all the other kids? No, I don't think so, for in general I have always enjoyed being different and separate and wanted to be nothing else. I did of course at various times want to be like a particular charming-the-pants-off-them guy, but I never envied anyone just for being native-born. Was I then maybe just resisting becoming a mongrel? No, that wasn't it either. I have always, as it were, understood what I will call the aesthetic principle that can make you prefer the pure-bred to the mutt, but in application to human beings I consider that to be no more than an insistence on marrying within the tribe, and so something like a Habsburg lower lip for an entire people. Ah!, did I then maybe just want to put some distance between myself and Rose and Leslie? Well, that may have had something to do with it, although I hope not for my own sake. Because in fact there *wasn't* any such distance, or not enough anyway. For, as you already know, in America through the decades you would have needed a crowbar to separate us, except of course that we were hardly close. I mean I was neither confiding nor dependent nor really affectionate with them, but just dutifully filial beyond all reason.

So, you see, I pretty much rejected all these scenarios, but after a while it became clear to me that I let my Hungarian identity slip away mostly because I did not care enough to hold onto it. Maybe when we left I didn't yet have much of it, you can think of it that way too, but whatever I did have I was not attached to firmly enough. The same old story. Like I haven't been much attached to anything else either. I knew that other things would take its place and even if the wonders of childhood and first experiences cannot be duplicated, that was good enough for me. Good bye! I let go of it without much thought or just about any pain. Right there I think, by that row of trees on top of that berm and under the half-murk of those *Wuthering Heights* skies. But now I find myself asking if maybe Miklós was right after all. Did I discard something of great value? And did I do so unnecessarily? Well, certainly, I cannot say that my careless frontier act made me eligible for a better American identity that I could not have had otherwise. I can say only that the identity I wound up with is the one I still want. And in any case, the divestiture *was* necessary in that it couldn't have been prevented. For what could have countered my cavalier attitude to loss, to suffering loss without suffering, that is? By then I had lived for years already without feeling the pain of loss, and that had made me only too ready to renounce like Alberich the Nibelung, and often do with less than what my heart really desired. In other words, I see no way that my Hungarian identity could have sidestepped its fate.

But even as I write this, I am consoled by knowing that things are different now. I could never shrug off my American skin the way I shrugged off the Hungarian one, or any other way either. Sometimes when a conversation with friends turns to the rising tide of right-wing sentiment in these United States and someone groans about having to find ourselves another country, I just shake my head, rejecting what for me would be actually impossible. I did that once, I then think, and would not do it again, as if that first time had been unbearably wrenching, which it had not been of course. But were I to do it again, this time it would be. Then I was not going into exile, but now I would feel banished plain and simple, like Ovid was to Tomis on the shores of the Black Sea, an outpost without a library even. Because to America I *am* attached. And good for me! How did this happen? How in this particular case did I rise above the neurosis, if that's enough of a word for it? Well, not as you would expect. Yes, in my personal life I did come finally after many years of trying to love a few people deeply enough to exterminate from my heart and mind forever the urge to leave them. No matter what. It was a question of feelings pure and simple, fear versus love I suppose, to put it simplistically. But aside from a deep gratitude for taking me in, an orphan of circumstances, my attachment to America did not begin with feelings at all. Instead, it began with rational analysis and evaluation rather, which apparently were a necessary prelude to emotional attachment. In other words, I loved America only after I had satisfied my thinking self that it *was* indeed better than the alternatives and worthy therefore of love.

It is embarrassing for me, given all my castigations of and disappointments with America, now to be singing its praises in such seemingly jingoistic terms. In my defense I can say only that my love for my country sprouted and grew in New York during the 1960s, a remarkably vibrant and free time and place, an America that is for the time being at least no more. That was when I first understood that America is the land of personal freedom and opportunity, where you can say and do and be whatever it pleases you to. That's an exaggeration I know, but in those days, the Vietnam War notwithstanding, so America seemed to me. Sure, it could have been and must yet strive to be better, I believed, but even as it was already it was the *best*. That was the America of those times, my twenties, when I became a historian and first considered myself to have a sufficient knowledge of history, by which I mean an outline of the career of our species, with more recent installments more or less sketched in – a sufficient knowledge to intelligently consider such matters. Indeed, when I first learned how to size up the world a little. And only then, when I saw America that way, when I saw her from a historian's perspective, only then did I love her. After that, as I came to know America more and more, then of course I also came to love many many other things about her: the natural beauty and grandeur, the diversity-in-unity that is the American people, the networks of roads, the institutions of higher education, the pre-European past and its remnants, the Founding Fathers, *Moby Dick*, William Faulkner, New York and San Francisco, the country's prosperity, intellectual and cultural life in New York, and I could go on. But knowing that America is the best came first.

Of course, America did not become my historical subject. My intellectual and professional interests did not let themselves be circumscribed by my new ethnic identity, or the old one either, as you know. For me America was and shall always be peripheral to the central themes and main story of Western civilization, my overarching interest. So in America I have lived as an American, even while I have devoted myself to excogitating various, although not the specifically excluded, Europes of the past. That has been one of the major preoccupations of my life. And it has been terrific. As for the division itself, that has also served me well by long ago becoming something like an identity-arrangement for me. Indeed, it has been very nice and comfortable for me to be one part American and another part European. There are so many things I like about that arrangement. For one, it's hyphenated in an interesting way, and not just in that it is not hyphenated at all in the actual writing of it. For it's also bisected, as it were, at a, well, elegant angle. For another, it makes me neither on the one hand and both on the other. And always just in the right proportions. And, finally, it's the best of everything. I live where it's the best to live, at least I'm pretty sure it is; and I also organize my intellectual life around what *to my taste* is without doubt the best. For me, it's all ideal, if I say so myself.

CHAPTER 9

Flotsam and Jetsam

THE FIRST THING I REMEMBER of December 14th is a gray street bordered by gray houses under a gray sky, very much like the one under which we had our adventures the previous day. Having had an unmemorable breakfast and been discharged from the reception center with lots of smiles and *österreichisch* fare-ye-wells, we six refugees, the four of us and the man and woman who had crossed with us, were carrying our bags and trudging along that gray street. Little did I know that we were on a collision course with the disgraceful miscarriage of my first adult responsibility. You see, despite the apparently simple directions we had received from the volunteers, we could not find the railroad station. "My son will ask," Leslie took charge readily, "he speaks German." And he proudly specified the number of years he had paid for German lessons, which I believe was four. So I stopped in front of the only passerby in sight, opened my mouth, "*bitte,*" mumbled, "*wo ist,... wo ist,...*" and there I got stuck. Miserably stuck. In a minute the word "*Bahnhof*" was on the tip of my tongue, but by then the unnamed man in our company had made himself understood with choo-choo sounds and gestures. I looked up at Leslie's apoplectic face, and swallowed my word instead of spitting it out.

We clambered onto the Vienna-bound train, ogled our fellow passengers and admired the manicured countryside. After about an hour we were welcomed by volunteers from the capital, who instantly turned us into Jews. That was rather surprising, but that's how it had to be, for it was mostly religious agencies that provided relief and immigration assistance to the refugees. The arrangement made perfect sense, given that sacred precincts had been offering asylum and care to wayfarers since time immemorial, and it was also practical. Never mind the false impression it created that only those with religious sponsorships were receiving American visas, an impression the director of resettlement for an American Catholic organization was compelled in late November to publicly deny; and never mind either that, according to Max Frankel, *The New York Times*'s lead reporter on the refugee crisis, the arrangement caused some confusion and unnecessary hardship, produced immigrants only haphazardly informed about the country's immigration laws and policies, and even disappointed refugees who had expected to be dealing with "the authority and prestige of the United States [itself], the romantic idol of many a Hungarian revolutionary...." In the overall context these were not very serious flaws, and though governments, the UN and non-governmental organizations also provided support, until a haven nation accepted responsibility for him or her, and in many countries even after that, the refugee relied mostly on religious agencies. So as early as possible the Austrians had you identify yourself as Christian or Jew and then handed you over to the appropriate organization. And for the time being then, Christian or Jew was pretty much your whole official identity.

Many Jewish refugees welcomed this. For them, and for Jews in general I believe, although not for Rose or Leslie, escaping from Hungary itself was a Jewish act and a way to partake of a historic Jewish national experience. Some understood that experience to be Zionism, others the Holocaust and still others the great geographical redistribution of European Jews triggered by the emergence of an especially virulent strain of antisemitism during the late 19th century. The refugee crisis, therefore, was *automatically* of interest to Jewish philanthropy, which in 1956, that is, on the heels of the period of greatest-ever Jewish persecution in Europe and still during the very infancy of the State of Israel, was vigorous and well-developed. Relief aid to the refugees in Austria began to be organized just a few days after the November 4th Soviet invasion, and the American Joint Distribution Committee, foremost among the Jewish agencies and what in Hungary and Austria too I had always heard referred to simply as the Joint, got promptly involved. On the 16th its head was reported by the *Times* to be expecting a new flood of Jews on the run, as distinguished from the recent postwar inundation. Then during the subsequent few days the Council of Jewish Federations praised Eisenhower for his commitment to the cause of the refugees, which evidently the Council saw as favorable to Jewish interests. And on December 3rd, the United Jewish Appeal was reported to have announced that altogether 5,000 Jews had reached Vienna. As you can see, the ethnic consciousness in its many well-institutionalized forms had its engines running immediately.

We ourselves benefited greatly and repeatedly from Jewish largesse, intended and labeled as such. And it was a great advantage to us I think that Jewish philanthropy was and had always been a largely American phenomenon. Of course, where but in America could Jews, before, during and after World War II, afford financially and in terms of their own security to worry about their brethren in faraway places? The Joint itself was founded by American Jews in 1914 to aid the settlement in Palestine, which was in mortal danger right then on account of complications occasioned by World War I. It housed and fed us too throughout our days in Vienna, and even kept us in the pocket-money that Leslie squirreled away in anticipation of needs sure to arise later, excepting only the small sum indulged on the chocolate he could not resist buying in a Vienna most remarkable it seemed for its coffee, chocolate and confectionary emporia. And once we reached America, HIAS, the Hebrew Immigrant Aid Society, an agency founded in 1881 to ease Jewish transplantation to America, took over where the Joint had left off, including free medical care, of which Rose at least availed herself for several years. And of course nothing was ever asked in return for all this, and except for a brief involvement by Leslie during the 80s I think in fund-raising for Israel, nothing ever was given. Since a Jewish identity never managed to stick to me, I myself was hardly ever subjected to even a solicitation for donations to a Jewish agency or cause, and I never felt the urge to repay something

I had never asked for *and* considered myself entitled to. In a word, I have been an ingrate.

For me the journey of transplantation started only in Vienna. All that had come before had just been a preparatory extrication, a breaking free of the bonds that had made life in the old country what it had been. But once we stepped down from that train, one after the other, each of us in his or her state of anxiety and bewilderment – then at once I was off. I had not expected it, but as if out of a starting block, I rushed out into the world, immediately looking, seeing, comparing and classifying, feeding my new-found curiosity. I was not exactly an explorer during the six weeks or so that then began, for I did not actually seek the unknown. The unknown was just there, everywhere all about me in a seemingly inexhaustible multiplicity, coming at me at a relentless pace, there to be perceived, noted and made sense of. And even less was I a conquistador, for I had no dreams of appropriating any of it as my own. Rather, I was just a humble and lone discoverer. For though I spent those days more tightly bound within the family unit than at any other time during the several preceding years, I discovered independently of my elders, who themselves were no more familiar than I with what awaited us. So in a sense for me the journey was a solitary experience. I was not able to communicate with Austrians or Americans, and when we mixed with Hungarians I was still a back-bench child in an adult environment. On some occasions, mostly on the ship crossing the ocean, I did horse around some with other kids my age, but as a rule I was as if invisible, absorbed in impressions of and thoughts about my surroundings, focusing on my own unshared experiences. I was present and not cheating anyone of the attention he or she or the situation deserved from me, but at the same time also always ready to get back to my discoveries. As you can imagine, the tendency for in-my-head isolation that I had already been cultivating for some time then was much reinforced by all this.

By late afternoon of our first Austrian day, we were installed in a comfortable Viennese hotel room and had a *carnet* of tickets good for meals in a chain of respectable working-class cafeterias. And we had been promised this life-support system until we left the capital. The hotel was named *König von Ungarn,* or King of Hungary. Nobody seemed to joke when we arrived that they had been expecting Leslie for some time, but the coincidence pleased us nevertheless. Ironically or perhaps appropriately given its name, the establishment was modest but for us also exciting just for being a hotel. In the room stood a large bed with heavy headboard and footboard for Rose and Leslie and a cot for Marika, and for me another cot in the bathroom with its own separate exit out to the hotel corridor. The room itself also had a dresser with a mirror in a gilt frame, a small round table where we could have snacks, night tables on either side of the bed, a pair of chairs against the wall and burgundy wallpaper all around. The bathroom had sufficient hot water for all our needs and porcelain fixtures that were well-worn but elegant. It was a pretty standard hotel room, a constricted space considering what we were used to, but a very satisfactory way-station. More importantly, it was the first time in my life I had my own room, even though I had it only at night. During the day it was a multi-purpose family facility of course, where Rose also took care of the laundry.

Pretty much everything else that mattered to me during those Vienna weeks took place outside that hotel. From the perspective of the way we live today, it seems hard to believe that all I knew then of how the world looks or how people live in it I had gathered from the pages of our encyclopedia and the postcard collection of one of our boarders. Aside from that I had seen nothing, pictures of places included. So for me, the city of Vienna served as an on-going revelation, a magical place, a prodigious display of an until-then-unknown man-made world. But don't imagine us sight-seeing. For even if our situation and our obsessive focus on a future discontinuous with that present had permitted it, we would have had no idea what there was to see in the city of the Habsburg emperor, the waltz king and the Ferris wheel on which Orson Welles and Joseph Cotton took a ride in *The Third Man.* Even by Rose and Leslie's standards later in life, and they were hardly cosmopolitan, back then we were ignorant of everything but our immediate surroundings. During our two weeks in the city, we did not visit a single museum, notable structure or historical monument, never even entered Stephan's Kirche, Vienna's cathedral, which was located only a few steps from our hotel. Going in or out, I never missed an opportunity to make contact with that cathedral by casting an admiring glance at the splendidly colorful tilework on its roof. The only thing we did make sure to see was the Danube, or actually the so-called *Donaukanal*, a tamed inner-city arm of the great river, which, disappointingly, was no bluer there than along its downstream stretch through Budapest. But that of course was not sight-seeing. It was just an effort to cling to something from a past that was utterly lost but for your memories. So my Viennese discoveries were simply of everyday phenomena visible and audible to an ordinary stroller who did not speak the local language and did not understand life as it was lived there or maybe anywhere at all.

I walked around open-mouthed. This, I understood early on, although I was not yet able, not for a long time, to think in such terms – this was a land of polymorphous riches. Here the things made by man and machines were, first of all, bountiful. In our strolls, we would enter, each time with more confidence, one or another of the stores of a fancy-foods chain called *Julius Meinl*. In the first one I saw a stack of identical chocolate bars about three feet tall arranged in a spiral and marveled at the cleverness of a form of display that gave you a glimpse of the delicacy over and over and even suggested its own heavens-bound extension. And then to my giddy delight I discovered that, as you would expect, each store had the same display. Then, second, here man's creations were not only bountiful but also multifarious. In Budapest already, walking around the block of the American Embassy with just this objective, I had become familiar with a few makes of automobile manufactured in the West. But in Vienna I was excited to see many more makes and models and colors, and also to notice minor variations in a given model, as if the evolution of species in the genus automobile was being demonstrated right before my eyes. And, finally, here man-made things large and small were not only bountiful and varied but also expertly designed, carefully made and beautifully adorned. I remember admiring something as ordinary as streetcars so new you thought the paint was still drying on them. I turned my head and followed their progress as they ran down wide avenues and snaked around corners decorated with glittering Christmas trees, their chimes discreetly warning pedestrians. After knowing only the monotonous poverty and shabby grayness of Communist Budapest, it was an encouragement to me and a source of optimism too to be in that opulent environment. I was dazzled to learn that the world can be otherwise, although, as you already know, afterwards I myself was never even tempted to join the consuming masses. You should see the cars I drive.

Secluded in the shabby-elegant housing provided for us, and on account of the kind of people Leslie and Rose were, and maybe also the state of uneasy truce between them – whatever the reasons, while in Vienna we did not have much contact with the great many other refugees there. I don't know how many Hungarian escapees might have been in the capital at any given time, but, as I've said already, by December 13th about 130,000 had made it across to Austria and only about 60,000 had departed to their countries of resettlement. In 1957, when the numbers were finally totaled, the refugee flood was estimated to have crested at 180,000. Throughout it all, Austria was never less than welcoming. The country's German name, *Österreich,* derives from a medieval designation meaning the eastern realm, that is, the eastern borderlands of the West, and as such Austria still saw herself after the war, when she offered asylum to all who might need it, and then continued to stand by the offer. Consequently, during the postwar demographic reconfiguration of Eastern Europe close to a million refugees passed through the country, with the last displaced-persons camp being liquidated only in 1952. And in 1956 there were still about 180,000 stateless people within her borders, a non-Hungarian 180,000, that is, with 130,000 of them in refugee camps. In a small country of less than 7.5 million, all this had to have felt more like a rolling invasion than national good-Samaritanism. And then came the new onslaught from the east. In haste thirteen reception centers were established, barracks and schools recently occupied by the

Red Army were reopened and quickly filled. Towards the end of the year the new refugees were huddling in 63 poorly equipped camps, squeezing into taverns and resorts and trying the hospitality of private citizens. And still the welcome mat was being brushed off for new arrivals.

Austria's generosity was especially notable because the situation she found herself in was difficult in at least two specific respects. First, she had to be concerned about her international status. She had declared neutrality just recently, and yet here she was taking up the cause of anti-Soviet hot-heads, as if she herself also entertained such sentiments. Was this perhaps a dangerous game? Yes, it was, but that did not shake the Austrians' commitment. It only confirmed their feeling that they shouldered an unfairly large share of what after all was the responsibility of all the countries of the free world. Why couldn't other Western powers for the moment at least dispense with quotas, time-consuming screening procedures, medical examinations and security checks, and deal instead with the situation as the daily emergency Austria knew it to be? Why did not the United States, the resettlement destination most desired, confirm that refugees would not lose their chances for a visa by accepting temporary asylum in another country? Finally, and this was the nub of the second specific difficulty, why was not more financial support forthcoming? Today Austria is one of the richest countries in the world, but such was not the case then. The war had devastated it and the Soviet occupiers had still further damaged the economic base in their sector. Without aid from abroad, and that meant the United States and the few international organizations, Austria feared not being able to prevent the refugee crisis from turning into a refugee disaster.

Of course, we were not aware of any of this and were preoccupied anyway with the refugee condition as it still pertained to us even after our own most essential needs had been taken care of. Leslie himself still had to attend to one final connection with the past. You see, he still had his wad in his pocket. He already suspected that it would not go very far, all this glitz and glamour did not bode well, but still it should put a few schillings in his wallet next to the small change provided by the refugee agencies, and it might even be a reserve of some sort. And, yes, it would be his own rather than a hand-out. So one of his immediate concerns was exchange of his forints. I don't recall how we found a bank appropriate for the transaction or how he made himself understood, but it couldn't have been too hard, what with the siege of the capital by the Magyar hordes going on for more than six weeks by then. But he was turned away. No schillings for forints. He then got some leads from refugees accosted on the street, but none of those panned out either. Since the descent of the Iron Curtain and the institution of a planned economy in Hungary, trade with the West had almost ceased and the forint had lost most of its value. The revolution had further aggravated this situation, and then on top of that the tens of thousands of refugees had flooded the Austrian market with the reddish bank notes. In late October, when the victory of the insurgents seemed a possibility, someone may still have been willing to pay a highway-robbery rate for Hungarian money. But in mid-December, in the midst of our very own spot-inflation, no one was foolish enough to take that bet anymore, and knowing that, some refugees had even given away all of their forints to those who helped them escape.

So in the early afternoon of December 15th, Leslie stood on the corner of a busy and glitterful shopping street in Vienna. The low winter sun was splashing its milky haze all over the city, but that offered no more heat than light. As he lifted his long coat on the right side and reached into his trousers pocket, he seemed a little bit stooped suddenly, not quite as tall as he had always been. With one emphatic motion then, he withdrew the wad and stuffed it into a garbage receptacle. In my imagination, his arm sank into the dross all the way up to the elbow, as if he were burying that money-only-in-name. Then he just stood there and stood there, looking into the abyss of waste. Now everything was gone. There was nothing left. What will be, he must have been asking himself. To have nothing again at age 44! He felt profoundly unhappy. He had no prospects, no hope. And he couldn't speak a word. Like that idiot, meaning me. Well, he had learned Russian, hadn't he? He'll learn English too. But he did have nothing. And he felt irremediably unloved.

Our two weeks in Vienna were overcast with uncertainty. All along our admission to the United States seemed quite likely, but it was not assured. Several mornings we languished in official places painted a non-committal beige, waiting to be interviewed and processed. From the sweaty-palmed rumors polluting the otherwise antiseptic corridors, Leslie had some idea of what the authorities were looking for by way of information and documentation, and he worried about not having something essential. And even aside from the brief membership in the Party, he worried that something he had done back home, as all at once we were referring to Hungary – something he had done to curry favor with the Communists may now be held against him. After all, he had just spent eight years doing what he could to make himself look like a friend to a regime that he was now claiming to have hated all along. And while in his mind there had never been any question about his actual sentiments, he had not in fact been a hero of the opposition, a man ready to stand up for his principles, or an outspoken critic of the system itself or its many petty and grand tyrannies. He had just been trying to get along. Maybe an application, even if it was rejected, to join a workers' union could now be viewed as an ideological stance inexcusable for an aspiring American? Remember, this was the Cold War! Should he be hiding anything? And if he did try to cover up something, might he be found out? Was there anybody here to denounce him? Because people are always ready to denounce you. What might the American authorities know already? Even if you're not the kind of person Leslie was, that is, given to anxiety and anticipation of all that's the worst, you are likely to have sleepless nights with everything at stake as it was then.

Although the screening of refugees applying for admission to the U.S. was not as meticulous all of a sudden as was customary during those early Cold-War years. The clamor for speed among the applicants themselves and also their champions on the other side of the Atlantic, President Eisenhower included, had been loud enough to cause an immediate relaxation of some of the requirements. Then on November 20th at a meeting in Vienna, Congressman Francis Walter, one of the two sponsors of the highly restrictive immigration law in effect at the time and chairman of the House Immigration Subcommittee, and General Joseph Swing, head of the Immigration and Naturalization Service, sat down with the U.S. ambassador to Austria and the deputy administrator of the American refugee relief program, and the four men agreed on the practical rules and streamlined working procedures to be applied under the circumstances. This was high-level, expeditious decision-making indeed. Leslie would not have been happy to learn that of the refugees with potentially disqualifying histories only those who had been *forced* by the need to support their families to enroll in Communist-dominated organizations were to be eligible for visas, while those who had voluntarily joined the Communist *party* itself were not, and those who had joined "involuntarily" were to be permitted to enter the country only as so-called parolees, if at all. If the conferees had also considered how any of this would be verified, their deliberations were not reported.

The basic sentiment that prompted all this activity and all these accommodations was expressed by Vice President Nixon's statement that assuring the right outcome to the refugee crisis was the responsibility of the *United States.* Nixon was speaking for at least a large segment of the American people, as evidenced by the widespread domestic expectation that the country would admit a much greater number than it actually did. And all of the free world seemed to agree. Indeed, it's fair to say that despite the invaluable contribution of other Western countries, the fate of the refugees in Austria was and was seen to be primarily in American hands. The reasons for this were obvious. There was of course the status of the United States as the leader of the free world, but there was also the many-layered historical context of the issue, most importantly America's self-image and reputation as a country of immigrants, her wealth, and the generosity she had recently shown Europe by the Marshall Plan. And the United States accepted the responsibility. It also made significant efforts to discharge it and did provide a haven to more refugees than any other country, but still it could not avoid being blamed for not doing an even better job. The criticism came, as Max Frankel reported in early

December, in the form of "the ill-will and bitterness that has been directed at the US in the last month" on account of the delays in the resettling of refugees, and also by way of the feelings of having been "betrayed" expressed by those still in the camps in the spring of 1957. Of course, the many rapidly processed and transported refugees, ourselves included, were quite pleased with the entire complex international operation.

I myself never even considered the possibility that we would not be invited to become Americans, but undoubtedly that possibility existed. And what would have happened then? We were stateless during those days, belonging nowhere, having no right to be anywhere or to call anyplace home. There was Israel of course, and surely some other country would also have taken us, one not as Cold-War-focused as America, not so particular about questionable acts in your past, not having such a throng pressing at its gates. Would our prospects have been less good if in the end we had had to proceed to Sydney or Stockholm? Obviously, Rose had no relatives in those places waiting for us and unable upon our arrival to slam the door in our face. That had to count for something, and Rose and Leslie must have considered it something significant. And then also we would not have been going to America, to AMERICA! America, the land of promises, the land with a mystique for the immigrant like no other. For no other place was, or had ever been, like America. And aside from all that, we also felt that our assets and status as we strolled along Vienna's boulevards were comprised of nothing more than our hope and intention to go to America. All we had was the mantra of our destination. Had that destination been denied us, we would have lost even the little we had not already thrown away. But if we did indeed go to America, then we would have hit the transplantation jackpot!

Most of the refugees, it seems, wanted to go to America, but most of them also realized that that would not happen. And so, quite a few accepted temporary asylum in Switzerland, Italy or the Netherlands, and many others received and accepted actual resettlement offers from one of what ultimately came to be 27 nations. In early November, one by one, most Western European and Latin American countries declared their willingness to grant asylum to a specified number of refugees, as did also the United States, Canada, Australia and New Zealand. Indeed, Canada offered to take an *unlimited* number, as did also France and Brazil. Then as the refugee ranks swelled, many nations, including the US, opened their gates and hearts to more and in some cases still more of the unfortunates on the run. Most of the haven countries considered the Hungarians desirable immigrants, and with good reason I think. And many of them, like the United States, relaxed or abolished routine procedures and also managed to move the new immigrants to their new homelands even faster than the leader of the free world. By the third week of November, moving at just about the speed of light, some refugees had reached Great Britain and France, and others would arrive soon in Switzerland and the Netherlands. By late December several countries had completely filled their quotas and, but for some delays occasioned by necessary preparations for dealing with the newcomers, had welcomed their new residents. An outpouring of international brotherliness combined with an amazing efficiency!

I have found little information on those who received temporary asylum, on how protracted their peregrinations were and how stretched-to-the-limit their sense of rootedness when finally they were resettled. Did some of them come twice to live in a country whose language they did not speak? For me that might have meant an additional enrichment in life, all other things being the same of course, haha, or it might have been lost years, as it was more or less for Nabokov, who between the time he fled Russia and his arrival in the United States lived an as-it-were temporary life of 15 years in Berlin, never learning German and writing still in Russian what by his own later standards were undistinguished novels. For Rose and Leslie it surely would have been something even worse, a further syntactical scrambling and general unhinging. In any case, interim asylum could represent a doubling of hardships, although it may also not have been much worse than many weeks in an Austrian camp. The scant evidence suggests that there were unusual problems aplenty. In early December members of a group were so unhappy with their temporary housing in the Netherlands that they walked off in protest. The Dutch, who then still seemed ever-tolerant, gave them the choice of returning or going back to Austria. At about the same time 300 refugees housed in a French Army camp near Besançon expressed their dissatisfaction with conditions by bolting for the Swiss border. Of course, the Swiss turned back the would-be twice-over refugees. I have also found a report from several months later about a hunger strike staged by refugees in a camp in Limerick, Ireland to protest delays in their movement on to the United States and Canada. We didn't know just how lucky we were to avoid traumas like these.

Looking now at the list of receiving countries, I immediately notice that the only nation offering asylum where the resettler might *not* have lived in a distinctively European community was Turkey. So Western civilization was at work here as usual, transforming the refugee crisis into, among other things, another episode in the history of European expansion and imperialism. Every haven country outside of Europe other than Turkey had at one time been colonized by Europeans, like all of the New World and Australia and New Zealand, and even Rhodesia-Nyasaland, today's Zambia and Zimbabwe, which offered asylum to a maximum of 30 children. To a remarkable extent, considered in a global context, the refugees were kinsmen of their neighbors-to-be, a relationship figuratively illustrated by the University of Sopron, which was transplanted in some part at least to British Columbia and affiliated there with the university bearing the name of that Canadian province. So, if you are inclined, as I am, to put the 1956 wave of Hungarian migration into some less often mentioned historical contexts, you can see it as a final incursion of the Magyars into Western Europe, following the immediately prior one that ended with the Battle of Lechfeld a millennium and a year earlier, and you can see it also as a miniature recapitulation of the expansion of Europe into much of the rest of the world between the 16th and 19th centuries.

Pearl and her daughter Eva had crossed the ocean as soon as they had heard that Erzsi and *her* daughter Ági had been among the first refugees to reach Vienna. They had taken advantage of Eva's employment by Sabena Airlines and had flown free or mostly so. Then Erzsi and Ági left for New York, and only after that did we arrive in the Austrian capital. It required some miracles and coincidences the specifics of which I don't recall anymore for Pearl and Eva to find us, but after more than a decade the sisters were reunited. I'm sure that for one of them it was a teary-eyed occasion. Then quickly it became obvious that helping Erzsi and then hopefully us had been pretty much just a pretext for the Bronx women's transatlantic trip. For whatever help they could provide definitely did not require their presence, and the real reason for their junket was to find Eva a proper husband. This, after all, was an unparalleled opportunity. The kind of young man Eva wanted, or was supposed to want, the kind that her parents, themselves still hardly Americans, definitely wanted for her, the kind that could not be found in New York, a nice young Hungarian Jew with prospects – during the early post-revolutionary days Vienna was supposed to be crawling with such candidates. The husband-hunting season had opened, and the game was good. The only thing missing was a 20th-century Jane Austin writing in... what? Hungarian, German, or maybe English? A week after our arrival the fairy godmother and god-cousin flew back to New York, having it seemed succeeded in their own mission, but really having not as it turned out not much later. Then we were still waiting in the capital and, as far as anyone could tell, our papers were being processed no faster or slower than they would have been even if the relatives claiming to be rescue-minded had not parachuted in to pretend to grant our wishes.

Pearl was a short woman, a little bit stout by that age. She looked like a smaller version of Rose, although without the beauty and the sternness in her appearance. Eva I figure to have been about 24 at the time, also sort of diminutive, with a lively look, and always ready to burst into laughter. I remember them, especially Eva, as tap-tapping around in what then was considered stilt-heels, wrapped in fur coats with wide upturned collars that could defy the iciest winds, swathed in elegant clothes that captivated with their bold patterns, adorned with gold jewelry, and sparkling in general. Sometimes they came to our hotel room at strange hours, or what seemed like strange hours to immigrants who had no money and still lived according to clock and calendar, keeping track of time as it was enforced in the cramped corners of the hive assigned to worker-bees. Unlike us, they were of that marvelous world I saw out on the boulevards and in the all-weather ambience of the shopping mall installed under one of the major intersections of the city and reached from the four corners by silently moving escalators, another new Western miracle! As if to dramatize our whole situation, just a few days after Leslie divested himself of all his suddenly worthless banknotes, Pearl made a present of a dollar bill to each of us children. Never before had I held or even imagined the existence of money so aggressively and haughtily foreign, of such great mystique, and of such great value that even a single unit of it was represented by an elaborately designed note rather than a scuffed-up aluminum coin.

One of the most emblematic incidents of the journey took place shortly before we left Vienna, as we were finishing lunch one day in our refugee-friendly cafeteria, a long large hall with windows above your head high up on the walls, factory-floor fluorescent illumination, and two rows of tables with eight or ten places each. Very Bauhaus. The tables were of the plainest kind, made of the plainest materials and as if with crude and blunt tools. The chairs were just right for the tables. The walls were clean but colored a dirty green. Very pleasantly proletarian actually. The cuisine itself was generic. At the end of the meal, we had already returned our trays, soiled dishes and cutlery to the appropriate counter in the front of the hall and were walking towards the exit at the other end, passing by clusters of diners involved with their midday repast *à la* George Grosz. The ambience was somber rather than noisy, and certainly when the knife and spoon slipped out of Leslie's sleeve and clattered a few times on the tile floor, everybody must have heard the reverberations caroming up and down the walls. A thief!? Leslie turned red, picked up the utensils, walked back to the front and put them on a tray. Were all eyes on him or did I just think so? He made the round trip back to us at a normal pace, carrying himself as ever, so that you might have thought he was returning things dropped by someone else. Or just doing a bit of helpful housekeeping. But about five feet from the door he so quickened his steps as to be almost running, which might have given him away to anyone who cared.

Once outside, he disappeared down the street so fast we couldn't catch up with him until the corner some distance away. He was out of breath and laughing raggedly. I never ever saw him like that, not before or after, in a state of exhilaration actually. Back in the hotel he withdrew an undershirt of some sort from a shelf of the large wardrobe, unfolded it and let the pale light feebly play on three very familiar sets of cutlery, stainless steel, with the name of the cafeteria chain, WÖK, stamped on each stem. He proudly pointed at the collection. Obviously, we would not be expected to eat with our fingers in New York, no matter how fabulous and instantaneous our good fortune. He was a little bit nervous in the evening walking back into that big hall, but he walked no differently than ever. Needless to say, there was no Javert in pursuit of this pseudo-*misérable* criminal. I say pseudo just to keep things in perspective. For Leslie was no Valjean: he stole only utensils for eating, not the bread itself. And he got the last setting just in time. Rose and Leslie still owned those well-worn pieces when they died.

Right around Christmas, at our last family appearance before the American officials we were informed that our visas had been granted. We had expected that all along, but still it was a time to be elated and relieved. And so it was settled: indeed we'd be Americans. Yanks! What everybody wanted to be, and especially everybody who was nobody. Now a new set of documents had to be completed, the last question of which concerned our preference for the mode of transportation to the New World: did we want to travel by air or by sea? For, you see, we received more than just permission to enter the country; it was an invitation rather, all expenses paid. Even the red carpet. We were to be delivered into our new lives somewhat like we had been delivered into the old: naked and helpless but well cared for. Rose thought she might have a fear of planes, so we chose the sea-route, which was okay with all of us. Then each of us was given, as if it were a pilgrim's satchel, a plastic navy-blue overnight bag, the size of a large loaf of bread with hand-straps and a detachable shoulder-strap, the kind that was, as I later learned, associated at that time in America with airlines and carried by their personnel, with the name of the airline, or maybe its logo, stamped into the plastic in white on the two sides. In large block letters our bags proclaimed: UNITED STATES ESCAPEE PROGRAM. I had seen such bags often on the shoulders of Vienna passersby without realizing that they represented the fate I too had been hoping for. I wish I could remember what those bags contained, but I can't. But I do recall how baffled I was by that double E at the end of escapee. Hungarian, then my only guide in such things, is written phonetically, and a phonetic approach here seemed to require nothing more nor less than a bit of bleating. It was only many months later that I first understood the meaning and use of that English suffix and was finally able to explain to the family exactly what kind of program we had been in.

Then promptly after New Year's we were snatched from the guardianship of the Joint and shipped out of Vienna. All on the same day we traveled from the capital by bus to Wienerneustadt, a ride of about an hour Rose was told when she inquired on my behalf, then from there by rail to Salzburg, a ride of no more than a few hours, and then again by bus to the Camp Roeder often mentioned in contemporary newspaper reports as a recently abandoned *American* army base outside that city that had been hastily reopened as a transit camp for the refugees. It had been dark for a while already when we rolled into the camp. My stomach hadn't acted up on either bus ride, and my anxiety suddenly gave way to hope, maybe finally I'm over it, for I knew well by then that I will sooner or later, like most everyone else, outgrow the motion sickness. The bus stopped just inside the wide gate set in the wire fence, which might have stretched into infinity in both directions. Sitting by the window, I saw a vast snowy landscape illuminated by little squares of yellow light that turned out to be the windows of the barracks, and big cones of it too streaming down from where the tops of the lampposts had to be. I saw wide tracks in the snow receding into a blackening distance, which I sensed to be crowded with mountains. The bus slowly backed up, turned at a sharp angle, then drove to a distant barracks, where we filed out with our bags, down to the packed snow, tiny figures scurrying from bus to building under a cone of light, then ducking inside for shelter from the winds sweeping down from among the stars above and beyond.

So now finally we were in a camp, which I would say is the right place for refugees not yet resettled to be. After all, living between two worlds sort of sums up the condition of such refugees, and almost by definition that's where camps are located. For a camp is a temporary settlement, an area dotted with structures of flimsy construction that cater only to needs and not to comfort or conveniences, a place suited only to being occupied overnight or for the duration of a fishing trip or at the most a seasonal sojourn. Of course, bivouacking in a hotel in Vienna and taking our mess in a cafeteria was also an unmistakably interim arrangement, one that certainly never let us succumb to the tempting illusion of having a home or being at home. But even for us that all by itself didn't turn the Austrian capital into a camp. For in addition camps must also *segregate* their occupants and thus foreground even more forcefully the between-two-worlds aspect of their experience. In order to function this way, camps are likely to be surrounded either by a fence, as indeed Camp Roeder was, or by uninhabited tracts of land, each of which can serve to keep the camp-dweller separate from the home-dweller. Which is as it should be, because those two are natural enemies and do not mingle peaceably. Gypsies are persecuted because they live in tents on wheels, nomads drifting in from the steppes are forcibly settled down, Jews are derided as wanderers, and migrants are confronted by walls, armed boat-men and the border patrol. Villagers and townspeople expect to be cheated and robbed by those without a permanent abode, and raped and abducted by them if not actually killed. The earth-bound always fear the footloose, and the rootless hate the rooted. In Camp Roeder even we, the most temporary of the homeless and territoriless, were therefore both rendered harmless and protected.

But to some at least riding with us on the bus, a camp must also have had additional connotations. History made it impossible for all Hungarians in their mid-twenties and older, and Jews especially, not to reflexively associate camps with the Communists and/or the Nazis before them. I don't think Rose had any personal experience of life behind a fence, but Leslie might very well have as a forced-labor conscript and then a prisoner of war. And they also knew about the concentration camps, I'm sure. After all, Leslie's parents had died in Auschwitz, and there were Bözsi's sufferings too. Did a shiver go down their spines then the next day when in bright daylight they saw the barbed wire? And what about a few days later when we heard that the previous evening a group of refugees was stoned as their bus was turning in through the camp's gate? The story, flea-jumping in hushed tones through the barracks, was terse and factual. Jews were thought to be receiving preferential treatment, it went, by being unfairly expedited through the transportation pipeline. So the Christian refugees seethed with anger and frustration, and when the next bus-load of Jews arrived, the stones flew. The incident was brief and nobody was hurt. The bus just drove on to a different part of the camp, and the hooligans didn't bother to follow it. I feel compelled to call them that, hooligans, although I do actually understand their anger. It's just its expression I object to. Although I admit that petitioning the authorities hardly seems to have been an acceptable alternative. Here we are in Austria, Rose or Leslie said in a low voice to somebody in our barracks, obviously another Jew, and even here it's the Magyars we have to fear.

The incident was a minor disturbance and of no consequence to me or probably to anyone. In its light, however, I suddenly see the entire emigration process as a perfect little social experiment, one with a special relevance to Jews. For how can you overlook the provocation inherent in the exclusivism, separatism and privilege-buying of the whole Jewish refugee operation? While we had been grand-hoteling it in the capital, many of our gentile fellow-escapees lay on their sacks of straw in camps throughout the country, staring at the ceiling as the light faded day after day, wondering, to quote one of them, if "we are running away [from] or chasing after [something]." For us the entire undertaking was all of one piece. From the very beginning we were going to America. For them the trajectory was scrambled, the momentum kept stalling and the severed roots dangled in midair, at risk of withering before they could be replanted. And on top of that, their living conditions too were often almost inhuman, as in the camp at Traiskirchen, which had only fifteen lavatories for 4,000 refugees. But the real hardships were psychological. Statelessness, the stripping away of identity and the loss of your usual adult independence were tolerable in the short term, while your hopes of regaining them continued to be actively nourished, as long as you continued to take one after another of the many small steps that were about to become the whole journey. But what was to nourish those hopes when you came up against a seemingly immovable roadblock? *We* had some psychological comfort, they didn't. Although they believed themselves as worthy of it as we were, or no less worthy in any case. And since the lifeboat wasn't big enough for everyone, it is true that every American visa issued to a Jew was one less available to a Magyar. Did we expect them to be saints? Indeed, would *we* have behaved any less hooliganishly?

Our own barracks was a comfortable enough place. Rows of bunk beds, two deep, stood along the walls all around except by the lavatories in the corners adjacent to the entrance door, with a wide open aisle down the middle. We had two stacks of beds next to each other, which allowed us to privatize the space between them. During the day, when we sat on the edges of the lower bunks, we faced each other as if pretending that we were sitting around our very own invisible table. Suitcases were under beds. Since all the occupants spent many idle hours sitting or lying about, stealing was not a problem or even a concern. Although if you had anything of value, it was still best not to advertise it. Quickly a rudimentary social life also sprang into being in the barracks. The refugees shared their dreams and trepidations. They also shared their grievances against the old country. This was the late moment when for us the transplantation finally became a mass phenomenon. And more than anything else, more than being at all times in a state of waiting, more than being utterly unsettled and ready to move on 15 minutes' notice, more even than the isolation from the outside world, it was the group experience that made me feel that a camp was really the right place for us to be. Of course, we would have preferred to had gone directly to the edge of the continent and gotten on a steamer of some kind and sailed immediately, but our actual condition was not at all out of line with, and indeed much better than, what you have to expect when you set out to escape from a police state and through the kindness of strangers are enabled to travel to a distant country where freedom prevails, there to make your new home. And we bore our condition patiently and even, as I recall, with mostly good humor.

The morning after our first night on the bunk beds we stepped out into brilliant sunlight, sparkling, shimmering, reflecting back from the snow all around, and in front of us and towering above us almost as if within reach in their crystalline and white majesty, the mountains. Yes, the Alps. I had never seen such mountains; indeed, aside from the hills of Buda, which at the most just transform the city into a lovely full-breasted maiden, I had never before seen any mountains at all. I had also never seen the ocean, or the tropics, or any dramatic geography, and no more even than just a few pictures of such things, and consequently had only a very stunted sense, if any at all, of landscape and of the beauty of panoramas. I now see on my map of Austria and adjacent Bavaria that there are some mountains almost 6,500 feet high near Salzburg. Maybe those too-big-even-for-Elizabeth-Taylor diamonds gleaming in front of me were as tall as that or maybe they weren't. I can't say, but in either case they were sufficiently overwhelming to shock into being that very sense of landscape within me, to awaken me to the beauty that can inhere in the arrangement of natural features. Ah, the magnificence of the world as man found it, more or less. I embraced those mountains. I welcomed them into my life. Them and all the mountains and all the wonders in the world. They were all gifts I had just received, the first of many I was to receive, from America. Because America not only allowed me to leave behind the ever-tending-to-flat, monotone-mired East, but also offered

478

me the freedom to go wherever in my natural surroundings I might find existence the most ecstatic. And all of that in *addition* to the marvels of the man-made world, some of which had already been flashed before my eyes.

Now that we were in an American environment and felt ourselves to be, well, almost American – now it was time to get acquainted with America. And first of all, that meant an introduction to abundance, which was to be found in one of the larger barracks in the camp, a barracks crammed with used garments and shoes arranged on racks standing in serried ranks. Many a day after breakfast in the cafeteria we would go to this building to see if a new shipment had arrived, for shipments were received frequently, and help ourselves to whatever caught our fancy. It reassured me to see that Americans in droves were discarding such beautiful things in such perfectly good condition, and the very quantity itself of clothes of such a vast variety suggested a country awash in riches. As often as you wished you could enter this little corner of America, try on things, take what you wanted, and then you could even bring back some items and take others, or bring back everything. Whatever you wanted to do. Even your own choices did not limit you. The whole arrangement seemed to proclaim that America is a country of fantasies. But, alas, you had to abandon your dreams of elegance or plenty or both, as Tantalus had to curb his appetite. The reality was that you could acquire things only very selectively, because now you were carrying your house on your back like a snail. So you could satisfy only your most concrete and immediate needs, only what you really had to have for the even colder conditions coming, although there was nothing to prevent you, if you were so inclined, from slipping into something more frivolous for an hour or a day and making believe.

Many years after that camp experience I saw a wonderful Vittorio de Sica film from 1951 called *Miracle in Milan*, a story about life in a postwar shantytown in the outer precincts of the shell-shocked city inhabited by a multitude of displaced people. Toto, the movie's hero, is a young man with no family and no possessions, who believes that people are good and that you should trust everybody and protect the weak from the strong. At one point, the spirit of the long-departed woman who had found baby Toto in a cabbage patch and had raised him plays hooky from heaven, comes back to Milan and gives him a white dove that will grant all his wishes. Soon Toto is besieged by his neighbors, each one with a wish for him to make come true, which he proceeds to do. Among the favor-seekers is a middle-class couple from beyond the shanties, who arrive with a pampered child in arms and a maid, wish for outfits suitable for a ball, and in a flash find themselves clothed in a fancy-pants suit and gown. They walk away, and you see them out of Toto's sight expressing their astonished delight and fingering the fine materials of their new garments with childish mirth. Even as I was watching that scene, I recognized that reaction as identical to how we ourselves had felt as we were walking out of that barracks in Camp Roeder. And we were not the only ones. In a sense, all of us refugees, for the moment at least true have-nothings, we were all very much like the residents of that makeshift Milanese slum and its middle-class intruders. Wishing and sort of getting. So for me that episode in the film has turned into a parody of get-rich-quick-and-easy America, although de Sica himself is very unlikely I think to have intended it that way.

In me the used clothing barracks created the impression that refugee relief was an exclusively American endeavor, but that was not the whole story. For the United Nations High Commissioner for Refugees was in Austria already on November 7th, assessing the situation and issuing a *worldwide* appeal for $10 million of aid money. The United States donated $1 million, the highest figure, with Canada second with $250 thousand, but smaller donations also came in from places as unexpected as Ethiopia and the Philippines, nations with at best attenuated connections to the matter at hand. Still, the response to the UN appeal was disappointing, and in the end it was indeed the efforts of the American government, organizations and people that made the difference. In mid-December the United States followed up its initial contribution with an additional $4 million, and even that amounted only to a fraction of the total ultimately given by all American sources. The National Council of

Churches organized a drive to raise $2 million, the American Friends Service Committee's drive aimed at $250 thousand, the Roman Catholic churches' drive sent 500,000 pounds of clothes and blankets to Vienna, the Methodist Council of Bishops opened a drive for $1 million, American Protestant churches provided $2 million for the "victims of oppression in Hungary," the International Ladies' Garment Workers' Union, to which Rose belonged subsequently for many years, donated 100,000 children's garments, the National Council of Disc Jockeys for Public Service set out to raise $5 million on the air, and the American Red Cross spent $5.4 million on its refugee operations. Most of this, of course, was to be achieved through donations by individual Americans and families.

The American predominance in providing aid is also striking if you consider the contributions of the four agencies that were devoted to the cause of refugees worldwide. There was the League of Red Cross Societies, founded in 1919 as an umbrella organization of national Red Crosses and Red Crescents. The American Red Cross contributed 37% of the total aid provided by the League. Very important work on behalf of the refugees was done by the Inter-Governmental Committee for European Migration, an agency dating back to only 1951. The Committee brought together 26 member nations, but 45% of its budget was provided by the United States. CARE, organized in 1945 as the Cooperative for American Remittances to Europe, was of course an American agency. It began distributing its well-known packages, each containing 22 pounds of powdered milk, cheese, rice, beans and other foods, to the Hungarian refugees on November 12th. And, finally there was the International Rescue Committee, another American agency, established on Albert Einstein's suggestion in 1939 in support of Germans victimized by the Nazis. So everywhere you looked it was Americans, opening their big hearts and their fat wallets. They were rich and they were doing good. I don't recall our actual encounters with Americans, but in the abstract at least we immediately loved and admired them all, and although now I know the real details of 1950s American attitudes to accepting refugees, then I considered them saviors one and all.

That barn-like place with the garments was our morning's introduction to America, and the English lessons, six days a week, in a classroom of sorts in another one of the barracks, were the afternoon's. The bewilderment started the very first day when the refugees were made to understand that English speech included some sounds not known in Hungarian and impossible for non-native speakers to pronounce, very foreign sounds, as if foreign words would not have been enough. Leslie was disgusted. What other tricks might the builders of the Tower of Babel have had up their sleeve? Having always and in everything favored the use of brute force, he found it more difficult than even others his age to make his facial muscles reproduce the indescribable nuances that turned Hungarian vowels into English ones, and had even less success with tee-aitches and double u's. The recommended placement of lips and tongue produced only pathetic results, compelling him to go through the same process again and again, until finally he would just contort his face into ugly caricatures of the required subtle muscular arrangements and force out a loud unclassifiable sound, as if to blame his ineptitude on a language that was fit more for animals than humans. He usually got a few laughs, suggesting that others were frustrated too and humiliated, as the learning of sounds and words, generally the job of children, will often humiliate adults. But the merriment never lasted long. Perhaps never before had the power of speech been demonstrated so forcefully to these immigrants-to-be. And how aware they were of not possessing it!

The difficulty of tuning into a strange language for even just a few words was illustrated by the need for our teacher to devote most of three hour-long sessions to the American system of money. Cash! Now, remember, the teacher spoke not a word of Hungarian. Her success in making us, or some of us I should say, understand that coins in America had names quite independent or not obviously related to their actual denomination, which is not the case in Hungarian, that alone amounted to a miracle of communication. But it had to be done. It was elementary and essential information. It was during that marathon mute-to-deaf encounter that I had my first inkling of what exactly transplanting yourself from one country to another entails, from one physical and cultural environment to another, from being at home in this world to hoping to be at home in that. You actually have to learn to think a new way. Well, I was ready. The penny-nickel-dime-quarter story intrigued me. As if I had just been made privy to some secret in the scheme of things, some Masonic mystery, knowledge of which amounted to a kind of insight. That of course was not Leslie's reaction. Although he very much wanted to be on a first-name basis with American money, the difficulty of acquiring the necessary familiarity with it only aggravated his fears of the difficulty of acquiring the thing itself. If only he could learn English fast, he wished. But it's impossible to pronounce those words. Those ridiculous sounds, with your tongue between your teeth. And you just stand there like an idiot, without any idea what they're talking about.

In general, the two weeks in the camp outside Salzburg was the time when concerns about the future and trepidations about what the new country would be like began to mount and nag. First the escape had commandeered all your emotional resources. Then the legal arrangements for entry into your adopted country had to be completed, and for a while the state of your nerves depended on that. But now that both of those matters had been brought to a successful conclusion, and you were moreover, although for the moment stalled, already on your way to your destination, now there was nothing to be anxious about aside from the new life itself, and so now your anxiety increased in direct proportion to the decrease in the distance that still separated you from it. Each element of the new country that you now encountered, like its money, only made your ignorance of the whole that much more concrete and frightening, and now everything tended to alert you to the likely strangeness and maybe hostility of, and certainly the difficulties represented by, the place you were so impatient to reach. However difficult daily life was at the moment, you knew that the necessary acculturation and the demands of creating a satisfactory new normalcy would be even more of an ordeal. These, of course, were not my own thoughts and feelings, but the thoughts and feelings of the adults only. I myself didn't worry. When I was reminded of difficulties I too was bound to encounter, I found instant comfort in the often-articulated wisdom that fourteen was a very good age for a transplantation. You'll be speaking English in three months, everybody was predicting.

A few days before being again shipped out, we had yet one more lesson to learn about American life. All the refugees waiting to depart had to undergo a cursory medical examination, or maybe you just had to have blood drawn again, I don't remember specifically. In any case, we were all standing on line, moving toward two men wearing the white coats of medical personnel. They were sitting at small tables on either side of the end of the line, in their hands professional instruments at the ready. But the refugees proceeded as if there were only one doctor available, with nobody stepping up to the other one, sleeve already rolled up, arm on offer. You see, the invisible doctor was black. But then along came Rose, the crooks of her elbows still black-and-blue a week after she had last had her blood siphoned off into a vial. As she neared the head of the line, she recognized the white doctor wielding the hypodermic as the man who had just recently tortured both of her arms with numerous painful probes, and swallowing her distrust and distaste, marched over to the black man, who confidently sank the needle through the skin and right into a vein, and after a few moments withdrew it and the blood-colored syringe with a gesture so elegant that it left no mark whatsoever on the apparently unpunctured epidermis. Rose stepped away from the table beaming, her left forefinger pressing a wad of cotton against her right arm. She had just had her first personal encounter with America, and it had been mutually satisfactory.

The waiting ended on January 17th. In a fairly orderly fashion, all of us from our own barracks and several others boarded buses for transportation to a railroad siding, where we then boarded a train. We were finally on our way, and excitement gripped the refugees. I just had time to throw a farewell glance at the mountains. The train ride itself lasted eighteen hours, not including the near-half-day wait for our departure, sitting on thinly upholstered benches in a stuck-in-time compartment.

Now I know that the Inter-Governmental Committee was in charge of that leg of our journey, but then everything seemed arbitrary and mysterious, as if no one had remembered to make arrangements. Our destination was unannounced; the doors to the train remained locked from the outside at all times, whether the train was in motion or idling at a siding; we sped through stations bearing strange but identifiably German names but stopped only at seemingly unpopulated spots; no food or drinks were distributed. At first the stateless passengers just grumbled, but then something about the situation unnerved them. What it was I cannot say. Nobody of course suspected foul play, so to speak, and that would have been preposterous anyway. But maybe somebody had made a mistake, confused this train with another or somehow just forgotten about us? Something was very wrong. You shot glances here and there, tried to curb the drift of your thoughts, went rigid at every unusual sound like a spooked dog. Were some people maybe reminded of other imprisoned train-rides they had had to endure not so many years earlier? Was it maybe the loss of control represented by the circumstances that overpowered your reason and threatened mass hysteria? Or was it the surrender to machines that awoke a primordial fear? I can't identify the cause, as I've said, but I do believe that something instinctive and almost animal-like about human nature was being displayed there.

At some point finally word reached us that our destination was Bremerhaven, a port in northern Germany, on the North Sea coast, not far from the large city of Bremen, which I knew of from poring over maps. We didn't know if the information was reliable, and I could not even guess from the speed-blurred names of the stations we passed, rattling everything like a thunderclap. In my mind I just saw a train shooting like an arrow loosed in the eastern heartland of the continent straight towards the ocean, cutting across mountains, forests and rivers, undeterred by settlements and frontiers, always west, west, west to... well, to Bremerhaven. This idea seemed to conform to the map of Europe I was carrying in my head even then. And through subsequent years too, whenever I thought about that ride, even if I could not resurrect the images I had perceived when the wheels were actually clacking under me, for the hundreds of cinematic trains my eyes have seen since then have both nourished and narrowed what my mind can see – whenever I thought about that ride, we refugees were rolling west, drawn to the ocean and the western coast as if by destiny. In other words, the forces of history all about me, everything always sweeping west, the barbarian invasions, the Mongols, the Turk, the Cold War – in my mind they completely overwhelmed geographical reality. For now that I am studying the atlas and scrupulously checking my recollections against the bedrock of facts, now I am confronted with our true course: Salzburg to Bremerhaven is due north-northwest, although back then a slight detour to skirt the Iron Curtain, about halfway, west-then-north where East Germany used to bulge out around Erfurt, would also have been in order.

Bremerhaven, founded in 1827 near settlements dating back well into the Middle Ages, first became a major port of departure for New-World-bound emigrants in 1837. Between that date and 1974, when seaports conclusively yielded this function to airports, 7 million seekers of a new country boarded ships there. Many of them were ethnic Germans, but there were also many emigrants from Eastern Europe. Most of the passengers sailed to the United States, but some did have Canadian, Brazilian, Argentine or Australian ports as their destination. It was this stream of humanity that we were about to join and thereby weave our lives more densely yet into the fabric of history, into the welter of events, that is, that sooner or later find a place for themselves in the historian's professional awareness. For already, as refugees of the 1956 Hungarian revolution we were deep in the ditch of history, clearing the banks just enough to be able to peer over them. But we were also Jews of the Holocaust and members of the Second Generation, and, as I've said already, part of the 20th-century Jewish exodus from Europe, and especially Eastern Europe, and participants in the European peopling of the New World, and the United States in particular, and among the ranks of those European emigrants too who had through the decades embarked on the transcontinental leg of the journey from this north-German port, and a lot of other things also I think that are neither as obvious as these nor ours to claim any more than everybody's, so to speak. Of course, among these undeniable historical connections we were very much aware of some, but not at all of others. And life is such that even the most historically molded experiences we lived primarily as personal events, as events lived as only we could and had to live them.

On the morning of January 19th the train rolled to a halt right by some docks. The refugees gathered their meager belongings and descended onto the pavement one by one, into a wintry North Sea day, another scene composed of nothing but gray. Before us the crooked limbs of cargo cranes seemed to be dangling from the leaden sky, as if a flock of prehistoric birds long ago turned to blackened cinders by a fiery extinction was about to land. Thrusting out from amongst them were the turrets, scaffolds, cables and rope-works of an immense ship, battleship-gray of course, with a funnel big enough to emit the clouds of soot and smoke rising above everything. Pushing and dragging bags, the line of refugees slowly moved towards the ship, which loomed larger with each step, its belly floating, it seemed against all probability, on the black water that splashed sluggishly against the dock.

Suddenly a booming sound of great intensity swept the docks. The deep, low vibrations seemed to turn both the air and your inner organs to liquid, and the momentary deafness filled you with alarm and foreboding. There was something intolerably sinister about this uncontrollable trembling and shaking of the world, to which your whole body responded despite all your efforts to the contrary. The first blast lasted for a long five seconds or so and unnerved everyone. Once it ceased, we began to come up for air, as it were, but then suddenly, still with a shock, the booming sound resumed. Now I could continue to breathe even while I was, like a martini too anxious to please, shaken *and* stirred, and now I could look around and help my ears identify that awful sound as the ship's horn. But unlike the rest of us, Marika could not look and could not assess and just burst into tears. The booming sound would have been frightening enough by itself and beyond your power to physically resist even if it had not, for most everyone, come on top of great anxiety and even fears about crossing the ocean on, or rather in, this hulking, machine-like ship, this steel container at once gigantic and woefully tiny. Rose herself was visibly nervous, plagued by the thought that we would be lost at sea, pitched down to the depths of the vast watery waste. So when the horn made us all jump the second time, Marika started to shake and sob. Leslie lashed out at her. "Be quiet! What are you crying for!" And that of course only made her cry all the louder. For the third time then the horn sounded. By now you were almost used to it and could certainly manage to calm the unavoidable fear of being startled, but this time the booming would not stop, or went on, I should say, a little bit longer than the previous two times. And that in itself was very frightening. So Marika continued to simper, and Leslie continued to fume. Nerves were shot all around.

The first planeload of America-bound refugees had landed at McGuire Air Force Base at Fort Dix, New Jersey on November 21st, only an amazing *seventeen* days after the Hungarian exodus had begun in earnest. There were 60 men, women and children on board for the 20-hour flight from Frankfurt. As they disembarked from the commercial airliner, the combined 19th and 172nd Army Bands played Brahms's Hungarian Dance No.5. Public interest was intense, as it had been all along since the very first shot of the revolution, and the landing produced what is known today as a media blitz. Picture it in black-and-white, like Lindbergh landing at Le Bourget or, better yet, a scene from *Superman*, the 1950s TV series: ranks of military police holding back ranks of newsmen, cameramen and radio reporters, and as No.5 is followed by No.6 the refugees being led to a temporary outdoor platform. From there the Secretary of the Army welcomes them, concluding his comments by turning to the military standard bearers, ordering them to raise high the stars and stripes, and then exhorting the refugees to "make it your first act on American soil to applaud the American flag." The standard bearers raise the flag, the interpreter interprets and the refugees applaud.

For ten days after that flights continued almost daily. Then on December 3rd the armed services got even more involved in the operation as the Air Force declared itself ready to begin what would be the largest air-transport undertaking since the Berlin airlift of 1948-49, to which the White House responded by urging a significant role for Navy planes and ships too. And so, a couple of days later the Department of Defense announced that henceforward the movement of the refugees out of Austria and into the United States would indeed be a military rather than a civilian operation, with military rather than commercial planes and ships. Private welfare agencies did not hide their disappointment. But they requested changes only to the proposed transport of 7,000 refugees from Bremerhaven in three troopships. They derided the American plan to pack 2,300 bodies into each military vessel by pointing out that Canada was booking space aboard Cunard Line ships.

Only three days later, on December 6th, President Eisenhower issued an apparently final statement on the Atlantic crossings arranged for the refugees. Among other things, he announced that three naval transports have been assigned to sail weekly from Bremerhaven starting on December 21st, each carrying about 1,600 passengers. The first of those ships was the *General Le Roy Eltinge*, a 10,000-ton former Army transport and veteran of World War II and Korea, "designed as a troop transport and distinctively carrying her funnel near the stern like a tanker." It actually carried 1,747 refugees on the first crossing, 1,500 of them young men or boys in their teens who had fought in the revolution. It had been scheduled to arrive in Brooklyn on December 31st, but was delayed one day by an Atlantic storm. The arrival was made all the more exciting by the birth on board of a baby boy, a new American *citizen*, just minutes before the ship entered New York's Upper Bay. Predictably, the parents named the infant Leroy Eltinge. As the ship docked at the Brooklyn Army Terminal, the Army Terminal Band played "rock 'n' roll and popular dance tunes," and then the Hungarian national anthem and the Star-Spangled Banner. The other two ships followed the *General Eltinge* as scheduled, and after the United States increased the number of refugee admissions, all three ships made additional crossings. Apparently, the *General Eltinge* herself returned to Bremerhaven without much delay, for she was the monstrosity waiting for us on January 19th.

We boarded by going up a steep gangway to the main deck, and there waited on line to be assigned bunks. Given the military nature of the accommodations, men and women had to be separated. So Leslie and I, following a sailor leading a group, entered the floating steel enclosure through one of those hatches that are actually holes left in the metal hide of the ship, while Rose and Marika entered it through another. Dragging our suitcase, our shoes resounding on the steps, we descended several flights of steep perforated-metal stairs. We were led into a dimly lit area, a section of one of the layers that comprised the ship's interior, a space created by gigantic plates of steel seamed together with tongues of flame, sealed off from other such spaces and from the oceans of the world, in which they were permanently immersed. The rows of bunks filling this space, something like sets of shelves, were actually lengths of hemmed canvas stretched inside metal frames, cantilevered off two end-posts and stacked four on top of one another. We got one set. Leslie occupied the second bunk from the bottom, I was above him, and the other two served as storage for our stuff. After we settled in, as it were – made contact with our neighbors, stowed our bags in a way we could consider safe, located the latrine and checked out its facilities, explored the area for corridors, stairways and exits – it was time to jostle our way through crowds no less anxious and disoriented than we were, bump against those descending the very stairs we were climbing, make way for the sailors who of course had priority and were always in a hurry, try not to bang our heads more often than necessary into all that came their way, and finally push our own way to the main deck and fresh air.

After some looking around, we found Rose and Marika. We reunited, and the freedom to be together on deck during the day made the separation imposed on us at night seem acceptable. Leslie had gathered from the suitcase we had by our bunks all that belonged to the women and now handed those things to Rose, and Rose had done and did likewise. So we were set up and tolerably comfortable for the ten days or so that we had been told would be needed for the crossing to New York. Bundled up against the cold, we strolled about and after a while found a spot to sit down on the metal ledge that protruded at sitting height from the sides of all the structures rising from the deck. The refugees, all along the port side and also the starboard, were conversing about seasickness. It seemed that nobody actually knew the phenomenon first-hand, but many had had acquaintances who had known it, and nobody hesitated to offer an opinion on who was more likely to get it and who less, which symptoms were the most to be feared, and what might help the sufferer get over it sooner rather than later. Apparently, Rose was not the only one nervous about the safety of an Atlantic crossing by boat, for many assurances were offered on that subject too. In any case, as someone pointed out, lifeboats lined both sides of the deck, hanging from frames equipped with winches that could in case of need swing them out over the ocean and then lower them onto the briny waves. But since our height above the liquid darkness seemed a good deal greater than what I had been used to from our fifth-floor window in Budapest, I shuddered even at the thought.

Of course, the ship was manned by sailors of the United States Navy. The young men in blue sailed the ship and fed us and attended to us otherwise too, like cleaning the latrines, for example, but all the while they remained elevated above the refugees by their uniformed uniformity, their coordinated tasks and their usefulness as demonstrated by the very orders that governed their every movement. They were obviously the vessel's crew, and we its passengers. They were busy, we were idle. They worked, we fretted. I remember only one crewmember, a very tall, burly black sailor, older than a draftee, with always a smile on his face. Amongst other things, it was his job to get the passengers to the mess halls at meal times, not an easy job when most of your charges are laid low, very low, by seasickness. By dinnertime the first day out of port, or possibly even on the prior crossing, he had learned the Hungarian words *"enni menni,"* which literally mean "to go to eat," with the phrase sounding no more grammatical in one language than in the other. But he apparently liked the brevity and the rhyme, and knew that his words got the message across. So three times each day he would walk from one end of the men's quarters to the other, ordering, tricking, cajoling with those words, and with a smile and a twinkle.

A couple of hours after we boarded a hum and a vibration ran through the ship. The engines had been fired up. A cheer went up from the crowd, but also a gasp. Soon the ship backed away from the dock, pivoted and began slowly to steam into the open port and out to sea. Once you managed to push the shaking and the noise into the background of your consciousness, it was not unpleasant to travel that way. We proceeded under a uniformly and unchangingly gray sky, southwest along the coast of the Netherlands then of Belgium, through the Straits of Dover, where land was visible first on the right and then on the left, and then through the English Channel. It took us a day and a half to reach the open Atlantic, beyond England and Ireland. Our progress was documented by a daily bulletin posted in a corridor off the main deck, which someone happened upon and then spread the news of. The bulletin indicated the distances that we had covered and that remained, our speed in knots, and our location in longitude and latitude and also by reference to geography when that was possible during this initial phase of the crossing. I assumed the responsibility of reviewing the postings regularly, after which I reported the information to the family, checked that it squared with that map of Europe in my head, and then I was free to return to my discoveries. During these days we learned about what the American armed forces considered suitable and acceptable as food for troops and others temporarily like them, explored the main deck of the ship, and had many repetitive and boring conversations with our fellow refugees about the United States, the English language and procedures generally relevant to people in our situation. Some people seemed aware of their ignorance regarding these matters, but the men especially had no difficulty expressing firm but most likely groundless opinions about them too. During the nights we slept in our bunks. We thought that crossing the ocean was boring but no worse.

During World War II and right through the mid-50s, large numbers of people throughout the world but mostly in Europe moved or were moved to destinations more or less distant from their homes. Troops and prisoners of war had of course to get to where the fighting and the camps were, as did people sent to concentration camps by the Germans and those collaborating with them and by the Soviets, but I am not concerned here with any such people because their movements were not migrations. Rather, I am focusing only on the millions who were on the move to new homes, as were we. Given the events of those times, it is not surprising that some people migrated willingly, others were forced to do so, while still others fell somewhere in-between. In addition to those so victimized by Stalin, there were also large populations of Poles expelled by the Germans during the early years of the war to be replaced by ethnic Germans living by then for a long time in the Baltic states, Romania and other eastern territories. At the same time, the Soviets were also deporting hundreds of thousands of Poles. Partly in retaliation, as it were, after the war an estimated 15 million Germans fled or were expelled – or, more euphemistically, transferred, evacuated or repatriated – from Eastern Europe to Germany. These movements, and there were others like them too, seem to have been mostly by rail. Also after the war perhaps as many as 20 million Europeans found themselves displaced from their homelands. Efforts at repatriation resolved the status of most of them, but about one million could not go back for fear of persecution. So-called DP, that is, displaced persons, camps, most of which were decommissioned by 1952, provided these people with a place to live until one or another foreign country accepted them as immigrants. Upon such acceptance, the migrants relied on their new homelands and refugee organizations to transport them to their destinations by trains, planes and ships. The movement of the refugees on the *General Eltinge* was a late and outstandingly well-managed example of this kind of arrangement.

But on the third day of our crossing, a force mightier even than history, namely, nature, began to make a mockery of that good management. That was when an unusually severe North-Atlantic winter storm first joined us on our journey and did not have the decency to leave until a full five days later. Conditions were probably not dangerous, but they were sure scary. For all those days the winds howled like wild animals. The waves seemed to rise like mountains, only to crash immediately into the abysses that opened up all about them. You had not a moment's doubt that you were about to be swept off the deck, for at times the ship listed so steeply that to look ahead amounted to actually looking straight into the depths. Wave after wave slammed into the side of the ship with a thunderclap, making everything creak and reverberate and shudder. One more blow, you kept thinking, will shatter this steel tub, the weight of the next wave crashing down will crush it, the slashing rain will simply swamp it and send it to the bottom of the ocean. Quickly someone figured out which numbers on the ship's bulletin indicated wind velocity, the information spread, and then, whenever you were able to, you crawled over to the corridor where the notice was posted to try to derive some comfort from a quantified description of conditions. But quickly the bobbing and yawing and rolling of the ship chased the comfort away, and then the fear visible on the other faces looking at those figures reconfirmed your own belief that a ship strong enough to withstand such a series of assaults had not yet been built, for a storm of such ferocity had to be an anomaly, an unexpected fluke, a freak of nature nobody had ever yet to plan for.

As soon as the ship started pitching, we all got seasick. I don't mean just the Hajdus, but all the refugees, with practically no exceptions. The nausea overwhelmed you during sleeping hours, and by breakfast time there was a retching man bent over every plumbing receptacle and garbage can, and others were shoving him out of the way. Ghostly looking creatures reeled with the movements of the ship, and hands seeking a grip slid down the metal walls, doors and posts painted yellow. When the fury of the ocean let up for a minute, all you could hear were groans and sighs. Leslie kept mumbling about Rose and Marika, but he no more than I had the strength to look for them. They have to be as sick as we are, I kept saying to him. I stumbled to the latrine, then stood there on trembling legs, amazed at the urge to vomit from an empty stomach.

Sailors dispensed Dramamine tablets in the morning and then again in the evening, and with each pill you waited for relief, but in vain. Slowly the conviction took hold that if there was a remedy at all, it was eating. Maybe it *was* true that the sooner you return to having normal meals, the sooner you'll feel okay. So the black sailor's siren song of *enni menni* sounded ever sweeter, but still you had no more command of your appetite than of the ocean itself.

On the second day of this suffering I wasn't quite as debilitated anymore, and I managed to prevail on Leslie to drag himself up to a vertical position so we could get some fresh air and maybe see if Rose and Marika were about. We pulled on our coats, cast a glance at our prostrate fellows and staggered towards the exit. But we didn't make it past a garbage can standing sentry there.

Sometime later we tried again. Slowly we climbed the stairs, at each landing passing wraith-like figures crumpled in defeat, but at the hatch we came face to face with the storm. When the ship pitched so as to lift the side of the deck to which we were hoping to exit, then we were thrown backwards and needed all our strength not to lose ground. When the ship pitched the other way, we could push the hatch open halfway, but then immediately the ocean, having just crashed over the edge of the deck, slapped us with a force we could not withstand. After several rounds of this Leslie retreated downstairs, but I persisted and finally did succeed in stepping outside, although by then the little strength I had had was already mostly spent.

Obviously, it wasn't the dead of night, but it could have been any other time of day. At first, the sky and the sea seemed to have interpenetrated, with the greens and grays and black running into each other, and all mottled with the spraying foam. Then I started to distinguish the clouds from the waves, although the pitching of the ship and the rapidly shifting shapes of the elements themselves made it impossible to find the horizon. After a few minutes, my body actually began to adjust to the constantly changing patterns of the wind and rain, bracing itself against assaults that could come from any direction. Ignoring the fear in my throat, I set out to traverse the deck. Head down, teeth clenched, muscles tense, one careful step, then another, and then finally I managed to get to the railing, grasped it with both hands and let myself sink into something like a quasi-ecstasy of discovery. I beheld the drama of enormous waves one after the other gathering their strength and rising to ominous heights, the wind knifing into the watery mountains, the sea rearranging itself every second into always new and yet more frightening shapes. The elements roared as if to express the rage of the gods against these presumptuous humans, and the ship seemed to bellow like a living creature being rent to pieces.

I was alone. Moving my hands along the railing, one over the other, as my feet moved along the deck, I laboriously made my way to a covered passageway between the two sides of the ship where a flight of stairs led down to a platform from which you could look yet further down into the engine room. Since the first day I had gone there daily, my condition permitting. There, to my relief, everything was proceeding as always. Of course, even the sailors had to keep fighting to maintain their footing, or again and again to regain it, but much less than I did, and in any case, that did not seem to interfere with their shoveling the coal or attending to the levers and dials and the many valve wheels attached to the engine. For a few minutes I watched the sweating, wobbling figures feed the fire, the flames swallowing the black nuggets being heaped and heaped on them. Then I lurched away reassured. The children of Prometheus were ever dauntless.

Now in the telling I see that for me the journey from Vienna to New York was a rite of passage, a ritual of transformation from being one thing to being another. More than anything else, more than the Bar Mitzvah certainly, it was that experience, and the eleven days of the crossing in particular, and the storm especially, that effectively ended my Hungarian and inaugurated my American life. As if the Old World had been utterly overwhelmed by the waters and buried in the bottomless liquid depths, as if it had yielded to the New World soon to appear out of the churning formlessness, rising in glory, in the splendid, rosy-fingered dawn of a new post-diluvian life. I can even see the days and nights I spent in the confines of the dimly-illuminated steel hull as a temporary descent into an underworld, where beings more dead than alive dragged themselves about, while little devils in blue cheered at their torments. And as there was no possibility of ever returning to the old country, so that journey too was something I would never be able to do in reverse. You could never undo that storm. The prior identity could never be regained. Never again would or could I be Hungarian. And never again could I be a child. I had entered adulthood, which very appropriately would come to me in its own language, English, and so would as a matter of course but without any condescension relegate Hungarian to being the language of my childhood. The crossing of the threshold between the two locations, states and identities – that was a rite of passage. It seems to me that the whole thing would not have lent itself to such fit-like-a-glove mythification had we just levitated across the ocean in 20 hours on the wings of an airplane.

A rite of passage is a ceremony and a *symbol* of transformation. For a teenager, such a rite is just the right thing, since it resonates well with normal development, including hormonal imperatives. As a teenager, shedding one status and taking on another corresponds to changes in your psychological reality and in what the world itself expects of you. So you *want* no longer to speak like a child, to paraphrase Saint Paul, and start putting away childish things. But what can you make of a rite of passage if you're like Leslie and Rose were, in the middle of your life, no longer as flexible, malleable or psychologically plastic as you may have been in your youth, at an age when you no longer have the need or the desire to change your feelings or behavior? When, consequently, a change in status can actually deepen rather than lighten any attendant pain or alienation. In retrospect, I have to admire their grit for pretty much just submitting to all the experiences awaiting them that you can characterize as rites of passage – the crossing, the changing of names, the English classes in the local high school, the taking of the oath as American citizens, and many less typical ones too no doubt. Especially since for them the passage remained permanently occluded. For them the storm was more deformative than transformative: it did mark the wrecking of the old identity, but it could not at the same time also open the path to a possible satisfactory replacement. After all, what is it exactly that they could or did become?

On the third day of the storm, our sixth day at sea, I finally felt okay. It still rained torrentially at times and the wind still howled, but after what we had just been through all that seemed hardly more than a little inconvenience. Leslie too was now sufficiently better to go up to the deck with me. Even Rose and Marika appeared at our usual meeting place, finally we saw them, after three days of being apart, after three days of anxiety for Leslie. Rose looked ghastly. She related how for two whole days the crashing of the waves against the ship, which was especially intense in the bows where she and Marika bunked, had nearly driven her out of her mind. The fear that such battering would splinter the vessel would not release her. In her youth she had heard about the *Titanic* and now imagined submerged icebergs everywhere, ready to dent and gash and crack the hapless *General Eltinge* pinballing through them. Together, the fear and the seasickness had utterly debilitated her. And she was still feeling sick. And if that is possible, Marika looked even worse. She was weak and seemed terrorized.

Finally, on the fourth day of the storm Leslie felt restored to physical well-being and Rose did too. The rain had stopped, although the ocean remained very wild and still the wind continued occasionally to crescendo to a scream-like gust. And conditions kept improving. The fifth day of the storm we spent mostly on the deck despite the continued near-violent weather – on and off slashing rain, scudding clouds, icy wind – with the intermittent conversation among the refugees now being immovably stuck on the question of how many more days we needed to reach New York, with all relevant factors being discussed in detail. Only poor Marika's suffering refused to abate. She just seemed unable to recover from the repeated assaults on her body and psyche during the last week, or maybe the last month.

That afternoon she was sitting next to Rose on that metal ledge as if wilted, vacantly staring ahead, conspicuous even in an environment where everything was still gray. The ship, all its exterior surfaces, that is, retained of course the color that epitomized the visual experience of the northern seas, and to it conformed the sailors in their blues and blacks, the immigrants in their drab, Communist-issue winter garments, and also the sky and the sea. But suddenly out of this unrelieved visual mono-tone emerged a tall male figure dressed in white, from his white peaked cap with the glittering gold stars and bands, which were complemented by similar judiciously placed stars and bands on the shoulders and sleeves of his jacket, to his white shoes, which for me were the most startling component of his attire. Never before had I seen a man wearing white shoes. He could have been a prince, a savior, a heavenly messenger, but ordinary mortal he was not. And he was walking directly towards us. In his hand, indeed on the upturned palm of his extended right hand, his extended *white-gloved* right hand it seems to me now, he carried a pear. I am tempted to say that it was a golden pear, but of course it only seemed to be so. In fact, it was an ordinary pear, of a color between green and yellow, which he presented to an astonished Marika with a slight bow.

How perfect it all was! Fruit given as a gift we understood very well. Over the years, between us Marika and I had received probably a half-dozen oranges as presents. One at a time, and no, not as treats, but as presents from the tropics. And there was also the unforgettable case of the banana my Uncle Misi, Gyuri's father, had given me a few years earlier. During the early 50s Misi was the commercial attaché at the Hungarian Embassy in East Berlin, and one Christmas season when he and his family came back to Budapest for a holiday he brought me a gift of a banana. I was ten years old I would say, but, like the refugee twin boys in the Eisenstadt reception center mentioned in the *Times*, who had been offered the same fruit, I had never seen a thing like that and had to be told first that it was a fruit and second, and as I was about to take a bite, that it had to be peeled before eaten. So the pear was a perfect gift because we were good fruit-receivers and also because of the circumstances of the moment. All of us packed into this boat as we were, in the middle of the Atlantic Ocean in the middle of winter, with the ship sailing under naval discipline, packed to the bursting and carrying only the absolute necessities for passengers and an all-male crew – here we were, under circumstances that may fairly be said to have constituted a world with nothing in it for giving. How ingenious then of this splendid personage despite all that to discover something to give, and a gift no less that conjured up a soft, easy life in the midst of all this harshness and hardship, and a gift that was also nearly golden.

The materialization of the captain on the deck, for that is whom we understood the bearer of the gift to be – I'd call him Captain America if the name were not taken already – his appearance, his demeanor, his wordlessness, even the ragged chorus of *sank you*s we mumbled in our first English-language interaction, all of this drew a crowd from amongst our fellow refugees, who of course were no less susceptible to the spell being cast than were we. So it took a few seconds after the captain turned on his heels and disappeared before one of them finally produced a pocket knife. Rose then cut the fruit into quarters, and we ate it. I remember the scene well, and would even if it didn't take me back again to Milan and Toto and that patently unrealistic work of neorealism, and in particular to the sequence in the film about a raffle that had been organized in the shantytown, with a roast chicken as the first prize. All the homeless-but-for-corrugated-tin gather in a circle in the urban field at the edge of the settlement to watch the drawing. An old man wins and proceeds to consume his prize right there in the middle of the circle. The hungry crowd watches him rudely dismember and devour that fowl, as if the right to ogle at the lucky one and imagine yourself in his shoes were the consolation prize for the chickenless. Surely, I now see, this was another parody of America, and this one may even have been intentional. By the way, Marika had no need to eat that pear or even just taste it. She had revived instantly on the captain's appearance, as if transported to an orchard of delights, and was living a fairy tale and anxious that reality not spoil it as we munched.

Although we didn't share that pear with our fellow passengers on the *General Eltinge,* our sufferings on land and on sea had brought us all together and, much more effectively than Communism, had made us all into equals. We were literally in the same boat, without distinction but for that which arises from age or family. Or so I used to think anyway. For now I find that in fact we were not. You see, all the refugees entering the United States had not been extended the same invitation: some of us had visas to come and settle down and become citizens, while others, and not only "involuntary" party members, were to enter only as parolees, that is, individuals who could reside in the States indefinitely under the supervision of the Attorney General, but would have to leave at some future date unless their status was "regularized" by Congressional action. And that, obviously, was a fundamental difference. Undoubtedly, the parolees considered themselves fortunate to be *en route* to New York, probably more fortunate than refugees who had accepted asylum in a less desirable haven and definitely more so than those still cooling their heels, as it were, in the slush and snows of Austria. But for parolees America was to be limbo only, which as you well know is the first circle of hell, whereas a visa automatically turned the place into *paradiso* itself. Since I never heard anything about our being parolees, I have to assume that we ourselves had visas. The phalanx of sisters in the Bronx may have accounted for our good luck, or more specifically Pearl and Hugo, who I later found out had sponsored us, that is, guaranteed that we'd have a place to live and Leslie a job. For that meant a lot I now understand, it may even have been dispositive. I'll never know. But on each of the few occasions I heard the matter referred to, Leslie snapped back only that it had never cost them a penny, which tells me that Pearl and Hugo do actually deserve some credit here.

The two-tier system reflected the two laws in effect in the United States that both empowered the government to admit immigrants and constrained it in exercising that power. There was, first, the McCarran-Walter Immigration and Nationality Act of 1952; and there was, second, the Refugee Relief Act of 1953. The former established the general framework within which, with some modifications of course, immigration into this country takes place even today, including the principles of national origins, quotas, and overall limits. The latter created a special program that operated only through the end of 1956 and provided for the admission of a separate cohort of 214,000 immigrants, 45,000 of them specifically from Communist countries. The spots still available in this special contingent were allocated to the Hungarians immediately upon outbreak of the refugee crisis – and not a minute too soon either, given the expiration date on the label. This amounted to 6,400 visas or so, a number that did not go very far, and not nearly far enough, most people seemed to agree. So President Eisenhower ordered officials to stretch the laws however they could. And thanks to their efforts, at the beginning of December to the number of potential visa-recipients the administration could add 15,000 who would receive the legal status of *parolees,* as the McCarran-Walter Act designated immigrants permitted outside regular quotas in case of emergencies. And there you have the two-tier system. In his 1957 State of the Union message the president urged Congress to regularize the parolees' status, but I have not been able to find out whether or not that ever happened.

At one point in his efforts to establish a basis for admitting an always greater number of refugees, President Eisenhower claimed merely to be giving "practical effect to the American people's intense desire to help the victims of Soviet oppression." That desire and the sense of American responsibility I've already mentioned were indeed evident everywhere. Admiration and sympathy for, and the eagerness to help, the refugees resounded in voices raised throughout the country. In mid-November already the White House announced that the American people's response to the government's invitation to sponsor admissions had been "overwhelming" and "very heartening." George Meany, head of the AFL-CIO, argued for admittance of 100,000, declaring that they would not have an adverse effect on the labor market. The United Steelworkers Union sponsored 1,000 refugees. And in early January popular sentiment seemed actually to overwhelm the legal situation. Eisenhower ordered the parole admission of an additional 6,800, and as of the end of March 1957 the United States had accepted almost 28,000 of the Hungarian refugees, more than any other country. And had given $5 million of aid money, also more than any other country. Yes, still more could have been done, but the actual response was generous anyway. Certainly, I am grateful for it as a Hungarian and proud of it as an American.

With the passing of the storm, the crossing and indeed the journey to America seemed to be behind us. Never mind that we still had two or two-and-a-half days left on board, it was time now to prepare for arrival. So the next morning, as sparkling winter light glazed the deck, Leslie called a family conference to discuss names. He announced that we would not change our family name to accommodate English-speakers, although we knew that Hajdu promised to be a phonetic and ortho-graphic handicap. But he had already changed the family name once, and that was enough for him. Given names were a different matter, however, and now it was time to conclude discussions long pending. Leslie understood that the English version of László was Leslie and an-nounced that so he would be known. Unfortunately, we knew nothing more about the new name, neither its popularity in Britain rather than in the States nor its double-gendered nature, which surely would have seemed a distasteful ambiguity to him and would likely have prevented the exchange of László, which is like a square jaw, and which fit him well, for Leslie, which is like a pair of house slippers. Rose's name had been Rózsa, which is also the name of the flower in Hungarian, so her choice was obvious. Marika's formal name had been Marianna, and that she could keep in one of several forms. In the end she chose Marion. But my name, Tibor, presented a problem, for it had no English cognate. So I could keep it or choose a substitute. I did not want to keep it, but also knew very little about possible replacements. What I did know was that at the Melbourne Olympics a couple of months earlier a spectacular American sprinter named Bobby Morrow had won both the 100- and 200-meter dashes. So I chose Bobby. But Rose would not hear of it; she thought it silly. My second choice then was Robert, which I honestly did not know to be the same name. And so Robert it became, I became, and of course Bob and even Bobby.

As you can see, on arrival in America I wanted to be an Olympic champion, but instead I was *expected* to be a young Hungarian freedom fighter. Congressman Walter had made that expectation clear just about the time we had been embarking in Bremerhaven, when rhetorically he asked "how the public interest was served by the admittance of perhaps thousands of persons who 'obviously were not refugees' and 'had not engaged in the Hungarian revolution against communism.'" But maybe I should not take this personally, since Walter had *never* been a friend to the immigrant and was still one of the leaders of the so-called restrictionists in the interminable congressional wrangling over immigration. The status of that very battle, as relevant to our situation, was brought up to date by Max Frankel at just about the time of our arrival. His February 3, 1957, article entitled *Refugees Confront U.S. with Basic Decisions: Case of Hungarians is One Example of a Problem as Yet Unresolved* began with praise for the effort on behalf of the refugees. "With emotions fired, much was done. The refugees were fed, clothed and housed and moved on to other Western countries with little thought of the bills being accumulated. Immigration laws were stretched." But, he continued, the confused state of the immigration laws was itself evidence that the underlying issue, *did* the United States want refugees from Communism, still divided the country. For we Hungarians constituted a very special case. We not only encapsulated the view of Communism that put the United States and its Cold-War stance in the best possible light, but also focused attention on one of the fundamental elements of America's self-image and role, and perhaps most importantly provided a means for America to assuage its guilt about its actions and omissions during the revolt itself. So it seems that after I failed to join the fight for freedom, I may even have benefited from its defeat.

But as the crossing neared completion, I had no regrets or feelings of being unworthy, but only excitement building hour by hour. The distance remaining to be covered suggested that now we had no more than a day and a half left on the ship. The daily bulletin promised that in a few hours we would be informed about rules of entry to the United States and the plans that were in place for processing and housing the immigrants until they could launch their new lives and be allowed to stand on their own two feet again. The pleasant winter weather continued. Groups of passengers were already on look-out detail on the main deck near the bow, their eyes, without the spyglasses I now find myself imagining them to have had, trained on the western horizon, not yet expecting to see New York but just some foretaste maybe of the New World or some sign that we were approaching land. As promised, the instructions for disembarkation were posted just before lunch. And perhaps the most prominent among the rules declared that anyone attempting to enter the country with any foodstuffs would be quarantined and the offending items confiscated and disposed of as required by law. In the course of a heated discussion at lunch between Leslie and Rose, I found out that all along Leslie had been secreting sausages in his suitcase.

Leslie, and Leslie alone of us all, was *egy igazi magyar ember,* that is, a true Hungarian. And so the sausages proved. We all took along mementoes of what had so abruptly become the severed past, things we imagined would keep it alive and prevent it from withering to dust and being scattered by the wind. But all those things, like the photographs, documents, knick-knacks, and the lace doilies and tablecloth that Rose was carrying in *her* suitcase, and my songbook – they all addressed only our personal lives and had only personal meaning. Leslie alone took along something that for him created a visceral connection also with the homeland itself and was bound to remind him of it, something that smacked of Hungary and could not, as far as he could imagine, be had beyond its borders. Hungarian smoked sausages are a common delicacy for Hungarians. They happen to be similar to pepperoni, although far superior to it I think, but Leslie did not know about pepperoni then and believed Hungarian smoked sausages to be *unique.* So he put two pairs of them, each sausage about a foot and a half long, in the bottom of his suitcase, knowing that they would not spoil in any season. Thinly sliced and consumed like a treat, which is how to my then knowledge it was always consumed, a sausage could last a month or two. So he would have sausage, even if only a taste, for a year, and as the sausage dwindled and eventually ran out, so would his and his taste-buds' most painful longings for the old country. And maybe by then he could even bear no longer to be truly Hungarian. For how can you be so if you don't live in Hungary and don't even eat sausages?

But, obviously, his assertion of this Hungarian identity, or actually Hungarian Jewish identity, was not being tolerated. And so, after lunch he continued his preparations for arrival and demonstrated that the sausages in his suitcase rather than that wad of 100-forint bills lately in his pocket were in fact the last connection he had to break with back home. From the mess hall we had gone down to our bunks to retrieve the items in question, and then after we made our way back upstairs I watched him as he took a single long stride from the topmost step inside the hatch, over the very high threshold and right onto the deck, and then in a blind determined hurry strode across the metal expanse, right up to the railing. He then reached inside the front of his leather coat where he was carrying his contraband treasure, stopped for a moment as if to ready himself, then ripped one pair of sausages as if from his heart and flung it into the ocean, then the other pair, but flung them not actually into the ocean but into the milky void only, because the water was much too far below to see or to hear the splash of the first stowed-away and now cast-away foodstuffs landing in it. He had not cut off a piece to have right then or later. He had not offered any of it to anyone. But had he wanted to, I would have gladly lent him my Swiss army knife for the deed.

Then he just stood there, and as a swell lifted our side of the vessel and put him, as it were, on ground a couple of inches higher than where I was standing, the hazy sunshine breaking through the clouds fell on him and I felt compelled to take a naked-eye snapshot of him that after all these years I still carry in my mental wallet. In a word, he looked awful. His cap, acquired in the used clothing barracks in Salzburg, a workingman's cap with a crescent-shaped visor, what we used to call a Lenin-cap back home, had during the worst days of the crossing when nothing else was handy been used too often as a towel, and so it had completely lost it shape and now just hugged his head like a woolen stocking might have. His face bristled with a blond growth of six or seven days. His coat, which covered him almost to the ground, had become encrusted all over by the salt that remains when seawater dries. It was a yellowish kind of salt that did not hide the brown of the leather but did turn its wearer into a hoar-covered ghost. He was looking aft, towards the Old World and the hard-to-part-from sausages, and visibly his feelings were weighing him down. The old life was becoming as faint now as it was distant. He couldn't see how all that could be so completely and utterly finished, and so suddenly. He now had to hold on more fiercely than ever to what he had, because there was no possible way to get anything else. He had, yes, through his own actions, committed himself to this, to be satisfied with Rose and the children, to suppress or at least learn to ignore the clamoring inside him, the yearning for love and acceptance and kindness from a woman. He took off the cap, turned his gaze ahead and rubbed his stubbly chin, then he put the cap back on. He was both weary and ready.

The ocean was placid the morning after the next, January 29, 1957, when the *General Eltinge* cut its engines. The sun had hardly started its daily climb yet, and the air was crisp. We were within sight of a continent. In steady streams those refugees not on the deck already emerged from below, walked to the railing on the landward side, stood there two and three deep and gazed at the New World. Risen from the waters, motion-less and unperturbed – but not at all different from the European shores they had last seen. Momentarily crestfallen, they were scanning the ho-rizon in search of the Statue of Liberty and not finding it. I too was per-plexed by its absence. Maybe this wasn't really America? But then what? The delay was annoying. There had been too much waiting already. Finally, the humming and vibrations started again. The vessel began to glide through the mirror-like surface, soon the outbuildings of a human settlement came into view, other ships and boats, prospective terminal points, nodes of activity, the first stirrings of a new life, the New World.

In about an hour we docked at Pier 4 in the Brooklyn Army Terminal, a gigantic installation that had sent out and received altogether three million soldiers during World War II. Finally, in the distance, small, fading-into-the-blue but also unmistakable, you could see the Statue. It was America after all. We had arrived at the beginning. We would soon find ourselves replanted, well or not so well.

CHAPTER 10

The New and the Old

WHEN WE ARRIVED, LESLIE HAD already for some time been suffering from gum disease, and a couple of years later he was receiving treatments for it from a dentist in the neighborhood of Penn Station. One day on the way home from there, he was waiting on the subway platform during rush-hour. I imagine him miserable after the protracted torture, gently cradling his chin in one hand as if to calm the wounds, when suddenly an ooze began to collect around his tongue. And then all at once, as he recounted it, his mouth filled with blood. Carefully he removed one soaked piece of gauze packing, then another, and then regretfully he also dropped a bloody handkerchief into a garbage can. But still his mouth was full of the salty, sickening liquid. He had no more absorbents then and also could not stomach the thought of swallowing, so ashamed but also desperate, he spat the stuff down onto the tracks. A big bloody gob! Immediately a policeman appeared, his accusing finger pointed at a sign prohibiting littering and spitting, and then, as if the guardian angel of immigrants were napping on the job, slapped a ticket for a fine into the miscreant's hand. Anger, self-pity and pain vied for supremacy within Leslie now, woes rained down on him, but he just stood there like a mute animal, unable to defend his dignity. You see, even if he had been able to communicate, he couldn't have spoken because of the blood again filling his mouth. – That's how it was for Rose and Leslie those days. The photograph on her naturalization certificate from 1962 shows a woman with eyes dull and features blurred, as if she were unable to bring the world into focus and had just about run out of strength trying.

It was awful, even if you consider it in the context of what may be normal for immigrants. Now that I think back on it, for at the time I was neither willing to drown in the swamp of their misery nor able just to stand to the side and observe, and so I just turned away – now it seems to me as if the cumulative pressures of the successive persecutions, self-erasures and everything-on-the-line gambles they had endured for nearly two decades had finally crushed all personal infrastructures, individual and familial. It's not that now the threats to existence were greater still or the chances of survival more circumscribed than they had been during the war or under the Communists. Indeed, quite the contrary. But neither of the two earlier crises had been lived down enough to now make it irrelevant to the new devastation. It's true that at least when the factory had been thriving, say, in 1947, the horrors of the war must have seemed safely sealed in a subconscious sinkhole for nightmares. But the psyche being the temporal labyrinth that it is, in fuller retrospect it turned out that in each previous instance a full recovery had been blocked by both the severity of the damage sustained and the timing of the next assault. To Leslie and Rose's credit, and to America's credit as well, this particular descent into near-desperation lasted only five or six years, after which there was an easing and a revival and though nothing like a rebirth, certainly a new and quite tolerable normalcy. In later photographs they tend to smile, and usually not just pasted-on smiles either.

Two or three years after we arrived, Rose had something like a nervous breakdown, and after regaining some of her health at least, she had another. As part of her condition, for about a year and a half she was subject to such disabling vertigo that she could hardly get out of bed for fear of falling down. And in general she was overcome by fears. Not at all like your usual Rose. Undoubtedly a physical ailment of some sort afflicted her, but it was so undefined and intermittent and unresponsive to treatment, and so unexplained first in its apparent and then its pretty much complete withdrawal, that as soon as Marika and I understood a little bit about these things, we confirmed to each other our common suspicion that it had actually been a breakdown.

For Rose the loss of will, courage and vitality was terrible to experience; for the rest of the family it was terrible just to witness. And on the marital relationship it had an even greater impact than the transplantation itself. For the last quarter of the 20th century, Rose lived as an imperious but actually quite able invalid and Leslie as her aggressively solicitous caretaker. He went around like her advance guard, harm-proofing the world for her, like Max von Mayerling does for Norma Desmond in *Sunset Boulevard*, planning the transportation for the next doctor's visit, trying to spare her from all exertion, all the time worrying about her health. He protected her and she needed him. Finally, his lifelong yearning for her love was being satisfied, even though, as I've said, till his final illness she continued to insist that she had never loved him. But, unquestionably, it was symbiosis, mutual satisfaction, a crazy intimacy. In any case, Rose's breakdowns were improvisatory preparations for that quarter-century, practice rounds by way of temporary impressments into servitude.

Except for the periods of Rose's illness, they both always had work, and we always had proper clothes and a roof over our heads, and always three meals a day. It was never a question of survival. But relentlessly the world exploited them, and they could not stand up for themselves. They just kept their heads down like cart horses under the whip, pulling, pulling. He usually worked under horrible circumstances, like the shoemaker's shop, for example, where his bench was in an unheated attic. Winter evenings he used to come home half frozen, hands blue. She worked in sweatshops, piece work on the sewing machine Bangladesh-style, overtime each day as long as she could take it, and then lugging the groceries up five flights, never sure if she had been cheated in the market. He lost his bluster and his self-esteem. He was bitter and silent. She just broke down and suffered. Of course, they had nothing and owned nothing except the stuff from the two suitcases, the used garments from the Red Cross barracks at Camp Kilmer, the way-station between the Brooklyn docks and the Bronx where we spent about two weeks, and the used furniture and kitchen items they had bought with the starting allowance from the HIAS. And there was no way to know how they would spend the rest of their working lives, if they could pull themselves up by their bootstraps, if ever again they would give orders or at least be independent. Of the various economic levels they had occupied at one time or another, which one would they manage to clamber up to again? Would they be successful? If ever Leslie had an unworried moment, did he allow himself to dream of another factory? I'm certain he knew that ten years earlier he had been a different man and, among other things, had not had to suffer being talked down to. Years later, after some unremarkable ups and downs, they retired in modest comfort, but until then they continued straining all sinews at all times, obsessively focused on making a living, scrimping and saving.

Generally speaking, the unfamiliarity of the new world overwhelmed Leslie and Rose, even though to broad-brush it now as I am tempted to by exclaiming that subjectively everything in America was new, I mean new to us, would be a vast exaggeration. For a lot was not. Just think about it – many many fundamental things were quite similar to how they had been and were therefore familiar. The flora and the fauna, the seasons, the climate, not the language but certainly the script used to write it, a very significant matter, and urban existence, the basic arrangements of family life, the schooling of children, the religious institutions, the political organization of nations, the Western culture that prevailed both before and after. That's a lot, indeed it is almost everything. In the kingdom of human life the old and the new were very much two species of the same genus. That's why the adults could start working immediately using their established skills, the children could go to school to *continue* their education, and we could shop for groceries, use public transportation, and even understand street noise in most of its registers.

But personal identity was a different matter. Even with so much of the world the same, what you had always been you could no longer be. So until Rose and Leslie could become something new, something appropriate to their new situation, they were again aliens. And this time aliens in an alien land, to paraphrase *Stranger in a Strange Land,* a classic science-fiction title from those times. In other words, they had to transform themselves, or at least allow themselves again to be transformed, after having already suffered several identity-wrecking transformations. From small-town young people to sophisticated urbanites, from Hungarian Jews with impeccable bourgeois instincts to a Catholic housemaid and a Red Army private, and then to would-be members of the proletariat. Who and what would they be now? How would they fit into the new world? Well, of course, the new world already had them pegged: they were immigrants. And indeed their silence or incoherent mumbling, and everything else about them too, confirmed that.

And as if the situation weren't difficult enough already, the identity-loss was further aggravated by Leslie and Rose's continued inability to have friends, either together or even sort of separately. As you know, this handicap had hobbled them already in Hungary, and the immigration just magnified the problem. In America for many years separate friend-ships would have been unthinkable, and from the beginning all joint at-tempts at social contacts misfired. In our first apartment in the Bronx we lived quite near some other refugees, so there were encounters and suitable opportunities, but Rose and Leslie never became friends with any of those people. During the first few years at the most, they also tried to participate in the Hungarian-Jewish social life that flourished among the many immigrants in the metropolitan area, but that didn't work out either. They also joined a synagogue as soon as they could afford to, an undistinguished place in the neighborhood of our second apartment where I could pretend to pray next to many of my classmates, but that also didn't produce any connections. You could say that, alas, their social skills spanned the entire spectrum from reject to repel. In the new coun-try they came to have a strange, sad, friendless life.

So for them, being immigrants meant having not only no identity-narrative yet in the new country, but also no audience for the identity-narrative from the old. And the latter they missed maybe even more than the former. If an interpreter was around, like, say, your son, then Leslie especially could never resist launching into an explanation of what *he* had been back there. But as considerate as people were, no one ever was willing to listen to that, and no one wanted to hear about your grieving for yesterday either, or your torments of isolation and nothingness, or your new habit of just turning away from the sight of the grim beaten-down creature in the mirror.

Of course, of all the new things, the new language was the most persistently problematic, with an impact on every aspect of life. Until you've been an adult trying to carry on a responsible existence without being able to communicate in a local tongue, you can't really appreciate why the English word "dumb" has the two meanings it does. The world of the lack-language, which is what Rose and Leslie were, is drastically reduced. Not understanding shuts you out from this and that, and chases you away, while the new language follows you wherever you go and oppresses you. It monopolizes your attention, frustrates your intentions, blocks your moves, leads you into error, exposes you to ridicule, builds you up and knocks you down, sets traps for you and plays tricks on you, it ambushes you, and it pollutes your words and thoughts with nonsense masquerading as near-sense, and with outright nonsense too. Without ever any respite, you are both its captive and its victim. Learning English was slow and painful for my parents. Everyone we encountered assured us that watching TV would be helpful, and surely it was better than it would have been just to sit around mouthing awkward-sounding phrases. So immediately after we were settled in the Bronx we bought a television set, which Marika and I watched avidly, Rose diligently, Leslie only rarely, and even then only after much pleading. Now that I recall those times I feel for him. He must have found the stream of incomprehensible syllables utterly dispiriting. Watching a telecast delivered in a foreign language is like trying again and again to jump on a train speeding by. How many misses or fractured bones before you give up from mental exhaustion, or from disgust, or just because there is blood in your mouth?

After some years, I can't say how many, maybe ten, maybe twenty, they could speak English after a fashion. Rose, and in this I am like her when attempting a new language, was always too concerned with being correct and hesitated to speak. Leslie, on the other hand, just charged ahead, damn his interlocutor. But, unmistakably, they had also been rendered more or less inarticulate, or linguistically broken you might say. Right to the end, language remained an issue. For example, the gender distinction of the third-person singular pronoun, which is foreign to Hungarian, always gave them a lot of trouble and at times also caused wild confusion and even hilarity. After all, it can catch you off guard to suddenly encounter this or that uncle in drag. Had they ever been subtle thinkers? I wouldn't think so, although they were intelligent people. But surely they had been more nimble-minded about things even beyond the practical, which they *always* until then had managed astutely – more nimble-minded than they became in the new language and the new language environment. Still, in later years they had only occasional moments of difficulty watching television. And Rose also became an avid consumer of literary classics, could swallow a tome like *Nicholas Nickleby* while already reminding me that she needed something else to read, and was not at all a superficial reader. The dictionary was always by her side, and she made lists of words she could not grasp even after looking them up and made sure to ask Marika or me what exactly they meant. Leslie also read some romance novels in later years, but in keeping himself occupied he always favored the small screen.

My own experience was utterly different from my parents'. I too of course had to contend with all that was unfamiliar in the New World, and so my discoveries continued and maybe even intensified. But in addition, since I was an adolescent, my subjective new, that is, what *per se* was not new but was just new to me, also encompassed everything you first encounter with the onrush of adulthood. For coming of age really is a passage into a new existence, obvious prior exposure to what that existence looks and sounds like notwithstanding. For me the usual difficulties of the process were compounded by the fact that the adolescence in question was to be of the 1950's urban American variety rather than what Leslie and Rose had gone through during their own prehistoric Hungarian youths. Still,

I dealt with it all with ease in some respects and anguish, frustration and stupidity in others, not unlike, I daresay, any 14-year-old white middle-class-background immigrant boy of those times might have. And Jewish, of course. I had the usual adolescent urges and the frequently accompanying anxieties, and I had dreams. I suffered through part-time jobs, and summer jobs, but life was mostly enjoyment and excitement. I especially loved attending school with girls. That was new for me too. I also bore my share of family and household burdens, and maybe even more than the usual teenager's share, but I ignored the awfulness at home as much as I could and from the parental disintegration, not the hardships but the illness and the defeat, I looked away. And, to their credit, Rose and Leslie didn't try *too much* to turn my head back. My assistance they demanded but not my emotional support. Were they being considerate, tactful or sensitive to adolescent needs to separate? Definitely not. For one, Rose was just too proud. But more importantly perhaps, they were just too preoccupied I think, consumed by the effort to keep the ship of family existence afloat on the strange American seas.

Learning English itself gave me no trouble at all. Mind you, I am not at all good at learning to speak foreign languages, as you have seen already with German and Russian, and I can also add French to the list, although I do *read* French well and could also *read* German and Latin well enough to do the historical research I wanted to. But English was a resounding exception. No, it required more than three months, but no more than six if you're talking just about being comfortable in everyday matters. And English of course I went on to get very good at, I think I can say without bragging, and also to fall in love with both as a spoken and a written medium. My success I attribute to the extraordinary urgency of the situation and to the manner of my acquisition of the new language. Dante is usually credited with having been the first to note the difference between the way you learn your mother tongue and the way you learn other languages, namely, that the mother tongue is acquired by imitation, whereas you come by other languages through book-learning, through the grammatical rules for conjugating verbs, using relative pronouns, sidestepping the sins of syntax, etc. Even if that distinction is not absolute, since some people, many immigrants among them, do need to or often just prefer to go the imitation route with second and even subsequent languages, in my case it goes to the heart of the matter. For to a very great extent I did learn English without books and without grammar too, although definitely *not* without the little green pocket dictionary that for a year at least accompanied me everywhere and initially was in my hands a hundred times a day. And in a few years the new language became for me something like a second mother tongue.

Acquisition of English was only the most notable instance of the ease with which I handled the new. For unlike Rose and Leslie I took to the new world of the New World in a spirit of adventure and challenge. In particular, I immediately embraced popular entertainment in its newest and most devastatingly American form. Since we had a TV set, we wanted to know what was being telecast, so Rose established the weekly routine of digging 15 cents out of her emaciated purse, the cost of a subway ride, to buy a *TV Guide*, then still a new but already wildly successful phenomenon and the authoritative popular publication on the medium. In every issue I read all the articles and studied all the pictures, and so became acquainted with the kinds of programs being produced and stars being promoted, and learned about the all-powerful networks, the idea of commercial messages, the rhythms of the entertainment seasons, the connections between stardom and money, and other wondrous and to me new aspects of the business too. The information was exciting, and as if I were making the continent my own one meridian's worth a week, immediately I started saving back issues, stacking them on the uppermost shelf of the kitchen cupboards. Although I never referred back to an old issue, I loved my collection. It was America. After about two years, we were ready to move to a bigger and better apartment, and after some resistance Rose acquiesced to my taking my *TV Guides* along. When the time came I climbed up on a stool, but as soon as I began to remove the stacks of little magazines, a nauseating army of cockroaches swarmed out of it and launched an infantry charge, landing on my head and shoulders, emergency-crawling all over my hands and arms, and dropping to the floor with a loathsome clacking as their tiny folded wings hit the linoleum. I surrendered at once.

A short while later, I also got acquainted with American popular music. Since I played the piano a little, one of the boys in school showed me something known as a fake book, a thick, cheaply-bound volume of well-known songs, with just the melody lines, basic chord symbols and lyrics printed two per page. To double its allure, the book, as an item pirated in the teeth of copyrights, was also reputed to be unavailable in stores. Somehow I acquired my own copy of this treasure trove, and banging on the old upright we got somewhere, I plunged into what then was called Tin Pan Alley and today the great American songbook. I introduced myself to the Gershwins, Cole Porter, Rodgers and Hart, Harold Arlen, Irving Berlin and many lesser masters too, including Frank Loesser of course. I learned the standards. Sitting in front of the TV, I got mesmerized by Fred Astaire's renditions of them. I committed the melodies and the lyrics to memory, enriching my immigrant's vocabulary along the way and picking up a good many turns of phrase. I was in heaven, and my heart beat so that I could hardly speak. At the same time, I also got to know rock'n'roll and Broadway show tunes. So in musical terms at least I quickly felt more of a native than many a Bronx-born-and-bred hummer.

And it was all a thrill. I had never done anything like that before, I mean, never before had I on my own acquired a body of knowledge or become familiar with an artistic genre or movement. It was my first adventure of, let's call it, cultural discovery. Through the decades, as I've hinted already here and there, many others were to follow, and that kind of activity was to become a source of much enjoyment and happiness for me. That first one was prompted by the transplantation, although it also tapped into some pre-existing proclivities. Somehow, without even understanding what I was doing, I had groped my way around the aesthetic standards applicable to my subject, discovered the possible approaches to it, traced its geographical and temporal boundaries, and compiled a list of its main characters and decisive events. It was an important step in my intellectual maturation and the development of my sensibility. It was also my earliest experience of the many opportunities for pleasure available in the contexts of artistic beauty and knowledge.

Leslie did not cheer me on in my avid embrace of American ways. Indeed, he saw it as a defection of sorts, as a rejection of the Old World, of his own ways, of what he himself seemed to value more than ever simply because now he had nothing else to value. He saw it as the loss of a son even, I suspect, or more accurately, a still further loss of the son he had never much had. In retrospect I see that it would have been a miracle if he hadn't felt that way, even though he and Rose did truly want the children to do better than they themselves had, readily forgetting that they had actually done pretty well when the whole world wasn't against them. But I really didn't care about any of this either. Like I said, I was an adolescent and would most likely have had conflicts with my father even if we had still been in the old country and he didn't have blood in his mouth. Certainly, it never occurred to me that he might feel rejected. I mean, wasn't whirlwind Americanization the game plan? By each according to his or her own abilities? What were you supposed to do if not make the fastest and best possible accommodation with the new? But I have to admit that because at first, and maybe even later, Rose and Leslie were not so good at that, I, fortified with the bravado and callousness of youth, did quickly cease to perceive their lives as having any relevance to mine. Obviously, I was playing on a bigger and more splendid field than had ever been open to them, and that made my little accomplishments and even the fun-and-games achievements of a new American identity seem *categorically* worth more than all their old-country adult assets. So I stopped seeing them as parents to look up to or even take seriously. And, finally, I became ashamed of them and hid those feelings even from myself, I am now ashamed to admit. For the time being, all that remained between us was the blood-connection.

The clashes at home were many and bitter, although in retrospect I recognize them to be no more than pretty ordinary age-appropriate clashes. Leslie thundered at me for being a dependent minor too big for his breeches, a hooligan, a know-it-all. A dependent still unable to provide for myself I definitely was of course, but never anything like a hooligan or even a wild teenager even by the still sedate standards of those days. And I don't think I was a know-it-all, even if at times it did seem that way to him since I knew a lot more about the new country than anybody else around the dinner table and often was asked about things and thanked for any answers I could give. On the other hand, I have to confess that I neither felt nor faked the kind of respect for him that he believed his due simply as my father. Indeed, I did not appreciate his sufferings and sacrifices, and did not recognize them as being endured on my account. He was making whatever he could of his own life, and I wanted to make whatever I could of mine. What would you expect of a teenager fixated on independence and on putting the Old World behind him?

It was only in the late 90s, when in preparation for moving into a so-called senior residence Rose and Leslie were downsizing, that I realized how utterly thorough my rejection of Hungary had always seemed to them. Included among the things to be sold were some paintings by Hungarian artists they had acquired on a trip back to the old country around 1970. When I heard about a dealer coming back for a second look at the canvases, for a minute I was at a loss how to feel about not having been asked if I wanted any of them, but then, ever true to form, I stifled whatever was threatening to bubble to the surface and just offered to pay more for the one I liked very much, a harvest scene, than the dealer would. Rose was shocked to hear that I wanted it at all. She said they had not offered it to me only because I never had any interest in Hungary, and then they gave it to me gladly as a present. Well, I was shocked too.

But, unfortunately, the problems at home went well beyond my Americanization and the reaction it provoked. Something like a generational dislocation also occurred, a shift that produced aftershocks through the decades. I now became sort of the responsible adult and Leslie and Rose turned into the dependents whose needs I had to attend to. I had to accompany them to the post office, to the immigration offices, on visits to doctors, at first even on relatively simple shopping expeditions where something ordinary, no more than a winter jacket, for example, was to be purchased, but I was needed nevertheless to put questions to the sales person about size and quality and usually, ugh, to try to haggle *in a department store.* I hated doing that, and indeed many of those things, and consequently did not do them well, or not to Leslie's satisfaction in any case. I was never shrewd enough or forceful enough, or I didn't know the value of money or didn't respect his hard work. So he, the dependent adult, scolded me for not wanting to be an inarticulate immigrant like himself, for not completely identifying with his pain and indirectly at least for being ashamed of him in ways I had always been already in Hungary and in specifically American ways now too. Why didn't he leave me alone? Or at least let me, the would-be adult, do his bidding in my own maybe overly deferential way, in the way that suited me as I was, with my own personality, according to my own irresponsible, cavalier ideas that made me talk politely to others, wait for my turn and pay the set price for things like everybody else? Well, maybe he was right in some of his condemnations of me, or maybe half-right, but I was who I was!

Still, even if it wasn't pleasant, life at home for me as a teenager was far from anything terrible. That I had the urge to neutralize it with doses of both the immigrant-new and the adolescent-new doesn't prove otherwise. But so I did. During the last year and a half of high school, and throughout my years at the City College of New York, while continuing to live in one and then another family apartment in the Bronx, I had a friend whom I'll call Ross Kaufman. Ross's parents were big-hearted, fun-loving, comfortable-in-their-skin, intelligent but only high-school-educated – I think that covers it – middle-class people. Until I got to know them, the Hajdus' Sunday routine was a special midday meal, with Rose's delicious fried chicken usually the *pièce de résistance*, in the company of my only ever Hungarian friend, whom I'll call Robert Vermesi, a boy my age who had come to America after the revolution by himself and was informally entrusted to the care of a distant uncle, a man of some means with the Dickensian name of Sunshine. For a couple of years at the most, Rose adopted Robert as a Sunday stepson, an arrangement that worked well for everybody, providing him with a semblance of family life and the senior Hajdus with a chance both to be generous while still compulsively tight-fisted and to be showered with a semblance of the gratitude for a free meal they never really got from their own children, who, I won't deny it, considered themselves actually entitled to be fed three times a day. Robert and I got along well enough, and liked each other enough, but we never developed feelings of true friendship. Or at least I didn't for him. And not long after I met the Kaufmans, Robert was at first mostly and then entirely sidelined, and a new Sunday routine took shape.

Ross was a very competitive guy and liked to make a contest out of everything. We were together in many classes in high school and he was always comparing our test scores and grades, and apparently also doing the play-by-play for his parents. Soon enough this led to an invitation to a Sunday dinner *chez* Kaufman, to be preceded by watching a then popular weekly TV show called *College Bowl*, in which brainy teams from two colleges tried to rack up the most points by answering questions like: what are the four largest moons of Jupiter, or name the 18th-19th-century English radical philosopher and father of the author of *Frankenstein*. You get the idea? The game at the Kaufmans' was to see who could beat the contestants themselves to the answers they declared after hitting the buzzer and being acknowledged, with Ross keeping a running score. We were joined in front of the set by Ross's parents, who were friendly and casual, so the wisecracks were flying, there was bonhomie all around, and the feeling between the generations was something I had never seen, especially since I was treated like an older and wiser brother to Ross, whom week after week I left in the brain-teaser dust. When the show was over, we had a copious dinner brought up from the local Jewish delicatessen, with ice cream and cookies for dessert, and Coca-Cola without end. All along the conversation was lively and clever, the Kaufmans took a genuine personal interest in me, and soon this became a Sunday *afternoon* routine. At home it was accepted that after sharing Sunday dinner with my own family, I would go over to the Kaufmans a few blocks away and spend the rest of the day there. I was happy in their company and they in mine, I called Lew and Pearl by their first names, Ross and I shot pool with Lew, I confided in Pearl about my girlfriends, we listened to Frank Sinatra and Louis Armstrong LPs, I got invited to Kaufman family affairs and met aunts and uncles and cousins, and for some years they were a surrogate family to me. My American family. To this day I think of them very fondly.

But then that ended too, as maybe it had to. After college, when I went on to succeed in graduate school and Ross to be defeated by it, we drifted irrevocably apart. I also didn't need an American family anymore. I was almost 23 and felt plenty grown up. But at home, with my Hungarian family – with them things did not progress so conventionally. The break you would expect to have happened between Rose and Leslie, on the one hand, and me, on the other, or call it an adjustments of relationships, did not happen. After all, the adolescent separation turned out to have been pathetically incomplete. In fact, it did not really transpire until they died, or maybe almost. True, I moved out, got married, started making a decent living at the earliest possible time, then got divorced and married again and raised two children. But throughout all this, a dutiful attachment to my parents – yes, I know I've mentioned this already – prevailed. It was not emotional intimacy, and not joy in their company, and not even the satisfaction of being there for loved ones in need. Only an unquestioned dutiful attachment. The services I used to perform for them when they were the greenest of greenhorns and I a just-a-shade-riper teenager I continued to perform: helped with tax returns, read and translated official correspondence they received, dealt with landlords, made telephone calls to lodge complaints about this or that. And maybe those things were even okay. But I was also drawn deeply into health matters and other kinds of emotionally difficult situations, turned to as the one who could be called upon sometimes daily and counted on always to fall for the save-our-souls anxiety. In addition, I visited them frequently, although never frequently enough it seemed, often arriving with things they could have obtained for themselves but just preferred to receive from me. I did all these things, and did them mostly without participation by Barbara or the kids, almost as if pursuing a life as a son side by side with a life as an independent adult with a wife and family. Worse than that, if ever for whatever reason I failed in carrying out my duties, I was stricken with anxiety as if I had committed some unspeakable sin. And what I really regret is that I allowed a jealous Rose to treat Barbara badly.

For many years I dismissed Barbara's anger about my extramarital loyalties by saying that I was only doing what was filially right, but now I understand things differently. Now I know that there was something very wrong with my Hajdu relationships, something very neurotic. I came to my senses, as it were, only recently, only after death had done its work. And even then I still needed a crucial assist from Eva Hoffman's *After Such Knowledge*. It was Hoffman who made me see that, *as a rule*, emigration confuses the generational order of families. Adolescents will suffer the growing pains of their stage of life whether they are transplanted or not, but usually adults can be counted on to maintain their adult perspective and powers and dignity. Unless something traumatic interferes, that is, like the disintegrating force of emigration or, even more so, the Holocaust. When such a force does crush them, and more yet when two such forces do, then the relationships of parent and child are likely to get twisted. Hoffman talks mostly about survivors of the worst atrocities of the Holocaust rather than more peripheral victims like Leslie and Rose, and mostly about such survivors rather than emigrants. But her observations apply very well to my case too: "The [second-generation adolescent's] ideal of autonomy is undercut by claims of loyalty and compassion that cannot be easily dismissed or gainsaid. The need to stay [with the parent] acquires the force of an imperative; the need to get away becomes freighted with the risk of betrayal and perhaps justified guilt.... The quandaries involved in relations between survivor parents and second-generation children are affective and familial; but as the children reach fuller consciousness,... the conflicts acquire a moral valence." That is, come to be experienced in terms of *duty*.

Not more than a year after we arrived, Marika and I started speaking to each other exclusively in English. The only two words we never could or would replace with English equivalents were *Anyu* and *Apu*. For us their bearers could be spoken of only as "she" and "he," and even more frequently "they." To me, and I daresay to Marika too, for reasons and with consequences I cannot disentangle any more than I have already, to the end Leslie and Rose remained our Hungarians parents. And I remained their Hungarian child.

Until at least a year after our arrival, when he learned about the form of television entertainment known as professional wrestling, the only show Leslie enjoyed watching was *Your Hit Parade*, a much-liked and fondly remembered Saturday evening confection. I wonder if he was taken with Gisele Mackenzie, one of its four stars; I know I was. Gisele was pretty and lively, and sang and mugged and danced and played the violin, but more interestingly she loved to show off her fabulous legs and her whole body clad in the black outfit of a magician's assistant. Or was he maybe amused by the preposterous dramatizations of the best of the day's popular music, little vignettes he could understand no more and no less than he understood Huntley and Brinkley? In other words, not at all? I myself was actually the most fascinated by the weekly count-down of hits – will *A White Sport Coat and a Pink Carnation* be number one again? – which I came slowly to understand to be the format of the show. I don't recall ever wondering how the rankings themselves were determined, probably because too many other more overt phenomena were also claiming my attention, but the fierce struggle of the new challenging the old and the urge to discover the rules and patterns of change, as if to formulate a species of social calculus, possessed me.

In the 1950s, to the new arrival from Eastern Europe, America presented itself as a land of an overwhelming variety of *things*. In the effort to comprehend this strange new reality, stranger still than what I had already been discovering and to be taken more seriously, indeed taken every bit as seriously as adult life itself – as part of that effort I automatically resorted to a kind of cataloging of the material world, trying I suppose to impose order on the teeming multiformity. And so, with the aid of whatever sources of information I could command, I drew up what I thought were exhaustive mental lists of all the makes of automobile running on the roads, the brands of beer brewed, the major league baseball teams, the different brands of cigarettes vying to assuage the nicotine cravings of a tobacco-crazed world, the subway lines in New York City, and so on. Of course, I understood nothing of marketing or distribution, of labor unions and public services, of local or national brands, of the cachet of a product or its lack thereof, or whatever other economic or social meanings these things could have had. I was just pleased with myself to know that Chevys were made by General Motors, that they came in three models or four or whatever, and that GM also made Buicks, Oldsmobiles and the rest. I had, I believed, something of a grip on the universe of things, and that gave me some self-confidence. Until one Saturday evening, that is, when the much-anticipated song-fest shattered my illusions. During a break between yodeling Swiss mountaineers and fraternity boys delivering their adulterated versions of the week's hit tunes a commercial aired for cigarettes named *Hit Parades*. What? How was I to understand this? To all appearances, this promotion had a genuine brand of cigarettes as its subject, except that, knowing all the brands of cigarettes, I knew that no such brand existed. To boot, the brand went by the very name of the television program on which it was being advertised. Was this then a spoof? A dramatization, so to speak, of a commercial message amidst dramatizations of popular songs?

It was a few weeks before I accepted the obvious: Hit Parades had just been added to the list of cigarette brands, joining Chesterfields and Lucky Strikes and Pall Malls and all the other smokes whose pedigree I had imagined reaching back to Sir Walter Raleigh. Of *course*, I finally understood, that list had never in fact been final but only provisional. It could always change. And it did change. In fact it *had* to change now and then. And as the roster of cigarette brands changed, and of top hits, so all other lists had to change too. Ford created the Edsel at just about this time, so it too joined the list of Ford makes to which it belonged, and then very soon it dropped off. Three of the then major daily newspapers in town, *The New York Herald Tribune*, *The New York Journal-American* and *The New York World-Telegram and Sun*, were themselves also not timeless entries on *their* list, as I had first assumed, but items created over the years by the merger of other papers, with the original names mashed into the ones prevailing in my then present. So finally I understood. The material world is always in flux, taste is fickle and capitalism thrives on innovation. What you valued yesterday you discard today, and who knows how you'll feel about it all tomorrow. You leave one country, one language, one identity, and you take another as now your own. And so it goes.

Hit Parades and the Edsel, or its front end anyway, were instances of a form of change much esteemed and long pursued in America, in which some newly invented thing is added to an existing repertoire. I, and all Hungarian immigrants I suppose, encountered this form of change both in its subjective and in its objective modes. There were things and ways of doing things familiar from the old country and new to me only to the extent of having American versions or equivalents. Apples, for example, I had eaten always, but not McIntoshes or Cortlands. There were also things entirely new to me but already well established in America, string ties, for example, to mention something much more trivial than fruit, which I first ever saw around the neck of some of my classmates on schooldays when boys were not allowed to enjoy open collars. Obviously, for me these two kinds of things belonged to the subjectively new. In contrast, the objectively new were things *literally* new, that is, new not just to immigrants but to everyone. And I don't mean just newly made either, like a new pair of the same old sneakers. I mean new in being previously unknown, unseen, unheard-of, unexpected, and until recently un-existent and maybe even unimagined, like Hit Parades and the Edsel. I realized pretty early on that the status of the objectively new in the Old World as opposed to the New represented a profound difference between the two places. An imaginary American emigrating *to* Hungary around 1956, passing us on the high seas going in the direction Wrong-Way Corrigan claimed mistakenly to have gone, would have been right to anticipate that of the new things he was to find there, the proportion constituted by the objective would be negligible in comparison to the proportion of it we ourselves were finding here.

America's intense encounter with the new started right at the beginning. When the first Europeans paddled ashore, they believed themselves to have found a continent still in its natural state, as it was when newly made by God Almighty. After all, the native peoples had not yet even plowed up the land. So the Pilgrims at Plymouth Rock, for example, sophisticated people from an advanced civilization, were starting out in a land supposedly still new, and they were intent upon doing things there that were *in* that land also new. And what they were intent upon was settling this continent and building upon it a civilization. And as they intended so they did, they settled and built, and how they did it, as you know, is an utterly thrilling and also shocking story. From one perspective then, the enterprise of the white man in North America began with the introduction into a pristinely *new* natural environment of *new*ly made things, for the newcomers had to make almost everything from scratch, and the introduction of *new* ways, for the way they did things had never before been done here, and maybe nowhere else either, for in some cases so their new habitat required. And then that enterprise continued with the conquest of successive portions of the continent and the spread of settling and building, until the Europeans and their African slaves had turned the whole supposedly virgin landmass into a newly fabricated, often newly conceived and so objectively new, and always suited-for-American-needs human environment, including the later-filled-in spots, which they had left blank during their early far-grasping and leapfrogging efforts.

And the encounter with the new had only begun once the white man had planted himself in a given place. For the first houses, churches and fortifications had been thrown up in haste and fear, and once life became more secure were repeatedly replaced by better-made things. So on account of many things, including very much its *own* shortcomings, destruction of what should have become the physical evidence of a newly accumulating historical past also began early on, and quickly with it a second form of change also became typical of America: the process of some newly made thing taking the place of another thing like it but no longer new. I estimate that there are no more than a few hundred edifices from the 17th and 18th centuries still standing in what were the thirteen colonies. Many of them are simple dwellings, like Bowne House in Queens, New York (c.1661), for example. They are plain and modest because they were built by members of communities unusual for their egalitarian ethos, ruthlessly circumscribed by the log-cabin necessities of pioneer and immigrant life, and in New England at least in the grip of an aggressively unostentatious Protestantism. Only a few of them, built of stone or brick rather than wood, with Jefferson's Monticello (1772) in all its neoclassical splendor perhaps foremost, stand out as creations notable for their style or construction, or their relationship to the human or natural environment. As for surviving public buildings, commercial structures and churches, although some of them are admittedly more imposing, even they are in the so-called First Period and Colonial Georgian building styles, which are not known for producing palaces, cathedrals and town halls of the magnificence usually associated with the earlier, and later revived for this very reason, Gothic, Renaissance and Baroque architectural styles. All these circumstances tended to invalidate any possible reason for preserving initial efforts and promoted a continuing focus on the new.

The history of Federal Hall in Manhattan is a striking demonstration of the practice of pulling down what had been erected not long before to make way for an improvement or just because it was no longer needed for its intended purpose. The original structure on the site was erected in 1700 to serve as New York's city hall and quickly became a historic public place. In 1765 representatives of the thirteen colonies gathered there as the Stamp Act Congress to lead the protest against taxation without representation. In 1788 the building was enlarged and remodeled to become the first structure built in the Federal style. Between 1785 and

1789 it served as the meeting place of the congress convened under the Articles of Confederation, and then under the new name Federal Hall for a year or so it became the first capitol of the United States. Here the First Congress met and as its first act counted the votes that elected George Washington the first president of the country. Federal Hall was the site of Washington's inauguration and also the place where in 1789 the Bill of Rights was drafted and proposed as a set of amendments to the Constitution. Surely, this was not only an architecturally important structure but also one of the two or three places that could be considered the birthplace of the nation. And yet, in 1812 it was razed, and so a richly expressive piece of the historical past was destroyed just to yield its place to something new, namely, the first US Customs House. And as if the process of birth had to be prolonged.

But this potentially decisive beginning notwithstanding, it is fair to say that the physical evidence of the historical past in America came under direct attack from the new only around the middle of the 19th century. The new enemy was an alliance of three historical developments. The first of them, the technological and manufacturing revolution known as industrialization, included a cascade of innovations that had a transformative impact on construction materials and methods. Concrete had been known to the Romans, but was forgotten after them and reinvented only in the late 18th century. In 1824 Portland cement, to this day the favored binding agent in concrete, was patented, and in 1849 reinforced concrete made its first appearance. A few years later Elisha Otis invented the elevator brake, in 1858 Henry Bessemer invented his method for the mass production of steel, which soon allowed the substitution of steel frames for load-bearing masonry walls, and finally in the early 1880s, thanks to the efforts of Thomas Edison and George Westinghouse, electrical service on a scale sufficient for large edifices became available. In 1884, with construction of the ten-story Home Insurance Building in Chicago, all of these innovations together made the dream of skyscrapers a reality. And also, I should add, gave birth to an American architecture of extraordinary and in some cases beautiful structures. Building tall, often in locations already built, soon became a commercial and civic imperative. The second historical development, industrial capitalism, inflicted on America what Marx first called creative destruction, which manifested itself as planned obsolescence and other less premeditated practices of the kind. Industrial capitalism also brought about ever greater concentrations of wealth, which further spurred extravagant new construction. And finally, there was the new artistic movement and cultural attitude known as modernism, which proclaimed its hostility to the old with its very name. Altogether these three things devastated the physical evidence of the historical past.

The casual destructive replacement may be said to have culminated in 1963. It was in that year that Pennsylvania Station in New York City, which I myself saw once or twice as an avid young immigrant but know much better now from the many images of it still in existence – it was in that year that Pennsylvania Station was bulldozed and its operations relocated underground, with a cash-cow office building erected atop and a hideous new Madison Square Garden behind it. The magnificent structure had been built during the first decade of the 20th century, with a glass-and-steel train shed and a grand concourse that puts me in mind of the spirit-rising-from-stone naves of Gothic cathedrals, going so far as to even draw your gaze upward towards the heavens. Vociferous protests had gone unheeded at the time, but then contributed greatly to establishment of the New York City Landmarks Preservation Commission, which in 1968 conferred landmark status on Grand Central Terminal, another railroad station that itself had been the object of proposed demolition and redevelopment schemes since 1954. A few months after the landmark designation, the Terminal's new owner, the Penn Central Railroad, as if reading from the same old script, announced its intention to replace the station with a large office tower. Again, there was a public outcry, with the most prominent and insistent voice being that of Jacqueline Kennedy. Of course, the city denied permission to proceed, whereupon the Railroad filed a lawsuit claiming that the Commission's action had amounted to a taking of private property for public use in violation of the

Fifth Amendment to the Constitution. When it eventually ruled on the case, the progressive Supreme Court of the times rejected the Railroad's claim, and since then historic preservation has been a respected part of American public life.

During the 19th century there was little historical preservation in the United States, and even what there was was not an end in itself. In 1850 Washington's Headquarters, a stately fieldstone farmhouse in Newburgh, New York, where the general and his wife had lived and worked during the last sixteen months of the Revolutionary War, was declared a historic site by the State of New York, which restored it and opened it to the public. In 1858 the Mount Vernon Ladies' Association – I picture a hall with thirty state-delegate ladies in dueling crinolines – bought George Washington's home in Virginia, with the intention to restore it and to open it to those who wished to see where the nation's greatest hero had "lived and died." The idea that some things in themselves are worthy of preservation or restoration began finally to gain some traction in 1889, when the Association for the Preservation of Virginia Antiquities, the first statewide organization of its kind, was founded. Then in 1925 the French Quarter in New Orleans became a focus of preservation activities, and in 1930 Charleston, South Carolina, adopted the first historic preservation ordinance. In 1949 the National Trust for Historic Preservation, a non-profit organization, extended the movement's field of operations to the entire country, and then finally came the decisive Penn Central case. As a result of all this, and of a consciousness raised by so many decades of slash-and-burn redevelopment, today the physical destruction of the past is less wanton. Maybe the former First Lady was right after all when she said that "Americans care about their past...." I know that she was definitely right when she added that nevertheless "for short term gain they [do] ignore it and tear down everything that matters."

In any case, it is Jacqueline Kennedy who gets the credit for raising the larger questions: How *do* Americans feel about the past? And what *is* the role assigned to the past by American culture and society? A sense-of-being-in-time, as Heidegger might have put it, is part of human apprehension of the world, a phenomenon that is universal but takes diverse forms. Even among Western societies, where a conception of time as something that moves forward in linear fashion prevails unchallenged, the emphasis placed on each of the three temporal segments of past, present and future is not the same. Americans, for one, are recognized as having a sense-of-being-in-time that is lopsidedly forward-looking. To discover why this is so, you have to look no further than the formative elements of the country's history. To begin with, emigration is often a shrugging off of the past, and the immigrant experience of building a future from nothing also both encourages and justifies a front-loaded approach to collective time. The imperative – manifest *destiny*, really? – to expand across the continent functions similarly. Also significant in this respect has been the brief career of the white man in North America, a brevity that itself makes the past seem like something that belongs to the Old World, that *is* indeed the Old World. Finally, the split by the spanking new beginning of the period 1776-1789 of even that brief 350-year career into another before-and-after occasions an emphatic restart that makes the country feel even younger and in its more persistent youth even less able to value the past. As a result of this particular sense-of-being-in-time, the ill-treatment of the American historical past has not been limited to destruction of the physical evidence, but has also included a denigration of the historical past as a dimension of reality itself.

Of course, I don't mean to suggest that America does not know its historical past at all, for that is hardly the case. First of all, there is Independence Hall and Faneuil Hall and historic state-houses and other historic edifices, including Thoreau's tiny cottage at Walden Pond. Despite the sad fate of Federal Hall, I think it's fair to say that today no one would propose to pull down any such structures. There are also all the past-evoking museums and monuments in Washington, the almost sacred battlefield at Gettysburg, and also other Civil War sites dedicated to historical memory. In general, throughout the country military encounters are commemorated where they had occurred, as are other collective efforts and notable events in the history of the nation or one of its constituent states. There is also the splendid Freedom Trail in Boston, and the equally splendid Black Heritage Trail. And above all, there are the national holidays particular to America, namely, Martin Luther King Day, Presidents' Day, Memorial Day and the Fourth of July, the feast-days, as it were, of the nation's canonized past, and to some degree also Columbus Day, Armistice Day and Thanksgiving. All in all an impressive line-up, but still only a very constrained historical past. For all these things are in the service of national or state identity, or in some cases ethnic identity. Now, I do love the Fourth of July and applaude efforts to promote awareness of the country's founding principles. And community-building is a laudable objective, and within reason – love of country, not jingoism – a necessary undertaking even. But as an attitude to the past, all this puts me in mind of the socialist realism of the Communists. For just as propaganda in slogan-plays and bold graphics was not art for art's sake, so reminders of key moments in the nation's history are not the past for the past's sake.

In 1963 I understood very little of all this, and even that but vaguely, but the whole question of how exactly the New World is new was already on my mind. Then that summer I returned to Europe for the first time. I went with two friends, traveling now together, now alone, through France, England, Italy, Spain, the Netherlands, the Rhineland and Switzerland, staying mostly in youth hostels, almost three months on a shoestring budget, spending $825 altogether, including the charter flight back and forth across the ocean. Nineteen hours or something like that in a propeller plane going, refueling in Shannon, Ireland, and about a thousand and nineteen it seemed coming back, refueling this time in Gander, Newfoundland, where walking out of the terminal I saw the sun rising out of the watery horizon, discovering the New World, golden yellow and, miraculously, about three times its size in lower-latitude skies. In Genoa, sitting at the counter in a café, I heard a 30-ish couple next to me speaking Hungarian. I was astonished. Who could these people be? They told me they were Hungarian tourists on a summer vacation and assured me that traveling abroad from Hungary was now possible, as was visiting the country by one such as myself. Well, that was the last thing I ever expected. That was hardly forever. Had the world been re-made during the previous six-and-a-half years, while I was becoming an American? So I scratched all my immediate plans, took the next train to Venice, and from there the overnight express to Vienna. In the morning I was at the Hungarian embassy applying for a visa. I thought I'd spend four or five days, look up old friends, tramp through old haunts, flaunt my new identity. But the visa processing was going to take three weeks, which I obviously could not spare. I was both disappointed and relieved. I actually had bigger fish to fry.

For I was seeing the Old World for the first time. The Old World at its best and most glorious. Yes, technically Hungary is part of the Old World, but in fact there is not much there that is really old. For one, Hungary was, as I've said before, always something of a backwater. Even during the Renaissance, in the days of King Matthias Corvinus (1443-1490), which were definitely among the country's best days, the most notable components of the local splendor were imports from the West. For another, whatever was notably old in the Hungary of those days, and much also of what was far from notable and just old, was destroyed during the 150 years of the subsequent Turkish occupation and the wars related to it. So when it comes to the man-made environment, Budapest is actually less old and has fewer historic structures or even just remnants of such structures than New York. Yes, there is Aquincum, as I've mentioned already, a 1st-century AD Roman settlement in northern Buda. Certainly nothing like that exists anywhere in America, the things closest to it in age being Pueblo sites, like Chaco Canyon for example, which are both much more recent and incomparably more grand than the few stubs of walls and foundation stones along the Danube. In any case, in Hungary the past that thrills me in the Old World is a very real feeling but hardly a reality. At the most you will find only something like Hollókő, a village about 50 miles northeast of the capital, a UNESCO World Heritage Site, which includes the ruins of a 13th-century castle

and about a hundred other old structures, the oldest of them built partly of wood in the 18th century after the Turkish withdrawal and repeatedly rebuilt after the many fires that devastated the settlement through
subsequent years.

In contrast, Western Europe is a place where the historical past
stretches far back, especially in comparison to America, and is present
everywhere. Italy may be the most remarkable in this respect, with
Rome itself offering an extraordinary display, as if almost around every corner, of the history of the last two thousand years and more, but
France is steeped in a long past too and is the European country I
know best and love the most. In France, the outbreak of the Revolution
in 1789 both exacerbated the long-standing practice of vandaliz-
ing ancient structures and elicited protests of what now had become
wholesale destruction of buildings associated with the old regime and
especially the Church. These protests were the first signs of an awareness that the past had to be protected. Napoleon followed up on them
by launching some preservation projects, Victor Hugo drew attention
to the destructive force of industrialization with an 1825 article entitled "War on the Demolishers," and the public pressure to preserve,
generated in part at least by the anti-industrial spirit of romanticism,
produced a breakthrough in 1830 with the creation of a national preservation office. As a result of all this, today in France the past is present *qua* past in splendid pieces representative of the lost whole, and
is in most instances neither overwhelmed by the present nor emptied
of its original meaning by cheap imitations. Of course, the country *is*
overrun by tourists, and surely no fewer miniature Eiffel Towers are
sold than miniature Statues of Liberty, but the historical past is too
multifarious and too intricately woven into the fabric of everyday life to
be seriously threatened by the annual hordes. So still today, although
maybe no longer as generously as in 1963, Western Europe constitutes
a social environment that invites you to live with the past as well as the
present, a social environment that responds positively should you *want*
to live that way. If you care about such things, then you cannot when

in France help but be struck at just about every turn by the immersion in and easy mindfulness of the historical past.

French history begins with Julius Caesar's conquest of Gaul, and sure enough, Gallo-Roman structures and ruins dot the country's Mediterranean coast and regions inland from it. Among them is a great favorite of mine, the spectacular Pont du Gard, a 1st century AD aqueduct across a river gorge, an exemplary Roman public works and another UNESCO World Heritage Site. Only a few fragmentary remains represent the subsequent barely-civilized, thinly-populated centuries of the first millennium, such as the thermal baths of Cluny in Paris (3rd century), sections of the ramparts of the city of Carcassone (5th century), and parts of the crypt of the Carolingian church of Saint-Denis outside Paris (8th century). But starting with the 11th century, the survivals and remainders and reminders of the past get more and more numerous and ubiquitous. In addition to the great Romanesque basilicas and Gothic cathedrals, built successively throughout the remaining centuries of the Middle Ages, there are also many other ecclesiastical buildings, smaller churches of course and abbeys and priories and others, as well as forts and castles, civic structures, and then from the 13th century on even private dwellings like the half-timbered houses in Rouen and Bourges. And structures from and after the Renaissance, that is, the 16th century, are everywhere. And there are many other things too that transport you to the historical past. For example, streets named after people not illustrious enough to have their image imprinted on legal tender. And so, in Chartres a street near the cathedral is named after Bishop Fulbert (c.960-1028), a leading man of learning from those days; and in Poitiers there is a Rue Dom Fonteneau, named after the 18th-century Benedictine monk and scholar who preserved the records of the religious houses of the province by copying their charters into 87 folio-size manuscript volumes, a good portion of which I read while doing research for my Ph.D. dissertation. The vineyards of Bordeaux and Burgundy continue a tradition of cultivation stretching back to just about the Roman invasion; in Reims and on the way there, you can see plaques on the western façades of churches announcing that Joan of Arc stopped on this spot and this in 1429, on her nigh-miraculous march at the head of the royal army, leading Charles VII to his triumphant coronation; and there are the royal tombs at Saint-Denis, which all by themselves amount to a guided tour of the French centuries, and so on.

One of the most remarkable French examples of an accumulating past-in-the-present is the royal château of Fontainebleau southeast of Paris, another one of my favorite places. A royal hunting lodge was in existence here already during the reign of Louis VII (1137-80) and portions of the keep from those times are part of today's château. But the true history, as it were, of the place begins only in the 1520's, when Francis I (1515-47) had the earlier elements, including a monastery founded by Louis IX (1226-70), a king canonized soon after his death and since then commonly known as Saint Louis, incorporated into a new complex. Francis made the château into one of the main royal residences – "it was," reported Benvenuto Cellini, "the place in his kingdom where [the monarch] most enjoyed being" – and, connoisseur of Renaissance art that he was, invited several Florentine and Bolognese artists to carry out the magnificent decorations of the place. From Francis through Louis-Philippe (1830-48), every French monarch who reigned longer than just a few years contributed to the exterior or interior of the château and the grounds you can still admire today. Napoleon (who was crowned Emperor of the French in 1804) called Fontainebleau a "house of the centuries," rebuilt some of its galleries badly damaged during the Revolution, and in 1814 memorably bid farewell to his guard in one of the château's courtyards before going into exile on Elba. Throughout the centuries, numerous other significant state events also took place here and further enhanced the historical aura that allows the wide-eyed visitor to ground his or her imaginary tour of the past in a physical reality very present indeed.

Here is Proust, a master of this theme, speaking of such an experience in the church of Saint-Hilaire, the simple semi-fictional parish church of the semi-fictional town of Combray, near Chartres, where the family of his semi-fictional protagonist, Marcel, used to spend their Easter holidays.

Having described the church in great detail, Proust says that "all this, and still more the treasures which had come to the church from personages who to me were almost legendary figures (such as the golden cross wrought, it was said, by Saint Eloi and presented to [King] Dagobert [7th century]),... made of the church for me something entirely different from the rest of the town: an edifice occupying, so to speak, a four-dimensional space – the name of the fourth being Time – extending through the centuries its ancient nave, which... seemed to stretch across and conquer not merely a few yards of soil, but each successive epoch from which it emerged triumphant, hiding the rugged barbarities of the eleventh century in the thickness of its walls,... raising up into the sky above the square a tower which had looked down upon Saint Louis, and thrusting down with its crypt into a Merovingian darkness, through which... [Marcel's guide] Théodore would light up... with a candle the tomb of Sigebert's [King of the Franks, mid-6th century] daughter."

This passage is not unusual for Proust, who, incidentally you have to say, fashioned *À la recherche du temps perdu* into a marvelous showcase for how the French past fits, or could fit until at least World War I, into French life. Of course, this French past is not the lost time Proust was searching for. He is quite clear that his quarry is his *own* prior experiences rather, what you would usually call your memories, but what he likens instead to the vivid and involuntary reliving of the kind that transpired when the taste of the madeleine dipped in the herb tea brought his childhood experiences miraculously alive. Recollections like that revealed to him what he considered the essence of things, and they proved to him that the materials for the literary work he longed to create "were [actually his] own past life." Now, obviously, the historical past is something else entirely. But the fact that the historical past is not the explicit subject of *À la recherche* suits my purpose here all the better, in that it lends still further support to the argument that in France the historical past is as it were ever-present and just an ordinary part of daily life. True, Proust was not *le français moyen*, that is, the average Frenchman, and that by dint of his vocation, sensibilities and intellectual gifts he was probably more aware of the historical past than that pollster's dummy might be. Still, time after time characters in the book convince you that not only the author, who finds just about everything that engages him equipped with a historical background, context or parallel, but all the French, all the men and women of his times from all walks of life, lived in both the past and the present, even if they did so in different ways and to different degrees.

"The aristocracy embodies all our history," says Proust, commenting on the genealogical near-obsession of the Baron de Charlus, one of his most vividly drawn aristocratic characters. And indeed, throughout *À la recherche*, the mention of one or another ancestor of an aristocrat Marcel encounters at a party or a summer outing conjures up before him figures or events from French history. Conversely, his detailed knowledge of the famous *Mémoirs* of the Duc de Saint-Simon, a voluminous record of court life at Versailles during the last twenty years or so of the reign of Louis XIV (1643-1715), and of the equally renowned letters written between 1671 and 1696 by the Marquise de Sévigné to her daughter in Provence, which had long been Marcel's grandmother's, and after her death, his mother's favorite reading – his thorough familiarity with these classics and with French history in general provides Proust with a huge cast of real people and a vast store-house of real events against whom and which to play off his own characters and the situations he finds them in. And so, here, there and everywhere, his thoughts detour to the past. Here is an example. Marcel, who always has trouble falling asleep in unfamiliar rooms, says of his first visit to the Grand Hôtel de la Plage in Balbec that the violet curtains "gave to [this] room with its lofty ceiling a quasi-historical character which might have made it a suitable place for the assassination of the Duc de Guise [1588]... but for me to sleep in – no."

The author also leaves no doubt that the past deposited its residue in simple folk too. Upon arriving at the Guermantes' and being graciously received by the Duke, he comments: "Just as some common expression coming from the lips of a peasant may delight us if it points to the survival of a local tradition or shows the trace of some historic event, unknown, it may be, to the person who thus alludes to it, so this politeness on the part of the [Duc] de Guermantes… charmed me as a survival of habits many centuries old, habits of the seventeenth century in particular." And *à propos* the porch of an old church he notes that: "The sculptor has… recorded [here] certain anecdotes of Aristotle and Virgil, precisely as [Marcel's family's cook] Françoise in her kitchen was wont to hold forth about Saint Louis as though she herself had known him, generally to deprecate, by contrast with him, my grandparents, whom she considered less 'righteous.' One could see that the notions which the medieval artist and the medieval peasant (who had survived to cook for us in the nineteenth century) had of classical and of early Christian history, notions whose inaccuracy was atoned for by their honest simplicity, were derived not from books, but from a tradition at once ancient and direct, unbroken, oral, distorted, unrecognizable, and alive." What's obviously missing from this sociology of historical survival is the middle class. But it is missing only because during the 17th century and before there was hardly such a thing. For *À la recherche* demonstrates that by the end of the 19th the many members of the bourgeoisie, especially overeducated ones such as Marcel himself, his family and some of his friends, had all come to participate in the defining Old-World phenomenon of continuing to live the historical past in the present.

I could go on, obviously, but I will indulge in just one more bit of Proustiana, in order to note that in addition to people, places and events, for Proust the historical past also persists in words. Brichot, a professor at the Sorbonne, is one of the scores of what I like to think of as third-rank characters in *À la recherche*. Such men and women are drawn in sufficient detail and possess distinctive enough personalities to make you feel that you know them, but they are hardly required for the progress of the plot, such as it is, or for Marcel's artistic, emotional or intellectual development. For most everyone in the book on almost all occasions, Brichot is nothing more than a butt of jokes, but for a fascinated Marcel, sitting across from him as they travel through the Normandy countryside on a local train, he is an explicator of the etymology of French place-names. Marcel loves how Brichot's derivations strip away the centuries from the villages and country towns, until the capitalized words themselves reveal a living Norman, Saxon or even Moorish past. As a medievalist, I myself had often discovered the French past in such derivations, and when reading *À la recherche* I am thrilled to accompany the professor and his would-be student on their historical journeys. Often Proust also detects a historical past in just ordinary words as spoken by his characters. He comments especially on Françoise, who speaks now the language of Mme de Sévigné, now of La Bruyère (1645-96) and now of Saint-Simon, who were of course pretty much contemporaries. Or he just generalizes as in the following: "As the glass cases in a local museum are filled with specimens of the curious handiwork which the peasants still carve or embroider in certain parts of the country, so our flat in Paris was decorated with the words of Françoise, inspired by a traditional and local sentiment and governed by extremely ancient laws."

Here again the contrasts between the respective social enterprises carried on in America and in Western Europe are unmistakable. Sure, American place-names also have interesting origins, if not etymologies, and I don't mean names like Truth or Consequences, N.M., which is actually a case of anecdote trying to compensate for historical poverty. There are place-names derived from Native American sources, but they memorialize only a past that has from the beginning been strenuously disowned and cut off. And there are also place-names like Rotterdam, Amsterdam, Utica, Rome, Syracuse, Geneva, Rochester, for example, in upstate New York, which seek to create the New World in the image of the Old, and others like New York, New Bedford, New Brunswick or indeed New England, which achieve no more than a wished-for continuity between places on this side of the Atlantic and on the other. In each case, an unintended result is an emphasis actually on the *absence* of any historical past beyond the bare fact of recent discovery and settlement. The same lack of temporal depth is also revealed when you venture into the past of the language or its literature. When Proust likens an encounter between Marcel's grandmother and one of her aristocratic friends to a scene from Molière, he is connecting the ladies to the French past and to

17th-century ways of life that still resonate in the late 19th. But if I were, for example, to find parallels between the story of a contemporary fortune-hunter getting his comeuppance and some tomfoolery in a Restoration comedy, I would only be showing off my stuffy academic taste for obscure theatrical entertainment. Even though the language of my analogy, both going in and coming out, would be English, the past I was harkening back to would in no way be American.

I myself was probably eleven when I first started reading stories set in a historically specific past, when, in other words, I first encountered any kind of historical narrative. Several times during my last Hungarian years I read Dumas's two best-known works, both written around 1840, *The Three Musketeers*, which is set in the time of Louis XIII (1610-1643), and *The Count of Monte Cristo*, which is set mostly in Dumas's own lifetime but was by the 1950s richly historical. More important though for the development of my proto-historical imagination were three novelized multi-volume biographies Rose and Leslie recommended to me in response to my constant requests for more and more grown-up books to read. The biographies were by a prolific Hungarian writer and dramatist of the first half of the 20th century named Zsolt Harsányi. Their subjects, in the order of the works' impact on me, were Rubens (1577-1640), as I've mentioned already, Bach (1685-1750) and Galileo (1564-1642). Each life was set in a vast historical panorama populated by scores of intriguing and well-documented figures, especially the life of Rubens, who in addition to being a tireless genius of a painter had also been a busy diplomat. So I read accounts of various episodes of the scientific revolution and the Counter-Reformation, and of life in the princely courts and guild-halls of Baroque Germany. How I loved those books! How I loved to consult the 24-volume family encyclopedia, climbing on a chair to reach the top shelf of the glass-fronted bookcase to pore over maps of Antwerp, Leipzig and Padua, or study the Habsburg family tree, or read about Giordano Bruno and Copernicus. But all of this of course was no more than just a sort of enthusiasm for knowledge about the past and really had nothing to do with the academic discipline known as history.

My enjoyment of history as such, that is, of reading low-calorie fiction-free narratives about the past, dates back to my last months in Budapest. As you would expect, the first-year history course in the *gymnasium* was a survey of Western civilization. When I first went home with my new history book I immediately sat down and read the chapters on Greece and Rome. I don't recall what if anything I knew already about antiquity, but I knew enough to be greatly curious about it and to be fascinated by the thoroughly textbook-ish although ideologically twisted beginning-middle-and-end account of it I found there. I still recall that the Gracchi were played up as Communists *avant la lettre*, but I don't think that either bothered me or made me skeptical. Among other things, I was first of all in a quest for chronology, and enthusiastic as I was, I readily overlooked the narrative's political agenda. Again, I just wanted to know about the past, and especially, as I had learned already from the biographies, about the makers of history most often invoked with admiration and respect.

But then came a break, a brief let-up in what had not yet been a real passion anyway. After coming to America, I promptly forgot about historical narratives. There was too much else to pay attention to I suppose, some of it even historical in nature. In any case, I was apparently satisfied with what the school curriculum offered, first in high school, then during the first year of college. At various times during that year I thought of majoring in mathematics or philosophy or chemistry, but though nothing clicked, I was aware of no particular attraction to the study of history. But then, during the spring semester of my sophomore year, in a class on Western civilization, I had a *eureka* experience. The subject for the day or the week was the Reformation. Prior to this encounter, I had always found historical eras and major phenomena to be pretty much what their names advertised them to be. But not so this time, as I realized during the discussion about the formative impact on the modern state of the hundred years of war triggered by the breaking apart of Western Christianity. The Reformation was indeed a continent-wide religious revolution, but wasn't it also, I now thought, a continent-wide *political* revolution? And *voilà*! There it was, just for the pleasure of it, the first historical idea I ever came up with on my own. I had found it! For afterwards I noted how much I had enjoyed that bit of simple analytical thinking, and a few days later I declared my intention to become a historian.

And then in the summer of 1963 came the European tour, if so I may call it. Of course, by 1963 it wasn't Marcel Proust's France anymore. And even if it had been, I would not have been hobnobbing with aristocrats. Still, there in the Old World I found something I had not known myself to be missing, needing or wanting: the historical past. A past that in Western Europe infused everything and was everywhere plain for me to see, and was actually the main attraction for a tourist like me, although I hadn't thought of it that way when planning the trip. But once there I immediately felt that this was the world as I love it! As it should be! America was the only place to live, but this, I saw, really was the proper stage of operations for the intellectual thrill vouchsafed me by the Reformation analysis, and a subject to which I could passionately devote myself. Choosing a field of specialization, which had to be done quite promptly, was easy now. European history it would be, and European history *not* of the recent past. The recent past seemed too present-bound to me, of interest too much as just an overture. Early modern Europe then remained a possibility, as did also the Middle Ages. At that time, remarkable pioneering work was being done in both of those fields, including the introduction of new kinds of evidence and new approaches to the old kinds, the formulation of questions never before asked and the adoption of amazingly productive social-science concepts, so they were both appealing. In the end I chose the Middle Ages because the undergraduate courses available to me did more justice to it than to early modern Europe, and because all in all I found the actual historical developments of that time period the more exciting of the two. And within Europe I chose France and England. France because I had fallen in love with it, and England as almost integrally related to the France of those times and sort of for good measure.

But contrary to what I came to believe after years of occasional musings, that was not the end of the story or even the end of its beginning. In 2001 I was reading Sebald's *Austerlitz*. By profession, the novel's protagonist is an architectural historian. Well into the book, in a long passage where he relates how he finally began to discover and piece together details of his own early years, Jacques Austerlitz says: "I realized then how little practice I had in using my memory, and conversely how hard I must always have tried to recollect as little as possible, avoiding everything which related in any way to my unknown past." Then he tries to spell out how exactly he managed to do that, and confesses that "I had constantly been preoccupied by that accumulation of knowledge [of architectural history] which I had pursued for decades, and *which served as a substitute or compensatory memory.*" For a moment I stopped, for the words I just italicized had blotted out everything else from my mind, like a command that you account before it's too late for how you have lived your life. Of course, I could not really apply to myself Austerlitz's words regarding the stifling of the personal past, and I was not about to suffer the kind of personal disintegration that awaited him. I was just sitting in a comfortable armchair in my living room, reading a remarkable book, sipping a cup of tea and trying to make out the print blurred by the tears in my eyes. But have I not been preoccupied by an accumulation of knowledge that came to serve as a substitute or compensatory memory? Yes, I have. And did I not swear allegiance to a part of the Old World's historical past that did not touch me *personally*, and did I not do so just after I had lost my *personal* connection to the Old World? Yes, I did, I did.

And so, in Sebald's words I apprehended a never-before recognized but fundamental truth of my life, personal and professional, emotional and intellectual. A truth that finally had to be acknowledged. A pithy and compelling interpretation of the events of my life and of how I have lived. An interpretation I believe myself now to have proved right. For as I have presented myself here, in so many words and also between the lines, is exactly how I feel myself and believe myself to be.

Appendices

Cast of 20th-Century
Historical Characters

ANDROPOV, YURI VLADIMIROVICH (1914-1984) – Soviet ambassador to Hungary, 1954 – 1957.

DONÁTH, FERENC (1913-1986) – Communist sentenced to 15 years in prison in 1951 show trial; later rehabilitated and became one of Nagy's supporters; member of Hungarian Workers' Party's Central Committee Secretariat, October 24 – November 4, 1956; subsequently interned in Romania with Nagy; sentenced to 12 years in prison in 1958; amnestied in 1960.

EICHMANN, ADOLF (1906-1962) – Lieutenant Colonel in the German SS. Organizer and director of the deportation of Hungarian Jews to Auschwitz in 1944. Captured by Israeli agents in Argentina in 1960, tried in Jerusalem in 1961, hanged in 1962.

GERŐ ERNŐ (1898-1980) – first secretary of the Hungarian Workers' Party, July 17 – October 25, 1956; fled to Moscow on October 28, where he remained until 1960.

GIMES, MIKLÓS (1917-1958) – Hungarian journalist; Communist from 1945; excluded from the Party after Nagy's dismissal in 1955; executed along with Nagy in 1958.

HORTHY, MIKLÓS (1868-1957) – Austro-Hungarian naval officer and from 1920 to 1944 conservative head of state, as Regent of Hungary. He resigned and was arrested in October 1944, testified at the Nuremberg trials in 1946 and lived out his life in Portugal.

KÁDÁR JÁNOS (1912-1989) – Minister of the Interior, 1948 – 1950; imprisoned, 1951 – 1954; regional party secretary, 1954 – 1956; Hungarian Workers' Party's first secretary and Minister of State in last Nagy cabinet; head of the Hungarian Socialist Workers' Party and *de facto* ruler of the country, November 1956 – May 1988.

KHRUSHCHEV, NIKITA SERGEIEVICH (1894-1971) – first secretary of the Communist Party of the Soviet Union, 1953 – 1964.

KOPÁCSI, SÁNDOR (1922-2001) – chief of the Budapest police in 1956; sentenced to life in prison as a co-defendant at Nagy trial; released in 1963.

KUN, BÉLA (1886-1938) – leader of the Hungarian Communists during the Hungarian Soviet Republic of 1919. Upon fall of the Republic emigrated to the Soviet Union, where he lived until tried and executed in Stalin's Great Terror.

MALÉTER, PÁL (1917-1958) – Minister of National Defense from October 31, 1956; arrested by KGB, November 3, 1956; tried with Nagy and executed on June 16, 1958.

MIKOYAN, ANASTAS IVANOVICH (1895-1978) – member of the CPSU Presidium, 1935 -1966; first deputy chairman of the Soviet Council of Ministers, 1955 - 1957; emissary of the Presidium to Hungary, October 24 – 31, 1956.

MINDSZENTY, CARDINAL JÓZSEF (1892-1975) – Prince Primate of Hungary and Archbishop of Esztergom, 1945 – 1973.

MÜNNICH, FERENC (1886-1967) – Hungarian ambassador to the USSR, September 1954 – August 1956; ambassador to Yugoslavia, August 1956 – October 25, 1956; member of the Hungarian Workers' Party's Central Committee from October 24, 1956; Minister of the Interior in Nagy's government from October 27 – November 3, 1956; deputy premier in the Kádár government from November 4, 1956; prime minister, 1958 – 1961.

NAGY, IMRE (1896-1958) – member of the Hungarian Workers' Party's Central Committee, 1945 - 1955 and October 23 – 31, 1956; member of the Politburo, 1945 – 1949, 1951 – 1955 and October 23 – 30, 1956; prime minister, July 4, 1953 – April 18, 1955; expelled from the Party, December 1955; readmitted on October 13, 1956; again named prime minister, October 23, 1956; took refuge in Yugoslav Embassy, November 4, 1956; deported to Romania, November 22, 1956; arrested, April 14, 1957; tried, sentenced to death and executed on June 16, 1958.

RAJK, LÁSZLÓ (1909-1949) – Communist Minister of the Interior and then Foreign Minister in the immediate postwar government of Hungary; sentenced to death in a show trial and executed in 1949; rehabilitated in 1956 and reburied on October 6, 1956.

RÁKOSI, MÁTYÁS (1892-1971) – first secretary of the Hungarian Workers' Party, 1949 – July 18, 1956, and *de facto* ruler of the country throughout most of those years; lived out forced retirement in the Soviet Union, in what is known today as Kyrgyzstan.

SUSLOV, MIKHAIL ANDREIEVICH (1902-1982) – member of the CPSU Presidium, 1955 – 1982; emissary of the Presidium to Hungary October 24 – 31, 1956.

SZÁLASI, FERENC (1897-1946) – leader of extreme right-wing Arrow Cross Party, and from October 16, 1944, Leader of the Nation and Prime Minister of Hungary. In 1946 he was tried for war crimes and high treason, sentenced to death and executed.

TILDY, ZOLTÁN (1889-1961) – leader of the Smallholders' Party and president of Hungary, 1946-1948; under house arrest, 1948 – 1956; Minister of State in Nagy government, October 27 – November 4, 1956; sentenced to 6 years of imprisonment, 1958; amnestied, 1959.

TITO, MARSHAL (1892-1980) – president of Yugoslavia, 1945 – 1980.

Outline of Hungarian History

896   Migrating from the east under the leadership of Árpád, the first Magyar tribes arrive in the Carpathian Basin, where they settle down. Gradually they conquer the whole Basin.

899-968   Like the numerous Germanic peoples before them, the Magyars make marauding and plundering incursions into Central and Western Europe as far as Spain and Italy. Other than the Turkic Cumans who arrive in Hungary during the 13th century, the Magyars are the last of the wave of so-called barbarian invaders to settle in Europe.

975   Bavarian monks are invited into the country. Increasing numbers of conversions to Christianity.

995   Prince Vajk, a descendant of Árpád, is baptized as Stephen.

1000   Under Roman auspices, Stephen is crowned King of Hungary, and is venerated thereafter as St. Stephen. Catholicism rather than Greek Orthodoxy becomes the country's official religion.

1102   The Hungarian crown extends its suzerainty over the Dalmatian coast and parts of Croatia and the country acquires a port on the Adriatic Sea. German influence in the country and an orientation to the West are already well established.

1222   Andrew II enacts the Golden Bull, granting nobles the right of armed resistance if the king infringes on their prerogatives, thus weakening the central authority for a long time.

1241   Invading Mongols devastate and depopulate the country. In addition to the nomadic Cumans, new settlers also arrive from France, Flanders and the Rhineland.

1301   Extinction of the male line of the House of Árpád.

14th-15th centuries are characterized by (i) frequent conflicts among claimants to the throne from the Angevin ruling family of Naples, the Polish kings, and the Austrian rulers and Holy Roman Emperors of the Habsburg dynasty, (ii) the growing Turkish threat as the Ottoman Empire expands north through the Balkans, and (iii) the increasing power of the magnates.

1342-1382   King Louis the Great extends Hungary's control over Dalmatia.

1458-1490   Matthias Corvinus, son of a powerful Prince of Transylvania (the easternmost region of the Carpathian Basin) is elected king and proves to be a victorious military leader against northern and western neighbors and the Turks, an able administrator and a prominent Renaissance figure. Briefly Hungary becomes the strongest power in Central Europe.

1526   Hungarian forces suffer a devastating defeat at the hands of the Turks at the Battle of Mohács. The Turks capture Buda and Pest, and the country is divided into three parts: Royal Hungary under the

Habsburgs in the west, a Turkish vassal state in the center, and a largely independent Transylvania.

1598   Beginning of religious conflict between Catholics and Protestants.

17th century is characterized by warring against the occupying and expansionist Turks, rivalry for the crown between the Habsburgs and the Princes of Transylvania, and continued religious discord, with Protestantism powerful in eastern parts of the country.

1687   Transylvania and Royal Hungary are reunited.   The Habsburgs proclaimed hereditary kings.

1699   Peace of Karlowitz ends Turkish presence. Country is under Austrian control now.

1711   Peace of Szatmár concludes Transylvanian rebellions against Habsburgs and restores the privileges of the nobility.

1722   Habsburg emperor pledges constitutional autonomy for Hungary.

1767   Emperor Joseph II issues the Patent of Toleration, bringing official religious discrimination to an end, and abolishes serfdom.

1825 marks the beginning of the "Era of Reform," during which Hungarian gains as the country's language, a national movement arises, economic reforms are instituted, and mechanization and modernization begin.

1840   Kossuth Lajos (Louis Kossuth) becomes leader of the national movement and the political liberals.

1848-1849   Revolution breaks out in Pest on March 15, 1848. Its leader is Kossuth; its other inspirational voice is the poet Sándor Petőfi. Soon the revolution turns into a war of independence. For almost a year the Hungarian armies are successful against the Austrians and the forces of the ethnic minorities that had risen up against Magyar domination, but in August 1849 the Hungarians are decisively defeated with the help of a Russian army invited by the young Emperor Francis Joseph.

1848-1916   Francis Joseph, Emperor of Austria and Apostolic King of Hungary.

1867   The Great Compromise creates the Dual Monarchy of Austria-Hungary, putting the Hungarian realm on an equal footing with Austria.

1914-1918   In the First World War Austria-Hungary is one of the Central Powers. Practically no fighting takes place on Hungarian soil.

1916   Charles I succeeds Francis Joseph as Emperor of Austria and (as Charles VI) King of Hungary.

1918   October 17, Hungary declares independence; November 16, Charles abdicates and the National Assembly declares a republic.

1919   Led by Béla Kun, the Communists create a Hungarian Soviet Republic. After four months of Communist rule, the White Army led by Admiral Miklós Horthy overthrows the Republic.

1920   Horthy restores the Kingdom of Hungary. The throne remains vacant, and Horthy becomes the elected Regent. In the effort to promote ethnic self-determination, the Peace Treaty of Trianon reduces Hungary to one-third of its size, stripping it of Croatia, Slovakia and

Transylvania. Hungarians are embittered and an irredentist movement that still flourishes today comes into being.

1931   Banks collapse as the Great Depression hits the country.

1938   Southern Slovakia and southern Carpatho-Ruthenia are re-annexed to Hungary by the Axis powers.

1939   Hungary signs Anti-Comintern Pact with Germany, Italy and Japan.

1940   Further re-annexations.

1941   Hungary declares war on the Soviet Union.

1944   March 19, German troops occupy Hungary. The Hungarian Holocaust claims a half a million Jewish victims. October 16, under the leadership of Ferenc Szálasi an extreme-right Arrow Cross government takes control of the country.

1945   The Red Army expels German forces from Hungary. Hostilities end on April 4.

1946   Hungary declared a republic.

1947   Paris Peace Treaty once again reduces Hungary to Trianon borders.

1948   Communists take over.

Recipe for Hungarian Goulash

Gulyás, MADE AS A HEAVY soup and not as a stew or a casserole, is a traditional dish very popular in Hungary. It is made in many different ways, according to regional styles and personal tastes. Usually, but not always, it includes tiny white-flour dumplings known in Hungarian as *csipetke*. The best I can recall, the recipe below represents a dish very much like the one my mother used to make.

<u>Ingredients</u> (will serve 4 persons)

1 ½ lbs. of any tender part of beef cut into ¾-inch cubes
2 tablespoons oil or lard
2 medium onions, chopped
2 cloves of garlic
1-2 carrots, diced
1 parsnip, diced
1-2 celery leaves
2 medium tomatoes, peeled and chopped, or 1 tbs. tomato paste
2 fresh green peppers
2-3 medium potatoes, sliced
1 tbs. Hungarian paprika
1 bay leaf
ground black pepper and salt according to taste
water

Instructions

Heat up the oil or lard in a pot and braise the chopped onions in it until they get a nice golden brown color.

Sprinkle the braised onions with paprika powder while stirring them to prevent the paprika from burning.

Add the beef cubes and sauté them till they turn white and get a bit of brownish color.

Let the beef-cubes simmer in their own juice while adding the grated or crushed and chopped garlic, some salt and ground black pepper, and the bay leaf. Add enough water to cover the contents of the pan and let it simmer on low heat for a while.

When the meat is half-cooked (approximately 1 ½ hours), add the diced carrots, parsnip, potatoes, celery leaves and some more salt if necessary. You'll probably have to add some more (2-3 cups) water too.

When the vegetables and the meat are almost done, add the tomato cubes and the sliced green peppers. Cook on low heat for another few minutes. You can remove the lid of the pan if you want the soup to thicken.

Bring the soup to a boil and add the *csipetke* dough (pinched into small pieces and rolled with the finger), which needs about 5 minutes to cook.

Jó étvágyat!